D0081319

REFERENCE

Encyclopedia of Sleep and Dreams

Encyclopedia of Sleep and Dreams

THE EVOLUTION, FUNCTION, NATURE, AND MYSTERIES OF SLUMBER

VOLUME I: A–L

Deirdre Barrett and Patrick McNamara, Editors

GREENWOOD

AN IMPRINT OF ABC-CLIO, LLC
Santa Barbara, California • Denver, Colorado • Oxford, England

PRAIRIE STATE COLLEGE
LIBRARY

Copyright 2012 by ABC-CLIO, LLC

All rights reserved. No part of this publication may be reproduced, stored in a retrieval system, or transmitted, in any form or by any means, electronic, mechanical, photocopying, recording, or otherwise, except for the inclusion of brief quotations in a review, without prior permission in writing from the publisher.

Library of Congress Cataloging-in-Publication Data

Encyclopedia of sleep and dreams : the evolution, function, nature, and mysteries of slumber / Deirdre Barrett and Patrick McNamara, editors.

   2 v.
  Includes bibliographical references and index.
  ISBN 978-0-313-38664-0 (alk. paper) — ISBN 978-0-313-38665-7 (e-ISBN)
  I. Barrett, Deirdre. II. McNamara, Patrick, 1956–
  [DNLM: 1. Sleep—Encyclopedias—English. 2. Dreams—Encyclopedias—English.
3. Sleep Disorders—Encyclopedias—English. WL 13]
  616.8'498003—dc23   2011045470

ISBN: 978-0-313-38664-0
EISBN: 978-0-313-38665-7

16 15 14 13 12   1 2 3 4 5

This book is also available on the World Wide Web as an eBook.
Visit www.abc-clio.com for details.

Greenwood
An Imprint of ABC-CLIO, LLC
ABC-CLIO, LLC
130 Cremona Drive, P.O. Box 1911
Santa Barbara, California 93116-1911

This book is printed on acid-free paper ∞

Manufactured in the United States of America

To Ina Livia McNamara on her fourth birthday

Contents

List of Entries

Guide to Related Topics

Many of the cross references that appear after the entries refer to the following topics and their related entries. For example, after the "Achuar" entry: **See also**: entries related to Cross-Cultural Dreams.

Animal Sleep

Comparative Sleep Regulation
Sleep and Bird Songs
Sleep in Aquatic Mammals
Sleep in Insects

Brain Stimulation

External Sensory Stimulation as a Technique to Study Dreaming
Use of Noninvasive Techniques in the Study of Dreaming

Comparative Sleep Databases

Comparative Sleep Databases
Phylogeny of Sleep Database

Consciousness and Dreams

Cognitive Expertise and Dreams
Consciousness in Dreams
Self-Consciousness and Dreaming

Cross-Cultural Dreams

Aboriginal Australia: Dreams and "the Dreaming"
Achuar
African American Dream Beliefs and Practices
Ancient Egypt and Dreams
Anthropology and Dreams
Asian Americans and Dreamwork
Bedouin Dream Traditions
Conceptions of Dreaming in the Western Desert of Australia
Co-Sleeping
Cross-Cultural Approaches to Dreams
Cultural Diversity and Dreaming
Native American Dreams
Quaker Culture and Dreams
Shamanism and Dreams
Significance of Dreams in Western Australian Desert Aboriginal Worldview
Traditional Korean Dreams

Dream Content

Animal Figures in Dreams
Central Image (of the Dream)
Characters in Dreams
Color in Dreams
Content Analysis of Dreams: Basic Principles
Counterfactuals in Dreams
Delusions and the Classification of Typical Dreams
Depictions of Dreams

Disconnection from the External Environment during Dreaming
REM Sleep across the Lifespan
Serotonin in the Regulation of REM Sleep
Sleep Intensity and the Homeostatic Regulation of Sleep

Sleep-Wake Continuum

Bizarre Imagery and Thought in Sleep and Waking
Logical Structure of Dreams and Their Relation to Reality
Subjective Experience across States of Sleep and Wakefulness

Social Psychology of Dreams

Church Dream Groups
Group Work with Dreams
Journaling of Dreams
Leading Dream Groups
Safety in Dream Groups
Social Network Analysis of Dream Content
Teaching Courses on Dreams
Television Consumption and Dreaming

Theories of Sleep

Activation Synthesis Hypothesis of Dreaming
Reverse Learning Theory

Preface

Although sleep and dreams have been studied for centuries, no fundamental break-throughs in the study of sleep and dreams occurred until 1953, when Aserinsky and Kleitman discovered and accurately described rapid eye movement, or REM, sleep. That discovery made it clear that there were two fundamental forms of sleep in humans: a classical, quiet form, and a paradoxically active form of sleep characterized by rapid movements of the eyes under the closed eyelids (thus rapid eye movement sleep), desynchronized electroencephalography (EEG) patterns, very active brain activity, autonomic nervous system storms, penile erections in males, clitoral engorgement in females, and paralysis in the antigravity muscles. The classical quiet form of sleep was subsequently called non-REM (NREM). In the decades since the landmark 1953 discovery, subsequent investigations have clarified the role of both forms of sleep in a multitude of sleep disorders and in maintenance of overall health and well-being. The field of sleep medicine was born and grew to maturity, and the study of dreams became more rigorous focusing on standardized dream content investigations and bringing to bear paradigms of the emerging technologies of the cognitive neurosciences to bear on old questions of content, function, and meaning.

We have sought in this encyclopedia to capture some of the breadth and depth of findings in all of these areas of sleep medicine and sleep and dreams research. We have sought to include representative findings from the field of sleep medicine, as well as cutting edge findings on sleep and dreams research. We have asked our authors to cite specific findings in addition to citing general principles and concepts concerning their topic. Delineation of specific findings from the sleep medicine clinic or the cognitive lab will allow the reader to draw his own conclusions in cases where knowledge is still provisional and conclusions can only be tentative.

Acknowledgments

We would like to thank Debbie Carvalko, Mike Nobel, and Christian Green for their advocacy and assistance on this enormous project. We owe a special debt of gratitude to Ms. Erica Harris who very professionally handled the huge task of coordinating correspondence with authors and tracking entries received as well as deadlines for each phase of the project. This book would not have been possible without Erica's expert help on all the things necessary in creating a book of this size and complexity. The International Association for the Study of Dreams and its conferences, publications, and Web site, www.asdreams.org, have been an invaluable resource for connecting with the dream researchers and topics covered in these volumes. And, of course, thanks to all of our entry authors.

A

Aboriginal Australia: Dreams and "the Dreaming"

Australian Aboriginal people do not generally take dreams to be subjective experiences generated by the mind or brain, but as real events in which the dreamer's spirit visits other places and meets malevolent spirits, totemic ancestors or spirits of the dead, or in which other people or spirits visit the dreamer (Glaskin, 2005). As Poirier (2003) has pointed out, this conception of dreams and dreaming contrasts with the Western view of dreams as manifestations of unconscious processes of the individual mind. Indeed, Kukatja people of the Western Desert believe that they can share in each other's dreams.

A link between the experience of dreams and cosmology in Aboriginal Australia is suggested by the English words dreaming and dreamtime to denote the ancestral era. The expressions are derived from dream times, which was a translation of the Arrernte word *altjerrenge* (in or at dream or dreaming) suggested by Baldwin Spencer and F. J. Gillen (Morphy, 1996). Aboriginal cosmogonies and cosmologies generally posit a creative ancestral period long, long ago (*baman'* in Yolngu languages) when totemic beings, often with the identities of other-than-human species and entities such as water, the sun, or rock, lived and created the conditions for subsequent human existence. They left, or were transformed into, features of the land and waters, and left behind the spirit essences that enter women to become the newly born (Munn, 1970). By no means do all Aboriginal names for the creative period relate to a word meaning dream, however. For example, *tjukurrpa* in the Kukatja language signifies the creative period while *kapukurri* means dream (Poirier, 2003). Many languages, such as Bardi, lack a specific name for the creative era but speak of ancestral events long ago (Glaskin, 2005). The idea of a connection between the experience of dreaming and contact with the spirit world is, however, widespread. Mardu people, for example, believe that a *mabarn* clever man can meet with others during dreams and protect them from harm from the spirit world; a group of dreamers accompanied by the *mabarn* may fly through the air on a raft of sacred objects.

A belief in a distinction between a person's body and spirit is very general among Aboriginal people: a spirit child enters a woman when she becomes pregnant, a person's spirit may leave the body during dreams, and the spirit leaves the body to haunt the living, travel to the totemic waterhole from whence it came or to a distant land of the dead—which in the cosmology of the Kurnai people of Gippsland is above the clouds (Howitt, 1904). It is a common belief that a spirit child will enter the wife's body when she becomes pregnant— an event that is related to dreaming. The husband or wife will encounter a spirit child in a dream or through the experience of some strange event, such as seeing a fish of extraordinary size. The event links the newly born to the place and spirit child's species (see, e.g., Tonkinson, 1984).

Dreams are also linked with the spirits of the dead. A person's soul leaves the body at death to travel to a land of the dead or return to the totemic waterhole, according to Aboriginal belief, and dreamers may encounter the dead in their dreams. Some particularly gifted individuals are thought to be able to travel in spirit in a dream and perform powerful actions such as healing the sick, visiting ancestral realms, or visiting sacred places to perform rituals. It is common for dreams to be taken post hoc as having predicted events, but Glaskin (2010) provides a striking example of the relationship of dreams to everyday activities. She reports a case in which a woman's deceased father appeared to the woman in a dream and told her that carrying photographs and hair of the dead to bring luck in card games brought torment to the dead.

In many regions, dreams are taken to be the source of revelation of designs, sacred objects, songs, and dances (e.g., Munn, 1973, p. 113). In some areas, such as Western Arnhem Land, revealed songs belong to the dreamer and may be transmitted by gift or inheritance. In others, such as northeast Arnhem Land, the Western Desert, and the Dampier Peninsula, dreamt songs have legitimacy only when accepted into the corpus of a group's ritual (Keen, 2003). Bardi people assert that revealed songs and designs are not new, but ones that the ancestors have not previously revealed (Glaskin, 2005). Thus it is not the case that

there is no innovation in ritual, but rather that innovation is ascribed to revelation from the totemic ancestors, ghosts of the dead, or other beings. Tiwi people of Melville and Bathurst Islands differ from the general pattern, however, in attributing innovation in the design of burial poles to individual creativity (Goodale, 2003, p. 162). Revelation may take other forms: young men, for example, may claim that the meaning of totemic symbolism was revealed to them during a daydream or reverie (Keen, 2004).

In these and other ways, dreams in Aboriginal Australia link the individual to other people, to religion and ritual, and to cosmology.

Ian Keen

See also: entries related to Cross-Cultural Dreams

References

Glaskin, K. (2005). Innovation and ancestral revelation: The case of dreams. *Journal of the Royal Anthropological Institute, 11,* 297–314.

Glaskin, K. (2010). On dreams, innovation, and the emerging genre of the individual artist. *Anthropological Forum, 20*(3), 251–267.

Goodale, J. (2003). Tiwi Island dreams. In R. Lohmann (Ed.), *Dream travelers: Sleep experiences and culture in the Western Pacific* (pp. 149–167). New York: Palgrave Macmillan.

Howitt, A.W. (1904). *The native tribes of South-east Australia.* London: Macmillan and Co.

Keen, I. (2003). Dreams, agency and traditional authority in northeast Arnhem Land. In R. Lohmann (Ed.), *Dream travelers: Sleep experiences and culture in the Western Pacific* (pp. 127–147). New York: Palgrave Macmillan.

Keen, I. (2004). *Knowledge and secrecy in an Aboriginal religion: Yolngu of Northeast Arnhem Land*. Oxford, UK: Clarendon Press.

Morphy, H. (1996). From empiricism to metaphysics: In defence of the concept of the dreamtime. In T. Bonyhady & T. Griffiths (Eds.), *Prehistory to politics: John Mulvaney, the humanities and the public intellectual*. Carlton Victoria, Australia: Melbourne University Press.

Munn, N. (1970). The transformation of subjects into objects in Walbiri and Pitjantjatjara myth. In R. M. Berndt (Ed.), *Australian Aboriginal anthropology* (pp. 141–163). Nedlands: University of Western Australia Press.

Munn, N. (1973). *Walbiri iconography: Graphic representation and cultural symbolism in a Central Australian Society*. Ithaca, NY: Cornell University Press.

Poirier, S. (2003). This is good country. We are good dreamers. In R. Lohmann (Ed.), *Dream travelers: Sleep experiences and culture in the Western Pacific* (pp. 107–125). New York: Palgrave Macmillan.

Tonkinson, R. (1984). Semen versus spirit-child in a Western Desert culture. In M. Charlesworth, H. Morphy, D. Bell, & K. Maddock (Eds.), *Religion in Aboriginal Australia: An anthology* (pp. 107–123). Brisbane: University of Queensland Press.

Achuar

The Achuar are an indigenous people living in the rain forests of southeastern Ecuador, near the border with Peru. Closely related to two neighboring tribes, the Shuar and the Shiwiar, the Achuar lived in relative isolation from the outside world until the latter part of the 20th century. As a result, their dream-based culture has survived in its traditional form, though the survival of the tribe is now being threatened by the destruction of the rain forest.

Dreams are central to the worldview of the Achuar. Daily life is built on dream sharing (*wayusa*). Each morning, several hours before dawn, the adults gather in small groups in family households to drink an herbal infusion called *wayús*, a mild stimulant. After a ritual purging, both men and women take turns sharing their dreams, which will affect the decisions they make and shape their waking activities. Children tell their dreams, too, but learn how to understand their meaning by listening to the elders, who have seniority over the interpretation.

The Achuar distinguish different types of dreams, including dreams that foretell future events; dreams that announce a successful hunt; dreams that presage illness, conflict, or misfortune; and dreams in which spirits, ancestors, or absent relatives communicate important messages for the tribe. Because they believe that individuals dream not only for themselves but also for the community, some dreams are taken to the tribal elders or the shaman for further interpretation. The Achuar also distinguish night dreams from vision-dreams, which are induced by ingesting hallucinogenic plants, including *ayahuasca*. Vision-dreams are considered sacred and are always shared with the community.

The close interrelation between dream life and waking life implicit in the practice of *wayusa* runs through Achuar life. Since actions are shaped by the information given in dreams, the failure of some predictive dreams to come true is taken as indication that the correct course of action was not followed.

Today, the survival of the Achuar and their traditional way of life is threatened by the encroachment of Western civilization and the destruction of the rain forest. Prompted by their dreams, the Achuar sought partnership with outsiders sympathetic to their plight, which resulted in the creation of the Pachamama Alliance, whose mission is to "empower indigenous people of the Amazon rainforest to preserve their lands and culture."

Richard A. Russo

See also: entries related to Cross-Cultural Dreams

References

Barber, S. (2003). Amazon tribes and collective dreams: Interview with Marilyn Schlitz. *Spirit of Ma'atSpirit of Ma'atSpirit of Ma'atSpirit of Ma'at*

Descola, P. (1996). *The spears of twilight: Life and death in the Amazon Jungle* (Trans. from French by Janet Lloyd). London: Harper Collins.

Pachamama Alliance. (n.d.). Retrieved from http://www.pachamama.org/

Schlitz, M. (1998, Spring). Amazon dreaming. *Noetic Sciences Review*.

Schlitz, M., & Pascoe, F. The Achuar dream practices. Mystic Mountain Center for Healing Arts. Retrieved from http://www.mysticalcompany.com/Achuar.php

Actigraphy and Sleep

The term *actigraphy* refers to the monitoring and collection of data produced by movement. Actigraphy devices contain accelerometers that measure acceleration due to movement. Data can be collected continuously for one week or more. Devices vary depending on manufacturer by modes of operation, length of recording, two or three axes of detection, and levels of sensitivity. In most devices, the detected movements are translated into digital counts across predetermined epoch intervals and stored into device memory.

Actigraphy has received much attention in recent years because of its simplicity of use and utility outside of a sleep lab for studying sleep quality. The acceptance of actigraphy into sleep research and sleep medicine was initiated by the commission of the American Sleep Disorders Association (ASDA) task force that evaluated the role of actigraphy and resulted in a report and guidelines for use of actigraphy in sleep (American Sleep Disorders Association [ASDA], 1995).

Although actigraphy cannot be used to specifically diagnose sleep disorders, it has been used over the years for both research and clinical purposes to determine an individual's sleep–wake cycles and circadian sleep rhythms and to evaluate the severity of insomnia (Ancoli-Israel et al., 2003). Actigraphy is not the gold standard for studying sleep, because the history of sleep research has revolved around the ability to determine sleep staging through electroencephalography, muscle activity, and heart rate, together known as polysomnography (International Classification of Sleep Disorders, 2005). There are various problems that present themselves in polysomnographic studies of sleep. First, polysomnography is very expensive, as it involves complex technology, an overnight hospital stay, and a technician who is hired to spend the night monitoring the patient. Second, overnight sleep studies are quite burdensome to the patient who is required to sleep in a hospital bed with various electrodes attached to him or her, as bodily functions are monitored (Riedel, Winfield, & Lichstein, 2001). Finally, polysomnography often lacks ecologic validity as few patients report sleeping the same in the lab as they do at home; further, it is difficult to capture a patient's true sleep patterns in a single-night study. Actigraphy enables multiple-night recording, allowing for a more thorough investigation of sleep patterns, in comparison to polysomnography, which is limited to one or two nights because of the reasons stated previously. In this view, actigraphy may be a viable alternative to polysomnography as it has been found to be a reliable method of determining sleep and wake time (Van de Water, Holmes, & Hurley, 2010).

Reliability and validity studies in healthy adults have shown that actigraphy is highly correlated with polysomnography for differentiating sleep from wake states and for measuring sleep fragmentation and sleep-efficiency variables (Blood, Sack, Percy, & Pen, 1997; Jean-Louis et al., 1996). The original ASDA report found that for laboratory-based studies validity estimates of sleep duration using actigraphy are relatively high. Most recent studies have come to similar conclusions. The major drawback of actigraphy has been found in populations for whom nighttime awakenings are frequent, such as those of patients with insomnia, and quiet wakefulness has been coded as sleep. Detailed documentation using sleep diaries and more sensitive/precise scoring algorithms in recent years have lead to greater improvement of sleep scoring using actigraphy. In older adults, actigraphy has been shown to have good validity but does vary depending on the individual's general health status. However, even in those older adults who are demented, actigraphy has shown good accuracy when validated with polysomnography. Normative studies using actigraphy have been undertaken in various populations including infants and children; aging populations; and individuals with breathing-related disorders, insomnia, periodic leg movements, and shift-work disorders (Ancoli-Israel et al., 2003). There have been few studies examining the accuracy of actigraphy in other clinical populations such as in individuals with psychiatric conditions and with neurological disorders. Given the frequency of sleep disturbances in these populations, in more recent years, studies have begun to use actigraphy more frequently to examine sleep-related factors. For example, in those with Parkinson's disease (PD), sleep problems are extremely common. In PD, actigraphy has been used to study the impact of dopamine agonists on sleep (Comella, Morrissey, & Janko, 2005; van Hilten et al., 1993, 1994), the efficacy of melatonin on improving sleep onset and circadian sleep drive (Dowling et al., 2005), and nocturnal motor activity (Nass & Nass, 2008). Actigraphy in PD has also been used to demonstrate improvement of sleep efficiency and decrease in sleep fragmentation after treatment with transcranial magnetic stimulation (van Dijk, Most, Van Someren, Berendse, & van der Werf, 2009). Only one study has examined the validity of actigraphy in PD, by comparing sleep-quality measures to those self-reported by the patient, and found that actigraphic measures of sleep were highly correlated with subjective measures of sleep (Stavitsky, Saurman, McNamara, & Cronin-Golomb, 2010).

In summary, actigraphy is gaining attention in the sleep-medicine and sleep-research field as an ambulatory method of recording sleep that allows for longer-term, less-intrusive recording of sleep–wake activity. It has been used to examine sleep–wake patterns in various clinical populations and has shown good validity in many of these when compared with polysomnography. Ambulatory monitoring companies are constantly working on improving the algorithm for differentiating sleep from wake states to improve the accuracy of actigraphy recording. Clinical and research studies need to continue the investigation of the utility of actigraphy in a variety of clinical populations, in particular those with psychiatric conditions and neurological disorders. The usefulness of actigraphy for medical interventions and for use in individuals who are unable to spend a night in the sleep lab is particularly important.

Karina Stavitsky

See also: Basics of Sleep Recordings; entries related to Sleep Assessment

References

American Sleep Disorders Association (ASDA). (1995). Practice parameters for the use of actigraphy in the clinical assessment of sleep disorders. *Sleep, 18*(4), 285–287.

Ancoli-Israel, S., Cole, R., Alessi, C., Chambers, M., Moorcroft, W., & Pollak, C. P. (2003). The role of actigraphy in the study of sleep and circadian rhythms. *Sleep, 26*(3), 342–392.

Blood, M. L., Sack, R. L., Percy, D. C., & Pen, J. C. (1997). A comparison of sleep

detection by wrist actigraphy, behavioral response, and polysomnography. *Sleep, 20*(6), 388–395.

Comella, C. L., Morrissey, M., & Janko, K. (2005). Nocturnal activity with nighttime pergolide in Parkinson disease: A controlled study using actigraphy. *Neurology, 64*(8), 1450–1451.

Dowling, G. A., Mastick, J., Colling, E., Carter, J. H., Singer, C. M., & Aminoff, M. J. (2005). Melatonin for sleep disturbances in Parkinson's disease. *Sleep Medicine, 6*(5), 459–466.

International Classification of Sleep Disorders. (2005). *International classification of sleep disorders: Diagnostic and coding manual* (2nd ed.). Westerchester, IL: American Academy of Sleep Medicine.

Jean-Louis, G., von Gizycki, H., Zizi, F., Fookson, J., Spielman, A., Nunes, J., . . . Taub, H. (1996). Determination of sleep and wakefulness with the actigraph data analysis software (ADAS). *Sleep, 19*(9), 739–743.

Nass, A., & Nass, R. D. (2008). Actigraphic evidence for night-time hyperkinesia in Parkinson's disease. *International Journal of Neuroscience, 118*(2), 291–310.

Riedel, B. W., Winfield, C. F., & Lichstein, K. L. (2001). First night effect and reverse first night effect in older adults with primary insomnia: Does anxiety play a role? *Sleep Medicine, 2*(2), 125–133.

Stavitsky, K., Saurman, J. L., McNamara, P., & Cronin-Golomb, A. (2010). Sleep in Parkinson's disease: A comparison of actigraphy and subjective measures. *Parkinsonism & Related Disorders, 164,* 280–283.

Van de Water, A. T., Holmes, A., & Hurley, D. A. (2010, March 30). Objective measurements of sleep for non-laboratory settings as alternatives to polysomnography—a systematic review. *Journal of Sleep Research.*

van Dijk, K. D., Most, E. I., Van Someren, E. J., Berendse, H. W., & van der Werf, Y. D. (2009). Beneficial effect of transcranial magnetic stimulation on sleep in

Parkinson's disease. Movement Disorders, 24(6), 878–884.

van Hilten, B., Hoff, J. I., Middelkoop, H. A., van der Velde, E. A., Kerkhof, G. A., Wauquier, A., . . . Roos, R. A. (1994). Sleep disruption in Parkinson's disease: Assessment by continuous activity monitoring. *Archives of Neurology*, 51(9), 922–928.

van Hilten, J. J., Kabel, J. F., Middelkoop, H. A., Kramer, C. G., Kerkhof, G. A., & Roos, R. A. (1993). Assessment of response fluctuations in Parkinson's disease by ambulatory wrist activity monitoring. *Acta Neurologica Scandinavica*, 87(3), 171–177.

Activation Synthesis Hypothesis of Dreaming

Based on our observations of neuronal activity in cats, Robert McCarley and J. Allan Hobson formulated the activation synthesis hypothesis of dreaming in 1975 and first published a detailed account of this theory in 1977. Originally designed to contrast critically with Sigmund Freud's disguise censorship theory of dreams, activation synthesis has since evolved in light of subsequent findings at both the neurophysiological and psychological levels, but the essence of the model is unchanged. In this entry, I will sketch the origin and subsequent development of the activation synthesis idea and conclude with the suggestion that it can now help us move beyond Freud in the understanding of consciousness itself.

Activation

The fundamental concept is that cognitive activation is the direct and unaltered expression of brain activation. In this sense, activation synthesis has kinship with Anderson's ACT * model, a generally accepted notion of brain–mind isomorphism in the understanding of waking cognition. Similarity of form is thus assumed by activation synthesis to link the physiological and psychological domains. The undesirable vestiges of Cartesian dualism are thus avoided and, with them, the Freudian assumption of defensive transformation of mind-to-mind or brain-to-mind information. From a philosophical point of view, activation synthesis is a proud example of neutral monism, which asserts that brain and mind are two sides of the same coin, where one side is objective (the brain) and the other side is subjective (the mind). Dissociation is possible, however, and one should avoid the trap of identity theory (see the entry on "Functional Theories of Dreaming").

Activation of the brain–mind is a clear manifestation of Eugene Aserinsky and Nathaniel Kleitman's (1953) discovery of rapid eye movement (REM) sleep and its correlation with dreaming. As such, it is uncontroversial. But Foulkes's (1962) discovery of dreaming in non-REM sleep raised still-unresolved questions about this idea. Neurophysiological evidence clearly supports the concept of diminished but still substantial residual brain activation even in deep sleep Stages 3 and 4 (when the brain is 50% to 80% active), so it should come as no surprise that some form of mental activity may persist even in the depths of sleep. Added to this fact is the long transition period between waking, non-REM, and REM sleep, leading Mark Mahowald and Carlos H. Schenck (1999) to posit state dissociations and Tore Nielsen (2000) to suggest that covert REM sleep processes may contribute to non-REM dreaming.

These subtleties notwithstanding, it is important to recognize that the relationship between brain and mind activation is quantitative, not qualitative. This fact is both acknowledged and accounted for in the three-dimensional activation–input–modulation model, a descendent of activation synthesis, which was formulated in 1990. The correlation between REM and dreaming remains robust, however, and REM sleep remains the most favorable physiological substrate for hallucinoid dreaming (see following text for definitions of different forms of dreaming).

Since the seminal work of Foulkes, most authors have accepted the correlation of REM sleep brain activation with internally generated and vivid visuomotor perception, with the delusional conviction that the dreamer is awake despite gross orientational instability (commonly recognized as dream bizarreness), with the scenario-like narrative construction of dream experience, and with memory impairment within and upon awakening from REM sleep dreams. By contrast non-REM sleep mentation is relatively more thought-like, more perseverative, and more impoverished.

Recently, the development of imaging techniques has advanced the activation argument by showing brain regional differences in blood flow during REM and non-REM sleep. While non-REM sleep manifests global inactivation, REM sleep reveals a striking and meaningful combination of activation and inactivation of brain regions. Most interestingly, the pontine tegmentum, forebrain emotion centers, and the parietal operculum of the cerebral cortex are turned on (isomorphic to the perceptual and emotional intensification of REM sleep dreams) while the frontal cortex is turned off (isomorphic to the deficits in thinking, insight, and memory of REM sleep dreaming).

Synthesis

In our original model, it was asserted that the brain makes the best of a bad job in fabricating dreams from the relatively noisy information sent up to it from the brain stem.

Today, I would still suppose this element to be a factor in creating dream chaos, but I would add that aminergic demodulation contributes to this impairment of cognitive synthesis. I would also emphasize that raw emotions (especially anxiety, elation, and anger) shape forebrain synthetic processes in such a way as to make dreaming salient as well as chaotic. To this crucial point, I would add that I never suggested that dreams were entirely meaningless, only that dreams reveal, rather than conceal meaning. Furthermore, it could just be that the hyperassociative quality of dreaming signals the reorganization of memory despite our difficulty in recalling the process by which it is achieved.

Studies of dream mentation take advantage of physiology insofar as they are formal. Dream-content analysis is inappropriate if one is hoping to advance the cause of brain–mind correspondence. For example, it is to be emphasized that one sees and moves (rather than exactly what one sees or how one moves), that one fails to reason (rather than what it is that escapes cognitive analysis), and that one forgets almost everything unless one awakens from REM without moving. (See the entry on "Functional Theories of Dreaming" for additional consideration of these points). The formal analysis of dream consciousness (and waking consciousness for that matter) is in its infancy and promises to be enlightening for decades to come.

Summary and Conclusions

The activation-synthesis theory of dreaming, originally designed to contrast critically with the disguise-censorship paradigm of Sigmund Freud, is now poised not only to help scientists understand the brain basis of dreaming but also to abet progress in the psychophysiological study of consciousness itself.

J. Allan Hobson

See also: Functional Theories of Dreaming

References

Anderson, J.R., Bothell, D., Byrne, M.D., Douglass, S., Lebiere, C., & Qin, Y. (2004). An integrated theory of the mind. *Psychological Review, 111*(4), 1036–1060.

Aserinsky, E., & Kleitman, N. (1953). Regularly occurring periods of ocular motility and concomitant phenomena during sleep. *Science, 118,* 361–375.

Foulkes, W.D. (1962). Dream reports from different stages of sleep. *Journal of Abnormal and Social Psychology, 65,* 14–25.

Hobson, J.A. (1990). Activation, input source, and modulation: A neurocognitive model of the state of the brain-mind. In R. Bootzin, J. Kihlstrom, & D. Schacter (Eds.), *Sleep and cognition* (pp. 25–40). Washington, DC: American Psychological Association.

Mahowald, M., & Schenck, C.H. (1999). Dissociated states of wakefulness and sleep. In R. Lydic & H.A. Baghdoyan (Eds.), *Handbook of behavioral state control: Molecular and cellular mechanisms* (pp. 143–158). Boca Raton, FL: CRC Press.

Nielsen, T.A. (2000). A review of mentation in REM and NREM sleep: "Covert" REM sleep as a possible reconciliation of two opposing models. *Behavioral and Brain Sciences, 23*(6), 851–866.

Acute Sleep Deprivation

Sleep deprivation refers to wakefulness that is extended beyond the 16 hours that is considered a normal day. Acute sleep deprivation is a single episode of extended wakefulness. Chronic partial sleep deprivation is covered in another section (see the entry "Partial Sleep Deprivation"). The degree of sleep loss can vary from just extending the wakefulness part of the way into the night (so that total wake time would be between 16 and 23 hours) to total deprivation of sleep for one or more nights. Most research with total sleep deprivation has examined changes in function after one or two nights without sleep, but some studies and observations exist from humans who have been awake for up to 10 days. Understanding of sleep loss is important because it is a common occurrence and also because extending wakefulness is a major tool in understanding the function of sleep (Bonnet, 2010).

Behavioral Effects

The initial sign of acute sleep deprivation is sleepiness that becomes increasingly persistent as time awake accumulates. This sleepiness can be quantified subjectively, by using nap tests, or by observing the ability to maintain performance on a number of tasks. Figure 1 plots sleepiness, as measured by time to fall asleep in a nap, across two nights and days awake. In general, sleepiness, as measured by all of these means, increases as time awake increases but is also modulated by time of day (circadian time). It can be seen that sleepiness increases rapidly between 1 and 7 A.M. but then decreases across the normal daytime until just before the normal time of going to bed. This same pattern repeats at an increased level of sleepiness on the next night. Performance of many tasks that include components of reaction time, attention, or memory follows a similar pattern (Pilcher & Huffcutt, 1996). Effects are more extreme on long or boring tasks. On these tasks, momentary lapses in attention called *microsleeps* occur with increasing regularity as time awake increases. However, loss of performance may be less on tasks that are interesting, motivating, or contain a challenge. Recently, loss of performance has also been shown on executive tasks, which require complex thinking or creativity.

Arousal Influences

Environmental factors such as activity, drugs, social interaction, bright light, noise, posture, and stress can modulate the level of sleepiness. Most individuals use these sources of arousal increasingly as wake time accumulates to attempt to balance the increasing pressure for sleep. It becomes

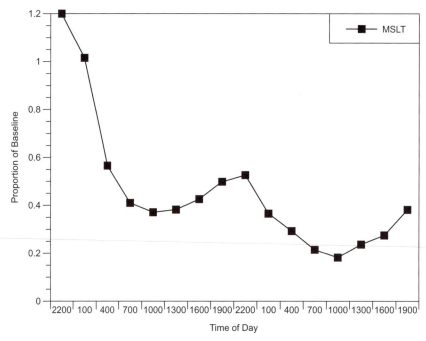

Figure 1: Latency to sleep in relation to baseline during 64 hours of sleep deprivation. Adapted from Bonnet, M.H., et al. (1995). *The use of caffeine versus prophylactic naps in sustained performance* (Vol. 18, pp. 97–104).

very difficult to keep a person awake even by the end of the first night of total sleep deprivation if the person is kept inactive in the dark. While manipulations such as standing up or walking can improve alertness acutely, such effects dissipate after individuals have been sedentary for a while. Caffeine or other stimulants such as modafinil, armodafinil, amphetamine, or methylphenidate are sometimes used to maintain wakefulness for longer periods of time. Caffeine and other stimulants are effective in reducing sleepiness and improving performance on many tasks that require attention or rapid responses. However, the stimulants may be less effective on tasks that require complex or creative responses. The length of medication benefit depends on active life and dose. This implies that benefits from caffeine, while continuing for three to five hours, may be shorter than those from some prescription medications.

As stimulants can improve alertness during sleep deprivation, sedatives, such as alcohol, can potentiate the effects of sleep deprivation. The effects of alcohol on response speed and driving are similar to the effects associated with sleep deprivation such that performance is decreased by a similar amount near the end of one night of total sleep deprivation as from a blood alcohol level of 0.05 to 0.08 percent (legal criterion for drunken driving) (Williamson & Feyer, 2000).

Physiological Influences

Many types of physiological function have been measured during total sleep loss in humans and animals. Changes in humans have generally been relatively small and are easily reversed when sleep resumes. Changes in function in small animals are quite different and are discussed in more detail in a separate section on animal models of sleep deprivation. In humans, there is probably a small overall decrease in body temperature and some change in hormone excretion related to continuing activity. Other more stress-related changes become apparent in chronic partial sleep-loss paradigms.

Individual Differences

Recent studies have shown that some individuals appear more sensitive to sleep deprivation than others and that these individuals may have a different genetic composition (Viola et al., 2007). It also appears that older individuals may be less sensitive to accumulating sleepiness during the night as compared with young adults.

Recovery

Sleep is all that is needed to reverse the negative effects of acute sleep deprivation in humans. The first night of recovery sleep is typically longer and contains increased deep sleep as compared with normal sleep. However, total sleep time on this night may be no more than 12 to 14 hours even after extended total sleep deprivation. REM sleep also increases above baseline levels, but this is more common on the second or following nights of recovery sleep, particularly in young adults.

Michael H. Bonnet

See also: Partial Sleep Deprivation; entries related to Sleep Assessment

References

Bonnet, M.H. (2010). Acute sleep deprivation. In M. Kryger, T. Roth, & W.C. Dement (Eds.), *Principles and practice of sleep medicine*. Philadelphia: Saunders.

Bonnet, M.H., Gomez, S., Wirth, O., & Arand, D.L. (1995). The use of caffeine versus prophylactic naps in sustained performance. *Sleep, 18,* 97–104.

Pilcher, J.J., & Huffcutt, A.I. (1996). Effects of sleep deprivation on performance: A meta-analysis. *Sleep, 19,* 318–326.

Viola, A.U., Archer, S.N., James, L.M., Groeger, J.A., Lo, J.C.Y., Skene, D.J., . . . Dijk, D.J. (2007). PER3 polymorphism predicts sleep structure and waking performance. *Current Biology, 17,* 613–618.

Williamson, A.M., & Feyer, A.M. (2000). Moderate sleep deprivation produces impairments in cognitive and motor performance equivalent to legally prescribed levels of alcohol intoxication. *Occupatioal and Environmental Medicine, 57,* 649–655.

Adolescent Cell Phone Use and Sleep

Children's bedrooms have become multimedia rooms. In their rooms, they have access to the Internet, to game computers, to music, and to television. Parents are becoming increasingly aware of the potential dangers to healthy sleep posed by these attractive, but time consuming, devices. Because cell phones are not mass media (they are commonly used for person-to-person communication), they have largely escaped notice.

A study of 1,656 Flemish 13- and 17-year olds, who were observed for a year, showed that 62 percent used their mobile phone after lights out at least occasionally. The majority used their phone right after lights out, although it went on until 3 A.M. in about a fifth and all through the night in another fifth. The risk of being very tired throughout the day increased dramatically with the use of the phone. The study attributed 35 percent of the incident cases of those scoring high on a tiredness score to the nightly use of the mobile phone (Van den Bulck, 2007).

Adolescents use their mobile phone at night for making and receiving calls and for sending and receiving text messages. This behavior is extremely difficult to police because it can be done with little or no noise. There are other popular uses of the mobile phone that do not show up on phone bills and that are therefore very hard for parents to detect. The simplest form is called ringing. One adolescent dials another's number and interrupts the call the moment the connection is made. This produces a missed call message, which is a way of saying "I was thinking of you" (Prezza, Pacilli, & Dinelli, 2004). Bombing is a practice whereby the number of times the phone rings is used to send prearranged messages. A missed call at a certain hour may mean "what time do you leave for school?" The number of rings before the responder hangs up may signal the number of quarters of an hour after a prearranged time, for example, three rings means 8:45 (Oksman & Turtiainen, 2004). All kinds of combinations may occur, sometimes including chain messages to certain groups of friends. Oksman and Turtiainen (2004) found similar patterns in different European countries, suggesting that these behaviors are common among adolescents in many cultures.

More and more young people get a mobile phone, and they do so at younger ages. More research is needed to understand what kinds of needs are being gratified by the behaviors they display at night. Given that Van den Bulck (2007) believes there is no safe dose and no safe time for mobile phone use at night, parents and caregivers should be made aware of the potential impact of this device. Future research should study whether and how parents try to police the use of their children's phones and which types of guidance achieve the most. Research on other forms of media use suggests that restricting media use is the least effective form of guidance.

Mobile phones have become multimedia platforms giving access to movies, television, computer games, and music. Apart from the threat they pose as nightly communication devices, they are likely to magnify the effects of the entertainment media on sleep. Whichever other threat the mass media currently pose for sleep will start to be channeled by the mobile phone at increasing rates. It is therefore hard to underestimate the impact of this little device.

Jan Van den Bulck

See also: Increasing Sleep Complaints

References

Oksman, V., & Turtiainen, J. (2004). Mobile communication as a social change. *New Media & Society, 6,* 319–339.

Prezza, M., Pacilli, M. G., & Dinelli, S. (2004). Loneliness and new technologies in a group of Roman adolescents. *Computers in Human Behavior, 20,* 691–709.

Van den Bulck, J. (2007). Adolescent use of mobile phones for calling and for sending text messages after lights out: Results from a prospective cohort study with a one-year follow-up. *Sleep, 30,* 1220–1223.

Adolescent Dreams

Adolescence covers the second decade of a human's life, occurring between puberty (at around 12) and the beginning of emerging adulthood (18 to 20). Neuropsychology research shows that the brain continues its development, differently in males and females, throughout young adulthood (20 to 30). From a developmental psychology perspective, the study of dreams considers the specific features of dreams during each stage of a human's life.

Beginning with the longitudinal studies carried out by Foulkes (1982) from childhood to adolescence (up to 15), a number of studies on the typical contents of dreams in adolescence used Hall and Van de Castle's method (Avila-White, Schneider, & Domhoff, 1999; Domhoff, 1996), combined with the study of the relationship between daydream and dreams (Strauch & Meier, 1996).

Empirical research shows that adolescents' capacity to remember dreams (and to describe them in a laboratory setting) is similar to adults. The length of the report of dreams progressively increases during adolescence and females tend to produce longer reports. Some content of dreams remains the same throughout childhood, adolescence, and adulthood. Constants include the distribution of indoor and outdoor settings and the percentage of male and female characters. By contrast, other elements of dreams do change with development.

Between adolescence and adulthood, dreams become more complex: interactions between the characters in dreams increase and the dreamer becomes more involved, active, and interactive. The occurrence of unrealistic content, imaginary characters, and animals decreases. A remarkable change involves the decrease in aggression in general and physical assault in particular, and situations where the dreamer is the victim of an assault, while at the same time anxiety tends to decrease in favor of anger. During the first phase of adolescence, it is common to experience dreams in which a success is achieved, especially among boys (e.g., winning a sport competition). In the second phase of adolescence, there is an increase in the number of dreams involving failure or trying to do something with no success. Such data show that throughout adolescence, while the dreamer feels less threatened and under attack, a sense of agency is achieved, even though it often takes the shape of obstacles or inability to carry out an activity.

Even though during adolescence gender identity and an individual sexual self are defined, sexual content in dreams is rare. Sexual content progressively increases but remains less frequent than aggressive content.

Concerning gender issues, boys' dreams are usually less complex than girls'. Girls are more creative in the structure of their dreams. Boys catch up and achieve the same ability a few years later. The characters of boys' dreams tend to be male peers, while the dreams of girls more frequently include males and other familiar people, including family members. Girls dream more often about school and family relationships (in particular the relationship with their mothers), while boys dream more often about success, performance, and tests of their competences, often in group, with behaviors anticipating adulthood (such as driving a car) and with a higher prevalence of aggressive contents (Maggiolini, Azzone, Provantini, Viganò, & Freni, 2003).

Adolescent dreams develop in parallel with changes in daily life. For instance, as boys' aggressive behavior decreases, aggressive content in dreams also diminishes. However, it is important to emphasize that in dreams passivity, impotence, and bewilderment are relevant, while daily reports describe more friendly relationships and situations where the adolescent is more active.

Future research, from a developmental psychopathology perspective, could explore changes in dreams occurring in the first and second phases of adolescence and in both phases of young adulthood, that of emerging adulthood (20 to 25), and consolidating adulthood (25 to 30), both informing how dreams develop through such phases and as a basis for a comparison with other phases of a human's life. Another interesting trend of the research will study neuropsychological development in adolescence and the development in the contents of dreams.

Alfio Maggiolini

References

Avila-White, D., Schneider, A., & Domhoff, G. W. (1999). The most recent dreams of 12–13 year-old boys and girls: A methodological contribution to the study of dream content in teenagers, *Dreaming, 9,* 163–171.

Domhoff, G. W. (1996). *Finding meaning in dreams: A quantitative approach.* New York: Plenum Press.

Foulkes, D. (1982). *Children dreams: Longitudinal studies.* New York: Wiley-Interscience.

Maggiolini, A., Azzone, P., Provantini, K., Viganò, D., & Freni, S. (2003). The words of adolescents dreams. A quantitative analysis. *Dreaming, 13*(2), 107–117.

Strauch, I., & Meier, B. (1996). *In search of dreams: Results of experimental dream research.* Albany: State University of New York Press.

Adolescent Sleep, the Electroencephalogram, and Brain Development

Teenagers and their parents are all too familiar with changing sleep habits during adolescence. Adolescents shorten their sleep period during the week and extend sleep on the weekend. The reduction in sleep duration is accompanied by electroencephalogram (EEG) changes that provide information about brain maturation during this critical period of human development.

During adolescence, bedtimes become later with age. In our longitudinal study of sleep and EEG changes across adolescence, average school night bedtime advanced from 9 P.M. at age 9 to 11 P.M. at age 17 (Feinberg & Campbell, 2010, pp. 56–65). The later bedtimes produce a shorter sleep period because rise times, largely determined by school start times, either do not change or become earlier. A recent meta-analysis of studies from 20 different countries found that average weekday sleep time decreases by 14 minutes per year between 9 and 18 years of age (Olds,

Blunden, Petkov, & Forchino, 2010, pp. 371–378). Although this decline is true for adolescents internationally, there are geographic differences in sleep duration, with adolescents in Asian countries sleeping about an hour less than American teens and nearly two hours less than their European and Australian counterparts (Olds et al., 2010, pp. 371–378). This weekday–sleep time reduction across adolescence is accompanied by increasing sleep extension on the weekends from about 1/2 an hour at age 9 to about 1-1/2 hours at age 18 (Olds et al., 2010, pp. 371–378).

The delay in bedtime and the preference for later rise times seen on weekends are indicators of a circadian phase delay in adolescents. This delay is further evident hormonally in the daily rhythms of melatonin release and behaviorally in adolescents' preference for later timing of activities (Carskadon, Acebo, & Jenni, 2004, pp. 276–291). It is not yet clear whether this phase delay is produced by endogenous alterations of the circadian timing systems of the brain or by changing environmental factors such as relaxed parental control and increasing scholastic and social demands.

In adolescence, the EEG during sleep changes even more dramatically than does sleep schedule. Sleep scientists are particularly interested in the slow-wave EEG that characterizes the deeper stages of nonrapid eye movement sleep because these waves are thought to reflect a restorative process that counteracts the effects of waking-brain activity. Early cross-sectional studies showed that slow-wave EEG activity decreases across late childhood and adolescence (Feinberg & Campbell, 2010, pp. 56–65). A recent longitudinal study has firmly established the timing and trajectory of this decrease (Feinberg & Campbell, 2010, pp. 56–65). EEG activity in the 1–4 Hz frequency band is maintained at late childhood levels until it begins to decline around 11 or 12 years of age. Slow-wave activity then drops by 66 percent by age 17, when the rate of decline begins to slow. Slow-wave activity continues to decline during adulthood, but the reduction in the six years of adolescence far exceeds the drop over the remainder of life. It has been proposed that the adolescent decline in slow-wave activity represents a late brain maturation produced by synaptic pruning. Connections between brain cells overproliferate in early childhood, and during adolescence these excess synapses are trimmed. Synaptic pruning would decrease slow-wave EEG activity by shrinking the size of neuronal populations that oscillate in unison during deep sleep and also by decreasing the need for sleep-dependent recuperation via a reduction of the brain activity during waking. The parallel ontogenetic curves of slow-wave EEG activity, synaptic density, and waking cerebral metabolic rate support this proposal (Feinberg, Thode, Chugani, & March, 1990, pp. 149–161).

In high school classrooms, the adolescent asleep with his head on his desk is a far too common sight. The increase in daytime sleepiness across adolescence is typically attributed to inadequate nighttime sleep duration. However, adolescent brain maturation also contributes to daytime sleepiness. A ground-breaking study found that an objective measure of daytime sleepiness was higher in a group of older adolescents than in less mature adolescents even when time in bed was held constant at 10 hours for both groups (Carskadon et al., 1980, pp. 453–460). In our longitudinal study, the increase in subjective daytime sleepiness ratings was related to the brain maturation reflected in the slow-wave EEG decline even when changes in sleep schedule and duration were statistically controlled (Feinberg & Campbell, 2010, pp. 56–65). We proposed that, in younger children, high waking-brain activity produces a high arousal level precluding daytime sleepiness and that, in adolescents, declining waking-brain activity allows daytime sleepiness to emerge. Thus, adolescents are biologically susceptible to daytime sleepiness, and insufficient sleep only exacerbates the problem.

Sleep deficiencies in adolescence are associated with emotional, behavioral, and health problems. Furthermore, reduced sleep duration is related to poorer scholastic performance (Carskadon et al., 2004, pp. 276–291). Most alarmingly, sleepiness affects teenagers' driving skills already impaired by inexperience and risk taking. The 8.5 to 9.25 hours of sleep per night recommended by The National Sleep Foundation of the United States may not be appropriate for all adolescents, but sleepiness that impacts daytime performance certainly reflects a need for additional nighttime sleep.

Ian G. Campbell

See also: Basics of Sleep Recordings; entries related to Sleep Assessment

References

Carskadon, M. A., Acebo, C., & Jenni, O. G. (2004). Regulation of adolescent sleep: Implications for behavior. *Annals of the New York Academy of Sciences, 1021,* 276–291.

Carskadon, M. A., Harvey, K., Duke, P., Anders, T. F., Litt, I. F., & Dement, W. C. (1980). Pubertal changes in daytime sleepiness. *Sleep, 2,* 453–460.

Feinberg, I., & Campbell, I.G. (2010). Sleep EEG changes during adolescence: An index of a fundamental brain reorganization. *Brain and Cognition, 72,* 56–65.

Feinberg, I., Thode, H.C., Jr., Chugani, H.T., & March, J.D. (1990). Gamma distribution model describes maturational curves for delta wave amplitude, cortical metabolic rate and synaptic density. *Journal of Theoretical Biology,* 142, 149–161.

Olds, T., Blunden, S., Petkov, J., & Forchino, F. (2010). The relationships between sex, age, geography and time in bed in adolescents: A meta-analysis of data from 23 countries. *Sleep Medicine Reviews, 14,* 371–378.

Adopted Women's Dreams

Adoptees are individuals who were relinquished at birth, or anytime prior to 18 years of age by their biological parents, or as a result of parental death and then entrusted to another set of parents either directly or indirectly via an adoption agency, foster care, or an orphanage. It is apparent that adoptees have experienced loss. What is not so apparent is the internal loss or intrapsychic experience of being adopted. Dream research investigates the psychic experiences of adopted individuals. Adhering to Freud's model of the dream as a psychic experience, psychoanalysts believe that dreams are a portal to the unconscious. Through repetitive primary process imagery, which is frequently unknown or hidden from the dreamer due to the dream's symbolic nature, the dreamer's deepest conflicts are revealed.

Since the inception of psychoanalysis and Freud's (1900) seminal work—*The Interpretation of Dreams*—clinicians have analyzed dream material from reports given to them by their patients in treatment. Very early conflicts are repeated in dreams, of which the meanings are oftentimes unknown to the dreamer. Conflicts emerge from experiences laid down during development, which are frequently beyond conscious memory. Much of the first two years of life—prior to the acquisition of language, experiences, sensations, and emotions—return to the adult through dream material. And the meaning is usually unclear to the dreamer.

To date, the dreams of adopted women have not been systematically studied. In fact, very few studies exist that have examined the dreams of adult adopted men or women. However, there exists an enormous amount of literature on the topic of loss in adoption, which has been a starting point for some dream studies. Early researchers such as Kirk (1964) investigated the loss incurred by both adoptive parents and their adopted children. He believed that these losses were central to the adoption experience but that they were not necessarily conscious and/or discussed openly—sometimes to the detriment of the adoptive family. Lifton (1994) has spent the major part of her life writing about unconscious as well as conscious experiences of adoptees. She reports that loss is at the very core of an adoptee's psychic conflict. Partridge (2006) qualitatively studied the dreams of adopted adults. She categorized the dreams into three types: (1) dreams of separation and loss; (2) dreams concerning connections with birth relatives; and (3) dreams about integrating all members of the triad. Partridge was among the first researcher to suggest that the loss experienced in adoption can be found in dreams.

Her study was pivotal for the subsequent work of this author.

Clinicians report dreams from patients they are treating. Numerous psychoanalysts have corroborated the adoption literature with dreams from adopted patients that purport the symbolization of loss and the various and particular psychic conflicts bound in relinquishment and adoption. One dream at a time from an individual analyst's journal articles have hardly constituted dream research of adopted women; however, they have laid the foundation for other researchers to build on.

In an early pilot study utilizing 33 dreams from adopted and nonadopted patients in psychoanalysis, this author first explored whether differences in dream content existed between the two groups. I found the presence of several themes in dreams from both adopted and nonadopted patients in treatment. The theme of loss was equally present in both groups along with birth, death, aggression, control, identity, ambivalence, and denial. Within the theme of death and aggression, adopted dreamers tended to be the victims of aggression to a larger degree than nonadopted dreamers who participated in this investigation. And adopted dreamers tended to take little or no defensive action against imminent danger or threats, whereas nonadopted dreamers tended to take defensive action. In a subsequent quantitative study that examined more than 200 dreams from adopted and nonadopted women and utilizing the *Dream Threat Scale* (Revonsuo & Valli, 2000), several findings suggested that adopted women had more severe losses in their dreams. Adopted women were more likely to have unhappy dream endings in which the dangerous threat was realized and were less likely to participate or react to aggressive threats, in which they did not or could not attempt to escape, in their perilous dreams.

The process of reunion, locating, and or meeting with a birthmother was not a variable that demonstrated any significant difference between the dreams of adopted women who had been reunited with their birthmothers and those who had not. Surprisingly, the process of searching for a birthmother suggested that adopted women who were still searching were more likely to suffer severe consequences (resulting from the threats in their dreams) than those who were not searching or had no intention of searching. Using a psychoanalytic model of unconscious conflict, the findings suggest that adopted women may experience relinquishment as a loss that needs to be worked through and resolved throughout the life span. Searching, specifically, arouses deep emotions that may manifest in their dreams. Much further research is needed on the dreams of adopted adults, whether it falls outside or within the parameters of psychoanalysis.

Barbara D'Amato

References

Freud, S. (1900). *The interpretation of dreams. Standard edition* (Vols. 4–5). London: Hogarth Press.

Kirk, H.D. (1964). *Shared fate*. New York: Free Press.

Lifton, B.J. (1994). *Journey of the adopted self*. New York: Basic Books.

Partridge, C.P. (2006). What adoption looks like in dreams of the adopted. *Smith College Studies in Social Work, 76,* 39–51.

Revonsuo, A., & Valli, K. (2000, October). Dreaming and consciousness: Testing the threat simulation theory of the function of dreaming. *Psyche, 6*(8). Retrieved January 2011 from http://psyche.cs.monash.edu.au/v6/psyche-6–08-revonsuo.html

African American Dream Beliefs and Practices

Among the separate ethnic traditions surrounding dreams that persist in contemporary America, the dream culture of African Americans stands out as relatively rich and long-lasting, thanks to the special circumstances of its history. Slavery inadvertently created a separate American melting pot, one of African cultures. The slave owners were motivated by pragmatism and religious conviction to eradicate African practices; nevertheless, certain African essentials endured. Regarding dreams, while only scattered details of beliefs survived, several themes common to African cultures came through. Periodic infusions from the Caribbean, where African beliefs remained more intact, reinforced those fundamentals. Admixtures from the slave-owner cultures (notably English and Irish) and from Native Americans flavored the mix without overwhelming the African essence. Then after emancipation, segregation allowed the resulting new tradition to continue and evolve. Today most persons would probably dismiss as country a grandmother's belief that dreaming of fish is a sign of pregnancy, yet might retain a broadly traditional orientation to dreams, with which a psychological understanding may well coexist.

Dreams Matter

One likely African survival in contemporary African American dream culture is the general idea that dreams matter for the conduct of waking life. All of the themes to follow come under that widely held conviction, one taken for granted in traditional African societies.

Ancestor Visitation Dreams

Traces of African ancestor veneration can be detected in the respect shown to elders, the importance of funerals, and elsewhere. The African belief that ancestors are concerned for the living shows up in the affirmation by most African Americans, as many as 70 percent, that they have themselves experienced ancestor visitation dreams, which moreover are typically distinguished from dreams merely about dead relatives. Most visitations are perceived as benevolent, something consistent with the African pattern while contrasting with the mostly sinister aspect of visitations in Euro-American traditions. However, physical contact with the dead in dreams is feared by some African Americans as life-threatening.

Ancestor visitations exemplify the persistence of traditional dream beliefs into the era of integration: reports come from all ages, and if anything correlate to prosperity more than poverty, due in part perhaps to conscious Afrocentrism among the educated.

Predictive Dreams

While no straight line between them can be drawn, probably the widespread use of dreams for divination in Africa reaches to the belief held by more than 90 percent of African Americans that dreams can predict the future. Predictions may come in literal or symbolic form; usually hinge on one central image or symbol; most often bring bad news (commonly death); and have a spiritual basis; that is, they are not merely the product of a psychic faculty of the mind. Experiencing such a dream as well as telling the dream may be seen as causally implicated in bringing about the predicted outcome. Lastly, dreams were once commonly consulted for numbers and policy betting, often with the aid of interpretive dream books. The practice survives in weakened form for lottery and street numbers (illegal betting on lottery).

Spirituality and Boundaries

Ancestor dreams and predictive dreams are traditionally regarded as originating from a spiritual source: the ancestor's spirit or perhaps God—even numbers dreams were sometimes said to come from God. Dreams are still cited during testimony and preaching in church, if less often than in the past. Some individuals think of the unconscious as a spiritual organ for receiving communications from outside.

Spiritual dreams and waking visions (voices, presences) are thought to arise from the same authentic sources. Therefore boundaries between such phenomena are less sharply drawn than by a skeptical mainstream. This accords with the African pattern. Thus the usage "I dreamed" sometimes refers to a waking experience, and "I saw so-and-so" to either a sleep state or a waking vision. Liminal events such as visions are more frequently experienced by African Americans (and Africans) than by white Americans.

Dreaming for Others

Another quasi-African theme is the communal function of dreams. A dream predicting pregnancy or death, for example, often signifies for someone other than the dreamer herself, usually a family member, but occasionally a wider community. Parents have been known to consult their children's dreams, held reliable for themselves thanks to their offspring's spiritual innocence. Half of African Americans report having had a dream meant for someone else. Dream sharing within families, predominantly among women, is widespread, encouraging transmission of African American dream culture to the next generation.

Anthony Shafton

See also: entries related to Cross-Cultural Dreams

Reference

Shafton, A. (2002). *Dream-singers: The African American way with dreams*. New York: John Wiley & Sons.

Aging and Dreams

It has always been said that dreams vanish in old age, a claim that modern dream researchers have explored with varied methods during the last decades. Several retrospective questionnaire studies confirmed that reported dream-recall frequency decreases with age, and a negative correlation between age and dream recall has been found. More precisely, this decline in dream-recall frequency has been shown to begin from early adulthood, and to continue to the sixth decade of life. These findings were corroborated by some prospective studies with dream diaries, though other studies of this kind did not find any difference in the frequency and length of dream reports between young adults and aged persons. Finally, laboratory studies of sleep mentation reported after nighttime awakenings showed that dream frequency elicited from REM sleep was higher for young adults than elderly persons, whereas dream frequency from non-REM (NREM) sleep was found to be comparable in both populations.

In addition to changes in dream-recall frequency, studies have also documented modifications in the content of dream reports across ages. First, dreams become less vivid perceptually from the fourth decade of life. It is particularly the case for visual imagery, whose quantity, clarity, and color attenuate in dream reports. There is also a decrease in the amount of emotional content, and the intensity of affect in dreams is inversely correlated with age. Qualitatively, dream-diary studies have shown that dreams of the elderly contain more joy and pleasure than those of younger people, and less fear and other negative effects. This relative disappearance of fear and aggressive thoughts could account by itself for most of the quantitative

modifications of dream content with age. In the same vein, questionnaire and diary studies showed a lower nightmare frequency in the elderly. Finally, some evidence suggests that dreams could be less and less bizarre with age.

As for young adults, gender differences are observed in oneiric activity in the course of aging. The main difference involves dream-recall frequency, which remains higher in women across the life span. Chronologically, the decrease in dream-recall frequency and vividness mostly occurs during the third decade of life in men, but is much more progressive in women, from the beginning of adulthood to the sixth decade. Higher dream-recall frequency in aged women than men has been confirmed from awakenings during REM sleep in the laboratory setting, which suggests that gender differences in sleep physiology partly underlie differences in dream recall.

Several explanations can be put forward to account for the modifications of dream psychology across the life span. First, it is well known that dream-recall frequency depends in great part on the interest that the individual attaches to his or her dreams, which has proven to decline after midlife. Morning dream recall is also influenced by the circumstances of awakening. Indeed, remembrance of a dream after awakening will be lesser in presence of any distractor. Thus, it is possible that adult life, with its morning constraints, brings on interferences that hamper dream memorization. Also, late sleeping, which highly favors morning dream recall, becomes increasingly less frequent during adulthood; this could impact the evolution of dream-recall frequency with age in questionnaire studies. Moreover, the decrease in perceptual and emotional vividness of dreams with age makes them less salient and thus less prone to be memorized. Finally, laboratory studies have shown that qualitative modifications of REM sleep physiology that occur with aging greatly account for the decrease in dream-recall frequency during life.

As we mentioned, aged persons attach generally little importance to their dreams. Only a small minority of them consider dreams as a means to self-understanding and possibly seek dream interpretation or dream sharing. However, working with dream reports in psychotherapy or psychological support is a well-tried practice, and numerous reports show that considering the dream material can enrich a comprehensive approach and also contribute to psychic elaboration in the aged. This should be taken into account given the growing interest for psychotherapy and psychological support in the aged.

Fabian Guénolé

References

Fein, G., Feinberg, I., Insel, T. R., Antrobus, J. S., Price, L. J., Floyd, T. C., & Nelson, M. A. (1985). Sleep mentation in the elderly. *Psychophysiology, 22,* 218–225.

Funkhouser, A. T., Hirsbrunner, H. P., Cornu, C. M., & Bahro, M. (1999). Dreams and dreaming among the elderly: An overview. *Aging and Mental Health, 3,* 10–20.

Giambra, L. M., Jung, R. E., & Grodsky, A. (1996). Age changes in dream recall in adulthood. *Dreaming, 6,* 17–31.

Kahn, E., Fisher, C., & Lieberman, L. (1969). Dream recall in the normal aged. *Journal of the American Geriatric Society, 17,* 1121–1126.

Zepelin, H. (1981). Age differences in dreams, II: Distortion and other variables. *International Journal of Aging and Human Development, 13,* 37–41.

Alcohol and Sleep

Since ancient times, alcohol has been an integral part of human civilization. Although the word *alcohol* in organic chemistry refers to any organic compound where the carbon atom of an alkyl group or a substituted alkyl group is bound to a hydroxyl group (–OH), in normal usage, the word *alcohol* is commonly used to describe ethanol or any beverage that contains ethanol. Alcoholic beverages, including wine and beer, were believed to possess heavenly spirit and were routinely used as euphoriants on various cultural, ceremonial, and religious occasions. While the evil side of alcohol became evident when seizures and insomnolence were described as clinical features in alcoholics by Hippocrates in 400 BCE, it was not until the middle of the 20th century when a systematic examination of alcohol and its effects on human sleep was performed by Dr. Nathaniel Kleitman, the father of sleep research (Keller, 1979; Kleitman, 1963).

In subsequent years, with the progress of sleep medicine as an independent field, ample evidence has accumulated describing the effects of alcohol on sleep. It is now believed that alcohol-related sleep disorders have profound socioeconomic consequences. In fact, within the United States alone, alcohol-related sleep disorders are estimated to cost $18 billion (Brower, 2003).

Strong evidences suggest that alcohol intake has a profound impact on sleep. Acute alcohol intake in healthy nonalcoholics reduces sleep latency, coupled with an increase in the amount of time spent in NREM sleep (Stages 3 and 4) and electrographic (EEG) power density in the delta frequencies (0.3 to 4 Hz, a putative measure of sleep intensity). This somnogenic property of alcohol makes it one of the most commonly used sleep aids to self-medicate sleep disturbances. It has been estimated that approximately 12 percent of the general population and 20 percent of insomniacs use alcohol to promote sleep, while 50 percent of alcoholics use alcohol to self-medicate sleep disorders. However, the sleep-promoting effects of alcohol intake are short-lived and last for four to five hours. During the remaining nocturnal sleep time, sleep is profoundly disturbed with the predominance of REM sleep and sleep fragmentation. Furthermore, repeated alcohol use for as little as three days produces tolerance to the sleep-inducing effects, resulting in increased propensity toward the development of physiological dependence (Brower, 2003; Roehrs & Roth, 2001).

Alcoholics, both during drinking period and during alcohol withdrawal, suffer from severe sleep disruptions. In fact, sleep disruptions are among the most severe and protracted symptoms and are observed for several years during sustained alcohol withdrawal. The acute alcohol withdrawal phase is accompanied by classical symptoms of profound insomnia, including difficulty in falling and staying asleep, reduced sleep efficiency, and increased wakefulness after sleep onset. It is

the worsening of insomnia symptoms that leads to early return to alcohol drinking. During post-acute withdrawal or protracted withdrawal phase, recovering alcoholics suffer from severe insomnia along with sleep fragmentation, excessive daytime sleepiness, and increased REM sleep. The persistence of insomnia and other symptoms of sleep disruptions deserve special interest because of their association with relapse. Sleep disturbances including insomnia and increased REM sleep pressure are major predictors of relapse to alcoholism (Brower, 2003; Roehrs & Roth, 2001). Acamprosate, an FDA-approved drug to treat alcoholism, reduces symptoms of insomnia and increases sleep in recovering alcoholics. This further strengthens the importance of relapse to alcoholism and its link with sleep disruptions.

Alcoholics also display major changes in brain activity (EEG) during normal resting awake conditions. The most predominant EEG changes include increased energy in theta (3.5–7.5 Hz) and beta frequencies (12–28 Hz), suggestive of hyperexcitability coupled with dysfunctional neurophysiology. Genetically predisposed high-risk populations with family history of alcoholism display several changes in resting electrophysiological indices, which may help in determining the vulnerability toward development of alcoholism (Porjesz et al., 2005).

Animal studies also support clinical studies. Acute alcohol treatment in alcohol-naive rodents reduces sleep latency and increases NREM sleep. In contrast, insomnia and REM sleep changes have been reported in animals during alcohol withdrawal. High alcohol–preferring inbred rats and mice strains display reduced sleep following acute ethanol intake, rapid tolerance development toward sleep-promoting effects of alcohol, and insomnia during alcohol withdrawal. In recent years, efforts have been made to determine the neuronal substrates responsible for mediating the effects of acute and chronic ethanol exposure on sleep. These studies implicate adenosinergic mechanisms in the wake-promoting basal forebrain region as a major neuronal substrate responsible for mediating the effects of alcohol on sleep (Sharma, Engemann, Sahota, & Thakkar, 2010; Thakkar, Engemann, Sharma, & Sahota, 2010).

Sleep disturbances are commonly observed during use and withdrawal of various addictive substances, including alcohol, nicotine, cocaine, and cannabis, and are believed to be a common risk factor for relapse to psychoactive drugs (Brower & Perron, 2010). However, little research exists describing the potential relationship between sleep disturbances and relapse to psychoactive drugs. This area of research is still in its infancy and the mechanisms defining a clear relationship between sleep disturbance and relapse to psychoactive drugs are relatively unknown.

Rishi Sharma, Pradeep Sahota, and Mahesh M. Thakkar

See also: entries related to Sleep and the Brain; entries related to Sleep Disorders; entries related to Sleep Physiology

References

Brower, K.J. (2003). Insomnia, alcoholism and relapse. *Sleep Medicine Reviews, 7,* 523–539.

Brower, K.J., & Perron, B.E. (2010). Sleep disturbance as a universal risk factor for relapse in addictions to psychoactive substances. *Medical Hypotheses, 74,* 928–933.

Keller, M. (1979). A historical overview of alcohol and alcoholism. *Cancer Research, 39,* 2822–2829.

Kleitman, N. (1963). *Sleep and wakefulness.* Chicago: The University of Chicago Press.

Porjesz, B., Rangaswamy, M., Kamarajan, C., Jones, K.A., Padmanabhapillai, A., & Begleiter, H. (2005). The utility of neurophysiological markers in the study of alcoholism. *Clinical Neurophysiology, 116,* 993–1018.

Roehrs, T., & Roth, T. (2001). Sleep, sleepiness, and alcohol use. *Alcohol Research and Health, 25,* 101–109.

Sharma, R., Engemann, S., Sahota, P., & Thakkar, M.M. (2010). Role of adenosine and wake-promoting basal forebrain in insomnia and associated sleep disruptions caused by ethanol dependence. *Journal of Neurochemistry, 115,* 782–794.

Thakkar, M.M., Engemann, S.C., Sharma, R., & Sahota, P. (2010). Role of wake-promoting basal forebrain and adenosinergic mechanisms in sleep-promoting effects of ethanol. *Alcoholism: Clinical and Experimental Research, 34,* 997–1005.

Alexithymia and Sleep

Alexithymia is marked by four central characteristics: (1) the inability to recognize emotions in others' and one's own emotions, which includes trouble distinguishing physical sensations in the body from emotions; (2) the inability to communicate one's emotions through difficulty, describing what emotions are being experienced; (3) more concern with the details of external events than one's own inner experiences; and (4) reality-based, systematic, or overly logical thinking that lacks fantasy, imagination, or abstract thought. The instrument most often used to measure alexithymia has become the 20-item Toronto Alexithymia Scale (TAS-20; Bagby, Parker, & Taylor, 1994). This questionnaire contains 20 items that are separated into three subcategories: difficulty identifying feelings, difficulty describing feelings, and externally oriented thinking. The scores for the TAS-20 range between 20 and 100, with a score of 61 and above typically used as the cutoff score indicating the presence of alexithymia.

The prevailing belief is that alexithymia is a personality trait, though it has been found to be highly correlated to stress. To elucidate the relationship, Mikolajczak and Luminet (2006) measured alexithymia in a group of subjects prior to a stressful situation and after. They found that alexithymia remained relatively stable despite the increased stress, indicating that alexithymia is more of a personality trait than transient state. Many other studies have found strong associations between psychiatric disorders and alexithymia, but many of these studies were correlation studies and were unable to determine causation. Mikolajczak and Luminet (2006) suggest that alexithymia may predispose one to these disorders and not merely act as a symptom of them. Additionally, researchers have examined the presence of alexithymia in all types of patient populations, both those with psychological disorders (such as anxiety, depression, substance abuse, obsessive compulsive disorder, and eating disorders) and organically based disorders (such as autism, stroke, heart disease, and Parkinson's disease), suggesting

alexithymia may be clinically relevant for many diseases and disorders. Studies have also shown that alexithymia may be correlated with seemingly unrelated factors such as gender, age, obesity, socioeconomic status, education, and life satisfaction. Since alexithymia can influence one's emotional health and quality of life, researchers continue to try to understand how all these factors are related, though a great deal still remains unknown.

Given the characteristics of alexithymia, one would predict that an alexithymic would also have altered cognitive processing of emotions. Studies have found that emotional words are remembered and recalled differently in alexithymics (Luminet, Vermeulen, Demaret, Taylor, & Bagby, 2006; Meltzer & Nielson, 2010). Furthermore, with the use of an fMRI, researchers were able to show significantly different activation patterns in alexithymics compared to nonalexithymics (Moriguchi et al., 2009). Specifically, researchers found that alexithymics have distinctly different cognitive processing for certain emotionally charged words. This altered cognition not only influences daytime functioning, but also may have implications for sleep since during the REM phase of sleep, some of the same neural networks that process emotion are also highly activated. Gujar, McDonald, Nishida, and Walker (2011) postulated that REM sleep may be responsible for maintaining emotional balance. In their study, a subject who had napped and had entered REM sleep had less reactivity than those who did not nap, or napped but did not enter REM.

Emotionally intense dreams are thought to primarily occur during REM sleep. Since one major component of alexithymia is limited imagination or use of fantasy, one hypothesis is that this paucity would carry over to dreaming. More specifically, those with higher alexithymia scores would exhibit less vivid dreams, and because of having less vivid dreams, would also have a decreased ability to recall dreams compared to those who are not alexithymic. De Gennaro et al. (2003) found that alexithymics rarely recalled their dreams, and when they were remembered, their dreams lacked detail. Lumley and Bazydlo (2000) found that externally oriented thinking correlated with an increase in nights without dream recall, shorter dreams, and dreams that were considered not vivid and boring, and the dreamers more often believed that dreaming was not important. Difficulty identifying feelings and difficulty describing feelings, however, correlated with the number of nights participants had disturbing dreams or nightmares, and bizarre and aggressive dreams. Still, other studies have found no differences in dreams between alexithymics and nonalexithymics besides dreams involving less fantasy (Parker, Bauermann, & Smith, 2000). Dreaming is thought to act as an emotional outlet and Taylor (1987) suggests that alexithymics who do not experience this emotional outlet from dreams will have unexpected bursts of emotion of which they are seemingly unaware.

This altered pattern of dreaming may indicate altered REM sleep or just altered cognitive patterns when awake that are associated with dream recall. To investigate whether sleep architecture is impacted, researchers have conducted studies with alexithymics in sleep labs. Bazydlo, Lumley,

and Roehrs (2001) found that high alexithymia scores correlated with an increase in light sleep and a decrease in deep sleep. Additionally, they found that alexithymia was correlated with a decreased REM latency (when controlling for depression) and an increase in the number of REM episodes. De Gennaro et al. (2002), however, only found a correlation with externally oriented thinking and REM latency, and many studies have found no correlations at all. Bazydlo et al. (2001) believe the alteration in light and deep sleep may contribute to poor sleep quality and sleepiness, thus affecting daily functioning. High TAS-20 scores have also been associated with increased self-report of insomnia, excessive sleepiness, sleep walking, and nightmares (Bauermann, Parker, & Taylor, 2008). Overall, the impact alexithymia has on sleep architecture and sleep behaviors is relatively inconsistent.

One of the reasons that results are inconclusive may relate back to the instruments used to obtain them. Many studies use the TAS-20 exclusively as a measure of alexithymia. On reviewing the studies using the TAS-20, Kooiman, Spinhoven, and Trijsburg (2002) have cautioned that it has a low internal consistency for the externally oriented thinking subscale and lacks the fantasy component that is fundamentally part of alexithymia. This skepticism about the tool is supported by the literature, as some studies only have significant results with only the externally oriented thinking subscale or only with the difficulty identifying feelings and difficulty describing feelings subscales. In addition, Lundh and Simonsson-Sarnecki (2002) point out the inconsistency within the tool itself. While the question format of the difficulty identifying feelings and difficulty describing feelings subscales ask the subject to assess his or her own abilities ("I am often confused about what emotion I am feeling"), the externally oriented thinking subscale is composed of questions that ask about direct experience ("I prefer talking to people about their daily activities than their feelings"). There are inherent problems with asking someone to assess an ability that he or she has never experienced—a subject may not be aware of a deficiency in understanding the emotions of others unless directly informed or placed in a situation where he or she has been made aware of the deficit. Lundh and Simonsson-Sarnecki (2002) go on to suggest that because of the difference in question structure, the externally oriented thinking subscale will remain stable while the difficulty identifying feelings and difficulty describing feelings subscales will be impacted by the subject's mood.

Methods may also be a reason for inconsistent results. In almost every study, there are severe limitations that make the results questionable. Many studies use a small random sample, despite the prevalence of alexithymia ranging from 4.3 to 18 percent in the general population. Therefore, when examining these data, correlations are often derived from skewed data caused by the low occurrence of alexithymia or low scores of the subscales of the TAS-20. Additionally, not all researchers account for depression and anxiety in alexithymics, despite the high prevalence in those with psychiatric disorders. Lundh and Broman (2006) found that several depression and anxiety measures, along with measures

of perfectionism, concerns over mistakes, doubts about actions, and personal standards, were all correlated with both the difficulty identifying feelings and difficulty describing feelings subscales, but not the externally oriented thinking subscale. When this study examined the relationship between insomnia and alexithymia, all components were found to be significant. However, when they controlled for trait anxiety, only the externally oriented thinking subscale remained significant. Even when studies control for psychiatric illnesses, it is most often for depression and not trait anxiety. This study may demonstrate not only the disparity between the subscales, but also that the presence of other psychiatric disorders can confound results.

Since alexithymia is still a developing concept, there is much about it that is still unknown. It is generally accepted to be a trait that occurs in a small proportion of the population. While we know there is a link between alexithymia and psychiatric illnesses, such as depression, the nature of the connection is still unknown. Alexithymia may predispose a person to depression or it may be a reaction to depression. Regardless, altered cognitive processing with emotional words has been found to be present in alexithymics. There have also been many aspects of sleep and sleep behaviors that have been found to be related to alexithymia. Specific dream content, poor sleep hygiene, impaired daytime functioning, and altered sleep architecture have all, though inconsistently, been found to be related to symptoms of alexithymia. Alexithymia, therefore, not only affects daytime functioning, but also extends into sleep behaviors that may further influence emotional health and well-being. Though these relationships have been investigated many ways, studies often fail to replicate previous findings, and in the end, too few studies have been conducted to draw any firm conclusions. Future studies must consider the complexities of alexithymia and make an effort to control for the many factors that have been overlooked in the past.

Patricia Lynn Johnson

See also: Nightmares; entries related to Sleep Disorders

References

Bagby, M., Parker, J.D.A., & Taylor, G.J. (1994). The twenty-item Toronto alexithymia scale—I: Item selection and cross-validation of the factor structure. *Journal of Psychosomatic Research, 38,* 23–32.

Bauermann, T.M., Parker, J.D.A., & Taylor, G.J. (2008). Sleep problems and sleep hygiene in young adults with alexithymia. *Personality and Individual Differences, 45,* 318–322.

Bazydlo, R., Lumley, M.L., & Roehrs, T. (2001). Alexithymia and polysomnographic measures of sleep in healthy adults. *Psychosomatic Medicine, 63,* 56–61.

De Gennaro, L., Ferrara, M., Cristiani, R., Curcio, G., Martiradonna, V., & Bertini, M. (2003). Alexithymia and dream recall upon spontaneous morning awakening. *Psychosomatic Medicine, 65,* 301–306.

De Gennaro, L., Ferrara, M., Curcio, G., Cristiani, R., Lombardo, C., & Bertini, M. (2002). Are polygraphic measures of sleep correlated to alexithymia? A study on laboratory-adapted sleepers. *Journal of Psychosomatic Research, 53,* 1091–1095.

Gujar, N., McDonald, S.A., Nishida, M., & Walker, M.P. (2011). A role for REM sleep in recalibrating the sensitivity of the human brain to specific emotions. *Cerebral Cortex, 21,* 115–123.

Kooiman, C.G., Spinhoven, P., & Trijsburg, R.W. (2002). The assessment of alexithymia: A critical review of the literature and psychometric study of the Toronto Alexithymia Scale-20. *Journal of Psychosomatic Research, 53,* 1083–1090.

Luminet, O., Vermeulen, N., Demaret, C., Taylor, G.J., & Bagby, R.M. (2006). Alexithymia and levels of processing: Evidence for an overall deficit in remembering emotion words. *Journal of Research in Personality, 40,* 713–733.

Lumley, M.A., & Bazydlo, R.A. (2000). The relationship of alexithymia characteristics to dreaming. *Journal of Psychosomatic Research, 48,* 561–567.

Lundh, L.-G., & Broman, J.-E. (2006). Alexithymia and insomnia. *Personality and Individual Differences, 40,* 1615–1624.

Lundh, L.-G., & Simonsson-Sarnecki, M. (2002). Alexithymia and cognitive bias for emotional information. *Personality and Individual Differences, 32,* 1063–1075.

Meltzer, M.A., & Nielson, K.A. (2010). Memory for emotionally provocative words in alexithymia: A role for stimulus relevance. *Consciousness and Cognition, 10,* 1062–1068.

Mikolajczak, M., & Luminet, O. (2006). Is alexithymia affected by situational stress or is it a stable trait related to emotional regulation? *Personality and Individual Differences, 40,* 1399–1408.

Moriguchi, Y., Ohnishi, T., Decety, J., Hirakata, M., Maeda, M., Matsuda, H., & Komaki, G. (2009). The human mirror neuron system in a population with deficient self-awareness: An fMRI study in alexithymia. *Human Brain Mapping, 30,* 2063–2076.

Parker, J.D.A., Bauermann, T.M., & Smith, C.T. (2000). Alexithymia and impoverished dream content: Evidence from rapid eye movement sleep awakenings. *Psychosomatic Medicine, 62,* 486–491.

Taylor, G. J. (1987). Alexithymia: History and validation of the concept. *Transcultural Psychology, 24,* 85–95.

Alexithymia in Renal Disease

End-stage renal disease is associated with severe sleep problems hitherto thought to be secondary to atypical depression. In order to more adequately characterize the mood dysfunction associated with end stage renal disease, sleep medicine specialists have proposed that these patients exhibit key characteristics of alexithymia.

Alexithymia, a term derived from a Greek stem meaning lacking words for feelings, was coined in 1973. It is a personality construct reflecting difficulties in affective self-regulation and is characterized by difficulties in experiencing and verbalizing emotions, limited imaginal capacity, scarce capacity for symbolic thought, an externally oriented cognitive style, and tendency to somatize (Lumley, Lynn, & Burger, 2007).

Alexithymia has been associated with physical and mental health problems, substance abuse and alcohol disorders, depression, chronic pain, impaired immune function, bulimia and anorexia, erectile dysfunction, rheumatoid arthritis, chronic itching, and can be the result of a severe stress and of a life-threatening illness. It probably contributes to unhealthy behavior, symptom reporting, and health-care utilization (Lumley et al., 2007).

In the general population, alexithymia correlates with health-related quality of life and mortality and is regarded as a way of dealing with disease-generated stress (Taylor & Bagby, 2004). Its scores correlate with sleep complaints in community samples. The correlation is dependent on depression. It is satisfactorily measured by the Toronto Alexithymia Scale (TAS-20), which explores (1) difficulty identifying feelings, (2) difficulty describing feelings to others, and (3) externally oriented thinking.

Alexithymia has been studied in patients treated with hemodialysis (HD), peritoneal dialysis (PD), and after renal transplantation (TX) in adults, children, and adolescents. In a study of more than 300 HD patients (Fukunishi, 1997), a 49 percent overall prevalence of alexithymia was disclosed. The prevalence was 36.4 percent in patients with a nephritic etiology, 60 percent in diabetics, 66.2 percent in diabetics with bulimia nervosa, and 37.7 percent in patients with other etiologies. Alexithymia was regarded as a consequence of stress generated by a demanding machine-dependent life, causing many losses and dependencies. A defense mechanism was suspected. The higher prevalence in bulimic diabetics was discussed as an additive effect of the eating habit and diabetes. In addition, Kojima, Hayano, and Tokudome (2007) disclosed significant associations between baseline depression, alexithymia, and unsatisfactory social support in HD patients. Such associations were also found in PD patients in whom higher TAS-20 scores were measured in those more-severely ill.

De Santo et al. (2010) compared TAS-20, depression measured by the Beck Depression Inventory (BDI), and the Pittsburg Sleep Quality Index (PSQI) in HD patients requiring parathyroidectomy (PTX) because of hyperparathyroidism not controlled by medical therapy. HD patients not requiring PTX were used as controls. TAS-20, BDI, and PSQI were significantly higher in patients needing surgery. Eighty percent of them were alexithymic and had higher concentrations of serum parathyroid hormone (PTH), calcium, and phosphate, and lower hemoglobin and albumin concentrations, and a higher prevalence of hypertension. BDI, TAS-20, and PSQI improved after PTX as did anemia; albumin, calcium, and phosphate concentrations; and systolic and diastolic blood pressure. The variables predicting reduction of TAS-20 were the reduction in the number of patients requiring antihypertensive drugs, PSQI, BDI, and hemoglobin concentration. Thus, alexithymia was regarded as a depression-driven construct, a finding previously disclosed in epidemiological studies in healthy people and in various clinical settings.

The studies in TX patients demonstrate that a successful transplantation does not reduce the prevalence of alexithymia below 30 percent. In addition, data from available studies in HD and after TX in children and adolescents are not at variance with those in adults and point to high prevalence of alexithymia independently associated with depression and social support. Finally, alexithymia was associated with untreated elevated blood pressure, independent of sodium and alcohol intake, body mass index, and physical fitness, and was therefore defined as a facet of essential hypertension.

High TAS-20 scores are not unexpected in persons who have a depressed immune system and live with bone pain, itching, high blood pressure, constricted eating and drinking habits, erectile dysfunction, depression, insomnia, and a life expectancy lower than that of patients with cancer. Deprived as they are of very simple pleasures, patients in end-stage renal disease live day by day.

Rosa Maria De Santo

See also: Alexithymia and Sleep; entries related to Sleep Disorders

References
De Santo, R.M., Livrea, A., De Santo, N.G., Conzo, G., Bilancio, G., Celsi, S., & Cirillo, M. (2010). The high prevalence of alexithymia in hemodialyzed patients with secondary hyperparathyroidism unsuppressed by medical therapy is cured by parathyroidectomy. *Journal of Renal Nutrition, 20,* S64–S70.

Fukunishi, I. (1997). Alexithymic characteristics of bulimia nervosa in diabetes mellitus with end stage renal disease. *Psychological Reports, 81,* 627–633.

Kojima, M., Hayano, J., & Tokudome, S. (2007). Independent association of alexithymia and social support in hemodialysis patients. Journal of *Psychosomatic Research, 63,* 349–356.

Lumley, M.A., Lynn, C., & Burger, J.A. (2007). The assessment of alexithymia in medical settings: Implications for understanding and treating health problems. *Journal of Personality Assessment, 89,* 230–246.

Taylor, G.J., & Bagby, R.M. (2004). New trends in alexithymic research. *Psychotherapy and Psychosomatics, 73,* 68–77.

Ancient Dream Theories

Archaeological explorations undertaken in Mesopotamia, the cradle of civilization, have revealed that dreams were of considerable interest to members of all the various kingdoms inhabiting the region, such as the

Assyrians and Hittites. Nearly 25,000 clay tablets dating back almost the third millennia BCE were unearthed from the Royal Library at Nineveh. Among them were cuneiform engravings on a group of 12 broken tablets describing the adventures of the legendary hero—King Gilgamesh. This famous tale included references to a series of sequential dreams experienced by several dreamers. The comments made about these dreams revealed considerable skill in dealing with the symbolic and metaphorical nature of the imagery associated with the dreams that had been reported.

A well-known biblical example of the ability to offer meaningful dream interpretation is provided when Joseph dealt with two troubling dreams that the pharaoh of Egypt experienced. Joseph interpreted the seven lean cows who replaced the seven fat cows, and the seven stalks of withered grain that destroyed the seven stalks of ripe wheat, as signifying that the current abundance of food would disappear in seven years and would be replaced by a famine of equal length. He recommended that the pharaoh begin to immediately build storage houses to stockpile the rich harvest currently available to have an adequate supply of food when the predicted famine occurred. The pharaoh was so grateful for this insightful interpretation that he placed Joseph second in command over all of Egypt, with only the pharaoh having greater power over the administration of his country.

As has been true throughout recorded history, unpleasant dreams are experienced more frequently than pleasant ones. Attempts to minimize their expected negative outcomes have varied greatly in different cultures. Sometimes the dreamer might make a sacrifice to a god hoping to create a favorable outcome. Another alternative was to tell the disturbing dream to a lump of clay that had been rubbed over the dreamer's body. This incorporated dream was then tossed into a nearby stream so it could be dissolved and carried away from the dreamer.

The power of incubated dreams to heal physical or emotional problems was strongly accepted in ancient Greece and Rome. Aesculapius was a legendary figure who lived in Greece during the 11th century BCE and was later deified. The first shrine to Aesculapius was established in the fifth century BCE in Athens by Sophocles. Eventually more than 300 active temples were located throughout Greece and the Roman Empire by the second century CE. The dream seeker would journey to a temple, often from a considerable distance, to participate in various preparatory rituals, such as bathing, sacrificing an animal, and then singing or praying before going into the temple. On entering, the supplicant often encountered an impressive statue of the god, surrounded by plaques testifying to the healings that previous dreamers had received there. Sometimes snakes, who symbolized Aesculapius, crawled about on the floor. Often the god, or a member of his family, such as his daughters, Hygeia or Panacea, would appear directly in the dream of the seeker, and healing would occur. Later, the priests became more active and would provide interpretations to the participants. A remnant of this healing tradition survives in the appearance of the modern caduceus, displaying a pair of snakes entwined around a staff, as a symbol of the medical profession.

Many other famous Greek thinkers recognized a close link between dream imagery and imbalances in somatic functioning. In the third century BCE, Aristotle conjectured that the reduced attention to external stimuli present during sleep may enable greater awareness of minimal internal sensations to be reflected. Galen, a Greek physician born around 130 CE, who authored a medical book more than 800 pages long, nicely summarized this psychosomatic linkage when he wrote, "it is necessary to observe dreams accurately both as to what is seen and what is done in sleep in order that you may prognosticate and heal satisfactorily." An impressive statement about the principles underlying successful dream interpretation was made by Aristotle: "the most skilled interpreter of dreams is he who has the faculty of observing resemblances."

The most prominent dream interpreter in early times who displayed this skill was Artemidoris of Daldis, who was born in Greece. His book, *Oneirocritica* (the *Interpretation of Dreams*), was published in five books around 150 CE. The first book covers 82 units (ranging from a few sentences to four pages in length) mostly dealing with the human body, and some with physical activities like pruning vines, eating, and types of sexual activity. In unit 52, he comments that tools that cut and divide things signified disagreements. Book 2 contains 70 units about objects and events in the natural world. In unit 8, he notes that a clear and bright sky is a good sign, but a gray, gloomy sky signifies failures. In unit 68, he proposes that flying at will foretells great ease and skills in one's business affairs. In book 3, the 66 units are

rather loosely organized. In unit 8, he notes that bugs are symbols of cares and anxieties because they keep people awake at night and in unit 33 he suggests that thorns signify grief because they are sharp and capable of holding onto objects.

The 84 units in book 4 explain that his son should approach dreams by inquiring about the dreamer's identity, occupation, birth, financial status, and state of health and age, and the habits of the dreamer should also be considered. There are many suggestions about how to examine the structure and relationship between items within the dream. Book 5 contains accounts of 95 dreams that Artemidoris collected from his travels around the world. He had elicited the personal histories, and with regard to their dreams, verified the accuracy of how his interpretations corresponded to what later happened to the dreamers. In his preface to his 1975 English translation of *Oneirocritica,* which he undertook as his doctoral dissertation at Yale University, Robert White proposed that, "Freud, Jung, and others were not so much innovators as restorers, since they were reassigning to dreams and dream-readings the importance they held in antiquity, and which they had lost in more recent centuries."

Dreams played a prominent role in the development of all of the world's major religions. The births of Buddha and of Jesus Christ were foretold in dreams that their mothers experienced when they were pregnant. In the Talmud, there are 217 references to dreams. Mohammed received his divine mission in his famous nocturnal journey dream, and the Koran asserts that the science of dreams was "the prime science since the beginning of the world." Arab-Muslim acceptance of the importance of dreams is reflected in one historian's estimate that 7,500 dream interpreters existed in the 10th century. In Europe, emphasis on the potential benefits of Christian dreams declined when the Church began to dominate intellectual areas, and a connection was forged to Satan as a primary source of dreams by the Church Fathers. Divulging sinful dreams with sexual, psychic, or aggressive content could lead to being burned at the stake. It became much safer to not acknowledge any form of dream recall.

Robert Van de Castle

See also: entries related to History of Dreams/Sleep

References

de Becker, R. (1968). *The understanding of dreams: And their influence on the history of the World.* New York: Hawthorn Books.

Moss, R. (2009). *The secret history of dreaming.* Novato, CA: New World Library.

Van de Castle, R.L. (1994). *Our dreaming mind.* New York: Ballantine Books.

White, R. (Trans.). (1975). The interpretation of dreams: *The oneirocritica of Artemidorus.* Park Ridge, NJ: Noyes Press.

Ancient Egypt and Dreams

Dreams played a complex role in ancient Egyptian life (Szpakowska, 2003). The earliest currently known references to dreams are found in letters to the dead that were left in or near the tomb of the addressee. The majority date from the late Old Kingdom to the Middle Kingdom (2345–1773 BCE). In one of these, the writer complains to his deceased father that he is being watched by a dead servant in a dream. The bad dream may have arisen due to a guilty conscience on the part of the author, for in the letter he vociferously denies having harmed or assaulted the man in life. In another letter a husband records his hopes to be able to see his deceased wife acting on his behalf in a dream.

From the Middle Kingdom onward, rather than being presented as desirable visions, dreams appeared as malignant forces or nightmares to be repulsed and avoided and, indeed, nightmares are referred to more often than dreams (Szpakowska, 2010). They are attested in execration texts, medical spells, and prescriptions to be used alongside artifacts, such as headrests and figurines of cobras, that would offer the vulnerable sleeper a modicum of protection. Literary texts such as the *Tale of Sinuhe* and the *Teachings of Ptahhotep* employed the metaphor of dreams to emphasize that which was ephemeral, untrustworthy, and potentially dangerous. Other texts suggest that the dream was perceived as a sort of liminal space that lay somewhere between the world of the living and the world beyond. Its boundaries were translucent thus allowing visual contact between the dreamer and those who inhabited the afterlife, including the gods and the dead. Unfortunately, the boundaries were also permeable from the other side, thus allowing the damned to come through and assault the dreamer as nightmares. A few texts recount the characteristics of terrors in the night that match modern psychological descriptions of anxiety dreams.

From the time of the New Kingdom (1550 BCE), gods began to appear in the dreams of pharaohs, such as Amenhotep II and Merneptah, whose divine visions occurred during respites in battle. The best known of the royal dreams are those of Tuthmosis IV, who recorded his dream on a stele that is still visible today at the foot of the Great Sphinx of Giza, and of Tanutamani, the last Nubian pharaoh. A few rare descriptions of nonroyal individuals having divine visions also exist. None of these dreams, however, were symbolic, nor did they require a specialist to interpret them; it is clearly stated within the texts that the dreams were instantly understood by the dreamers.

The earliest-surviving dream dictionary (P. Chester Beatty III) is attested in the Ramesside Period (1200 BCE) and thereafter their incidence increases (Quack, 2006). The beginning and the end of the Ramesside dream dictionary are missing, but enough remains to indicate that this was not a small composition. The surviving portion of the manuscript is organized into three sections. The first consists of lists of dreams and their interpretations—139 dreams that are interpreted as good omens are listed first, followed by 83 negative omens. This is followed by the second section consisting of a protective spell to ward off the effects of a nightmare. The third section provides a description of a type of man called a *follower of Seth,* and four more good dreams. The follower of Seth is described as being a hot-tempered, violent, debauched, red-haired man whose sexual prowess was enjoyable to women. This type of character can be contrasted with that of the ideal ancient Egyptian man: one who was quiet, humble, modest, and pious. A demotic dream dictionary (Volten,

1942) organizes dreams by categories, including dreams of numbers, games, drinking (beer), snakes, speaking out, animal excrement and flesh, swimming with other people, accepting wreaths and other plants, and crocodiles. In addition, there were categories of dreams that the authors conceived that a woman might dream of: sexual dreams, women giving birth to animals, and women suckling animals. Many of the links between the image seen and its interpretation in the dream manuals are based on puns—a device commonly used in Mesopotamian dream interpretation and Egyptian religious texts. By the time of the Greco-Roman period, oneiromancy had become well established, as evidenced by the archives of priests whose duties included the interpretation of dreams (Ray, 1976).

Kasia Szpakowska

See also: entries related to Cross-Cultural Dreams

References

Quack, J. (2006). A black cat from the right, and a scarab on your head: New sources for ancient Egyptian divination. In K. Szpakowska (Ed.), *Through a glass darkly: Magic, dreams and prophecy in ancient Egypt* (pp. 175–187). Swansea: The Classical Press of Wales.

Ray, J. D. (1976). *The archive of Hor.* London: The Egypt Exploration Society.

Szpakowska, K. (2003). *Behind closed eyes: Dreams and nightmares in ancient Egypt.* Swansea: The Classical Press of Wales.

Szpakowska, K. (2010). Nightmares in ancient Egypt. In J.-M. Husser & A. Mouton (Eds.), *Le cauchemar dans l'antiquité: Actes des journées d'étude de l'UMr 7044* (15–16 Novembre 2007, Strasbourg) (pp. 21–39). Paris: de Boccard.

Volten, A. (1942). *Demotische Traumdeutung (Pap. Carlsberg XIII and XIV Verso)*, Analecta Aegyptiaca Iii. Kopenhagen: Einar Munksgaard.

Ancient Greek Dream Beliefs

Archeological evidence indicates the caves of mainland Greece were first occupied by *Homo sapiens* at least 30,000 years ago, and perhaps much earlier than that. Over the millennia, these people developed vibrant cultural practices that revolved around hunting, seafaring, and war. After the collapse of the Mycenaean civilization around 1100 BCE, there followed a period of social disarray in which the written language was lost. During this bleak era, when the Greek people were struggling to rebuild their culture, they told each other epic tales about heroes of the past. The best known of these stories, the *Iliad* and the *Odyssey,* are attributed to a blind poet named Homer, who lived sometime after 1000 BCE. Originally there was no written text of these stories, just the oral versions sung by bards at public festivals and royal celebrations. When writing was reinvented by the Greeks, Homer's versions were recorded and became the literary foundation for the development of classic Greek culture. Dreams play a significant role in both the *Iliad* and the *Odyssey*, which means that a general understanding of ancient Greek dream beliefs needs to start with these two epic poems. It also indicates that a sophisticated interest in dreams reaches far, far back into the prehistory of the Greek people.

The *Iliad* and the *Odyssey* recounted the adventures of an army from Greece who attacked the distant city of Troy (the *Iliad*) and then embarked on a perilous journey home (the *Odyssey*). The *Iliad* contains important dream scenes at the beginning and end of the story. At the beginning, the Greek leader Agamemnon is sent an evil dream from the god Zeus to deceive him about the next day's battle and thereby help the Trojans. At the end, Achilles, the greatest Greek warrior, receives a poignant visitation dream from his dead friend Patroklos, who asks Achilles to perform his funeral rites. In the *Odyssey*, the goddess Athena appears in different guises in people's dreams to influence their feelings and behavior. An especially dramatic scene comes at the end of the *Odyssey,* when Odysseus finally returns home disguised as a beggar and meets privately with his wife Penelope. She tells the beggar about a strange dream, and as they discuss its meaning, she says, "Two gates there are for our evanescent dreams,/One is made of ivory, the other made of horn." In this view, the gate of ivory is for false dreams and the gate of horn for true, or potentially true, dreams. This conceptual duality about the nature and meaning of dreams carries throughout ancient Greek culture: some dreams are valuable, heaven-sent revelations, but others are false, misleading, and dangerous.

Early Greek philosophers took note of dreams, and in some cases used them to advance their self-understanding. Heraclitus defined dreams as inherently personal experiences: "[F]or those who are awake there is a single, common universe, whereas in sleep each person turns away into his own, private universe." Socrates mentioned two of his own dreams to his students: one was a recurrent dream that told him all his life to "practice the arts," and the other was a prophetic dream accurately foretelling the day of his death. Plato, one of Socrates's disciples, argued in *The Republic* that dreaming reveals an irrational, bestial realm of instincts within the psyche that should be controlled by the waking, rational mind. Aristotle, a student of Plato, led Greek philosophy in more empirical directions, and he analyzed dreams in terms of mental activity during sleep, specifically the residual impressions from daytime experiences.

In terms of the ancient Greek people's actual dreams and practical efforts to interpret them, the primary venue was the cult centers of Asclepius, the god of healing. Countless temples devoted to Asclepius were spread throughout Greece and eventually the whole Mediterranean, attracting people with various physical and mental illnesses. Visitors to the temple practiced dream incubation, that is, seeking a special healing dream from the god, in which their illnesses could be diagnosed and curative measures revealed. Hippocrates, one of the founders of Western medicine, was trained as a priest at the Asclepian temple in Cos, and his writings include several discussions of the role of dreams in healing. The animal companion of Asclepius is the snake, which can be seen in the symbol of the serpent-entwined staff that adorns every doctor's office and hospital in present-day society.

Kelly Bulkeley

References

Bulkeley, K. (2001). Penelope as dreamer: The perils of interpretation. In K. Bulkeley (Ed.), *Dreams: A reader on the religious, cultural, and psychological dimensions of dreaming* (pp. 223–245). New York: Palgrave.

Devereux, G. (1976). *Dreams in Greek tragedy: An ethno-psycho-analytical study*. Berkeley: University of California Press.

Dodds, E. R. (1951). *The Greeks and the irrational*. Berkeley: University of California Press.

Kingsley, P. (1999). *In the dark places of wisdom*. Inverness, CA: Golden Sufi Center.

O'Flaherty, W. D. (1984). *Dreams, illusion, and other realities*. Chicago: University of Chicago Press.

Animal Figures in Dreams

The presence of animal figures in dreams raises many intriguing questions about what their possible significance might be. One consistent finding among all studies investigating the topic is that there is a much higher percentage of animal figures present in the dreams of younger children. In one study, I examined the frequency of animal figures appearing in the dreams of 741 children aged 4 to 16. A single dream was obtained from each child (383 girls and 358 boys). A steadily decreasing percentage of animal figures appeared as chronological age increased: the percentage figure was 39 percent for 4- to 5-year-old children, 35 percent for 6- to 7-year-olds, 34 percent for 8- to 9-year-olds, 30 percent for 10- to 11-year-olds, 22 percent for 12- to 13-year-olds, and 14 percent for 14- to 16-year-olds (Van de Castle, 1983).

In the normative material for the Hall–Van de Castle content scales (Hall & Van de Castle, 1966) that involve 500 dreams from 100 American male college students, only 6 of the 1,180 characters were animals, and for the 500 dreams from 100 female college students, only 4 of the 1,423 characters were animals.

In terms of the type of animals appearing in the 741 children's dreams, the most frequently appearing were dogs (30), horses (28), cats (15), and snakes (15). In a study involving 2,000 dreams from 485 male college students and 2,000 dreams from 316 female college students, a similar ranking of types of animal figures appeared. A total of 66 dogs, 59 horses, 27 cats, 27 birds, and 24 snakes appeared among the 397 animal characters tabulated. A modest, but interesting, phylogenetic difference was also found. Out of the 217 animal dreams reported by the 741 children previously cited, mammals appeared in 78 percent of the girls' dreams and only 61 percent of the boys' dreams, while nonmammals appeared in 39 percent of the boys' dreams and only 22 percent of the girls' dreams. This difference was statistically significant. Among the 397 animal characters reported in the dreams of the 4,000 college students, women reported 128 mammals and the boys reported 98; and in the nonmammal category, the boys reported 92 nonmammals while the girls reported 54. This difference was also statistically significant. In another type of analysis, children reported more dreams of large and threatening wild animals such as bears, lions, tigers, gorillas, and so on, and these appeared in 27 percent of their dreams, but similar animals were found only in 7 percent of the college student dreams.

The wild animals appearing in dreams may be linked to emotions of fear, apprehension, and aggression. An impressive example of the attributes associatively linked to animals in general is provided in a contingency analysis I carried out with some dreams of American college students. I divided these dreams into several groupings. One group consisted of 907 dreams (454 from males and 453 from females) in which only human characters were present. Aggressive interactions were present in 44 percent of these dreams. I also examined three other groups in which animal figures were involved to varying degrees. One group involved 54 dreams in which both human and animal characters appeared, but the number of human characters was greater than the number of animal characters. Aggression was present in 59 percent of these dreams. The second group involved 40 dreams in which an equal number of human and animal characters appeared. Aggression was present in 72 percent of these dreams. The remaining group contained 56 dreams that had more animal characters than human characters, or involved exclusively animal figures. An aggressive interaction appeared in 79 percent of these dreams. Thus, as the density or predominance of animal figures became more prominent in the dream, there was a steady increase in the amount of aggressive interactions present, as well as the emotion of fear and the outcome of a misfortune. These results are discussed at greater length in *Our Dreaming Mind* (Van de Castle, 1994).

The reader should not conclude that all dreams involving animals are going to be strongly associated with an aggressive component or other negative features. It obviously depends on who the dreamer is. In her article "Dream reports of animal rights activists," Jacquie Lewis (2008) describes how she collected dream reports from 284 activists who attended the Animal Rights Conference held in Washington, DC, in 2004. (Approximately 1,000 people attend this conference every year.) Participants were asked to record their most recent dream, whether it was last night, last month, or last year. A surprising 38.4 percent of their dreams included animal figures. These dreams also included human characters, but they all involved at least one animal figure. In these dreams, the animal characters comprised 29.4 percent of all characters. Lewis made a detailed breakdown of the nature of the aggressive and friendly interactions in these dreams. She found that the highest percentage of aggression was perpetrated by someone other than the dreamer on an animal (31.3%). The second-most prevalent form of aggression (17.6%) was committed by a human character, other than the dreamer, on another human. The dreamer experienced aggression from another human in 15.6 percent of interactions, but aggressiveness from an animal character only appeared in 11.7 percent of the dreams. Friendliness toward animals was reported in 60.4 percent of the 52 friendly interactions that were present in these dreams. The most frequent types of animals appearing in her sample were cats (25) and dogs (7). One of her provocative findings was that 14.7 percent of the dreams obtained involved a deceased companion animal. Overall, this highly original and important study by Lewis confirms the validity of the continuity theory of dreams, that is, that there is a marked similarity in content between waking preoccupations and dreaming preoccupations. She noted "a typical animal rights activist dream report involves an animal that is found suffering, either at the hands of another person or through environmental circumstances, and then the dreamer steps in to help the animal." Lewis acknowledges that her study findings need to be considered within the context of the setting—they were gathered at an animal rights conference, and the subjects "may have felt compelled to record positive animal dreams in which they are the rescuer of animals, rather than record dreams in which an animal showed aggression to them or they were aggressive to an animal" (Lewis, 2008, p. 197).

Another example of the continuity hypothesis in action is shown when one considers the types of animals that are reported in the dreams of members of indigenous cultures. I examined the dreams of Australian aborigines (246 dreams), South Pacific islanders (118 dreams), North American Indians (190 dreams), and Peruvians (448 dreams). Fish or other forms of aquatic animals were the most frequent type of animal figures for those groups living near the water, but were almost totally absent in dreams of inland dwelling groups (Central Australia and Hopi Indians). Kangaroos, wallabies, crocodiles, and sting rays were exclusive to Australian dreams; the only cats were in Truk Islanders' dreams; and the only exotic jungle animals (lion, tiger, elephant) were found in the dreams of Peruvian students. The particular types of animals we employ in our dreams will clearly be a function of what we have learned from cultural behavioral sources (needed for food or clothing) or from understanding symbolic referents associated with animal attributes (strong as a bull, free as a bird, etc.).

Robert Van de Castle

See also: entries related to Dream Content

References

Hall, C.S., & Van de Castle, R. (1966). *The content analysis of dreams.* New York: Appleton-Century-Crofts.

Lewis, J. (2008). Dream reports of animal rights activists. *Dreaming*, 18, 181–200.

Van de Castle, R. (1983). Animal figures in fantasy and dreams. In A.H. Katcher & A.M. Beck (Eds.), *New perspectives on our lives with companion animals* (pp. 148–173). Philadelphia: University of Pennsylvania Press.

Van de Castle, R. (1985). Animal figures in dreams. *Dream Network Bulletin, 4*(6), 10–14.

Van de Castle, R. (1990). Animal figures in dreams: Age, sex, and cultural differences. *ASD Newsletter, 7*(2), 1–3.

Van de Castle, R. (1994). *Our dreaming mind.* New York: Ballantine Books.

Animation and the Dream

Like the dream, animation is often overlooked as trivial, but has the power to illuminate interior worlds. And animation has some intrinsic qualities that make it especially suitable for illustrating or evoking dream experience.

Animation is present in many apparently live action films and can be defined as any moving image that is created or mediated on a frame-by-frame basis. Common methods of animating include drawing the phases of movement (either on paper or digitally); moving objects, puppets, or human actors frame by frame; and creating models in a digital environment. These methods share a control and mediation of movement and image that can create an alternative reality that may obey some or none of the rules of reality. A sort of film making is created where the imagination is the only limitation, where anything that can happen inside the head can be projected onto the screen. Animation is the realm of fantasy played out without guilt. This irresponsible playfulness may be what associates it so strongly with the world of childhood.

Animation, in the shape of optical toys and vaudeville phantasmagoria, actually predates live action film and is at the root of the more fantastical, imaginative strand of film history. Some of the most visually inventive film directors—for example, Terry Gilliam, David Lynch, Jean-Pierre Jeunet, and Tim Burton—began their careers as animators.

Like the dream, animation speaks the language of condensation and distortion. Maybe because it is so time-consuming to produce, the animated image tends to be freighted with multiple meanings. Animation's unique capacity for metamorphosis allows the shifting and collapsing of identities, spaces, and realities.

Animation tends to use the language of symbolism and metaphor. Things routinely stand in for other things, and narratives play out in multiple layers. *Black Dog,* by Alison De Vere, originated in a dream and adds elements from mythology to make a resonant symbolic narrative.

Movement is essential to animation and to the dream. Allan Hobson (2004) avers that when a dream is still, we are about to wake up. Animation allows the exploration of the particular qualities of dream movement. In *La Joie de Vivre* by Hector Hoppin and Anthony Gross, the characters are real enough to allow identification, but stretch, distort, and defy gravity in a recognizably dreamlike way. Another film to evoke the sensation of dream movement is the live action–animation hybrid *Avatar*.

Animation has the capacity, and the social permission, to transgress the boundaries that demarcate life and death, cleanliness and obscenity, human and animal, subject and object. Robert Morgan's *The Cat with Hands* originated in an image

Still from *The Cat with Hands*, directed by Robert Morgan. (Robert Morgan)

from his sister's dream of a horrifying animal/human chimera, and builds from it an uncanny horror story.

Of course, dreams are not completely reproducible by animation. Most dreams have at least some of the texture of the real. Maybe the most successful attempts at reproducing dream experience are hybrid combinations of animation and live action. Richard Linklater worked with Bob Sabiston to create a liminal world between reality and animation for *Waking Life,* an investigation of the altered consciousness of dreaming. The film is based on live action footage, but animated into a queasily shifting world into which impossible events insinuate themselves.

Many qualities of animation that allow the communication of dreams are held in common with film in general. The creation of a morally neutral space for trying out possible behaviors is something we see in film in general, where extreme violence often has no real consequences. But animation takes this one step further—it allows us to express transgressive ideas that are unacceptable as conscious thoughts.

Surrealism is still a vital force in contemporary animation, as evidenced by the work of the great Czech filmmaker Jan Svankmajer, who sees dream and reality as communicating vessels. In his films "the dream plane fuses with harsh reality."

Short Life, a film that draws directly from the dreams of painter Johanna Freise, animation by Daniel Suljic, mixes several dreams with one memory to make a story that resonates with the viewer's dream experience.

Sleep, a music video by Tibor Banoczki and Sarolta Szabo for Ethav, contains images straight from the directors' dreams.

Still from *Short Life, Where are You Going*, directed by Daniel Šuljić and Johanna Freise. (Daniel Šuljić and Johanna Freise)

Still from *Sleep*, directed by Tibor Banoczki. (Tibor Banoczki)

Filmography

What follows is a selection of animated films inspired by or explicitly referencing dreams:

Anderson, David. *Dreamland Express,* UK, 1982, 14 min, National Film and Television School, UK.
Ashwood, Dan. *Fever Dreams,* US, 2007, 5 min, Harvard University VES Department.

Banoczki, Tibor, and Sarolta Szabo. *Sleep* music video for Ethav, UK, 2009, Domesticinfelicity.

Brothers Quay. *The Comb*, UK, 1990, 17 min, Koninck Studios, Zeitgeist Films.

Cameron, James. *Avatar*, USA, 2009, 162 min, Twentieth Century Fox.

De Vere, Alison. *Black Dog*, UK, 1987, 18 min, Malinka Films.

Freise, Johanna, and Daniel Suljic. *Short Life*, Austria, 2007, 9 min, Sixpack film.

Gross, Anthony, and Hector Hoppin. *La Joie de Vivre*, France, 1934, 8 min 50 sec, Animat Production Company; Europa Film Treasures.

Kon, Satoshi. *Paprika*, Japan, 2006, 90 min, Sony Pictures Entertainment.

Linklater, Richard. *Waking Life*, Detour Films.

Lobser, David. *Elephant Girl*, US, 2007, 4 min 30 sec, dlobser.com.

Morgan, Robert. *The Cat with Hands*, UK, 2001, 4 min, Animus Films, London.

Shynola, *Pyramid Song*, UK, 2001, RSA UK.

The following films have a distinctly dreamlike quality:

Laloux, Rene. *Fantastic Plane*, France/Czechoslovakia, 1973, 72 min, Argos Films.

Miyasake, Hayao. *Spirited Away*, Japan, 2001, 125 min, Studio Ghibli, Walt Disney Pictures.

Svankmajer, Jan. *Alice*, Czechoslovakia, 1988, 86 min, First Run Features.

Ruth Lingford

Reference

Hobson, A. (2004). *13 dreams Freud never had: The new mind science*. New York: Pi Press.

Anthropology and Dreams

Anthropology is the holistic study of humans and other primates in all times and places. It incorporates four subfields: biological, linguistic, archaeological, and cultural anthropology. Anthropology generates the richest understandings of the phenomena, including dreams, by combining the findings of all its subfields and other relevant disciplines.

Our species, *Homo sapiens*, evolved heavy adaptive reliance on culture and language. Branching cultural lineages have led to diverse ways of thinking, acting, and communicating. Anthropology's main contribution to the study of dreams so far has been to document this variation in how dreams are experienced, are understood, and affect behavior in different cultures, allowing us to identify universal patterns of human dreaming.

In one of anthropology's foundational works, Tylor (1877[1871]) suggested that meeting people in dreams likely led our ancestors to believe in separable, immortal aspects of persons—spirits—implicating dreams in the origins of religion. For a dream to be taken as evidence requires a cultural belief about dreams that they are not merely imaginary; various beliefs of this sort have been historically and ethnographically documented. Many anthropologists in the 20th century collected dream narratives in diverse cultural settings and documented how particular cultural dream theories influenced how dreams were interpreted. Later, emphasis moved from studying dream narratives as objects to investigating dream sharing and communication (Tedlock, 1991).

Several rich ethnographies have appeared on how particular dream traditions and other cultural institutions influence one another (e.g., Poirier, 2005). Some of these works include sophisticated linguistic analyses of how dream-related phenomena are differently represented in particular languages. These studies have demonstrated that dreaming and waking life profoundly influence one another in a diversity of ways depending on prevailing cultural assumptions.

Despite anthropology's holistic ideal, almost all anthropological studies of dreams have been conducted by cultural anthropologists using ethnographic methods. Participant observation and interviews among living peoples to collect dream narratives and find out how dreams and dreaming work in different living cultures are the easiest methods available for anthropologists to make a distinctive contribution to our understanding of dreams and dreaming (Lohmann, 2007). Relatively undeveloped in the discipline is the study of the relationship between dreams and language, the biology of dreaming, how biological and cultural factors interact in generating dreams and their consequences, how dreaming has evolved and varies among primates, and how dreams leave their mark on the material record through which archaeologists study past peoples.

The ethnography of dreams can advance by showing how anatomy and physiology enable the learning of distinctive cultures of dreaming, while shaping some of their observed patterns. As biological anthropology concentrates more on brain and sense functioning as these relate to culture and language, and as psychological and neuroscience findings are further incorporated into the anthropological purview, we will develop a more sophisticated biocultural understanding of human dreaming and its evolution.

Improving archaeological methods of reconstructing past people's subjective experiences from the material they left behind can provide a long-term perspective on dreams in past cultures. This counteracts presentist stereotypes of human dreaming in the same way as ethnographies help correct culture-bound misunderstandings in the science of dreaming. Examples of the potential for this are best developed in studies of iconography, including Houston and Stuart's (1989) decipherment of an ancient Maya glyph meaning a personal dream spirit, which significantly altered anthropologists' understanding of ancient Maya culture. This finding was made possible by drawing on archaeological, linguistic, and cultural anthropology and illustrates the potential for the coming general anthropology of dreams.

The sparse attention to dreams and dreaming by anthropologists working outside cultural anthropology and insufficient efforts to incorporate all four subfields and other disciplines into the anthropology of dreams have left a gap in our knowledge that is just beginning to be addressed. Building the general anthropology of sleep experiences is the next frontier for dream research in the discipline.

Roger Ivar Lohmann

See also: entries related to Cross-Cultural Dreams

References

Houston, S., & Stuart, D. (1989). The way glyph: Evidence for "co-essences" among the classic Maya. In *Research reports on ancient Maya writing* (p. 30). Washington: Center for Maya Research.

Lohmann, R. I. (2007). Dreams and ethnography. In D. L. Barrett & P. McNamara (Eds.), *The new science of dreaming, volume 3, cultural and theoretical perspectives* (pp. 35–69). Westport, CT: Praeger.

Poirier, S. (2005). *A world of relationships: Itineraries, dreams, and events in the Australian Western Desert.* Toronto: University of Toronto Press.

Tedlock, B. (1991). The new anthropology of dreaming. *Dreaming, 1*(2), 161–178.

Tylor, E. B. (1877[1871]). *Primitive culture: Researches into the development of mythology, philosophy, religion, language, art and custom* (2 vols.). New York: Henry Holt and Company.

Anthropology of Sleep

Anthropology aims to document and understand the full sweep of human diversity. As such, an anthropological account of sleep should include evolutionary, comparative, and descriptive cultural and biobehavioral evidence about the what, why, and so what of this most common of behaviors. Yet the account is incomplete because anthropology, so concerned with people's waking lives, has scanted sleep but now is waking up to its importance. Sleep is a product of biology and culture: emerging material on the diversity of human sleep practices questions some assumptions of sleep science and contrasts with Western sleep cultures even as it confirms others. Along with evolutionary analysis, this material provides new ideas about old problems concerning why we sleep, how it works, what it does, what affects it, and what can go wrong.

Evolutionary Considerations

A comprehensive anthropology of human sleep begins by looking at its place in the species' adaptive complex. Humans flourish under widely differing conditions in an enormous range of environments, by relying on a suite of cultural and biological adaptations. Culture and social life are indispensable for human survival and integral to development and function. Consequently, culture shapes the worlds that humans inhabit. Children grow up and adults survive by living in social groups structured and operating through culture, composed of shared modes of thought, perception, and behavior, including beliefs, values, and practices. The dependence on culture is built in to organic design, as exemplified by the ability to acquire language.

Thus, culture gets under the skin. Sleep is no exception, and a survey of key human features suggests how. First, intense sociality mandates that sleep is social, designed to accommodate and likely to rely on the presence of others for physical, social, and emotional security. Infants depend completely on adult care, for example, and the historic ethnographic record documents that cultures consistently placed babies in the bed or room with caregivers, in contrast to societies today that place infants in separate rooms, alone. Although the brain regulates sleep, and its development and function rely heavily on context, the effects of sleeping arrangements and patterns throughout life remain unstudied. Second, enormous cultural and ecological diversity requires behavioral flexibility, including sleep, that accommodates ongoing social, subsistence, and other survival demands. Humans can adjust sleep schedules or restrict sleep as demands or opportunities require. For example, documented cases of bush- or forest-living foragers relate that mobile groups stalked by big cats can collectively maintain 24-hour vigilance for days or weeks at a time. People stay up for positive reasons, too: virtually all societies observe festive occasions that curtail sleep, often for extended periods. Third,

behavioral flexibility comes at a cost: curtailed sleep triggers a suite of adaptive stress responses that reallocate mental and physical resources. This is fine in the short term, but can mount up from sustained sleep shortages to increased mental and physical health risks such as depression, obesity, or diabetes. Thus, lifestyles that erode sleep are sustainable but costly to health.

Sleep Ecology

Although cross-cultural systematic studies of sleep behavior are scant, ethnographic and historical accounts describe sleeping conditions (where, when, how, and with whom) as well as cultural, demographic, and climatic factors that pattern sleep

Sleeping man, Kathmandu, Nepal 2007. (Klaus Roesch)

behavior. Such cross-cultural evidence yields a general profile of sleep as integrated in the flow of daily life, as occurring in more than one daily episode if needed, and as best done in the same bed or room with others rather than alone. Relatedly, bedtimes are fluid rather than fixed and napping is common. Bedding (mattresses, coverings, pillows) commonly is minimized to curb pests or parasites and reduce cleaning burden. Fire usually is present for warmth, light, and safety; sleeping conditions could be relatively noisy from people, domestic animals, and little or no acoustic and physical barrier such as solid walls or sealed windows to shut out disturbances.

Therefore, traditional sleep settings typically featured rich and dynamic sensory qualities including security and contact comfort from integration in social settings and relationships; fuzzy boundaries in time and space; and little climate control. Typical sleep settings in contemporary industrial societies, by contrast, appear to have more stable, comparatively impoverished sensory qualities, including solitary or low-contact sleeping arrangements; scheduled bedtimes and wake times with sleep compressed into a single block at night; padded bed and profuse bedding; absence of fire; darkness; silence; and high acoustic as well as physical boundaries to sleep spaces. Properties of the more static modernized sleep conditions that may make sleep regulation more difficult include sleeping alone or with limited contact from infancy onward; a lie down and die model of sleep that mandates a single nighttime block as normative; and sensory deprivation of physical and social cues in sleep settings.

Sleep across the Life Course

Cross-cultural evidence documents sleep conditions throughout the life course that are common across ethnographic records but different from prevailing Western practices. First, co-sleeping and co-rooming is extensive and sustained for life. As noted previously, infants and most children are normatively provided with sleeping partners from birth onward, and solitary sleep is an exception rather than a rule. As family formation evolves across the life course, the elderly are most at risk for losing sleep partners, so grandchildren or other kin often are recruited. Second, fixed bedtimes are absent for children, as with adults: daily routines are usual, but also highly flexible. Sleep commonly occurs as needed, interspersed with daily life. Thus, for instance, young children may watch, listen, or snooze during family meal preparation and conversation, or elderly may drift during community meetings or rituals. Third, the absence of fixed bedtimes and ability to accommodate individual sleep needs around the clock support a lack of rules about specific, stage-graded developmental needs for sleep. Thus, diverse and changing sleep patterns with age can be accommodated, including people who do not sleep through the night or elderly who fall asleep and wake up earlier.

Sleep Beliefs, Norms, and Values

That people devote a third of their time to sleep establishes it as a core element of daily life. The diversity of sleep settings and practices across societies reflects their diversity in the shared beliefs, values, and experiences that form the culture of each society. People sleep alone or with others, experience night fears or insomnia, or ration sleep or not, depending on what they understand about sleep, its value, and its qualities in relation to shared goods about health, status, survival, development and aging, gender, or spiritual and moral virtue. Hence, cultural perceptions, priorities, norms, and practical constraints shape when, how, and how much people sleep, and how they experience it, whether as restful, difficult, meaningful, or disturbed. Sleep science commonly overlooks this critical fact and assumes its Western cultural views and practices are universal and normative. Cross-cultural evidence can illuminate these assumptions.

Cultures differ in their accounts of what sleep is and how it happens. Sleep may be seen as produced and regulated by countervailing forces that oversee flows in life or energy, as manifested in diurnal light–dark cycles. Many regard this as a period of diminished energy and life force, to be navigated until the energy of day returns. Sleep's association with low life force or energy also may increase accessibility or vulnerability to other realms of existence. This association, plus the dramatic bodily changes in sleep, fosters linking sleep with death (Greek mythology and contemporary Islam name sleep as the brother of death). Or it may be seen as a product of sheer physical tiredness that wells up to overwhelm the sleeper, an assertion of physical needs like hunger. Sleep also may be viewed as a delicate state requiring quiet and privacy (as in North America) or as robust and compatible with noise and company. Exemplifying the latter, many Balinese rituals occur when spirits are most active, at night, and communities may stay up for days attending nightly performances of epic shadow plays. People attend from infancy onward and learn to drowse amid the din. Western science provides materialist explanations regarding sleep physiology and regulation that pervade globalizing views of sleep.

Cultural accounts also differ on what sleep does, what it is for. Sleep may serve spiritual, physical, and even practical needs. For example, many societies see sleep as a time of enhanced connection or vulnerability to nonhuman dimensions that can provide valuable information about existence and human's place or action within it. Sleepers may walk in other spirit realms or witness scenes that interpret the present or foretell the future. Dreams ground such views. Thus, sleep may enable communication with totem animals, ancestors, or spiritual entities that can guide decisions or behavior (hunting, travel, conflicts), or provide a moral compass in personal or social life. Sleep also may be viewed as protective or restorative, a means to block out and rest from external demands, to save physical and emotional energy. Effects of sleep on waking performance (tasks, emotions, memory) reinforce perceived importance of sleep.

Cultural accounts of how sleep happens and what it does also relate to what it means. Sleep commonly is allied with physical and spiritual vulnerability and danger, a time when low life-energy slides toward death or when inimical forces might consume or pervert the soul or life force. Many practices relate to sleep safety. Co-sleeping ties sleepers to the human world and reduces response time for illness or danger. Thus, the Gebusi in New Guinea believed that the ill must have continuous attendants, and that sleeping alone risked soul loss or witchcraft. Amulets, prayers, and other practices to bolster moral strength and alliance with protective forces or deter evil ones also are common. Moreover, deep sleep may be viewed as particularly risky while lighter, more easily reversed sleep is more valued and is cultivated through dynamic sleep settings or extended rituals. The meanings and emotions associated with sleep (danger, fear, worry) also can foster insecurity and heighten vigilance and lighten sleep (analogous to when a bad storm is predicted, or fearing to miss the alarm clock). Contrarily, some Western societies, such as the United States, value deep, uninterrupted slumber and readily label inability to sleep through the night as insomnia. Sleep furthermore is imbued with morality. Sleeping arrangements and sleep behaviors, for example, are judged and sanctioned or pathologized based on local codes. Thus, sleeping with the wrong person may be punished, oversleepers may lose their jobs, sleep paralysis may be treated as possession, and infants who sleep through the night may be called good babies, depending on cultural norms. Similarly, a few societies value babies' sleeping alone, while others regard it as child abuse.

Globalization and Culture Change

Globalization and the forces of rapid social change are transforming sleep in many ways. These forces include changing daily schedules for new forms of labor and universal schooling; introduction of mass media and technologies; shifts in family and household structure; altered settlement patterns (particularly urbanization), infrastructure, and housing; and uptake of Western scientific and biomedical accounts of human function, behavior, and health. Ever more people use Western beds, sleep alone, have alarm clocks, and stay up with TV, computer chat, or online games. Such structural, technical, and behavioral changes have altered beliefs, priorities, and practices related to sleep. What difference does this make for sleep behavior, sleep experiences, and health? Are sleep physiology and sleep needs everywhere the same? Anthropology is deeply interested in these questions. However, researchers lack a robust database on sleep before globalization to illuminate which characteristics are due to cultural diversity, lived experience, capabilities, welfare, and disparities. Opportunity to document sleep culture, behavior, biology, and their correlates before these changes is vanishing rapidly: systematic field studies of sleep in remote settings are needed now.

Carol M. Worthman

See also: entries related to Evolution of Sleep

References
McKenna, J. J., Ball, H. L., & Gettler, L. T. (2007). Mother–infant cosleeping, breastfeeding and sudden infant death syndrome: What biological anthropology has discovered about normal infant sleep and pediatric sleep medicine. *American Journal of Physical Anthropology, 132*, 133–161.
Worthman, C. M. (2008). After dark: The evolutionary ecology of human sleep. In W. R. Trevathan, E. O. Smith, & J. J. McKenna (Eds.), *Evolutionary medicine and health: New perspectives* (pp. 291–313). New York: Oxford University Press.

Worthman, C.M. (2011). Developmental cultural ecology of human sleep. In M. El-Sheikh (Ed.), *Sleep and development: Familial and socio-cultural considerations.* New York: Oxford University Press.

Worthman, C.M., & Melby, M. (2002). Toward a comparative developmental ecology of human sleep. In M.A. Carskadon (Ed.), *Adolescent sleep patterns: Biological, social, and psychological influences* (pp. 69–117). New York: Cambridge University Press.

Antiquity and Dreams

From third-millennium Mesopotamia to the Christians of the Roman Empire, one encounters the conviction that dreams came from gods or from the dead; they were exogenous communications, rather than inner psychological productions. A characteristic form of such dreams throughout antiquity was the epiphany dream in which an authoritative figure appeared and gave advice to the dreamer as in the *Iliad* (2.1ff.), where Zeus sends a destructive dream to Agamemnon. This dream took the form of the trusted advisor Nestor, who stood above the head of the sleeping general, and encouraged him to attack Troy without delay to achieve swift victory. In the *Odyssey* (19.562ff.), we learn that such false dreams passed through a gate of ivory, while true dreams came through a gate of horn.

Incantations and rituals proliferated to cultivate good dreams or defuse bad dreams. In late second-millennium Egypt, the sufferer of a bad dream would utter the words, "Hail, o you good dream, which is seen in the night and in the day. Drive out all the deep-rooted filth and bad things which Seth, son of Nut, created" (Szpakowska, 2003, p. 197). Then the dreamer's face was rubbed with a paste of bread and fresh herbs marinated in beer and myrrh. The clay cobras found at Egyptian sites may have been set up in the four corners of a bedroom in order to repel any evil demons, including nightmare demons. An Assyrian compendium contains a ritual text instructing recipients of evil dreams how to invoke the god Shamash to "turn the dream which I saw into good luck!" The ritual culminated with the dreamer throwing a lump of clay into the river to dissolve just like the bad dream (Butler, 1998, p. 294).

Although gods and demons presided over dreams, the practice of incubation (*incubatio* sleeping in), the ritual of sleeping in a temple in order to receive beneficial dreams from the god, is not much attested before the first millennium BCE. A Hittite cure for male infertility, or one who is "not a man vis-à-vis a woman," presents an early case (Mouton, 2007, p. 135). The patient was instructed to proceed to an uncultivated field. There he passed through a portal made of reeds while holding a spindle and a distaff, which he then exchanged for a bow and an arrow while the healer, named Paškuwatti, intoned, "I am going to remove your femininity and restore your virility" (Mouton, 2007, p. 136). Paškuwatti then prayed for the goddess Uliliyašši to appear to the patient as he slept on the floor before her altar. Each day the patient narrated the content of his dreams. If the goddess approached, this indicated that the dreamer was ritually pure, that is, not repellent on account of some fault. If she revealed her

PRAIRIE STATE COLLEGE
LIBRARY

3 2783 00123 1581

eyes, this was even better, and a dream of sex with the goddess was consummate. The ritual ended after such a dream, otherwise it continued.

Incubation dreams in Greco-Roman antiquity became more common as shrines to Asclepius and Serapis proliferated. At the temple of Asclepius at Epidaurus, pilgrims performed sacrifices and then slept in the precinct of the temple, hoping to be healed or to be shown the location of missing objects. The miraculous cures of the god were carved on stone columns for all to read: "Euhippos carried about a spear point in his jaw for six years. While he was sleeping here the god extracted the spear point and placed it in his hands. When day came he walked out healthy"; "A man with a stone in his penis. He had a dream. He dreamt that he was having intercourse with a beautiful boy, and in ejaculating he ejected the stone, picked it up and emerged holding it in his hand" (Lewis, 1976, pp. 38–39).

Ancient approaches to dreams could be narrated entirely as a phantasmagoria of exotic customs such as those considered previously. Such an approach, however, obscures the fact that the ancients also approached dreams with systems of logic, empirical observation, and naturalist explanation. Not everyone walked around convinced that dreams always and only came from gods and revealed the future. The situation was complex and contextual, as it is in contemporary society where neuroscience and psychoanalysis cohabit with supermarket dream books that teach one how to understand interpersonal relations or predict the future according to key dream symbols.

In ancient Mesopotamia as among the Homeric Greeks, dream divination (oneiromancy) was but one means of predicting the future. Alongside it ranged other modes of interpretation such as observing the flight of birds, astrology, and tocomancy (birth anomalies). Extispicy (inspection of animal entrails) was generally considered the most robust divinatory method. These practices required reasoning and the assemblage of databases correlating signs with outcomes. In Mesopotamia, the marshalling of this information fell to the *bârû*, examiners, who operated as proto-scientists. Their assumptions about causation would not pass muster today, but the systematicity with which they collected correlations does take a first step in the direction of scientific method.

The largest surviving ancient treatise on dream interpretation, Artemidorus's *Oneirocritica* (second century CE), follows the precepts of the empiricists, who emphasized personal experience, the collation of past experience (*istoria*), and reasoning by analogy. In other words, the researcher, Artemidorus, advanced his ideas about dream interpretation based on his long career as a practitioner, reference to the historical record of predictions and outcomes, and he addressed novel phenomena based on analogy with known cases.

Artemidorus held that only allegorical (i.e., symbolic) dreams could be used to interpret the future. A professional had to differentiate such dreams (*oneiroi*) from physical dreams (*enypnia,* a term often transliterated in the more recognizable form *enhypnion,* something seen in sleep), which only reflected the present condition of the body or the current desires of the person: "the fearful person sees what he fears; or again, the hungry man dreams of eating" (Lewis, 1976, p. 54). In making this distinction, and writing a whole volume about predictive *oneiroi,* Artemidorus confirmed that the ancients were very interested in the futurity of dreams. At the same time, his recognition of the *enypnia* showed that they understood that dreams could also arise from human physiology and psychology. A similar distinction can be traced back to Mesopotamia where symptomatic dreams such as nightmares and erotic dreams did not yield prognostications.

In Herodotus's *History* (7.16), the Persian king Xerxes momentarily wavers over going to war against the Greeks and he sees an epiphany dream much like that of Agamemnon. A figure appeared to him and urged him to wage war forthwith. His advisor, Artabanus, however, counseled him to ignore this dream, stating that dreams merely refigure what one has been thinking about during the day; they should not be taken as divine communications or predictions of the future. In order to prove this beyond a doubt, Artabanus dressed up as Xerxes and slept in his bed in order to trick the dream, and expose the sham of prophetic dreams. That night, not only did the dream appear again, but it recognized Artabanus as the man blocking the command of the earlier dream. In anger, the dream threatened to burn out Artabanus's eyes with hot iron rods if he did not agree to wage war on Greece.

A physical approach to dreams developed in the Hippocratic medical corpus, notably in the text *On Regimen* (book 4) where dreams of natural phenomena such as the stars or the moon indicated the state of the body leading to the prescription of health regimes: "Springs and wells relate to the bladder and in these cases diuretics should be employed. A rough sea indicates disease of the bowels. Light and gentle laxatives should be used to effect a thorough purgation" (Lewis, 1976, p. 30). This physiological tradition continued over the centuries and is reflected again in the writing of Artemidorus's contemporary, Galen, thus indicating that the enypnion, marginalized in the prophetic dream book tradition, enjoyed a separate, parallel tradition of theory and practice. This observation puts the brakes on a view of antiquity as exclusively entertaining an exogenous, future-oriented view of the dream. The ancients were of two incompletely reconciled minds.

In his perceptive treatise *On Divination through Sleep,* Aristotle remarked of oneiromancy that "it is not easy to despise it or to believe in it" (462b13, in Aristotle, 1996, p. 107). He ultimately espoused a view that coincides with the modern view of prophetic dreams: if they come true, they do so strictly by coincidence. The gods do not send dreams, the philosopher decided, but they are, nonetheless, demonic (463b15, in Aristotle, 1996, p. 111). This enigmatic term does not mean that they come from supernatural demons, nor should they be written off as mysterious, but rather, as he goes on to say, "that nature is demonic." In other words, nature stands beyond human as well as divine control; it is not completely predictable. If one rolls the dice enough times (his example), one will get the result one predicted. That is the most one may say for divinatory dreams.

If previous studies of dreams in antiquity have largely concentrated on a body of ideas and practices utterly different from those found in the contemporary Western world, texts such as Aristotle's or the appearance of deductive reasoning in Mesopotamia mobilize a different genealogy, one more continuous with contemporary thought. Current research on dreams in antiquity (e.g., Harris, 2009) focuses more on understanding the plurality and contradictoriness of ancient ideas, while exploring the development of naturalistic and physiological explanations.

Charles Stewart

See also: entries related to History of Dreams/Sleep

References

Aristotle. (1996). On sleep and dreams (Ed. & Trans. D. Gallop). Warminster, UK: Aris and Phillips.

Butler, S.A.L. (1998). Mesopotamian conceptions of dreams and dream rituals. Münster: Ugarit Verlag.

Harris, W. V. (2009). Dreams and experience in classical antiquity. Cambridge, MA: Harvard University Press.

Lewis, N. (1976). The interpretation of dreams and portents. Toronto: Samuel Stevens.

Mouton, A. (2007). Rêves hittites: Contribution à une histoire et une anthropologie du rêve en Anatolie ancienne [Hittite dreams: Contribution to a history and anthropology of dreams in ancient Anatolia]. Leiden: Brill.

Oppenheim, A. L. (2008 [1956]). The interpretation of dreams in the ancient Near East (New introduction by S. Noegel). Piscataway, NJ: Gorgia Press.

Szpakowska, K. (2003). Behind closed eyes: Dreams and nightmares in ancient Egypt. Swansea: The Classical Press of Wales.

Antrobus's (1983) Word Information Count (WIC)

Word information count (WIC) is an estimate of the amount of information about the sleep experience in each dream report—a count of the words that describe the content of the dream. WIC excludes redundancies in the report, commentary, and connections made to the mentation after the participant has awakened. John Antrobus (1983) and colleagues claim that it is an estimate of the degree of activation of those brain regions that generate cognitive information during sleep. If these WIC scales demonstrate a positive skew (as they have in many studies), thus violating the standard assumptions of analysis of variance, all of the WIC scores need to be log transformed ($\log_{10}$(WIC + 1)) to remove their positive skew.

Patrick McNamara

Reference

Antrobus, J. S. (1983). REM and NREM sleep reports: Comparison of word frequencies by cognitive classes. Psychophysiology, 20, 562–568.

Art Therapy and Dreams

Art Therapy

Art therapy expresses internal imagery through creative materials to improve an individual's mental, emotional, and spiritual well-being. Traditionally, art therapy asks clients to use familiar media—paint, crayons, and clays—to translate inner experiences into external elements. This translational process, as well as the images and objects that result, is then used in the therapeutic dialogue.

Engaging clients' creativity enriches traditional talk therapy by adding non-verbal communication, shifting it to art therapy. Art therapy can be less analytical and more interactive as clients express deeper issues and their resolution through art-making. With the need to choose materials and qualities that best represent their feelings, clients must separate far enough from those experiences to investigate and learn about them. In creating art projects from their feelings, clients now can give a tangible form to previously intangible feelings.

Increasing objectivity toward their feelings leads clients to understand and take control of their emotional responses. This process naturally develops their sense of power and safety toward the situation and players involved. So begins a positive feedback loop: from investigation to knowledge, to objectivity, to an increasing sense of control, to wider investigation. Through this creative process, art therapy presents rich information, deep psychological content, and enhanced emotional and mental resources for its clients. With more resources, the individual can heal more effectively and rapidly. Art therapy speeds and strengthens this healing.

Dreams and the Therapeutic Process

Dreams arise directly from the deep subconscious, illuminating feelings and beliefs that we may not acknowledge consciously. By opening a window on the subconscious,

dreams show us the network of interacting beliefs that run below the surface of daily life. These beliefs compel our waking behavior. At the same time, they seem to lie beyond our conscious control.

In dreams, beliefs appear as impressions that are mysterious, tantalizing, or promising—as well as terrifying or baffling. Laden with metaphor and symbolism, dreams' insights often remain hidden from us. We might even rebel or deny their content. Yet dreams are holograms of information, conversations between different faces of our awareness, intent on communicating and bent on healing.

They encode raw information from our subconscious, offered to us for mental, emotional, physical, and spiritual health.

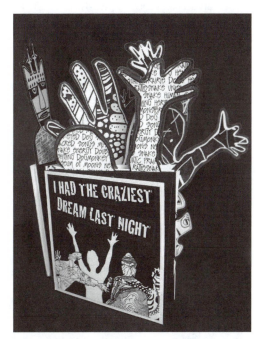

I Had the Craziest Dream Last Night, hand crafted pop-up book with pen and ink illustrations, by Victoria Rabinowe. (Victoria Rabinowe)

Through dreams, feelings are brought into our waking awareness to be healed and cleared or used as resources for greater well-being. Accessing this encoded information, learning its language, and using it to heal is the basis of dream art therapy.

Dream Art Therapy

Dream art therapy uses dream imagery as the basis for art-making. Giving form to the dream imagery becomes the basis for a creative project. This might be straightforward expressions: "Draw the images of the dream," "Write down the story of your dream and add what happened next," or "Physically act out the characters' actions."

The project might also be more exploratory. An interpretive overlay can be added to the creative project. Questions such as "If this dream was a map, what would it look like?" "If these people were animals what kind would they be?" take dreamers further into the power of knowledge held with their dreams, as they search for answers.

Traditional therapies rely on conversations with the conscious mind, awash in imprinted programming and verbally adept at defending itself. Yet our actual behavior is triggered by deeper, nonconscious feelings. Dream imagery arises uncensored from our subconscious awareness.

In dream-based art-making, clients inhabit two worlds at the same time. They are at once within the world of the dream, with its nonlinear narratives, wild and often-disturbing imagery, highly charged relationships, and intense experiences as well as in the art studio world of the waking. Dreamers access and use information directly from their subconscious as they stay centered in this creative space. They keep this dual connection open as they examine, choose, and act on their art materials.

Standing in this powerful position between known and unknown, dreamers deliberately link their waking, conscious mind to their deeper subconscious awareness. Dream artists become the intermediary between these worlds, the shamans of their own transformational processes. This potent union of cognitive knowledge and deep, dreaming wisdom integrates within the dream artists and adds new resources. Dreamers guide themselves to shift their relationship to dream imagery with gentleness, compassion, and humor.

This powerful integration can be quite therapeutic. For those with recurring and particularly distressing dream imagery, using dreams for ongoing art therapy may heal long-standing issues at their source. Art-making empowers dreamers to face the darkest aspects of their soul's journey in a positive and proactive way. Dreamwork by its nature is transformational. Using dreams as our inspiration for art-making amplifies the healing that art therapy brings on its own.

Victoria Rabinowe with Victoria Hughes

See also: entries related to Dreams and Therapy

Reference

Rabinowe, Victoria. (2008). I had the craziest dream last night! Twelve creative explorations into the genius of the night mind. Sante Fe, NM: Bright Shadow Press.

Asian Americans and Dreamwork

Dreams have long been an important part of Asian culture and daily life. Like other ethnic groups, Asian people have respected and used dreams for important purposes including foretelling the future of one's life and the nation. There is evidence that the ancient Chinese used dream dictionaries to interpret their dreams beginning around 1020 BCE (e.g., dreams about teeth falling out foretell possible danger to your parents; Van de Castle, 1994). Ancient Japanese politicians are also known to have used dreams to govern the nation (Tsuruta, 2005). In ancient Korea, stories exist that suggest important historical figures had accurate predictive dreams about their own futures. For example, a Korean story suggests that a young woman in ancient Korea bought a dream from her sister in which her sister urinated and made the town flood. She thought the dream would bring her good luck because flooding in dreams was believed to be related to earning power or money in Korean culture. The next day the young woman met the king and later became a queen. Some speculated that this might be a result of the dream she bought. In modern days, Asian people respect and use dreams in more personal ways. Many Koreans have a tradition of birth dreams, which is a dream had by a mother while pregnant. It is believed that the dream foretells the gender and future of a baby.

Dreamwork may be a helpful tool to facilitate comfort and disclosure about personal experiences in therapy with Asians and Asian Americans. Asian Americans are known as emotionally restrained (i.e., think that one should not show emotions to other people), and it may not be easy for Asian peoples to disclose personal or familial concerns to therapists because their disclosing may indicate weakness and bring shame to their family (Kim, Atkinson, & Yang, 1999). However, Asians might feel more comfort and less shame in disclosing their dreams to therapists. Ultimately, this can lead to spontaneous discussions about personal and familial problems related to their dreams (Hill et al., 2007; Sim et al., 2010; Tien, Lin, & Chen, 2006). Asians who value finding meaning in their dreams (e.g., Koreans) may be particularly willing to seek psychological help through dreamwork.

There have been only a few empirical studies that examined dreamwork with Asians or Asian Americans. In a single session of dreamwork with Asian American therapists and clients, Hill et al. (2007) examined the impact of different levels of therapist input (i.e., high or low) and found that Asian American clients did not prefer either high or low therapist input during dream sessions, in general. However, clients with high Asian values tend to prefer high-input dream sessions, while clients with low Asian values tend to prefer low-input dream sessions. In addition, clients with low attachment anxiety reported better session outcomes in the high-input dream sessions, whereas clients with high attachment anxiety reported better session outcomes in the low-input dream sessions. In another study, Tien and her colleagues (2006) found that participants reported more positive attitudes toward dreams after participating in dream sessions. In addition, even Taiwanese participants with less positive attitudes toward dreams still reported gains from dream sessions.

Sim et al. (2010) conducted a qualitative study on problems and action ideas (i.e., changes that clients want to make based on their understanding of their dreams; Hill, 2004) of female East Asian Americans during dream sessions and compared problems and action ideas of first-generation and second-generation female Asian Americans. Both first- and second-generation female Asian Americans typically discussed interpersonal issues and academic or career issues during dream sessions. Immigration- and adjustment-related issues and physical/health issues were discussed more often by first-generation female Asian Americans than by second-generation participants. In terms of action ideas, interpersonal behavioral changes were typical action plans for both first- and second-generation female Asian Americans. Changes in thoughts and feelings were discussed more frequently by first-generation female Asian Americans than by second-generation participants.

In conclusion, using dreams may be an effective way to make therapy accessible and less daunting to Asian Americans and possibly increase utilization of mental health services among Asian Americans. In dreamwork with Asian Americans, it is important that therapists tailor their therapy styles to each individual client's preferences because not all Asian Americans like directive dreamwork. Therapists may need to assess their clients' levels of Asian values and attachment anxiety and seek feedback from their clients throughout dream sessions (Hill et al., 2007). If clients do not have positive attitudes toward dreams but are willing to try dreamwork, using dreamwork can improve their attitudes toward dreams and may still provide some benefit (Tien et al., 2006). In addition, therapists may also want to attend to generational differences as first-generation and second-generation Asian Americans might share similar problems, but also present differences due to the different contexts in which they were born and raised (Sim et al., 2010).

Wonjin Sim

See also: entries related to Cross-Cultural Dreams

References

Hill, C.E. (Ed.). (2004). Dream work in therapy: Facilitating exploration, insight, and action. Washington, DC: American Psychological Association.

Hill, C.E., Tien, H.S., Sheu, H., Sim, W., Ma, Y., Choi, K., & Tashiro, T. (2007). Predictors of outcome of dream work for East Asian volunteer clients: Dream factors, attachment anxiety, Asian values, and therapist input. Dreaming, 17, 208–226.

Kim, B.S.K., Atkinson, D.R. & Yang, P.H. (1999). The Asian Values Scale: Development, factor analysis, validation, and reliability. Journal of Counseling Psychology, 46, 342–352.

Sim, W., Hill, C.E., Chowdhury, S., Huang, T., Zaman, N., & Talavera, P. (2010). Problems and action ideas discussed by first- and second-generation female East Asian students during dream sessions. Dreaming, 20, 42–59.

Tien, H.-S., Lin, C.-H., & Chen, S.-C. (2006). Dream interpretation session for college students in Taiwan: Who benefits and what volunteer clients view as most and least helpful. Dreaming, 16, 246–257.

Tsuruta, M. (2005). Dreaming in Japan. Dream Time, 22, 16–19.

Van de Castle, R.L. (1994). Our dreaming mind. New York: Ballantine Books.

Asklepieia and Asklepian Rites

For close to a thousand years, from around 600 BCE to 400 CE (the archaic through the Hellenistic and Roman periods), the god Asklepios was one of the most popular deities in Mediterranean antiquity. Even within his cult, he was said to have been originally a human being—a physician who was born and lived in Homeric Trikka, in northern archaic Greece. The earliest mention of Asklepios is found in Homer's Iliad, compiled no later than the mid-eighth century BCE, although on textual grounds demonstrably incorporating narratives and traditions as far back as the Bronze Age. In the Iliad, Asklepios is mentioned simply and reverentially as "the blameless physician" (amunos ieteros, Iliad 11.518), extremely skilled in the healing arts. Later divinized, the healing god practiced his healing arts on hopeless cases, mostly through the supervised incubation of dreams at his sanctuaries. The greatest of these was at Epidauros on the Argive Peninsula, where his grave was said to be.

There were more than a hundred Asklepios shrines, or healing centers, in the ancient world, including the famous ones at Epidauros, Athens, Corinth, and Pergamon in Asia Minor, but they were also found as far away as Spain and Algeria. These were largely outdoor clinics, defended not only against intrusion from without but also pollution from within. The sanctuary, or temenos, but especially the Asklepieion, was a place set apart, literally cut apart (from temnein, to cut), from normal collective life. With only the rare exception (such as the god's famous healing shrine on the Isola Tiberi in the middle of the putrid river running through Rome), Asklepieia were established in places of great natural beauty, far beyond the polis with its bustling agora and distracting life of constant transaction. As the Roman traveler Pausanias wrote of Epidauros in the second century CE, "The sacred grove of Asclepius is surrounded by bounds on every side. No men die or women give birth within the enclosure; the same rule is observed in the island of Delos" (Descriptio Graecae 2.27.1). The temple, altar, and incubation building, and associated structures, including theaters, athletic stadia, and extensive networks of cisterns, conduits, and healing wells, typically completely enclosed within a high retaining wall, were sacred to the god Asklepios, whose shrine was the telos of the pilgrimage of the desperate. These were places where evidence attests that fountains flowed; snakes and dogs, healing animals, roamed and licked the wounds of the suffering; festivals, processions, and dramatic performances, also held to be therapeutic, were staged in monumental theaters; and artificial lakes allowed regimens of swimming, boating, or hypothermic exposure (if the god prescribed it). The largest Asklepieia also had gymnasia for exercise. Central temples were adorned with inscribed accounts of healing, like that of Aeschines the Orator, bearing witness to the god's compassion and power. Pausanias says, "Tablets (stelai) stood within the enclosure. Of old, there were more of them: in my time six were left. On these tablets are engraved the names of men and women who were healed by Asclepius, together with the disease from which each suffered, and how he was cured" (Descriptio Graecae 2.27.3). The healing dream was incubated—hatched, as it were—in a therapeutic building, the abaton, the place of no-walking, usually close by the god's own temple. In the classical period, patient preparations for dream incubation were relatively simple: purification in water, using the extensive system of sacred springs and wells within the walls, and sacrifices, some bloodless; by the Roman period, more elaborate torchlight processions may have developed. Porphyry (On Abstinence 2.19) and Clement of Alexandria (Stromateis 5.1.13) repeat the carved inscription over the entrance to Epidaurus, "Pure must be he who enters the fragrant temple; purity means to think nothing but holy thoughts" (Edelstein & Edelstein, 1945[1998]: I, T. 318, 163–164; I, T. 336, 177–78). This, however, is an ethicized descendent of an earlier, older prohibition, which was very much about physical purity and lack of contamination.

The suppliant to Asklepios was never alone. She was cared for from the outset of her visit by attendants, who showed her where to sleep, on a kline (couch) or directly on the floor. She slept nearby others like herself, who sought healing and help. She slept nearby the god to be tended by him. The dream was the consulting room in which one encountered the god-physician. It was itself the theater of healing. Asklepios visited the individual sufferer privately and often immediately undertook to alleviate her symptoms with his own hands.

Aelius Aristides, a hypochondriac orator from second century BCE Pergamon in Asia Minor, presents in his Sacred Tales one of the most striking accounts of a dream epiphany and of the magnetic, tender shock it induced in the dreamer.

> For there was a seeming, as it were, to touch him and to perceive that he himself had come, and to be between sleep and waking, and to wish to look up and to be in anguish that he might depart too soon, and to strain the ears and to hear some things as in a dream, some as in a waking state. Hair stood straight, and there were tears of joy, and the pride of one's heart was inoffensive. And what man could describe these things in words? If any man has been initiated, he knows and understands. (Aelius Aristides, The Sacred Tales 2. 32–33 in Behr, 1968, p. 230)

The god's coming was the fulcrum of all the ritual activity preceding it and all that would ensue afterward. It was an iconic encounter. It was the goal of the sought dream.

In these ancient accounts, Asklepios the dream surgeon, at times taking the form of a snake or a dog, healed the afflicted organ during the dream, or else prescribed therapeutic regimens to be undertaken in the confines of the sanctuary after the dreamer awoke. In dreams, the accounts tell us, the god did predictable things, like removing abscesses or extracting embedded weapons. He also did weird things, surreal things, godlike things. He once cut open an abdomen to remove an abscess in one dream, covering the floor of the abaton with blood, or excised an eyeball and inserted drugs into the open socket. He even severed a head and reattached it.

On waking, unlike the experience of our modern hospitals, although similar to that of our modern hospices, the sufferer found the healing environment of the dream reinforced by the sanctuary in which it was dreamed. The dream would have been retold to cult attendants and fellow patients as an interior event of great value with exterior consequences. The patient was offered an interpretation of her dream at once. Whatever length of time the divine prescriptions required, she was free and indeed expected to stay until she was well, sharply deviating from the managed care of today that often ejects sick people back to the undifferentiated chaos of secular life before they are ready to leave the liminal space of the hospital. The incubated dream was thus also the centerpiece of a concentric series of circles that encompassed both dreaming and waking states.

Certainly cures at these shrines included recognizably contemporary holistic therapies such as rest, exercise, psychology, bathing, and engagement in music and drama. But they also included bizarre measures such as the eating of figs mixed with ashes from the god's altar, naked marathons in freezing rain, abstinence from bathing for weeks, and bodily suspension upside down for long periods of time. As we have said, dream cures often entailed graphic accounts, including radical surgery, challenging any facile assumption of sublimation. An entire set of surgical instruments has been excavated at Epidauros. Its purpose may have been to enact a surgery stipulated in an incubated dream,

pace assertions such as Carl Alfred Meier's: "Nor were there any physicians in the sacred precinct and no medical therapy of any kind" (Meier, 1967, p. 216). This we cannot say with certainty; indeed, the evidence contravenes.

Often the divine prognosis or even the ailment itself may seem to us to be so fantastic as to be unintelligible, locked in the foreign country that is the past. A number of inscriptions of this kind, called iamata, survive from the classical period, which were dictated by recovered patients to sanctuary scribes, most likely the priests. These describe in the first person the original illness or injury and its miraculous cure at the Asklepieia. The most famous and complete were the six Pausanias saw at Epidauros; two of the six were excavated, along with fragments of two others. They are encyclopedic, listing multiple stories of complaints and cures. From Stele I: "Cleinatas of Thebes with the lice. He came with a great number of lice on his body, slept in the Temple, and sees a vision. It seems to him that the god stripped him and made him stand upright, naked, and with a broom brushed the lice from off his body. When day came he left the Temple well" (I. 28). Gorgias of Heracleia was in a worse way: "Gorgias of Heracleia with pus. In a battle he had been wounded by an arrow so badly that he filled sixty-seven basins with pus. While sleeping in the Temple he saw a vision. It seemed to him the god extracted the arrow point from his lung. When day came he walked out well, holding the point of the arrow in his hands" (I. 30). And some are beyond the pale: "Aristagora of Troezen. She had a tapeworm in her belly, and she slept in the Temple of Asclepius at Troezen and saw a dream. It seemed to her that the sons of the god, while he was not present but away in Epidaurus, cut off her head, but, being unable to put it back again, they sent a messenger to Asclepius asking him to come. Meanwhile day breaks and the priest clearly sees her head cut off from her body. When night approached, Aristagora had a vision. It seemed to her the god had come from Epidaurus and fastened her head on to her neck. Then he cut open her belly, took a tapeworm out, and stitched her up again. And after that she became well" (I. 23) (Edelstein & Edelstein, 1945[1998], pp. 221–237).

Ancient incubations, no matter how elaborated their symbolic expression, usually produced very practical dream recommendations or predictions, and this was most markedly true in the case of dream cures. However these were enacted, they were not merely symbolic. Mystery continues to surround what went on in these centers, but we know a great deal about what people believed went on. The primary goal of such epiphanies was, in fact, healing—not, as might be easier for the postmodern mind to digest, spiritual transformation, but clinical cure—in which the god who came in the dream was an expert physician whose expertise far outstripped that of any mortal. So the ancient writer Diogenes Laertius distinguishes: "Phoebus Apollo gave to mortals Asclepius and Plato, the one to save their souls, the other to save their bodies" (Vita Philosophorum 3.5). Rather than revealing the healing dream as a sublimated entity whose efficacy was purely psychological or spiritual, centuries of evidence from antiquity instead repeatedly attest to literal cures of dire physical illnesses or traumas. Sometimes these were partial or temporary, and relapses sent the sufferers back to Asklepios. Sometimes, or so the claims ran, they were total and permanent.

The sufferers, relieved of the disease or affliction that had been tormenting them, the suppurating wound or the pregnancy gestating for years, saw the god doing things to their dream bodies. But their waking bodies walked out of the sanctuary holding the long-buried arrow point or the endlessly unborn baby.

Payment was always due: money if possible, although the poor were subsidized. Offerings and inscriptions told the world what happened in the dream and its real-life consequences. The grateful patient of Asklepios who successfully implemented his advice dedicated iatra or sostra, thank offerings, according to his or her wealth. These could take, among other things, the form of sacrificed cock (as in Socrates's final words to Crito), a composed paean, the erection of a stone stele with an account of the incubation and its aftermath, or a sculpted image of the healed body part to show the world what the god had done for the suppliant in her dreams. Cases of god-sent relapse in the event of tardy payment are known. Again, the bottom line was actual cure, undertaken or envisioned in the therapeutic dream in graphic detail.

The aftermath of an intense or prolonged incubation could be a degree of possession by or absorption into the deity; after the incubation, if it produces the desired dream of the god, one's life is no longer entirely one's own. It is as though the prolonged contact through dreams with the holy place, and thus with the god that lives there, has blurred the edges of the distinct and socially defended personality; the god has infested the dreamer. This is understandably especially true of healing dreams, and the worse the illness or wound, the truer it is. There can be said to be a kind of fusion of the smaller self with the larger, and this might even be asserted without psychoanalytic overtones. That fusion can be forged by gratitude alone, and it is the result of the invasion of the personal world of one's dreams by the transpersonal godhead.

Later these extreme cases might stay at the healing shrine and become permanent fixtures, dream hangers-on; in Hellenistic Greek cultures, they were called katochoi, literally, voluntary prisoners, such as the notorious and prolific Aelius Aristides, who took up residence at the Asklepieion at Pergamon intermittently for a total of 12 years. This condition is not a pathology separate from that of a normal seeker of dreams at the shrine. Rather, it simply represents a more extreme existential condition and behavior on the spectrum of incubation; that spectrum inevitably mandates identification with the god who dreams through and thus into the sufferer. One belongs to the goddess by dint of having dreamed her; this is made manifest by those who remain at the incubation shrine instead of going home.

Although they are no more, Asklepieia are linked by heritage to other dream-incubation sites and healing dream traditions throughout the world, including those still in use at the present time. Were these the predecessors of the foreign clinics of Stage IV cancer patients, vendors of extreme diets and wild promises of cure? The difference is that the Asklepieia represented a time-honored and accepted institution not only woven into the social fabric of ancient Greece, but also embraced by more orthodox healers. The path to the shrine of Asklepios was culturally legitimate. There was a lack of skepticism on the part of ancients toward the Asklepieia as valuable places of genuine medicine, in particular, an odd (to us) unwillingness on the part of Hippocratic and other doctors directly to challenge the authority of the god, since he would take on himself what they could not cure. In fact, most ancient Greek physicians who practiced in their communities joined priests of the Asklepian sanctuaries in considering themselves his followers. On Kos and elsewhere, Hippocratic physicians were actually called Asklepiadai, or sons of Asklepios. If they were at all able, the ill made their way, or were carried, to those sanctuaries where they could seek the help of the god. And largely, unlike any therapeutic model practiced today in the West, that help was dispensed only through dreams.

Kimberley C. Patton

Note

This entry is in part adapted from the two sources by the author listed in the following references. Translations of ancient Greek sources are from Edelstein and Edelstein, Asclepius, with some amendments by the author.

References

Behr, C. (Trans. and Ed). (1968). Aelius Aristides and the sacred tales. Amsterdam: Adolf M. Hakkert.

Edelstein, E., & Edelstein, L. (1945[1998]). Asclepius: Collection and interpretation of the testimonies (Vols. I & II). Baltimore: Johns Hopkins University Press.

Kearney, M. (2000). A place of healing: Working with suffering in living and dying. New York: Oxford University Press.

Meier, C.A. (1967). Ancient incubation and modern psychotherapy (Trans. Monica Curtis). Evanston, IL: Northwestern University Press.

Miller, P.C. (1994). Dreams in late antiquity: Studies in the imagination of a culture. Princeton, NJ: Princeton University Press.

Patton, K. (2004). "A great and strange correction": Intentionality, locality, and epiphany in the category of dream incubation. History of Religions, 43(3), 194–223.

Patton, K. (2009). Ancient Asklepieia: Institutional incubation and the hope of healing. In S. Aizenstat & R. Bosnak (Eds.), Imagination and medicine: The future of healing in an age of neuroscience (pp. 3–34). Dallas: Spring Journal Books.

Attention Deficit with Hyperactivity: Dreaming in Children with ADHD

Sleep complaints have often been reported by children and adults with attention deficit/hyperactivity disorder (ADHD); however, polysomnographic studies in the sleep laboratory yielded inconsistent results for ADHD children and only provided evidence for a link between ADHD and periodic limb movements during sleep (Sadeh, Pergamin, & Bar-Haim, 2006). Regarding dreaming, the continuity hypothesis of dreaming simply stating that waking life is reflected in dreams would predict that waking-life symptoms are reflected in the dreams of patients with psychiatric disorders (Schredl & Engelhardt, 2001). For example, Schredl and Engelhardt (2001) reported a direct relationship

between daytime depressive mood and negative dream emotions in patients with major depressive disorder as well as in patients with other disorders. As the major symptoms of ADHD are described as inattention, difficulty in performing tasks, hyperactivity, and impulsivity, it was expected that dream content would reflect these areas. In the first and yet only study on this topic (Schredl & Sartorius, 2010), 103 children with ADHD and 100 controls completed a dream questionnaire eliciting dream-recall frequency and the most recent dream. In contrast to the expectation, the dreams of the children with ADHD did not show a heightened occurrence of activities but were more negatively toned and included more misfortunes/threats, negative endings, and physical aggression toward the dreamer. General dream characteristics such as dream length and dream bizarreness as well as dream-recall frequency did not differ from children without ADHD. As this is the first study, methodological issues should be considered. Finding hyperactivity within dreams might need more specific self-rating scales because an external judge might not be able to infer hyperactive behavior from the dream report alone. The negatively toned dreams reflect the child's distress often associated with having ADHD, especially the impulsivity. It would be very interesting to study whether the negatively toned dreams change during pharmacological and/or psychotherapeutic treatment in a way similar to how sleep quality improves (Sobanski, Schredl, Kettler, & Alm, 2008).

To summarize, the waking-life symptoms affect the dreams of children with ADHD to a considerable amount. Two clinical applications of these findings might benefit these children. First, questions regarding dreams should be included in the diagnostic interview and, second, specific treatment techniques such as the imagery rehearsal treatment might be helpful for the children with ADHD by reducing the frequency of negatively toned dreams and, thus, alleviating the negative effects of these dreams on daytime mood.

Michael Schredl

See also: entries related to Sleep and Development

References

Sadeh, A., Pergamin, L., & Bar-Haim, Y. (2006). Sleep in children with attention-deficit hyperactivity disorder: A meta-analysis of polysomnographic studies. Sleep Medicine Reviews, 10, 381–398.

Schredl, M., & Engelhardt, H. (2001). Dreaming and psychopathology: Dream recall and dream content of psychiatric inpatients. Sleep and Hypnosis, 3, 44–54.

Schredl, M., & Sartorius, H. (2010). Dream recall and dream content in children with attention deficit/hyperactivity disorder. Child Psychiatry and Human Development, 41, 230–238.

Sobanski, E., Schredl, M., Kettler, N., & Alm, B. (2008). Sleep in adults with attention deficit hyperactivity disorder (ADHD) before and during treatment with methylphenidate: A controlled polysomnographic study. Sleep, 31, 375–381.

Awake, Frozen with the Most Awful Fears, but Also Asleep

The protagonist in Herman Melville's 1851 novel Moby Dick, Ishmael, describes an experience in which he awakens, "half steeped in dreams," but is "frozen with the most awful fears," thinking that if he "could but stir it one single inch, the horrid sleep would be broken" (Melville, 1851, p. 29). Here, Melville describes the classic hallmarks of sleep paralysis, 25 years before it was recognized by the medical community (Mitchell, 1876). According to the International Classification of Sleep Disorders, sleep paralysis is a period of inability to perform voluntary movements either at sleep onset or on awakening, either during the night or in the morning, that is usually accompanied by terrifying hallucinations (American Academy of Sleep Medicine, 2001). How can individuals be awake, and yet paralyzed, and what can we learn from the nature of the hallucinations that are commonly reported?

Researchers have found that sleep paralysis occurs when the inhibitory directives that the brain sends during REM sleep to suppress movements (and muscle activity) continue to be active even after an individual awakens. Thus, individuals experiencing sleep paralysis, although consciously aware that they are no longer asleep, are still subject to the active suppression of motor activity (atonia) that is normally confined to REM sleep. Under these conditions, the boundaries that separate sleep from wakefulness no longer exist, and brain processes that are normally confined to only one or the other of these states occur simultaneously. The breakdown of these boundaries between sleep and wakefulness, which results in sleep paralysis, is not a rare event. In fact, instances of sleep paralysis affect a significant percentage of healthy adults: between 40 and 50 percent of all individuals experience at least one episode of sleep paralysis, lasting from seconds to a few minutes, during their lifetime (American Academy of Sleep Medicine, 2001).

Not only is sleep paralysis a relatively common occurrence, but the hallucinations that individuals experience during sleep paralysis share marked similarities in different cultures; namely, the presence of an unusual or foreign being who is threatening and induces fear in the individual. For example, in Fiji, the experience of sleep paralysis is interpreted as *kana tevoro* or being eaten or possessed by a demon. In Chinese culture, the hallucinations of sleep paralysis are often referred to as a ghost pressing on body. The Muslims of South Asia consider sleep paralysis to be an encounter with evil jinn and demons who have taken over one's body, while in African cultures it is commonly referred to as a witch riding your back. In Newfoundland and Labrador, people believe that there is an old hag that sits on one's chest and prevents one from breathing, and certain individuals are thought to be capable of hagging someone or causing an old hag episode to occur. In contemporary Western culture, reports of alien abduction are often attributed to the hallucinations that arise in conjunction with sleep paralysis. The way in which individuals react to the experience of being awake yet unable to move provides insights into how cognitive processes are influenced by cultural determinants. The consistency of hallucinations during sleep paralysis, despite cultural differences, also contrasts with the content of dream narratives, which vary greatly among individuals and are subject to personal experience (Cheyne, 2005).

How can one explain the constant occurrence of frightening hallucinations during sleep paralysis? If we all of a sudden found ourselves unable to move one single inch, despite our intent to do so, it seems natural to assume that feelings of profound anxiety would arise. In fact, similar terrifying sensations have been documented in experiments wherein individuals are awake, but paralyzed due to the administration of neuromuscular blocking agents, such as curare. Patients awakening from surgery, who find themselves unable to move, also report feelings of terror (Mainzer, 1979). These data indicate that the terrors of sleep paralysis occur as a consequence of being awake but immobile. Clearly, sleep paralysis provides us with a great deal of information about sleep, wakefulness, and what occurs when the boundaries that separate these states are no longer present.

Daniel R. Bronson and
Michael H. Chase

See also: entries related to Sleep Disorders

References

American Academy of Sleep Medicine. (2001). International classification of sleep disorders, revised: Diagnostic and coding manual. Chicago, IL: American Academy of Sleep Medicine.

Cheyne, A. (2005). Sleep paralysis episode frequency and number, types and structure of associated hallucinations. Journal of Sleep Research, 14(3), 319–324.

Mainzer, J. (1979). Awareness, muscle relaxants and balanced anesthesia. Canadian Anesthetists' Society Journal, 26, 386–393.

Melville, H. (1851). Moby dick. London: Richard Bentley.

Mitchell, S.W. (1876). On some of the disorders of sleep. Virginia Med Monthly, 2, 769–781.

Awakenings Protocol

One of the tried and true ways to investigate mentation that might occur during sleep is to wake people up and ask them about what they were experiencing while asleep. Of course, like any other method that relies on self-report, there are problems with this method. What if the individual's knowledge of his or her own mental states while asleep is faulty? What if people cannot remember what they were thinking about while asleep? What if people intentionally deceive researchers? There are no definitive answers to any of these concerns, regarding the awakenings method or protocol. But we can supply some provisional responses to these concerns. Most people in fact claim that they do sometimes remember experiencing thoughts and feelings while asleep. They call these experiences dreams. Thus, it is reasonable to suppose that some form of mentation occurs while asleep. What about people's knowledge or ability to report on that mentation? Well, people manifestly do report on mentation that they believe occurred while they were asleep. We can increase our confidence that these reports are true, or veridical, by analyzing thousands of such reports from thousands of people who vary in their backgrounds and abilities. It is now clear after a hundred years of such research that self-reported dreams contain some pretty common themes and content indicators. Most people report that they dream about social interactions with people they know like family members. Males report slightly different themes than females and certain dream figures (like male strangers) are typically associated with fear or anxiousness in dreams and so forth (see entries related to Dream Content). There can be little doubt that we are dealing with relatively reliable reports when people share their dreams. The fact that dreams contain unusual content relative to waking thought processes should not be surprising given that brain activation patterns are different from those seen in the waking state.

In addition to all the evidence gathered from dream content studies concerning the reliability of the awakenings protocol, there is now evidence that when a person is awakened from a particular sleep state, brain-state activation patterns associated with that state persist for several minutes (Balkin et al., 1999; Walker, Liston, Hobson, & Stickgold, 2002). Thus when we sample mentation within a 20-minute window after an awakening, we are actually sampling from the brain state obtained right before the awakening. These findings support the key assumption of research with the awakenings protocol that selected REM sleep brain-state effects persist for some 20 minutes after awakening. The existence and properties of potent brain-state carryover effects from REM sleep have been reviewed by Balkin et al. (1999), Bertini and Violani (1992), and Reinsel and Antrobus (1992). In one of the earliest studies demonstrating carryover effects, Fiss, Klein, and Bokert (1966) found that stories given in response to thematic apperception test cards were more visual and complex after REM versus NREM sleep awakenings. Lavie (1976) reported that perceptual effects induced by the spiral aftereffect and the beta or phi phenomenon persisted for up to 15 minutes after awakenings and were easier to induce after REM than NREM sleep awakenings. Stones (1977) demonstrated that word list learning tasks given after REM versus NREM sleep awakenings yielded excellent recall rates. In the case of REM sleep awakening, recall rates remained high even after a 20-minute delayed recall window. In the 1980s and 1990s, researchers vigorously pursued the possibility that carryover effects demonstrated laterality effects but dozens of experiments failed to convincingly demonstrate any such lateralized performance effects after REM versus NREM sleep awakenings. Nevertheless, consistent REM sleep carryover effects were demonstrated on affect and cognitive tasks. More recently several groups have reported carryover effects on varying types of tasks such as anagram solving (Stickgold, Whidbee, Schirmer, Patel, & Hobson, 2000) and memory processing (Walker et al., 2002).

Thus, we can to some extent probe the neurocognitive properties of a sleep state via the awakenings procedure. To illustrate use of the procedure to study sleep mentation effects, I summarize the method of Walker et al. (2002), as their method allows for sampling from both REM and NREM sleep states. To control for circadian and time-of-night effects, the order of awakenings from REM and NREM sleep is counterbalanced as described by Walker et al. (2002; see Figure 2).

All subjects are tested before lights out (PRE), and after REM and NREM sleep awakenings, and then in the morning (POST). If the investigators are interested in dreams, then participants are asked to report dreams (if any) and then to perform cognitive tasks after each awakening. Half of the subjects receive the tests after awakening from the second REM sleep period (REM$_a$) and fourth NREM sleep period (NREM$_a$); half receive the tests after the third NREM sleep period (NREM$_b$)

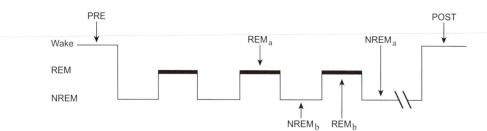

Figure 2: Awakenings protocol. Walker et al. Cognitive flexibility across the sleep-wake cycle: REM-sleep enhancement of anagram problem solving. *Cognitive Brain Research, 14*, 314–324. Copyright © 2002, Elsevier.

and the third REM sleep period (REM$_b$). After awaking in the morning, all subjects are given the tasks again (POST) (Figure 1 from Walker et al., 2002).

Patrick McNamara

See also: entries related to Sleep Assessment

References

Balkin, T.J., Braun, A.R., Wesensten, N.J., Varga, P.B., Carson, R.E., Belenky, G., et al. (1999). Bi-directional changes in regional cerebral blood flow across the first 20 min of wakefulness. Sleep Research Online, 2(Suppl. 1), 6.

Bertini, M., & Violani, C. (1992). The post awakening testing technique in the investigation of cognitive asymmetries during sleep. In J.S. Antrobus & M. Bertini (Eds.), The neuropsychology of sleep and dreaming (pp. 47–62). Hillsdale, NJ: Lawrence Erlbaum Associates.

Fiss, H., Klein, G.S., & Bokert, E. (1966). Waking fantasies following interruption of two types of sleep. Archives of General Psychiatry, 14, 543–551.

Lavie, P. (1976). Ultradian rhythms in the perception of two apparent motions. Chronobiologia, 3, 214–218.

McNamara, P., Auerbach, S., Johnson, P., Harris, E., & Doros, G. (2009). Impact of REM sleep on distortions of self concept, mood and memory in depressed/anxious participants. Journal of Affective Disorders, 122(3), 198–207.

Reinsel, R.A., & Antrobus, J. (1992). Lateralized task performance after awakening from sleep. In J.S. Antrobus & M. Bertini (Eds.), The neuropsychology of sleep and dreaming (pp. 63–87). Hillsdale, NJ: Lawrence Erlbaum Associates.

Stickgold, R., Scott, L., Fosse, R., & Hobson, J.A. (2001). Brain–mind states: I. Longitudinal field study of wake–sleep factors influencing mentation report length. Sleep, 24(2), 171–179.

Stickgold, R., Whidbee, D., Schirmer, B., Patel, V., & Hobson, J.A. (2000). Visual discrimination task improvement: A multistep process occurring during sleep. Journal of Cognitive Neuroscience, 12(2), 246–254.

Stones, M.J. (1977). Memory performance after arousal from different sleep stages. British Journal of Psychology, 68(2), 177–181.

Walker, M.P., Liston, C., Hobson, J.A., & Stickgold, R. (2002). Cognitive flexibility across the sleep–wake cycle: REM-sleep enhancement of anagram problem solving. Cognitive Brain Research, 14, 314–324.

B

Basics of Sleep Recordings

As sleeping organisms generally take a characteristic posture, refrain from further movements, and lack responsiveness to most environmental events, one can assume the state of sleep by direct observation. Tools that record movements such as actigraphs—little watchlike devices worn for several days or weeks—reveal the regularity of rest–activity cycles and therefore hint at sleep–wake schedules. However, for true differentiation of sleep from rested wakefulness, for example, a comatose state, precise measures of sleep rely on electrophysiological recordings.

At the beginning of the 20th century, tools had been developed to record electric activity, for example, of the brain or the heart. Characteristic changes in brain neuronal firing during sleep have then been described, revealing that sleep is not a steady state but rich in dynamics. Stages of sleep, from the process of falling asleep to deep sleep, are still based on electroencephalographic (EEG) features such as slowing of the dominant EEG frequency (see the entry "Cortical EEG Oscillations, Local Sleep, and Dream Recall") and single graphic elements such as sleep spindles (see the entry "Sleep Spindles"). In 1953, an additional sleep stage was described with rapid eye movements (REMs), low-amplitude EEG, and high amounts of dream reports upon awakening (Aserinsky & Kleitman,

1953). This REM sleep is further characterized by atonia of voluntary muscles. To differentiate from REM sleep, the other sleep stages that take about 75–80 percent of sleep time were termed non-REM (NREM) sleep (Rechtschaffen & Kales, 1968). The various sleep stages alternate throughout the night in a cyclic, recurring pattern (see the entry "Stages of Sleep and Associated Waveforms").

The gold standard to record sleep in humans is therefore based on three core measures: a combination of EEG with recordings of eye movements (electrooculogram, EOG) and muscle tone (electromyogram, EMG) (Keenan & Hirshkowitz, 2011). Without information on eye movements and muscle tone, a clear distinction of REM sleep is hardly possible (see Figure 3).

How Exactly Are Sleep Recordings Performed?

Data are obtained using surface electrodes that are temporarily glued with a conductive gel or paste on the surface of the scalp or skin at the desired positions. Electrodes may be reusable (e.g., for EEG) or disposable ones (e.g., common for electrocardiogram, ECG, recordings). The skin where the electrodes are placed has to be cleaned to minimize impedance and ensure adequate conduction, as the goal is to measure tiny electric currents without interfering noise.

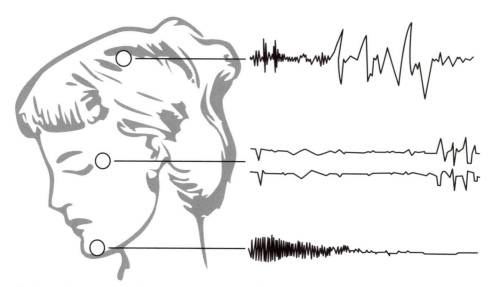

Figure 3: Recording of Sleep. To obtain information on sleep stages in humans, brain activity (EEG, top), eye movements (EOG, middle), and muscle activity (EMG, bottom) are recorded. The traces reflect signals typical for wakefulness (left), NREM sleep stages with slow and high amplitude EEG oscillations (middle), and REM sleep with rapid eye movements and muscle atonia (right). (Courtesy Renate Wehrle)

Electrode resistance should not exceed 5 kΩ at the beginning of the recording. All electrophysiological recordings measure the voltage between an electrode of interest and a reference electrode. Signal amplitudes are usually in the range of microvolts (?V, surface EEG) to millivolts (mV, subdural EEG or EMG) and are amplified. The sampling rate must be high enough—more than twice the highest frequencies of interest according to the Nyquist sampling theorem. Digital resolution should be at least 12 bits per sample. Filtering of very low and very high frequencies helps to reduce artifact load, but the frequencies of interest must be preserved: filters for EEG (e.g., 0.3 Hz and 35 or 70 Hz) are therefore different than the ones for EMG (e.g., 10 and 100 Hz). Additional notch filters eliminate artifacts caused by electric power at 50 or 60 Hz, depending on countries. Sleep recordings naturally last several hours and are scored based on evaluations of epochs lasting 30 seconds.

EEG

For EEG, an international standardized system—the 10–20 electrode system developed in the late 1950s—defines basic electrode positions and their names. The term 10–20 derives from subdividing the distance between anatomical landmark positions on the skull in intervals of 10 or 20 percent of the total front–back or left–right length. Letters identify the corresponding lobe, for example, F for frontal or P for parietal; odd numbers refer to the left hemisphere, even numbers to the right hemisphere. This system helps to guarantee consistency and reproducibility across different recordings. Although regional differences in brain activity during sleep exist and are an important focus of research, they are not critical for the scoring of sleep stages per se. Initially, sleep was defined at the C3 and/or C4 derivation over the central lobe, referenced against the contralateral ear (Rechtschaffen & Kales, 1968). Doing so, most changes of the dominant EEG frequency and graphoelements typical for sleep, such as K-complexes, sleep spindles, and saw tooth waves, can be recorded. However, K-complexes and slow waves are much more prominent over frontal regions. Recordings from occipital regions are more suitable to trace alpha rhythms and help to identify arousals or distinguish wakefulness from sleep onset. These electrode positions have therefore been added in a recent update on sleep scoring guidelines (Iber, Ancoli-Israel, Chesson, & Quan, 2007).

EOG

At least two channels are recommended to record eye movements unambiguously. The eye acts as an electric dipole, and eye movements therefore induce changes in electric voltage. Electrodes placed at the outer side of each eye may be referenced against a referential ear electrode (Iber et al., 2007; Rechtschaffen & Kales, 1968), against a frontocentral derivation (Iber et al., 2007), or against each other in pairs (Carskadon & Dement, 2011), resulting in records of horizontal and/or vertical eye movements. Blinks are vertical movements, whereas REMs are predominantly horizontal. Falling asleep is accompanied by slow rolling eye movements. For unambiguous detection, blinks and other eye movements, should be voluntarily performed at the beginning of the recording as a reference for later analysis. (Note: Sleep recordings in small animals such as rodents usually go without eye movement recordings.)

EMG

In humans, recordings from chin muscles are very suitable to detect changes in the tone of voluntary muscles occurring during sleep (neck muscles are used in most animal models). Electrodes are placed on mental and submental muscles and recorded bipolarly. They should be firmly fixed to avoid deterioration of signals across time.

Cardiorespiratory Polysomnography

Brain activity is not the only physiological phenomenon undergoing changes during sleep. Many bodily functions alter their behavior in sleep. Most systems, for example, heartbeat or breathing, generally go at slower regular rhythms during NREM sleep and display irregular activity during REM sleep (Carskadon & Dement, 2011). Therefore, polysomnography may include recordings of multiple further bioparameters to capture normal but also abnormal physiologic activity such as in diagnostic recordings performed in sleep medicine.

Classically, recordings of the heart rhythm (ECG) and of respiration are added. Breathing parameters are obtained by measuring movements of the thorax and abdomen to record the respiratory effort, by measuring airflow at the nose/mouth to record the effective breathing, and by measuring the oxygenation of the blood via pulsoxymetry. For clinical purposes, snoring is also recorded, and EMG electrodes are attached at the legs to detect periodic leg movements. Video surveillance with infrared is recommended.

Depending on capacity, methodology, or research/diagnostic question, polysomnographic recordings may be extended by, for example, regular sampling of blood pressure, body temperature for information on circadian rhythms, esophageal pressure, penile tumescence, or regular sampling of blood drawings via intravenous catheters to measure hormonal levels and so on.

Common Artifacts

In addition to artifacts caused by electric currents, many more sources of artifacts may blur underlying electrophysiological recordings: the most prominent artifacts are caused by muscle activity and movements. It is not possible to reliably judge underlying electrophysiological signals in the presence of such distortions as they strongly affect a large range of frequencies. When targeting sleep-related movement disorders such as sleepwalking, video surveillance is mandatory. Artifacts with very low frequencies such as hardware drifts or drifts induced by sweat may be reduced by good grounding of electrodes and can be suppressed with filtering. EEG derivations close to the eyes often have EOG artifacts, and artifacts created by heartbeat pulses may occur at any derivation.

Good electrode contact, the use of a conductive paste that can last long recording hours, and an alert monitoring to ensure proper electrode connections can strongly reduce many artifacts. Periods dominated by movement artifacts cannot be analyzed and are scored as wake. More recently, correction methods for ECG and EOG artifacts have been developed.

Current Developments

Sleep recordings benefit from the development of new technologies and higher computer powers. For example, the EEG setup can be extended to high-density EEG recordings: instead of a few individual electrodes in the 10–20 system, caps containing up to 256 even-spaced recording sites can be used to measure fine-grained regional differences in electrical activity with the high temporal resolution as typical for EEG. Similarly, information from intracerebral recordings using depth electrodes— implanted to identify epileptic foci—can be recorded during sleep and reveal valuable facts about sleep-related activity in deeper brain structures. Superior spatial information about the sleeping brain can be further assessed by sleep recordings performed simultaneously with other imaging techniques such as positron emission tomography or functional magnetic resonance imaging (see the entries "Functional Neuroimaging during Human Sleep" and "Neural Metaphor and Dreams"). Future techniques and findings will doubtlessly expand and modify our understanding of sleep.

Renate Wehrle

See also: entries related to Sleep Assessment

References

Aserinsky, E., & Kleitman, N. (1953). Regularly occurring periods of eye motility, and concomitant phenomena, during sleep. *Science, 118*(3062), 273–274.

Carskadon, M. A., & Dement, W. C. (2011). Normal human sleep: An overview. In M. H. Kryger, T. Roth, & W. C. Dement (Eds.), *Principles and practice of sleep medicine* (pp. 16–26). St. Louis: Elsevier Saunders.

Iber, C., Ancoli-Israel, S., Chesson, A., & Quan, S. F. (2007). *The AASM manual for the scoring of sleep and associated events. Rules, terminology and technical specifications.* Westchester, IL: American Academy of Sleep Medicine.

Keenan, S., & Hirshkowitz, M. (2011). Monitoring and staging human sleep. In M. H. Kryger, T. Roth & W. C. Dement (Eds.), *Principles and practice of sleep medicine* (pp. 1602–1609). St. Louis: Elsevier Saunders.

Rechtschaffen, A., & Kales, A. (1968). *A manual of standardized terminology, techniques and scoring system for sleep stages of human subjects* (NIH Publication No. 204). Washington DC: NIH.

Bedouin Dream Traditions

The Bedouins are the nomadic peoples inhabiting the deserts of the Arab world. They include many tribes that once roamed the land freely before borders were constructed and countries were identified. In the country known today as Jordan, only a small number of Bedouins have maintained the nomadic lifestyle. The majority of Jordanian Bedouin have settled down and replaced pastoralism with cultivation. Although some Bedouins have combined the two lifestyles, most of them presently live in houses instead of tents; they drive pick-ups and use cell phones. The camel still holds an important role in Bedouin culture but is no longer relied on as the main source of food or transport.

Like most native peoples of the world, the old spiritual traditions of the Bedouins are becoming extinct. However, the ancient knowledge is not completely lost—it still lives in the memory of the few remaining elders and in the documentations by scholars and researchers. Adhering to the prominent religion of the region, the Bedouins of today have buried their old deities and rituals and converted to Islam. However, traces of pre-Islamic beliefs can still be seen. One such example is the tying of green fabric on the branches of sacred trees, used as an offering to the spirits in hopes of healing or fertility.

Ancient Bedouin traditions are earth-based. Deities were associated with sacred trees, which in turn were worshipped. Today's Bedouins believe that spirits reside by sacred trees, which are used as portals to connect to higher levels of consciousness and to other realms. Dreams still play an important role in Bedouin culture, with special brews and tools to enhance dreaming.

Bedouin dreams are functional; they are regarded as a sixth sense and serve several purposes important to survival. Dreams warn of danger or raids by other tribes, foretell the future, and provide insight into people's characters. Dreams are also used to find lost or stolen objects and to locate treasure. In the past, dreams guided the Bedouin to water wells, oasis, and lush places for grazing.

Diet, Incense, and Psychoactive Plants

Bedouin dream traditions are bound to the landscape and lifestyle. Traditional Bedouins live in the desert, away from civilization and the distractions of modern-day life. They sleep close to the earth, eating from the land, making fire from local twigs, leaves, and branches, and inhaling the smoke that arises.

Bedouin dreaming is characterized by three primary components: diet, incense/smoke, and psychoactive plants. When combined, in their natural setting, they lead to a heightened dreaming capacity and greater dream recall.

The diet of the Bedouin is simple; it is primarily composed of goat or camel milk. In the hottest periods of summer, camel milk is used as an alternative for water. Since the animals eat the local plants, which absorb the microelements in the earth, their milk is imbued with the plant properties in the area. Most of the desert plants are alkaloids, which are poisonous and entheogenic. Thus, drinking the milk changes the metabolism of the body. With minimal processing and storing of food in the desert, the Bedouin's staple foods include fennel roots, bush tomatoes, wild figs, capers, desert onion, mushrooms, truffles, oak acorn, honey, nuts, and the seeds from some grasses. Tea is drunk heavily, and is mixed with local herbs, including desert thyme and Artemisia. A member of the daisy family, Artemisia herba-alba (wormwood or Bedouin *Sh'eh*) produces hallucinogenic effects if taken in large quantities.

Bedouins report more vivid and lucid dreams in the early spring. This is accredited to the Broom plant, which is the first flower to bloom in the desert during the first two weeks of March. The White Broom shrub (known as Bedouin *Ratam*) contains terpene and cytosine. The goats eat the plant, and the Bedouins drink the goat milk, which is infused with the plant's active components.

There are certain locations in the desert that are regarded as good dreaming places. These power spots are usually under or near sacred trees. The twigs, sap, and branches scattered on the ground are used for making a fire. Depending on the source of these plants, the smoke emitted from burning them could be psychoactive, inducing visions and dreams. A powerful combination is composed of *Ratam* twigs, Terebinth gum, and Harmala seedpods (commonly known as Syrian Rue).

The Harmala plant (Bedouin *Hamal* or *Harjal*) contains harmaline, a central nervous system stimulant with psychoactive properties likened to the Amazonian Ayahuasca. Dried Harmala, mixed with other tree gum, is placed on top of hot charcoal, releasing a fragrant smoke that is inhaled. Harmala vapor is used in a similar fashion to the sweat lodge of the Native Americans. Bedouin women use Harmala seedpods to make spirit catchers, which are amulets similar to dream catchers.

The Tent as Dream Catcher

The Bedouin tent is seen as a portal for dreams; it is made of local goat or camel hair, and is thus called *Bait al-Sha'ar,* the house of hair. A protection amulet usually hangs on the tent guarding against the evil eye. The amulet resembles the dream catcher of the Native Americans, but it differs in design. The Bedouin amulet is of a composite geometric shape consisting of an inverted triangle held up by a piece of wood and hung by two strings forming an upright triangle. The Harmala seeds in the inverted triangle are stringed together and crisscrossed into a horizontal *mandrola*, the almond-shaped center of the Vesica Pisces. The Vesica Pisces is one of the simplest forms in sacred geometry and is also a symbol of the divine feminine.

Similar patterns composed of triangles and *mandrolas* are characteristic of Bedouin embroidery. The colors most commonly used are red and black, with green, white, or orange accents. These patterns appear on the Bedouin pillow, which was traditionally stuffed with balsam, a sweet-scented plant believed to aid sleep and enhance dreaming (R. Sajdi, personal communication, February 26, 2011).

A Symbol Interpreted

Unlike Islamic dream interpretation, there is no Bedouin dream dictionary or any written reference. In spite of the fact that Islam is now their primary religion, the Bedouins have maintained their own interpretations to some degree. The primary reference to Islamic dream interpretation is *Tafseer Al-ahlam Al-kabir* (The Big Dream Interpretation Book) by Ibn Sirin (2000). To give credibility to the interpretations, the book relies on verses from the Quran, sayings of the Prophet, stories about the Prophet's companions, or Arabic world meaning. For the purpose of this study, one symbol is explored herein, to shed light on the divergence between the Islamic and Bedouin interpretations.

The Snake

The snake is a primordial image that appears in dream reports cross culturally. It is as common to dreamers in Jordan as it is in America or Japan (Nasser & Bulkeley, 2009). The snake is a fact of everyday life for the Bedouin. It is likely to appear in waking as frequently as in dreams, if not more.

According to Islamic dream interpretation, snakes represent enemies, because of their close association to *Ibliss* (Lucifer) (Ibn Sirin, 2000). The snake is not specifically mentioned in the Quran as the form in which *Ibliss* appeared to Adam and Eve to tempt them. However, this is a common belief that stems from the biblical account and from the folklore association between *Ibliss* and the snake.

According to Ibn Sirin (2000, pp. 190–191), the snake might refer to infidels and sorcerers, because of the poisons they spread. It might refer to adulterers, because of their poisonous nature. Snakes could also refer to one's wife or offspring, because of God's saying "O ye who believe! Truly, among your wives and your children are (some that are) enemies to yourselves: so beware of them!" (64:14). A water snake could refer to money. The snake could also refer to water and streams, as the word for snake in Arabic is *Hayya,* which stems from Haya, meaning life, and God's saying "We made from water every living thing" (21:30). While not mentioned in Ibn Sirin's book, another association with snake and water comes from the word used to describe a large serpent, *Thu'ban,* which stems from *Tha'aba,* which means spilled a liquid, like water or blood.

According to the Bedouins, the snake in dreams could also be referring to water or life. However, they usually interpret it as a sign guiding to treasure. This interpretation stems from the belief that when treasure is buried, an animal (usually a snake) is sacrificed at the site to protect it. So when a snake appears in a dream, it is the spirit of the sacrificed animal (R. Sajdi, personal communication, February 26, 2011). This is congruent to jinn mythology of the Arab world. The jinn are pre-Islamic shape-shifting elemental beings made from fire. The jinn were incorporated in Islam, with a whole sura (chapter of the Quran) named after them. The jinn are believed to inhabit deserts and graveyards; they are assigned to treasures to protect them from intruders. The most common manifestation of the jinn is the dog or the snake (Nasser, 2009). The Bedouins believe in ghouls (another rank of the jinn), which assume the guise of animals, especially the hyena and the *hanash,* a large snake.

A Lost Tradition

Although several studies have been conducted about Bedouins, information on Bedouin dream interpretation is lacking. As more Bedouins settle in modernized villages and move away from their original way of life, the ancient teachings are likely to be lost. However, the belief in dreams as providers of information will remain, as the Bedouins belong to the line of Abrahamic tradition, which emphasizes the prophetic potential of dreaming.

As Muslims, the Bedouins are familiar with the prophet *Yusuf* (Joseph). Mentioned in the Quran, with a whole sura named after him, *Yusuf* is regarded as a master dreamer and interpreter. *Yusuf*'s dream of the stars bowing to him depicts the dream interpreter as a powerful person, and is thus respected. The Islamic practice of *istikhara* (dream incubation) is a common practice among modern-day Muslims; it is the greatest evidence that Muslims believe in dreams. In addition, the Prophet Muhammad interpreted dreams and placed them in high regard. It is believed that after the prophet Muhammad, the only prophecy available to humans is through dreams. All this suggests that dreams will always play an important part in the Bedouin consciousness.

Lana Nasser

See also: entries related to Cross-Cultural Dreams

References

Abdullah, Y. A. (1989). *The meaning of the Qur'an.* Beltsville, MD: Amana Corporation.

Ibn Sirin. (2000). *Tafseer Al-ahlam Al-kabir* [The big dream interpretation book]. Beirut: Dar Al-kutub Al-ilmieh.

Nasser, L. (2009). The jinn: Companion in the realm of dreams and imagination. In K. Adams, K. Bulkeley, & P. M. Davis (Eds.), *Dreaming in Christianity and Islam: Culture, conflict, and creativity.* New Brunswick, NJ: Rutgers University Press.

Nasser, L., & Bulkeley, K. (2009). Typical dreams of Jordanian college students. In K. Adams, K. Bulkeley, & P. M. Davis (Eds.), *Dreaming in Christianity and Islam: Culture, conflict, and creativity* (pp. 98–100). New Brunswick, NJ: Rutgers University Press.

Sajdi, R., Shamanic/desert plants. Retrieved from http://www.acacialand.com/Shamnic Plants.html

Belief in Dream Relevance and the Continuity Hypothesis

As key components of human personality, beliefs and attitudes make up a person's orientation to a particular object of appraisal. Attitudes represent the affective evaluations of objects, while beliefs represent the perceived probability of existence or truth. Today, both attitudes and beliefs are investigated in relation to a diverse range of objects and targets. As perceptions of fact and truth, beliefs provide unique insights into particular cultural domains. Although attitudes toward dreams have gained recent attention, research investigating beliefs about dreams is far more limited. Of particular interest to our understanding of dreams in modern culture is the belief in dream relevance (i.e., the importance of dreams) and waking–dreaming continuity (i.e., the degree to which our dreams reflect our waking lives). Such fundamental beliefs about dreams play critical roles in the work of dream researchers, clinicians, and anthropologists alike.

In 1986, American psychologist Mary Watkins suggested that Western culture tends to deem dreams as insignificant and meaningless. In 1992, anthropologist Barbara Tedlock argued that American minds waver between two differential beliefs regarding dreams: either dreams mean something or quite simply, dreams mean nothing. Such statements might be interpreted to indicate a lack of importance attributed to dreams by Western culture, and further suggest an inherent distinction between waking and dreaming lives. Unfortunately, such perspectives do not describe the extent to which either of these beliefs is true, or furthermore, how these beliefs have changed over time.

A small number of studies have recently emerged, involving direct investigations of popular beliefs about dreams. In a German sample, 36 out of 50 adults reported believing that daytime problems played an important role in their dreams, suggesting a majority-held belief in continuity between dreams and waking life (Schredl, Kleinferchner, & Gell, 1996). A subsequent investigation of laypeople's endorsements of popular dream theories found that postsecondary students from the United States, South Korea, and India were most likely to believe that dreams contained hidden truths or meanings about the self (Morewedge & Norton, 2009). This belief was more frequently endorsed than beliefs reflecting problem solving, learning, and by-product theories of dreaming. In addition, it was observed that participants perceived dreams to be more meaningful sources of information compared to similar waking thoughts, regardless of the endorsed theory. Findings by Morewedge and Norton suggest a popular belief in both dream relevance and waking–dreaming continuity that is not restricted to Western culture.

These findings were recently confirmed in a sample of Canadian university students, of whom the large majority (81%) believed that dreams contain important and relevant information, with 13 percent being unsure of their appraisal (King & DeCicco, 2009). When observed more closely, students were most likely to endorse the beliefs that dreams reflect relationships, decisions being made, and mood states, suggesting a common belief in waking–dreaming continuity. These findings, as well as those by Schredl et al. and Morewedge and Norton, indicate a popular belief in the continuity hypothesis of dreaming, which suggests that our dreams reflect our waking-life experiences, thoughts, and behaviors. This contrasts earlier claims by Watkins and Tedlock and constructs a perspective of Western culture, which places value on dreams (at least to some degree).

Preliminary evidence has also been offered for a link between dream-related beliefs and dream content (King & DeCicco, 2009). In particular, individuals endorsing the belief that dreams reflect physical health reported more body parts in their dreams. Given these findings, however limited, further research is warranted on the possible origins of dream-related beliefs. For example, these beliefs may be heavily influenced by either waking-life cognitions or past experiences; on the other hand, they may be directly impacted by the content of dreams. Some combination is also possible, wherein a dynamic interplay of waking and dreaming experiences may be shaping our beliefs about dreams. Larger cross-cultural studies are needed to more accurately account for the frequency and potential origins of specific dream-related beliefs.

David B. King

See also: entries related to Dream Theories

References

King, D.B., & DeCicco, T.L. (2009). Dream relevance and the continuity hypothesis: Believe it or not? *Dreaming, 19,* 207–217.

Morewedge, C.K., & Norton, M.I. (2009). When dreaming is believing: The (motivated) interpretation of dreams. *Journal of Personality and Social Psychology, 96,* 249–264.

Schredl, M., Kleinferchner, P., & Gell, T. (1996). Dreaming and personality: Thick vs. thin boundaries. *Dreaming, 6,* 219–223.

Tedlock, B. (1992). *Dreaming: Anthropological and psychological interpretations.* Santa Fe, NM: School of American Research Press.

Watkins, M. (1986). *Invisible guests: The development of children's imaginal dialogues.* Hillsdale, NJ: Analytic Press.

Bible and Dreams: Luther and Calvin, The

One of the major turning points in the history of Christianity is the Protestant Reformation of the 16th century. The two men who are seen as most influential in the history of Christianity from that point and into the present day are Martin Luther and John Calvin. To help with a fuller understanding of the role of dreams and dreaming in Christianity, a look at Luther's and Calvin's commentary on the dream texts of the Bible will make an important historical contribution. For our purposes here, dreams are those occurrences associated with sleep and the Biblical texts used here make clear that it is those experiences that are referred to, not visions, revelations, auditions, or other experiences. Nightly dreams are a universal human experience, often connected to religious experience; therefore, they provide a great vantage point from which to look at the history and varieties of religious experience. This article examines Luther's and Calvin's attitudes toward dreams, some theological points and parallels to modern understandings of dreams, and working with one's dreams.

Attitude toward Dreams

Both Luther and Calvin expressed specific attitudes toward dreams. Luther's attitude is more negative toward dreams: he comments on the concept of Sheol in Genesis 42:38.

> While the soul still lives in the body, it is deceived in various ways during sleep when the empty visions of dreams present themselves—visions that are not real.

Because they took the Bible so seriously, and because dreams are recorded in the Bible, Luther and Calvin were obligated to consider the value of dreams as part of their Biblical heritage.

Luther, commenting on Genesis 40:19, says:

> But other dreams, which do not have their origin from God, are ambiguous and deceptive. Therefore there is need of extraordinary wisdom to differentiate them. . . . Nevertheless, all dreams should not be completely despised, even though I take no pleasure in them. But the marks of true dreams must be observed. For an impression soon follows those that are sent by God, so that he who dreams cannot forget the dream; or if it has escaped him, it soon recurs, as can be seen in the history of Nebuchadnezzar.

Calvin shows a more open attitude. In commenting on Jeremiah 23:25–27, he says this:

> Dreams themselves are to be taken in a good sense, for God was wont to make himself known to his servants by dreams. Hence it is dreams that are from above that are to be understood here, not every kind of dream.

Theological Points

The attitudes of Luther and Calvin toward dreams were minor points in the theological challenges they faced shaping emerging Protestantism. When classifying them, they put dreams under the function of the Holy Spirit.

Luther, regarding Joel 2:28 and the reference to dreams there, says:

> These nevertheless, one understands when the Holy Spirit interprets them so that those who have seen them have no doubts that the dreams come from God.

For Luther it was important that dreams be in congruence with the words of the Holy Scripture. Regarding the dream of Jacob's ladder in Genesis 28, he states:

> you must compare your dream with the Word. If your dream differs from what the Word itself states, you must remember that it is false and vain. But this dream of Jacob is in very beautiful agreement with the divine Word which he hears being sent down from heaven: "I am the Lord . . . etc." Therefore the godless err in their interpretation and understanding of dreams, just as they talk nonsense when they explain signs and prodigies; for they neither observe nor have the Word.

Likewise Calvin associates dreams with the work of the Holy Spirit. Regarding Daniel 2:28, Calvin says:

> the king's dream was not subjected to human knowledge, for mortals have no such natural skill as to be able to comprehend the meaning of the dream, and God manifests those secrets which need the peculiar revelation of the Spirit. When Daniel says the Magi, Astrologers, and the rest cannot explain to the king his dream, and are not suitable interpreters of it, the true reason is, because the dream was not natural and had nothing in common with human conjectures, but was the peculiar revelation of the Spirit.

Parallels to Modern Understandings

There are some parallels to modern understanding about dreams that can be found in Luther and Calvin.

One principle of group dreamwork is for the participants not to let their own values or agendas get in the way of the work the dreamer needs to do. I believe Calvin may be referring to a principle like this in the following words, regarding Genesis 41:33:

> However, there is no doubt that God guided his tongue, in order that Pharaoh might entrust him with this office. For he does not craftily insinuate himself into the king's favor; nor abuse the gift of revelation to his private gain: but, what had been divinely ordained was brought to its proper issue without his knowledge; namely, that the famishing house of Jacob should find unexpected sustenance.

"Abusing the gift of revelation" is using one's experience of the revelation of God for personal gain.

Recurring dreams are experienced by most everyone who pays attention to their dreams. Calvin refers to Pharaoh's recurring dreams in Genesis 41. He says:

> God gave a second dream, succeeding the first, for two reasons. To rouse the mind of Pharaoh to more diligent inquiry, and to add more light to a vision which was obscure. This two-fold approach is something God does in our waking lives as well.
> But our dullness and inconstancy cause him to repeat the same thing the more frequently, in order that what he has certainly decreed, may be fixed in our hearts; otherwise, as our disposition is variable, so, what we have once heard from his mouth, is tossed up and down by us, until it entirely escapes our memory.

Carl Jung says one function of dreams is to compensate for things or feelings we lack in our waking lives. In his comments on Genesis 37:8, Calvin uses the term consolatory to say the same thing: "Perhaps, also, by this consolatory dream, he intended to alleviate the trouble of the holy youth."

Joseph's dreams of grandeur compensate (or are consolatory) for his being younger than, and despised by, his older brothers.

Another modern dreamwork technique is acting on our dreams, based on the insights we have gained from our dreams. Regarding Genesis 20:8, Luther says, "He doesn't put off from day to day making amends for his deed, as we procrastinators are in the habit of doing." Regarding I Kings 3:5, noting that Solomon asks for help from God, Luther says Solomon "follows his dream," or "acts on it."

Summary

If I am looking for help from Luther or Calvin in using my personal dreams in my own prayer life, I will not get much. If I want to be able to dismiss dreams as nonsense or garbage that is supposed to be thrown out, I could get support from the negative comments of Luther and Calvin about dreams. If I want to find helpful material in my dreams, I could use the positive comments from Luther and Calvin about dreams in the Bible. It is helpful for modern Christian dreamworkers, particularly those in the Lutheran or Reformed traditions, to know what Luther and Calvin have to say about dreams. Times and viewpoints change over the centuries and dreams can provide help for us in these modern times and we are better able to use our dreams in our spiritual life when we are aware of the attitudes of great Christian theologians toward dreams. I believe Luther and Calvin would agree with that.

Geoff Nelson

See also: entries related to History of Dreams/Sleep

Note

This article is a condensation of the chapter "Dreaming through the Bible with Luther and Calvin" from the book *Dreaming in Christianity and Islam*, eds. Kelly Bulkeley, Kate Adams, and Patricia M. Davis. New Brunswick, NJ: Rutgers University Press, 2009.

Big Dreams

While Freud can rightly be credited with ushering the dream into the awareness of the Western world at the outset of the 20th century, his approach to the dream kept the dream subservient to the rational ego, a move that comported well with the increasingly radical individualism of the West. More recently, the continuity hypothesis of dreaming similarly binds the dream to the personal psychology of the dreamer. Couched within a normative epistemology, this view is buttressed by extensive data showing that the content of the typical dream, and indeed of the overwhelming majority of all dreams, is continuous with the experiences and concerns of the dreamer's waking ego consciousness.

These views of the dream, however compatible with the mechanistic mentality of modernity, are sharply at odds with human experience. Humans have always experienced some dreams as extraordinary—terror arousing, awe-full, rich with portents, epiphanic. Jung (1974) made this point forcefully in his essay, "On the Nature of Dreams":

> Not all dreams are of equal importance. Even primitives distinguish between "little" and "big" dreams, or, as we might say, "insignificant" and "significant" dreams . . . little dreams are the nightly fragments of fantasy coming from the subjective and personal sphere, and their meaning is limited to the affairs of everyday . . . . Significant dreams, on the other hand, are often remembered for a lifetime, and not infrequently prove to be the richest jewel in the treasure house of psychic experience. (p. 76)

Two major implications emerge from this latter assertion. First, whereas Jung's characterization of the "insignificant" dream closely corresponds with the continuity hypothesis, the phenomenology and ongoing influence of the "significant" dream point toward an entirely different class of dreaming that dramatically transcends the daily concerns of the dreamer. Second, the methodologies applied to significant dreams cannot be restricted to those who seek the normative, as the exceptional case cannot be understood by accumulating or amplifying the typical.

Relatively few researchers have taken up these conceptual and methodological challenges, though in recent years attention to the significant dream has been increasing (see, e.g, Adams, 2003; Bulkeley, 2006; Knudson, Adame, & Finocan, 2006; Kuiken, Lee, Eng, & Singh, 2006; but see also the work of Harry Hunt, Deirdre Barrett, and Stanley Krippner among others). The results emerging from these various lines of inquiry clearly support the existence of multiple dream types. There is clear evidence that some, though not all, dreams involve exceptionally vivid, emotionally evocative imagery that is frequently characterized as bizarre or otherworldly. Work has been progressing on various taxonomies of dreams, showing not only that there is a multiplicity of dream types but also that dreams differ in their impact on the experience of the dreamer. Big or significant dreams may touch on fundamental issues of human existence and as a result may be deeply transformative in their effect on the dreamer, may aid the dreamer in responding to a crisis, and in at least some research, there is the suggestion that significant dreams may be linked to an impulse toward a moral response. For some dreamers, extraordinary dreams are experienced as numinous, constituting in and of themselves religious experiences.

In terms of methodology, inquiry into significant dreams has increasingly employed qualitative methods appropriate to the study of unique life experiences. Qualitative inquiries using narrative methods have begun to describe in detail the ways that significant dreams can have ongoing significance in the dreamer's experience. Given that big dreams are polyvalent in meaning, narrative methods are eminently conducive to future depth inquiry into the phenomenology of such dreams. As a natural extension of this work, the use of performative writing as a method of inquiry appears to hold great promise. Performance texts may prove particularly suited to evoke the exceptionally vivid imagery and uncanny or numinous emotions associated with big dreams as well as their transformative influence on the dreamer.

Roger M. Knudson and
Jeffrey R. Schweitzer

See also: Little Dreams

References

Adams, K. (2003). Children's dreams: An exploration of Jung's concept of big dreams. *International Journal of Children's Spirituality, 8,* 105–114.

Bulkeley, K. (2006). Revision of the good fortune scale: A new tool for the study of "big dreams." *Dreaming, 16,* 11–21.

Jung, C.G. (1974). On the nature of dreams. In R.F.C Hull (Ed. and Trans.), *Dreams* (pp. 1–23). Princeton, NJ: Princeton University Press.

Knudson, R.M., Adame, A.L., & Finocan, G.M. (2006). Significant dreams: Repositioning the self narrative. *Dreaming, 16,* 215–222.

Kuiken, D., Lee, M., Eng, T., & Singh, T. (2006). The influence of impactful dreams on self-perceptual depth and spiritual transformation. *Dreaming, 16,* 258–279.

Bizarre Imagery and Thought in Sleep and Waking

Bizarre imagery and thought (IT) has long been the defining characteristic of dreaming sleep. Indeed, the sequential discontinuities and improbable combination of features of such IT are defined as bizarre because they are so rare in the waking state. Indeed, bizarre IT is the major subjective cue that people use, when aroused from sleep, to judge whether they were, in fact, asleep. Although the EEG criteria are widely assumed to define some form of subjective sleep, people aroused from State-2 sleep in the early night tend to report they were awake, and only later in the night as their mentation becomes more dreamlike tend to say they were asleep (Sewitch, Pollack, Weitzman, Antrobus, & Clark, 1982).

When Dement proposed that dreaming occurs exclusively in EEG-defined Stage-1 REM sleep, Hobson (1990) quite reasonably proposed that inasmuch as bizarre IT was the primary characteristic of REM sleep, it must be elicited by the unique neurological processes of that REM sleep. He proposed that pontine-geniculate–occipital (PGO) cortical spikes of REM sleep produce bizarre IT by interrupting ongoing cortical production of otherwise normal IT. Subsequent research found that while PGO activity was associated with eye movements and vivid visual imagery, it was not related to bizarre IT (Reinsel, Antrobus, & Wollman, 1992).

One might assume that bizarre IT is produced by a cortex that is only partially activated so that it cannot correct its own inconsistencies. But using report length—log(word recall)—as an indirect index of cortical activation, bizarre IT actually increases, rather than decreases, with increased cortical activation—both within and between sleep stages. Indeed, report length accounts for most of the cognitive difference between REM and Stage-2 reports (Antrobus, 1983). Obviously, the more elements generated during a sleep episode, the more likely some may appear inconsistent with others. But if cortical activation and report length are positively associated with bizarre IT, then in contrast to our everyday experience, the greater cortical activation of the waking state should produce even more bizarre IT. Inasmuch as IT had never been studied in waking with the same procedures used to collect sleep reports—reclining in a dark room for an hour, Reinsel et al. (1992) did just that. And they found that waking reports are not

only just as dreamlike as REM reports, but they are substantially more bizarre!

Although this finding flies in the face of the REM-dreaming orthodoxy, one may note that many REM dreams are not remotely bizarre, and that the popular concept of the dream is based on those remembered spontaneously in the morning, which are the most dramatic of those produced during the night. Nevertheless, that waking IT in the sleep lab environment should be as bizarre as REM IT suggests that the sensory/perceptual events of one's normal waking environment may somehow suppress bizarre IT. Absent these sensory intrusions, waking IT may become just as bizarre as in REM sleep. To examine this idea, Wollman and Antrobus (1986) isolated sequential discontinuities from other features of bizarre IT. Proposing that the typical sensory events of the normal waking environment increased discontinuities in waking IT, they compared waking reports in the sleep lab environment during intervals with moderate versus minimal background auditory noise, including partial speech segments. As predicted, waking sequential discontinuities increased in the noise relative to quiet condition, while the latter was identical to that of REM sleep reports.

Improbable identities (e.g., It was my brother, but he was a girl) was the only class of bizarre IT that was substantially larger in REM than waking (7.8% vs. 1.7%). Note that Hall and Van de Castle (1966) found these in only 1 percent of their large study of home diary dream reports. We suggest that the dissociation among cortical regions in REM sleep (Braun et al., 1997), which are typically highly associated in waking, accounts for the improbable identities that are almost exclusive to REM sleep reports. A girl image in the waking state would strongly suppress the boy features of one's brother that are located in the nonvisual regions of the cortex. But to the extent that in REM sleep visual features can be created somewhat independently of other cognitive features, such coordination is weak. It is only upon awakening, at which time these semi-independent cortical regions become actively interconnected, that the dreamer notes the prior discrepancies and comments on their bizarreness. Unfortunately, the rareness of these improbable identities will make it difficult for future research to compare them to patterns of cortical activation.

John Antrobus

References

Antrobus, J. S. (1983). REM and NREM sleep reports: Comparison of word frequencies by cognitive classes. *Psychophysiology, 20,* 562–568.

Braun, A. R., Balkin, T. J., Wesenten, N. J., Carson, R. E., Varga, M., Baldwin, P., . . . Herscovitch, P. (1997). Regional cerebral blood flow throughout the sleep–wake cycle: An H20-O-15 PET study. *Brain, 120,* 1173–1197.

Hall, C. S., & Van de Castle, R. L. (1966). *The content analysis of dreams.* New York: Appleton-Century-Crofts.

Hobson, A. (1990). Activation, input source, and modulation. In R. R. Bootzin, J. F. Kihlstrom, & D. L. Schacter (Eds.), *Sleep and cognition* (pp. 25–40). Washington DC: American Psychological Association.

Reinsel, R., Antrobus, J., & Wollman, M. (1992). Bizarreness in dreams and waking fantasy. In J. Antrobus & M. Bertini (Eds.), *The neuropsychology of sleep and dreaming* (pp. 157–184). Hillsdale, NJ: Erlbaum.

Sewitch, D. E., Pollack, C. P., Weitzman, E. D., Antrobus, J. S., & Clark, W. C. (1982). The alteration of sleep–wake perception by sleep and wake biasing suggestions and partial feedback given to normal sleepers. *Sleep Research,* 11, 96.

Wollman, M., & Antrobus, J. (1986). Sleeping and waking thought: Effects of external stimulation. *Sleep, 9,* 438–448.

Body Dreamwork

Dream interpretation is famously controversial. There are many theories, and even practitioners of the same theory usually differ about a given dream. The mere dream report cannot be interpreted without the participation of the dreamer. But the dreamer's interpretations are not reliable either.

The purpose of Freud's free association and Jung's daydream was to engender something to break through "directly from the 'unconscious.'" Working with the body is a further development of their methods.

The body responds to attention. With a little training, people can learn to put their attention inside their bodies and to let a *physical quality* come there. What comes might be expansive, or constricted, heavy, jumpy, or no word for it, just *this* quality.

Then, if the person thinks of something else, the quality changes. The body responds with a uniquely different quality to anything, whether large or tiny. The question *How is my life going these days?* will bring a unique bodily quality, but so *will noticing this little crease on the dress.*

If one attends in the body and awaits a unique quality until it actually comes, then little steps come *from* it. They can answer questions.

Where did you ever see a door like that?

Nowhere.

Wait for the quality it makes in your body.

(*silence*) . . . Oh, it's like the door at my grandmother's.

A whole field of information is implicit in that nameless bodily quality. Very strikingly, *what one answers from within the body can be utterly different from what one said before.*

This variable, the bodily quality called the *felt sense*, was first identified in the *Philosophy of the Implicit* (Gendlin, 1986, 1997, 2009, in press). It led to a widely used research instrument, the *Experiencing Scale* (Hendricks & Cartwright, 1978; Klein, Mathieu, Gendlin, & Kiesler, 1969).

Speaking from attention in the body is observable. People speak, then pause and say "Hm. Is that right? Hm . . . (*silence* . . .) No, it's not what I said, it's more like . . ." Then, "Let's see, is *that* right? (*silence* . . .) Yes, (*audible exhale*) that's what it is." Then, "Oh, another thing about it is . . ." More specific detail comes up.

This *bodily* checking is quite different from mere talk or self-doubt. It requires some actual time, 5 to 30 seconds. The pacing of speech and silences is characteristic. The glance becomes distant. As long as people continue to look right at you, they are not attending in the body.

Why does a bodily felt quality contain so much more information than one

knows? Our bodies *interact directly* in our situations in many intricate ways that we do not (are not able to) think about separately. The word *body* is acquiring a much wider meaning, not only what physiology defines.

Why are dreams special? They process our situations on a primitive level where perceptions of trees, animals, and stones are still being formed. But our individual history and situations also participate in the formation of the images. This very odd chair and this oddly behaving pig are freshly formed by the self-healing impetus of the basic organismic process. That is why in bodywork the images go beyond our stuck problems (Gendlin, 1986, see theoretical appendix).

The practice works observably regardless of theory. We ask questions; we show people how to let the unique quality come and to wait for answers that come from it.

One's usual energy may be, for example, constricted, constantly agitated, largely immobile dragging oneself along, or a guarded withdrawal. A sudden shift to a positive life-forward energy is quite observable in body posture, face, and breath.

People tend to interpret their dreams very negatively, but we find that a dream is *code* for a hidden life energy that leads to solving life problems. It opens a direction that we cannot otherwise provide.

The new energy is often invisible within the dream. It comes when the conscious person *lives bodily from the dream images.*

Letting the life-forward energy actually come in the body is the chief purpose of body dream interpretation. When it comes, we work to ensure that it is fully experienced and can be taken home and practiced. Then, if the dreamer wants, we go on interpreting.

The Questions

We derive questions from many sources, especially Jung and Freud.

First, we let the dreamer freely tell associations. Then, *most safely,* we begin with the place in the dream. If no place was mentioned (some people report no detail), we ask:

Where did this happen?

I don't know.

Was it in a room or outside?

An ordinary living room.

Where were the windows?

Tall windows on the right side.

In your body, please get the feel of that room.

Then we ask:

Where did you ever see a room that felt like that, with tall windows on the right side?

How to Use Questions

Dreamers first answer, "Nowhere. I don't know. Nothing comes." So we explain:

We aren't really asking you. The question is for you to take down and ask your body. Let the feel of that place come again. Then wait and see what the question brings down there.

Until they experience the bodily coming a few times, people can't be sure they are doing this.

When a place is remembered:

What happened there? What was it like to be at your grandmother's house?

When an earlier time is mentioned:

What was happening to you during those years?

Maximizing and Practicing the New Energy

Actually having and keeping the new energy require special work. After a minute, the energy might no longer be there, only remembered. We need to let it come again and again.

We say:

Come around to it again. You said . . . and then we asked . . . and then it came. Lead up to it again and let it come again in your body. This time stay with it for a little while.

Before we end, we let it come again:

Can you have it again? Come around to where it came.

Then:

With that image and those steps do you think you can let it come whenever you want, and practice it?

Getting Help from the Dream

If we go to the most troubling spot right away, we work as if there were no dream. We want the help of the dream before we tackle the problem. In bodily terms help means anything that brings life-forward energy.

In a dream, what sort of things bring help? Anything beautiful, also children, animals, anything living and green. Also, very odd objects unique just to this dream. We ask about those early on.

Tell me more about those funny bowls.

They were sculptured with animals and plants that stuck out . . . (more detail followed)

Now, in your body, be the sculptured bowls with animals and plants sticking out from you.

Help can also come unexpectedly. For example:

Where did you ever see a bed like that?

I don't know, um . . . (*long pause*) Oh, it's like the bed I used to go and sit on, while my parents were fighting. I was safe there.

Now please go and sit on that bed. Feel yourself sitting on that bed as we work further. Let the being safe flow through your whole body. Take a few minutes just for that.

When no help is found, we can ask for the body's positive version directly:

How would your body be if this changed and were just right? Don't make it up; wait.

Example:

There was a sick turtle going down a road with its entrails hanging out, dragging on the road behind it.

(This was in a dream group. Some people gasped at the vivid horror of that scene.)

The questions brought no help. So we asked directly:

What would a healthy turtle be like?

A healthy turtle? (*She straightened up.*) A *healthy* turtle?

Her whole body changed. A new energy flowed visibly through her body. We worked to keep it, then went on to the next person. Suddenly she interrupted:

I want everybody to know my turtle is up on her hind legs, and she's dancing!

Another example:

Can I tell you only just a part of my dream? (*Then shaky voice*) It's about something painful.

Sure, but have the whole dream with you.

When the questions brought little,

In the rest of the dream is there perhaps an animal or a plant, or a baby, or some living thing or some beautiful thing?

(*silence*) There was a child.

Yes, that's what I mean. A child is always a good thing.

I think there were more children.

Can we have those children with us as we go on? Maybe we could have them all around us? Would that be all right?

(*Sigh.*)

Her whole body changed. It eased from her extreme tension. Then she said:

I could use a whole army of children around me!

Working with the Dream Characters

Safely and gently:

What does Bob mean to you? How does he make you feel in your body?

More effectively:

Could that person stand for a part of you that you don't know very well?

How is that person your opposite?

What would come in your body if you had a little bit of . . .? Not really that, but something in that direction?

What new way of being in your body might come?

People often dream of someone chasing them or of a beautiful but fearsome animal. By being it bodily, they can feel it as a part of them.
Most effectively:

Let's say you are acting in a play—next week. Now you're only preparing. It's theater for children; everything is exaggerated. Imagine yourself standing in the wings, ready to come on stage.
Now, in your body, be that person. How would you come on stage? Would you march, crawl, stomp, sneak . . . how? Don't tell me yet. Do it inside first.

By not asking people to act visibly, we avoid performance anxiety and merely inventing what to say. Our way was Stanislavski's training for actors. But we do ask:

Please sit forward on the edge of the chair. (We model this.) Loosen your body and move a little bit.

Once people become experienced, a short phrase replaces the elaborate instructions. We just say:

Please be that. Or: Could your body do that?

Anything can be asked about in this way:

Wear the necklace. How does it feel on your body?
Be your body with this dress on.

Example:

What does your brother bring now in your body?

He always does whatever he wants. My parents let him get away with everything. Not like me. I was the good one.

What would it feel like in your body, if you had a little bit of doing whatever you want?

Please body him.

(*Visible shift*) In all these years that never occurred to me.

Another example:

The others in the club asked me to let Bill sleep with my wife. It was supposed to be a birthday present for Bill . . . That dream is really crazy. I wouldn't let them ask me something like that. I don't know what club this is.

What's Bill like?

Bill does only the part of a job he likes. He is unscrupulous and imposes on everybody.

One theory says everything in a dream is part of you. Of course we don't know if that fits here. See in your body, might there be a part like that?

That part of me? Well, yes (laugh). But I don't like that. I'm glad I'm not like Bill. But, um, sure, there is that part of me . . .
I'd run over everybody . . . I don't let it come up much, even inside.

Now he fills that into the dream story:

She should sleep with that part of me? (*silence*) Hmm . . .

Now he feels that part active in his sexuality.

Body Dreamwork | 89

The Dream Story

The story plot needs to be summarized in three parts: what first happened, *how the dreamer responds,* and what then happens. This lets one see one's typical patterns as determining the outcome.

For example:

Lying on the seat was a child's ring with different color stones. I knew it wasn't worth anything, it was plastic with glass stones. It was definitely a child's ring. It then slipped down between the seat and the wall. I left it there.

Story: *Can it mean something if we say: First there was a colorful ring. Then you thought it wasn't worth anything. Then it slipped down.*

Now he feels how the colorful ring could continue.

Let the Dream Continue

Be inside your body and have that image before you. Now let the dream continue. Wait and see what will happen.

For example:

There was a dead man lying on his back on an altar . . . I know, that's my creative spirit. It's dead.

Wait, Let the dream continue. Watch and see what he will do.

. . . He got right up!!

Various Important Considerations

- A broader method (bias control, not discussed here) enables interpretations of one's own dream.
- Sixteen dreamwork questions are in use. Each is a formula for countless questions,

since countess specifics can be asked about in any dream.

- Awakened during REM, people report a flood of material. Home dreams are the organism's selection that lab dreams miss.
- This life-forward process from the body has been used in advanced trauma work and hands-on bodywork. While working from outside, it is more effective to work also from *inside* the body (Levine & Frederick, 1977; Van der Kooy & McEvenue, 2006).
- Dreams can seem to picture only what one already knows. But the odd images and figures can indicate a new direction.
- An archetypal devil in *your* dream knows *your* particular situation. For Freud, all energy is sexual. For Jung, sexuality provides analogies for other problems. Your individual body can say how the universals function in *this* dream.
- Looking to a dream to make the right decision can be badly misleading. Dreams react to the previous day. Today's dream might seem to favor one side; the next dream may favor the other side. But the hidden positive energy points to a new constellation, a change in the person, not the decision.
- Many people spend life stuck at the edge of a life-forward change. They may envision the change as unsafe or losing essential needs. The new constellation is different.
- For inexperienced people, a safe relationship with their dreams is most important. More dreams will come. We help them love the dream, admire its intricacy and uniqueness. *That's a wonderful dream!* we exclaim when we feel it. Or, *That's so interesting!*
- Dreaming is a living process, not just frozen pictures. When we let the pictures bring their bodily quality, dreamwork continues the living process.

Eugene Gendlin

See also: entries related to Dreams and Therapy

References

Bierman, R. (n.d.). *Focusing in changing abusive fighting to constructive conflict interactions*. Paper presented at the 11th International Focusing Conference, Ottawa, Ontario, Canada. Retrieved from http://www.focusing.org/rwv/article/rwv-presentation.html

Gendlin, E. T. (1986). *Let your body interpret your dreams*. Wilmette, IL: Chiron Publications.

Gendlin, E. T. (1996). Experiential dream work. In Eugene T. Gendlin (Ed.), *Focusing-oriented psychotherapy*. New York: The Guilford Press.

Gendlin, E. T. (1997). *A process model*. New York: The Focusing Institute. Retrieved from http://www.focusing.org/process.html

Gendlin, E. T. (2009). What first and third person processes really are. *Journal of Consciousness Studies, 16,* 10–12, 332–362.

Gendlin, E. T. (in press). Implicit precision. In Z. Radman (Ed.), *Knowing without thinking: The theory of the background in philosophy of mind*. Basingstoke, UK: Palgrave Macmillan. Retrieved from http://www.focusing.org/gendlin/pdf/gendlin_implicit_precision.pdf

Hendricks, M., & Cartwright, R. D. (1978). Experiencing level in dreams: An individual difference variable. *Psychotherapy: Theory, Research and Practice, 15*(3). Retrieved from http://www.focusing.org/research_expdream.html

Klein, M. H., Mathieu, P. L., Gendlin, E. T., & Kiesler, D. J. (1969). *The experiencing scale: A research and training manual*. Madison: University of Wisconsin Extension Bureau of Audiovisual Instruction.

Levine, P., & Frederick, A. (1977). *Waking the tiger: Healing trauma: The innate capacity to transform overwhelming experiences*. Berkeley, CA: North Atlantic Books.

Van der Kooy, A., & McEvenue, K. (2006). *Focusing with your whole body*. Toronto: Marlborough.

Brain Correlates to Lucidity

Dreaming and waking are two states of consciousness with similarities and differences. In both states, the thinker is aware of objects, events, and themselves (Cicogna & Bosinelli, 2001). In waking, however, the thinker typically has insight into his or her own mental state. This insight is called meta-awareness or self-consciousness. Generally, meta-awareness is the awareness of being aware; specifically, meta-awareness includes the awareness that one is awake and not, for example, dreaming (Pace-Schott, 2011). In contrast, such insight is largely absent from a typical dream. Some dreams, however, do contain this insight to varying degrees. In what are called lucid dreams, the dreamer is fully aware that he or she is dreaming and can typically control the course of the dream (LaBerge, 2007). The awareness in lucid dreams is akin to that during normal waking, in that the thinker can distinguish that he or she is dreaming or awake with little confusion. This similarity between lucid dreaming and wakefulness, and its contrast to typical dreaming, suggests that the phenomenon of lucid dreaming can be used as a scientific tool to determine what patterns of brain activity are associated with meta-awareness, and hence provide insight into its neural basis. Although functional neuroimaging of lucid dreaming has not yet been performed, comparison of brain activity during waking and sleep, electro-physiological measurement of lucid versus nonlucid dreaming, and neurocognitive correlates of lucidity have all been explored experimentally and have shed light on this interesting problem.

Patterns of brain activity associated with and common to waking and typical dreaming consciousness include forebrain activation by ascending arousal systems of the brain stem, diencephalon, and basal forebrain (Hobson, Pace-Schott, & Stickgold, 2000; Muzur, Pace-Schott, & Hobson, 2002). The routes of these activations are not identical neurochemically or anatomically, but ultimately may produce what is similar about the awareness of waking and typical dreaming. Along the same lines, differences in brain activation between dreaming and waking consciousness indicate which brain regions and circuits may be associated with aspects of consciousness that are present in waking but not dreaming. In particular, the lack of meta-awareness during typical dreams has been attributed to the deactivation of frontolateral executive regions of the brain during sleep (Hobson et al., 2000; Muzur et al., 2002). Positron emission tomography has shown that frontolateral and posterior multimodal association areas remain deactivated during sleep, including rapid eye movement (REM) sleep, when most dreams occur (Braun et al., 1997, 1998; Maquet et al., 1996, 2005). It has been hypothesized that frontolateral deactivation inhibits working memory such that the ability to compare the current experience to the immediate past is lost, and meta-awareness is consequently suppressed.

Whereas frontolateral cortex remains deactivated during both REM and non-REM sleep, other brain areas that are deactivated during non-REM sleep reactivate during REM sleep, when most dreams occur. Regions that reactivate during REM sleep include the ventromedial prefrontal and anterior cingulate cortices, as well as much of the subcortical limbic system and paralimbic cortices (Nofzinger et al., 2004; Nofzinger, Mintun, Wiseman, Kupfer, & Moore, 1997). These regions, called the anterior paralimbic REM activation area, can be activated in REM sleep to levels exceeding that during waking. Activation of the ventromedial prefrontal cortex during waking is associated with self-related, social, and emotional cognition, types of cognition that are present in dreaming (Pace-Schott, 2011). In addition, activation of ventromedial prefrontal cortex is associated with affectively guided decision making. Hence, increased activation of ventromedial prefrontal cortex could lead to lucid dreaming, wherein perceived control over decision making is relatively heightened compared to typical dreaming.

In addition to functional brain-imaging studies that suggest possible connections between lucid dreaming and regional brain activation, direct neurophysiological evidence supports the role of specific brain regions in lucidity. In a recent study, Ursula Voss and colleagues confirmed that lucid dreams are a real-time event and not simply a consequence of how dreams are remembered (Voss, Holzmann, Tuin, & Hobson, 2009). They demonstrated this by observing prearranged eye-movement signals that study participants made during lucid dreams. In the same study, they characterized electrophysiological signals made by the brain during lucid and nonlucid dreams. They found that brain signals during nonlucid REM sleep and lucid dreaming were similar in many respects, and different from waking. They also found that brain signals during lucid dreams were distinct from those during nonlucid REM sleep, and similar to waking. Specifically, they found that gamma frequency (30 to 80 Hz) signals were higher during lucid dreaming than during nonlucid REM sleep, and that these signals were strongest in frontolateral regions. Similarly, overall coherence was highest in waking and lucid dreaming, compared to nonlucid REM sleep, and coherence during lucid dreaming was highest in frontolateral regions. Hence, they established lucid dreaming as a distinctly measurable phenomenon and implicated frontolateral activity as something that distinguishes it from nonlucid dreaming and is in accord with waking.

A less direct but accessible approach to correlate regional brain activity with lucidity is to compare neurocognitive performance in individuals with a high propensity for lucid dreaming to those with a low propensity for lucid dreaming. Michelle Neider and colleagues used this approach in high school students with no prior training in lucid dream induction (Neider, Pace-Schott, Forselius, Pittman, & Morgan, 2010). In this study, students followed a dream awareness protocol for one week after performing two cognitive tasks, the Wisconsin Card Sort Task and the Iowa Gambling Task. These tasks were chosen because performance on these tasks engages the dorsolateral prefrontal cortex and ventromedial prefrontal cortex, respectively. They found that students who reported experiencing lucid dreams during the study week performed significantly better on the Iowa Gambling Task than students who did not, with no difference in Wisconsin Card Sort Task performance, and no demographic differences between groups. This result suggests a connection between dream lucidity and neurocognitive performance and indirectly implicates ventromedial prefrontal cortical function in lucidity.

Although the neural basis for lucidity in dreams is not yet known, important progress has implicated frontolateral brain regions as well as ventromedial prefrontal cortex in its genesis. Future studies will ideally combine direct confirmation of lucidity with anatomical, physiological, and neurocognitive measures to distinguish which functions of which brain regions are necessary and sufficient for lucidity to occur. Such work may promote understanding of meta-awareness and the neural bases for distinct states of consciousness such as waking, nonlucid dreaming, and lucid dreaming.

Peter Morgan

See also: entries related to Sleep and the Brain

References

Braun, A. R., Balkin, T. J., Wesenten, N. J., Carson, R. E., Varga, M., Baldwin, P., . . . Herscovitch, P. (1997). Regional cerebral blood flow throughout the sleep–wake cycle. An H2(15)O PET study. *Brain, 120*(Pt 7), 1173–1197.

Braun, A. R, Balkin, T. J., Wesensten, N. J., Gwadry, F., Carson, R. E., Varga, M., . . . Herscovitch, P. (1998). Dissociated pattern of activity in visual cortices and their projections during human rapid eye movement sleep. *Science, 279,* 91–95.

Cicogna, P.C., & Bosinelli, M. (2001). Consciousness during dreams. *Consciousness and Cognition, 10,* 26–41.

Hobson, J.A., Pace-Schott, E.F., & Stickgold, R. (2000). Dreaming and the brain: Toward a cognitive neuroscience of conscious states. *Behavioral and Brain Sciences, 23,* 793–842, 904–1121.

LaBerge, S. (2007). Lucid dreaming. In D. Barrett & P. McNamara (Eds.), *The new science of dreaming, vol. 2: Content, recall, and personality correlates* (pp. 307–328). Westport, CT: Praeger.

Maquet, P., Péters, J., Aerts, J., Delfior, G., Degueldre, C., Luxen, A., & Franck, G. (1996). Functional neuroanatomy of human rapid-eye-movement sleep and dreaming. *Nature, 383,* 163–166.

Maquet, P., Ruby, P., Maudoux, A., Albouy, A., Sterpenich, V., Dang-Vu, T., . . . Laureys, S. (2005). Human cognition during REM sleep and the activity profile within frontal and parietal cortices: A reappraisal of functional neuroimaging data. *Progress in Brain Research, 150,* 219–227.

Muzur, A., Pace-Schott, E.F., & Hobson, J.A. (2002). The prefrontal cortex in sleep. *Trends in Cognitive Science, 6,* 475–481.

Neider, M., Pace-Schott, E.F., Forselius, E., Pittman, B., & Morgan, P.T. (2010). Lucid dreaming and ventromedial versus dorsolateral prefrontal task performance. In *Consciousness and Cognition,* 563–574.

Nofzinger, E.A., Buysse, D.J., Germain, A., Carter, C., Luna, B., Price, J.C., . . . Kupfer, D.J. (2004). Increased activation of anterior paralimbic and executive cortex from waking to rapid eye movement sleep in depression. *Archives of General Psychiatry, 61,* 695–702.

Nofzinger, E.A., Mintun, M.A., Wiseman, M., Kupfer, D.J., & Moore, R.Y. (1997). Forebrain activation in REM sleep: An FDG PET study. *Brain Research, 770,* 192–201.

Pace-Schott, E.F. (2011). The neurobiology of dreaming. In M.H. Kryger, T. Roth, & W.C. Dement (Eds.), *Principles and practice of sleep medicine* (5th ed., pp. 563–574). Philadelphia, PA: Elsevier.

Voss, U., Holzmann, R., Tuin, I., & Hobson, J.A. (2009). Lucid dreaming: A state of consciousness with features of both waking and nonlucid dreaming. *Sleep, 32,* 1191–1200.

Brain Damage: Effects on Dreams

Cessation of dream experiences has long been observed in patients who suffer from brain damage. The history of such observation can be traced back to Hermann Wilbrand's clinical report in 1887. The ventromesial frontal region and the inferior temporal cortex are two major structures in the forebrain that are most strongly associated with this neurological symptom (Yu, 2006, 2007a, 2007b). The primary function of the ventromesial frontal region is to motivate an organism to seek out and engage with external objects that can satisfy its inner biological needs. Many psychobehavioral routines, including all basic instinctual functions and gratifications, are governed by this brain pathway. The anatomical situation of the inferior temporal cortex equips it with compact neuroanatomical and functional associations with the motivational system in the ventromesial frontal region on the one hand, and the visual representation system in the occipital cortex on the other. Patients' reports of dream cessation following neurological insults circumscribed to the ventromesial frontal region or the inferior temporal cortex suggest that these two brain structures play critical roles in the neural network for dream formation.

Notwithstanding the extensive, repeated clinicoanatomical evidence, an argument can be made that patients' reports of dream cessation can be conceived of as a secondary effect of memory failure, rather than as a direct consequence of neurological insults. There are two arguments within this criticism. First, dream recall is difficult in nature, even in normal people. Second, neurological patients' memories, and therefore their dream recall, are poor.

Dream recall of normal people has been widely investigated in different ethnic settings. As indicated in numerous studies, dream-recall frequency is susceptible to the effects of both methodologies—including retrospective self-rating scale, dream diary or nightly log, and REM awakening—and individual factors, such as gender, neuroticism, openness to experience, visual memory, and imagery abilities. Overall, the dream-recall frequency obtained by the retrospective self-rating method is the most conservative estimate in comparison with those obtained with the other two methods. The average dream-recall frequencies documented by the studies using the retrospective self-rating method are two to three times per week (see Yu, 2006, 2010, for details). The discrepancy of dream-recall frequencies between individual studies is somehow conceivable in view of the fact that the term *recall* can be interpreted differently by different people. It is difficult to standardize how many details of a dream narrative are remembered and how long the memory for a dream is retained in order to consider it a valid recall of a dream vignette. Indeed, when dream recall is conceptualized as any dream experience of which people are aware, whether or not they remember the dream content, very high frequencies of dream recall are obtained. In Yu's (2010) retrospective study, for instance, more than 40 percent of participants were aware of their dream experiences at least several times a week, and cases completely devoid of any awareness of dream experiences were extremely rare—namely, 0.3 percent. The overall evidence indicates that most neurologically healthy people are regularly aware of their dream experiences, even though they may not remember the details of their dream narratives.

In stark contrast to what was mentioned previously, neurological patients who suffer lesions in the ventromesial frontal region or the inferior temporal cortex consistently exhibit a cessation of dream experiences. Not only do they lack the ability to recall their dreams, but more dramatically they also sustain complete unawareness of dream experiences beginning with the onset of their neurological insult. This clinical presentation cannot be properly explained by the normal tendency to forget dreams.

Considering the symptomatological characteristic that memory is a fragile system that can be affected by many neuropathologies, it is not surprising to find that most patients who have been unaware of their dream experiences since the onset of their neurological illness simultaneously suffer memory deficits. It is important to note, however, that the ability to recall dream experiences is often preserved even in patients who present with profound memory difficulties (Yu, 2006, 2007b). Because of the neuroanatomical layout that pictorial memory is predominantly processed by the right hemisphere and verbal memory by the left hemisphere, memory disorders can be limited to a specific modality or material. Moreover, autobiographical or episodic memory is multifaceted rather than confined to a single modality. Therefore, although many neurological patients display profound memory disorders, which are always specific to a certain modality, they are still able to retrieve personal or dream experiences via many other channels or cues. This is especially true when considering that the phenomenology of dreaming, and therefore the retrieval of a dream experience, is, in essence, emotional. In view of the evidence that (1) dream recall is not difficult in nature, and (2) profound memory deficits do not necessarily result in cessation of dream experiences, memory failure does not appear to constitute a convincing explanation for defective dream experiences as a consequence of neurological insult.

Calvin Kai-Ching Yu

See also: entries related to Sleep and the Brain

References

Wilbrand, H. (1887). *Mind-blindness as a focal symptom and its relationship to alexia and agraphia*. Wiesbaden: Bergmann.

Yu, C.K.-C. (2006). Memory loss is not equal to loss of dream experience: A clinicoanatomical study of dreaming in patients with posterior brain lesions. *Neuro-Psychoanalysis, 8,* 191–198.

Yu, C.K.-C. (2007a). Cessation of dreaming and ventromesial frontal-region infarcts. *Neuro-Psychoanalysis, 9,* 85–92.

Yu, C.K.-C. (2007b). Dream recall and the dissociation between dream cessation and neurological memory disorders. *Neuro-Psychoanalysis*, 9, 213–221.

Yu, C.K.-C. (2010). Dream Intensity Scale: Factors in the phenomenological analysis of dreams. *Dreaming*, 20, 107–129.

Brain Energy, Metabolism, and Sleep

The brain is a high energy–requiring organ as it continuously consumes metabolic energy. Although the brain constitutes only 2 percent of body mass, it receives 15 percent of the cardiac output, consumes 20 percent of total body oxygen, and utilizes 25 percent of total glucose. However, brain tissue is unique in that it does not store large amounts of energy; instead, energy-expensive biosynthetic processes (protein/lipid/cholesterol biosynthesis) are carried out when activity (action potential/neuronal excitability)-dependent energy consumption is at its minimum. The direct relationship between neuronal activity and energy consumption was suggested as early as 1890 by Roy and Sherrington and confirmed by numerous studies. An overall reduction in neuronal activation during sleep led to the long-lasting hypothesis that one of the functions of sleep is to restore brain energy. Studies that associated the sleep–wake related changes in neuronal activation with brain energy metabolism date back to the mid-20th century and used a number of techniques for estimation of brain metabolites.

In 1954, Tom Seki described a close correlation between factors involved in brain energy metabolism, cerebral circulation, and neural activation recorded on the EEG. In humans, ^{18}F-2-DG administration followed by brain imaging by positron emission tomography (PET) showed a 23 to 44 percent decrease in the metabolic rate during sleep across the entire brain, whereas measurements of $CMRO_2$ reported a reduction of 25 percent in brain metabolism (Maquet, 2000).

Biochemical assays to measure changes in brain metabolites were initiated in animal models in the 1970s. Stanley Van den Noort and Katherine Brine in 1970 observed a 10 percent decrease in lactate and a slight rise in phosphocreatine and adenosine triphosphate (ATP) in the brains of sleeping rats. These studies were difficult to interpret because of lack of information on the electrophysiological confirmation of sleep. Indirect assessments of cerebral metabolic rate were done with use of radioactive 2-DG in sleep–wake studies. One study examined 75 regions in the monkey brain and showed statistically significant decreases in metabolic rate in 44 of these regions during sleep (Kennedy et al., 1982). Later similar decreases in metabolic rates were also noted in rats and cats using 2-DG autoradiography in whole brain during sleep. Thus, by the turn of the century, ample evidence was available in support of the idea that cerebral metabolism is reduced during sleep, leading J.H. Bennington and H.C. Heller to postulate the hypothesis that sleep and the accompanied reductions in neuronal activity is essential for replenishment of cerebral glycogen stores that are depleted during waking (Benington & Heller, 1995). The direct proof of this hypothesis was, however, difficult due to differences in the measures of glycogen during sleep and sleep deprivation, as well as the limited contribution of glycogen toward total brain energy.

Another major hypothesis derives from studies of extracellular adenosine, a metabolic by-product of ATP breakdown (Basheer, Strecker, Thakkar, & McCarley, 2004). Pharmacological studies showed that adenosine as well as the agonists of adenosine receptors induced sleep, whereas adenosine antagonists including the classic stimulant, caffeine, decreased sleep. One of the best functional theories for adenosine's role in sleep–wake behavior derives from the fact that adenosine progressively rises during waking and sleep deprivation with increases in metabolism, and neural activity and has an inhibitory effect on wake-promoting neuronal networks thus promoting sleep.

The adenosine studies prompted us to examine the currency of cellular energy, ATP, since adenosine itself might reflect ATP breakdown. We recently reported that cellular ATP is well balanced during the wake period in rat brain, but shows a surge in the initial hours of sleep. This surge can be prevented if the rats are kept awake. The ATP surge was strongly correlated with the non-REM slow-wave EEG delta activity (0.5–4.5 Hz), a well-recognized marker of sleep homeostasis. Our results also show that the increased levels of ATP correspond with an increase in nonphosphorylated form of AMP-activated protein kinase (AMPK), a well-known sensor and regulator of cellular energy that potentiates anabolic processes. On the contrary, the levels of phosphorylated AMPK increase during wake and sleep deprivation and potentiate catabolic processes to generate more ATP. These results suggest that sleep-induced surge in ATP and decreased phosphorylation of AMPK set the stage for increased anabolic processes during sleep (Dworak, McCarley, Kim, Kalinchuk, & Basheer, 2010).

Taken together, there is intriguing evidence that wakefulness is an energetic challenge to the brain and that the reduced neuronal activity during NREM sleep might play an important role in restoring brain energy balance. However, further studies are needed to clarify the role of the brain energy metabolism in sleep regulation and especially its functional implications.

Markus Dworak and Radhika Basheer

See also: entries related to Sleep and the Brain

References

Basheer, R., Strecker, R. E., Thakkar, M. M., & McCarley, R. W. (2004). Adenosine and sleep–wake regulation. *Progress in Neurobiology, 73,* 379–396.

Benington, J. H., & Heller, H. C. (1995). Restoration of brain energy metabolism as the function of sleep. *Progress in Neurobiology, 45,* 347–360.

Dworak, M., McCarley, R. W., Kim, T., Kalinchuk, A. V., & Basheer, R. (2010). Sleep and brain energy levels: ATP changes during sleep. *Journal of Neuroscience, 30,* 9007–9016.

Kennedy, C., Gillin, J. C., Mendelson, W., Suda, S., Miyaoka, M., Ito, M., . . . Sokoloff, L. (1982). Local cerebral glucose utilization in non-rapid eye movement sleep. *Nature, 27,* 325–327.

Maquet, P. (2000). Functional neuroimaging of normal human sleep by positron emission tomography. *Journal of Sleep Research, 9,* 207–231.

Brain Mechanisms of Vision in Dreams

Vision is a function of brain/mind that requires very large, interconnected brain systems and extremely complicated mechanisms, including visual scanning. When we see, the brain automatically chooses informative targets and scans them rapidly (three to four eye movements per second) (Yarbus, 1967). The neural system that controls the scanning eye movements during the waking state has been well characterized. The same system may be used to scan what we see in waking imagination and dreaming. Rapid eye movements (REMs) very likely coincide with dreaming and may reflexively scan what we see in dreaming.

Furthermore, unexpected findings of a recent functional magnetic resonance imaging (fMRI) study (Hong et al., 2009) suggest that the sharing in waking and dreaming goes beyond the visual scanning mechanism and extends to the subsequent processing of the visual information obtained by scanning (Hong et al., 2009). (1) REMs, which are presumably visual events, were associated with activation not only in the cortex (outer surface of the brain) involved in sight, but also in those for hearing, smell, touch, balance, and control of body movements. Comparison with waking study findings supports the view that the waking brain functions essentially the same way. That is, visual stimuli may trigger activation of non-visual sensory and motor systems in wakefulness as well, perhaps for faster detection and response to the stimuli. (2) Extraordinarily robust activation in the thalamic reticular nucleus (TRN) associated with REMs sheds light on its mechanism. It was suggested that TRN new primes the nonvisual sensory and motor cortices in response to visual stimuli, whether they are linked to scanning eye movements in dreaming or awake state. The anatomy and organization of the TRN are suitable for this role. (3) Findings from this study support that REMs are associated with the recruitment of the binding mechanism (Llinas & Ribary, 1993), which integrates various sensory data into a unified experience in the waking state. To see a bird flying, its images on

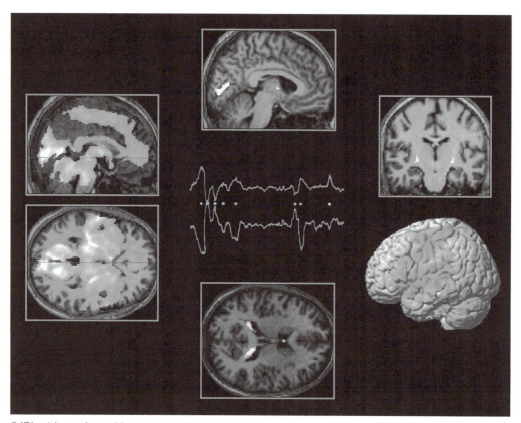

fMRI evidence for multisensory recruitment associated with rapid eye movements during sleep. In this fMRI study these authors studied the neural correlates of rapid eye movement (REM) during sleep by timing REMs using video recording rather than using the traditional EOG methodology (central figure with yellow dots indicating REMs) . They detected approximately four times as many REMs. The results demonstrate that REM-locked activation could be well localized: the peak of activation was clearly in the striate cortex (top figure) and the thalamic reticular nucleus (top upper right figure). The 3D surface rendering figure (lower right) shows REM-locked activation in the motor and the somatosensory cortices around the central sulcus and in the superior temporal lobe. The two figures on the left, upper and lower, show distributed REM-locked activation. The bottom figure shows the surprising and unexpected REM-locked periventricular deactivation. (Human Brain Mapping, vol. 30, issue 5, 2009, cover. Copyright 2009 Charles Chong-Hwa Hong. This material is reproduced with permission of John Wiley & Sons, Inc.)

the retina are broken down into three basic components: shape, movement, and color. Different parts of the brain process those different components. If the bird sings, the auditory system is also involved. The distributed sensory data in various parts of the brain need to be bound so that we can see and hear the flying bird in a cohesive fashion. (4) Other areas that are activated in association with REMs include the language areas of the brain, as well as the area that is the major source of cholinergic input to the entire cortex and profoundly affected by Alzheimer's disease. Language and cholinergic systems may play roles in visual perception in both waking and dreaming states.

These findings have important practical implications (Hong & Harris, 2009). REMs may be used as a natural, ideal, task-free probe into several major brain systems: the eye-movement-control system, visual and nonvisual sensory system, the binding system, the language system, and the cholinergic system. Some of these systems are reported to be abnormal in schizophrenia, Alzheimer's disease, and other major mental disorders. A single fMRI scan may allow examination of all of these important brain systems. Additionally, there are a few key advantages to this fMRI method employing REMs as a probe. (1) The probe being task-free, it may be useful in cognitively impaired persons who cannot cooperate fully with conventional brain activation studies and even in infants. In typical waking studies, research participants need to understand and cooperate with instructions to perform specific tasks. (2) Muscle tone is greatly suppressed in REM sleep. Head movements create false results in MRI studies. Thus, this method

may be useful for people who tend to move more during waking MRI studies, such as persons with schizophrenia or movement disorders such as Parkinson's disease. (3) Much of the external sensory input to the brain is blocked in REM sleep. Thus, REM sleep may be an ideal state to study internal sensory mechanism. During waking studies on the effect of visual stimuli, research participants will hear sounds and may sense itching on the nose and these nonvisual sensory stimuli may obscure the results. (4) Whereas multiple subjects are usually needed to produce reliable results, data from a single participant (only six minutes in duration) produced reliable results about REMs. The ability to draw results from a single person allows comparison with other data that is specific to an individual patient. Changes over time can also be analyzed within a single person. This method may become a powerful tool to study the development of the brain/consciousness beginning at birth.

Charles Chong-Hwa Hong

See also: entries related to Sleep and the Brain

References

Hong, C.C.-H., & Harris, J.C. (2009). Study of neural correlates of rapid eye movements in dreaming sleep using video camera for timing of REMs and functional MRI: Its implications (editorial). *Sleep and Hypnosis, 11*, 1–4.

Hong, C.C.-H., Harris, J.C., Pearlson, G.D., Kim, J.-S., Calhoun, V.D., Fallon, J.H., . . . Pekar, J.J. (2009). fMRI evidence for multisensory recruitment associated with rapid eye movements during sleep. *Human Brain Mapping, 30*, 1705–1722.

Llinas, R., & Ribary, U. (1993). Coherent 40-Hz oscillation characterizes dream state in humans. *Proceedings of the National Academy of Sciences of the United States of America, 90,* 2078–2081.

Yarbus, A.L. (1967). *Eye movements and vision.* New York: Plenum Press.

Brief History of Sleep Medicine

Perhaps the best place to start with a history of sleep is with a description of the recognition of the neurophysiology of sleep. In 1875, Caton first recorded the brain electrical activity of animals (Caton, 1875), but it was not until 1929 that Berger reported the electroencephalogram (EEG) of humans (Berger, 1929). Subsequently, in 1937, Loomis described the EEG features of what is now known as NREM sleep (Loomis, Harvey, & Hobart, 1937). He described five levels of NREM with vertex waves, sleep spindles, K complexes, and delta slowing. The next major breakthrough came in 1953, when Kleitman and Aserinsky described REM sleep and the proposed correlation with dreaming (Aserinsky & Kleitman, 1953). Finally, in 1957, Dement and Kleitman provided a description of sleep cycles and a classification system of sleep stages with four stages of NREM and REM (Dement & Kleitman, 1957). This system of description withheld the test of time until some recent modifications offered in 2007 by the American Academy of Sleep Medicine (AASM; Iber, Ancoli-Israel, Chesson, & Quan, 2007).

Narcolepsy

Narcolepsy was first described in 1880 by Gelineau. The first breakthrough in understanding the disease came in 1960 when Vogel recognized the characteristic early onset REM sleep as a feature of this disorder (Vogel, 1960). This led to the concept that cataplexy and sleep paralysis were associated with the muscle atonia of REM sleep while hypnagogic hallucinations are dissociated dreams. The next step was the observation of the relationship between HLA-DR2 and narcolepsy (Juji, Satake, Honda, & Doi, 1984). A lower frequency of HLA-DR2 in African Americans led to the conclusion that the actual predisposing antigen was DQ1 rather than DR2 (Matsuki et al., 1992). Finally, the responsible subtype was identified as HLA DQB1*0602 (Mignot et al., 1994) present in 85 to 90 percent of narcoleptics who have cataplexy (Mignot, Hayduk, Black, Grumet, & Guilleminault, 1997). The major breakthrough, however, occurred with the description of the hypocretin–orexin system (de Lecea, Kilduff, Payron, Gao, et al., 1998; Sakurai et al., 1998). These molecules were found to arise from a precursor, preprohypocretin, synthesized by a small number of cells in the posterior and lateral hypothalamus, especially the perifornical area. They project to a diverse set of targets in the brain and spinal cord, especially the monoaminergic and cholinergic fields of the brain stem tegmentum comprising the ascending reticular activating system (Kilduff & Peyron, 2000; Marcus et al., 2001). Subsequently, narcolepsy in dogs was found to be transmitted as an autosomal recessive trait and was caused by a deletion in the Hcrt receptor-2 gene (Lin et al., 1999), and that Hcrt-1 was associated with human narcolepsy (Nishino, Ripley, Overeem, Lammers, & Mignot, 2000).

REM Sleep Behavior Disorder

REM sleep behavior disorder (RBD) is a striking parasomnia that was first described in 1986 (Schenck, Bundlie, Ettinger, & Mahowald, 1986). It has been suggested that the physiology underlying RBD is impairment in the normal muscle atonia associated with REM. In cats, lesions to the descending inhibitory pathway from cells of the pedunculopontine nuclei in close proximity to the primary REM-sleep generator in the dorsal pons produce varying degrees of motor activity during REM sleep (Hendricks, Morrison, & Mann, 1982). At least 50 percent of RBD patients carry diagnoses of Parkinson's disease, multiple system atrophy, or dementia with Lewy bodies (Olson, Boeve, & Silber, 2000). Thus, RBD appears to be associated with those neurodegenerative disorders with alpha synuclein positive inclusion bodies.

Obstructive Sleep Apnea

Although earlier literary references to obstructive sleep apnoea (OSA)/Pickwickian syndrome are often cited, the first modern reference is attributed to Burwell and colleagues' (Burwell, Robin, Whaley, & Bickelmann, 1956) description of the obesity hypoventilation (Pickwickian) syndrome in 1956. Initially, the associated excessive daytime sleepiness (EDS) was attributed to alveolar hypoventilation, but subsequently, it was demonstrated by polysomnography monitoring that upper airway obstructions were punctuated by brief arousals (Gastaut, Tassinari, & Duron, 1966) and the EDS was then assigned to the fragmented sleep.

Later, the importance of obstructive apneas was expanded to include hypopneas and even upper airway resistance. By 1978, the pathophysiology of upper-airway collapse in the pharyngeal segment of the airway was established (Remmers, deGroot, Sauerland, & Anch, 1978) and tracheostomy was recognized as an effective treatment. Within a few years, it was demonstrated that continuous positive airway pressure could prevent airway collapse and provide an effective treatment option for OSA (Sullivan, Issa, Berthon-Jones, & Eves, 1981). Certainly, it was the discovery of this effective treatment that resulted in a gradual increased interest in establishing the diagnosis and the associated growth in clinical sleep laboratories. The first major epidemiologic study of the prevalence of OSA showed a prevalence of 2 and 4 percent in middle-aged women and men, respectively (Young et al., 1993). Subsequent epidemiologic studies confirmed the role of obesity and the relationship to hypertension (Peppard, Young, Palta, & Skatrud, 2000) and an increased prevalence of coronary heart disease, heart failure, and stroke (Shahar et al., 2001).

Restless Legs Syndrome

Restless legs syndrome (RLS) was first described by Ekbom in the 1940s, but for many years it was thought to be a rare curiosity. However, current epidemiologic studies suggest it may be one of the most common sleep-related disorders, with a prevalence as high as 10 percent (Phillips et al., 2000). Pharmacological studies have indicated that levodopa and dopamine-receptor agonists are effective therapies for RLS, indicating that the disorder is associated with a decrease in dopaminergic function in the brain. However, contradictory results have been obtained with 18-fluorodopa positron emission tomographic scans (Trenkwalder et al., 1999). Functional magnetic resonance imaging of patients with RLS suggests involvement of the cerebellum and the thalamus with additional activation of the red nucleus, pons, and midbrain when periodic leg movements are also present (Bucher, Seelos, Oertel, Reiser, & Trenkwalder, 1997). Physiologic studies have suggested that a disturbance of inhibitory subcortical pathways, such as the reticulospinal tract, may allow expression of a normally suppressed neural generator at the level of the spinal cord (Bara-Jimenez, Aksu, Graham, Sato, & Hallett, 2000). About 50 percent of patients with RLS have a family history of the condition (Winkelmann et al., 2000), and a recent report has described a family with linkage to chromosome 12q (Desautels et al., 2001). Another advance in our understanding of RLS has been the observation of a relationship with low iron stores in the brain (Sun, Chen, Ho, Earley, & Allen, 1998).

Sanford Auerbach

See also: entries related to Sleep Disorders

References

Aserinsky, E., & Kleitman, N. (1953). Regularly occurring episodes of eye mobility and concomitant phenomena during sleep. *Science, 118*(3062), 273–274.

Bara-Jimenez, W., Aksu, M., Graham, B., Sato, S., & Hallett, M. (2000). Periodic limb movements in sleep: State-dependent excitability of the spinal flexor reflex. *Neurology, 54,* 1609–1616.

Berger, H. (1929). Über das Elektrenkephalogramm des Menschen. *Archiv fur Psychiatrie und Nervenkrankheiten, 97,* 6–26.

Bucher, S. F., Seelos, K. C., Oertel, W. H., Reiser, M., & Trenkwalder, C. (1997). Cerebral generators involved in the pathogenesis of the restless legs syndrome. *Annals of Neurology, 41,* 639–645.

Burwell, C. S., Robin, E. D., Whaley, R. D., & Bickelmann, A. G. (1956). Extreme obesity associated with alveolar hypoventilation—Pickwickian syndrome. *American Journal of Medicine, 21,* 811.

Caton, R. (1875). The electric currents of the brain. *British Medical Journal, 2,* 278.

Dement, W., & Kleitman, N. (1957). Cyclic variations in EEG during sleep and their relation to eye movements, body motility and dreaming. *Electroencephalography and Clinical Neurophysiology, 9,* 673–690.

Desautels, A., Turecki, G., Montplaisir, J., Sequeira, A., Vernet, A., & Rouleau, G. A. (2001). Identification of a major susceptibility locus for restless legs syndrome on chromosome 12q. *American Journal of Human Genetics, 69,* 1266–1270.

Gastaut, H., Tassinari, C. A., & Duron, B. (1966). Polygraphic study of the episodic diurnal and nocturnal (hypnic and respiratory) manifestations of the Pickwick syndrome. *Brain Research, 2,* 167–186.

Hendricks, J. C., Morrison, A. R., & Mann, G. L. (1982). Different behaviors during paradoxical sleep without atonia depend on pontine lesion site. *Brain Research, 239,* 81–105.

Iber, C., Ancoli-Israel, S., Chesson, A., & Quan, S. F. (2007). *The AASM manual for the scoring of sleep and associated events: Rules, terminology and technical specifications.* Westchester, IL: American Academy of Sleep Medicine.

Juji, T., Satake, M., Honda, Y., & Doi, Y. (1984). HLA antigens in Japanese patients with narcolepsy. All the patients were DR2 positive. *Tissue Antigens*, 24, 316–319.

Kilduff, T. S., & Peyron, C. (2000). The hypocretin/orexin ligand–receptor system: Implications for sleep and sleep disorders. *Trends in Neurosciences,* 23, 359–365.

Lin, L., Faraco, J., Li, R., Kadotani, H., Rogers, W., Lin, X., . . . Mignot, E. (1999). The sleep disorder canine narcolepsy is caused by a mutation in the hypocretin (orexin) receptor 2 gene. *Cell, 98,* 365–376.

Loomis, A. L., Harvey, E. N., & Hobart, G. A. (1937). Cerebral states during sleep as studied by human brain potentials. *Journal of Experimental Psychology,* 21, 127–144.

Marcus, J. N., Aschkenasi, C. J., Lee, C. E., Chemelli, R. M., Saper, C. B., Yanagisawa, M., & Elmquist, J. K. (2001). Differential expression of orexin receptors 1 and 2 in the rat brain. *Journal of Comparative Neurology, 435,* 6–25.

Matsuki, K., Grumet, F. C., Lin, X., Gelb, M., Guilleminault, C., Dement, W. C., & Mignot, E. (1992). DQ (rather than DR) gene marks susceptibility to narcolepsy. *Lancet, 339*(8800), 1052.

Mignot, E., Hayduk, R., Black, J., Grumet, F. C., & Guilleminault, C. (1997). HLA DQB1*0602 is associated with cataplexy in 509 narcoleptic patients. *Sleep, 20,* 1012–1020.

Mignot, E., Lin, X., Arrigoni, J., Macaubas, C., Olive, F., Hallmayer, J., . . . Grumet, F. C. (1994). DQB1*0602 and DQA1*0102 (DQ1) are better markers than DR2 for narcolepsy in Caucasian and black Americans. *Sleep, 17*(8 Suppl.), S60–S67.

Nishino, S., Ripley, B., Overeem, S., Lammers, G. J., & Mignot, E. (2000). Hypocretin (orexin) deficiency in human narcolepsy. *Lancet, 355*(9197), 39–40.

Olson, E. J., Boeve, B. F., & Silber, M. H. (2000). Rapid eye movement sleep behaviour disorder: Demographic, clinical and laboratory findings in 93 cases. *Brain, 123*(Pt 2), 331–339.

Peppard, P. E., Young, T., Palta, M., & Skatrud, J. (2000). Prospective study of the association between sleep-disordered breathing and hypertension. *New England Journal of Medicine, 342,* 1378–1384.

Phillips, B., Young, T., Finn, L., Asher, K., Hening, W. A., & Purvis, C. (2000). Epidemiology of restless legs symptoms in adults. *Archives of Internal Medicine, 160,* 2137–2141.

Remmers, J. E., deGroot, W. J., Sauerland, E. K., & Anch, A. M. (1978). Pathogenesis of upper airway occlusion during sleep. *Journal of Applied Physiology, 44,* 931–938.

Sakurai, T., Amemiya, A., Ishii, M., Matsuzaki, I., Chemelli, R. M., Tanaka, H., . . . Yanagisawa, M. (1998). Orexins and orexin receptors: A family of hypothalamic neuropeptides and G protein-coupled receptors that regulate feeding behavior. *Cell, 92,* 573–585.

Schenck, C. H., Bundlie, S. R., Ettinger, M. G., & Mahowald, M. W. (1986). Chronic behavioral disorders of human REM sleep: A new category of parasomnia. *Sleep, 9,* 293–308.

Shahar, E., Whitney, C. W., Redline, S., Lee, E. T., Newman, A. B., Javier Nieto, F., . . . Samet, J. M. (2001). Sleep-disordered breathing and cardiovascular disease: Cross-sectional results of the Sleep Heart Health Study. *American Journal of Respiratory and Critical Care Medicine, 163,* 19–25.

Sullivan, C. E., Issa, F. G., Berthon-Jones, M., & Eves, L. (1981). Reversal of obstructive sleep apnoea by continuous positive airway pressure applied through the nares. *Lancet, 1*(8225), 862–865.

Sun, E. R., Chen, C. A., Ho, G., Earley, C. J., & Allen, R. P. (1998). Iron and the restless legs syndrome. *Sleep, 21*(4), 371–377.

Trenkwalder, C., Walters, A. S., Hening, W. A., Chokroverty, S., Antonini, A., Dhawan, V., & Eidelberg, D. (1999). Positron emission tomographic studies in restless legs syndrome. *Movement Disorders,* 14, 141–145.

Vogel, G. (1960). Studies in the psychophysiology of dreams, III: The dream of narcolepsy. Archives of General Psychiatry, 3, 421–428.

Winkelmann, J., Wetter, T.C., Collado-Seidel, V., Gasser, T., Dichgans, M., Yassouridis, A., & Trenkwalder, C. (2000). Clinical characteristics and frequency of the hereditary restless legs syndrome in a population of 300 patients. *Sleep, 23,* 597–602.

Young, T., Palta, M., Dempsey, J., Skatrud, J., Weber, S., & Badr, S. (1993). The occurrence of sleep-disordered breathing among middle-aged adults. *New England Journal of Medicine, 328,* 1230–1235.

C

Cancer Patients and Dreamwork

Since the late 1990s, members of the International Association for the Study of Dreams (IASD) have concentrated on creating and implementing a dreamwork program for people who are facing cancer. Tallulah Lyons has facilitated a weekly dream group at The Wellness Community (TWC) in Atlanta, Georgia, since 1998. Wendy Pannier facilitated a group twice a month at TWC in Philadelphia, Pennsylvania, from 1995 to 2009 and is now offering dreamwork programs for cancer patients at TWC in Cincinnati, Ohio. In 2005, Lyons and Pannier collaborated and received grants to develop and direct a cancer dreamwork project, the Healing Power of Dreams, which includes a three-hour workshop, guidelines for dream groups, a participants' manual, and a set of evaluation questions. In 2006, the grants were extended to enable the creation of a facilitators' manual and the training of additional dreamwork facilitators. With the participation of other IASD members, workshops have been offered in more than a dozen facilities across the country, periodic ongoing dream groups have been established, several hundred participants have received the dreamwork manual, and countless queries about dreams have been answered through the Healing Power of Dreams website (www. healingpowerofdreams.com).

Integrative Approach

Dreamwork with cancer patients begins in a group setting with the teaching of basic symbol work and projective techniques. Facilitators then incorporate basic principles of several well-researched mind/body practices that are at the core of the fast growing field of integrative oncology, which combines standard medical care with complementary approaches. Guided imagery is key to the IASD dreamwork approach. We also incorporate the basic principles of mindfulness meditation and encourage participation in expressive arts, particularly collage, clay work, mandala work, and journaling. For embodying healing dream imagery, we encourage meditative movement, particularly yoga and Qi Gong, and energy work in the form of focused visualizations.

All the practices mentioned in the preceding text are well documented as having not only positive effects on quality of life but also positive effects on the immune system. Key studies are cited in a recent comprehensive book on integrative oncology (Abrams & Weil, 2009).

Many complementary practices are now offered in a growing number of cancer facilities but rarely is dreamwork

Artist Diane Urban says of her piece *Heart*: "This piece commemorates connection to cosmic harmony and balance. The pink [center] symbolizes universal feminine love. This image from my dream also helps me tap into the feminine art energy of my grandmother and cousins." (© Diane Urban)

existing programs, underscoring the need for more relevant dream studies in integrative medicine.

Healing Dreams

We define healing dreams as dreams that carry a felt sense of reconciliation; a sense of resolution of conflict; a sense of meaning and purpose; and a sense of balance, harmony, and peace. Healing dreams always bring a sense of new possibility and hope. For many who are facing cancer, healing dreams offer guidance, commenting on medical treatment options and outcomes as well as perceptions, attitudes, and behaviors that need attention in order for healing to occur. In the IASD cancer project, the word *healing* describes a process of returning to a state of balance and harmony from a state of imbalance and disease. Healing is differentiated from cure, which means disappearance of the cancer. Healing and cure sometimes occur together, but there can be healing on multiple levels of mind, body, and spirit no matter the outcome of the disease.

Healing dreams usually fall into one of four categories. First and often the most powerful is dreams of numinous encounter. In such dreams, the dreamer encounters a being, person, animal, or object that elicits a total positive shift in mind, body, and spirit. The second type is dreams of resolution and renewal. There is no numinous encounter, yet the dreamer awakens with certainty that everything is going to be all right. Dreams of guidance comprise the third category. Dreams bring guidance and clarity about health-care providers and treatment options, about lifestyle changes

included. To gain acceptance for dreamwork within medical settings, it is imperative that dream group facilitators be able to demonstrate that dreamwork is linked to well-researched mind/body practices. Contemporary dream research, including neurological insight into the dreaming brain (Hoss, 2005), the clinical nightmare research of Earnest Hartman (1998), and new re-scripting approaches with PTSD nightmares (Moore & Krakow, 2007), offers additional credence to the inclusion of dreamwork as an integrative oncology practice. Unfortunately, this body of work is not well known or implemented in most and finances, about every imaginable conflict that accompanies the diagnosis of cancer. The fourth type of healing dream arises as the culmination of long-term dreamwork. Often after being disturbed by a nightmare, the dreamer may be able to shift the imagery and energy in a positive direction through working with a series of dreams and meditative sessions. All types of healing dreams offer imagery and energy that can be embodied through intentional meditative practice for enhancement of the body's innate healing systems and for living life to the fullest.

Dreams and Healing Imagery

Mind/body research demonstrates that any imagery that is perceived as positive correlates with indicators of enhancement of the patient's immune system. For research findings on the positive effects of imagery with cancer patients, see the work of Martin Rossman (2003) and Belleruth Naparstek (2004).

Our basic hypothesis is that dreams connect the dreamer with imagery of specific aspects of body, mind, and spirit that need special attention and care. We contend that the use of healing dream imagery for guided-imagery exercises and meditative focus is more powerful, personalized, and targeted than the imagery that arises from most waking states of consciousness.

Goals

The primary goals of the Healing Power of Dreams project are (1) to facilitate participants in transforming nightmare imagery/energy into imagery and energy that is

perceived as healing, and (2) to facilitate participants in integrating healing dream imagery/energy into all aspects of their lives.

Process

Participants learn basic dreamwork techniques in a group setting using a projective approach. With help from the group, the dreamer identifies aspects of mind, body, and spirit the dream is highlighting. If the imagery feels disturbing, the group helps create a plan for allowing the imagery to transform through a series of guided-imagery exercises, art, or meditative movement. When a dreamer receives a particularly healing dream or when healing imagery is experienced as the culmination of meditative work, then the healing imagery is recorded in a personal guided-imagery CD. The CD is then used to integrate the imagery through daily meditation and during chemotherapy and radiation treatments.

Dream Reentry

Key to our approach for nightmare transformation and healing dream integration is a dream reentry technique that utilizes a full-sensory, guided-imagery experience to help the dreamer create a safe place in the presence of supportive companionship. First, the dreamer is guided into a deep state of relaxation by focusing on the breath and on progressively relaxing parts of the body. When fully immersed in safety and support, the dreamer reenters the dream in order to allow transformation of the imagery and energies and finally to embody and integrate healing imagery that has evolved as powerful dream medicine for the healing journey.

Outcomes

Each year since 2005, we have conducted a survey of participants in ongoing dream groups. Consistently the surveys have shown:

- Decreased feelings of anxiety and stress
- Increased sense of connection with others
- Increased sense of connection to inner resources
- Increased understanding of healing at multiple levels
- Increased sense of quality of life, particularly emotional, social, and spiritual
- Increased feelings of confidence and control over life and health issues
- Increased feelings of hope
- Increased feelings of how to live fully now, despite cancer

In 2009 and 2010, members of an ongoing dream group participated in a pain-management study. They used healing dream imagery for guided imagery with personal CDs. They combined the CD exercises with other pain-management approaches. The study was informal and without rigorous controls, so there was not enough data for empirical conclusions. Individual accounts, however, were consistently positive and controlled studies are planned for the future.

Another area ripe for research is the role of trauma. In workshops and ongoing groups, participants report many dreams that reactivate past personal traumas. The feelings in the dreams, however, are often different from those associated with the past and allow many dreamers to use past experiences in symbolic ways to reconnect with enduring strengths and capacities that can be used to move through present illness and future crises.

Another thread requiring more scrutiny is the potential role of dreams in alerting the patient to his or her condition. Over the years, in line with research from others, many participants in the cancer project have reported dreams about their disease before diagnosis. Sometimes these dreams have enabled the dreamer to begin early treatment.

Effects of Healing Dreams

Many participants report dreams that guide them in making decisions about health-care options and lifestyle changes. Many report an increase in dreams and an increase in the intensity of their dreams throughout treatment and the recovery process.

Dreamers report that they often connect with a unique sense of meaning and purpose. They report frequent dreams of support, renewal, and reconciliation. They report dreams that bring a sense of wholeness and of being loved. They report dreams of knowing they are healed no matter the outcome of the disease.

Many survivors and caregivers who work with their dreams over time report that cancer becomes a turning point in which they begin to see challenges as opportunities to learn and grow. Many begin to relate to the cancer situation as teacher and guide. The dream group is an ideal setting for experiencing these shifts in perception and attitude.

The IASD cancer project is dedicated to expanding the number of dream groups in integrative oncology facilities, to expanding the training program for facilitators, and to expanding the understanding of the healing potential of dreams within the entire growing field of integrative medicine.

Tallulah Lyons

References

Abrams, D., & Weil, A. (2009). *Integrative oncology: Weil integrative medicine library.* Oxford: Oxford University Press.

Hartman, E. (1998). *Dreams and nightmares: The origin and meaning of dreams.* Cambridge: Perseus Publishing.

Hoss, R.J. (2005). *Dream language: Self-understanding through imagery and color.* Ashland, OR: Innersource.

Moore, B.A., & Krakow, B. (2007, April). Imagery rehearsal therapy for acute posttraumatic nightmares among combat soldiers in Iraq. *American Journal of Psychiatry, 164,* 683–684.

Naparstek, B. (2004). *Invisible heroes: Survivors of trauma and how they heal.* New York: Bantam Dell.

Rossman, M.L. (2003). *Fighting cancer from within.* New York: Henry Holt.

Central Image (of the Dream)

The central image (CI) of the dream refers simply to the most powerful or striking image in a dream. The CI has turned out to be very important in recent dream research; it appears to carry the chief emotional power of the dream.

The basic idea of the CI was introduced by Ernest Hartmann and his many collaborators in 1997. It derived originally from powerful dreams noted soon after a traumatic event, such as the famous tidal wave dream, considered paradigmatic: an adult, after escaping from a fire, an accident, a rape, or an attack, often has a dream such as "I was on the beach and this huge tidal wave came and swept me away." The tidal wave dream is considered important because it so clearly demonstrates a key aspect of the nature of dreaming: the dream does not picture what happened (the fire or attack) but the emotion (I am overwhelmed, I am terrified). Thus, the powerful image pictures, or contextualizes, the underlying emotion. In fact, the central image was first called the contextualizing image (CI). This term was difficult for some and never became popular. It was then changed to the easier central image, keeping the abbreviation CI.

Research on the CI uses a very simple CI score sheet, which can be applied to any dream, usually in the form of a written dream report. The scorer is asked first to decide whether there is a CI, defined as "a is a striking, arresting, or compelling image—not simply a story—but an image, which stands out by virtue of being especially powerful, vivid, bizarre, or detailed." After identifying the CI, the scorer then gives it an intensity score from 0 (no definite CI) to 3.0 (about as powerful an image as you have encountered). Finally, the scorer is asked to decide what basic emotion (from a list of 18 emotions) was pictured by this CI. Inter-rater reliability in studies using the CI has been very high, with correlations between .75 and .90 for CI intensity.

Using the CI score sheet, a CI can be identified in more than 50 percent of dreams in most dream series. CI intensity has been shown to be significantly higher after trauma than before trauma, and higher in adults who have recently experienced traumatic events than in those who have not. It is significantly higher in students who report having experienced abuse of any kind than in those who report no abuse. CI intensity also appears to be high in students who have suffered a recent loss or a traumatic loss.

In a systematic study of dreams before and after 9/11—presumed to represent mild trauma or at least emotional arousal for everyone in the United States—880 dreams were collected from 44 people who had recorded their dreams for years: the last 10 dreams before and the first 10 after 9/11. All dreams were scored on CI intensity and other measures. It was found on blind scoring that the dreams after 9/11 were characterized by higher CI intensity ($p < .001$) but not by any other measure tested, such as length, dreamlikeness, vividness, presence of planes or tall towers, and so forth.

In a number of studies, CI intensity has also been shown to be significantly higher in memorable dreams and in dreams considered important or significant by the dreamer as compared to ordinary or most recent dreams from the same dreamer.

In all these studies, the change in CI intensity was the clearest and most significant change. The other changes were more difficult to summarize in brief, but overall there was a shift in the emotions pictured toward more fear/terror and helplessness/vulnerability after various forms of trauma or stress.

Since the CI appears so sensitive to underlying emotion in psychological studies, it is likely that the CI will also be related to brain changes such as activity in the amygdala and related pathways during rapid eye movement (REM) sleep. This should be especially evident in dreams with powerful CIs, such as nightmares.

Ernest Hartmann

See also: entries related to Dream Content

References

Hartmann, E., & Kunzendorf, R. (2005–2006). The central image (CI) in recent dreams, dreams that stand out, and earliest dreams: Relationship to boundaries. *Imagination, Cognition and Personality*, 25, 383–392.

Hartmann, E., Zborowski, M., Rosen, R., & Grace, N. (2001). Contextualizing images in dreams: More intense after abuse and trauma. *Dreaming, 11,* 115–126.

Characters in Dreams

Next to the occurrence of the dream self, representations of other characters are one of the most prevalent and stable features of dream content. They are consistently present in dreams, appearing in more than 95 percent of adult reports (Dorus, Dorus, & Rechtschaffen, 1971); there are an average of 2.6 to 3.7 characters in every dream in addition to the dream self in adults (Kahn, Stickgold, Pace-Schott, & Hobson, 2000) and an average of 2.2 per dream for children aged 4 to 10 (Kahn, Pace-Schott, & Hobson, 2002). Dreamed characters are spatially and temporally stable, especially in the lengthy dreams of REM sleep. Spatially, they show a lower overall incidence of distortion than do other features of dreams, such as settings (Foulkes & Schmidt, 1983). Only 14 percent show any sign of bizarreness (Foulkes & Schmidt, 1983), but more than 60 percent of recognizable characters deviate in some way from their waking counterparts—usually in how they behave or in the feelings they evoke (Kahn et al., 2002). Over time, characters from REM sleep dreams demonstrate less moment-to-moment variation relative to actions performed than do characters from non-REM sleep dreams (Hall & Van de Castle, 1966). In fact, the longer a dream report from REM sleep, the less a character's composition will vary (Hall, 1955).

Dream characters are often highly realistic in quality, acting with apparent autonomy and inciting emotional reactions from the dreamed self. They evoke emotions whether they are known (81%) or unknown (69%) to the dreamer, and feelings of caring and affection are the most frequently evoked (Cartwright, Agargun, Kirkby, & Friedman, 2006; Klinger, 1977). Content analyses of aggressive and friendly interactions (Bilu, 1989; Cartwright et al., 2006; Eudell-Simmons, Stein, Defife, & Hilsenroth, 2005; McNamara, McLaren, Smith, Brown, & Stickgold, 2005; Popp et al., 1996) indicate that among aggressive encounters, 68.2 percent are perpetrated by other characters—only 31.8 percent by the dreamed self. Friendly interactions are also frequently initiated by other characters (52.4% vs. 47.6%). In the case of attack nightmares, where the dream self is chased, threatened, or assaulted, 59 percent of the time the intention of the attacker is clearly apparent; moreover, 75 to 85 percent of the time the dream self does nothing to clearly incite the attack (McNamara et al., 2005).

Social interactions are even more frequent in dream reports than they are in reports of randomly selected daytime experiences (Kahn et al., 2002). Characters are more often familiar than unfamiliar in both children's dreams (70% vs. 30%, respectively) (Dorus et al., 1971) and adults' dreams (52% vs. 48%) (Kahn et al., 2000), although the proportion of unknown characters may be as low as 22 percent if generic characters—for example, a policeman, a friend—are separately tallied (25%) (Kahn et al., 2002).

That dream characters are usually depicted in some form of social interaction with the dreamed self supports the notion (Nielsen & Lara-Carrasco, 2007) that a primary function of dreaming is the realistic simulation of *character-self interactions* that frequently depict one's predominant social relationships and conflicts, including one's most salient emotional concerns (Hall, 1951; Hall & Van de Castle, 1966; Kahn et al., 2000). Activation of these socially contextualized emotions may be privileged during dreaming and may play a role in regulating negative emotions at this time. McNamara and colleagues (Resnick, Stickgold, Rittenhouse, & Hobson, 1994) found from a random sample of REM and NREM sleep and wakefulness reports that REM sleep reports were twice as likely as waking state reports ($p < .04$) to simulate social interactions but were not different from NREM sleep reports. Also, REM sleep reports contained more aggressive interactions than did either waking state ($p < .02$) or NREM sleep ($p < .06$) reports.

Characters communicate their emotional meanings through channels resembling those used by real individuals in the waking world. They display facial expressions and emotional gestures, they express concerns in speech rich with inflection and prosody, and they touch or manipulate the dreamed self in provocative and intimate ways. One study of 635 REM sleep dream reports (Foulkes, Sullivan, Kerr, & Brown, 1988) found that almost every interaction between the self and another character involved talking. The simulated emotional expressions of dream characters appear to be as subtle or overt, as direct or indirect, or as simple or complex as the expressions that are used daily on the social stage. Moreover, these expressions appear to incite the dream self to react emotionally. Such reactions may be in sympathy with those of the character, or they may be appropriately complementary, but rarely are they judged by subjects themselves to be *inappropriate* to the waking-state situation depicted by the dream (Popp et al., 1996).

The notion that dream characters may be a necessary feature of an emotion-regulation function of dreaming is supported by a variety of findings showing that the nature of these characters is affected by the changing emotional concerns of the individual while awake. Clinically, dreams are used regularly to clarify interpersonal relationships, for example, object relations and patient–therapist transference situations (Luborsky, 1977). A patient's level of object representations can be identified in dream narratives as they can be in other measures. Popp and colleagues (Popp et al., 1996) used a validated system for content analysis of repetitive relationship patterns to demonstrate that a person's most frequent relationship patterns are expressed in their dreams as they are in their waking psychotherapy narratives. Emotionally negative themes are predominant in both types of report. In a similar vein

(McNamara et al., 2005), dream narratives can be reliably assessed using measures of interpersonal behavior on the Social Cognition and Object Relations Scale; the categories of *affect* and *relationships* are rated with particularly high reliability.

These findings are generally consistent with laboratory and home studies that have attempted to identify dream content related to an individual's current concerns (Cartwright, 1974). To illustrate, when subjects are asked to rehearse a statement about wishing to attain a desired personality attribute, the wished-for attribute appears in dreams more often than nondesired attributes and manifests as a feature of both other characters and the self (Arkin & Antrobus, 1991).

The nature of dream characters changes with age. Animal characters decrease consistently in prevalence with increasing age (Foulkes, 1985; Seidel, 1984; Van de Castle, 1994, p. 307). The frequency of generic animal characters and strangers diminishes with age while the frequency of familiar and family characters increases (Seidel, 1984). However, in older children, the presence of dreamed animals is associated with social immaturity (Domhoff, 1993). The more predominant animal characters are in dreams, the greater the likelihood that these dreams also contain aggression. In the dreams of 11- and 12-year-olds, aggression is present more often when an animal character is also present (74%) than absent. In fact, children are four times as likely as adults to be victims of aggression in their dreams, and animal characters are the source of this aggression. Such findings support the possibility that the increasing differentiation of emotions and emotional control through childhood is accompanied by a consistent change in the nature of dream characters and how they relate to the dreamed self.

Tore Nielsen

References

Arkin, A. M., & Antrobus, J. S. (1991). The effects of external stimuli applied prior to and during sleep on sleep experience. In S. J. Ellman & J. S. Antrobus (Eds.), *The mind in sleep* (2nd ed., pp. 265–307). New York: John Wiley & Sons.

Bilu, Y. (1989). The other as a nightmare: The Israeli–Arab encounter as reflected in children's dreams in Israel and the West Bank. *Political Psychology*, 10, 365–389.

Cartwright, R., Agargun, M. Y., Kirkby, J., & Friedman, J. K. (2006). Relation of dreams to waking concerns. *Psychiatry Research, 141*, 261–270.

Cartwright, R. D. (1974). The influence of a conscious wish on dreams: A methodological study of dream meaning and function. *Journal of Abnormal Psychology, 83*, 387–393.

Domhoff, G. W. (1993). The repetition of dreams and dream elements: A possible clue to a function of dreams? In A. Moffitt, M. Kramer, & R. Hoffmann (Eds.), *The functions of dreaming* (pp. 293–320). Albany, NY: SUNY Press.

Dorus, E., Dorus, W., & Rechtschaffen, A. (1971). The incidence of novelty in dreams. *Archives of General Psychiatry, 25*, 364–368.

Eudell-Simmons, E. M., Stein, M. B., Defife, J. A., & Hilsenroth, M. J. (2005). Reliability and validity of the Social Cognition and Object Relations Scale (SCORS) in the assessment of dream narratives. *Journal of Personality Assessment, 85*, 325–333.

Foulkes, D. (1985). *Dreaming: A cognitive-psychological analysis*. Hillsdale, NJ: Lawrence Erlbaum Associates.

Foulkes, D., & Schmidt, M. (1983). Temporal sequence and unit composition in dream reports from different stages of sleep. *Sleep, 6*, 265–280.

Foulkes, D., Sullivan, B., Kerr, N. H., & Brown, L. (1988). Appropriateness of dream feelings to dreamed situations. *Cognition & Emotion, 2*, 29–39.

Hall, C., & Van de Castle, R. I. (1966). *The content analysis of dreams*. New York: Appleton-Century-Crofts.

Hall, C. S. (1951). What people dream about. *Scientific American, 184*, 60–63.

Hall, C. S. (1955). The significance of the dream of being attacked. *Journal of Personality, 24*, 168–180.

Kahn, D., Pace-Schott, E., & Hobson, J. A. (2002). Emotion and cognition: Feeling and character identification in dreaming. *Consciousness and Cognition, 11*, 34–50.

Kahn, D., Stickgold, R., Pace-Schott, E. F., & Hobson, J. A. (2000). Dreaming and waking consciousness: a character recognition study. *Journal of Sleep Research, 9*, 317–325.

Klinger, E. (1977). *Meaning and void: Inner experience and the incentives in people's lives*. Minneapolis: University of Minnesota Press.

Luborsky, L. (1977). Measuring a pervasive psychic structure in psychotherapy: The core conflictual relationship theme. In N. Freedman & S. Grand (Eds.), *Communicative structures and psychic structures* (pp. 367–395). New York: Plenum.

McNamara, P., McLaren, D., Smith, D., Brown, A., & Stickgold, R. (2005). A "Jekyll and Hyde" within: Aggressive versus friendly interactions in REM and non-REM dreams. *Psychological Science, 16*, 130–136.

Nielsen, T. A., & Lara-Carrasco, J. (2007). Nightmares, dreaming and emotion regulation: A review. In D. Barrett & P. McNamara (Eds.), *The new science of dreams* (pp. 253–284). Westport, CT: Praeger Greenwood.

Popp, C. A., Diguer, L., Luborsky, L., Faude, J., Johnson, S., Morris, M., . . . Schmidt, K. (1996). Repetitive relationship themes in waking narratives and dreams. *Journal of

Consulting and Clinical Psychology, 64, 1073–1078.

Resnick, J., Stickgold, R., Rittenhouse, C. D., & Hobson, J. A. (1994). Self-representation and bizarreness in children's dream reports collected in the home setting. *Consciousness and Cognition, 3,* 30–45.

Seidel, R. (1984). *The relationship of animal figures to aggression and ego immaturity in the dreams of eleven and twelve year old children.* Unpublished work.

Van de Castle, R. L. (1994). *Our dreaming mind.* New York: Ballantine Books.

Children's Dreams and Nightmares

From our first nap as a newborn to our last night, we always spend part of sleep in cycles of rapid eye movement (REM), which are associated with dreaming. The duration of REM at birth is 50 percent of sleep or eight hours of dreaming and even higher in premature babies (Hartmann, 1998). During the first year, the time in REM falls off rapidly and is about 25 percent of sleep time by young adulthood and less than 20 percent in old age (Foulkes, 1979). Why do babies spend so much time in REM? One explanation is that extended episodes of REM in the early weeks of life stimulate the maturation of the central nervous system—during a rapid expansion of the brain's sophisticated capacities. Thus, REM appears to play a special time-limited role in brain development during the first year (Fiss, 1979).

Until some future technological breakthrough allows us to directly observe or record babies' dreams, we will not be sure they are dreaming in the first months of life. However, children can begin to report dreams as soon as their language skills allow them to describe the vivid experiences they have while sleeping. Sigmund Freud wrote that his daughter, Anna, at the age of 19 months, reported her first dream about some of her favorite foods. She called out: "Anna Fweud, wild strawbewwies, omblets, pudden" (Freud, 1965). My own daughter had been fascinated by the flight and sounds of birds during walks in the park. Just before she turned two, she woke up and pointed toward the window. It was dark so I was sure she had not seen a bird outside but more likely in her dream. Just after the age of two, she woke up sobbing that a spider had bitten her leg and she was calling out for help in vanquishing the spider. There were no spiders in her bed and no bites on her leg (Siegel, 2002).

Younger children's dreams are brief with minimal plot development. They are frequently populated by animals and characters that threaten or victimize others (Foulkes, 1979). These ominous dream dangers are often met with passivity and reflect the young child's nightly internal struggle to understand and gain control over confusing or upsetting waking experiences. When young children have been exposed to trauma, they are more likely to experience sleep disturbances than to report dreams (Terr, 1990). For preschoolers, limited verbal communication skills, difficulties distinguishing dream and reality, and anxiety connected with upsetting dreams make it difficult to research the content of these early dreams.

Foulkes (1979) argued in favor of scientific studies of children's dreams using a sleep laboratory and standardized dream-collection procedures. Children are woken up during REM and asked about their dreams. Although laboratory studies produce invaluable data, they are expensive and rare. In addition, a lab setting can be intimidating and alienating to a child and may inhibit dream recall. In contrast, naturalistic collections of dream reported to parents, psychotherapists, or researchers have revealed occasional reports of much more elaborate dream narratives from young children (Siegel & Bulkeley, 1998). These home dreams are less inhibited by the impact of the lab experience and are closer to the way children experience and share dreams with family members, friends, and helping professionals. Because of the additional risk of bias in case studies, researchers using home dreams must strive to use standardized procedures for soliciting and collecting children's dreams. In addition, because funding for lab studies of children's dreams is scarce, dream researchers will have to rely on a combination of collection techniques (lab and home dreams) that will ultimately lead to increasing understanding of the biology and psychology of children's dreams.

In children aged 6 to 10, dream recall, reporting, and length increase as verbal skills improve and the ability to distinguish fantasy and dreams from waking reality becomes more solidified. Gender differences in dream content are detectable with girls remembering more dreams and characters having more complex social interactions. Boys' dreams have more victimization themes and aggression themes during this period (Oberst, Charles, & Chamarro, 2009).

Adolescents' reported dreams become longer and have more complex narratives. More characters speak and more emotions are expressed in their dreams. There is less passivity and victimization and more evidence of active struggles to grapple with dream adversaries. This reflects increased waking capacity for independent functioning. Teen dreams also reflect concerns about peer relationships, identity, sexuality, and their changing bodies. During adolescence, boys begin to report just as many dreams as girls and the gender distribution of dream characters more closely mirrors that of adults; boys' and men's dreams tend to have more male characters and girls' and women's dreams have a more balanced gender distribution of characters. Although some teens may become more inclined to keep their dreams private as they establish their sense of separateness from their parents, they are also more curious and can begin to appreciate the intriguing and sometimes disturbing symbolism and bizarre narrative twists.

What are the common dream themes of children? Many children have dreams that closely parallel universal themes in adults' dreams (Siegel, 2002). These include falling, flying, paralysis or the inability to move, appearing naked or partially clad, losing valuables, test anxiety dreams, and natural disaster dreams such as tidal waves and earthquakes. For very young children, animal characters may appear in many or even the majority of their dreams and often symbolize aspects of their relationships with important family members or caregivers. Additional themes that are very common for children include dreams of being chased or threatened by animals, insects, or other bad guys such as ghosts, monsters, or characters from games or movies and dreams of being abandoned, kidnapped, or separated from family members. These dreams symbolize both specific and general anxieties that are common as children struggle to understand and master their inner and outer experiences (Siegel & Bulkeley, 1998).

During life passages and crises, nightmares and vivid dreams are more common. Jung reported that very memorable or archetypal dreams occur during these turning points (Mattoon, 1978). The week before kindergarten started, Ariel had a nightmare about being chased by a menacing unicorn. Her preschool was called Unicorn Preschool and had been a place of security and creative learning for her. On the surface, the whole family was excited about Ariel's upcoming first day of kindergarten. Her nightmare was the first clue that she was anxious. The aggression of her dream unicorn symbolized her worries about starting at a new school and was a reversal in the metaphoric meaning of the mythic creature that was linked to school in Ariel's unconscious. The dream helped her parents understand her anxiety about starting kindergarten and allowed them to reassure her and take steps to psychologically prepare her for the transition (Siegel, 2002).

A considerable part of the children will experience a divorce in their family, and they frequently dream about it for months, years, or even decades afterward. Common postdivorce dream themes include wished-for reunifications of parents who have split up and themes of separation and loneliness. In high-conflict divorces, where the tension and parental squabbling may go on for years, children's loyalty conflicts and emotional turmoil can be exacerbated by nightmares of rejection or symbols of general anxiety that are not overtly related to divorce. A 10-year-old whose divorced parents were at odds and whose father constantly cursed and threatened his ex-wife had recurrent dreams of carrying a ticking time bomb as he struggled to cope with the conflict. When he was able to tell the bad dream to his psychotherapist and his mother, not only did he feel great relief, but his mother better understood the depth of his anguish and took steps that led to reducing visitation with his enraged and out-of-control father (Siegel, 2002). Another example is a psychologist in training who recounted a recurrent childhood nightmare of being trapped between giant fingers and unable to move. She called her mother who remembered the dream well and reminded her that the dream began when her mother and father were battling over custody of her when she was nine years old. Understanding the dream's metaphor of being emotionally paralyzed, and a pawn in the conflict between her parents, helped her resolve lingering upsets stemming from this traumatic period of her childhood (Siegel, 2002).

When children of divorced parents share their nightmares with parents, the crisis of the bad dream opens an opportunity for the family. Without dismissing or interpreting the dream, parents can welcome the dream by reassuring their child emotionally and even physically for younger children. Reassuring a child that nightmares are both normal and related to important worries may help transform the acute distress that lingers after a nightmare. Potential benefits of family dream sharing include an increased understanding of emotional distress that the child may not be able to communicate verbally or directly, an emotional catharsis, and an actual reduction in subsequent nightmares, anxieties, and sleep disturbances. Sharing crisis dreams can be a vehicle for emotional quality time that may be especially important during periods of crisis or transition (Siegel & Bulkeley, 1998).

Most adults remember few, if any, of the many thousands of dreams they had during childhood. Two reasons for this stand out. First, nightmares typically wake up the dreamer, making it more likely he or she will remember the dream. Second, many children are told to dismiss the nightmare because it is only a dream. Without more attention to dreams, nightmares predominate as the only dreams remembered because they cause awakening. In contrast, in families where dreams are valued and shared as a source of inspiration, insight, and intuition, children will remember more dreams with a lower percentage of nightmares.

Not only do the different schools of psychotherapy interpret dreams differently, every culture and religion has unique perspectives and often divergent ways of understanding the nature of dreaming and interpreting dream symbolism. For helping professionals and educators who listen to or work with children's dreams, it is important to learn more about how the child's culture affects his or her experience of dreams. Caution should be exercised in interpreting dream symbolism because in many cultures symbols are considered

reversals and mean the opposite of what they seem. Many people and many cultures interpret dreams literally as predictions of future events or as omens or messages from divine or diabolical sources. These attitudes shape how children experience their dreams. For psychotherapists and parents, analysis and interpretation of younger children's dreams should be avoided. Reassurance and creative and artistic exploration of the dreams are more advisable and less likely to clash with family and cultural beliefs about dreams or to inadvertently reinforce anxieties.

What is the difference between a nightmare, a night terror, and a posttraumatic nightmare? Night terrors are one of the most frightening experiences parents may encounter. Shortly after falling asleep, a child wakes up screaming, flailing its arms, panicking, and acting as if its life is being threatened. Terrified parents often do not realize that in the morning, their child may not even remember the night terror. Physical and verbal reassurance will usually suffice to help the child drift back to sleep. Night terrors differ from nightmares in a few key ways. Night terrors are a form of sleep disturbance and occur primarily in preschool and school-age children and only rarely in adults (Mack, 1974). They occur during the first non-REM sleep phase shortly after the child falls asleep. The dream story is often very brief and expressed by a seemingly awake and terrified child. Night terrors are linked to a family history of sleep disorders and are most likely partly physiological and partly triggered by illness or stress. In contrast, nightmares usually occur during REM sleep, later in the night, or toward the morning.

They have more of a story line with symbolism and imagery, are more likely to be remembered in the morning, and the child does not usually scream or appear physically agitated when he or she wakes up. A posttraumatic nightmare may occur in a child who has experienced an overwhelming and unresolved trauma such as child abuse, death of a family member, an accident, or injury. Normally nightmares gradually lessen in intensity as the child begins to heal emotionally. In cases where a trauma is profound or does not move toward resolution, children or adults may experience wrenching posttraumatic nightmares that are repetitive reenactments, metaphoric of some aspect of the trauma that was most overwhelming—like a cliff-hanger that never has an ending (Siegel, 2002). Novelist Virginia Woolf was sexually abused by her half-brother when she was five years old (Terr, 1990) and had posttraumatic nightmares that repeated throughout her childhood and for most of her adult life. Many abuse victims and survivors of war or disasters suffer ongoing nightmares with content metaphorically linked to the trauma. Psychologically, nightmares show the enduring impact of unresolved trauma. Therapeutically, supportive dream sharing as part of a comprehensive treatment plan may be a vehicle that helps children express and resolve seemingly unbearable emotional wounds.

How can parents and psychotherapists respond to children's nightmares? Nightmares are one of the main symptoms of posttraumatic stress disorder and can contribute to psychological distress that may be expressed as anxiety or presleep fears and can exacerbate tendencies toward sleep disorders. The most important first step for parents, psychotherapists, and helping professionals is to reassure a child without dismissing the importance of the dream's painful emotions and distressing symbols and characters. Reassurance will go a long way toward calming the child's immediate distress and may reduce the frequency and intensity of the nightmares. It is important for a child to know that nightmares are common and often symbolize worries that can be discussed and worked out. Beyond the stage of reassurance, if a child is encouraged to explore the dream further, the next step is using fantasy for imaginary rescripting (Halliday, 1995) and rehearsing new outcomes for the nightmare. In Ariel's dream, rescripting might have involved taming the unicorn or limiting its evil powers with a magic wand or an invisible force field. Rescripting may include imagining a more resolved ending or creating an alternate direction for the dream narrative (Siegel, 2002). Especially for younger children, the focus should be on a creative approach that emphasizes exploring the dream through visual and expressive arts, drawing, painting, role-playing dream characters, making collages or masks, or decorating dream journals or dream pillows with their dream images. In addition, when parents keep a journal or record of their child's dreams, it may be cherished along with their baby book and childhood photos. Giving dreams titles and adding some documentation of recent family events may help with later understanding and appreciation (Siegel & Bulkeley, 1998).

Although many themes and symbols may be universal, every dream is a unique product of the mind. Encouraging children to share and explore their dreams and nightmares will help them feel pride in their creative powers, can alert parents and helping professionals to emotional conflicts and unresolved traumas the child might not otherwise be able to articulate, and will give families an enjoyable way to communicate about feelings.

Alan Siegel

References

Fiss, H. (1979). Current dream research: A psychobiological perspective. In B. Wolman (Ed.), *Handbook of dreams: Research theories and applications* (pp. 20–75). New York: Van Nostrand Rheinhold.

Foulkes, D. (1979). Children's dreams. In B. Wolman (Ed.), *Handbook of dreams: Research theories and applications* (pp. 131–167). New York: Van Nostrand Rheinhold.

Freud, S. (1965). *The interpretation of dreams* (Trans. James Strachey). New York: Avon (Original work published 1900).

Halliday, G. (1995). Treating nightmares in children. In C. Schaeffer (Ed.), *Clinical handbook of sleep disorders in children* (pp. 149–176). New York: Jason Aronson.

Hartmann, E. (1998). *Dreams and nightmares: The new theory on the origin and meaning of dreams.* New York: Plenum Press.

Knapp, S. (1987). Night terrors in children and adults: Emotional and biological factors. In Henry Kellerman (Ed.), *The nightmare: Psychological and biological foundations* (pp. 185–192). New York: Columbia University Press.

Mack, J. (1974). *Nightmares and human conflict.* Boston: Houghton Mifflin.

Mattoon, M. (1978). *Applied dream analysis: A Jungian approach.* Washington, DC: V. H. Winston.

Oberst, U., Charles, C., & Chamarro, A. (2009). Influence of gender and age in aggressive dream content of Spanish children and adolescents. In Children's Dreams and Nightmares: Emerging Trends in Research [Special Issue]. *Dreaming: Journal of the Association for the Study of Dreams, 15*(3), 170–177.

Siegel, A. (2002). *Dream wisdom: Uncovering life's answers in your dreams.* Berkeley, CA: Celestial Arts.

Siegel, A. (2009). Children's dreams and nightmares: Emerging trends in research dreaming. In Children's Dreams and Nightmares: Emerging Trends in Research [Special Issue]. *Dreaming: Journal of the Association for the Study of Dreams, 15*(3), 147–154.

Siegel, A., & Bulkeley, K. (1998). *Dreamcatching: Every parent's guide to exploring and understanding children's dreams and nightmares.* New York: Three Rivers.

Terr, L. (1990). *Too scared to cry: How trauma affects children and ultimately all of us.* New York: Basic Books.

Chinese Sex Symbols in Dreams

Sexual symbolism in China has an extraordinarily long and rich history that dates back to the late Old Stone Age (18,000 years ago). Many sex symbols that are commonly used by Chinese people today have their roots in ancestral symbolism. In ancient Chinese times, it was very popular to symbolize male genitals with birds (see Yu [2008] for details), possibly because they have telescopic necks and lay eggs, which are taken together to resemble the penis and testicles (Zhao, 1993). Birds (鳥; *niao*) are considered as penile symbols even today. In everyday language, Chinese people often replace the word penis (陰莖; *yin jing*/陽具; *yang ju*/陽物; *yang wu*) with the words sparrow (雀; *quel*雀仔; *que zai*), birdie (小鳥; *xiao niao*), or chickling (小雞; *xiao ji*/小雞雞; *xiao ji ji*), and substitute for the word testicles (睪丸; *gao wan*) the word eggs (蛋; *dan*/蛋蛋; *dan dan*). An ancient Chinese curse word, 屌 (*diu*; colloquially written Cantonese: 閪), which literally refers to the male genital organ, has long been used interchangeably with the Chinese word bird. The classical and literary word for the sacrum, 尻/屍 (*kao*; colloquially written Cantonese: 閪), which has been turned into a Cantonese rude word for the male genitals, is often written as 鳩 (*jiu*), which means turtledoves. The Chinese word for the female genitals, 屄 (*bei1*; colloquially written Cantonese: 閪), is formed by the radical 尸 and the part 穴. The part 穴 (*xue*) itself is a word used to describe caves, holes, and fissures. Both ancient and modern Chinese people symbolize the female genitals with cavities, such as black hole (黑洞; *hei-dong*) and water-curtain cave (水簾洞; *shui-lian-dong*).

Although the sex symbols utilized by Chinese people today largely originate from ancient symbolism, the focus of sex symbolism has shifted from reproductive function to sexual behavior itself and the precise symbols have undergone major transformations over thousands of years of evolution. For instance, frogs (青蛙; *qing-wa*) and toads (蟾蜍; *chan-chu*) are no longer seen to correspond specifically to the uterus but, in the broader sense, they refer to the female genitals. Moreover, the female genitals are far more often associated with edible frogs (田雞; *tia-ji*) than with frogs and toads, in keeping with modern Chinese people's inclination toward

sexualizing foods to create sex symbols. Similarly, contemporary Chinese people perceive abalones (鮑; *bao*/鮑魚; *bao-yu*) or black abalones (黑鮑; *hei-bao*) to bear a resemblance to the female genitals. Different from the ancient symbols, which are perceived today as merely loosely linked with the sexual concepts that they once signified, contemporary sex symbols are far more substantively meaningful and familiar to the Chinese people in the modern era. Usually, those contemporary symbols are folk adages, slang terms, or coarse words, which can be easily accessed via the mass media. Some sexual metaphors are so regularly used that they have become a virtually universal language that can be communicated among Chinese people, for example, using the metaphors of striking something with a tool (扑嘢; *bog ye*), combating with a real army (打真軍; *da zhen-jun*), hitting the aircraft (打飛機; *da fei-ji*), soybean curd grinding (磨豆腐; *mo dou-fu*), and blowing a vertical bamboo flute (吹簫; *chui xiao*) to denote copulation, sexual intercourse without using a condom, male masturbation, excitation of the female genitals by manual contact, and oral sex for men, respectively.

In contrast to ancient Chinese symbols, such as birds eating fish and offering burning incense sticks, which rarely occur in dreams, some contemporary Chinese sex symbols—especially those involving aggressive behavior and weapons, including guns or cannons, shooting (e.g., firing a gun, shooting an arrow, etc.), and hitting someone or something, for example—are prominent dream themes for Chinese people (Yu, 2008, 2010). Similar to sexual experiences, these specific contemporary

Chinese sex symbols are more frequently dreamed by men than women. Moreover, the frequencies of dreaming sexually explicit material and sex symbols correlate positively with each other and inversely vary with the degree of social desirability. Accordingly, the more defensive the people are, the less likely they are to report dreaming sexual experiences and sex symbols. This suggests that although sex analogies in modern Chinese colloquial language do not serve the dynamic function of substituting for sexual scenes in dreams, they carry socially taboo connotations, as do sexually explicit material, and facilitate sexual expression in dreams. However, it is difficult to establish direct evidence that objects and activities typically borrowed to connote sex during the waking time retain their implicit sexual meanings over the process of dream formation. Different from their surrogate function in the daytime, the Chinese sex symbols might simply represent the aggressive impulses that the dreamer acts out.

Calvin Kai-Ching Yu

References

Yu, C.K.-C. (2008). Ancient Chinese sex symbols in dreams. *Dreaming, 18,* 158–166.

Yu, C.K.-C. (2010). Contemporary Chinese sex symbols in dreams. *Dreaming, 20,* 25–41.

Zhao, G.H. (1993). China's culture of reproduction worship. *Journal of Popular Culture, 27,* 101–111.

Chronotype

Within the human population, there is significant interindividual variation in preferred sleep/wake times. Classification on this basis is termed *chronotype,* spanning those who wake and sleep relatively early (morning types) through to those who wake and sleep relatively late (evening types). At the extreme ends of this spectrum, individuals may have difficulties complying with standard work times and social commitments. Currently, little effort is made to optimize work schedules for performance on the basis of chronotype. Furthermore, chronotype exhibits significant variations with age, including a shift to evening preference during adolescence and a shift to morning preference in old age. Understanding the physiological mechanisms that contribute to an individual's chronotype is thus a problem of great practical importance.

Experimental studies have demonstrated the importance of intrinsic circadian period in determining chronotype. Longer intrinsic periods have been shown to correlate with evening preference, and genetic mutations that shorten or lengthen intrinsic period have been shown to associate with advanced or delayed sleep-phase disorders, respectively. These results can be understood in terms of the light phase response curve (PRC); those with shorter circadian periods require more daily exposure of the delay portion of their PRC to entrain to a 24-hour day than those with longer periods, resulting in an earlier entrained phase (Brown et al., 2008).

Contrary to early thought on the topic, chronotype is not purely determined by circadian mechanisms. Recently it was shown that the kinetics of the homeostatic sleep drive also affect chronotype. Individuals with slower homeostatic dynamics are found to exhibit evening preference, and this trend is exhibited across different stages of adolescence, suggesting a possible mechanism for adolescent eveningness (Jenni, Achermann, & Carskadon, 2005). However, the physiological basis for such differences remains unknown.

In the case of age-related morningness, changes to both the circadian and homeostatic sleep-regulatory systems appear to contribute (Dijk, Duffy, & Czeisler, 2000). Experimental evidence suggests a decline in circadian amplitude with age, which is most prominent in males. This could plausibly be due to decay in suprachiasmatic nucleus volume with age, although more detailed studies are required to confirm this hypothesis.

Recent developments in neurophysiology have enabled the development of physiologically based mathematical models of sleep/wake and circadian rhythms. Such models provide a means of interpreting and quantitatively predicting how the experimentally identified mechanisms interact to produce chronotype. Moreover, models may be used as tools to identify and potentially even diagnose pathologies underlying sleep-phase disorders on an individual basis.

Mathematical modeling has been used to confirm the mechanisms observed experimentally. Longer intrinsic circadian period results in delayed sleep/wake timings, as do slower kinetics for homeostatic clearance and decay. Furthermore, reducing circadian amplitude has been shown to quantitatively reproduce the advanced sleep/wake timings of the elderly (Phillips, Chen, & Robinson, 2010).

Since many different mechanisms can be responsible for delayed or advanced sleep/wake timings, developing a methodological framework for differentiating which are involved on an individual basis is a problem with important clinical applications. Mathematical modeling suggests that differences in entrained circadian phase may provide an important clue. In populations where chronotype differences are primarily determined by interindividual variations in intrinsic circadian period, entrained circadian phase is predicted to closely track sleep/wake times. However, in populations where chronotype differences are primarily determined by interindividual differences in homeostatic kinetics, entrained circadian phase is predicted to differ relatively little between morning types and evening types (Phillips et al., 2010). These predictions are supported by experimental findings that show the existence of two such populations (Mongrain, Lavoie, Selmaoui, Paquet, & Dumont, 2004).

With knowledge of daily activity and light-exposure patterns, as provided by actigraphy and light-monitoring technologies, it is thus possible to use mathematical models to infer the underlying physiology on an individual basis. In the future, this may become an important tool in diagnosing and treating abnormal chronotypes.

Andrew J. K. Phillips

References

Brown, S. A., Kunz, D., Dumas, A., Westermark, P. A., Vanselow, K., Tilmann-Wahnschaffe, A., . . . Kramer, A. (2008). Molecular insights into human daily behavior. *Proceedings of the National Academy of Sciences, 105,* 1602–1607.

Dijk, D.J., Duffy, J.F., & Czeisler, C.A. (2000). Contribution of circadian physiology and sleep homeostasis to age-related changes in human sleep. *Chronobiology International, 17,* 285–311.

Jenni, O.G., Achermann, P., & Carskadon, M.A. (2005). Homeostatic sleep regulation in adolescents. *Sleep, 28,* 1446–1454.

Mongrain, V., Lavoie, S., Selmaoui, B., Paquet, J., & Dumont, M. (2004). Phase relationships between sleep–wake cycle and underlying circadian rhythms in morningness–eveningness. *Journal of Biological Rhythms, 19,* 248–257.

Phillips, A.J.K., Chen, P.Y., & Robinson, P.A. (2010). Probing the mechanisms of chronotype using quantitative modeling. *Journal of Biological Rhythms, 25,* 217–227.

Church Dream Groups

Humans spend an average of five years of their lives watching the little movies that come to us each night while we sleep. Many are the religious practices in cultures around the world that use these nightly occurrences as guides in their religious lives. The Bible itself has several instances and stories where dreams play a significant role. So, how can the modern Christian Church use dreams to find guidance in the individual lives of church members?

There are specific ways that dreams can help Christians. First, they provide a picture of our true emotions. Being honest with our feelings is a major step in practicing our faith. Second, our dreams can help us prioritize our life. If we dream about something or someone that we have encountered recently, that may be a signal that we need to pay closer attention to that event or person than we might ordinarily have done. This can help with our decisions, our plans, and our prayers. A third way we can relate our dreams to our faith is through the way dreams and prayer seem to work. Dreams can relate seemingly unrelated events (this experience is called *synchronicity*), and if we pay attention to our dreams, we find a-causal events related to each other. This is the way prayer works, according to Biblical stories (Acts 10) and the experiences of believers throughout history. The final way that dreams may help Christians is by helping them become more familiar with the use of symbol and image to communicate. Most religious language uses symbols and images in the same way that dreams do. This is the case for the Christian Bible. We will be more comfortable with Biblical books like Ezekiel or Revelation if we are more comfortable with our dreams.

One of the most helpful ways to do so is with dream groups, small gatherings of people devoted to sharing and exploring their dreams together. Small groups have been a method of Christian education and formation for centuries and the format fits well for doing dreamwork. The dreamer will gain more insight when there are several other people reflecting on the dream.

Dreams can help the church by adding means for a variety of experiences that are desired by believers. Personal growth can come as one becomes more understanding of themselves through their dreams. When participating in a dream group, a sense of community is achieved that exists on a deep level. Dreamwork adds a variety of qualities to a person's life and these qualities will help with a person's spiritual life as well. Inspiration may be given in whatever the dreaming believer is involved in, whether in family, work, or church life. There can be new creativity from dreams that helps one with work, including work in the church. We become more aware of the world around us, a quality emphasized in many religious practices. We grow in our tolerance for others when we are more comfortable with the characters and events in our dreams. Tolerance for others is another quality emphasized by many religions. Paying attention to our dreams may give us new reasons to pray or new foci for our prayers. Doing dreamwork may expand the variety of images we use in prayer. We may develop our own personal symbol dictionary based on the characters and events that appear in our dreams. This can be a helpful guide for us as we live out our faith in our waking life.

There are some cautions that church members need to be aware of as they begin to do dreamwork. Dreamwork is not for everyone. Beyond the curiosity that all humans have about their dreams, doing dreamwork in the context of personal faith and church involvement takes an ability to reflect on one's self in deep and honest ways. This is not something everyone is comfortable with. We must be willing to work with symbols of death, sex, and violence that will occasionally be in our dreams. We must also be willing to live with the extrasensory experiences of precognition (dreams that seem to tell the future) or synchronicity (referred to previously).

Many of these benefits and cautions about dreamwork are applicable to people who are not Christian and not involved in churches. But the values are the same for church-going Christians, with the added benefits of Biblical and historical continuity of dreams and religious experience. It is in the group format where dreams have their most benefit, and people share these deep experiences in a context of like-minded believers.

Geoff Nelson

Cinema and Dreams

Despite the obvious differences between dreams—generally considered the epitome of private, subjective, mental phenomena—and the very public, collaborative, capital-intensive art of cinema, the similarities are just as intriguing and provocative, though they have proved more inspiring and productive for makers and theorists of film than for scholars and researchers of dreaming.

The relation between dreaming and cinema may be pursued along two lines of inquiry: first, the analogy between dreaming and the experience of viewing films, and second, the capacity of film to represent dreams in a more sensorially convincing form than any other art medium. Both have been touchstones of cinema theory and practice almost since the invention of the art (conventionally assigned to the brothers Auguste and Louis Lumière's innovation of the *cinématographe*, which both captured moving images on film and projected them, in 1895).

Although in the early days of silent cinema, reviewers and filmmakers incidentally noted that films could portray fantastic events, imitate the structure of dreams, and apparently operate on the viewer like a waking dream, Hugo Münsterberg (1863–1916) was the first to theorize that films "obey the laws of the mind rather than those of the outside world," and that therefore the representation of the dream state, not of exterior reality, is the true aesthetic capacity of the new art of cinema (Münsterberg, 1916). The first psychologist to investigate the film medium in any detail, Münsterberg thus implicitly argued against the already-developing realist paradigm in cinema theory: that is, that film art most fully realizes its fundamental formal and technical properties, and thus its true aesthetic potential, when it reproduces exterior reality as faithfully as possible. The prestige of this position, which implies an austerely documentarian program for cinema, with the human artist in service to the recording capacity of the motion-picture camera, has at least to some extent influenced the popular perception that only film dramas can be serious art, and that dream-based films and other forms of fantasy, as well as genres like musicals and comedy, are anomalous and frivolous uses of the medium.

In "A Note on the Film" appended to her influential treatise on aesthetics, *Feeling and Form*, the American philosopher Susanne Langer (1895–1985) emphasized the phenomenological experience in film viewing of a virtual present marked by an intense sensation of the centrality of the observer to the scene—characteristics that suggest the dream rather than waking experience as the model for cinematic art (Langer, 1953). Significantly, she noted also that in cinema as in dreams, the perception of time and of space may seem to blend and fuse, and that both may feel emotionally charged in ways that are difficult to convey in words. Langer's observations are in line with her expressionist theory of art, which has perhaps influenced artists more than critics.

The American experimental filmmakers Maya Deren (1917–1961) and Stan Brakhage (1933–2003) both offered significant statements on the relation of dreaming and cinema, invoking the concept of the mind's eye in defense of the view that films generally express an artist's vision rather than recording existing reality. Deren particularly emphasizes the capacity of film to create representations of artists' actual dreams, while Brakhage declares that film art can promote the expressive over the objective in especially vivid and compelling forms and takes the extreme avant-gardist position that even hallucinations are valid perceptions for the artist to explore. The critic Parker Tyler (1904–1974), a major theorist of experimental film, who made substantial use of psychoanalytic concepts in his essays on film, argued *contra* Freud that the irrational impulses motivating the creation of art should be celebrated and explored rather than explained away, and that dreams, like films, are better understood as poetry than as symptoms (Tyler, 1960). Therefore, disjunctions in narrative, puzzling symbolism, and other common features of avant-garde film should be appreciated for their enactment of a dream aesthetic, derived from an overlooked but valid aspect of human experience, rather than devalued as failures to maintain the conventions of realism.

The most extensive exploration as yet of the phenomenological and cognitive dimensions of the dream–film analogy has been undertaken by the philosopher Colin McGinn in *The Power of Movies: How Screen and Mind Interact* (McGinn, 2005). Following Langer, McGinn notes the distinctively dreamlike spatiotemporal disjunction of films, along with the fusion of perception and affect. In addition to maintaining that films, like dreams, create a fundamentally solipsistic world in which every perception relates to the primary concerns of the self, McGinn emphasizes as well the intensity of emotion associated with the narrowing of the field of attention in both, and the quality of absorption into both the film and the dream. The genres of film are compared to types of dreams—as the horror film has often before been compared to the nightmare—with the interesting implication that comparative study might illuminate both. McGinn's is the first summation of the implications of the dream–film analogy that draws on post-Freudian developments in dream psychology.

The most influential use of the dream–film analogy in academic film theory, on the other hand, has been its adoption by the French film theorist Christian Metz (1931–1993) to advance the psychoanalytic theories of Jacques Lacan (1901–1981) as a means of understanding and interpreting film. Metz went beyond the application of classical Freudianism to art, theorizing that the Lacanian concept of the mirror stage—in which the subject is held to be structured *as* a subject around the experience of recognizing one's own virtual image—helps explain the psychological and ideological power of films, particularly because the conditions of film viewing mimic the psychologically receptive, even passive, experience of dreaming (Metz, 1986). (Metz's dense and abstruse argument at the very least calls attention to how often other critics apply Freud's ideas about dreaming to art without even bothering to establish the validity of the equation.) Another significant variation of psychoanalytic theory is Bertram Lewin's (1896–1971) notion of the dream screen, elaborated in detail by Robert Eberwein (1985). Lewin held that the mental screen of the film internalizes the actual vision of the breast on which the preverbal infant lies suckling and projecting its fantasies, and Eberwein applies this idea ingeniously to the curiously infantilizing, passive experience of watching a film projected on a standard theatrical screen.

Noël Carroll, an outstanding authority on mass art, has argued cogently that such speculations are both illogical and unnecessary: illogical because we actually understand the cognitive processes of film viewing better than we understand the unconscious mind or the minds of infants, and unnecessary because films, like dreams, display so many features that fascinate for obvious reasons that require no explanation (Carroll, 1991). (The impact of the dream–film analogy in film theory is extensively reviewed in Rascaroli [2002].)

Certainly the depiction of dreams is a significant and intriguing factor in the development of early film conventions and syntax (the term generally used in film criticism for the rules by which shots, scenes, and films are structured to convey ideas to the viewer). When early films were still conceived as literally moving pictures—photographs with the quality of motion added—the magician Georges Méliès (1861–1938) was already experimenting with simple cinematographic effects to transform objects and persons, change settings instantly, and introduce spectacular elements such as anthropomorphized heavenly bodies. The dream provided a convenient naturalizing framework for fantastic scenes in Méliès's early short films such as *The Nightmare* (1897) and *The Astronomer's Dream* (1898). Although these fantasy films essentially used film merely as an extension of Méliès's bag of tricks, they alerted other filmmakers to the unexplored potential of film editing. G. A. Smith's *Let Me Dream Again* (1900), which cuts from a scene of a man cavorting in a café with a young woman, through a short soft-focus shot, to the same man in bed with his much less alluring spouse, is one of the earliest films to use an edit to change scene. The fact that the edit in this early film shifts us from dream to reality, rather than from one real-world setting to another, provides an interesting perspective on the realist paradigm in film history. Another early dream film, Edwin S. Porter's *Dream of the Rarebit Fiend* (1906), adapted from Winsor McCay's popular comic strip, is a virtual textbook of special effects and editing

Scene from the 1906 film *Dream of a Rarebit Fiend*, produced by the Edison Manufacturing Company. (Edison Manufacturing Company/Photofest)

practices, extemporized by Porter to depict a dream scene, but soon incorporated by himself and many others into the developing conventions of more naturalistic films.

As narrative motion pictures evolved from the early vignettes of pioneers such as Porter, Smith, Méliès, and the Lumière brothers, to two-reelers (10 to 15 minutes in length), to feature-length films, dream sequences provided imaginative directors and cinematographers with opportunities to transcend the boundaries of realism. Traditional uses of the dream in literary narrative were adapted, and a typology may be discerned in cinematic dream sequences and dream plots, beginning with the ancient motif of the dream journey or dream quest.

Buster Keaton's 1924 comedy *Sherlock Jr.* styles the quest as a farcical detective story, with the dream occupying nearly the whole of the motion picture. A simple boy-gets-girl plot serves as the pretext for several highly innovative features: double exposure is used to depict a dream body emanating from Keaton's sleeping figure; characters in the hero's waking life are transformed as characters in his dream; magical or improbable events are facilitated by special effects, as in Méliès and Porter. Elements such as these become standard tropes of dream sequences, and of dream films such as *The Wizard of Oz* (Victor Fleming, 1939), which, like *Sherlock Jr.*, also depicts the dream journey as a means for the central character to resolve, in symbolic form, the transient or fundamental conflicts of his or her life. An underappreciated classic—and the only live-action film to embody the vision of Dr. Seuss— *The 5000 Fingers of Dr. T.* (Roy Rowland,

1953), explicitly employs the dream-journey plot to convey the idea that children may achieve autonomy through the power of their imagination, and so find their place in a world dominated by grown-ups. At the other extreme of the life cycle, Isak Borg, the elderly protagonist of Ingmar Bergman's *Wild Strawberries* (1957), finds new balance and meaning in his life as a result of a series of dreams that mix fantasy and memory. (The resemblance in theme and structure to Charles Dickens's *A Christmas Carol*, which has been adapted to film many times, suggests an unconscious influence.) The hero of Federico Fellini's *8½* (1963), a film director universally understood as a stand-in for Fellini himself, confronts his doubts about his creative and sexual potency through plunging himself into dreams, and emerges once again able to make films.

Sherlock Jr. also introduces the dream–film analogy to cinematic representation: its hero is a silent-movie projectionist, whose dream literally projects him into the film that is playing when he falls asleep in the booth. A justly celebrated sequence follows, in which the hero must negotiate the rapidly changing landscape of the film as backgrounds shift behind him—an indelible cinematic image of the frequently disjunctive, involuntary experiential world of the dream, while at the same time a canny satire of film conventions. Aside from Fellini's celebrated exploration of the dream–film parallel in *Juliet of the Spirits* (1965) and *City of Women* (1980) as well as *8½*, many films use a complex dream-journey story to expose the artifices of film plotting to inspection and contemplation, notably *Dead of Night* (Cavalcanti and others, 1945), *Eternal Sunshine of the Spotless Mind* (Michel Gondry, 2004), and *Inception* (Christopher Nolan, 2010). *Living in Oblivion* (Tom DiCillo, 1995) finds an especially witty form, contrasting the dreams (and dreams within dreams) of cast and crew on a film set to bring the characters' inner lives to the screen as well as comment on independent-film culture and conventions.

A subsidiary topic within the dream journey is the permeability of the dream and external reality—as when characters, like shamans, or for that matter, experienced lucid dreamers, effect their goals by establishing a connection between the dream and waking worlds, as in the case of the dream detectives, artists, and warriors of *Dreamscape* (Joseph Ruben, 1984), *A Nightmare on Elm Street* (Wes Craven, 1984), *Paprika* (Satoshi Kon, 2007), and again, *Inception*. A negative form of the dream journey occurs when a character is overwhelmed by dream content, as in Stanley Kubrick's *Eyes Wide Shut* (1999—adapted from Arthur Schnitzler's *Dream Story*), in which the great director expresses his misgivings about the appeal of fantasy in film and in life; and *Vanilla Sky* (Cameron Crowe, 2001), with a script rewritten by Alejandro Almenábar from his 1997 film, *Open Your Eyes*. Plots such as these suggest another category of dream films, in which the cinema is used to elaborate a metaphysical fantasy, culminating with the protagonist, or the plot, ultimately cut adrift from the security of the waking world, as from the conventions of mainstream narrative cinema. *Inception* and the highly innovative *Waking Life* (Richard Linklater, 2001) trap their dreamers within a dream. Luis

Buñuel's *The Discreet Charm of the Bourgeoisie* (1972) refuses to settle the question of where dreams end and reality begins and seems to strand the viewer along with the dreamer in an inescapable circuit of embedded representations. The same might be said of David Lynch's *Mulholland Dr.* (2001) and *Inland Empire* (2006), among his many dreamlike films, although most viewers have found the plots of these films too disorienting to hazard even this view. The prototype for this genre of metaphysical fantasy is *Dead of Night*, in which the protagonist wakes from a nightmare into the opening moments of the same nightmare. (The recursive structure of this horror film is said to have inspired the steady state [or infinite loop] model of the universe.) Although these are variations on the theme of the dream journey, their preoccupation with existential anxiety renders them as distinct from other dream films as tragedy is from comedy, or as nightmares are from ordinary dreams.

The horror film is widely understood to be derived from the nightmare, and the popularity of *A Nightmare on Elm Street* and its sequels has encouraged application of the dream plot and the explicit representation of dreams within the genre. *Paperhouse* (Bernard Rose, 1988) and *In Dreams* (Neil Jordan, 1999) are interesting examples of directors exploring the uncanniness of dreams to unsettling effect. More generally, John E. Mack's treatment of nightmare imagery as expressive of preoedipal anxiety concerning persecution and annihilation of the self yields significant insight into the defining themes, as well as the popularity, of the horror genre, as does Patrick McNamara's understanding of the essentially creative nature of the nightmare vision (Mack, 1970; McNamara, 2008).

The challenge that dreaming presents to our commonsense accounts of reality has been taken up enthusiastically by avant-garde filmmakers, along the lines associated with Deren, Brakhage, and Tyler, as cited previously. The most famous instance, and one of the most celebrated of all films, is Luis Buñuel and Salvador Dalí's *Un chien andalou* (1929), which provides the model for surrealist film. However, although it was said to have been inspired by dreams, and the surrealist project was certainly promoted in terms of introducing the irrationality of dreams not only into art but into life, *Un chien andalou* does not explicitly use the fiction of the dream, even if its imagery and structure are almost always considered dreamlike. Deren explicitly uses the dream as format in *Meshes of the Afternoon* (1943), as does Kenneth Anger in *Fireworks* (1947) and James Broughton in *The Bed* (1968), among American experimental filmmakers often counted among the surrealists. These films share the notion of the dream as a gateway to transcendental vision (as opposed to the mere perception of the appearance of things), and significantly for American avant-gardists, a guide to sexual openness and diversity of options.

The psychoanalytic program of the therapeutic analysis of dreams inspired a distinctive if limited genre of dream films: the dream-interpretation plot, in which the audience is shown how a Freudian approach to dreams—and to one key dream in particular, which encodes a whole life's mysteries—can resolve the protagonist's conflicts and overcome symptoms and

inhibitions that have disrupted his life. The prototype is G. W. Pabst's *Secrets of a Soul* (1926), still a truly remarkable *tour de force* in the cinematic depiction of dreams and of what we make of them. With the collaboration of Freud's associates, Karl Abraham and Hans Sachs (though Freud himself kept his distance, as he did from cinema generally), Pabst developed three stylistically differentiated means of representing the dream—first, for its initial appearance; second, for the recounting of the dream to the psychoanalyst; and third, for the therapist's item-by-item investigation and explanation of the significant features of the dream.

The best-known instance of the dream-interpretation plot, however, is Alfred Hitchcock's *Spellbound* (1945), in which psychoanalyst Ingrid Bergman not only cures Gregory Peck of amnesia but solves the murder of which he has been accused, by following the clues laid in his dream—as limned, in perhaps the cinema's most famous dream sequence, by Salvador Dalí. The dream in *Spellbound* is both a stunt and a game—Hitchcock intended to exploit the surrealist artist's notoriety (without including in his film anything that would alarm the censors or the public), and the great director and his screenwriter, Ben Hecht, conceived the clever notion that psychoanalysis styled the search for identity as detective work (something that might have occurred to Sophocles as he was writing *Oedipus the King*, if only he had read Freud).

Hitchcock is well known as one of many film artists who have expressed a fascination with dreams, dream studies, and the capacity of films to represent dreams and the dream state. Among other significant examples are Jean Cocteau, Ingmar Bergman, Federico Fellini, Luis Buñuel, Akira Kurosawa, Robert Altman, David Lynch, Richard Linklater, Michel Gondry, and the screenwriter Charlie Kaufman, all of whom may be said to have gravitated toward oneiric cinema and expanded the boundaries of cinema into the landscape of dreams.

Bernard Welt

References

Barrett, D. (n.d.). *Index of films and documentaries.* http://www.asdreams.org/video fil.htm

Carroll, N. (1991). *Mystifying movies: Fads and fallacies in contemporary film theory.* New York: Columbia University.

Eberwein, R. (1985). *Film and the dream screen.* Princeton, NJ: Princeton University Press.

Langer, S. K. (1953). *Feeling and form.* New York: Prentice Hall.

Mack, J.E. (1970). *Nightmares and human conflict.* New York: Columbia University Press.

McGinn, C. (2005). *The power of movies: How screen and mind interact.* New York: Pantheon.

McNamara, P. (2008). *Nightmares: The science and solution of those frightening visions during sleep.* Westport, CT: Praeger.

Metz, C. (1986). *The imaginary signifier: Psychoanalysis and the cinema.* Bloomington: Indiana University Press.

Münsterberg, H. (1916). *The photoplay: A psychological study.* New York: Appleton.

Rascaroli, L. (2002, Fall). Like a dream: A critical history of the oneiric metaphor in film theory. *Kinema.* Retrieved January 15, 2011, from http://www.kinema.uwaterloo.ca/rasc022.htm

Tyler, P. (1960). *The three faces of the film: The art, the dream, the cult.* New York: T. Yoseloff.

Circadian Rhythms

Most terrestrial organisms evolved in an environment that changed rhythmically according to a 24-hour light cycle. Humans are no exception. Our physiologies cycle through peaks and troughs tied to the 24-hour light cycle. Diurnal variation in temperature, hormones, autonomic nervous system discharges, and even complex behavior is now well established. The source of this circadian rhythmicity in humans appears to be retinal–hypothalamic transfer of light information from the eyes up to the suprachiasmatic nucleus in the hypothalamus. The hypothalamus then sends efferents to the pineal gland, which secretes melatonin. Melatonin itself exhibits circadian rhythmicity and is intimately associated with the waxing and waning of sleepiness over the 24-hour cycle. Lesioning the retino-hypothalamic-pineal tract in animals destroys the animal's circadian physiology.

The regular daily oscillation between sleep and wake states is one example of circadian rhythmicity. An internal circadian clock operates in interaction with homeostatic control mechanisms that regulate daily sleep amounts and sleep intensity. A series of clock genes such as Cry2 and Per2 and their protein products regulate the internal clock. During wakefulness, neurochemicals controlled by genes that compose the circadian clock are thought to accumulate in proportion to the length of the wake period. One such possible chemical is adenosine, which acts in a sleep center (possibly the basal forebrain) to inhibit arousal/increase sleepiness and then dissipates at a rate depending on sleep intensity until it returns to baseline during sleep. In the two-process model of sleep regulation, a sleep-need process (process S) increases during waking (or sleep deprivation) and decreases during sleep. This part of the model indexes restorative aspects of sleep and explicitly predicts that sleep is required for some restorative process of the brain or the body or both. Process S is proposed to interact with input from the light-regulated circadian system (process C) that is independent of sleep and wakefulness rhythms. Slow-wave activity (SWA) is taken as an indicator of the time course of process S, because SWA is known to correlate with arousal thresholds and to markedly increase during the previous waking period and during the rebound period after sleep deprivation in all mammals studied. Once a threshold value of process S is reached (i.e., once the appropriate amount and intensity of slow-wave sleep is reached), process C will be activated. Simulations using the model's assumptions show that the homeostatic component of sleep falls in a sigmoidal manner during waking and rises in a saturating exponential manner during sleep.

This exquisitely regulated circadian sleep-regulatory system can break down in patterned ways. In both advanced and delayed sleep-phase syndromes, the circadian sleep system is shifted such that it is out of phase with the sleep propensity rhythm, and sleep onset therefore occurs too soon or too late to achieve optimal sleep. The sleep circadian system is known to be disrupted in a range of disorders from autism to Alzheimer's disease.

Patrick McNamara

See also: entries related to Sleep Physiology

Clinical Aspects of Nightmares

A nightmare is usually defined as a frightening dream that awakens the dreamer. This is not a perfect definition, but no better one has been devised. The typical nightmare, as defined in the preceding text, needs to be distinguished from night terror, and hypnagogic or hypnopompic imagery, which can sometimes be quite nightmare-like.

A night terror, sometimes called sleep terror, is not a dream. It is an arousal from stage 3 or 4 non-REM sleep, usually early during the night. It is characterized by feelings of intense terror, and by autonomic arousal, but little or no dream imagery. Night terrors are especially common in children aged three to six, but persist into adulthood in up to 1 percent of the population.

Hypnagogic imagery is defined as imagery during sleep onset, while hypnopompic imagery is imagery at sleep offset (during awakening). Most often such imagery is brief and fleeting, without the detailed plot of a typical dream. However, dreamlike and even nightmare-like episodes do occasionally occur at sleep onset and offset.

People often ask how a nightmare can be distinguished from a dream. It cannot. The true nightmare or typical nightmare *is* a dream—a frightening dream that awakens the sleeper. An anxiety dream is defined as a dream involving or picturing anxiety that does not awaken the sleeper. However, there is no absolute distinction between the content of an anxiety dream and that of a nightmare, though the nightmare is usually thought of as more terrifying—characterized by the powerful emotions of terror or fear, rather than only anxiety.

There have been numerous research studies of nightmares. It is well established that nightmares are more frequent in children than in adults. Also, nightmares are more frequent in persons who have experienced trauma and more frequent after a traumatic event than before. A number of studies have examined persons who have frequent nightmares that are not apparently related to trauma. These turn out to be people with thin boundaries (qv) in many different senses. They are sensitive in many ways, they let things in more easily than most, they experience in-between states of many kinds, and they see reality in shades of gray rather than in black-and-white. Studies using a well-established Boundary Questionnaire have shown, for instance, that art students have relatively thin boundaries, while naval officers, accountants, and lawyers have relatively thick boundaries.

Studies also show that nightmare distress is quite different from nightmare frequency. Some people are very upset about their nightmares, while others may have very frequent and powerful-sounding nightmares and show little distress. In fact, in the studies of persons with frequent nightmares, more than half said they considered their nightmares as part of them,

did not want to change the nightmares, and did not want any treatment for them. For those who do experience distress, and who consider their nightmares a problem to be treated, a simple cognitive-behavioral treatment called *imagery-rehearsal therapy* has been shown to be very useful.

Ernest Hartmann

See also: Lucid Dreaming Therapy for Nightmares; entries related to Sleep Disorders

References

Belicki, K. (1992). Nightmare frequency versus nightmare distress: Relations to psychopathology and cognitive style. *Journal of Abnormal Psychology, 101*(3), 592–597.

Hartmann, E. (1984). *The nightmare: The psychology and biology of terrifying dreams.* New York: Basic Books.

Cognitive Approach to Dreaming

The cognitive approach to dreaming consists in analyzing the form or content of dream reports and in explaining them with references to cognitive processes involved in waking and sleep mentation. This approach disappeared during the first half of the 20th century because dreams became almost exclusively a psychoanalytical topic and because of the ban on the study of mental states by behaviorism. After the pioneering work of Hall (1953), the resurgence of experimental dream psychology took place in the 1960s as a consequence of the discovery of REM sleep. Toward the end of the 1970s, dream researchers, somewhat disappointed by the limited explanatory value of sleep neurophysiology, started to study dreams as cognition (Antrobus, 1978; Foulkes, 1978). The concern of basing explanations on empirical findings as well as the references to cognitive processes stood in complete contrast to the psychoanalytical approach. The results and conclusions changed the traditional conception of dreaming.

The argument in favor of adopting a cognitive view of dreaming is that the main processes enabling us to dream are primarily cognitive. First, we need the ability to evoke things by means of substitutes like words, mental imagery, and so on. In order to dream, this semiotic function must be well developed (whence the impossibility of a dream experience similar to ours in babies and animals). Second, many cognitive processes must be activated: memory and general knowledge provide the dream content; mental imagery, speech production processes, and so on represent this content; organizing processes assemble the representations to form a step of a dream scene and give a more or less narrative form to the sequence of scenes. References to semantic organization, logical consistency, attention, and perception are also relevant in dream studies. Research conducted within the cognitive approach provided more information on aspects of dreaming such as the following:

- Dream imagery, which undergoes intra- and interindividual variations in terms of vividness, complexity, and, to a lesser extent, color. Mental imagery abilities are not impaired during sleep.
- General categories of dream content and the rate of dream recall, which is higher upon awakenings in REM sleep, in the later part of the night, in persons with good visual–spatial abilities, and in women.
- The sequential organization of dreams, which is more organized than expected. Abrupt narrative breaks occur in most dream reports of some length, but they constitute a small minority of the relationships between temporal units.
- Other aspects, such as the integration of perceptual stimuli during dreaming, speech in dreams, and the nature and frequency of memory sources or of bizarre content.

The main changes in the conception of dreaming brought by these findings were, first, that the commonalities between dreaming and waking thoughts became at least as striking as the differences. Some productions of the waking mind share many features with dreams and the latter have a larger degree of organization than expected. Second, cognitive processes are helpful to analyze and explain dreaming: for example, story grammar or the distinction between episodic and semantic memories helped respectively to analyze the sequential aspect or the nature of memory sources of dreams. General stages of cognitive development permitted distinguishing stages of children's dream development, and visual–spatial skills positively correlate with dream recall and vividness in adults and with the complexity of the form of dreams in children. Third, dreaming can occur in every stage of sleep and not only in REM sleep. The time of night has a greater influence than sleep stage on the narrative structure and creativity of dreams. Fourth, dreams display very important within-subjects and between-subjects variations in terms of topics, narrative structure, realism, vividness, and emotionality.

A definition of dreaming must take into account that variability.

There is no exclusion between a cognitive approach and the study of emotions. As far as the meaning of dreams is concerned, this issue was ignored by most cognitive researchers, but it is reintegrated in some recent studies (see the entry "Using Dreams in Cognitive-Behavioral Therapy"). Future research should specify laws involved in dream production (for instance, in the semantic and sequential organization) and show the relationships between dream psychology and the psychology of creativity.

Jacques Montangero

See also: Using Dreams in Cognitive-Behavioral Therapy

References

Antrobus, J. (1978). Dreaming as cognition. In A. Arkin, J. Antrobus, & S. Ellman (Eds.), *The mind in sleep: Psychology and psychophysiology* (pp. 569–581). Hillsdale, NJ: Erlbaum.

Foulkes, D. (1978). Dreaming as language and cognition. *Scientia, 113*, 481–499.

Hall, C. (1953). A cognitive theory of dreams. *Journal of General Psychology, 49*, 273–282.

Cognitive Expertise and Dreams

Dream recall and dream reporting are cognitive skills. The development of these skills—the acquisition of cognitive expertise—influences the content and completeness of verbal reports of dreaming. Hence, cognitive expertise is an important consideration in dream research, especially when verbal reports constitute the primary data source in studies of how dreams are generated.

Background

Any study of the phenomenological qualities of human experience poses challenges, not the least because measures are indirect and verbal descriptions of these experiences may omit important features such as emotion or sensory–perceptual qualities. Studies of waking subjective experience include the opportunity to control the conditions associated with an individual's report. This permits investigators to explore how phenomenological reports relate to an experimental manipulation (e.g., exposure to a violent vs. a neutral film or to instructions that vary the quality of waking imagery an individual is meant to focus on). In the study of dream phenomenology, however, it is not possible to control the stimulus conditions. This makes it especially challenging to investigate factors that influence the generation of subjective experience in sleep (see the entry "Methodological Challenges in the Scientific Study of Dreams").

Dreaming Mind, Waking Mind

Why endeavor to systematically chronicle the relationship between dreaming and waking experiences? For one, studies of how the mind functions in sleep can provide important insights into the development of cognition and consciousness. Indeed, laboratory studies have established that mental activity occurs throughout the night. The phenomenological qualities of this mental activity vary—from singular images and thoughts most often associated with the hypnagogic state (the transition from waking to sleep) to the elaborate, multisensory, and storylike experiences most often associated with experimental interruptions of late-night REM sleep in the sleep laboratory and spontaneous morning awakenings in the home setting. Many investigators consider only the latter to be bona fide dreaming; others include any instance of mental activity reported from sleep in their definition of dreaming. (In the present discussion, the latter—more inclusive— definition of dreaming is used.)

The precise relationship between cognition in sleep and waking has yet to be determined, however. Investigators often base their inferences about the relationship between dreaming and waking cognition (and experience) on data obtained from experience-sampling procedures. Typically, an individual's ongoing experience (dreaming or waking) is interrupted with an alarm or other signal. The participant first provides a complete verbal description of the just-interrupted experience. He or she then responds to specific questions that target specific sensory, affective, cognitive, or structural features of the experience.

Evidence from studies that use experience-sampling procedures has produced seemingly conflicting results. Some investigators have presented data showing that individuals are less likely to notice unusual events (anomalies) in dreams (e.g., Kahn & Hobson, 2005), suggesting that high-order cognitive skills such as those involved in error monitoring are absent or attenuated in sleep. Others have presented data showing that dreaming and waking include the same range of high-order cognitive skills, including focused attention and reflective awareness (awareness or evaluation of one's ongoing thoughts, feelings, or behavior) (e.g., Kahan & LaBerge, 1996, 2010).

Individual differences may well account for some—perhaps a great deal—of the variation in results obtained concerning high-order cognition in dreaming.

Expertise and Dream Studies

Expertise denotes a high level of mastery or skill in a specific area (domain). Examples of individuals with expertise include concert musicians, elite athletes, linguistic translators, and chess masters. Expertise begins with an aptitude that is fully developed through the acquisition and organization of extensive knowledge relevant to a particular domain and the disciplined practice of domain-specific skills. Experts and novices differ in many respects. For example, experts are faster and more effective (than novices) in discerning patterns in their area of specialization. Experts are better able to select appropriate strategies for accessing long-term memory and using this information to assimilate new information. Experts also have better self-monitoring skills—"they seem to be aware of their own errors and are able to make in-course corrections" (Solso, Maclin, & Maclin, 2008, p. 436).

Individuals with *cognitive* expertise demonstrate a high level of skill in areas such as memory, attention, problem solving, imagery, language, or metacognition (knowledge of how one's cognitive processes work).

Dreaming Is a Form of Cognitive Expertise

The substantial methodological challenges in dream research often obscure the importance of considering how a participant's cognitive expertise influences the evidence obtained in dream studies. The extent of this influence varies with the question of interest in a dream investigation. For example, a minimal level of cognitive expertise is needed to investigate *whether* people dream (i.e., factors that predict dream recall or the frequency with which dreams are recalled from different sleep stages). Similarly, minimal cognitive expertise is needed to investigate variations in how people use dreams (e.g., for self-exploration, self-understanding, problem solving, creativity). Cognitive expertise (of participants) is more important in studies of dream content (i.e., of *what* people dream). In order to study variations in dream content and how this content relates to factors such as personality, gender, waking concerns, or attitude toward dreams, dreams must be recalled as completely (and accurately) as possible.

Cognitive expertise is of particular importance in studies of the dream-generation process. Investigations of how subjective experiences are generated rely heavily on the a priori assumption that verbal reports of subjective experience provide valid information concerning the underlying cognitive and perceptual processes. Thus, the *accuracy* of claims made about how dreaming (or waking) experiences are generated is tied to the quality of the evidence provided in the verbal report. Cognitive expertise influences the content and completeness of reports of dream experience.

A dream experience must be recalled from the *waking* (or awakening) state. Hence, investigators interested in the cognitive-perceptual processes involved in dream generation, especially, must consider how cognitive skills contribute to the accessibility of subjective experiences generated in one state and recalled from another. Even with the minimum delay between an experience and the requested report (or rating) of that experience, the verbal report is also affected by one's attention, working memory, and metacognitive skills. For example, the content and completeness of the verbal report are influenced by the strategies one uses to retain the dreaming experience through the awakening process (i.e., by one's working memory skills and one's visual imagery ability).

The verbal report is also influenced by the organizational structures or schemata that one activates to guide verbal recall, or better yet, the verbal *translation*, of what is often a complex, multimodal sensory experience. Numerous studies have demonstrated that practice in recalling and reporting dreams increases the number of dreams recalled as well as the qualities of those dreams.

Attention skills also influence the verbal report of a dreaming (or waking) experience. These include the individual's expertise in noticing specific qualities of subjective experience—such as sensations, feelings, thoughts, or reflections on the ongoing experience. For example, in an investigation of whether vision is the dominant sensory modality of dreaming experience—as is the case in waking—it is critical that the study participants be skilled in noticing the particular sensory qualities of their dreaming experience and that they be practiced in reporting on those qualities in a consistent manner. Similarly, an investigation into whether individuals experience self-reflective awareness in dreaming (i.e., think about or evaluate their ongoing thoughts, feelings, or behavior *in* the dream) must involve participants who have cultivated the ability to notice and report on instances of reflective awareness (in waking and in dreaming). Studies in which participants' skill in reflective awareness was increased via attentional training have revealed an increase in reports of reflective awareness in dreaming. The practice of attention skills in waking increases the ability to notice where one's attention is drawn and redirect attention to present-moment experience. Such attention practices increase the ability to monitor and regulate current experience—in both waking and in dreaming (e.g., Purcell, Moffitt, & Hoffmann, 1993).

The participants' expertise in metacognition is another important contributor to the validity of data obtained on the dream-generation process (as recorded by the verbal report or by ratings of the phenomenological qualities of subjective experience). Simply put, metacognition is one's knowledge and understanding of how his or her cognitive processes work. One metacognitive skill that is critical to investigations of dream-generation processes is the participant's ability to distinguish the qualities of a targeted subjective experience from the interpretive, analytic, or other constructive processing one is inclined to add in the course of recollection. Participants thus need the ability to discriminate what was experienced prior to the experimental interruption of a dreaming (or waking) experience from what is experienced in the course of recollection; in other words, participants need expertise in *source monitoring* (Johnson, Hashtroudi, & Lindsay, 1993).

Conclusion

Dreaming is not merely an imagined experience in sleep that happens to us. Rather, dreaming is a skill that can be developed. Like any form of expertise, the level of skill one develops is influenced by his or her initial aptitude and, perhaps more importantly, by the commitment of intention, attention, and practice.

Dream researchers are therefore encouraged to consider the level of *cognitive expertise* participants bring to their investigations and, especially, what level of cognitive expertise is a necessary prerequisite to address their question of interest.

Tracey Lea Kahan

References

Foulkes, D. (1999). *Children's dreaming and the development of consciousness.* Cambridge, MA: Harvard University Press.

Johnson, M.K., Hashtroudi, S., & Lindsay, D.S. (1993). Source monitoring. *Psychological Bulletin, 114*(1), 3–28.

Kahan, T.L. (1994). Measuring dream self-reflectiveness: A comparison of two approaches. *Dreaming, 4*(3), 329–344.

Kahan, T.L., & LaBerge, S. (1996). Cognition and metacognition in dreaming and waking: Comparisons of first and third-person ratings. *Dreaming, 6*(4), 235–247.

Kahan, T.L., & LaBerge, S. (2010). Dreaming and waking: Similarities and differences revisited. *Consciousness and Cognition.* doi:10.1016/j.concog.2010.09.002

Kahn, D., & Hobson, J.A. (2005). State-dependent thinking: A comparison of waking and dreaming thought. Consciousness and *Cognition, 14*, 429–438.

Purcell, S., Moffitt, A., & Hoffmann, R. (1993). Waking, dreaming, and self-regulation. In. A. Moffitt, M. Kramer, & R. Hoffmann (Eds.), *The functions of dreaming* (pp. 197–260). Albany: State University of New York Press.

Solso, R.L., Maclin, O.H., & Maclin, H.K. (2008). *Cognitive psychology* (8th ed.). Boston, MA: Pearson.

Cognitive Theory of Dream Meaning, A

Three different types of unexpected research findings from inside and outside the sleep laboratory since the 1950s have led to a cognitive theory of dream meaning, as first outlined in work by Calvin S. Hall (1953), John Antrobus (1978), and David Foulkes (1985, 1999).

First, the many laboratory studies of adult dreams in the 1960s and 1970s led to a very surprising result: the dreams reported from REM awakenings are usually reasonable simulations of the waking world that deal with everyday topics and contain relatively few fantastic, bizarre, or highly emotional aspects. One of the most comprehensive studies of REM dream content in the sleep laboratory, based on 635 dream reports from 58 young adult men and women, reported that "dreaming consciousness" is a "remarkably faithful replica of waking life"; a prototypical REM dream report is a "clear, coherent, and detailed account of a realistic situation involving the dreamer and other people caught up in very ordinary activities and preoccupations, and usually talking about them" (Snyder, 1970, pp. 133, 148). Overall, as many as 90 percent of the dream reports "would have been considered credible descriptions of everyday experience" (Snyder, Karacan, Tharp, & Scott, 1968, p. 375). Many other studies showed the relatively low degree of bizarreness and the appropriateness of emotions to dream content in laboratory reports (see Domhoff, 2007, for a summary).

Second, longitudinal and cross-sectional studies of children aged 3 to 15 in the sleep laboratory reveal that dreaming gradually develops beginning late in the preschool years in ways that parallel waking cognitive development. The content in the few REM reports from preschoolers was static, undeveloped, and lacking in any emotion. Reports became more dreamlike (in terms of characters, themes, and actions) in the five- to six-year-olds, and the dreamers themselves began to play a more central role in their dreams by ages seven to eight. Dreaming became adultlike in its cognitive complexity at ages 9 to 10, but it was not until the children were 11 to 13 years old that their dreams began to resemble those of adult laboratory participants in frequency, length, content, and emotions, or to have any relationship to personality variables (Foulkes, 1982; Foulkes, Hollifield, Sullivan, Bradley, & Terry, 1990).

Third, numerous studies of dream reports from throughout the world use several different systems of content analysis, but in particular the system resting on nominal categories developed by Calvin S. Hall and Robert Van de Castle (1966) has provided a replicable body of descriptive empirical findings that reveal cross-cultural, gender, age, and individual similarities and differences of the kind that might be expected on the basis of studies of waking psychological variables. There are also several studies of lengthy individual dream series showing that most people are consistent over several months or years in what they dream about and that the most frequent characters, social interactions, and social and recreational activities in their dreams are continuous with their waking interests and emotional concerns (Domhoff, 1996, 2003).

Based on the evidence for parallels in the contents and complexity of dreaming and waking cognition, a cognitive approach to dream meaning begins with the fact that thinking and imagining develop as part of a conceptual system, that is, a system of schemas and scripts, which is the organizational basis for all human knowledge and beliefs. From a cognitive perspective, dreams are imaginative simulations that express people's conceptions, which are also the basis for action in the waking world (Hall, 1953). Starting with the idea that dreams often reveal highly personal conceptions, it is possible to build a picture of a dreamer's overall conceptual system, which is usually very complex.

In particular, many dream scenarios express the several different conceptions people hold of themselves, which often seem contradictory because people see themselves and their roles differently with, for example, parents, teachers, or friends.

In terms of findings with the Hall/Van de Castle coding system, self-conceptions may manifest themselves in the varying proportions of success and failure experienced by the dreamer, the degree to which the dreamer suffers misfortunes in various situations, and the degree to which the dreamer is an instigator or victim in aggressive interactions with different classes of characters.

Dreams also express conceptions of family and friends, which once again can be complex because, to use another example, people may conceive of their parents in one way when they need help or advice and in another way when they want to be independent of parental demands. More generally, the relative frequency of aggressive and friendly interactions with a given person, which can be expressed as an aggression/friendly percentage in the Hall/Van de Castle coding system, when considered along with the degree to which the dreamer is an initiator or recipient in social interactions with that person, has been shown through blind analyses of dream reports to be highly predictive of a dreamer's waking conceptions of his or her relationship with that person (Domhoff, 2003, chapter 5).

The highly personalized nature of dreams can also be seen in the fact that they far less often involve politics, economics, or other current events that might be of interest to the person in waking life. However, there is a significant minority of dreams, perhaps as many as 25 to 30 percent for some adults, which have no easily discernible connections to the person's waking life (Domhoff, Meyer-Gomes, & Schredl, 2005–2006). They are more like sagas or adventure stories; in keeping with a cognitive approach, Foulkes (1999, p. 136) calls such dreams narrative-driven to contrast them with dreams that seem to be based on personal concerns.

A cognitive approach also contains a way to assess the weight to be given to the conceptions expressed in dreams: by determining the relative frequency of their occurrence. Several studies show that the frequency with which a person, action, or activity occurs in a series of dreams reveals the intensity of the concern with that person, action, or activity in waking life, which means that dreams are dramatized enactments of both conceptions and concerns. The emphasis on concerns links dreaming with the fact that the drift of waking thought is shaped to a great extent by underlying concerns (Klinger, 1999, 2009).

The availability of open-access dream archives and analytic software on the Internet, at www.dreambank.net, for the analysis of lengthy dream journals makes it possible to test and refine a cognitive theory of dream meaning in more detail than was ever possible before. In addition, there is software (DreamSAT) on www.dreamresearch.net that can be used in conjunction with the Hall/Van de Castle coding system to determine values for 19 content indicators and compare them with normative findings for men and women. Such studies lead to detailed inferences that then can be corroborated or rejected by the dreamer and people who know the dreamer well, with the people who know the dreamer sitting as judge and jury to adjudicate any differences between the dream researcher and the dreamer on specific inferences. (For a detailed example based on the analysis of thousands of dream reports as well as interviews with the dreamer and four of her friends, see Domhoff, 2010.)

Similarly, there are now 40 standardized word strings for specific types of perceptions, emotions, cognitive processes, characters, social interactions, and cultural activities that can be used to study dream journals in conjunction with normative findings for men and women with each word string. Findings with these word strings using the dream report archives on DreamBank.net are consistent with the waking conceptions and concerns of the men and women, ranging in age from 23 to 80, who have been studied using this approach (Bulkeley, 2009a, 2009b; Bulkeley & Domhoff, 2010).

G. William Domhoff

See also: entries related to Dream Theories

References

Antrobus, J. (1978). Dreaming as cognition. In A. Arkin, J. Antrobus, & S. Ellman (Eds.), *The mind in sleep: Psychology and psychophysiology* (pp. 569–581). Hillsdale, NJ: Erlbaum.

Bulkeley, K. (2009a.) Seeking patterns in dream content: A systematic approach to word searches. *Consciousness and Cognition, 18,* 909–916.

Bulkeley, K. (2009b). The religious content of dreams: A new scientific foundation. *Pastoral Psychology, 58,* 93–106.

Bulkeley, K., & Domhoff, G. W. (2010). Detecting meaning in dream reports: An extension of a word search approach. *Dreaming, 20,* 77–95.

Domhoff, G. W. (1996). *Finding meaning in dreams: A quantitative approach.* New York: Plenum.

Domhoff, G. W. (2003). *The scientific study of dreams: Neural networks, cognitive development, and content analysis*. Washington, DC: American Psychological Association.

Domhoff, G. W. (2007). Realistic simulation and bizarreness in dream content: Past findings and suggestions for future research. In D. Barrett & P. McNamara (Eds.), *The new science of dreaming: Content, recall, and personality correlates*. Westport, CT: Praeger.

Domhoff, G. W. (2010). Barb Sanders: Our best case to date. In *The quantitative study of dreams*. Retrieved from http://psych.ucsc.edu/dreams/Findings/barb_sanders.html

Domhoff, G. W., Meyer-Gomes, K., & Schredl, M. (2005–2006). Dreams as the expression of conceptions and concerns: A comparison of German and American college students. *Imagination, Cognition & Personality*, 25, 269–282.

Foulkes, D. (1982). *Children's dreams*. New York: Wiley.

Foulkes, D. (1985). *Dreaming: A cognitive-psychological analysis*. Hillsdale, NJ: Erlbaum.

Foulkes, D. (1999). *Children's dreaming and the development of consciousness*. Cambridge, MA: Harvard University Press.

Foulkes, D., Hollifield, M., Sullivan, B., Bradley, L., & Terry, R. (1990). REM dreaming and cognitive skills at ages 5–8: A cross-sectional study. *International Journal of Behavioral Development*, 13, 447–465.

Hall, C. (1953). A cognitive theory of dreams. *Journal of General Psychology*, 49, 273–282.

Hall, C., & Van de Castle, R. (1966). *The content analysis of dreams*. New York: Appleton-Century-Crofts.

Klinger, E. (1999). Thought flow: Properties and mechanisms underlying shifts in content. In J. Singer & P. Salovey (Eds.), *At play in the fields of consciousness*. Hillsdale, NJ: Erlbaum.

Klinger, E. (2009). Daydreaming and fantasizing: Thought flow and motivation. In K. Markman, W. Klein, & J. Suhr (Eds.), *Handbook of imagination and mental simulation*. New York: Psycholoy Press.

Snyder, F. (1970). The phenomenology of dreaming. In L. Madow & L. Snow (Eds.), *The psychodynamic implications of the physiological studies on dreams*. Springfield, IL: Thomas.

Snyder, F., Karacan, I., Tharp, V., & Scott, J. (1968). Phenomenology of REM dreaming. *Psychophysiology, 4*, 375.

Coleridge, Samuel Taylor, and Dreaming

Samuel Taylor Coleridge (1772–1834) was an English poet, critic, and philosopher who played a seminal role in the foundation and development of English Romanticism. Through his poetry and other writings, he contributed penetrating insights into the complex interrelationships between dreaming, the imagination, creative writing, and the unconscious mind.

One of his most significant motivations for exploring the topic of dreaming was his own personal dreams. Throughout his life, Coleridge suffered from debilitating and baffling nightmares that impelled him to better understand the mysterious nature of dreaming. He used his nightmares as a direct source of creative inspiration for many of his poems, including "Christabel," "Dejection: An Ode," "The Pains of Sleep," and "The Rime of the Ancient Mariner." His struggles with nighttime terrors were exacerbated by his addiction to opium.

Coleridge was thoroughly versed in the dream literature of his age. A wide and varied range of sources informed his understanding of dreams (Ford, 1998, pp. 9–26). He was familiar with the dream theories of ancient writers such as Aristotle, Plato, and Artemidorus, the supernatural explanations of Baxter and Swedenborg, and the influential philosophical and physiological dream theories of such writers as Erasmus Darwin, John Locke, David Hartley, and others. At the same time, he was dissatisfied to varying degrees with all of the dream theories he encountered, and this fueled his desire to pursue his own creative investigations into the nature and significance of dreams.

Central to his understanding of dreaming was an analogy he drew between dreams and dramatic theatre (Allen, 1997, pp. 145–151). Coleridge believed that both required a suspension of disbelief. In dreaming, this loss of the power of the will and the capacity for judgment is sudden and involuntary. In theatrical drama, the audience voluntarily consents to being gradually led into a comparable state of passive surrender. Using this parallel between dreaming and drama, Coleridge theorized that both are driven by the same creative processes. The suspension of disbelief enables the unconscious imagination to emerge. However, other aspects of the unconscious may also come forth, such as the terrifying nightmares that persistently plagued Coleridge throughout his life.

Besides nightmares and ordinary dreams, Coleridge actively explored a range of mental states that existed on a continuum between waking and dreaming, including reverie, visions, ghost sightings, daydreaming, falling asleep, and poetic consciousness (Ford, 1998, pp. 84–97). Coleridge considered all these states to be types of dreams. He referred to poems as rationalized dreams, because in poetry a degree of reasoning is still present. Daydreams, visions, and reveries are prominent themes in many of his poems, including "The Picture," "Kubla Khan," "A Daydream," and "The Garden of Boccaccio." His literary exploration of dreams and partial dream states extended to the form as well as the content of his poetry. He experimented with unconventional beats and rhymes as a way of evoking a dreamlike effect upon the reader (Robinson, 1997, pp. 130–134).

"Kubla Khan" is perhaps Coleridge's most famous work, in part because of the extraordinary claims he made in the poem's preface about the origin of the poem (Wheeler, 1981, pp. 20–30). According to Coleridge, he received this poem in a dream and was able to recall upon awakening the 200 to 300 verses in their entirety. As he was writing down the poem from memory, a visitor interrupted him for about an hour. When he returned to writing the rest of the poem, he found that he could no longer remember the unwritten verses, which were forever lost. Some scholars and critics are skeptical about the authenticity of the poem's alleged origins.

Chris Olsen

References

Allen, B. J. (1997). The projected poet: Coleridge's use of dream in dramatic reception. *Dreaming, 7*(2), 141–156.

Coleridge, S. T. (1997). *The complete poems/ Samuel Taylor Coleridge* (W. Keach, Ed.). New York: Penguin Books.

Ford, J. (1998). *Coleridge on dreaming: Romanticism, dreams and the medical imagination.* Cambridge: Cambridge University Press.

Robinson, D. (1997). Coleridge, Mary Robinson, and the prosody of dreams. *Dreaming, 7*(2), 119–140.

Wheeler, K. (1981). *The creative mind in Coleridge's poetry.* London: Heinemen.

Color in Dreams

Although many people report that they rarely dream in color, researchers have reported color in the range of 80 to 100 percent of the time in laboratory awakening of subjects from the rapid eye movement (REM) state or when the subject is specifically asked to record the colors in their dream reports immediately upon awakening (Murzyn, 2008; Schredl, 2008, p. 54; Van de Castle, 1994, p. 254). In contrast, spontaneous dream reports (those reported some time after awakening or without specific questioning about color) typically yield explicitly mentioned color in the range of only 11 to 46 percent of the time (Schredl, 2008, p. 54; Van de Castle, 1994, p. 254). Reports of dreaming in color versus black and white (a term often used inaccurately to describe no color recall) are largely a function of how and when the dream was recorded and the focus on recalling specific colors. Memory decline for dream content and color over time is the likely contributing factor.

Although the colors in dream reports typically follow the continuity hypothesis, reflecting the norms of waking perception (grass is typically green and the sky typically blue, for example), in a dream an image can take on any color. The perception of dream imagery is in part a product of the visual association cortex, which is highly active during REM sleep, as it forms connections (visual associations) with information generated from within. The combining, or condensation, of a dream image and its color appears to be a connection of associations represented by the image with associations represented by the color. Our conscious associations with color are usually personal in nature, coming from our experience (the beauty of green countryside), our learning (red relating to stop), our cultural influences (the flag), or our beliefs (blue in relation to spirit). The colors generated in our dreams can arise from these conscious associations. However, dream color may be dominated to a greater degree by unconscious factors— our human physiological and emotional response to color.

Studies by Robert Hoss (2010, p. 87) suggest that our human emotional associations with color are a dominant factor and that color in essence paints our dreams with emotion. Bob Van de Castle also hypothesizes that there is a strong correlation between the emotional significance of a dream and the intensity of the color appearing in it (Van de Castle, 1994, p. 255). Studies in the field of color psychology have shown color to evoke an emotional response as well as a physiological response in the autonomic nervous system, which occurs below our threshold of awareness (Lüscher, 1971, pp. 12–14). For example, red illumination has been shown to excite the autonomic nervous system and increase heart rate, muscular tension, and respiration. Blue has the opposite effect, reducing heart rate and respiration, calming both the brain and the body. Recent neurological studies during REM sleep have shown that many brain centers involved with the autonomic process are very active when we dream (Hobson, Pace-Schott, & Stickbold, 2003, pp. 1–50). The limbic system, or emotional brain, and particularly the amygdala, is notably active in REM and is thought to selectively process emotionally relevant memories as well as to orchestrate the dream plot (Dang-Vu, Schabus, Desseilles, Schwartz, & Marquet, 2007, p. 102). The amygdala plays a waking state role in associating sensory information it receives (which would include color) with emotion, and therefore is likely to continue to play a role in associating emotion with color in dream sleep. The recall of a specific color in a dream may have much to do with the intensity and emotional significance of that color and its ability to draw our attention.

Further evidence that the appearance of specific dream colors may have a physiological origin comes from a content analysis of explicitly named dream colors in a database of 38,063 spontaneously reported dreams (Hoss, 2010, p. 86). This study revealed that the most dominant colors recorded from the dreams were black and white (reported as colors) with a grouping of red, blue, green, and yellow being the next dominant (all nearly equal in frequency of occurrence, with red slightly higher). While variations within this pattern existed between individuals, this basic pattern appeared present within almost all individuals, as it did across large populations, whether male or female. This pattern was shown to have little relationship to the color mix that dominates our waking environment, nor to global surveys of favorite colors, nor to the influence of color media change over time, nor to the more random pattern that might be expected if dream color was based on learned or memory associations alone (Hoss, 2010, pp. 83–86). It is of interest that these colors are the same six that the opponent process theory attributes to the physiology of color perception in the brain (Hoss, 2010, p. 86), and the same four hues often termed the *psychological primaries* because of the human tendency to perceive them as primary. They also represent a pattern that psychologist Carl G. Jung observed in dreams and attributed to the four orienting functions or consciousness (Jung, 1972, pp. 48, 78). This alignment of dream color patterns with neurological or physiological mechanisms may be an indication that dream color is related to our subliminal human response to color and the emotional associations that accompany it—a well-known phenomenon in the field of color psychology, but only hypothesized as it applies to dreams.

Robert J. Hoss

See also: entries related to Dream Content

References

Birren, F. (1978). *Color and human response.* New York: John Wiley & Sons.

Dang-Vu, T., Schabus, M., Desseilles, M., Schwartz, S., & Marquet, P. (2007). Neuroimaging of REM sleep and dreaming. In D. Barret & P. McNamara (Eds.), *The new science of dreaming* (Vol. 1, pp. 95–114). Westport, CT: Praeger.

Hobson, J. A., Pace-Schott, E. F., & Stickbold, R. (2003). *Sleep and dreaming* (E. F. Pace-Schott, M. Solms, M. Blagrove, & S. Harnad, Eds.). New York: Cambridge University Press.

Hoss, Robert J. (2010). Content analysis on the potential significance of color in dreams: A preliminary investigation. *International Journal of Dream Research, 3*(1), 80–90.

Jung, C. G. (1972). *Mandala symbolism.* Princeton, NJ: Princeton University Press.

Lüscher, M. (1971). *The Lüscher color test* (I. Scott, Ed. & Trans.). New York: Random House.

Murzyn, E. (2008). Do we only dream in colour? A comparison of reported dream color in younger and older adults with different experiences of black and white media. *In Consciousness and cognition, 17*(4), 1228–37.

Schredl, M. (2008). Spontaneously reported colors in dreams: Correlations with attitude towards creativity, personality and memory. *Sleep and Hypnosis, 10*(2), 54–60.

Van de Castle, R.L. (1994). *Our dreaming mind*. New York: Ballantine Books.

Comics and Dreams

The comic strip (also known as sequential visual art) has several formal aspects that make it a medium particularly well suited for dream art. Dreams are primarily *visual* experiences; so, too, are comic strips. Anything that can be drawn, including bizarre imagery seen in dreams, can be included in a comic strip. Dreams are experiences unfolding in time, generally with a narrative structure, overt or implied. Comics are *sequential*; individual panels are combined to form sequences, suggesting narrative—though the narrative arc may be linear, nonlinear, or absent. Although the appearance of written text is rare in dreams, dream texts are the primary medium through which researchers, dreamworkers, and individual dream journalers are able to record and work with dreams. Comic strips can include *text*. Texts within a comic strip may advance the narrative, supply information not contained in the pictures, offer commentary, or contain something entirely different from what is happening in the images. Text can be incorporated into the images in the form of dialogue (in voice bubbles), thoughts (in thought bubbles), or even as part of the graphic imagery. Finally, much variation is possible within the sequential art form. Comics may consist of a single box or a lengthy sequence of panels. Panels may vary in size, shape, and arrangement on the page; complex connections and interactions between individual panels in a sequence can be established using graphic techniques; text may vary in length (including none at all) and placement and can include actual dream texts. All these possibilities allow the dream artist to develop a unique form for each strip that reflects and enhances the dream content.

The pioneering artist in the field of dream comics is undoubtedly Winsor McCay (1869–1934). In the early part of the 20th century, McCay drew two dream-based comic strips that are classics and have influenced comic artists ever since. *Dreams of the Rarebit Fiend* ran in newspapers from 1904 to 1913 and featured the dreams (often nightmares) of a rarebit fiend whose identity changed from one week to the next (Little Nemo, who was soon to star in his own strip, first appeared in *Rarebit Fiend*). Each strip always ended the same way, with the dreamer waking up and blaming his disturbing dream on something he had eaten—usually Welsh rarebit.

Little Nemo in Slumberland debuted in October 1905 and ran until July 1914. (McCay revived it briefly from 1924 to 1927.) Unlike *Rarebit Fiend*, which was intended for an adult audience, McCay wrote *Little Nemo* with children in mind. Nevertheless, Little Nemo's adventures in the dream world were often dark and disturbing. The format was consistent: each strip plunged the viewer right into the dream, which would often start mildly but become wilder as it went on, until, in the final panel, Nemo would wake to find himself in his own bed and realize he had been dreaming. McCay's expert draftsmanship and masterful ability to capture the look and feel of dreams reached their height in the Little Nemo strips, as is evident in such classics as the famous "Walking Bed" episode, in which Little Nemo's bed grows legs and takes him for a stroll above the rooftops.

From its roots in the work of Winsor McCay to the dream sequences in the *Zap Comix* of the 1960s to the contemporary graphic novel, the evolution of the comic strip into a serious art form has opened many possibilities for artists interested in dreams. Neil Gaiman's immensely popular *Sandman* series is based on dreams. Other notable artists creating dream comics, who collectively illustrate the wide variety of approaches that are possible, include Pierre-François Beauchard, a French artist who (under the name David B.) draws long, stylishly elegant accounts of his dreams; Canadian artist Julie Doucet, whose autobiographical strips exploring gender issues include many dreams and fantasies; Jesse Reklaw, whose short four-panel strips are based on dreams sent to him by readers; and Rick Veitch, who draws visually complex strips based on his own dream life.

Richard A. Russo

References

B., D. (2008). *Nocturnal conspiracies: Nineteen dreams from December 1979 to September 1994*. New York: NBM/ComicsLit.

Doucet, J. (1997). *My most secret desire*. Montreal: Drawn and Quarterly.

McCay, W. (2000). *Little Nemo 1905–1914*. Cologne: Taschen.

McCay, W. (2007). *Complete dream of the rarebit fiend 1904–1913*. Hohenstein-Ernsttal, Germany: Ulrich Merkl.

Reklaw, J. (2000). *Dreamtoons*. Boston, MA: Shambhala Publications.

Reklaw, J. (2011). *Slow wave*. Retrieved from http://www.slowwave.com/

Veitch, R. (1996). *The dream art of Rick Veitch, volume 1: Rabid eye*. West Townshend, VT: King Hell Press.

Comorbidity between Epilepsy and Sleep Disorders

The comorbidity between epilepsy and sleep disorders is poorly investigated in the literature and rarely taken into consideration by clinicians in general practice, in spite of its high prevalence and potential clinical (Manni & Terzaghi, 2010) and pathophysiological consequences (Shouse et al., 1990).

There is growing evidence about the coexistence between obstructive sleep apnoea (OSA) and epilepsy (in 10% of adult patients and 20% of children).

The differential diagnosis between epilepsy and sleep apnoea may be challenging.

Syncope induced by OSA, sleep apnoea–related cyanosis, and motor behavioral episodes upon awakening after apnoeas may all be misinterpreted as epileptic seizures. Analogously nocturnal frontal lobe epilepsy (NFLE) seizures and pure sleep-related tonic seizures were reportedly misinterpreted as apnoeas.

There are concerns of potential mutual detrimental effects between epilepsy and

OSA. Indeed, a high prevalence (up to 30%) of OSA was reported in drug-resistant epilepsy patients, while poor seizure control was documented in older epilepsy patients with OSA compared with age-matched patients without epilepsy.

OSA-induced hypoxemia, nocturnal sleep disruption with nonrapid eye movement (NREM) sleep fragmentation, and REM sleep decrease as well as increased daytime sleepiness are the most likely mechanisms by which OSA may facilitate interictal EEG epileptiform abnormalities (IEAs) and seizure occurrences.

Accordingly, continuous positive airway pressure (CPAP) treatment of epilepsy with OSA was found to reduce IEAs. Furthermore, CPAP treatment proved to significantly improve seizure control in epilepsy patients with OSA (Malow et al., 2008).

Patients with epilepsy plus OSA have recorded poorer cognitive performances than those with epilepsy only. In fact, permanent attention, planning, and spatial learning deficits were documented in OSA patients, reflecting structural changes in the frontal and prefrontal areas of the brain at conventional and functional neuroimaging.

A few lines of evidence indicate that CPAP treatment of OSA in epilepsy patients improves cognitive performance.

Seizure recurrence in itself was recently suggested to exacerbate OSA. In an adult patient with intractable epilepsy and co-morbid OSA, the left frontal lobe resection led to remission of the OSA and of the seizures, while a significant increase in the apnoea–hypopnoea index following a sleep-related seizure was documented in an epilepsy patient with mild OSA.

The mechanisms by which epileptic seizures may exacerbate sleep apnoea may relate to the effects induced by seizures on sleep structure or on respiration. Indeed, seizures can facilitate the occurrence of apnoeas by inducing sleep instability and facilitating NREM 1 and 2 sleep stages, during which apnoeas are more likely to occur. On the other hand, the occurrence of epileptic discharges over frontal and temporal lobes may be detrimental to sleep-disordered breathing, as experimental animal models have shown that electrical stimulation of these cerebral areas provokes respiratory arrest via the descending projections to the brain stem respiratory centers.

In addition, antiepileptic drugs may worsen OSA by blunting the reactivity of respiratory centers, reducing the upper airway tone and inducing weight gain, all factors that can adversely affect OSA.

Parasomnias and epileptic seizures may coexist in a subject, making the differential diagnosis particularly challenging (Bazil, 2004). In childhood, a frequent association between epilepsy and NREM arousal parasomnias, enuresis, and rhythmic movement disorder was documented.

A particular pattern of association was found between NFLE and NREM arousal parasomnias, which were reported in the personal or family history of up to one-third of NFLE patients (Bisulli et al., 2010).

As far as REM parasomnias are concerned, REM sleep behavior disorder, unrecognized or misdiagnosed, has been found to co-occur in 12 percent of elderly epilepsy patients.

Patients with epilepsy often complain of poor, nonrestorative sleep; however, insomnia in epilepsy is poorly investigated, with the literature giving conflicting prevalence figures and no information on the actual impact of this disorder on seizure control.

A greater awareness, among clinicians, of the comorbidities between sleep disorders and epilepsy may help to prevent misdiagnosis and mistreatment.

Raffaele Manni and Michele Terzaghi

See also: entries related to Sleep Disorders

References

Bazil, C. W. (2004). Nocturnal seizures. *Seminars in Neurology, 24,* 293–300.

Bisulli, F., Vignatelli, L., Naldi, I., Licchetta, L., Provini, F., Plazzi, G., . . . Tinuper, P. (2010). Increased frequency of arousal parasomnias in families with nocturnal frontal lobe epilepsy: A common mechanism? *Epilepsia, 51*(9), 1852–1860.

Malow, B. A., Foldvary-Schaefer, N., Vaughn, B. V., Selwa, L. M., Chervin, R. D., Weatherwax, K. J., . . . Song, Y. (2008). Treating obstructive sleep apnea in adults with epilepsy: A randomized pilot trial. *Neurology, 71,* 572–577.

Manni, R., & Terzaghi, M. (2010). Comorbidity between epilepsy and sleep disorders. *Epilepsy Research, 90*(3), 171–177.

Shouse, M. N., King, A., Langer, J., Wellesley, K., Vreeken, T., King, K., . . . Szymusiak, R. (1990). Basic mechanisms underlying seizure-prone and seizure-resistant sleep and awakening states in feline kindled and penicillin epilepsy. In J. A. Wada (Ed.), *Kindling 4* (pp. 313–327). New York: Plenum Press.

Comparative Sleep Databases

Evolutionary biologists recognize two main approaches to studying functions of behavioral traits, such as REM or NREM. One is to conduct experiments aimed at determining the benefits and costs of the behavior to the individual's fitness. The other approach is to use comparative analysis to examine how, and in association with which other traits, the behavior evolved—for it is only through comparison that general inferences about the evolution of a trait can be drawn. One important way in which the comparative approach has been pursued is via the compilation of databases that contain data on as many species as possible so as to make comparative inferences as valid as possible.

Sleep Quotas

The primary types of data typically entered into these comparative sleep databases consist of what have become known as sleep quotas. These are measures of the relative proportions of REM and NREM or of the *duration* (percentage time of total sleep spent in a given sleep state) of each of the two major mammalian sleep states. There are several lines of evidence that point to the fundamental importance of sleep quotas for an analysis of sleep state function. First, duration of REM and NREM sleep states appears to be regulated by separate sets of genes in mammals. For example, mouse strains C57BL and C57BR are associated with increased REM and short slow-wave sleep episodes, while BALB/c is associated with short REM and long NREM episodes. Second, deprivation of or restriction in the amount of REM or NREM sleep leads to a sleep debt, as manifested by sleep rebound effects after a deprivation period. The rebound is proportional to the amount of sleep lost during the deprivation period. Thus, the phenomenon of an incurred sleep debt implies that mammals need a certain *amount* of sleep in order to function properly. Third, sleep times for a given bout of a particular sleep state vary considerably across mammalian species from a low of about 15 minutes to a high of about 2 hours. Fourth, sustained reductions in sleep times for either of the two major sleep states result in significant and increasing impairment in fundamental physiological functions and eventual death—at least in lab rats. Fifth, sleep quotas are reliably associated with physiologically significant measures of mammalian biology, including immunocompetence. Sixth, major human disorders of sleep manifest as changes in sleep *amounts* with either too little (insomnia) or too much (excessive daytime sleepiness) sleep. Seventh, changes in amount of sleep predict clinically significant physiological and mental health dysfunction. Thus, sleep quotas appear to be reliable and meaningful indexes of sleep biology and clinically significant sleep disorders in humans.

Data Quality

One of the major problems associated with these comparative sleep databases is the quality of the data. Sleep quota data are invariably acquired in nonuniform contexts and with varying techniques. There are no data at all for many taxa and what data there are for the few species that have been studied in depth have been acquired with widely divergent techniques and methods. Exhaustive reviews of the literature demonstrate that daily sleep quotas have been obtained for approximately

148 taxa (species and genera) representing 18 orders, 56 families, and 148 species. All extant orders of mammalia are represented, with more than one data source available for many species. In order to gauge the quality of these data, each study needs to be evaluated along the following lines: Was sleep studied for a full 24 hours? There is no other sure way to get a complete picture of the daily sleep cycle in an animal unless you study the animal for a full 24-hour cycle. Ideally, the animal should have received a 24-hour electroencephalography (EEG) recording. Very few studies, however, meet this requirement for obvious reasons. It is technically difficult to record EEG for 24 hours. Another difficulty is that to do EEG recordings one typically needs to be in a laboratory, but lighting conditions in the lab make normal sleep near impossible for most animals. The constant nature of the lighting and its intensity also perturb biological rhythms, which in turn disturb the true sleep cycle. Thus, whenever possible, EEG recordings should be conducted under normal (for the animal) light–dark schedules. Another problem is the artificiality of the lab environment. Animals are adapted for the wild, not the lab, so their behavior changes dramatically in the lab. Until the animal is adapted to the lab so that his fear subsides and his physiology stabilizes, no EEG studies can be trusted to measure the typical sleep pattern. Thus EEG sleep studies should be conducted only after the animal is adapted to the lab and recording procedure. The period of adaptation varies tremendously across species with some species not able to adapt to the lab at all. Another problem introduced via the choice

to study the animal in the lab is the animal's diet. Typically, the diet differs dramatically from what the animal eats in the wild. Food is also very often restricted in the lab. When attempting to obtain valid sleep quotas from an animal, it should not be starved or fattened up. Instead, it should be given a diet that matches as closely as possible its diet in the wild. Sleep is also affected by ambient temperature. The lab typically is maintained at temperatures that are not typical for the animal. Thus, before recording EEG sleep measures, the investigator should attempt to approximate normal ambient temperature (normal for the animal). Perhaps, the most important data-quality problem produced by recording in the lab is that animals are sometimes restrained in order to obtain recordings. This restraint of course dramatically influences brain functions and EEG recordings. Investigators therefore need to describe the degree and type of restraint they used when reporting sleep quotas and whenever possible record sleep under nonrestrained conditions. A final data-quality problem for comparative sleep studies is that most investigators fail to report behavioral sleep data. Does the animal lie down in a recumbent position when sleeping? Is there REM-related paralysis? Are there REM-related penile erections? What about autonomic nervous system signs? All of these behavioral data help to differentiate sleep expression across species. Studies on data quality of extant comparative sleep databases tend to demonstrate that data quality is a serious issue but not a fatal shortcoming. Clearly, studying sleep in the lab needs to be supplemented with studies of sleep in the wild.

Laboratory-Obtained Sleep Values versus Sleep Values Obtained in the Wild

Are lab-obtained sleep values representative of sleep processes that occur in the wild or of sleep values obtained under more natural conditions? The consensus among sleep scientists seems to be that sleep values obtained in the lab represent the animal's maximum capacity for sleep. When sleep values obtained in the lab are compared to values obtained in the wild for the same species, the lab-obtained values are reasonably close to the values obtained in the wild, though they are typically slightly longer than those obtained in the wild. Thus, lab-obtained values are predictably related to the animal's natural sleep processes. The crucial condition for obtaining valid, nonarbitrary, and representative values is that lab conditions approximate (in terms of light–dark schedules, ambient temperature, diet, etc.) natural conditions for the animal in question. Most importantly, *the animal needs to be adapted to the lab and recording procedures before sleep recordings are made*. Analysis of existing studies suggests that adaptation to the lab before doing EEG recording was and is a standard, so this major data-quality issue is less threatening than originally assumed. The majority of available studies on sleep quotas in animals satisfy these criteria (i.e., lab recording procedures approximate natural conditions for the animal and recordings are virtually never conducted until the animal is adapted to the lab). Thus, we can be confident that available data obtained in the lab on sleep quota variation in mammals are often, though not invariably, reasonably representative of sleep variation in the wild. In addition, comparative sleep databases should whenever possible use data collected in the wild or natural conditions. This will typically entail the use of studies that utilized telemetry to measure sleep architecture and sleep times. Data from telemetric recordings obtained under natural conditions are available for a number of species (e.g., opossums, hedgehogs, baboons, lemurs, chimpanzees, rats, and rock and tree hyraxes). Telemetric techniques have also been used to study sleep of a number of marine mammals that were allowed to swim freely while recording was conducted. Despite the fact that lab-obtained sleep values (assuming values obtained after adaptation to lab procedures) do not appear to grossly distort natural sleep values, it is probably not the case that this is true of all animals. As mentioned previously, some animals never fully adapt to the lab.

Statistical Analyses of Comparative Sleep Expression

Once a comparative sleep database is assembled, the data need to be analyzed. A large proportion of the variance in comparative biological variables is commonly associated with two factors: body size and phylogeny. Allometry is the study of *how a trait scales with body size*. Previous studies of sleep quotas have found negative correlations with body size, but little attention has been paid to establishing quantitative scaling relationships, despite the fact that regularities in these relationships may be important for understanding sleep variation in general.

The other issue that needs to be controlled is phylogeny or relations between species due to evolutionary descent. There are recently developed methods to quantify phylogenetic signal that use maximum likelihood and phylogenetic simulation. These methods are available in stand-alone computer programs that allow the investigator to reconstruct ancestral states, character polarity, and convergence, all standard evolutionary techniques.

One purpose of the comparative method is to reveal how biological traits such as sleep have evolved. Thus, we are interested in whether particular sleep traits have evolved together with various functional measures such as aspects of physiology, immunity, brain anatomy, ontogeny, behavior, ecology, and maternal investment. Modern comparative methods allow one to reconstruct the evolution of traits, such as sleep quotas, by mapping trait variation among extant species onto their phylogenetic relationships (established from DNA and fossil studies). With such information, it becomes possible to test whether the evolution of one trait is statistically correlated with the evolution of another trait.

In past comparative studies of sleep quotas, researchers treated values for individual species as independent data points, without using any explicit evolutionary model. Implicitly, such analyses assume that the evolution of all species in the data set has come about from an equidistant common ancestor, as represented by a star phylogeny, but this of course is an error. To investigate correlated evolution in a phylogenetic framework, investigators can apply methods based on independent contrasts. The method of independent contrasts calculates evolutionary change as differences in trait values between pairs of species (or higher nodes) in a phylogeny. By calculating nested comparisons up the tree, these differences are, by definition, statistically independent of one another. A test using independent contrasts therefore addresses the question, does evolutionary change in trait X_1 correlate with evolutionary change in X_2? It is possible to assess the effects of multiple independent variables using independent contrasts.

In order to carry out these analyses, the investigator first needs to develop a tree or a phylogeny for the species in his data set. Much work has already been done in producing detailed and suitable phylogenies of specific mammalian groups and on relationships among mammalian orders, and these data are available in various forms and in various phylogenetic software packages. But trees still need to be tailor-made to some extent to fit the particular data set you are working with. Output values from phylogenetic methods such as independent contrasts can be analyzed by standard statistical methods, such as linear correlation and regression, subject to satisfying evolutionary and statistical assumptions.

Patrick McNamara

See also: entries related to Evolution of Sleep

Comparative Sleep Regulation

Many studies have addressed the large variation of sleep duration between mammalian species, and more recently also in birds. This variability has led to much speculation regarding the function of sleep (e.g., Siegel, 2011). A more promising avenue toward the understanding of sleep function is the recognition that sleep is strictly regulated by its duration and intensity. Sleep is typically defined as a homeostatically regulated, easily reversible state of sustained quiescence accompanied by reduced sensory responsiveness. This is a useful definition because it can be applied to a broad diversity of species, including species whose brain activity cannot be compared to the mammalian electroencephalogram (EEG).

The term *sleep homeostasis* was coined in 1980 by Alexander Borbély on the basis of studies in rats. He observed that their sleep propensity is maintained within a certain range (reviewed in Achermann & Borbély, 2011, p. 37). This sleep-regulatory system enables organisms, including humans, to compensate for the loss of sleep or surplus sleep: a sleep deficit leads to a predictable increase in sleep intensity and duration of subsequent sleep, whereas excess sleep has the opposite effect. Thus, deviation in either direction leads to a compensatory response.

EEG slow-wave activity, that is, EEG power in the range of 0.25 to 4.0 Hz in nonrapid eye movement (NREM) sleep is the most important correlate of sleep intensity. Historically, the early experiments of Blake and Gerard (1937) in human subjects showed that across the sleep episode slow waves in sleep decline progressively, in parallel with the arousal. Subsequently, a slow wave–dependent arousal threshold was published for the rat (reviewed in Tobler, 2011, p. 10).

Since the timing and duration of sleep and wakefulness behavior are regulated within the relatively strict boundaries set by the circadian clock, the intensity dimension of sleep provides larger response flexibility to deviations. Interestingly, in dolphins, which engage in deep sleep for several hours only with one hemisphere at a time, while the other hemisphere shows a wakefulness EEG pattern, sleep loss is also compensated preferentially in the hemisphere that was sleep deprived, indicating a local need for recovery.

The relative independence of sleep homeostasis from the circadian clock was shown in rats whose circadian organization of the sleep–wake cycle had been disrupted and which still showed a compensatory increase in slow waves during recovery from sleep deprivation. Guinea pigs, which have only a weak circadian sleep–wake rhythm, confirmed this independence by compensating for sleep deprivation with the same amount of slow waves, independently of the timing of the sleep deprivation. Recent studies identified the neuronal correlate of EEG slow waves in NREM sleep of the rat, but the mechanisms leading to the intensity increase after sleep deprivation are still not fully understood (Vyazovskiy et al., 2009).

A further correlate of sleep intensity was found in the rat and in several mouse strains: the number of brief awakenings within the sleep period, a measure of sleep continuity, increases when slow waves diminish in the course of the main sleep period or after sleep deprivation when the drive for sleep dissipates (Franken, Dijk, Tobler, & Borbély, 1991).

Species, including mammals, birds, reptiles, fish, and invertebrates, such as cockroaches, scorpions, honeybees, and Drosophila, respond to changes in sleep drive attained by sleep deprivation, by homeostatic regulatory mechanisms. In birds, a homeostatic increase in EEG slow waves was found in pigeons and sparrows, but a correlation between arousal threshold to stimuli and the amount of EEG slow waves is still lacking. Investigations of the effects of sleep deprivation in amphibians are lacking and a correlation between sleeplike behavior and changes in arousal threshold is not established, whereas in perch, disturbance of their sleeplike state by exposure to constant light elicited compensation of resting behavior during recovery, depending on the duration of previous light exposure, confirming the presence of sleep homeostatic mechanisms in the lowest vertebrate.

The definition of sleep in invertebrates includes a minimum duration of quiescence, which correlates with a lowering of the arousal threshold, and a homeostatic component consisting of an increase in the amount and continuity of sleep. Because sleep in mammals is a very complex behavior, the definition and identification of sleep in invertebrates was an important step enabling sleep research in simpler models. Especially, sleep research in the fruit fly Drosophila has complemented research in laboratory mice in identifying genes underlying sleep duration and sleep homeostasis.

Adverse circumstances can hinder an animal to rest at the species-appropriate circadian time. Therefore, sleep may have evolved from rest behavior by allowing organisms to recover more quickly from a period of wakefulness by intensifying biological processes during sleep.

Irene Tobler

See also: entries related to Evolution of Sleep

References

Achermann, P., & Borbély, A. A. (2011). Sleep homeostasis and models of sleep regulation. In M. H. Kryger, T. Roth, & W. C. Dement (Eds.), *Principles and practice of sleep medicine* (pp. 431–444). Philadelphia: Saunders.

Blake, H., & Gerard, R. W. (1937). Brain potentials during sleep. *American Journal of Physiology*, 119, 1937, 692–703.

Franken, P., Dijk, D.-J., Tobler, I., & Borbély, A. A. (1991). Sleep deprivation in rats: Effects on EEG power spectra, vigilance states, and cortical temperature. *American Journal of Physiology, 261*, R198–R208.

Siegel, J. M. (2011). Sleep in animals: A state of adaptive inactivity. In M. H. Kryger, T. Roth, & W. C. Dement (Eds.), *Principles and practice of sleep medicine* (pp. 112–123). Philadelphia: Saunders.

Tobler, I. (2011). Phylogeny of sleep regulation. In M. H. Kryger, T. Roth, & W. C. Dement (Eds.), *Principles and practice of sleep medicine* (pp. 126–138). Philadelphia: Saunders.

Vyazovskiy, V. V., Olcese, U., Lazimy, Y. M., Faraguna, U., Esser, S. K., Williams, J. C., . . . Tononi, G. (2009). Cortical firing and sleep homeostasis. *Neuron, 63*, 865–878.

Conceptions of Dreaming in the Western Desert of Australia

Numerous anthropological writings have stressed the fundamental role played by dreams in Australian Aboriginal life, thought, and cultural creation. Classic studies in the field have furthermore underlined the intimate relationships between the realm of dreams and that of the ancestral and cosmological order, the latter being translated as the dreamtime (Spencer & Gillen, 1927) or the dreaming (Stanner, 1956). Given the structurally distinct levels of reality that the two realms represent in aboriginal thought, they are not to be confused; there is nonetheless a clear ontological continuity between them. In Aboriginal Australia, dreams have a strong spiritual potential. Dream experiences and narratives also have a deeply embedded social dimension; they are valued as acts of communication and exchange and as a barometer of the state of the relationships among humans, the land, and the socio-cosmic environment. Dreaming, as a mode of experience, is an inherent part of aboriginal theories of human action in the world.

In the local dream theories of the Western Desert, a dream occurs when, while asleep, one's spirit, which is associated with the abdominal-umbilical area, leaves the body to pursue various experiences and encounters, thus becoming capable of acquiring knowledge. Dreams are often portrayed as a voyage, a journey of one's spirit out of the body. The spirit is associated with cognition, volition, and the expression of emotions, and the abdominal area, in turn, is the seat of emotion and spiritual (and curative) power. Western Desert Aborigines thus draw a close relationship among dream experiences, knowledge, understanding, emotion, well-being, and strength (spiritual power).

Dreams are regularly shared, usually between relatives. In this oral tradition, dream narratives have, among other things, an entertaining and aesthetic value: simply put, Aborigines enjoy hearing (and telling) a good story. Dream narratives usually begin by specifying temporal and spatial references; that is, when and where the dream actually occurred. Dreams are shared whenever the dreamer considers that his or her dream might be capable of providing information about past, current, or future events that may concern either himself or herself, his or her close relatives, the community, or significant sites on the ancestral territory. Even a dream that has left a negative or frightening impression on the dreamer might, upon awakening, be viewed positively for its informative, curative, or aesthetic value or potential. It is usually the role of elders—men and women well versed in ritual matters—to evaluate the meaning of dreams that leave a strong impression.

In the Western Desert, dream interpretation is flexible and open to multiple readings, depending on current events and contextual variables, and on the impression made on the dreamer by the dream. Dreams and dreaming are also considered as a prelude to significant or peculiar events (births, deaths, accidents, etc.), even though they might only be recalled and interpreted afterward. For example, in local theories of conception, a dream is necessary to validate the passage of a soon-to-be-born child (spirit-child) from the ancestral to the human realm. For the Aborigines, the dream realm plays a role in the unfolding of an emergent reality; they recognize the primacy of the activity of dreaming over dream content or dreams as simple objects.

Western Desert Aborigines value the relational, mediating, and communicative potential of dreams among human, non-human, and ancestral components of the world. Dream experiences are indeed considered to be the space–time par excellence for communication between humans and ancestral beings, and between humans and the spirits of the dead. It is likewise through the medium of dreams that the ancestral beings or dead relatives reveal new mythical and ritual elements to humans, which then contribute to enrich existing forms (Dussart, 2000). The Aborigines consider that all sacred knowledge comes from such revelatory dreams.

More research is needed in this rich field of investigation. A few possible avenues of inquiries would be dreaming as a mode of knowing and relating, the interactions between human and nonhuman agencies in the dream realm, and the place of dream inspiration in contemporary aboriginal art forms.

Sylvie Poirier

References

Dussart, F. (2000). *The politics of ritual in an aboriginal settlement: Kinship, gender, and the currency of knowledge.* Washington, DC: Smithsonian Institution Press.

Poirier, S. (2005). *A world of relationships: Itineraries, dreams, and events in the Australian Western Desert.* Toronto: Toronto University Press.

Spencer, B., & Gillen, F. (1927). *The Arunta.* London: Macmillan.

Stanner, W.E.H. (1956). The dreaming. In T.A.G. Hungerford (Ed.), *Australian signpost* (pp. 55–56). Melbourne: F.W. Cheshire.

Connection between Dreams and Mood, The

The link between dream images and the dreamer's mood stems from the continuity hypothesis of dreaming (Hall & Nordby, 1972), which states that dreams reflect one's waking-day life. Research examining the connection between dreams and mood has connected the two to specific dream imagery and has revealed the important relationship between mood disorders and dreams.

It has been found that waking-day mood and dreams are clearly connected when measuring mood with the Profile of Mood States (Shacham, 1983). It was found that people high in depression/dejection were also high in dream imagery of sadness, anger, aggressive acts, and aggression toward the dreamer (King & DeCicco, 2007). Those high in tension/anxiety, depression/dejection, anger/hostility, confusion/bewilderment, and total mood disturbance were also high in dream imagery of body parts (King & DeCicco, 2007). Total mood disturbance was also correlated with characters, human characters, and familiar characters. These findings suggest that higher levels of mood disturbance in waking day are reflected in specific dream images.

Research has extended these findings to the dreams of depressed individuals. It has been shown that higher levels of depression in waking day are related to more sadness, anger, aggressive acts, and aggression (King & DeCicco, 2007) in dreams. Previous findings also report higher levels of masochism, negative effect, and aggression in the dreams of depressed individuals (Bears, Cartwright, & Mercer, 2000; Cartwright, 1991; Schredl & Engelhardt, 2001). Similarly, anxiety has also been found to be related to dreams and dream imagery.

Research has found that dreams can cause anxiety or what is better known as anxiety dreams (Nejad, Sanatinia, & Yousofi, 2004). Few studies, however, have looked at the relationship between measures of waking anxiety and dream images.

One study found a significant relationship between general trait anxiety and the number of anxiety dreams children reported (Schredl, Pallmer, & Montasser, 1996). More currently, studies have looked at the relationship between waking-day anxiety scores and dream content (DeCicco, 2010; Jones & DeCicco, 2009). These studies have found those high in anxiety have more animal imagery, apprehension, body parts, and more scene changes in dreams. These findings are consistent with previous research where animals and apprehension/fear are correlated in dreams (DeCicco, 2007) and also, body parts and scene changes were correlated with total mood disturbance in waking day (King & DeCicco, 2007).

The relationship between mood and dreams is also illustrated with psychological disorders that have a mood component, such as addictions. Research has found very important connections between mood and addictions (Enoch & Goldman, 2002; Tice, Bratslavsky, & Baumeister, 2001) and between dreams and addictions (Choi, 1973; Christo & Franey, 1996; Denzin, 1988; Flowers & Zweben, 1998).

The connection between mood and addiction is particularly important as research has shown that addictions are related to negative mood and to psychiatric mood disorders (Santora & Hutton, 2008). Findings also show that people high in negative affect have higher rates of negative dream imagery (e.g., aggression, failures, misfortunes, etc.) (King & DeCicco, 2007), which can also include nightmares and sleep disturbance. Recent findings reveal that recovering alcoholics have more total emotions and characters than nonalcoholics (DeCicco &

Higgins, 2009) and recovering alcoholics are significantly higher in total mood disturbance than nonalcoholics (DeCicco & Higgins, 2009). This study also found that dream interpretation by recovering alcoholics leads to significant insights relating to waking-day mood and to sobriety. This makes dream interpretation a very useful tool for the treatment of alcohol addiction.

The relationship between mood and dreams has been found to reflect the waking-day mood and life situations of the dreamer, which confirms the continuity hypothesis of dreaming. Furthermore, mood and dream content have been shown to be clearly related. The more current investigations among dream content, dream interpretation, and mood have also shown that important waking-day insights regarding mood can be gained from the process. All these findings have revealed the important connection among dream imagery, dream moods, and the waking-day mood of the dreamer.

Teresa L. DeCicco

References

Bears, M., Cartwright, R., & Mercer, P. (2000). Masochistic dreams: A gender-related diathesis for depression revisited. *Dreaming, 10*, 211–219.

Cartwright, R. D. (1991). Dreams that work: The relation of dream incorporation to adaptation to stressful events. *Dreaming, 1*, 3–9.

Choi, S. Y. (1973). Dreams as a prognostic factor in alcoholism. *American Journal of Psychiatry, 130*(6), 699–702.

Christo, G., & Franey, C. (1996). Addicts' drug-related dreams: Their frequency and relationship to six-month outcomes. *Substance Use & Misuse, 21*(1), 1–15.

DeCicco, T. L. (2007). Dreams of female university students: Content analysis and relationship to discovery via the Ullman method. *Dreaming, 17*(2), 98–112.

DeCicco, T. L. (2010). Unpublished raw data.

DeCicco, T. L., & Higgins, H. (2009). The dreams of recovering alcoholics: Mood, dream content, discovery, and the storytelling method of dream interpretation. International *Journal of Dream Research, 2*(2), 45–51.

Denzin, N. K. (1988). Alcoholic dreams. *Alcoholism Treatment Quarterly, 5*(1/2), 133–138.

Enoch, M., & Goldman, D. (2002). Problem drinking and alcoholism: Diagnosis and treatment. *American Family Physician, 65*(3), 441–448.

Flowers, L., & Zweben, J. (1998). The changing role of 'using' dreams in addiction recovery. *Journal of Substance Abuse Treatment, 22*, 193–200.

Hall, C. S., & Nordby, V. J. (1972). *The individual and his dreams*. New York: Signet.

Jones, E., & DeCicco, T. L. (2009). Differentiating anxiety and depression using the storytelling method of dream interpretation and content analysis. Paper presentation at the 26th Annual Conference of the International Association for the Study of Dreams, Chicago, IL.

King, D. B., & DeCicco, T. L. (2007). The relationship among dream content, physical health, mood and self-construal. *Dreaming, 17*(3), 127–139.

Nejad, A. G., Sanatinia, R. Z., & Yousofi, K. (2004). Dream contents in patients with major depressive disorder. *The Canadian Journal of Psychiatry, 49*(12), 864–865.

Santora, P., & Hutton, H. (2008). Longitudinal trends in hospital discharges with co-occurring alcohol/drug diagnoses. *Journal of Substance Treatment, 35*, 1–12.

Schredl, M., & Engelhardt, H. (2001). Dreaming and psychopathology: Dream recall and dream content of psychiatric patients. *Sleep and Hypnosis, 3*, 44–45.

Schredl, M., Pallmer, R., & Montasser, A. (1996). Anxiety dreams in school-aged children. *Dreaming, 6*, 265–270.

Shacham, S. (1983). A shortened version of the profile of mood states. *Journal of Personality Assessment, 47*, 305–306.

Tice, M., Bratslavsky, E., & Baumeister, R. F. (2001). Emotional distress regulation takes precedence over impulse control: If you feel bad, do it! *Journal of Personality and Social Psychology, 80*(1), 53–67.

Consciousness in Dreams

What Do We Mean by Dream Consciousness

Dream consciousness is the quality and type of awareness experienced by an individual while asleep and dreaming. Like wake consciousness, dream consciousness incorporates varying levels of thought, feelings, and awareness of one's existence/experience, sensations, thoughts, surroundings, and so on. Consciousness both when awake and when dreaming reflects and is influenced by one's history, experience, and relationships.

It was once believed that during sleep we become unconscious, because when asleep we are (generally) not aware of the fact that our physical body is in bed and sleeping, and instead we accept the dream experience as the total and unquestioned reality. However, we now know that the dreaming mind is a great deal conscious and thinks much the same way as the waking mind does—however, within an often bizarre or altered environment. For example, one may dream of talking animals, interacting with deceased relatives, or flying high above the trees. But within these bizarre scenarios, the mind thinks, questions, reasons, reflects, and remembers (however, imperfectly by waking standards), in much the same way as during the day.

Dream consciousness can be seen as one state of consciousness along the spectrum of types of thinking accessible to people, awake and asleep, including logical directed thought, looser states of less-directed thinking, mind wandering or daydreaming, dreaming while asleep, and lucid dreaming, a unique state that allows us to experience dream and wake consciousness simultaneously.

Brain Basis of Dream Consciousness

Each state of consciousness is defined by alterations in brain chemistry and neuronal activity within and between specific regions of the brain. An alteration in brain chemistry occurs in the rapid eye movement (REM) stage of sleep. For one, the chemical balance of cholinergic and aminergic neuromodulators changes such that two of the neuromodulatory systems completely shut down—specifically, the locus coeruleus neurons and the dorsal raphe nucleus neurons, which, respectively, house norepinephrine and serotonin (Hobson, Pace-Schott, & Stickgold, 2000). These neuromodulators affect cognitive function, mood, attention, the ability to retrieve memories, and the ability to pay attention; their absence results in a reduced ability to direct the flow of the dream, to retrieve episodic memories, and to recognize implausibility (Kahn & Hobson, 2004).

In this REM stage, there is also reactivation of the limbic, paralimbic, and amygdala regions that had shut down in the early non-REM stages of sleep. The limbic, paralimbic, and amygdala areas are important for producing emotion, and hence, dreaming consciousness is often emotional. The medial prefrontal cortex, important for eliciting internally motivated behavior, is also reactivated; this reactivation contributes to the internally generated feelings and imagery of dream consciousness (Braun et al., 1997, 1998; Maquet et al., 1996; Nofzinger, Mintun, Wiseman, Kupfer, & Moore, 1997).

On the other hand, the dorsal lateral prefrontal cortex, a brain region important for executive decision making and for accurate autobiographical memory recall, remains deactivated in REM. Autobiographical memories that occur during dreaming may, therefore, not be accurate and remain so in the unfolding dream scenario.

What Are We Aware of in Dream Consciousness?

In dream consciousness, we are aware of many of the same things as when awake. Thoughts, feelings, and responses to dream events are strikingly familiar to the thoughts and responses of similar wake events, but there are significant differences, too. We are not generally aware of the location of our physical bodies when asleep, although we do develop, in many cases, a highly attuned awareness of our dream body.

We are not aware, by and large, of sensory stimuli in the environment of our sleeping body but are very aware of internal visual imagery and feelings as well as some distinct smells, sounds, and sensations in the dream environment.

REM sleep may also enhance other kinds of thinking, such as creativity and problem solving when awake. For example, studies have demonstrated that after a nap that contained REM there is a greater ability to solve problems requiring creative insight and there is an enhanced ability to make unusual associations (Cai, Mednick, Harrison, Kanady, & Mednick, 2009; Walker, Liston, Hobson, & Stickgold, 2002). We might say that consciousness in dreams adds to the consciousness we have in waking by giving us the awareness of things, events, and possibilities we do not, and often cannot, experience when awake.

Importantly, consciousness in dreams adds something entirely new and unique by allowing us to experience what we cannot when we have only our wake consciousness present (Kahn & Gover, 2010).

David Kahn and Tzivia Gover

References

Braun, A.R., Balkin, T.J., Wesensten, N.J., Carson, R.E., Varga, M., Baldwin, P., . . . Herscovitch, P. (1997). Regional cerebral blood flow throughout the sleep–wake cycle. *Brain, 120*, 1173–1197.

Braun, A.R., Balkin, T.J., Wesensten, N.J., Gwadry, F., Carson, R.E., Varga, M., . . . Herscovitch, P. (1998). Dissociated pattern of activity in visual cortices and their projections during human rapid eye-movement sleep. *Science, 279*, 91–95.

Cai, D.J., Mednick, S.A., Harrison, E.M., Kanady, J.C., & Mednick, S.C. (2009). REM, not incubation improves creativity by priming associative networks. *PNAS, 106*(25), 10130–10134.

Hobson, J.A., Pace-Schott, E.F., & Stickgold, R. (2000). Dreaming and the brain:

Toward a cognitive neuroscience of conscious states. *Behavioral and Brain Sciences, 23*(6), 793–842.

Kahn, D., & Gover, T. (2010). Consciousness in dreams. *International Review of Neurobiology, 92*, 181–195.

Kahn, D., & Hobson, J. A. (2004). State-dependent thinking: A comparison of waking and dreaming thought. *Consciousness and Cognition, 14*, 429–439.

Maquet, P., Peteres, J. M., Aerts, J., Delfiore, G., Degueldre, C., Luxen, A., & Franck, G. (1996). Functional neuroanatomy of human rapid-eye-movement sleep and dreaming. *Nature, 383*, 163.

Nofzinger, E. A., Mintun, M. A., Wiseman, M. B., Kupfer, D. J., & Moore, R. Y. (1997). Forebrain activation in REM sleep: An FDG PET study. *Brain Research, 770*, 192–201.

Voss, U., Holzmann, R., Tuin, I., & Hobson, J. A. (2009). Lucid dreaming: A state of consciousness with features of both waking and non-lucid dreaming. *Sleep, 32*(9), 1191–11200.

Walker, M. P., Liston, C., Hobson, J. A., & Stickgold, R. (2002). Cognitive flexibility across the sleep–wake cycle: REM-sleep enhancement of anagram problem solving. *Cognitive Brain Research, 14*, 317–324.

Contemporary Theory of Dreaming, The

The contemporary theory of dreaming, developed by Ernest Hartmann and his collaborators in a number of publications between 2000 and 2010, describes the nature and possible functions of dreaming.

The wording of the contemporary theory has varied slightly, depending on the emphasis of a specific publication, but the essentials have not changed. What follows is the latest version, from Hartmann (2010).

1. *Dreaming is a form of mental functioning.* It is not an alien intrusion, not material in a foreign language, and not separable from our other mental functioning. It is one end of a continuum of mental functioning (which means chiefly cerebral cortical functioning) running from focused waking thought at one end, through fantasy, daydreaming, and reverie to dreaming at the other end.

2. *Dreaming is hyperconnective.* At the dreaming end of the continuum, connections are made more easily than in waking, and connections are made more broadly and loosely. Dreaming avoids tightly structured, over-learned material. (We hardly ever dream of reading, writing, arithmetic.) Dreaming always involves new connections: dreaming is creation, not replay.

3. *The connections are not made randomly.* They are guided by the emotions of the dreamer. The dream, and especially the central image (CI) of the dream, pictures the dreamer's emotion or emotional concerns. The more powerful the emotion, the more powerful (intense) is the CI.

4. *The form or language of dreams is mainly picture metaphor.* But this is not a language restricted to dreaming. It is the way things are expressed toward the right-hand end of the continuum. At this end of the continuum, there is less serial processing, less task orientation, less functioning by formal rules, less constraint. The system relaxes into a default mode, functioning by similarity (metaphor), rather than formal rules, guided by whatever emotions or emotional concerns are present.

5. *Functions of dreaming.* This making of broad connections guided by emotion has an adaptive function, which we conceptualize as weaving in new material—taking new experiences and gradually connecting them, integrating them, into existing memory systems. In other words, the dream helps us to

build and rebuild a meaningful emotional memory system, which is the basis of our individual selves. This primary function occurs whether or not a dream is remembered. When a dream is remembered, the broad connections can also be adaptive in increasing self-knowledge and producing new insights and creations.

6. *Function of the continuum*. In addition to the functions of dreaming (stated previously), the entire focused waking-to-dreaming continuum has an adaptive function. It is obviously useful for us to be able to think in direct, focused, serial fashion at certain times, and at other times to associate more broadly and loosely—in other words, to daydream and to dream.

There is a great deal of research supporting the contemporary theory of dreaming, especially psychological research on many series of dreams after traumatic events and at other times. These support especially the tenets of the theory involving the CI of the dream as influenced by the dreamers' underlying emotion. Among the clearest findings are those from a systematic study of 880 dreams before versus after September 11, 2001. The dreams after September 11, a time of increased stress or emotional arousal, showed higher CI intensity (using a reliable measure). This difference was highly significant, whereas all other measures tested (length of dream, dream likeness, vividness, presence of towers, planes, etc.) showed no significant differences. There was also a shift in emotions pictured toward more fear/terror and helplessness/vulnerability.

The contemporary theory of dreaming is not based directly on brain studies, but it is consistent with all current studies of the brain, including PET and fMRI studies of REM sleep (when most but not all dreaming occurs) and of the default network underlying reverie and daydreaming.

Ernest Hartmann

See also: entries related to Dream Theories

Reference

Hartmann, E. (2010). *The nature and functions of dreaming*. New York: Oxford University Press.

Content Analysis of Dreams: Basic Principles

Dream content analysis is one of the basic methods applied in psychological dream research (Schredl, 2010). This method has the advantage that it suffices the common criteria of science such as possible replication by another research group, assessment of reliability and validity, and minimizing experimenter bias. The aim is to quantify particular aspects of the dream report, for example, bizarreness or emotional intensity, in order to carry out statistical analyses (Hall & Van de Castle, 1966).

The procedure of carrying out a dream content analytic study is as follows. First, specific hypotheses, for example, increased rejection rate in dreams of patients with depression, should be formulated to reduce expenditure and to increase statistical power because one needs not to correct for multiple testing. The next step is to select an existing scale (see Winget & Kramer, 1979), using a dream manual (e.g., Hall & Van de Castle, 1966) or developing a new scale depending on the study's hypotheses. The coding rules of the new scale should be as explicit as possible and—very important—developed before reading the study's dream material. Next, it should be very carefully documented how dream reports were elicited since the type of dream report (lab dreams, diary dreams, dreams from therapeutic sessions, etc.) used for the analysis might have a strong effect on the findings. For example, laboratory dreams are often less emotional than diary dreams or most recent dreams and they include very often laboratory references (Schredl, 2008). After the dream reports were collected, they usually were typed to facilitate blind rating and presented in randomized order. All information not reflecting the dream experience such as "I dreamed of my uncle whom I saw the day before" should be removed so the judges are not distracted by irrelevant information. The data has to be analyzed very carefully to avoid problems such as dependent observations due to multiple dreams per participant (statistical dependency) or multiple testing. For the interpretation of the results, the reliability and validity of the applied scales should be taken into account.

The reliability coefficient is determined as measures of correspondence between different judges, that is, two or more judges rate the same dreams and—according to the scales' measurement levels—coefficients of exact agreement, Spearman rank correlations, or Pearson correlations can be computed. Often, exact agreements exceed 80 or 90 percent, and correlation coefficients above 0.6 were reported (Schredl, Burchert, & Grabatin, 2004). However, guidelines or cutoff values classifying good and poor reliability do not exist in dream research. The problem of validity cannot be handled as easily as the reliability issue. Many rating systems (Hall & Van de Castle, 1966) rely on the so-called face validity, that is, one sees that the scale is measuring for what it has been constructed. However, the major validity problem arises because analyzed dream reports are more or less detailed reflections of the actual dream experience. Analyzing 133 dream reports, Schredl and Doll (1998) clearly demonstrated an underestimation of dream emotions if only explicitly mentioned emotions are measured; a good deal of information got lost because describing a dream with all its details is impossible.

To summarize, quantitative dream research relies on the dream content analytic method. Distinct differences in dreams of men and women have been shown in a variety of studies using different types of dream reports (Schredl, 2007). It is important to keep the methodological problems such as reliability, validity, multiple testing, and so on in mind to obtain a profound database on dream content.

Michael Schredl

See also: entries related to Dream Content

References

Hall, C. S., & Van de Castle, R. L. (1966). *The content analysis of dreams.* New York: Appleton-Century-Crofts.

Schredl, M. (2007). Gender differences in dreaming. In D. Barrett & P. McNamara (Eds.), *The new science of dreaming—Volume 2: Content, recall, and personality correlates* (pp. 29–47). Westport, CT: Praeger.

Schredl, M. (2008). Laboratory references in dreams: Methodological problem and/or evidence for the continuity hypothesis of dreaming? *International Journal of Dream Research, 1*, 3–6.

Schredl, M. (2010). Dream content analysis: Basic principles. *International Journal of Dream Research, 3*, 65–73.

Schredl, M., Burchert, N., & Grabatin, Y. (2004). The effect of training on interrater reliability in dream content analysis. *Sleep and Hypnosis, 6*, 139–144.

Schredl, M., & Doll, E. (1998). Emotions in diary dreams. *Consciousness and Cognition, 7*, 634–646.

Winget, C., & Kramer, M. (1979). *Dimensions of dreams*. Gainesville: University of Florida Press.

Continuity Hypothesis and Colors in Dreams

The continuity hypothesis of dreaming states that dream content reflects waking life. Given that our daily world is colored, one would expect that all dreams contain some kind of color. Studies carried out in the first half of the 20th century, however, yielded extremely low numbers of persons reporting that they dream in color (Schwitzgebel, 2002). Today, the number of persons who state that they dream completely in black and white is rather small (Schredl, Fuchedzhieva, Hämig, & Schindele, 2008). Dream content analytic studies yielded relatively small percentages of dreams (about 20%) with explicitly mentioned colors (Schredl, 2008); if dreamers were asked explicitly for colors in their reports, the percentage of dreams with colors increased to about 80 percent (Kahn, Dement, Fisher, & Barmack, 1962).

The most extensive study on color perception in dreams was carried out by Rechtschaffen and Buchignani (1992).

Immediately upon awakening, 129 variations, which included different combinations of color saturation, illumination, clarity (sharp vs. diffuse, fogged, out of focus), figure versus background differences, and overall color balance of a single photo (young woman sitting on a couch), were presented to the participants. Participants generally had little difficulties in matching one of the photos to the last dream scene: $N = 312$ matches were made by the 24 participants. Most dreams were comparable to waking-life color perception, but 20.2 percent of the chosen photos were achromatic. Taken altogether, the problem as to whether all dreams are colored is not yet solved and thus the question arises as to what factors affect the reporting of colors in dreams.

First, methodological issues have to be considered. Schredl et al. (2008) found that a considerable number of persons do not recall any colors of their dreams (about 35%), indicating that it seems difficult to remember colors retrospectively. The increase in colored elements in diary dreams where the person is asked about the color of the dream elements directly upon awakening supports this idea. In addition, waking memory for colors was negatively related to the percentage of black-and-white dreams (Schredl et al., 2008). As colors are not that important for the dream plot—because they are normal—they might be easily forgotten upon awakening.

Schwitzgebel (2002), however, hypothesized that dreams might be neither colored nor black and white, that the color modality is indefinite. That would explain why persons in the era of black-and-white movies attribute to their dreams only black and white (cf. Murzyn, 2008), whereas today most people say their dreams are in color. According to this hypothesis, watching black-and-white media does not affect the dream content per se but the people's concepts of dreaming.

To summarize, most persons in our days say that their dreams include some color. As the memory for colors is fragile, it would be necessary to train persons— by using dream diaries or repeated laboratory awakenings—to see whether all or almost all colors can be remembered even if they are not outstanding or important for the dream action, for example, the colors of the clothes of a person one talked to in the dream. This will render Schwitzgebel's hypothesis very unlikely and support the continuity hypothesis of dreaming like the study showing that wearing colored goggles during the day affects dream colors (Roffwarg, Herman, Bowe-Anders, & Tauber, 1978).

Michael Schredl

See also: entries related to Dream Theories

References

Kahn, E., Dement, W., Fisher, C., & Barmack, J. E. (1962). Incidence of color in immediately recalled dreams. *Science, 137*, 1054–1055.

Murzyn, E. (2008). Do we only dream in color? A comparison of reported dream color in younger and older adults with different experiences of black and white media. *Consciousness and Cognition, 17*, 1228–1237.

Rechtschaffen, A., & Buchignani, C. (1992). The visual appearence of dreams. In J. S. Antrobus & M. Bertini (Eds.), *The neuropsychology of sleep and dreaming* (pp. 143–155). Hillsdale, NJ: Lawrence Erlbaum.

Roffwarg, H. P., Herman, J. S., Bowe-Anders, C., & Tauber, E. S. (1978). The effects of sustained alterations of waking visual input on dream content. In A. M. Arkin, J. S. Antrobus, & S. J. Ellman (Eds.), *The mind in sleep: Psychology and psychophysiology* (pp. 295–349). Hillsdale, NJ: Lawrence Erlbaum.

Schredl, M. (2008). Spontaneously reported colors in dreams: Correlations with attitude towards creativity, personality and memory. *Sleep and Hypnosis, 10*, 54–60.

Schredl, M., Fuchedzhieva, A., Hämig, H., & Schindele, V. (2008). Do we think dreams are in black and white due to memory problems? *Dreaming, 18*, 175–180.

Schwitzgebel, E. (2002). Why did we think we dreamed in black and white? *Studies in History and Philosophy of Science, 33*, 649–660.

Continuity Hypothesis of Dreaming

That waking-life events are incorporated into dreams has been noted by many dream researchers (for an overview see Schredl, 2003). Sigmund Freud (1987), for example, used the word *tagesreste* (day residue) designating dream elements with clear relationship to the previous day or days. The term *continuity hypothesis* was formulated by Hall and Nordby (1972), saying "the wishes and fears that determine our actions and thoughts in everyday life also determine what we will dream about" (p. 104).

Empirical studies (for overviews see Domhoff, 1996; Schredl, 2003; Strauch & Meier, 1996) support the continuity hypothesis, but also identify factors that modulate the probability of incorporating a waking-life experience into subsequent dreams. The major factors found so far are exponential decrease with time, emotional involvement, type of waking-life experience, personality traits, and time of the night.

Many studies have shown an exponential decrease in the incorporation rate of waking-life experiences into dreams with elapsed time between experience and the subsequent dream, that is, events of the day before can be found more often than events that happened years ago (Schredl, 2003). The studies regarding the effects of traumas on dreams (Wittmann, Schredl, & Kramer, 2007) and a diary study (Schredl, 2006) testing this effect directly indicate that emotional involvement regarding the waking-life experience affects the probability of incorporation into dreams. Several studies (e.g., Schredl & Hofmann, 2003) have shown that focused thinking activity (reading, working with a computer) during dreams occurs less frequently than unfocused activities such as talking with friends, and so on. These results indicate that the type of activity is of importance for the continuity between waking life and dreaming. The time of the night or the time interval between sleep onset and dream onset has affected the incorporation rate of waking-life experiences in two studies (Verdone, 1965); dreams of the second part of the night comprise more elements of the distant past, while dreams of the first part of the night incorporate mostly recent daytime experiences (Schredl, 2003). The interaction between personality traits and incorporation of waking-life experiences has been rarely studied. Two studies (Baekeland, Resch, & Katz, 1968; Schredl, Kleinferchner, & Gell, 1996) indicate that personality dimensions such as field dependence or thin boundaries modulate the magnitude of continuity between waking and dreaming.

Based on these findings, Schredl (2003) postulated a mathematical model including the factors yet known to influence the continuity between waking and dreaming (see Table 1). The multiplying factor includes the effects of emotional involvement (EI), type of the waking-life experience (TYPE), and the interaction between personality traits and incorporation of experience (PERS). The relationships between these factors should be determined by future studies. The slope of the exponential function may be moderated by the time interval between sleep onset and dream onset (time

Table 1: Mathematical Model for the Continuity between Waking Life and Dreaming

Incorporation rate = a (EI, TYPE, PERS) $* e^{-b(TN)*t}$ + Constant

a (EI, TYPE, PERS)	Multiplying factor which is a function of emotional involvement (EI), type of the waking-life experience (TYPE) and the interaction between experience and personality traits (PERS)
b (TN)	Slope of the exponential function which is itself a function of the time interval between sleep onset and dream onset (TN)
t	Time interval between waking-life experience and occurre nce of the dream incorporation

of the night; TN). The basic idea behind the model is the fact that the continuity hypothesis in its general formulation is too imprecise for deriving specific hypotheses for dream research studies. The mathematical model might help to advance the research in this field because the factors can be specifically tested.

Detailed knowledge of the factors affecting the continuity between waking and dreaming might help in deciphering possible functions of dreaming because they show why waking-life experiences are so important to be incorporated into dreams.

Michael Schredl

References

Baekeland, F., Resch, R., & Katz, D. (1968). Presleep metation and dream reports: I. Cognitive style, contuiguity to sleep and time of the night. *Archives of General Psychiatry, 19*, 300–311.

Domhoff, G. W. (1996). *Finding meaning in dreams: A quantitative approach.* New York: Plenum Press.

Freud, S. (1987). *Die Traumdeutung (1900)* [The Interpretation of Dreams]. Frankfurt: Fischer Taschenbuch.

Hall, C. S., & Nordby, V. J. (1972). *The individual and his dreams.* New York: New American Library.

Schredl, M. (2003). Continuity between waking and dreaming: A proposal for a mathematical model. *Sleep and Hypnosis, 5*, 38–52.

Schredl, M. (2006). Factors affecting the continuity between waking and dreaming: Emotional intensity and emotional tone of the waking-life event. *Sleep and Hypnosis, 8*, 1–5.

Schredl, M., & Hofmann, F. (2003). Continuity between waking activities and dream activities. *Consciousness and Cognition, 12*, 298–308.

Schredl, M., Kleinferchner, P., & Gell, T. (1996). Dreaming and personality: Thick vs. thin boundaries. *Dreaming, 6*, 219–223.

Strauch, I., & Meier, B. (1996). *In search of dreams: Results of experimental dream research.* Albany: State University of New York Press.

Verdone, P. (1965). Temporal reference of manifest dream content. *Perceptual and Motor Skills, 20*, 1253–1268.

Wittmann, L., Schredl, M., & Kramer, M. (2007). The role of dreaming in posttraumatic stress disorder. *Psychotherapy and Psychosomatics, 76*, 25–39.

Continuous Positive Airway Pressure (CPAP) Therapy for Obstructive Sleep Apnea

Obstructive sleep apnea (OSA) is a common condition characterized by repetitive narrowing or closure of upper airway (Young et al., 1993). Substantive data demonstrate an association between OSA and diverse adverse outcomes such as increased daytime sleepiness, impaired daytime functioning, metabolic dysfunction, cardiovascular disorders, increased risk of traffic accidents, and reduced health-related quality of life. Among the cardiovascular outcomes, data are most compelling for OSA as a risk factor for hypertension (Budhiraja, Budhiraja, & Quan, 2010).

Continuous positive airway pressure (CPAP) therapy is widely considered the first-line treatment for OSA. It involves use of a mask and machine to prevent the characteristic recurrent upper airway narrowing. CPAP attenuates diverse cardiovascular risks associated with OSA. CPAP has an ameliorating effect on increased blood pressure (BP) in patients with resistant or severe hypertension. The BP lowering effects of CPAP are more pronounced in patients with daytime sleepiness than those without excessive sleepiness. Additionally, current data suggest that CPAP use in moderate to severe OSA helps retard the progression of atherosclerosis and coronary artery disease. Combined end points of cardiovascular death, acute coronary syndrome, hospitalization for heart failure, or need for coronary revascularization is significantly lower in persons treated for OSA compared to those with OSA who decline therapy. Large prospective trials are currently under way to provide more substantive evidence regarding the salutary effects of CPAP on coronary artery disease. CPAP also improves cardiac function and quality of life in patients with congestive heart failure comorbid with OSA. However, CPAP does not improve survival or significantly alleviate sleep-disordered breathing in patients with congestive heart failure who predominantly have central variety of sleep apnea. Finally, risk of arrhythmias is significantly increased in OSA. CPAP therapy alleviates this risk (Budhiraja et al., 2010).

Excessive daytime sleepiness is another major adverse consequence of OSA. CPAP alleviates sleepiness in a majority of patients with sleep apnea. CPAP therapy can improve daytime functioning and job performance. CPAP treatment in patients with coexistent OSA and Alzheimer's disease results in improved sleep and mood as well as slows the cognitive deterioration. OSA also has an adverse impact on intimacy and sexual relationships,

and these are improved with CPAP treatment. Finally, CPAP improves the quality of life not only of patients but also of their bed partners. Notably, there seems to be a dose–response relationship between hours of CPAP used at night and beneficial outcomes. On average, subjective sleepiness progressively improves with increasing CPAP use of up to four hours a night, while functional outcomes may continue to improve with CPAP use of up to seven hours a night.

The salutary effects of CPAP therapy are mediated through several complex pathways. Diverse mechanisms such as hypoxia, inflammation, sympathetic activation, obesity, metabolic dysregulation, sleep disruption, and endothelial dysfunction are responsible for adverse outcomes of OSA. CPAP therapy consolidates sleep, reduces systemic inflammation and oxidative stress, improves insulin sensitivity, decreases sympathetic activity, and improves endothelial function, thereby reducing the risk of cardiovascular disease in patients with sleep apnea (Budhiraja et al., 2010).

Despite the several demonstrated benefits of CPAP therapy, a significant proportion of patients do not use it regularly over the long term (Weaver & Grunstein, 2008). Several factors might compromise adherence to CPAP. This therapy utilizes a cumbersome device with an intrusive mask that needs to be used every night. Some people find the mask on the face disagreeable, while some others find it difficult getting used to the pressure with which the device blows air. Nose congestion, dryness of eyes, bloating, and claustrophobia are other common side effects that may impede regular CPAP use. Social, cultural, and racial factors as well as partner support, or lack thereof, are other factors that influence CPAP use.

Several interventions may help promote CPAP use (Weaver & Grunstein, 2008). Recent advances in CPAP and mask technology are primarily aimed at affording CPAP users a more comfortable experience. Many new devices incorporate algorithms that make each breath more comfortable at inhalation and exhalation. Other devices analyze patients' airflow in real time and adjust the pressure based on patients' needs. The newer machines are generally more compact and less noisy, allowing for portability and better sleep. Better-fitting masks made of better materials may provide more comfort. Heated humidifiers can help alleviate dryness of nose and eyes. Treatment of side effects such as nose congestion improves CPAP adherence. Finally, behavioral strategies such as proper patient education, positive reinforcement, and cognitive behavioral therapy have shown promise in augmenting CPAP adherence.

Rohit Budhiraja

See also: entries related to Sleep Disorders

References

Budhiraja, R., Budhiraja, P., & Quan, S.F. (2010, October). Sleep-disordered breathing and cardiovascular disorders. *Respiratory Care, 55*(10), 1322–1332.

Weaver, T.E., & Grunstein, R.R. (2008, February). Adherence to continuous positive airway pressure therapy: The challenge to effective treatment. *Proceedings of the American Thoracic Society, 15*(2), 173–178.

Young, T., Palta, M., Dempsey, J., Skatrud, J., Weber, S., & Badr, S. (1993, April). The occurrence of sleep-disordered breathing among middle-aged adults. *New England Journal of Medicine, 29*(17), 1230–1235.

Convergent Evolution of REM Sleep in Mammals and Birds

The various races of birds take to flight and startle the groves of the gods at dead of night with a sudden whirr of wings. Doubtless their restful slumber is disturbed by visions of hawks swooping to the fray in fierce pursuit. (Lucretius, 1994, p. 161)

Contrary to Lucretius's view, doubt persists over whether birds and nonhuman mammals experience the type of dreams that we experience during REM sleep. Our ability to examine dreaming in nonhuman animals is obviously constrained by their inability to verbally report on personal experiences. Nonetheless, several lines of evidence suggest that nonhuman mammals, and possibly birds, dream. Among mammals, with the exception of monotremes and cetaceans, which apparently lack cortical signs of REM sleep (Siegel, 2005), the neuroanatomy and resulting neurophysiology of REM sleep is highly conserved. Because a trait unique to humans responsible for dreaming has not been identified, from an evolutionary perspective alone, it seems likely that the capacity to dream predates the evolution of humans and is present in nonhuman mammals.

The observation of sleeping dogs twitching their paws and vocalizing, as if chasing rabbits in their dreams, is a line of evidence commonly invoked in favor of animal dreaming. However, phasic twitching persists in cats following separation of the forebrain from the brain stem (Villablanca, 1966). Hence, cortically generated dream mentation is not the cause of twitching. Moreover, the apparent enactment of dreams in cats with mesopontine lesions (Jouvet & Delorme, 1965) seems to reflect disinhibition of locomotor drive resulting in increased drive, rather than the simple release of normal dream-related motor drive resulting from the associated abolition of muscle atonia (Hendricks, Morrison, & Mann, 1982). Although phasic twitching in (and of) itself does not establish dreaming, twitching may nonetheless be related to dream content in intact animals. In line with the activation synthesis hypothesis (Hobson & McCarley, 1977), a relationship between dream content and phasic twitching may arise when the cortex attempts to incorporate both direct input from the brain stem and indirect sensory input resulting from brain stem–generated motor activity (Blumberg, 2010).

Another approach to examining dreams in nonhuman animals is to relate brain activity during REM sleep to previous waking activity. In rats, patterns of hippocampal neuronal activity that occur during wakefulness as the animal moves through a specific environment are replayed during subsequent REM sleep on an equivalent time scale, as would be expected if the rat was dreaming about previous experiences (Louie & Wilson, 2001). Although this finding is consistent with the notion that nonhuman mammals dream during REM sleep, in the absence of a verbal report of the conscious experience of dreaming, doubts remain.

As the only nonmammalian taxonomic group to exhibit unequivocal REM (and non-REM) sleep, birds are seemingly the most likely candidate for dreaming among nonmammalian animals. As in marsupial and eutherian (placental) mammals, all birds examined exhibit a REM sleep state characterized by activation in the electroencephalogram (EEG), REMs, reduced muscle tone, autonomic variability, twitching, and diminished thermoregulatory responses. In addition, ostriches, a member of a group of birds that retain several ancient traits, also exhibit periods of REM sleep without "cortical" activation such as that observed in monotremes (Lesku et al., 2011a). Also, like mammals, in at least some birds, episodes of REM sleep are more frequent and longer in duration toward the end of the major sleep period (Martinez-Gonzalez, Lesku, & Rattenborg, 2008). The time birds spend in REM sleep increases following sleep deprivation, indicating that as in mammals, avian REM sleep is homeostatically regulated (Martinez-Gonzalez et al., 2008; Tobler & Borbély, 1988). Pharmacological agents that decrease REM sleep in mammals also decrease REM sleep in birds (Fuchs, Siegel, Burgdorf, & Bingman, 2006). Finally, albeit not in the hippocampus, as in rats, during REM (and non-REM) sleep, neurons in the song system of finches replay patterns of activity that occurred during previous singing (Shank & Margoliash, 2009). As with neuronal replay occurring in sleeping mammals, it is unknown whether replay is associated with dreams of singing in finches.

Despite the marked similarities between avian and mammalian REM sleep, there are some potentially important differences. The avian hippocampus does not appear to generate a mammal-like theta rhythm during REM sleep or movement while awake, or sharp-wave ripples during non-REM sleep or quiet wakefulness (Rattenborg, Martinez-Gonzalez, Roth, & Pravosudov, in press). Given that these rhythms are involved in orchestrating communication between the hippocampus and cortex in mammals, communication between the avian hippocampus and forebrain regions homologous or analogous to the cortex may be fundamentally different in birds during wakefulness and sleep, a finding that could influence the quality of potential avian dreams. In addition, episodes of avian REM sleep are short (typically < 10 seconds) when compared to those in mammals (Martinez-Gonzalez et al., 2008), a feature that might necessarily limit the duration of potential dreams.

Birds independently evolved a REM sleep state in most respects similar to that in mammals. Interestingly, birds are also the only taxonomic group outside of mammals to exhibit non-REM sleep, a homeostatically regulated state characterized by high-voltage slow waves in the EEG (Lesku, Vyssotski, Martinez-Gonzalez, Wilzeck, Rattenborg, 2011b). Why were birds the only taxonomic group to independently evolve both mammalian-like REM and non-REM sleep? Although the answer to this question remains unknown, a starting point is to examine traits that birds share with mammals but not other taxonomic groups. For instance, mammals and birds also independently evolved large brains for their body size and an associated ability to perform complex cognitive tasks.

Given that large brains, complex cognition, and non-REM and REM sleep coevolved independently in mammals and birds, these traits may be functionally interrelated (Rattenborg, Martinez-Gonzalez, & Lesku, 2009), as suggested by recent studies implicating sleep in processes that support cognitive performance. The role of dreaming (if it occurs in birds and nonhuman mammals) in such processes remains a mystery.

Niels C. Rattenborg

References

Blumberg, M. S. (2010). Beyond dreams: Do sleep-related movements contribute to brain development? *Frontiers in Neurology*, 1, 140.

Fuchs, T., Siegel, J.J., Burgdorf, J., & Bingman, V.P. (2006). A selective serotonin reuptake inhibitor reduces REM sleep in the homing pigeon. *Physiology & Behavior, 87*, 575–581.

Hendricks, J.C., Morrison, A.R., & Mann, G.L. (1982). Different behaviors during paradoxical sleep without atonia depend on pontine lesion site. *Brain Research, 239*, 81–105.

Hobson, J.A., & McCarley, R.W. (1977). The brain as a dream state generator: An activation-synthesis hypothesis of the dream process. *American Journal of Psychiatry, 134*, 1335–1348.

Jouvet, M., & Delorme, F. (1965). Locus Coeruleus et Sommeil Paradoxal [Locus Coeruleus and Paradoxal Sleep]. *Comptes Rendus des Seances de la Societe de Biologie et de ses Filiales [Records of meetings of the Society of Biology and its Chapters], 159*, 895–899.

Lesku, J. A., Meyer, L. C. R., Fuller, A., Maloney, S. K., Dell'Omo, G., Vyssotski, A. L., & Rattenborg, N. C. (2011a). Ostriches sleep like platypuses. *PLoS One, 6*, e23203.

Lesku, J. A., Vyssotski, A. L., Martinez-Gonzalez, D., Wilzeck, C., & Rattenborg, N. C. (2011b). Local sleep homeostasis in the avian brain: Convergence of sleep function in mammals and birds? *Proceedings of the Royal Society B: Biological Sciences, 278*, 2419–2428.

Louie, K., & Wilson, M. A. (2001). Temporally structured replay of awake hippocampal ensemble activity during rapid eye movement sleep. *Neuron, 29*, 145–156.

Lucretius. (1994). *On the nature of the universe* (Trans. Ronald E. Latham). London: Penguin Books.

Martinez-Gonzalez, D., Lesku, J. A., & Rattenborg, N. C. (2008). Increased EEG spectral power density during sleep following short-term sleep deprivation in pigeons (*Columba livia*): Evidence for avian sleep homeostasis. *Journal of Sleep Research, 17*, 140–153.

Rattenborg, N. C., Martinez-Gonzalez, D., & Lesku, J. A. (2009). Avian sleep homeostasis: Convergent evolution of complex brains, cognition and sleep functions in mammals and birds. *Neuroscience & Biobehavioral Reviews, 33*, 253–270.

Rattenborg, N. C., Martinez-Gonzalez, D., Roth, T. C., & Pravosudov, V. V. (in press). Hippocampal memory consolidation during sleep: A comparison of mammals and birds. *Biological Reviews of the Cambridge Philosophical Society.*

Shank, S. S., & Margoliash, D. (2009). Sleep and sensorimotor integration during early vocal learning in a songbird. *Nature, 458*, 73–77.

Siegel, J. M. (2005). Clues to the functions of mammalian sleep. *Nature, 437*, 1264–1271.

Tobler, I., & Borbély, A. A. (1988). Sleep and EEG spectra in the pigeon (*Columba livia*) under baseline conditions and after sleep-deprivation. *Journal of Comparative Physiology, Part A: Sensory, Neural and Behavioral Physiology, 163*, 729–738.

Villablanca, J. (1966). Behavioral and polygraphic study of "sleep" and "wakefulness" in chronic decerebrate cats. *Electroencephalography and Clinical Neurophysiology, 21*, 562–577.

Cortical EEG Oscillations, Local Sleep, and Dream Recall

In the last decades, it has been demonstrated that sleep is a local and use-dependent process. The technical advances and higher spatial resolution obtained by using quantitative analyses of EEG sleep recorded from multiple cortical derivations allow for the assessment of the spatiotemporal EEG dynamics during sleep. In this way, it has been demonstrated that the homeostatic recovery process is mainly local and does not involve the whole cerebral cortex to the same extent, because the higher sleep need (expressed by the amount of slow-wave activity, or SWA) mostly affects the frontal cortex in both animals and humans (e.g., Marzano, Ferrara, Curcio, & Gennaro, 2010). Furthermore, experience-dependent plasticity in specific neural circuits during wakefulness induces localized changes in slow-wave activity (SWA) during subsequent sleep, highlighting the presence of specific regional effects of learning and plasticity on EEG sleep measures. In general terms, the local sleep theory indicates that sleep should be reconsidered in terms of their temporal and spatial characteristics. The extension of this theoretical framework to the study of dreaming may have a great heuristic potential to elucidate the mechanisms of dream generation and to shed light on the relationship between episodic memories, cortical activity, and dreaming. In fact, dream recall is a peculiar form of declarative memory—mostly episodic—encoded during sleep. Therefore, the retrieval of oneiric contents should share some electrophysiological mechanisms with successful episodic memory encoding of the awake brain. The current model of episodic memory states that cortical theta oscillations during wakefulness act to temporally order individual memory representations (Nyhus & Curran, 2010), and intracranial recordings showed that significant increases in frontal theta oscillations during encoding predict subsequent recall (Sederberg, Kahana, Howard, Donner, & Joseph, 2003).

Therefore, the integration of the notions that EEG sleep exhibits local changes according to the sleep stage, and learning, memory, and plasticity processes, and that successful memory retrieval is predicted by the preceding EEG oscillations, allows one to investigate innovatively the association between dreaming and cortical activity. Actually, recent findings with EEG topography provide electrophysiological evidence that cortical brain oscillations of sleep are predictive of a successful dream recall, and a higher frontal theta activity during sleep predicts subsequent dream recall upon the awakenings from REM sleep (Moroni et al., 2010). Differently, a lower alpha oscillatory activity in correspondence of temporo-parietal areas (Esposito, Nielsen, & Paquette, 2004) and of right temporal area (Moroni et al., 2010) predicts a successful dream recall upon awakening from stage 2 sleep.

Therefore, the intrinsic electrophysiological differences between REM and NREM sleep, and their regional changes, modulate the predictive relationship linking cortical oscillations of sleep and dream recall. The changes of cortical oscillatory activity, localized on the temporo-occipital and frontal regions in NREM and REM sleep, respectively, seem to indicate the presence of a recruitment of those regions that control successful memory encoding of dreams. This suggests an interdependent regulation of two neuronal circuits involved in the ability to recall a dream upon awakenings from REM and NREM sleep, respectively: the hippocampo-cortical circuit and the thalamo-cortical circuit.

In this novel view, specific brain oscillations in the last minutes of nightly sleep increase or decrease the probability of a successful recall, extending the continuity hypothesis (i.e., qualitative and quantitative aspects of dreams reflect waking-life experience and features) to the brain mechanisms mediating memory encoding and retrieval during wakefulness. It could be paraphrased: Dream recall belongs to both the sleeping and the awake brain.

Cristina Marzano and
Luigi De Gennaro

References

Esposito, M. J., Nielsen, T. A., & Paquette, T. (2004). Reduced alpha power associated with the recall of mentation from stage 2 and stage REM sleep. *Psychophysiology, 41*, 288–297.

Marzano, C., Ferrara, M., Curcio, G., & Gennaro, L. D. (2010). The effects of sleep deprivation in humans: Topographical electroencephalogram changes in non-rapid eye movement (NREM) sleep versus REM sleep. *Journal of Sleep Research, 19*, 260–268.

Moroni, F., Marzano, C., Mauro, F., Curcio, G., Ferrara, M., & De Gennaro, L. (2010). Theta and alpha oscillations during sleep predict subsequent dream recall. *Journal of Sleep Research*.

Nyhus, E., & Curran, T. (2010). Functional role of gamma and theta oscillations in episodic memory. *Neuroscience and Biobehavioral Reviews, 34*, 1023–1035.

Sederberg, P. B., Kahana, M. J., Howard, M. W., Donner, E. J., & Joseph, R. M. (2003). Theta and gamma oscillations during encoding predict subsequent recall. *Journal of Neuroscience, 23*, 10809–10814.

Co-Sleeping

Co-sleeping in the context of human-infant-care practices denotes any generic situation in which a caregiver, usually, but not always the mother, sleeps within sensory range of an infant on the same or different surface. Mother–infant sleep proximity permits mutual monitoring, sensory access, and physiological regulation and support, including (but not limited to) the delivery and ingestion of breast milk (McKenna, Ball, & Gettler, 2007). Mother–infant co-sleeping (both same and separate surfaces) is almost ubiquitous across human cultures and represents humankind's ancestral sleeping and nighttime breastfeeding arrangement. One survey of 127 cultural groups for whom ethnographic reports were available found that about 79 percent of the societies studied slept in the same room as their infants, with about 44 percent sharing the same bed or sleeping surface (Barry & Paxson, 1971).

Compared with other mammalian species, the breast milk of both human and nonhuman primates is relatively low in calories derived from fat and protein, reflecting the relative immaturity of the human infant's gastrointestinal system. Less calorically dense breast milk requires more frequent, usually infant-initiated, daytime and nighttime breastfeeding sessions to meet the infant's daily nutritional needs. Hence, many studies worldwide show a robust relationship between breastfeeding and mothers adopting some form of co-sleeping. Indeed, multiple laboratory- and home-based studies have demonstrated that when mothers bed share rather than place their infants in different rooms, breastfeeding sessions practically double and intervals between feeds can be reduced by as much as half of what they are when breastfeeding mothers and infants sleep apart (Ball & Klingaman, 2008; Gettler & McKenna, 2011; McKenna et al., 2007).

Alongside these intimate connections to breastfeeding, mother–infant co-sleeping likely evolved (or was adaptively maintained) among our ancestors because the human infant is the least neurologically developed primate of all, having only 25 percent of their adult brain volume at birth, compared to about 35 percent in chimpanzee infants and even higher among other non-human primates (Robson, Van Schaik, & Hawkes, 2006). Specifically, this high degree of altriciality results in human infants and children being comparatively more physiologically and socially vulnerable (i.e., to external threats by conspecifics and predators) for a longer period of time, extending into the second decade of life. Thus, throughout the course of human evolution, hominin infants would almost undoubtedly have slept near or on their mothers' bodies not only to feed but also to receive a variety of sensory stimulation (touch, sound, smells, movement) and protection, all of which likely helped compensate for the infants' extreme immaturity and helplessness in the challenging ecologies facing our ancestors over the last five million years (Ball & Klingaman, 2008; McKenna et al., 2007).

While mother–infant co-sleeping facilitates increased nighttime breastfeeding behavior and, thus, the two practices are assumed to be functionally interdependent, co-sleeping takes hundreds, maybe thousands, of different forms worldwide and is extremely heterogeneous even within cultures. To illustrate just a few sleeping arrangements: Aborigine infants from Australia co-sleep with their parents on the same surface without any furniture and with minimal bedding (on blankets or mats) intimately nestled up to or lying under the arms of their mothers' bodies, as do the Gusii of Kenya and the Bhils of the western Ghats, in southern India. Flores infants of Indonesia and Gund infants of northern China co-sleep next to their caregivers on bamboo benches, or mats and futons placed on an earthen floor, while the Semang of Malaysia co-sleep on split bamboo mattresses slightly raised off the ground, and the Nahaue of northwest India and the Cuna of Panama sleep with their babies in hammocks strung up between two trees. The Ainu of Japan from North Hokkaido and Yapese infants from Pacific Micronesia are placed alone in baskets hanging from a ceiling but lowered to within arm's reach of their mothers, while still other infants co-sleep by room sharing, such as what occurs in many Western cultures when infants remain within sensory access of their parents but on different surfaces such as in bassinets, cradles, or cribs (Murdock et al., 2006). In the United States, it is increasingly common for some infants to co-sleep in criblike extensions at the level of the parents' bed open on the mattress side, permitting the infant to slip easily in and out for easy breastfeeding (Ball & Klingaman, 2008).

The distance at which infants sleep from their mothers (or other caregivers) significantly impacts the immediate physiology and behavior of each member of the mother–infant dyad, especially their daily nighttime sleep architecture and arousal patterns as well as the degree of potential entrainment (i.e., percentage of sleep time co-sleeping partners spend simultaneously awake or in the same sleep stage). The general development of the infant's sleep patterns in the first few years of life is also dramatically different when routinely bed-sharing and solitary-sleeping infants are compared. Regarding sleep consolidation, for example, studies show that routine bed sharing, breastfeeding mothers and infants awake more frequently (simultaneously) but for significantly shorter periods of time, compared to solitary-sleeping mothers and infants, suggesting that mothers choosing to routinely bed share (and breastfeed) do not habituate to the presence of their infant in terms of arousal. Rather, routine bed sharing with breastfeeding leads to synchronization between mother and infant in terms of arousals and sleep-stage shifts. Furthermore, despite more frequent arousals, bed sharing, breastfeeding mothers and infants show significantly greater sleep duration compared to when they sleep separately (McKenna et al., 2007).

However, and likely as a result of more frequent arousals, bed-sharing infants also spend significantly less time in deep sleep (stages 3–4) over the course of the night than do routinely solitary-sleeping infants. Young, neurologically developing infants are most likely to experience prolonged central apneas that result in difficulties in arousing when they are in *deeper*-sleep stages (3–4) (McKenna et al., 2007). Thus, it has been argued elsewhere that less deep sleep combined with more frequent arousals in *lighter* sleep (stages 1–2) may prove particularly protective to infants with developmentally or congenitally based arousal (McKenna et al., 2007), which may be a primary factor in some SIDS (sudden infant death syndrome) cases (Byard & Krous, 2003), although these hypotheses await testing.

Moreover, perhaps contrary to expectations, bed-sharing mother–infant dyads sleep more than their solitary-sleeping counterparts and, in fact, routinely bed-sharing mothers report greater satisfaction with their sleep (McKenna et al., 2007). Intentional routine bed sharing shows no effect on maternal reports of marital satisfaction (Germo, Chang, Keller, & Goldberg, 2007; Messmer, 2009), unlike reactive bed sharing (i.e., bringing babies to bed not by choice but in an attempt by parents to solve ongoing infant sleep problems). In these situations, a significant negative association between time spent bed sharing and marital satisfaction has been demonstrated (Messmer, 2009). These results suggest that, for two-parent households, the decision to co-sleep in the form of bed sharing should be made jointly in order to maximize the emotional and psychological well-being of parents and infants alike.

Given that parental decisions regarding sleeping/feeding arrangements affect the nighttime physiological and behavioral experiences of infants and children, it is not surprising that an infant's developmental sleep trajectory (sleeping through the night without parental intervention or contact and the timing of sleep consolidation in general) will vary considerably among infants and children, depending on what feeding methods (bottle or breast) and routine sleeping arrangements are adopted. For example, Elias and colleagues compared the first-year development of sleep in infants who were raised following more traditional Western pediatric standard-care recommendations, which minimize parent–infant contact and feeding during the night, with the sleep of infants whose mothers practiced co-sleeping in the form of bed sharing with infant-initiated breastfeeding (Elias, Nicolson, Bora, & Johnston, 1986a; Elias, Nicolson, & Konner, 1986b). She found that for infants receiving minimal nighttime contact and care, the maximum sleep-bout length increased from an average of 6.5 hours at 2 months of age to 8 hours at 4 months and to greater than 8 hours during the second year. In contrast, bed-sharing–breastfeeding infants at 2 months of age only slept an average of 5 hours during their longest sleep bout, and it was not until they were 20 months old that these infants slept significantly longer than 5 hours during their longest sleep bout. An interesting question raised by these data is, regarding human infant sleep development, which of these trajectories might most closely represent what is normal or more optimal for the human infant from a species-wide, evolutionary biological perspective?

Studies using cross-cultural data might be insightful in trying to answer this question. For example, one study compared the development of sleep in the first year of life among 10 Kipsigis infants of rural Kenya who slept with their mothers and were breastfed throughout the night routinely with a group of Los Angeles infants who slept alone and were bottle-fed. The findings are consistent with the Elias et al. (1986b) studies insofar as the Kipsigis infants (co-sleeping and breastfeeding) continued to sleep for shorter periods throughout the night and did not consolidate their sleep (i.e., sleep continuously through the night), until well after the first year of life, unlike the Los Angeles babies who slept for longer and consolidated sleep at earlier ages. At about four months of age, the Los Angeles babies could be found sleeping about two hours longer than were the Kipsigis infants over a 24-hour period (Super & Harkness, 1987).

Because cross-species and cross-cultural data suggest that breastfeeding with co-sleeping represents the context within which human infant sleep evolved, it is likely that shorter sleep bouts with less consolidated sleep and more awakenings in the first year of life, as emerge in the context of co-sleeping with breastfeeding, are biologically appropriate and in the infant's best interest. Aside from maximizing the intake of breast milk, this may owe to infants needing time to develop the kinds of mature neural structures and mechanisms needed to manage prolonged sleep bouts and life-threatening apneas that require a quick and effective arousal during deep sleep, as mentioned previously. Moreover, the human infant's brain and immune system's growth and maturation, both at their critical period during the first year of life, are enhanced by, if not dependent on, breast milk, which is optimally delivered (during sleep bouts) in the context of mother–infant co-sleeping, when practiced safely (McDade & Worthman, 1998; McKenna et al., 2007; Robson et al., 2006).

In the United States and some European nations, there exists ongoing disagreements regarding whether or not the relative potential benefits and potential life-saving aspects of co-sleeping justify the risks of an infant being accidentally suffocated while co-sleeping on the same surface, especially in the form of bed sharing (Gettler & McKenna, 2010). Modern beds and bedding (e.g., mattresses, blankets, and pillows) and contemporary living arrangements (e.g., overcrowded households) transform an otherwise inherently protective arrangement, mothers and infants sleeping side by side for nighttime breastfeeding, into something risky or dangerous, as present data reveal. An infant sharing a bed with an adult (usually the mother) who smokes or has taken alcohol or other consciousness-affecting medications has been clearly shown in multiple studies to be at substantially increased risk of unexpected death, over and above the risk associated with maternal smoking alone (Fleming, Blair, & McKenna, 2006). Nonbreastfeeding, bed-sharing mothers also put their infants at increased risk (Ball & Klingaman, 2008).

However, recent studies have shown no increased risk for breastfed infants bed sharing with nonsmoking mothers (Fleming et al., 2006). Still, other studies have shown an increased risk for SIDS among infants bed sharing with an unimpaired mother compared to solitary-sleeping infants. For example, a large multicenter European study, which did not account for breast-feeding practices, showed a small risk increase, while a Scottish study showed a larger comparative risk for bed-sharing infants, particularly for younger infants, though that study did not take account of parental alcohol intake (Fleming et al., 2006; Gettler & McKenna, 2010; McKenna et al., 2007). Co-sleeping with an infant on a sofa is also associated with a particularly high risk, compounded by the circumstances in which sofa sharing often occurs (e.g., changes to normal sleep routines or socioeconomic deprivation). Clearly there are inappropriate circumstances or environments in which co-sleeping occurs with increased vulnerability of some infants and these deserve further investigation (Fleming et al., 2006; Gettler & McKenna, 2010; McKenna et al., 2007).

While evolved connections between human infant and maternal biology, including the biology of infant sleep development, have been relatively constant through time, cultural perceptions of what is normal, healthy, and appropriate, including how and where infants are supposed to sleep (and feed), are much more subject to social evaluations and rapid change. As is true for all domains of human life, parochial social values and cultural ideologies clearly underlie and explain the emergence of exceedingly diverse infant-care practices, including sleeping arrangements. Since beliefs change much faster than infant biology, culturally based practices can prove either more or less compatible with more conservative evolved needs of

human infants and parents. In many Western industrialized cultures, a major cultural shift toward more co-sleeping (both separate surface and bed sharing) has taken place over the last few decades, as the extraordinary health benefits of breastfeeding for mothers and infants continue to be confirmed, making breastfeeding, rather than formula- or cow-milk feeding, the preferred feeding practice. As new mothers learn how to breastfeed, they soon discover that breastfeeding is managed more easily in co-sleeping arrangements (either separate surface, bed sharing, or both) and that they and their infants can get more sleep (Ball & Klingaman, 2008). Insofar as this is true, traditional expectations and/or developmental models of infant sleep based on studies of formula- or cow-milk fed infants, sleeping separate from their mothers, are increasingly obsolete and inapplicable to the majority of infants in these cultures. The challenges ahead include resolving how pediatric sleep research can accommodate the powerful sets of biological factors that altogether make forms of co-sleeping and breastfeeding appropriate choices but, at the same time, how to educate parents to make choices relevant to their circumstances that can assure the health, development, and safety of infants and parents (Gettler & McKenna, 2010; McKenna et al., 2007).

Lee T. Gettler and James J. McKenna

See also: entries related to Sleep and Development

References

Ball, H. L., & Klingaman, K. P. (2008). Breast-feeding and mother–infant sleep proximity: Implications for infant care. In W. Trevathan,

E. O. Smith, & J. J. McKenna (Eds.), *Evolutionary medicine and health: New perspectives* (pp. 226–241). New York: Oxford University Press.

Barry, H., & Paxson, L. M. (1971). Infancy and early childhood: Cross-cultural codes, 2. *Ethnology, 10*(4), 466–508.

Byard, R. W., & Krous, H. F. (2003). Sudden infant death syndrome: Overview and update. *Pediatric and Developmental Pathology, 6*(2), 112–127.

Elias, M. F., Nicolson, N. A., Bora, C., & Johnston, J. (1986a). Sleep/wake patterns of breast-fed infants in the first two years of life. *Pediatrics, 77*(3), 322–329.

Elias, M. F., Nicolson, N. A., & Konner, M. (1986b). Two sub-cultures of maternal care in the United States. In D. M. Taub & F. A. King (Eds.), *Current perspectives in primate social dynamics* (pp. 37–50). New York: Van Nostrand Reinhold.

Fleming, P., Blair, P., & McKenna, J. (2006). New knowledge, new insights, and new recommendations. *Archives of Disease in Childhood, 91*(10), 799–801.

Germo, G. R., Chang, E. S., Keller, M. A., & Goldberg, W. A. (2007). Child sleep arrangements and family life: Perspectives from mothers and fathers. *Infant and Child Development, 16*, 433–456.

Gettler, L. T., & McKenna, J. J. (2010). Never sleep with baby? Or keep me close but keep me safe: Eliminating inappropriate "safe infant sleep" rhetoric in the United States. *Current Pediatric Reviews, 6*(1), 71–77.

Gettler, L. T., & McKenna, J. J. (2011). Evolutionary perspectives on mother–infant sleep proximity and breastfeeding in a laboratory setting. *American Journal of Physical Anthropology, 144*, 454–462.

McDade, T. W., & Worthman, C. M. (1998). The weanling's dilemma reconsidered: A biocultural analysis of breastfeeding ecology. *JDBP, 19*(4), 286–299.

McKenna, J. J., Ball, H. L., & Gettler, L. T. (2007). other–infant co-sleeping, breastfeeding and

sudden infant death syndrome (SIDS): What biological anthropology has discovered about normal infant sleep and pediatric sleep medicine. *Yearbook of Physical Anthropology, 50*, 133–161.

Messmer, R. L. (2009). *The relationship between parent–infant bed-sharing and marital satisfaction for mothers of infants aged 6–12 months* (Master of Arts dissertation, The University of British Columbia).

Murdock, G. P., Ford, C. S., Hudson, A. E., Kennedy, R., Simmons, L. W., & Whiting, J. W. M. (2006). *Outline of cultural materials* (6th ed.). New Haven, CT: Human Relations Area Files.

Robson, S. L., Van Schaik, C. P, & Hawkes, K. (2006). The derived features of human life history. In K. Hawkes & R. R. Paine (Eds.), *The evolution of human life history* (pp. 17–45). Santa Fe, NM: School of American Research Press.

Super, C., & Harkness, S. (1987). The infant's niche in rural Kenya and metropolitan America. In L. C. Adler (Ed.), *Issues in cross-cultural research* (pp. 113–162). New York: Academic Press.

Costly Signaling Theory

Costly signaling theory (CST) is one of a number of evolutionary approaches to dreams. CST was developed within the literature on animal behavior to explain signal exchanges between predators and prey or between potential mates. For example, why do moose or elk develop such unwieldy antler systems? Antlers are metabolically costly, and if they grow too large they can actually impede attempts to defend against or evade predators or competitors. CST accounts of the development of these physiological monstrosities treat them as signaling systems and then observe effects of variations in these systems on reproductive success or status competitions. If, for example, large antlers signaled the presence of robust parasite-resistant genes in a reindeer or elk, then the possessor of large antlers should outcompete males with lesser antler systems in the competition for high-quality matings with females who are assumed to wish to pair with high-quality males. Large antlers will, in effect, advertise presence of good genes—genes that can metabolically sustain costly and even wasteful physiological systems. This, in turn, creates selective pressures for displaying and enhancing such advertisements. Males without the parasite-resistant genes will not be able to display large antlers, as they will not be able to metabolically grow and maintain the antlers without paying a metabolic cost that in turn will make them more vulnerable to parasite infestation. Thus large antlers, although costly to produce and thus an expensive handicap, will nevertheless constitute an honest signal of good genes, and thus honest communication between potential mates will be possible. In short, the antlers were developed because of their capacity to signal information concerning genetic quality of the individual. The more costly, the more extravagant the signal, the more unlikely it could be faked by an inferior-quality individual. In short, possessing elaborate antler systems was a sure sign that the individual was a high-quality male. This sort of information is absolutely critical for females looking to avoid matings with an individual whose genes would prevent a healthy pregnancy or viable offspring.

What does CST have to do with dreams? REM clearly is associated with costly physiological processes. REM is also involved in intense limbic system activation—which suggests that REM contributes to development of emotional expressions. If REM functions to help produce costly signals (e.g., hard-to-fake emotional displays), then some of its paradoxical traits that actually are risky to the organism's health begin to make sense.

Many dreams are emotional and some theorists have treated emotions as signaling devices that are hard to fake. To the extent that emotions are hard to fake, they are taken as honest indicators of the individual's state of mind and the individual's ability to handle adversity. In short, emotions likely carry vital information about the genetic quality of the individual. If this is so, then people likely came under selective pressures to become excellent readers of emotion and masters at modulation of emotional displays, particularly facial displays of emotion. Over the millions of years that sapiens have evolved, they became adept at faking some emotional states and thus new signaling systems were brought in to do the work that facial displays of emotion or vocalizations once did. People needed additional information about an individual before accepting verbal reports or emotional displays at face value. Dreams were both emotional and involuntary. They nevertheless had to be verbally shared with others if they were to directly affect others. The fact that dreams were involuntary products of the mind made them valuable artifacts in the war for information about the quality of the individual who had the dream. When someone shares a dream with others, it is difficult to make up a dreamlike story on the spot. Dreams are to that extent difficult to fake. Thus they can theoretically become valuable signaling devices for people considering cooperating with one another. Dreams can be considered costly signals because they are metabolically costly, particularly when they include bizarre imagery. We now know from neuroimaging studies that brain-activation levels during REM sleep are sometimes higher than they are for the waking state. But do we have any evidence that ancestral populations treated people with frequent or unusual or intense dreams as special individuals of high status? Yes, ethnographic records of premodern tribal cultures round the globe show that dreams were accorded sacred status and that shamans were particularly interested in dreams.

Patrick McNamara

See also: entries related to Evolution of Sleep

Counterfactuals in Dreams

Many theorists have attempted to characterize the species of cognition one sees in dreams. One proposal that has received some preliminary empirical support is that many dreams specialize in processing counterfactuals. Counterfactuals in logic characterize conditions under which some state of affairs might have been true. In philosophy and in language, semantics counterfactuals have been used to characterize modal event logics and to use possible world scenarios to evaluate formal languages. In economics, counterfactuals are crucial to a range of theories concerning risk and decision-making rules under conditions of regret and attempts to avoid losses. In psychology and cognitive neuroscience, counterfactuals are treated as mental simulations of possible worlds or how things might have been if one variable in a mental model had been changed slightly. Regardless of the various ways in which counterfactuals are treated in these disparate intellectual disciplines, the common denominator is that they are mental simulations of what might have happened if I had chosen differently or performed slightly differently. For example, "If I had left 5 minutes earlier I would have not missed the plane and then I would have later been killed in the crash that destroyed that plane." Or: "If I had taken an umbrella I would not have gotten wet." Or "If I had studied harder I would have not failed the exam." In daily life, when we encounter an unhappy or frustrating event, we appraise the significance of the outcome by imagining alternatives or what might have happened if things had gone differently. We then cognitively generate simulations of imaginative scenarios (counterfactuals) that would allow or promote the alternative outcome. We do this typically by constructing a visual scenario of the events in question and then changing or mutating various causal antecedents of the outcome of the event. We next compare the simulations of what might have been to what actually happened in an attempt to restore the unwanted outcome to a more normative routine outcome. That is what dreams may be doing in many cases. The mental simulations that we call dreams are attempts to redress an unwanted outcome or to anticipate and avert a forthcoming unwanted outcome. The significance of this idea is that if it is true then people can learn via dreaming. That is because counterfactuals are a primary means of learning under normal conditions of life. When we encounter an unwanted outcome (I failed the test), we generate a counterfactual (If I had studied more) against which we compare the negative event. To the extent that the comparison process reveals that the counterfactual alternatives seem plausible or possible as compared to what actually happened (I indeed could have studied more), we feel tension, distress, or discomfort and are therefore motivated to try to redress the failure or negative event. Thus, by engaging in these counterfactual simulations, we may more easily learn how to avoid negative outcomes in the future, or we may learn how to strive more effectively for current unmet goals or desired outcomes.

Patrick McNamara

Creative Problem Solving in Dreams

The French surrealist poet St. Paul Boux would hang a sign on his bedroom door before retiring, which read: "Poet at work." John Steinbeck expressed a similar idea when he observed: "It is a common experience that a problem difficult at night is resolved in the morning after the committee of sleep has worked on it." Neither of these writers mentions dreams specifically but most of the examples of sleep contributing to creative problem solving are from dreams, and modern research on this also implicates dreams and the related state of REM.

More dream inspirations occur in the visual arts than any other, as visual imagery occupies so much of the content of dreaming. Archeologists have speculated that a bird-staff and some of the other fantastic elements painted on the cave walls of Lascaux, France, 10,000 to 40,000 years ago may represent dreams. Certainly, since we have records, innumerable artists have painted images from their dreams. German artist Albrecht Durer's 1525 watercolor of a savage storm bears an inscription indicating it was a nightmare about unearthly rain.

Visionary William Blake painted one of his own dreams as "Young Night's Thoughts" (1818) with himself lying on the ground dreaming, the action of the dream painted next to him, a poem based on the same dream beneath that, and finally a straightforward account of the dream. Blake also dreamed of an instructor telling him of new painting and engraving techniques that he employed in his real work. Pre-Raphaelite Sir Edward Burne-Jones once fell asleep and dreamed of the nine muses on Mt. Helicon so vividly that he felt compelled to paint them the moment he arrived at his destination as "The Rose Bower." Many surrealists painted specific dream images. A few titles that reflect this are Salvador Dalí's "The Dream," Frida Kahlo's painting of the same name, Max Ernst's "Dream of a Girl Chased by a Nightingale," Paul Nash's "Landscape from a Dream," Dalí's "The Dream Approaches," and Gil Bruvel's "The Sleep Goes Away." Dreams show up in other modes of visual art. Modern architects Lucy Davis and Solange Fabião have both dreamed numerous times of their building designs. Not all dream art looks stereotypical dreamlike: modern artist Jasper Johns's series of highly realistic giant American Flag paintings began when he dreamed of painting this on a giant canvas.

Dreams have frequently contributed to literature, narrative being the second-most prominent element of dreaming after visual imagery. Mary Shelley dreamed the two main scenes that became *Frankenstein* and Robert Lewis Stevenson did the same with *Dr. Jekyll and Mr. Hyde*. The Romantic writers were especially fond of dreams. Mary's husband, Percy Bysshe Shelley, published a collection of his nocturnal experiences in *The Catalogue of Phenomenon of Dreams, as Connecting Sleeping and Waking*. Cristina Rossetti used hers in poetry such as "The Crocodiles," which described a fanciful version of the animal encrusted with gold and polished stones. Modern writers who have written scenes from dreams include Anne Rice, Stephen King, Eudora Welty, and Jack Kerouac. Filmmakers including Ingmar Bergman, Frederico Fellini, Akira Kurosawa, Orson Welles, and Robert Altman filmed scenes or even entire films that they dreamed.

Music also has arrived in dreams. Musicians Billy Joel and Joseph Shabalala say they hear *all* their compositions—minus

Shirish Korde dreamed music for his chamber opera Rasa, based on Bharati Mukherjee's novel *Jasmine*, which in turn had its ending created in a dream. (Shirish Korde)

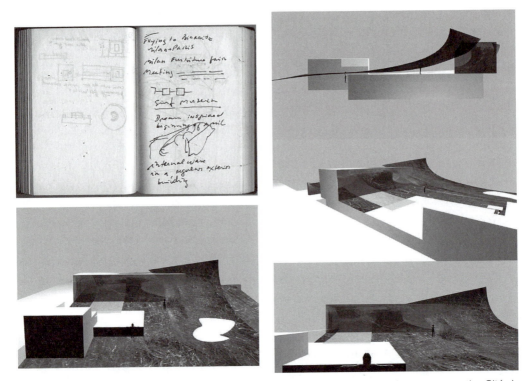

Architect Solange Fabião had decided to submit a design for the oceanography museum—the Cité de L'Océan et du Surf in Biarritz, France—but had not yet come up with her plan when she dreamed that she was in a huge retangular building with a swooping ceiling. She studied it and realized that the building was underneath a giant ocean wave. Solange awakened and sketched the building that she'd seen. Her dreamed design won the commission and was completed in June 2011. (Solange Fabião)

words—in dreams. More typically, Paul McCartney dreamed "Yesterday"—the most played song in the history of radio. Because of McCartney's unfamiliarity with the experience, he went around checking with people whether it was a known piece of music. "Because I'd dreamed it, I couldn't believe I'd written it," he told others. Classic composers such as Ludwig van Beethoven, Giuseppe Tartini, and Igor Stravinsky each dreamed one of their musical compositions.

Scientific discoveries have also come in dreams. August Kekulé dreamed the structure of benzene, Dmitri Mendeleev dreamed his final form of the periodic table of the elements, and Otto Loewi won a Nobel Prize for an experiment he saw in a dream. Modern engineers Paul Horowitz and Alan Huang dreamed designs for laser telescope controls and laser computing respectively. Inventions ranging from the automated sewing machine to the computerized anti-aircraft gun have originated in dreams.

Many non-Western cultures teach people to look at their dreams for solutions. These cultures seem to have higher rates of problem-solving dreams. While Western mathematicians have occasionally made major breakthroughs in their dreams, India's greatest mathematician, Srinivasa Ramanujan, said that all his mathematical proofs came to him in dreams, and he attributed them to the goddess Namagiri to whom he'd been taught to pray for dreams. Musician Joseph Shabalala said it was natural for him to write down the music he had heard in dreams as his parents had both been African healers who utilized their dreams for their work.

Research

The first retrospective study on dreams and objective problems was more than a century ago. In 1892, Charles Child asked 186 college students whether they had ever solved a problem in a dream. One third said they had. Examples included a chess game played in a dream, an algebra problem solved, a bookkeeping error detected, and a passage from Virgil translated.

Modern prospective studies have used dream-incubation techniques to attempt to induce dreams about particular problems similar to what some non-Western cultures do. In 1972, William Dement asked 500 college students to try to solve three brainteasers for 15 minutes at night, moving on to another problem if they were successful so that they fell asleep with an unsolved problem on their mind. Eighty-seven dreams were judged to address a problem. Seven dreams solved one of them.

In 1993, Deirdre Barrett had 76 college students incubate dreams addressing problems chosen by the dreamer nightly for one week. Approximately half recalled a dream that they judged to be related to their problem; a majority of these believed their dream contained a solution. Independent judges rated slightly fewer dreams as either addressing or solving the problems than did the dreamers, but the trends of their conclusions followed the same patterns as those of the dreamers.

Other researchers have approached the issue by examining whether rapid eye movement (REM) sleep, the stage closely associated with dreaming, has any effect on problem solving. Evidence is emerging that it does. In 2009, psychologists at the University California, San Diego, examined whether REM facilitated more than just memory when learning. They administered a test of creative problem solving and then primed subjects with some hints as to answers. They then had either a waking time-out period with non-REM sleep only or REM sleep before retesting on the problem solving. The group that had REM sleep showed more improvement on their creative solutions to the previously presented problems. The same year, in Robert Stickgold's lab at Harvard, a team led by post-doctorate student Ina Djonlagic gave subjects a task they could do in rote way that also had an aha-type insight for a general rule, which made the task easier. In this case, the conditions before retest were simply sleep versus wake. They found that the sleep group improved more—but improvement and explicit articulation of having grasped the general rule were correlated with amount of REM time specifically.

Deirdre Barrett

References

Barrett, D. (1993). The "committee of sleep": A study of dream incubation for problem solving. *Dreaming, 3*(2).

Barrett, D. (2001). *The committee of sleep.* New York: Crown/Random House.

Djonlagic, I., Rosenfeld, A., Shohamy, D., Myers, C., Gluck, M., & Stickgold, R. (2009). Sleep enhances category learning. *Learning Memory,* 16(12), 751–755.

Karni, A., Tanne, D., Rubenstein, B. S., Askenasy, J. J., & Sagi, D. (1994). Dependence on REM sleep of overnight improvement of a perceptual skill. *Science, 265,* 679–682.

Cross-Cultural Approaches to Dreams

When the term *cross-cultural* is used in disciplined inquiry, it refers to identifiable experiences and behaviors in the search for group similarities and differences. There are three cross-cultural approaches to dreams: case study comparisons, comparisons of dreams on a particular topic, and comparisons within several dream samples. The latter is often referred to as cross-cultural studies and uses enough dreams to test specific hypotheses statistically. For example, Krippner, Jaeger, and Faith (2001) examined 799 dream reports—one per participant—from Argentina, Brazil, and the United States in an attempt to test the continuity hypothesis that posits that dream content reflects the dreamer's daily activities, albeit in symbols and metaphors. More emotional content was discerned in female than in male dreams across countries, and more emotion in Argentine and Brazilian female dreams was detected than in U.S. female dreams. More activities were mentioned in male dreams across cultures. Family members were more often mentioned by female dreamers in all three cultures, especially by Argentine and Brazilian dreamers. These findings refute the notion that dreams differ from daily life, representing unfulfilled wishes or future expectations.

These data also affirm the usefulness of the Hall–Van de Castle coding system, which consists of some 50 categories (e.g., family members, sexual interactions) as a useful instrument in cross-cultural studies. Other systems are rarely applied and provide no norms. The Hall–Van de Castle system also allows for the computation of percentages such as animal percent; there are a greater percentage of animals among dreamers who live in hunter-gatherer societies, again supporting the continuity hypothesis.

The first type of cross-cultural approach, a comparison of case studies, is exemplified by T. Gregor's study of 18 men and 18 women from the Mehinaku tribe in the Amazon rainforest. Each contributed several dream reports, which were examined for aggressive and sexual content and compared with Hall and Van de Castle's (1966) U.S. sample. The results convinced Gregor that the dream experience is less variant than other aspects of culture; for these two content variables, there was a remarkable similarity among genders, between genders, and across the two cultures. Data of this nature support the hypothesis that dream content is rooted in a biological base with a cultural overlay.

Tyger by Dierdre Luzwick demonstrates how a dream image in one culture may have a different meaning than the same image reported by dreamers in another culture. (Reproduced from the original art of Dierdre Luzwick)

The Hall–Van de Castle system can be used in the second type of cross-cultural approach, that is, comparisons on a particular topic such as the impact of culture on dream content. D. Schneider studied several hundred dream reports from 13 traditional societies, concluding that there are certain regularities in the manifest content of groups of dreams across cultures and that the differences seem to be a function of the culture of the dreamer. For example, in all these groups, dreamers were more often victims than aggressors. Additionally, men dreamed more often about other men than they did about women. Sexual interactions of any type totaled less than 10 percent in almost all of these societies. However, J. A. Hobson and D. Kahn (2007) published the case of an engineer who had sexual relations in his dreams with 38 different women. However, he masturbated daily while engaging in sexual fantasies, suggesting that the continuity hypothesis might include imagined behavior as well as actual behavior. Some writers would assert that the preponderance of sexual dreams represented wish fulfillment; however, the engineer claimed not to be attracted to any of the women he dreamt about. An earlier study involved three Nigerian tribes, one constantly on the verge of famine, one enjoying bountiful harvests, and one in an intermediate condition. The tribe with dreamers who were well-fed reported the most dreams about food, refuting wish fulfillment as the primary function of dream content.

Not all dreams represent daily activities. Krippner et al. (2001) studied 1,666 dream reports from 6 different countries, providing definitions for creative dreams, lucid dreams, out-of-body dreams, and other unusual dreams. Russian participants reported significantly more unusual dreams than dreamers from most other countries, followed by Brazilian participants; U.S. dreamers reported the fewest. Krippner et al. used the same collection to identify spiritual dreams, using the six-category Casto Spirituality Scoring System (i.e., spiritual objects, characters, settings, activities, emotions, experiences). Brazilian dream reports included significantly more spiritual content than dreams from other countries; Japanese participants included the least.

Cross-cultural comparisons indicate that dream content is more often negative than positive. If a key function of dreams is to affect regulation, the downloading of negative experiences during the day may have been adaptive in the course of human evolution, allowing dreamers to awaken refreshed. People with posttraumatic stress disorder report nightmares in which their traumatizing experiences are repeated, usually without recourse to metaphor and symbolism common in other dreams. Perhaps they cannot download negativity, thus do not function well in their daily life.

There are drawbacks to cross-cultural approaches to dreams. Dream reports might not be translated accurately and a term from one culture might differ from the meaning of that term in another culture. Some participants will report daydreams and waking fantasies when asked to provide a dream. Nonetheless, cross-cultural approaches to dreams can yield information useful to several disciplines, including cultural anthropology, ethnography, the sociology of gender, evolutionary psychology, and clinical psychology.

Stanley C. Krippner

See also: entries related to Cross-Cultural Dreams

References

Domhoff, G. W. (2003). *The scientific study of dreams: Neural networks, cognitive development, and content analysis.* Washington, DC: American Psychological Association.

Domhoff, G. W., & Schneider, A. (2008). Similarities and differences in dream content at the cross-cultural, gender, and individual levels. *Consciousness and Cognition, 17*, 1257–1265.

Hall, C., & Van de Castle, R. L. (1966). *The content analysis of dreams.* New York: Appleton-Century-Crofts.

Hobson, J. A., & Kahn, D. (2007). Dream content: Individual and generic aspects. *Consciousness and Cognition, 16*, 850–858.

Krippner, S., Jaeger, C., & Faith, L. (2001). Identifying and utilizing spiritual content in dream reports. *Dreaming, 11*, 127–147.

Cultural Dimensions of Sleep

Sleep is a human universal. Like other biological imperatives, such as eating, there are cultural dimensions to how we sleep, when and where we sleep, and with whom, and to how we understand the experiences that we have while sleeping. We are socialized into ways of sleeping from infancy. Sleeping patterns vary through the course of a human life and are influenced by our gender, status, wealth, occupation, and health as well as our age and culture. Sleeping patterns may also be seasonally affected, as a consequence of daylight, weather, or work, or because of particular religious observances.

Different cultures have different ways of sleeping, and, like other aspects of our human experience, how we sleep tends to be naturalized in our thinking as the normal human way of doing things. Yet there are significant differences in the way that people sleep in different cultures throughout the world. In terms of when we sleep, Steger and Brunt (2003, p. 16) describe monophasic sleep cultures as those in which sleep occurs in one long period at night, as is fairly common in Western societies. Cultures having biphasic sleep patterns have two main sleep periods, a long nocturnal sleep and a shorter afternoon one; Spain typifies this sleep pattern. Japan and China have been described as having napping or polyphasic sleep cultures (Steger & Brunt, 2003, p. 16). Even in so-called monophasic sleep cultures, it is not uncommon for persons to experience all three kinds of sleep patterns over the developmental course of their life (Steger & Brunt, 2003, p. 16).

Variations in the social and cultural environments in which we sleep are related to concerns for safety as well as protection from the elements. Bedding materials and sleeping spaces vary considerably throughout the world (Worthman & Melby, 2002) and, within single cultures, may change considerably over time. It is not uncommon for humans in many societies to sleep close to their pets or domesticated animals.

It is not just when we sleep or where that differs cross-culturally though. In contemporary Western sleep settings, many people sleep alone or with a spouse or partner. Historical studies of sleep have shown that the tendency toward solitary sleeping in Western societies is fairly recent (Elias, 1978 [1939]). A survey of the ethnographic material available for a range of traditional societies in different continents, experiencing different climates and practicing different forms of subsistence living, revealed that in many non-Western societies, solitary sleeping is rare, co-sleeping is common, and the boundaries between sleeping and waking states are quite flexible (Worthman & Melby, 2002). The evidence suggests that in most cultures, co-sleeping with others is the norm. Whom one co-sleeps with will depend on cultural factors to do with relatedness and kinship, as well as emotional factors in interpersonal relations, and, in many cases, economic factors. Most of what we know about sleep in scientific terms comes from sleep research in settings that reflect Western sleep norms (Worthman & Melby, 2002, p. 107).

Sleep, or lack of sleep, may also be an integral part of a society's ritual activities, and the neurobiological effects of sleep deprivation may contribute to rituals involving trance and altered states of consciousness, which are often nocturnal (Worthman & Melby, 2002, p. 87). How persons worldwide conceptualize what happens when we sleep, especially in relation to how dreams are understood, reveals significant aspects of cultural beliefs about the nature of human existence, and the world (Tedlock, 1992). Less typical sleep experiences, such as sleep paralysis, are also culturally elaborated (Adler, 2011). While sleep then is a biological universal, the ways in which we sleep are socially, culturally, historically (and sometimes politically) constituted. As such, sleep is an important reflection of the societies in which we live, how they change through time, and our socialization within them.

Katie Glaskin

See also: Anthropology of Sleep

References

Adler, S.R. (2011). *Sleep paralysis: Nightmares, nocebos, and the mind–body connection.* London: Rutgers University Press.

Elias, N. (1978 [1939]). *The civilizing process vol. 1: The history of manners.* Oxford, UK: Basil Blackwell.

Steger, B., & Brunt, L. (Eds.). (2003). *Nighttime and sleep in Asia and the West: Exploring the dark side of life.* London: Routledge Curzon.

Tedlock, B. (Ed.). (1992). *Dreaming: Anthropological and psychological interpretations*: Santa Fe, NM: School of American Research Press.

Worthman, C. M., & Melby, M. K. (2002). Toward a comparative developmental ecology of human sleep. In M. A. Carskadon (Ed.), *Adolescent sleep patterns: Biological, social, and psychological influences* (pp. 69–117). New York: Cambridge University Press.

Cultural Diversity and Dreaming

Dreams in Diverse Cultures

Dreams have been a focus of interest in anthropology at least since the time of Tylor, who saw in them the origin of religion. The Dayaks, and many other cultures, hold "that dreams are incidents which happen to the spirit in its wanderings from the body" (Tylor, 1964 [1878], p. 5). "When the sleeper awakens from a dream, he believes that he has really somehow been away, or that other people have come to him" (Tylor, 1960 [1881], p. 203). "The Malays do not like to wake a sleeper lest they should hurt him by disturbing his body while his soul is out." Nocturnal encounters with the deceased may have engendered the notion of an immortal soul surviving after death (Kracke "Afterword" in Lohmann, 2003, pp. 213–215; Tylor, 1964 [1878], p. 6).

The study of dreams in antiquity and in primitive cultures was an inspiration to Sigmund Freud, who attributed to Artemidoris of Thebes and other classical dream commentators the stimulus for his idea that dreams have meaning and to popular folklore the idea that dreams represent wishes.

Later on, Bronislaw Malinowski cited Trobriand sexual dreams of Trobriand men about their sisters as evidence for his concept of a matrilineal Oedipus complex in which the forbidden childhood sexual object is not a boy's mother but his sister.

Anthropological Questions

What do people in another culture believe dreams are? What do they think causes them? When do they tell them, or refrain from telling them, and why? How do they interpret them?

Many cultures throughout the world are reported to have beliefs similar to those described by Tylor: that the dreamer's soul, or one kind of soul, wanders from the body in sleep and has experiences in the world. Indeed, the temporary muscular atonia (sleep paralysis) that takes place during REM sleep, when most dreams occur, may contribute to the impression that the sleeper's soul has left his body while he dreams. Tylor cited such beliefs for the Dayak (Iban of Borneo), the Malays, the Zulu, and the Ojibwa. Anthropologists have verified them in some of these cultures for the Iban; Hallowell [1966] for the Ojibwa). Hallowell noted that one man located a spot he had previously seen only in a dream. Others continue to report similar beliefs in the cultures they study: the Kalapalo (Basso, in Tedlock, 1987, p. 88; Tedlock, in Tedlock, 1987, pp. 113, 115), the Mehinaku (Gregor, 1981), and many others. Devereux (1951), who conducted therapy with a Plains Indian patient, stated that for his tribe the dream is a real event, though on a different plane from waking reality. In Morocco, Crapanzano recounts his conversations with Tuhami, nocturnally married to Aisha Qandisha—a female spirit who seduces men in their dreams and holds them jealously.

But more intensive study of dreaming in a culture—recording many dreams and noting the explanations dreamers give for different kinds of dreams—shows that the concepts and explanations of dreaming are often much more complex. The idea that dreams are portents, prognostications of future events, is one that recurs in many cultures around the world, as it does in many European folk cultures and in dream books in our own society. As Michael Brown (in Tedlock, 1987, p. 157) has aptly phrased it for the Aguaruna, a Shuar tribe of the Peruvian montaña, they "reveal emergent possibilities or likelihoods." In these beliefs about dream forecasting, dreams do not provide absolute predictions, but rather offer a glimpse of future possibilities that can be realized or averted by taking appropriate action.

Among the Parintintin of Amazonian Brazil, a dream with an undesirable portent can be canceled by telling it to someone by the fire or by performing a ritual act of breaking a piece of thatch in pieces, muttering "it will not happen—I dreamed in vain." An old man I worked with dreamed that the house my hammock was hung in burned down, but he saved me from dying of a fever by performing this ritual. On the other hand, a young man told me of an erotic dream he had once had that would portend the availability of tapir, but he thoughtlessly told the dream in the morning to his hunting companion. They saw a group of tapir during the day, but failed to kill one—because he had told the dream by the fire. "Anyone who dreams," they say, "has a little bit of shamanic power"

because they can either take advantage of the dream's prediction (by going hunting if it tells that a particular game animal is nearby—but not tell it by the fire!) or cancel it out if it predicts illness or death.

In most cultures that share this belief, a dream can be interpreted literally as a prediction, but more often the dream communicates in an esoteric language based on metaphoric analogy. For the Parintintin, a dream of an animated party portends the presence of white-lipped peccary available for hunting—because white-lipped peccaries travel in packs that charge through the jungle, and if they go through your camp, they can cause as much damage as a wild party. Many cultures have elaborate codes of dream portents of that sort, and much can be told about the anxieties, aims, and desires of the culture from the sorts of events in dreams that are predictive, and what kinds of conditions or events they portend. In Parintintin culture, shamans carry out their supernatural acts through their dreams: they will dream intentionally (in a lucid dream) of something that predicts what they want to carry out—but for them, the dream brings it about.

Another belief encountered in many cultures suggests self-observation of the process of forming a dream. The Parintintin say that thoughts in your mind as you go to sleep—often about events of the day—are taken into sleep with you and turned into your dream (Kracke, 1999). Barbadians likewise, as reported by Larry Fisher, feel that you dream of things that you study, that you dwell on with excessive intensity. Here, a number of cultures that value dreams have evidently observed the importance of day residues in the formation of dreams. Vishvajit Pandya has described among the Ongi of Little Andaman Island, east of India, a belief that each human being has a body internal associated with one's personal smell; in dreams, the body internal revisits each spot the sleeper has been to during the day, gathering up the bits of smell left there and reweaving them into the spider home of the sleeper's body internal. The Ongi have produced a metaphor for much of what dream therapists and dream researchers think dreams do for us in gathering our memories of the day, weaving them into our long-term memory, and repairing the rends left by the day's adversities.

Implications for Study of Dreaming

Other cultures have given dreams a much more exalted epistemological role than we do in our culture: as a view of emerging reality or a way to see through the screen to another reality on the other side of this one. In such cultures, dreams are taken seriously and contemplated. In some, ceremonial life is focused on dreams: Alfred Kroeber refers to a group of such cultures in native California as dream cultures. Wallace reconstructed old Iroquois practices in which a person's dreams must be ritually reenacted, fulfilling the wishes of his soul. Some languages have a special grammatical form in which dreams must be told— often one that groups dreams with myths and with events one knows about through being told about them, not from one's own direct experience. Parintintin has a special form that is just for telling dreams.

These dream-aware cultures may have reached a familiarity with aspects of dreams that we are only now feeling our way toward since we have rediscovered their importance. We may be able to look to the concepts those cultures have developed for new insights on dreams as well as affirmations of those we are groping for. Dreams in these diverse cultures, and their beliefs about them, form a rich field for examining dreams and how they are constructed.

Waud H. Kracke

See also: entries related to Cross-Cultural Dreams

References

Devereux, G. (1951). *Reality and dream: Psychotherapy of a Plains Indian*. Garden City, NY: Doubleday Anchor.

Gregor, T. (1981). Far, far away my shadow wandered: The dream symbolism and dream theories of the Mehinaku Indians of Brazil. *American Ethnologist, 8*, 709–720.

Hallowell, A. I. (1966). The role of dreams in Ojibwa culture. In G. E. Von Grunebaum & R. Caillois (Eds.), *The dream and human societies* (pp. 267–292). Berkeley: University of California Press.

Kracke, W. (1999). A language of dreaming: Dreams of an Amazonian insomniac. *International Journal of Psychoanalysis, 80*, 257–271.

Lohmann, R. (2003). *Dreamtravelers: Sleep experiences and culture in the Western Pacific* (Ed. Roger Lohmann). New York: Palgrave-MacMillan.

Tedlock, B. (1987) *Dreaming: Anthropological and psychological interpretations*. Santa Fe, NM: School of American Research.

Tylor, Sir E. B. (1960 [1881]). *Anthropology* (Abridged and edited by Leslie A White). Ann Arbor: University of Michigan Press.

Tylor, Sir E. B. (1964 [1878]). *Researches into the early history of mankind*. Chicago: University of Chicago Press.

Wallace, A. (1958). Dreams and wishes of the soul. *American Anthropologist, 60*, 234–248.

D

Definition of Sleep

Sleep is a behavioral state of reversible quiescence that arises from an interaction between the circadian system (which organizes functioning of biological rhythms that cycle on the order of every 24 hours) and a wake-dependent homeostatically controlled system of sleep pressure. During waking behavior some as yet unknown substance cumulates in the brain. As circadian pacemaker processes and indicators (e.g., body temperature) decline with the onset of the dark period, the wake-related substance in the brain reaches a threshold and the urge to sleep becomes intense. At the onset of sleep, the need to sleep gradually dissipates across the state as sleep cumulates and circadian indicators start to rise again. When circadian processes rise and sleep intensity diminishes, the individual awakens feeling refreshed. This homeostatically regulated process characterized by a reversible form of behavioral quiescence is called sleep.

Sleep in most animals is composed of behavioral, functional, physiological, and electrophysiological traits. For complex animals, electrophysiological measures of sleep are obtained via electroencephalography (EEG) and include both REM and non-REM (NREM) sleep. NREM in humans include N1 (a transitional form that occurs as we fall asleep) and N2/N3, which is characterized by high-voltage slow-wave forms on EEG. When an animal exhibits all four major components of sleep, including the behavioral, electrophysiological, physiological, and functional components, then it is said that the animal exhibits full polygraphic sleep. Full polygraphic sleep, in this sense, has so far been documented only in primates (including humans). Behavioral measures of sleep include a species-specific body posture and sleeping site, reduced physical activity (quiescence), reduced muscle tone, reduction in neck/nuchal muscle tone, paralysis of the antigravity muscles in some species, increased arousal threshold, and rapid reversibility to wakefulness. Physiological indices of sleep include significant reductions in temperature and metabolism during NREM and significant lability in autonomic nervous system, cardiovascular and respiratory measures during REM, along with increases in metabolism. Electrophysiological measures of REM include low-voltage fast waves, REMs, theta rhythms in the hippocampus, and pontine–geniculo–occipital or PGO waves. Electrophysiological measures of NREM include high-voltage slow waves, spindles, and k-complexes. Functional indices of sleep include increased amounts of sleep after sleep deprivation and increased sleep intensity after sleep deprivation.

—*Patrick McNamara*

See also: entries related to Sleep Assessment

Delusions and the Classification of Typical Dreams

The analogy between dreaming and psychosis has long been drawn because of their similar conscious manifestation. Some research evidence suggests that both phenomena are operated by similar brain mechanisms (see Yu, 2009b, 2010, for details). There are typical themes in psychosis. Among various typical delusions, themes showing persecutory and grandiose features are most frequently observed in people diagnosed with psychotic and schizophrenia-spectrum disorders. Just as there are typical delusions in psychosis, so there are typical themes in dreams, such as school, teachers, studying; being chased or pursued; falling; arriving too late; and a person now alive as dead. Not only are these typical dream themes shared by most people from vastly different cultures but they tend to recur within an individual (Yu, 2008, 2010, 2011).

It is interesting to note that typical dream and delusional themes overlap considerably. For example, prevalent dream motifs of being chased or pursued; being physically attacked; being smothered, unable to breathe; vividly sensing a presence in the room; and being tied, unable to move can be construed as persecutory delusions in psychosis. On the other hand, dream themes such as having magical powers and having superior knowledge or mental ability are interchangeable with grandiose delusions. Moreover, to some extent, classic bizarre themes pertaining to schizophrenia and psychotic disorders, including grandiose, persecutory, religious, somatic, jealous, and erotomanic delusions, and less bizarre themes characteristic of the paranoid suspiciousness that denotes paranoid personality disorder can be found in the dreams of ordinary people. Some classic delusions, such as being tracked, having a superior status, and becoming a big wheel or celebrity, occur even more prevalently than common dream motifs, such as teeth falling out and being nude (Yu, 2009a, 2009b, 2010). In Yu's (2010) study, 9 of the 26 most prevalent dream themes showing a prevalence rate of 50 percent or more were exemplary delusional themes.

On the strength of the replicated findings generated mainly from factor analyses, Yu (2009a, 2009b) developed a delusional model that classifies the most prevalent dream themes into the categories of grandiosity, persecution, and ego ideal. Dream themes subsumed under the first category, including the examples of having a superior status, having superior knowledge or mental ability, becoming a big wheel or celebrity, and becoming a certain form of deity, can be largely compared to those grandiose delusions illustrated by the *Diagnostic and Statistical Manual of Mental Disorders* (4th ed., text rev.; *DSM–IV–TR*; American Psychiatric Association, 2000). Similarly, dream themes allotted to the second category, such as being persecuted, being tracked, some people plotting against you, being chased or pursued, and being physically attacked, are the *DSM–IV–TR*'s exemplars of a persecutory delusion. The ego ideal category does not directly involve classic psychotic delusions but is concerned with issues surrounding dreamers' falling short of social expectations and paranoid suspiciousness, such as arriving too late, being inappropriately dressed, failing an examination, blaming others for making troubles, and some people are spying on or talking about you. This three-factor classification of dream themes can be conceived equally well as a measurement model for assessing the three delusional predispositions that modulate dream formation. In addition to the three major categories of dream themes, Yu (2010) has also developed the Paranoia, Erotomania, Appetite-Instinct, and Sensorimotor Excitement scales to supplement the classification and assessment of dream narratives.

The three-factor model is aimed at conceptualizing common dream narratives within an articulate, parsimonious framework. The actual relationships between the dream themes are more complicated and less definite than what this classification model presents in that each dream theme can be deciphered in multiple fashions. For instance, themes of people wanting to take advantage of you and something seriously wrong with your body can be clustered into both the ego ideal and persecution factors. As with most dream themes subsumed under the grandiosity category, the theme of living in a very big house may portray a pleasurable scenario in which a wish is fulfilled in a straightforward manner. Alternatively, it could be understood as an ego-ideal theme in which the very big house symbolizes an inflated ego. In a similar vein, the theme of entering or passing through a narrow space might be a metaphor for sexual intercourse, a projective image of the somatic pressure surrounding the body or a symbolic, regressive response

to the somatic stimuli through which the dreamer relives the scene of being born.

Calvin Kai-Ching Yu

See also: entries related to Dream Content

References

American Psychiatric Association. (2000). *Diagnostic and statistical manual of mental disorders* (4th ed., text rev.). Washington, DC: Author.

Yu, C.K.-C. (2008). Typical dreams experienced by Chinese people. *Dreaming, 18*, 1–10.

Yu, C.K.-C. (2009a). Delusions and the factor structure of typical dreams. *Dreaming, 19*, 42–54.

Yu, C.K.-C. (2009b). Paranoia in dreams and the classification of typical dreams. *Dreaming, 19*, 255–272.

Yu, C.K.-C. (2010). Recurrence of typical dreams and the instinctual and delusional predispositions of dreams. *Dreaming, 20*, 254–279.

Yu, C.K.-C. (2011). The constancy of typical dreams. *Asia Pacific Journal of Counselling and Psychotherapy, 2*, 51–70.

Depictions of Dreams

For at least 1,500 years, human beings have been creating visual artworks that depict their dreams. The current review of such depictions in sculpture, painting, dance, and film focuses on works accessible on Web sites at the time of writing.

One of the oldest dream depictions that still survives is the 660 CE carving of the *Dream of the Rood* on the Ruthwell Cross, a Northumbrian rune stone. The *Rood*, the Anglo-Saxon term for *cross*, is represented in the dream by a bejeweled tree, which tells the dreamer that it once signified death but now signifies redemption.

Through the remainder of the Middle Ages and up until the middle of the 19th century, most dream depictions continued to be religious. One of the more interesting depictions from medieval times is Hieronymus Bosch's (1491) *Flight through the Tunnel*—a painted panel that envisions heaven as light at the end of a tunnel and, thus, exemplifies dream imagery associated with near-death brain functioning. From the 19th century, three notable depictions of religious dreams are by William Blake: his 1800 watercolor of *Jacob's Ladder*, his 1810 watercolor of *The Great Red Dragon and the Woman Clothed with the Sun* illustrating his poem entitled *A Dream*, and his 1825 watercolor of *Queen Katherine's Dream*. Throughout this period, nightmarish dreams were typically attributed to religious demons, such as the incubus in Henry Fuseli's (1782) painting *The Nightmare*.

After photographic pictures gave rise to motion pictures in the latter half of the 19th century, religious themes gave way to psychosexual themes not only in movies depicting dreams but also in painted depictions and danced depictions of dream content. Dreams manifesting Oedipal content are portrayed in Birgit Jürgenssen's (1989) photographic image *We Are Near to Awakening, When We Dream* That We Dream, and in the opening dream sequence of Federico Fellini's (1983) movie *8½*. Other psychosexual dreams are pictured in Georges Méliès's (1898) silent film *The Astronomer's Dream*, in Andrei Tarkovsky's (1983) narrative film *Nostalghia*, in František Kupka's (1909) painting *The*

Black-and-white version of the full-color *Dream Frames,* which one art student digitally imaged for the forthcoming book by Kunzendorf and Veatch. (Anonymous art student)

Dream, and in Jerome Robbins's (1984) ballet *Afternoon of a Faun* about the male dancer's wet dream.

And whereas nightmare depictions before the middle of the 18th century manifested religious or mythical demons, nightmare depictions since then have visually expressed latent psychological demons. Nightmares expressing death-related fears are pictured in Maya Deren and Alexander Hamid's (1943) experimental film *Meshes of the Afternoon*, in the dream sequences of Ingmar Bergman's (1957) narrative film *Wild Strawberries*, and in Frida Kahlo's (1940) painting *The Dream*. Nightmares expressing other fears are painted in Helmut Middendorf's (1982) *Airplane Dream* depicting a warplane overhead, in the *Wolf Man*, and in Sergei Pankejeff's (1964) *My Dream* depicting the wolves that were present in his childhood dreams and were psychoanalyzed in his therapy with Sigmund Freud.

By the middle of the 20th century, the dream depictions of certain artists began to capture not only the dream's visual content and its emotional meaning but also its surreal spatial structure and its surreal logic. As Botz-Bornstein (2007) notes in this regard:

> To produce surreality means to create a new reason able to penetrate into a "reality more true than reality" (to use a phrase by Timbaud).
> The surrealist ideal to free itself from the tyranny of logic signified to free itself from the "inferior" consciousness as it exists in our waking life. Logic needed to be deconstructed into a dream logic. (p. 108)

Roberto Matta's (1941) surrealist painting *Invasion of the Night* abstractly captures the nightmare's inner space—its emotionally distressing, spatially surreal structure—as well as any artwork before or since. The surreal structure and surreal logic of dreams other than nightmares are well represented in two of Salvador Dalí's paintings: his 1939 panel *Dreams of Venus* and his 1944 canvas *Dream, Caused by the Flight of a Bumblebee around a Pomegranate a Second before Awakening*. In addition, Dalí designed the backdrops for Leonide Massine's (1939) dream-based ballet *Bacchanale* and designed the dream sequence for Alfred Hitchcock's (1945) film *Spellbound*. Seven short films depicting the dreams of surrealist artists Max Ernst, Fernand Leger, Man Ray, Marcel Duchamp, Alexander Calder, and Hans Richter are presented in Richter's (1947) movie *Dreams That Money Can Buy*.

Many other drawings and paintings of dreams—including Alfred Kubin's (1903) drawing *In a Dream* and Henri Rousseau's (1910) painting *The Dream*—are reviewed in Lynn Gamwell's (2000) edited book *Dreams 1900–2000: Science, Art, and the Unconscious Mind*. Additional filmed depictions of dreams—such as Edwin Porter's (1906) silent film *Dream of a Rarebit Fiend*, the dream sequence in Luis Bunuel's (1950) movie *The Forgotten Ones*, the collection of dreams in Akira Kurosawa's (1990) movie *Dreams*, and the feature-length dream in Victor Fleming's (1939) movie *The Wizard of Oz*—are also reviewed in Gamwell's book.

In a recent effort to produce the critical frames of dream-based movies without actually making movies, psychology professor Robert Kunzendorf and art professor James Veatch have instructed art students to revisualize one of their dreams as if they were seeing a movie, to notice dream scenes containing critical changes in their dream's action and to create a digitally imaged series of movie frames depicting each of the critical dream scenes—like the digitally imaged series of dream frames. The 100 students who contributed their digitized dream frames to the professors' forthcoming book also filled out two questionnaires measuring personality traits. Upon correlating the digitized dreams' visual characteristics with their dreamers' personalities, Kunzendorf and Veatch made several interesting discoveries, two examples of which concern dreaming of a faceless person and dreaming of the color yellow. The presence of a faceless person in the 100 digitized dreams was positively correlated with greater death anxiety in the dreamer. Accordingly, like the faceless-person nightmares in Deren and Hamid's film *Meshes of the Afternoon* and in Bergman's film *Wild Strawberries*, the faceless-person dreams in Kunzendorf and Veatch's book call to mind the existential maxim that "what man fear[s] most [is] a nameless and faceless death" (Becker, 1975, p. 92). On the other hand, a greater amount of yellow in the 100 digitized dreams was positively correlated with greater hostility in the dreamer—in accord with the ancient Greek association of yellow bile, one of the four humors, with a hostile temperament. Correlations other than those discovered thus far by Kunzendorf and Veatch can be computed by the book's readers, using indexed traits of the 100 dreamers.

Robert G. Kunzendorf

References

Becker, E. (1975). *Escape from evil*. New York: Free Press.

Botz-Bornstein, T. (2007). *Film and dreams*. Lanham, MD: Lexington Books.

Gamwell, L. (Ed.). (2000). *Dreams 1900–2000: Science, art, and the unconscious mind*. Ithaca, NY: Cornell University Press.

Kunzendorf, R. G., & Veatch, J. W. (in press). *Envisioning the dream through art and science*.

For images and video clips of the works of art mentioned in this article, see the following websites.

Afternoon of a Faun: Retrieved January 15, 2011, from http://video.google.com/videoplay?docid=1037730427355313168#

Airplane Dream: http://www.grec.net/cgibin/fotcl.pgm?NUMIL=0049698&COL=7

The Astronomer's Dream: http://www.youtube.com/watch?v=a_Mp0F0RE1A

Bacchanale:http://www.butler.edu/dance/br-drop-collection/bacchanale *and* http://www.flickr.com/photos/klausfehrenbach/4323035547/

The Dream: http://www.bochum.de/C125708500379A31/vwContentByKey/W278PE3B343BOLDDE

The Dream: http://www.frida-kahlo-foundation.org/The-Dream.html

The Dream: Retrieved January 15, 2011, from http://www.moma.org/collection/object.php?object_id=79277

Dream, Caused by the Flight of a Bumblebee around a Pomegranate a Second before Awakening: http://www.museothyssen.org/en/thyssen/ficha_obra/352

Dream of a Rarebit Fiend: http://www.youtube.com/watch?v=g0cmKpmLrJE

Dream of the Rood: http://www.dumfriesmuseum.demon.co.uk/ruthwellcross.html

Dreams:http://www.veoh.com/browse/videos/category/entertainment/watch/v6987516Be99YN75

Dreams of Venus: http://yametonart.com/2008/10/06/dreams-of-venus-1939-worlds-fair-pavilion.aspx

Dreams That Money Can Buy: Retrieved January 15, 2011, from http://video.google.com/videoplay?docid=-6885641304025620481#

8½:http://www.youtube.com/watch?v=jmEqBdde5H0

Flight through the Tunnel: http://rolfgross.dreamhosters.com/Bosch-Web-2005/Images/Last-Judgment-VeniceTunnel.jpg

The Forgotten Ones: http://www.dailymotion.com/video/xb3ypt_olvidados_creation

The Great Red Dragon and the Woman Clothed with the Sun: http://en.wahooart.com/A55A04/w.nsf/Opra/BRUE-7Z4Q6N

In a Dream: Retrieved January 15, 2011, from http://www.moma.org/collection/object.php?object_id=36916

Invasion of the Night: http://www.sfmoma.org/artwork/267

Jacob's Ladder: http://www.humanitiesweb.org/human.php?s=g&p=c&a=p&ID=2008

Meshes of the Afternoon: Retrieved January 15, 2011, from http://video.google.com/videoplay?docid=4002812108181388236#

My Dream: Retrieved January 15, 2011, from http://www.forteantimes.com/front_website/gallery.php?id=1824

The Nightmare: http://www.arts.uwaterloo.ca/~acheyne/Fuseli.html

Nostalghia: http://www.youtube.com/watch?v=VEnYT-kFuGc

Queen Katherine's Dream: http://www.tate.org.uk/britain/exhibitions/gothicnightmares/rooms/room6_works.htm

Spellbound: http://videosift.com/video/A-Dream-Sequence-from-Salvador-Dali

We Are Near to Awakening, When We Dream That We Dream: http://birgitjuergenssen.com/werke/ph892.php

Wild Strawberries: http://www.youtube.com/watch?v=zIQ-s6hwykM

The Wizard of Oz: http://www.popmodal.com/video/3633/Wizard-of-Oz-Trailer-From-the-1939-Movie-Classic

Depression and Dreaming

Several studies found reduced dream recall in patients with depression, and severity of depression measured by the Hamilton depression scale was associated with reduced dream recall (Schredl, 1995). The explanation of this relationship, however, remains unclear; that is, the question whether the reduced dream recall is due to the specific sleep architecture often found in depressive patients (e.g., advanced REM sleep), due to cognitive impairment often found in severely disturbed patients, or due to the specific symptomatology of depression has not yet been answered (Schredl, 1995).

The continuity hypothesis of dreaming states that dreams reflect waking life. For psychiatric patients, one would expect that waking-life symptoms such as depressive mood or bizarre thinking also can be found in the patients' dreams. The literature reviews of Kramer and coworkers indicate that the majority of empirical studies support the continuity hypothesis (Kramer, 2000; Kramer & Roth, 1978).

For depressive patients, Beck and Ward (1961) have found an increased amount of masochistic themes in their dreams. Masochistic dream content was defined as occurring negative emotions, weeping, and unfriendly interactions like rejection. Subsequent studies confirmed that dreams of depressive patients are more negatively toned and include unpleasant experiences more often than healthy controls (Schredl, Riemann, & Berger, 2009). Severity of depression was related to the intensity of negative emotions and to the occurrence of death themes in the dream reports (Schredl & Engelhardt, 2001).

Even though dream recall is already reduced in depressive patients, pharmacological treatment of depression was also often associated with a further reduction in dream-recall frequency (Armitage, Rochlen, Fitch, Trivedi, & Rush, 1995). Pace-Schott et al. (2001) found that SSRIs (fluvoxamine, paroxetine) decreased dream-recall frequency in healthy controls. The REM sleep–suppressing effect of most antidepressants might explain reduced dream recall since REM sleep is associated with intense dreaming. In a large outpatient sample, the effect of trimipramine on reducing dream recall was small and might be explained by the reduction of negatively toned dreams (Schredl et al., 2009).

Whereas Kramer, Whitman, Baldridge, and Ornstein (1968) found a decrease in hostility and anxiety in depressed patients treated with imipramine, other studies (Armitage et al., 1995) found no changes in dream content during pharmacological treatment despite clinical improvement. Hauri (1976) found increased negative dream topics even in patients completely recovered from their depressive episode. A four-week treatment with trimipramine yielded a considerable shift in dream emotions toward the positive end of the scale, which was paralleled by the decrease of symptom severity (Schredl et al., 2009). To summarize, the findings support the continuity hypothesis of dreaming by demonstrating a close link between waking-life symptomatology and negative dream emotions. Future studies should analyze dream content in order to support the hypothesis that improvement in daytime symptoms is directly reflected in the patients' dreams and whether working on dreams might be a valuable option in the psychotherapeutic treatment of patients with depression.

Michael Schredl

See also: entries related to Sleep and Development

References

Armitage, R., Rochlen, A., Fitch, T., Trivedi, M., & Rush, A. J. (1995). Dream recall and major depression: A preliminary report. *Dreaming, 5,* 189–198.

Beck, A. T., & Ward, C. H. (1961). Dreams of depressed patients. *Archives of General Psychiatry, 5,* 462–467.

Hauri, P. (1976). Dreams in patients remitted from reactive depression. *Journal of Abnormal Psychology, 85,* 1–10.

Kramer, M. (2000). Dreams and psychopathology. In M. H. Kryger, T. Roth, & W. C. Dement (Eds.), *Principles and practice of sleep medicine* (pp. 511–519). Philadelphia: W. B. Saunders.

Kramer, M., & Roth, T. (1978). Dreams in psychopathologic patient groups. In R. L. Williams & I. Karacan (Eds.), *Sleep disorders: Diagnosis and treatment* (pp. 323–349). New York: John Wiley & Sons.

Kramer, M., Whitman, R. M., Baldridge, B. J., & Ornstein, P. H. (1968). Drugs and dreams: III. The effects of imipramine on the dreams of the depressed. *American Journal of Psychiatry, 124,* 1385–1392.

Pace-Schott, E. F., Gersh, T., Silvestri, R., Stickgold, R., Salzman, C., & Hobson, J. A. (2001). SSRI treatment suppresses dream recall frequency but increases subjective dream intensity in normal subjects. *Journal of Sleep Research, 10,* 129–142.

Schredl, M. (1995). Traumerinnerung bei depressiven Patienten [Dream recall in depressed patients]. Psychotherapie, Psychosomatik und Medizinische Psychologie [Psychotherapy, *Psychosomatics, and Medical Psychology], 45*, 414–417.

Schredl, M., & Engelhardt, H. (2001). Dreaming and psychopathology: Dream recall and dream content of psychiatric inpatients. *Sleep and Hypnosis, 3*, 44–54.

Schredl, M., Riemann, D., & Berger, M. (2009). The effect of trimipramine on dream recall and dream emotions in depressive outpatients. *Psychiatry Research, 167*, 279–286.

Depression in Patients with Kidney Disease

Depression is a common, underdiagnosed, and understudied and probably undertreated problem in patients with end-stage renal disease (ESRD), treated with hemodialysis (HD) or peritoneal dialysis, and in patients with chronic kidney disease (CKD) (Fabrazzo & De Santo, 2006; Kimmel et al., 2000).

Patients on HD carry the risk of high frequency of moderate depression, which is a very important clinical psychiatric complication ranking second after hypertension as a comorbid condition. The prevalence of a current depressive disorder in HD varies between 20 and 30 percent. The variability depends not only on the methods used for assessment, but also on the difficulties of dissecting the overlapping of uremic and depressive symptoms. Higher levels of depressive affect in HD is a significant problem associated with the risk of decreased quality of life, of perceived low-quality life, of self-reported health status, an increased risk of cardiovascular disease death events, of cardiovascular events, and of all causes of death. In addition, depression increases the number of hospitalizations and their duration in 10 percent of the patients and is associated with decision to withdraw from dialysis. Persistent depression in HD is associated with poor outcome (Boulware et al., 2006; Kimmel et al., 2000). Depression is associated with difficulties in staying and falling asleep and restless legs syndrome.

Depression in ESRD impacts on immunological response, stress response, nutritional status, proinflammatory cytokines, poor compliance with dialysis and medical treatment, and dyadic relation. It has been calculated that a treatment capable of reducing by 8.1 point BDI (Beck Depression Inventory) scores would cause a 32 percent increase in survival time (Kimmel et al., 2007).

Boulware et al. (2006) made the case for a reverse causality between depression and medical conditions, suggesting that the worsening of the medical conditions precedes the worsening of the depressive affect, than vice versa. Thus, depression might represent an indicator of disease severity and comorbidities. In this case, treating depression would not reduce cardiovascular disease (CVD) deaths; however, treatment would still improve nutrition, physical symptom, and quality of life.

Depression was associated with sleeping disorders, stress, anxiety, and alexithymia in HD patients needing parathyroidectomy for secondary hyperparathyroidism, and high scores of the BDI were associated with the worst sleep disorder (SD). Nearly

100 percent of them did not experience a refreshing sleep. The association of SD and depression had been demonstrated in epidemiological studies in healthy university students at the University of L'Aquila in Italy and in many studies in ESRD.

In CKD, the prevalence of depressive disorders also exceeded 20 percent in cross-sectional studies and correlated with poor quality of life, which points to a continuum from early to late stage of renal disease (Hedayati, Minhajuddin, Toto, Morris, & Rush, 2009). In CKD, depression is associated with pain and SDs.

The gold standard to assess depression in HD and CKD is represented by Structured Clinical Interviews for the *Diagnostic and Statistical Manual of Mental Disorders* (4th ed.; *DSM-IV*), a tool known as SCID. BDI, which for the general population uses a cutoff of 10 or greater, uses a cutoff of 14 to 16 in HD patients and is a valid measure of major depressive disorder, because it correctly classifies more than 80 percent of SCID depression cases. Also the Patient Health Questionnaire (PHQ-9) is adequate and rapid. In CKD, the cutoff is 10 or greater.

Only few HD patients and CKD with depression are adequately treated. This needs to be changed since depression is curable. Simply improving nutrition and compliance reduces mortality. Social support is of paramount importance, because an increased perception of social support increases survival. A combination of medical treatment and psychotherapy might prove optimal.

Rosa Maria De Santo

See also: entries related to Sleep Disorders

References

Boulware, L. E., Liu, Y., Fimk, N. E., Coresh, J., Ford, D. E., Klag, M. J., & Powe, N. R. (2006). Temporal relation among depression symptoms, cardiovascular disease events, and mortality in end-stage renal disease: Contribution of reverse causality. *Clinical Journal of the American Society of Nephrology, 1*, 496–504.

Cukor, D., Cohen, S. D., Peterson, R. A., & Kimmel, P. L. (2007). Psychosocial aspects of chronic disease: ESRD as a paradigmatic illness. *Clinical Journal of the American Society of Nephrology, 18*, 3042–3045.

Fabrazzo, M., & De Santo, R. M. (2006). Depression in chronic kidney disease. *Seminars in Nephrology, 26*, 56–60.

Hedayati, S. S., Minhajuddin, A. T., Toto, R. D., Morris, D. W., & Rush, A. J. (2009). Prevalence of major depressive episode in CKD. *American Journal of Kidney Diseases, 54*, 424–432.

Kimmel, P., Cukor, D., Cohen, S., & Peterson, R. (2007). Depression in End-Stage Renal Disease Patients: *A Critical Review Advances in Chronic Kidney Disease*, Vol. 14, Issue 4, pp. 328–334.

Kimmel, P. L., Peterson, R. A., Wehis, K. L., Simmens, S. J., Alleyne, S., Cruz, I., & Veis, J. H. (2000). Multiple measurements of depression predict mortality in a longitudinal study of chronic hemodialysis patients. *Kidney International, 57*, 2093–2098.

Depth of Sleep

For many people, a night of deep sleep is associated with improved quality of sleep and improved alertness and function on the day that follows. However, sleep depth can be measured in many ways, and some may not be directly related to the common impression. One of the first scientific studies of sleep, performed by Ernst

Otto Heinrich Kohlschutter in 1862, used graded intensity sound to produce awakenings across the night to construct a depth of sleep curve. This initial curve showed that participants were very difficult to awaken during the first hour or two of the night but that sleep became progressively lighter as the night progressed. It was proposed, without supporting evidence, that the very deep sleep during the early part of the night was more restorative than the lighter sleep that occurred later during the night.

Many years later when it became possible to record ongoing EEG patterns while participants slept, high correlations were found between the depth of sleep as measured by arousal thresholds and the preponderance of low-frequency high-amplitude EEG activity, later called slow waves or delta (stage 4) sleep. In addition, in humans it was found that thresholds to awakening generally decreased from stage 4 to stage 3 to stage 2 to stage 1 sleep. In humans, but not animals, arousal thresholds from REM sleep were similar to those seen in stage 2 sleep. Once this relationship had been established, most research was based on EEG classifications, and deep sleep has become increasingly synonymous with delta sleep (Kleitman, 1963).

Determinants of Deep Sleep

When individuals are asked to rate a night of sleep based on depth of sleep, ratings of deep sleep are most strongly related to the amount of time spent awake on the night rated. Deepest sleep is most strongly associated with the least time awake during the night more consistently than with either sleep-stage parameters or measured

awakening thresholds during sleep. However, many factors affect subjective depth of sleep, EEG parameters, and the actual measures of responsiveness during sleep.

Depth of sleep as measured either by arousal threshold or by total amount of delta sleep is greatest in children (Busby, Mercier, & Pivik, 1994). Both delta sleep and arousal thresholds during sleep decrease with age so that the common conception of light sleep in the elderly is correct. Aging is also accompanied by an increase in arousals and awakenings during sleep. It has been found that arousal thresholds are reduced during sleep following movements or awakenings for up to 25 minutes. Therefore, increased movement and awakening with aging also are associated with both physiologically lighter sleep and subjectively lighter sleep. This means that methods used to lessen disturbance of sleep such as blackout curtains or noise abatement also improve depth of sleep by either criterion.

Sensory processing continues during sleep. Studies of nerve transmission indicate that auditory stimuli, for example, continue to be sensed and interpreted to some extent. This means that a meaningful stimulus, such as a child speaking one's name at a low intensity, can successfully produce an awakening during sleep while other external stimuli such as traffic noise can usually be ignored without disturbance to ongoing sleep. However, research has shown that neutral stimuli can become meaningful and then will also cause an awakening at a low-intensity level. This process is very adaptive in assuring that a mother awakens to the cry of a new infant. However, it can also sensitize us to aircraft noise or noisy neighbors if we allow those stimuli to produce a negative emotional association. However, some unwanted external disturbance can be masked by a more intense neutral noise such as a fan or white noise generator (Bruck, Ball, Thomas, & Rouillard, 2009).

Depth of sleep measured in any way is increased after sleep deprivation or significant sleep disturbance. We may react to sleep disturbance by becoming less sensitive to disturbance and this allows improved sleep. Sedative medications, such as sleeping pills, increase depth of sleep by both decreasing wake time and increasing arousal thresholds during sleep stages (Bonnet, Webb, & Barnard, 1979). Stimulant medications, such as caffeine, reduce depth of sleep directly by decreasing arousal thresholds during sleep and by increasing wake time (Bonnet et al., 1979). Data also suggest that depth of sleep decreases across a normal night of sleep irrespective of sleep stage. This effect may be related to either decreases in arousal threshold or increasing movement and awakening.

Patients with sleep disorders frequently complain of light sleep. This is probably related to increased wake time and movement time during the night rather than to specific reductions in sleep-stage amounts or increases in arousal thresholds when in stable sleep.

Michael H. Bonnet

See also: entries related to Sleep Assessment

References

Bonnet, M.H., Webb, W.B., & Barnard, G. (1979). Effect of flurazepam, pentobarbital, and caffeine on arousal threshold. *Sleep, 1*(3), 271–279.

Bruck, D., Ball, M., Thomas, I., & Rouillard, V. (2009). How does the pitch and pattern of a signal affect auditory arousal thresholds? *Journal of Sleep Research, 18*, 196–203.

Busby, K.A., Mercier, L., & Pivik, R.T. (1994). Ontogenetic variations in auditory arousal threshold during sleep. *Psychophysiology, 31*(2), 182–188.

Kleitman, N. (1963). *Sleep and wakefulness* (2nd ed.). Chicago: University of Chicago Press.

Development and Initial Validation of the Iowa Sleep Disturbances Inventory

There currently are a large number of questionnaires that are used in research and clinical practice to measure sleep disturbances. Although most focus on specific sleep complaints, such as insomnia or fatigue, some instruments have multiple scales assessing a range of sleep complaints and sleep disorders (e.g., insomnia, sleep apnea, restless legs syndrome). Many of the most widely used sleep questionnaires demonstrate good reliability and can discriminate between groups of poor and normal sleepers (Sateia, Doghramji, Hauri, & Morin, 2000, pp. 243–308). Two main limitations have been raised in regard to the existing sleep instruments. First, many instruments lack comprehensiveness in terms of both items and content areas. For example, several instruments propose to measure broad content areas (e.g., daytime dysfunction) with one or two items. A more fundamental problem with existing sleep instruments is that many are limited to a narrow range of content, most commonly insomnia and lassitude (e.g., fatigue, sleepiness). This becomes particularly problematic when trying to assess a wider range of sleep complaints, such as nightmares, vivid dreams, or narcolepsy symptoms.

A second limitation of existing sleep instruments is a lack of well-defined scales that measure specific content areas. Many sleep scales have been found to be multi-dimensional. For example, several widely used questionnaires combine nighttime sleep problems and daytime fatigue in a total sleep disturbance score, which is suggestive of a single, broad factor of sleep disturbances. However, structural analyses have established that daytime and nighttime disturbances represent distinct dimensions that are only moderately correlated (Koffel & Watson, 2009a, pp. 183–194); thus, it would be more informative to measure these dimensions with separate scales.

To address the limitations of existing measures of sleep disturbances, Koffel and Watson (in press) created the Iowa Sleep Disturbances Inventory (ISDI), using structural analyses. The ISDI provides a comprehensive assessment of 11 specific dimensions of sleep complaints, including nightmares, initial insomnia, fragmented sleep, anxiety at night, light sleep, movement at night, sensations at night, excessive sleep, irregular schedule, nonrestorative sleep, and fatigue. The ISDI has shown evidence of good internal reliability in psychiatric patients, sleep-disorder patients, and college students, with most coefficient alphas above 0.80. The ISDI scales show good convergent and discriminant validity with some of the most widely used sleep measures. In addition, the ISDI scales measure sleep disturbances not captured by traditional measures (e.g., sensations at night, nightmares, movement at night).

The ISDI scales have been used to define a hierarchical model of sleep disturbances. In this model, specific sleep disturbances cluster under two higher-order factors of insomnia and lassitude. The insomnia factor is defined primarily by the ISDI scales of fragmented sleep, initial insomnia, light sleep, and anxiety at night. The lassitude factor is defined primarily by the ISDI scales of fatigue, excessive sleep, and nonrestorative sleep.

It is important to note that several ISDI scales, including nightmares, movement at night, and sensations at night, do not load strongly onto either of these factors, raising the possibility that additional higher-order sleep factors exist. For example, the ISDI sensations at night and movement at night scales tend to cohere together when additional factors are extracted in psychiatric patients and sleep-disorder patients. These scales may define a factor of restless legs syndrome, although more research is needed. There is also evidence that measures of nightmares, vivid dreams, and narcolepsy symptoms are closely related and form a factor entitled unusual sleep experiences (Koffel & Watson, 2009b, pp. 548–559). Similarly, Watson (2001, pp. 526–535) found that items referring to narcolepsy symptoms, nightmares, recurring dreams, dream recall, and waking dreams (i.e., a dream in which the person dreams of waking up) load onto the same factor. Although these findings are encouraging, it is clear that additional research is needed regarding the content and correlates of the unusual sleep experiences factor.

Erin Koffel

See also: entries related to Sleep Assessment

References

Koffel, E., & Watson, D. (2009a). The two-factor structure of sleep complaints and its relation to depression and anxiety. *Journal of Abnormal Psychology, 118*, 183–194.

Koffel, E., & Watson, D. (2009b). Unusual sleep experiences, dissociation, and schizotypy: Evidence for a common domain. *Clinical Psychology Review, 29*, 548–559.

Koffel, E., & Watson, D. (in press). Development and initial validation of the Iowa Sleep Disturbances Inventory. *Assessment.*

Sateia, M.J., Doghramji, K., Hauri, P.J., & Morin, C.M. (2000). Evaluation of chronic insomnia: An American Academy of Sleep Medicine Review. *Sleep, 23*, 243–308.

Watson, D. (2001). Dissociations of the night: Individual differences in sleep-related experiences and their relation to dissociation and schizotypy. *Journal of Abnormal Psychology, 110*, 526–535.

Disconnection from the External Environment during Dreaming

A key feature of sleep that persists in dreaming is the profound disconnection from the external environment. Consider the following example: if we are to sleep all night in front of the television or in an airport, the stream of sounds that surrounds us does not elicit behavioral responses and our dreams have little, if anything, to do with the contents of those sounds. Why is this so, and what can we learn from this about dreaming and underlying brain activity?

Sleep is defined by behavioral unresponsiveness or a high arousal threshold. Accordingly, external stimuli fail to elicit a meaningful behavioral response unless they are strong enough to cause an awakening. During nonrapid eye movement (NREM) sleep, disconnection may be explained by the fact that the thalamocortical system is active in a mode that is drastically different than that of wakefulness. Hyperpolarized cortical neurons become bistable and alternate between active and silent periods, while the thalamus may not relay peripheral sensory inputs as effectively to the cortex. However, in rapid eye movement (REM) sleep when subjects are most likely to experience vivid dreams, the thalamocortical system is depolarized with a wakelike low-voltage electroencephalogram (EEG). Despite this strong cortical activation, a high arousal threshold persists in REM sleep. Moreover, stimuli largely fail to be incorporated in the content of the dream, although some stimuli such as a spray of water or pressure on the limbs have a slightly higher chance of incorporation. Remarkably, even when subjects sleep with their eyes taped open and objects are illuminated in front of them, their dream reports upon awakening do not relate to the external stimuli. While it is true that just before waking up stimuli such as the sound of an alarm clock can enter our dreams, when sleep is preserved dream consciousness is remarkably disconnected from the external environment. Given the strong cortical activation, such disconnection poses an intriguing unsolved paradox.

Disconnection could reflect the fact that typical signal propagation along ascending sensory pathways is disrupted so that external stimuli do not effectively drive the activity of high-order cortical regions. The available evidence suggests that in sleep responses to external stimuli such as sounds are largely preserved up to and including primary sensory cortices. Therefore, it could be that a functional disconnection occurs later between primary and high-order cortical regions.

If indeed dream disconnection reflects a closed cortical gate, multiple factors (which are not mutually exclusive) could potentially explain this scenario. The most obvious one is that levels of many neuromodulators including norepinephrine, serotonin, histamine, and hypocretin are greatly reduced in REM sleep compared to wake. Histaminergic tone in particular may be necessary for facilitating full-fledged transmission of feed-forward sensory inputs. In contrast to other neuromodulators, levels of histamine are also high in cataplexy, a symptom of narcolepsy in which muscle tone loss is transiently lost, awareness of external stimuli is preserved, while the neuromodulatory environment is largely similar to that in REM sleep. Put simply, levels of histamine seem to be correlated with one's ability to incorporate sensory stimuli into conscious experience. Another possibility is that phasic discharges of noradrenergic neurons in the locus coeruleus, typically triggered by sensory stimuli during wakefulness, are a necessary condition for external events to elicit behavioral orienting responses and for them to enter our stream of consciousness. In addition, converging evidence from developmental and neuropsychological studies suggests that dreaming might be closely related to imagination and that during dreaming brain activity is likely dominated by a top-down flow as may occur during mental imagery. Such a top-down mode of cortical transmission could obstruct the processing of incoming stimuli and disconnect one from the environment. Another possibility is that nodes of internally oriented, default networks such as the medial prefrontal cortex dominate cortical activity at the expense of the processing of external stimuli. A final consideration is that disconnection reflects alterations in attention as may be the case in visual neglect.

Future research is needed to further understand what underlies our disconnection from the external environment during dreaming. It is important to examine whether, where, and how typical sensory processing may be disrupted in REM sleep. For example, one could simultaneously monitor activity in primary and high-order sensory regions in animals as stimuli are presented and focus on signal propagation between distinct cortical layers that are known to reflect bottom-up versus backward signal propagation. It is also important to establish whether specific neuromodulators are necessary for signals to reach high-order cortices as they typically do in wakefulness. In humans, one can apply directional measures of signal propagation such as Granger causality to high-density EEG data and to REM sleep recordings obtained in neurosurgical patients. The answer to the disconnection mystery might be instrumental for understanding dreams, related domains such as the preservation of sleep in the face of external distractions, as well as other states of dissociation such as hypnosis, absorption, and autism. More generally, it could help shed light on the relation between consciousness and neuronal activity.

Yuval Nir and Giulio Tononi

References

Dement, W., & Wolpert, E. A. (1958). The relation of eye movements, body motility, and external stimuli to dream content. *Journal of Experimental Psychology, 55*(6), 543–553.

Issa, E.B., & Wang, X. (2008). Sensory responses during sleep in primate primary and secondary auditory cortex. *Journal of Neuroscience, 28*(53), 14467–14480.

Nieuwenhuis, S., Aston-Jones, G., & Cohen, J.D. (2005). Decision making, the P3, and the locus coeruleus–norepinephrine system. *Psychological Bulletin, 131*(4), 510–532.

Nir, Y., & Tononi, G. (2010). Dreaming and the brain: From phenomenology to neurophysiology. *Trends in Cognitive Sciences, 14*(2), 88–100.

Rechtschaffen, A. (1978). The single-mindedness and isolation of dreams. *Sleep, 1*(1), 97–109.

Rechtschaffen, A., & Foulkes, D. (1965). Effect of visual stimuli on dream content. *Perceptual and Motor Skills, 20*(Suppl.), 1149–1160.

Steriade, M. (2003). *Neuronal substrates of sleep and epilepsy*. Cambridge: Cambridge University Press.

Discovery of REM Sleep

Although detailed behavioral characteristics of dreaming had already been described by Lucretius (circa 98–55 BC), the neurobiological study of the REM dreaming sleep stage began only 60 years ago. In 1953, Aserinsky and Kleitman discovered a sleep stage with rapid eye movements and low-voltage electroencephalographic (EEG) activity, during which subjects reported to have dreamed upon awakening (Aserinsky & Kleitman, 1953). This discovery opened the door to an explosion of research devoted to the electrophysiological, neuroimaging, pharmacological, neurochemical, and genetic properties of this sleep stage.

However, numerous observations also preceded Kleitman's laboratory discovery.

As early as several centuries ago, philosophers had already highlighted various characteristics of dreaming. Immanuel Kant (1724–1804) observed that "the madman is a waking dreamer," and Arthur Schopenhauer (1788–1860) said that "Dreams are short madness and madness a long dream." Alfred Maury (1817–1892) also wrote that "dreaming is a kind of delirium." Finally, the neurophysiopathologist John Hughlings Jackson (1835–1911) beautifully anticipated: "find out all about dreams and you will find out all about insanity." Therefore, one of the main characteristics of dreaming, that is, a psychotic-like mental activity, was known long prior to any neurobiological findings related to REM sleep.

The description of several other isolated criteria of REM sleep, however, only came gradually, over time. Hervey de Saint Denys (1822–1892) described erection during sleep. This was, surprisingly, ignored by Freud (1856–1939), who was familiar with de Saint Denys's 1867 book *Les Rêves et les Moyens de les Diriger*, and whose theory about sexuality should have been supported by the finding—albeit a false support, since sleep erection is independent of libido (Schmidt, Valatx, Sakai, Fort, & Jouvet, 2000).

Describing another characteristic of REM sleep, Weed and Hallam (1896) reported that, "The dreams occurring from 5:00 to 6:30 are the most frequent, most interesting, most vivid and most varied." Moreover, they noted that more than half of dreams contain disagreeable emotions, an observation that was then quantified by de Manacéine (1897) (29 pleasant vs. 57 unpleasant dreams in a study). This observation was recently confirmed by Revonsuo (2003).

Finally, the last significant result of the 19th century was the description of pupillary dilation during dreaming by Duval (1882) and by Berger and Loewy (1898). This mydriasis during REM sleep was more recently confirmed in cats (Berlucchi & Strata, 1965).

In the last century, Jacobson (1930) recorded eye movements by "connecting one electrode near the orbital bridge and another behind the ear . . . this arrangement tended to yield . . . marked galvanometric variations." He later wrote (Jacobson, 1938) that, "when a person dreams . . . most of his eyes are active. When the sleeper whose eyes move under his closed lids . . . awakes . . . you are likely to find . . . that he had seen something in a dream."

At around the same time, Derbyshire, Rempel, Forbes, and Lambert (1936) recorded low-voltage EEG periods during sleep in cats: "when sleep was apparently less tranquil judging by twitching of the vibrissae, there were only small rapid waves as in the alert waking state."

The year 1937 brought three major findings for the further discovery of the dreaming sleep stage. First, Blake and Gerard confirmed the previous EEG phenomena in humans: "feeble irregular potentials . . . yet the test sound (auditory stimuli threshold) evokes no response" (Blake & Gerard, 1937). Thus, in this observation, the most important criterion for the subsequently discovered REM sleep (low-voltage EEG) was coupled with an increased arousal threshold; this was later confirmed by Dement (1958) in cats. Second, Loomis, Harvey, and Hobart (1937) not only presented the first hypnogram showing the nighttime

progression of the different EEG stages, but also found that dreaming occurs during EEG stage B, that is, during a low-voltage activity period. Finally, in the same year, Klaue described a deep sleep stage in cats (*tiefer Schlaf*) with a cortical "quiet electrical current," "complete muscular relaxation . . . and numerous jerks of single extremities" (Klaue, 1937).

In the final relevant report of the decade, Blake and Gerard (1937), with the participation of Nathaniel Kleitman, confirmed the existence in humans of a sleep period with low-amplitude beta waves, "called 'null' (or low voltage)."

During the Second World War, McGlade (1942) observed a relationship between twitches and dreaming in two subjects: "When they were again awakened, after the first large body movement at the end of the group of twitches, they invariably stated they had dreamed."

Finally, Ohlmeyer, Brilmayer, and Hüllstrung (1944) observed periodic erections in humans, with a mean duration of 25.5 minutes and with a 79.7-minute periodicity of occurrence.

In view of all this previous work, Kleitman, with his remarkable knowledge of the sleep literature (1,434 references in his 1939 edition of *Sleep and Wakefulness*), certainly had some anticipation of results when he instructed Aserinsky (see Lufkin, 1968, but also Aserinsky, 1996) to perform the research that led to the first full description of the REM dreaming sleep stage (Gottesmann, 2010).

Claude Gottesmann and Hartmut Schulz

See also: entries related to History of Dreams/ Sleep; entries related to Sleep Assessment

References

Aserinsky, E. (1996). The discovery of REM sleep. *Journal of the History of the Neurosciences, 5*, 213–227.

Aserinsky, E., & Kleitman, N. (1953). Regularly occurring periods of eye motility, and concomitant phenomena during sleep. *Science, 118*, 273–274.

Berger, E., & Loewy, R. (1898). L'etat des yeux pendant le sommeil et la theorie du sommeil [The state of the eyes during sleep and the theory of sleep]. *Comptes Rendes Des Seances De La Societe De Biologie Et De Ses Filiales [Record of the Meeting of the Society of Biology and its Chapters]*, 448–450.

Berlucchi, G., & Strata, P. (1965). Ocular phenomena during synchronized and desynchronized sleep. Aspects Anatomo- Fonctionnels de la physiologie du sommeil. [Anatomical-Functional Aspects of the Physiology of Sleep]. *CNRS, Paris*, 285–307.

Blake, H., & Gerard, R.W. (1937). Brain potentials during sleep. *American Journal of Physiology, 119*, 692–703.

de Manacéine, M. (1897). *Sleep: Its physiology, pathology, hygiene and psychology*. London: Walter Scott.

Dement, W.C. (1958). The occurrence of low voltage fast electroencephalogram patterns during behavioral sleep in the cat. *Electroencephalography and Clinical Neurophysiology, 10*, 291–296.

Derbyshire, A.J., Rempel, B., Forbes, A., & Lambert, E.F. (1936). The effects of anesthetics on action potentials in the cerebral cortex of the cat. *American Journal of Physiology, 116*, 577–596.

Duval, M. (1882). Sommeil. In E. Jaccoud (Ed.), *Nouveau dictionnaire de médecine et de chirurgie pratique* (Vol. 33, pp. 262–288). Paris: J.B. Baillière.

Gottesmann, C. (2010). The development of the science of dreaming. *International Review of Neurobiology, 92*, 1–29.

Jacobson, A. (1930). Electrical measurements of neuromuscular states during mental activities. III. Visual imagination and recollection. *American Journal of Physiology, 95*, 694–702.

Jacobson, A. (1938). *You can sleep well: The ABC's of restful sleep for the average person*. New York: Whittley House.

Klaue, R. (1937). Die bioelektrische Tätigkeit der Grosshirnrinde im normalen Schlaf und in der Narkose durch Schlafmittel. [The bioelectrical activity of the cerebral cortex during normal sleep and during sleep induced by anesthesia]. *Journal of Psychology and Neurology, 47*, 510–531.

Loomis, A.L., Harvey, E.N., & Hobart, G.A.I. (1937). Cerebral states during sleep, as studied by human brain potentials. *Journal of Experimental Psychology, 21*, 127–144.

Lufkin, B. (1968). Letter to the editor. *Psychophysiology, 5*, 449–450.

McGlade, H.B. (1942). The relationship between gastric motility, muscular twitching during sleep and dreaming. *American Journal of Digestive Diseases, 9*, 137–140.

Ohlmeyer, P., Brilmayer, H., & Hüllstrung, H. (1944). Periodische Vorgänge im Schlaf. *Pflüg Arch, 248*, 559–560.

Revonsuo, A. (2003). The reinterpretation of dreams: An evolutionary hypothesis of the function of dreaming. In M. Pace-Schott, M. Solms, M. Blagrove, & S. Harnad (Eds.), *Sleep and dreaming: Scientific advances and reconsiderations* (pp. 85–109). Cambridge: Cambridge University Press.

Schmidt, M.H., Valatx, J.L., Sakai, K., Fort, P., & Jouvet, M. (2000). Role of the lateral preoptic area in sleep-related erectile mechanisms and sleep generation in the rat. *Journal of Neuroscience, 20*, 6640–6647.

Weed, S., & Hallam, F.M. (1896). A study of the dream consciousness. *American Journal of Psychiatry, 7*, 405–411.

Dissociated States of Being and *Agrypnia Excitata*

Biological sciences traditionally recognize the existence of three states of mammalian being: wakefulness, rapid eye movement (REM) sleep, and nonrapid eye movement (NREM) sleep. They have their own neuroanatomical, neurophysiological, and neurochemical substrates. Video-polygraphic studies, which allow contemporaneous monitoring of many biological parameters, have shown distinctive patterns for wakefulness and different stages of sleep. When behavioral, polygraphic, and cellular variables occur in substantial synchronization, a state becomes fully declared.

Nevertheless, these conditions are not always mutually exclusive (Mahowald & Schenck, 1992). Evidence for only partly defined or mixed states of being is available from both animal experimentation and human clinical studies (Mahowald & Schenck, 1992).

Furthermore, numerous studies have replicated the finding of mentation not only in REM but also in NREM sleep. About 50 percent of subjects appear to have noticeable degraded recall of mentation from NREM sleep. Indeed, a possible theory is that sleep mentation is tightly coupled to REM sleep processes, but that some of these processes under certain circumstances may dissociate from REM sleep and stimulate mentation in NREM sleep in a covert fashion. Covert REM sleep is thus defined to be "any episode of NREM sleep for which some REM sleep processes are present, but for which REM sleep cannot be scored with standard criteria" (Nielsen, 2000).

According to Mahowald and Schenck (1992), areas of overlap among states can be classified into: (1) wake–NREM combinations (A. Disorders of arousal such as sleepwalking, sleep terror, confusional arousals; B. Psychogenic dissociation); (2) wake–REM combinations (A. Cataplexy, hypnagogic hallucinations, sleep paralysis; B. REM sleep behavior disorder [RBD]; C. Lucid dreaming; D. Delirium); (3) wake–NREM–REM combinations (A. Status dissociatus; B. Parasomnia overlap syndromes); (4) NREM–REM combinations that are theoretically possible but not accompanied by conscious awareness.

The study of RBD and narcolepsy has been instrumental in promoting the concept of state dissociation: patients with RBD show violent dream-enacting behaviors, which represent the acting out of dream mentation and are possible because of the absence of typical somatic muscle atonia during REM sleep; in narcolepsy, the sleep attacks and hallucinations represent an intrusion of REM sleep into wakefulness and the paralysis in the morning is when REM atonia persists after awakening. Very often, these two state boundary dyscontrol conditions overlap (Raggi, Cosentino, Lanuzza, & Ferri, 2009).

An even more complex condition within the broader concept of *Status Dissociatus*, as primarily defined by the presence of ambiguous, multiple, rapid oscillation of state-determining variables, is certainly represented by the syndrome named *Agrypnia Excitata*, which has been suggested by Lugaresi and Provini (2001) to account for the association of slow-wave sleep (SWS) loss (*agrypnia* that means

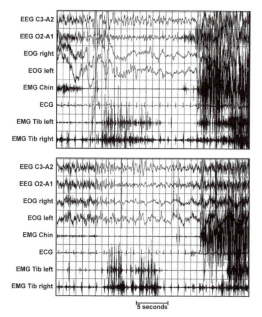

Examples of polysomnographic recording of undifferentiated sleep attacks in a patient with Fatal Familial Insomnia. The contemporary presence of sawtooth waves on the central EEG lead, muscle twitches on the tibialis anterior muscles, and flattening of the EMG from the chin muscle are suggestive of REM sleep. Abbreviations: EEG C3-A2 and EEG O2-A1 = electroencephalogram from the C3-A2 and O2-A1 derivations; EOG = electrooculogram; EMG = electromyogram (surface electrodes); ECG = electrocardiogram; Tib = tibialis anterior muscle. (Alberto Raggi)

to chase sleep away) and abnormal REM sleep (*excitata*).

Fatal familial insomnia (FFI; a human prion disease), Morvan's chorea (an autoimmune limbic encephalopathy), delirium tremens (an alcohol or benzodiazepine withdrawal syndrome), and Mulvihill–Smith syndrome (a hereditary disease causing premature aging, multiple pigmented nevi, microcephaly, short stature, mental retardation, and immunodeficiency) share

this clinical phenotype largely consisting in an inability to sleep associated with motor and autonomic activation (Ferri et al., 2005; Lugaresi & Provini, 2001).

FFI is an exemplary form. Its symptoms arise in the midlife and leads to death within 8 to 72 months. Most patients complain of initial disturbances of vigilance, such as being no longer able to nap or falling asleep at night. They may also display some personality changes such as apathy. These complaints coincide with the development of visual fatigue with diplopia and sympathetic activation, in the form of unexplained evening pyrexia, subtle hypertension, perspiration, sweating, and tachycardia/tachypnea. Patients become progressively somnolent during the daytime and may lapse into peculiar episodes of dream enactment, whereby they display complex jerklike movements possibly mimicking the content of dreams. In the middle stages of the typical forms of this disease, patients start having a motor impairment, spontaneous and evoked myoclonus, pyramidal signs, dysmetria, dysartria, dysphagia, sphincter loss. They may also show occasional convulsive seizures. The following clinical course leads sufferers to death in a state of akinetic mutism and emaciation (Lugaresi & Provini, 2001).

Imaging and pathological studies show prominent thalamus pathology. The thalamus plays a fundamental role in SWS generation. The dorsomedial (DM) and anterior (A) thalamic nuclei are interposed in the circuitry connecting the limbic areas to the hypothalamus and the basal forebrain. The DM nucleus represents an intermediate station in the trans-basal ganglionic circuit of the limbic system, linking the ventral striatum and pallidum with the prefrontal cortex. Studies in cats demonstrate that the DM nucleus receives inputs, with direct gamma-aminobutyric acid (GABA)ergic projections, from the hypothalamus and the basal forebrain. The DM also forms part of the central autonomic network, which integrates all autonomic functions. Finally, the medial thalamus contributes in setting the sympathetic tone through hypothalamic neurons (Lugaresi & Provini, 2001).

Moreover, severance of cortical–subcortical limbic structures may depend on autoantibodies blocking voltage-gated potassium channels within the limbic system in Morvan's chorea and the sudden changes in GABAergic synapses downregulated by chronic alcohol abuse within the limbic system in delirium tremens. The pathogenetic mechanisms occurring in Mulvihill–Smith syndrome is unknown.

In *Agrypnia Excitata*, the appetite for sleep is preserved, but true sleep cannot be consumed and intrusions of REM sleep, which seems to be indispensable for the organism's survival, are responsible for the behavioral manifestations of vivid dreams and oneirism. A plentiful research agenda may arise from the previously reviewed concepts about status dissociatus; in particular, basic and clinical sciences could provide important information concerning genetic influences on sleep patterns.

Alberto Raggi and Raffaele Ferri

References

Ferri, R., Lanuzza, B., Cosentino, F. I., Iero, I., Russo, N., Tripodi, M., & Bosco, P. (2005).
Agrypnia excitata in a patient with progeroid short stature and pigmented nevi (Mulvihill–Smith syndrome). *Journal of Sleep Research, 14*, 463–470.

Lugaresi, E., & Provini, F. (2001). *Agrypnia excitata*: Clinical features and pathophysiological implications. *Sleep Medicine Reviews, 5*, 313–322.

Mahowald, M. W., & Schenck, C. H. (1992). Dissociated states of wakefulness and sleep. *Neurology, 42*(7 Suppl. 6), 44–51.

Nielsen, T. A. (2000). A review of mentation in REM and NREM sleep: "Covert" REM sleep as a possible reconciliation of two opposing models. *Behavioral and Brain Sciences, 23*, 851–866.

Raggi, A., Cosentino, F. I., Lanuzza, B., & Ferri, R. (2009). Behavioural and neurophysiologic features of state dissociation: A brief review of the literature and three descriptive case studies. *Behavioural Neurology, 22*, 91–99.

Distinctive Dream Content Associated with REM Sleep Behavior Disorder

Rapid eye movement (REM) sleep behavior disorder (RBD) is an intriguing parasomnia formally identified in humans in 1986 (Schenck, Bundlie, Ettinger, & Mahowald, 1986, pp. 293–308). The subjects, usually men older than 50 years, show complex and often explosive motor behaviors during REM sleep associated with vivid dreams. Although nonviolent behaviors may occasionally be observed, subjects appear to be frequently involved in aggressive dream-enactment behaviors, as they may scream, grasp, punch, or kick a fictive character or object, and sometimes jump out from bed. Arousal from episodes is rapid and followed by a dream recall that usually matches the observed activity (e.g., one patient may wake up hitting the wall with his feet and report he was dreaming of being attacked by a dog and to be kicking him back). Episodes are potentially harmful and injuries are reported by more than 75 percent of patients or bed partners. Polysomnography recording in RBD shows electromyographic (EMG) abnormalities during REM sleep, namely a sustained or intermittent loss of the physiological REM sleep muscle atonia and an increased EMG phasic activity. RBD may be idiopathic (e.g., when no other neurological signs are associated) or symptomatic. The latter is often associated with neurodegenerative diseases, mostly alpha-synucleinopathies (Parkinson's disease, dementia with Lewy bodies, and multiple system atrophy). There is a growing body of evidence suggesting that the apparently idiopathic RBD may represent an early marker of the aforementioned neurodegenerative diseases (Boeve et al., 2007, pp. 2770–2788).

For reasons not yet fully understood, the increased motor activity during REM sleep in RBD is paralleled by a higher rate of aggressiveness in dreams, as shown by a study employing the Hall and Van de Castle method (Fantini, Corona, Clerici, & Ferini-Strambi, 2005, pp. 1010–1015). Indeed, a significant increase in all aggressiveness indicators was found in RBD dreams versus controls, with particular representation of physical aggression (29.3% vs. 3.8%). A higher rate of animal characters (19% vs. 4%) was also observed, habitually threatening or attacking the dreamer. Despite this result,

no difference in daytime aggressiveness, as assessed by the total Aggression Questionnaire scores, was found between RBD patients and controls, with RBD showing even lower scores in the subscale of physical aggressiveness.

One may also be surprised by the high frequency of certain dream scenarios, almost stereotypically reported by the RBD population. Those include an unfamiliar people entering the dreamer's house, strangers threatening the dreamer or his relatives, or the dreamer being attacked by animals, with the dreamer usually fighting back in self-defense or attempting to flee. Fear and anger are the most common associated emotions. In a large unpublished series of 154 dreams collected in 82 either idiopathic or symptomatic RBD patients at the San Raffaele Hospital Sleep Center in Milan (Italy), we found that only 36 dreams (23%) contain pleasant or neutral emotions, while the majority of them (118/154, 77%) fell into the following categories: (1) *fighting with humans* ($n = 72/154$, 47%; 63% of which involved the dreamer responding to an aggression perpetrated to self or to a beloved person); (2) *dangerous situations* (29/154, 19%), most containing vestibular sensations (falling from a precipice, to be swiped away by water, etc.); (3) *threatening animals* (23/154, 15%), mostly dogs, snakes, or other wild animals; (4) *physical activities* (0.5% of the total dreams), mostly sports such as soccer playing and biking.

The physiopathological mechanism underlying this change in dream content is unknown. According to the activation–synthesis model of dream generation, phasic discharges from brain stem generators simultaneously activate motor, perceptual, affective, and cognitive pathways and these impulses are then synthesized into dreams by the forebrain (Hobson & McCarley, 1977, pp. 1335–1348). Thus, in RBD, the increased motor activity and the action-filled dreams may be the expression of the hyperactivity of a common neuronal generator. In favor of this hypothesis stand the frequent dream changes after administration of clonazepam, which is known to decrease EMG phasic motor activity. Besides a dramatic reduction in frequency and intensity of behavioral episodes, patients usually report normalization of their dreams that become less violent and stereotyped and more variegated and bizarre. Other possible explanations for altered dream content in RBD take into account the evolutionary theory of dreaming. The latter suggests that the biological function of the dreams would be to simulate threatening events and to rehearse threat avoidance (Revonsuo, 2000, pp. 793–1121). Previous studies found that children's dreams contain a higher rate of aggression and animal characters compared to adult dreams, and that both elements decrease as a function of age, suggesting that dream activity may be useful to the development of threat-avoidance skills. Dreams in RBD share similar increased percentages of aggressiveness and animal characters with children's dreams, compared to same-age and gender controls. Therefore, it may be hypothesized that chronic idiopathic RBD, as a frequent marker of an underlying neurodegenerative process, may originate by the release of ontogenically early dream patterns. The peculiar alteration of dreams in RBD may provide us a key to expand our understanding about the mechanisms of physiological and pathological dream synthesis.

Maria Livia Fantini

See also: entries related to Sleep Physiology

References

Boeve, B. F., Silber, M. H., Saper, C. B., Ferman, T. J., Dickson, D. W., Parisi, J. E. . . . Braak, H. (2007). Pathophysiology of REM sleep behavior disorder and relevance to neurodegenerative disease. *Brain, 130,* 2770–2788.

Fantini, M. L., Corona, A., Clerici, S., & Ferini-Strambi, L. (2005). Aggressive dream content without daytime aggressiveness in REM sleep behavior disorder. *Neurology, 65,* 1010–1015.

Hobson, J. A., & McCarley, R. W. (1977). The brain as a dream state generator: An activation-synthesis hypothesis of the dream process. *American Journal of Psychiatry, 134,* 1335–1348.

Revonsuo, A. (2000). The reinterpretation of dreams: An evolutionary hypothesis of the function of dreaming. *Behavioral and Brain Sciences, 23,* 793–1121.

Schenck, C. H., Bundlie, S. R., Ettinger, M. G., & Mahowald, M. W. (1986). Chronic behavioral disorders of human REM sleep: A new category of parasomnia. *Sleep, 9,* 293–308.

Disturbed Sleep and Posttraumatic Stress Disorder

Nightmares are one of the key symptoms of posttraumatic stress disorder (PTSD), a disorder that 8 to 20 percent of people develop after experiencing a traumatic event. Posttraumatic nightmares are highly distressing since they are often exact replications of the original traumatic event, although they may get more symbolic over time. Although nightmare treatment is not yet part of standard PTSD treatment, their role may be central to the development and persistence of PTSD. Specific nightmare treatment, whether cognitive-behavioral (e.g., imagery rehearsal) or pharmacological (e.g., prazosin), reduces not only nightmare frequency but also PTSD symptom severity, suggesting that nightmares specifically—or disturbed sleep in general—are critically involved in the persistence of PTSD.

A role for nightmares and disturbed sleep in the extinction of conditioned fear (fear extinction) has been proposed (Germain, Buysse, & Nofzinger, 2008; Levin & Nielsen, 2007), in line with evidence from animal studies showing that rapid eye movement (REM) sleep deprivation impairs fear extinction and consolidation of fear extinction. According to this view, the function of sleep is disrupted when sleep is terminated prematurely, fragmented, or interrupted. In human studies, fear conditioning and extinction are studied by first repeatedly pairing a stimulus (e.g., visual image of a geometric form) with an electrical shock administered to the right hand, which constitutes the fear-conditioning part. Another stimulus, the safety stimulus, is never paired with shocks, and as a result, the skin conductance response to the fear-conditioned stimulus should be higher than the response to the safety stimulus. In the extinction session, the fear-conditioned stimulus is repeatedly presented but without any following shocks, and the physiological response extinguishes. If this novel knowledge about the former fear-conditioned stimulus is consolidated successfully, subjects will again have no or

little physiological response to the former fear-conditioned stimulus during the recall of extinction session.

Interestingly, the brain regions involved in fear extinction and consolidation of fear extinction (Sehlmeyer et al., 2009), such as the ventromedial prefrontal cortex and the dorsal anterior cingulate cortex, are also the brain regions that show increased levels of activity during REM sleep (Maquet et al., 1996). This points to overlap in the neural circuitry of fear extinction (consolidation) and REM sleep. Moreover, those are also the regions that show differential activity in PTSD patients, which have impaired fear extinction and consolidation of fear extinction (Milad et al., 2009). Moreover, although older studies have noted few, if any, sleep disruptions in PTSD in polysomnographic recordings, a meta-analysis that controlled for confounding factors such as age, gender, co-morbid depression, and alcohol abuse noted altered polysomnographic parameters, among others an increased REM density in PTSD patients (Kobayashi, Boarts, & Delahanty, 2007).

The question is whether disturbed sleep precedes posttraumatic stress complaints. When young healthy subjects have a 90-minute afternoon nap after a fear-conditioning and fear-extinction session, about half of them show a normal afternoon nap consisting of one sleep cycle with slow-wave sleep, light non-REM sleep, and ending with a 5- to 10-minute period of REM sleep (Spoormaker et al., 2010); the other half shows a pattern of disrupted sleep with a longer sleep latency, more wake-after-sleep-onset, and less or no REM sleep, while the amounts of non-REM sleep stages are similar. This depends on how much subjects habituate to electrical shocks: the ones who keep responding (relatively) intensely to the mild electrical shocks are also the ones who show a disrupted sleep pattern and, crucially, impaired recall of fear extinction (Spoormaker et al., 2010). Note that this impaired recall of fear extinction (i.e., increased physiological responses to the former fear-conditioned stimulus) is associated with decreased activity in the ventromedial prefrontal cortex, one of the fear-extinction hotspots.

In conclusion, these studies suggest that disturbed sleep is not an epiphenomenon of PTSD, but that it may be a central mediating factor in the development and persistence of this debilitating anxiety disorder. This has consequences for the scientific study and the clinical treatment of PTSD, as the cognitive and emotional impairments following REM sleep disruptions point to a relevant affective function of this sleep stage, and clinical sleep complaints such as nightmares and insomnia can be treated with cognitive-behavioral treatments. Future studies should examine whether a brief, sleep-focused treatment administered in the beginning of treatment enhances treatment effects of standard PTSD therapy and increases patients' well-being.

Victor I. Spoormaker

See also: entries related to Sleep Disorders

References

Germain, A., Buysse, D. J., & Nofzinger, E. (2008). Sleep-specific mechanisms underlying posttraumatic stress disorder: Integrative review and neurobiological hypotheses. *Sleep Medicine Reviews, 12,* 185–195.

Kobayashi, I., Boarts, J. M., & Delahanty, D. L. (2007). Polysomnographically measured sleep abnormalities in PTSD: A meta-analytic review. *Psychophysiology, 44,* 660–669.

Levin, R., & Nielsen, T. A. (2007). Disturbed dreaming, posttraumatic stress disorder, and affect distress: A review and neurocognitive model. *Psychological Bulletin, 133,* 482–528.

Maquet, P., Péters J., Aerts, J., Delfiore, G., Degueldre, C., Luxen, A., & Franck, G. (1996). Functional neuroanatomy of human rapid-eye-movement sleep and dreaming. *Nature, 383,* 163–166.

Milad, M. R., Pitman, R. K., Ellis, C. B., Gold, A. L., Shin, L. M., Lasko, N. B., & Rausch, S. L. (2009). Neurobiological basis of failure to recall extinction memory in posttraumatic stress disorder. *Biological Psychiatry, 66*(12), 1072–1074.

Sehlmeyer, C., Schöning, S., Zwitserlood, P., Pfleiderer, B., Kircher, T., Arolt, V., & Konrad, C. (2009). Human fear conditioning and extinction in neuroimaging: A systematic review. *PLoS ONE, 4,* e5865.

Spoormaker, V. I, Sturm, A., Andrade, K. C., Schröter, M. S., Goya-Maldonado, R., Holsboer, F., . . . Czisch, M. (2010). The neural correlates and temporal sequence of the relationship between shock exposure, disturbed sleep and impaired consolidation of fear extinction. *Journal of Psychiatric Research, 44,* 1121–1128.

Dream Interview: A Client-Defined, Metaphor-Based Interpretation

Dream interpretation began when experts thought to be wiser than the dreamer offered interpretations based on tradition, religious revelations, or superstition. By the 19th and 20th centuries, priests and other wise ones were joined by psychotherapists who, like Freud and Jung, added certain associations elicited from the dreamer to their interpretations, which were based on their own psychological theories. Because the metapsychologies of the therapists varied, and because each therapist used various interpretative systems based on a variety of convictions, or myth, or intuition, interpretations from different therapists could easily conflict. In an effort to standardize interpretations by incorporating relevant and crucial information from the dreamer and diminishing the role of other factors that can drive inappropriate projections, we developed the dream interview (Flowers, 1993).

The dream interview is an existential approach that elicits the dreamer's descriptions of major dream images and asks the dreamer if the verbal description of the image or action in the dream reminds him or her of anything, anyone, or any aspect of himself or herself in waking life. The role of the interviewer can be played by the therapist or the dreamer. The interviewer is to keep all his interpretive ideas, intuitions, and special knowledge to himself and use only the dreamer's words to assist the dreamer in finding a parallel to waking life. The key skill for the interviewer is that of asking nonleading questions to elicit rich descriptions that contain relevant facts and feelings from the dreamer's unique perspective. This process is highly organized and contains basic questions that often require follow-up questions tailored to the given dream. The key element of these questions is that they are asked from the point of view of a person from another planet who knows very little about life on earth. This perspective keeps the interpreter out of the dreamer's way. The dreamer is asked to describe first, interpret later. The interviewer follows three basic steps: description, recapitulation, and bridge.

> Sample dream: A cat was on the windowsill. It came into my room, raised a ruckus, and left.
> Sample interview:

Interviewer: Pretend I come from another planet. What are cats like? (Elicit description)

Dreamer: They are sleek, agile, distant, aloof; they love you when they want and leave you when they want.

I: What was the cat in your dream like? (Specific to generic description)

D: The same, gorgeous, black, and sleek.

I: What room did the cat enter? (Elicit more detail)

D: My bedroom.

I: How did you feel when it raised a ruckus and left? (Elicit description of feelings)

D: Awful, I was in tears.

I: Is there anything, anyone, or any part of yourself like a gorgeous, black, sleek, agile cat that raises a ruckus in your bedroom, is distant, aloof, loves you when it wants and leaves you when it wants, and you feel awful, end up in tears when it leaves? (Recapitulation in the dreamer's words combined with an invitation to bridge to waking experience)

D: Oh my boyfriend! He is sleek and black and gorgeous and has exactly that personality.

Upon reflection, the dreamer said that she had always chosen men like cats and that what she really needed now was a dog—faithful, loyal, and attached. Had the interviewer assumed that cats represent the mother, the feminine principle, or an Egyptian goddess, it would have been easy to lead the dreamer away from her own meaning.

If the dreamer does not see a strong parallel between the dream descriptions recapitulated by the interviewer, one asks for a more detailed description, or goes to the next image and returns to the difficult ones later. Working with longer dreams with several scene changes, the interviewer methodically asks about the major images and their mutations, scene by scene. Major images are to be bridged and linked so that the dynamic thrust of the dream is respected and the images are understood in the dramatic context of the dream, which acts as a control mechanism discouraging tangential and inaccurate interpretations. This replicability facilitates research.

Gayle M. V. Delaney and
Loma K. Flowers

References

Delaney, G. (1998). *All about dreams.* San Francisco: HarperSanFrancisco.

Delaney, G. (2009). Modern dream interpretation. *San Francisco Medicine,* 82(3).

Flowers, L. K. (1993). The dream interview method in a private outpatient psychotherapy practice. In G. Delaney (Ed.), *New directions in dream interpretation* (pp. 77–101). New York: State University of New York Press.

Flowers, L. K. (1995). The use of presleep instructions and dreams in psychosomatic disorders. *Psychotherapy and Psychosomatics, 64,* 173–177.

Flowers, L. K., & Zweben, J. E. (1998). The changing role of "using" dreams in addiction recovery. *Journal of Substance Abuse Treatment, 15*(3), 193–200.

Dream Sharing as Social Interaction

Beliefs in U.S. society regarding the importance of dreams tend to fall into one of two views: dreams are imbued with great meaning, or dreams are perceived to be meaningless. This dichotomy reflects a perceived distinction between waking life and nocturnal dreaming, the latter being less important and perhaps not worth talking about. Cross-culturally, both the Zuni and Momostenango, for example, share dreams informally among family members and friends, and formally in social groups (Tedlock, 1992). In U.S. society, however, sharing dreams is not an ordinary public communication, as there is little reward for remembering one's dreams, much less presenting them to others. As interest in studying dream sharing in U.S. society has increased, researchers have come to consider dream reports as public social performances worthy of consideration. Much can be learned from studying those who recount their dreams and about the social process of dream sharing, including social rules pertaining to issues of gender, social relationships, and context.

Fine and Leighton (1993) present a model that describes dreams as: (1) external to the individual (i.e., socially produced and mediated by the self); (2) reflective of cultural/societal content; (3) shared socially with others; and (4) connected to social organization. Their model complements other approaches to the study of dream sharing, focusing on the ways in which the dream world becomes reintegrated socially into the waking world. The process of dream recounting is dialectical in that interaction is not just internal, as when one says, "I had a dream and this is what it means," but is also external, as one only sometimes chooses to share dreams with others. A dream that is remembered becomes part of the individual's waking social agenda and as such the dream becomes socialized, which refers to the use of language, feelings, and memories that embellish the dream in preparation for sharing. Through the process of remembering and subsequent socialization, the dream becomes more deeply embedded in our ongoing social existence (Ullman, 1990, pp. 126–127). Dreams that are shared therefore are socially and culturally constituted or perhaps reconstituted. Reporting and interpreting dreams is a distinctly social event motivated by the value of presenting a dream to others in the context of the culture's valuation of dreams.

There is much to learn about dream sharing as social interaction. First, dreams are a gateway not only to the unconscious, but they are the stories within the culture. One of the ways that culture and society are maintained is through storytelling. However, in Western culture, so heavily dominated by mass media and popular culture, storytelling takes on an additional role as dreams that are recounted may be appreciated for their entertainment value. A mundane or banal dream may be one not worth repeating, but one that is exciting or involves a celebrity may be worth telling to others (Alperstein & Vann, 1997). Similarly, individuals sometimes phrase the sharing of a dream in the language of hyperbole. The individual may begin by saying something like: "You wouldn't believe the dream I had last night" or "I had the wildest dream last night." Such emphatic statements preceding the telling of a dream elevate the discourse to the level of entertainment, something valued in the culture.

Second, through dream sharing, individuals demonstrate their connectedness to the culture by including references to media content, including references to media figures—celebrities, fictional characters, newsmakers, and newscasters—as well as references to other cultural artifacts, such as products and brands. Demonstrating such cultural knowledge provides the individual with social status. A dream that involves a character from a television program or movie, for example, may be one that is worth telling to others because as a media figure that character is part of our shared culture (Alperstein & Vann, 1997). Presenting such a dream to others is one means by which individuals create and maintain cultural connections.

Third, dream sharing is a process through which individuals maintain or enhance social identity. As individuals choose which of their dreams to recount to others, and which dreams not to share, they may utilize this opportunity to present themselves in a particular way that affirms or enhances their identity. Fine and Leighton (1993) describe dream sharing as a "collective attempt . . . made to maintain and appropriate presentation of self, [in which] the narrator and audience collaborate in creating an acceptable meaning for these ideas" (p. 99). Prefacing dreams with a disclaimer such as "I had the weirdest dream last night" signals to the listener that what he or she is about to hear is clearly attributable to dreaming and not the responsibility of the dreamer and therefore should not reflect negatively on the dreamer.

Just as there are rules of presentation of self in dream sharing, Tedlock (1992) suggests that in finding the proper context for the speech event, choice of audience, and discourse frame, the social rules of dream sharing vary among cultures. Both the Zuni and Raramuri, for example, privilege the telling of bad dreams. Members of the Zuni culture do not share good dreams for fear of thwarting the potential good luck they may hold. Other rules of dream sharing, which vary cross-culturally, pertain to context, as in Raramuri culture dreams may be shared during morning visits. In Sambian culture, individuals tell dreams privately and publicly. Shamans tell dreams; elders tell dreams; adult men tell dreams with regard to hunting and trading; and, others might tell dreams only to close friends.

Researchers who have studied rules of dream sharing in American culture emphasize the importance of personal risk and safety, as dreams are shared in social, perhaps group, settings. Individuals seek assurance of risk reduction when assessing the safety of sharing a dream that may reveal that which is intimate and personal, potentially exposing the individual to embarrassment. To ensure the safety of the dreamer, "The dreamer who shares a dream should be in control of the process" (Ullman, 1990, p. 127). The feeling for personal safety is a requirement for dream sharing that extends beyond the therapeutic milieu to a more public context. Herdt describes three discourse frames regarding the cultural and social nature of dream sharing. These include public, secret, and private talk (Herdt, 1992, p. 59). As applied

to dream sharing, these three discourse frames suggest that implicit and explicit rules governing society determine which dreams get told in a public setting, secret setting, or perhaps not at all. Within this framework, sexually suggestive dreams, for example, may not be appropriate for sharing in a public setting, but may be told among close friends.

In a study of dream sharing, Vann and Alperstein (2000) found that individuals tell dreams for the following reasons: in order to entertain; to share something that is of intimate value; or, to elicit a reaction. In other words, the telling of a dream is clearly a calculated social interaction, the intended outcome being self-presentation. As with any other social interaction, some calculation is made as to the degree of risk involved and the benefits derived. Telling a dream is a complex social process, which goes beyond mere reporting of dream content, when, for example, a shared dream serves as a means to bring individuals closer together. That is, individuals only tell dreams, or a particular dream, to people or individuals they know well or want to know well and in contexts that bring about greater intimacy among those individuals involved, ultimately enhancing social relationships. Vann and Alperstein (2000) found that dreams are shared informally as a part of private discourse. Their respondents generally did not formally share their dreams in a dream-sharing group or in the course of psychotherapy. The majority of their respondents reported telling dreams to those whom they defined as intimates, in zones they considered safe. The respondents in the Vann and Alperstein study (2000) recognized zones of safety and danger in dream sharing, with the majority reporting that there were social situations in which it would not be safe to tell a dream. "Zones of safety and danger refer to the social geography of dream sharing" (Wagner-Pacifici & Bershady, 1993, p. 134). For example, dreams in which the listener was in danger would be less likely to be shared with that individual. Thus, in dream sharing, individuals employ strategies of self-protection that may provide panoply of protection through which the individuals may maintain their reputation. In this case, although the institutional context—friendship—is a safe zone, in which it should be safe to tell a dream, protective practices may ensure personal safety by prohibiting dream sharing. Within various social contexts, dream sharing follows the same rules of social interaction as other aspects of everyday life.

The same reasoning applies to one other response given for hesitancy in dream sharing: women hesitate to share dreams in which they have done something wrong, whereas men hesitate to tell dreams that reveal weakness on their part (Vann & Alperstein, 2000). Given the gender expectations of contemporary U.S. society, it is not surprising that men would be more hesitant to share dreams that reveal weakness (perhaps threatening their masculinity) and women are more likely to worry about revealing something that may be perceived as socially inappropriate. In either case— female or male—the dreamer is engaging in a form of self-protection, hesitating to reveal an aspect of the self that may impact their self-presentation. The telling of a sexual dream was identified by the majority of respondents in the Vann and Alperstein study as a type of dream they would never tell.

Vann and Alperstein (2000) describe four general principles about dream sharing in contemporary American culture: (1) dreams are shared for entertainment; (2) gender influences the sharing of dreams; (3) individuals are selective in determining which dreams are deemed safe or unsafe to share, and; (4) dreams generally are shared with friends and intimates in private. Dream sharing, therefore, is reflective of a culture's general attitudes toward dreams. Where dreams are highly valued and where the distinction between the dreaming and waking worlds is not so clearly delineated, dream sharing affects aspects of everyday social and spiritual life. As mentioned, the Zunis, for example, will not share good dreams for fear of spoiling good fortune that may be coming their way, while in American culture, dreams are shared for social purposes.

Although psychologists and anthropologists have maintained a keen interest in researching dreams and dream sharing, it has remained an area of secondary importance among sociologists. Hilbert (2010) points out an unresolved paradox in which individuals experience the dream and dream telling as objective reality, which he contends is problematic given the subjective nature of dreams and dream telling. Future research on dream sharing needs to consider both the external constraints—dream telling as social production—in the context of internal—psychological—constraints that impact whether or not an individual chooses to recount a dream to others and under what circumstances and in which contexts one should or should not tell a dream.

Neil Michael Alperstein

References

Alperstein, N., & Vann, B. (1997). Star gazing: A socio-cultural approach to studying media figures in dreams. *Communication Quarterly, 45*(3), 1–11.

Fine, G., & Leighton, L. (1993). Nocturnal missions: Steps toward a sociology of dreams. *Symbolic Interaction, 16*(2), 95–104.

Herdt, G. (1992). Selfhood and discourse in Sambia dream sharing. In B. Tedlock (Ed.), *Dreaming: Anthropological and psychological interpretations* (pp. 55–85). Santa Fe, NM: School of American Research Press.

Hilbert, R. (2010). The anomalous foundations of dream telling: Objective solipsism and the problem of meaning. *Human Studies, 33*, 41–64.

Tedlock, B. (1992). *Dreaming: Anthropological and psychological interpretations*. Santa Fe, NM: School of American Research Press.

Ullman, M. (1990). Guidelines for teaching dreamwork. In S. Krippner (Ed.), *Dreamtime and dreamwork: Decoding the language of the night* (pp. 122–128). New York: Jeremy P. Tarcher/Perigee.

Vann, B., & Alperstein, N. (2000). Dream sharing as social interaction. *Dreaming, 10*(2), 111–119.

Wagner-Pacifici, R., & Bershady, H. (1993). Portents or confessions: Authoritative reads of a dream text. *Symbolic Interaction, 16*(2), 129–143.

DreamBank.net: An Online Archive for Studying Dream Content

DreamBank.net, or the DreamBank, is an open-access, web-based dream report archive and research site that is constantly growing. As of early 2011, it included more than 26,000 dream reports, approximately 19,200 of which are in English and 6,900 in German. They were collected in a variety of settings, ranging from the sleep laboratory to the classroom to personal dream journals kept for varying reasons. About 5,000 of the dream reports are from groups, such as children, teenagers, college students, and blind adults. The rest are in dream series from individual teenagers and adults, including 86 dreams written down by a physiologist in 1897–1898, 900 dreams from a woman who periodically recorded them between 1912 and four days before her death in 1965 at age 78, and 1,093 dreams from a factory worker in the northern Pennsylvania–Ohio area who kept a detailed dream diary between 1949 and 1964, because he thought they provided useful clues in picking winners in horse races.

The DreamBank is useful for researchers who need large representative samples of carefully written reports on which to test their ideas and methods, or as control groups for comparison with dream reports they have collected. Random samples can be drawn from DreamBank search results for these purposes. For control groups, perhaps the most useful dream reports are the 500 dreams from men and 500 dreams from women that were used in establishing the norms for every category in the Hall–Van de Castle coding system. In addition, the Hall–Van de Castle codings for the normative dreams and more than 1,000 other dream reports are available at http://dreambank.net/coding_search.cgi.

The search engine can be used to study the dream reports by entering individual words, long strings of words, or phrases into the query box. There are detailed instructions on the site on how to make accurate and efficient searches. Most searches take only a few seconds to complete, even with long word strings. The results are converted into frequency counts and percentages that are presented in tables. It is possible to determine the consistency of elements per a given number of dream reports in an individual series and to find contingencies between two elements in a collection of dream reports. The dream reports retrieved by the search engine can be viewed in full or in an abbreviated form that displays only the sentences containing the requested words, with the requested words highlighted and in boldface in either case. When scrolling through the dreams, those that are not relevant can be eliminated before the dreams are printed or analyzed. Researchers who want to put their own dream reports in a password-protected space can use the search engine. Dream reports in any Western language can be searched.

Systematic studies using dream reports from the DreamBank reveal that the social networks in dreams have the same properties as waking social networks, that religious and spirit elements are rare in dreams (less than 4%), and that flying under one's own power, falling through space, and other unusual events are even more rare (less than 1%). DreamBank studies also show that the major characters and activities in a person's dream journal are very consistent over time. For example, in a comparison of the first 3,116 dream reports in the Barb Sanders series with 1,138 that were added later, at least one of the 13 main people in her life (parents, ex-husband, three siblings, three children, granddaughter, and three best friends) appear in 33.6 percent of the dreams in the first set and in 35.1 percent of the second set. The everyday nature of perhaps as many as 70 to 75 percent of dream reports is shown in a study of 2,022 dreams from a college student, Kenneth. His small circle of friends appear in 53.9 percent of the dream reports, his mother or father in 23.9 percent, driving his car or truck in 24.5 percent, going fishing or camping in 17.0 percent, eating in 13.7 percent, and playing or watching sports in 6.1 percent. Overall, 76.7 percent of the dream reports mention at least one of the 18 words that have to do with the dreamer's friends, parents, driving, camping/fishing, eating, or sports (Domhoff & Schneider, 2008).

Studies using 40 standardized word strings that relate to perception (e.g., the five senses, colors), cognition (e.g., awareness, planning, reading/writing), emotions (e.g., fear/apprehension, sadness, anger, happiness), social interaction (e.g., friendliness, physical aggression, sexuality), common culture (e.g., schools, money, technology), and the natural world (e.g., weather, fire, water) discover the same gender differences found with the Hall–Van de Castle coding system (Bulkeley, 2009a). When the results of word searches in 192 dream reports from a young adult male were compared with normative findings for the 40 word strings, researchers correctly predicted many aspects of the dreamer's personality (socially outgoing, even-tempered, thoughtful), the activities in which he or she is involved (works with newspapers, swims, sexually active), relationships (family members, animals), and cultural preferences (nonreligious, a

science fiction fan) (Bulkeley & Domhoff, 2010).

It is also possible to make thematic studies of the dream reports that are found through the use of word strings. In the case of the 315 dream reports on DreamBank from Merri, an artist in her late 30s, it was inferred through a qualitative analysis of the interactions and emotions in dream reports containing the words God, Jesus, Christian, and Bible that (1) the dreamer was brought up in a strict Protestant tradition, which (2) she had rejected with considerable hostility. In addition, it was further inferred that (3) she nonetheless continued to have strongly held spiritual beliefs that were expressed in a nontraditional way. All three of these inferences, along with several others, proved to be correct according to the dreamer (Bulkeley, 2009b).

However, there are limitations to computerized searches, starting with the fact that it is highly unlikely that complex coding categories for characters, social interactions, successes and failures, and misfortunes could be duplicated with word strings. The best that can be accomplished with such categories is to use word strings to find subsets within a larger dream collection that could then be examined by trained coders. Then, too, it is sometimes necessary to scroll through the dream reports uncovered in a search to see if any of them are false positives due to possible multiple meanings for one or more of the words in newly created word strings that of necessity had to be used.

Even with these limitations, the fact remains that the DreamBank makes possible studies that never could have been done in the past because of the difficulties of collecting large samples of thorough dream reports and the labor-intensive nature of systematic coding systems with high levels of interrater reliability. When used in conjunction with the 40 standardized word strings, for example, it is possible to study dream content that was seldom quantified in the past because it appeared with such extreme frequency that analyzing it would have been extremely time consuming (e.g., the many types of thinking in dreams; activities such as talking, walking, and running; and the many natural and humanly constructed objects found in most dream reports). Worldwide access to the DreamBank also makes it possible for researchers in many different regions of the world to work together to do studies of the same collection of dreams. Such highly detailed studies by groups of researchers might lead to a level of specificity in the study of dream meaning that has not been reached in the past.

G. William Domhoff

See also: entries related to Dream Content

References

Bulkeley, K. (2009a). Seeking patterns in dream content: A systematic approach to word searches. *Consciousness and Cognition, 18*, 909–916.

Bulkeley, K. (2009b). The religious content of dreams: A new scientific foundation. *Pastoral Psychology, 58*, 93–106.

Bulkeley, K., & Domhoff, G. W. (2010). Detecting meaning in dream reports: An extension of a word search approach. *Dreaming, 20*, 77–95.

Domhoff, G. W., & Schneider, A. (2008). Studying dream content using the archive and search engine on DreamBank. net. *Consciousness and Cognition, 17*, 1238–1247.

Dreaming: **The Journal of the Association for the Study of Dreams**

Dreaming is a scholarly journal devoted specifically to dreams. It is international and interdisciplinary—publishing academic articles related to dreams from many approaches and viewpoints. *Dreaming* covers biological aspects of dream and sleep/dream laboratory research; psychological articles of any kind related to dreaming; clinical work on dreams regardless of theoretical perspective (Freudian, Jungian, existential, eclectic, etc.); anthropological, sociological, and philosophical articles related to dreaming; and articles about dreaming from the arts and humanities. Most issues include a mixture of these topics, but *Dreaming* occasionally has special issues devoted to a particular aspect of dreaming. These have included Dreaming and the Arts, Children's Dreams and Nightmares, Historical Studies of Dreaming, and Anthropological Approaches to Dreaming.

Dreaming was started in 1991 by The Association for the Study of Dreams (now the International Association for the Study of Dreams), which appoints its editor and oversees editorial content. Ernest Hartmann, MD, was the first editor serving from 1991 to 1998; Don Kuiken, PhD, was its second from1996 to 1998, Jayne Gackenbach, PhD, served as acting editor from 1998 to 1999; and Deirdre Barrett, PhD, has been editor from 1999 to the present. The journal has had three publishers and is now published by the American Psychological Association (APA). *Dreaming* is a quarterly, with volumes coming out in March, June, September, and December of each year. As with most scholarly journals, articles submitted to *Dreaming* are peer-reviewed before a decision is reached.

Dreaming is available by individual or library subscription and is included in many of APA's electronic rights packages. All abstracts and some back articles can be found at the journal's websites listed in the reference section that follows, along with instructions for authors on how to submit articles to the journal.

Deirdre Barrett

See also: International Association for the Study of Dreams

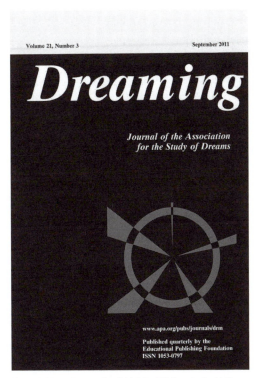

Dreaming: Journal of IASD (Richard C. Wilkerson/International Association for the Study of Dreams)

Reference

Dreaming: Journal of the Association for the Study of Dreams. http://www.asdreams. org/idxjournal.htm and http://www.apa.org/ pubs/journals/drm/index.aspx

Dream-Lag Effect

The dream-lag effect refers to the finding that memory elements contributing to the formation of a dream often stem from events that took place about a week prior to the dream, whereas memory elements from events that took place two to four days earlier are much less frequent. The dream-lag effect is often studied in conjunction with the day-residue effect,

which refers to the appearance in dreams of memory sources stemming from events occurring the day prior to the dream. The extent of reappearance of events in dreams is often of about the same magnitude for both the dream-lag and day-residue effects (see Figure 4).

The term dream-lag effect was proposed in 1989 by Nielsen and Powell who first demonstrated its occurrence with a controlled experimental protocol. This group subsequently replicated the effect (Nielsen, Kuiken, Alain, Stenstrom, & Powell, 2004; Nielsen & Powell, 1992; Powell, Nielsen, Cheung, & Cervenka, 1995), with the first independent replication of it appearing in 2010 (Blagrove, Henley-Einion, Barnett, Edwards, &

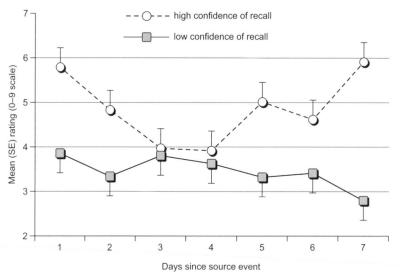

Figure 4: Day-residue and Dream-lag Effects. Subject self-ratings of the extent to which home dreams reflect events occurring from 1 to 7 days prior to the dream. Only subjects who had high confidence in their recall of source memories (dotted line) showed evidence of both effects. These subjects gave higher correspondence ratings to events taking place 1 to 2 days prior to the dream (day-residue) and 5 to 7 days prior to the dream (dream-lag) than to events taking place 3 to 4 days prior to the dream.

Heidi, 2010). French researcher Michel Jouvet had earlier described and theorized about a similar type of effect in samples of his own home dreams; results from the original, French-language, publication (Jouvet, 1979) were subsequently reprinted in an English book translation (Jouvet, 1999 [1993]).

The occurrence of day-residue and dream-lag effects has never been satisfactorily explained although researchers involved agree that both phenomena support the view that sleep and dreaming are involved in memory consolidation functions. Nielsen et al. (Nielsen, 2004) suggested that the curvilinear pattern of ratings exemplifying the day-residue and dream-lag effects (see Figure 4) may reflect the implication of a circaseptan (approximately one week) timer or oscillator in the processing of source memories, a notion consistent with the fact that dreaming is regulated by other types of chronobiological rhythms, for example, circadian and ultradian rhythms.

While research supports the robustness of both of these temporal factors, it remains unknown if they are associated with the same or separate underlying memory processes. Part of this uncertainty has to do with a lack of research comparing attributes of the two memory effects.

A qualitative difference between day-residue and dream-lag memory elements is suggested by judge ratings of the nature of these elements; dream-lag memory elements are more likely to concern spatial imagery and the solving of socioemotional problems than are day-residue elements (Nielsen et al., 2004). However, an interdependence between the two phenomena was suggested by evidence that the two are delayed in parallel by stressful or impactful events. When participants viewed a stressful film on two occasions in the sleep laboratory, peak incorporations of the film appeared on post-film days 3 and 10 rather than on days 1 and 7 (see Figure 5) (Nielsen & Powell, 1995).

The systematic variation in processing of memory elements in the day-residue and dream-lag effects may reflect an underlying process by which newly acquired experiences are transferred from short-term into longer-term memory. The temporal pattern of the two effects appears similar to the time course of new memories that rely initially on the hippocampus processes then increasingly (over a period of about a week) on neocortical structures, including medial prefrontal and anterior cingulate cortices, in a complementary fashion. Dreaming may thus participate in the relocation of memory storage from hippocampus to neocortex over time.

Tore Nielsen

References

Blagrove, M., Henley-Einion, J., Barnett, A., Edwards, D., & Heidi, S.C. (2010). A replication of the 5–7 day dream-lag effect with comparison of dreams to future events as control for baseline matching. *Consciousness and Cognition, 20.* (2), 384–91.

Jouvet, M. (1979). Mémoire et "cerveau dédoublé" au cours du rêve a propos de 2525 souvenirs de rêve. [Memory and "split brain"in the dream and 2525 memories of the dream.] *L'Année du Praticien [Year of the Practioner], 29,* 27–32.

Jouvet, M. (1999 [1993]). *The paradox of sleep: The story of dreaming.* Cambridge, MA: Bradford, The MIT Press.

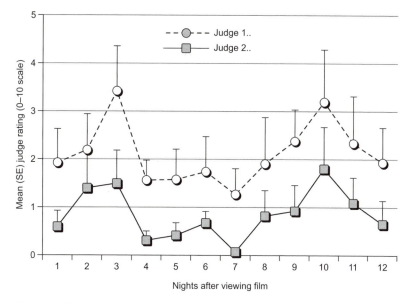

Figure 5: Parallel Delays of the Day-residue and Dream-lag Effects Following Viewing of a Stressful Film. Judge ratings of the extent to which home dreams reflect elements of the film reveal peaks at days 3 and 10 following the film rather than at the expected days 1 and 7.

Nielsen, T. A. (2004). Chronobiological features of dream production. *Sleep Medicine Reviews, 8,* 403–424.

Nielsen, T. A., Kuiken, D., Alain, G., Stenstrom, P., & Powell, R. (2004). Immediate and delayed incorporations of events into dreams: Further replication and implications for dream function. *Journal of Sleep Research, 13,* 327–336.

Nielsen, T. A., & Powell, R. A. (1989). The "dream-lag" effect: A 6-day temporal delay in dream content incorporation. *Psychiatric Journal of the University of Ottawa, 14,* 561–565.

Nielsen, T. A., & Powell, R. A. (1992). The day-residue and dream-lag effects: A literature review and limited replication of two temporal effects in dream formation. *Dreaming, 2,* 67–77.

Nielsen, T. A., & Powell, R. A. (1995). Temporal delays in dream content incorporation of a distressful film: A replication. *Sleep Research, 24A,* 259.

Powell, R. A., Nielsen, T. A., Cheung, J. S., & Cervenka, T. M. (1995). Temporal delays in incorporation of events into dreams. *Perceptual and Motor Skills, 81,* 95–104.

Dreamwork in Counseling

When Sigmund Freud (1856–1939) published his groundbreaking work on *The Interpretation of Dreams* in 1899/1900, he considered dreamwork together with the interpretation of transference to be the core of counseling. Dreamwork enables self-awareness because dreams are the "royal road to a knowledge of the unconscious activities of the mind" (Freud 1953 [1900], p. 608). Building on Freud's insights, scholars from various disciplines engaged in dream research and its relevance to psychic issues have come to a multifaceted understanding of the therapeutic benefits of dreamwork in counseling. Empirical studies show the effect of dreamwork on the counseling process, most notably on the session quality and the therapeutic alliance (e.g., Hill & Goates, 2003). Dreams and dreamwork can elucidate inner conflicts, struggles, and yearnings of the counselee; shed light on the state of the therapeutic relationship; help to understand relationships to significant others; open hitherto unknown paths into life; and touch deep levels of understanding of self, other, and transcendence.

Remarkably, it is mainly the rise of interest in spirituality that has led to a new revival of dreamwork, in the realization that "focusing on dreams in counseling may be a useful framework to explore clients' spiritual values and beliefs" (Crook, Lyon, & Wimmer, 2005, 35). In accordance with their own psychological method and their experiences with their own dreams, clinicians working with client's dreams define their role differently. Spiritually minded counselors—of whatever psychological school—and their clients will tend to reflect spiritual concerns. Based on their findings and on their observation that "little is known . . . about how counselors and clients integrate spirituality and dreamwork in practice" (Crook et al., 2005, p. 36), Crook, Lyon, and Wimmer offer five recommendations for therapists who want to integrate dreamwork in counseling: that they (1) become acquainted with a dream model that accords to their own psychological background, (2) communicate to their clients their willingness to work with dreams, (3) become familiar with

their clients' beliefs—for example, in regard to an imputed source of their dreams, (4) allow dreamwork to take up discussion time in the session, and (5) realize that dreamwork "may not be appropriate for all clients" (Crook et al., 2005, p. 43).

Dreamwork implies a hermeneutical process, whereby the presumptions of both counselor and counselee, the context, the fields of possible application interact with the dream itself (Morgenthaler, 2008). Of paramount importance is the therapeutic relationship and the counselor's attitude (Lemke, 2000). Counselors should act on the maxim that it is not they who interpret the dreams of their patients, but rather that they accompany their patients in reflecting on their dreams. Counselors should strengthen their clients' confidence that they will be able to find an autonomous interpretation of their own dreams and that it is they themselves who are responsible for finding a meaning.

How to integrate dreamwork into counseling practice remains an important question. Much empirical and hermeneutical research is yet to be done.

Isabelle Noth

References

Crook, R., Lyon, R. E., & Wimmer, C. L. (2005). Spirituality and dream work in counseling: Clients' experiences. *Pastoral Psychology, 54*(1), 35–45.

Freud, S. (1953 [1900]). The interpretation of dreams. In J. Strachey (Ed. and Trans.), *The standard edition of the complete psychological works of Sigmund Freud* (Vols. 4–5, pp. 1–627). London: Hogarth Press.

Hill, C. E., & Goates, M. K. (2003). Research on the Hill Dream Model. In C. E. Hill (Ed.), *Dream work in therapy: Facilitating exploration, insight, and action* (pp. 245–288).

Washington, DC: American Psychological Association.

Lemke, H. (2000). *Das Traumgespräch. Umgang mit Träumen nach klientenzentriertem Konzept. [The dream interview: Client centered approach to dealing with dreams.]* Stuttgart: Kohlhammer Verlag.

Morgenthaler, C. (2008). Trauminterpretation als Modell einer pastoralpsychologischen Hermeneutik. [Dream interpretation as a model of pastoral psychology.] *Wege zum Menschen, 60*(3), 248–262.

Dynamic Structure of Reptilian EEG versus Mammalian Sleep EEG

Do reptiles sleep like mammals? When analyzing mammalian sleep from an EEG (electroencephalogram) point of view, there are four different phases but with two main phases that alternate and are prevalent throughout the whole sleep: the slow-wave sleep (SWS) and the rapid eye movement REM phases. The SWS appears to have a nonlinear structure from the perspective of signals and system analysis while REM and the other two phases exhibit a random fractal structure: a behavior that coincides with that theoretically predicted for a stochastic system with power-law spectra, as is the case of linearly correlated noise (Pereda, Gamundí, Rial, & González, 1998). The EEG of reptiles at rest is of very low amplitude, very close to linear correlated noise without any changes throughout the resting period (González et al., 1999). Thus, if the existence of SWS and REM are the EEG traits of mammalian dreams, it must be concluded that reptiles do not have mammalian sleep patterns. However, during reptilian wakefulness at its preferred temperature, the reptilian EEG has a nonlinear structure similar to the mammalian SWS; in addition, while mammalian synchronized activation is particularly observed during sleep, synchronize activation in reptiles occurs in awake, attentive animals (Rial et al., 2010). These and other similarities constitute the fundamental argument for claiming that reptilian wakefulness has evolved toward mammalian sleep.

Julián Jesus González

See also: entries related to Evolution of Sleep

References

González, J. J., Gamundí, A., Rial, R., Nicolau, M. C., De Vera, L. M., & Pereda, E. (1999). Nonlinear, fractal, and spectral analysis of the EEG of lizard, Gallotia galloti. *American Journal of Physiology Regulatory, Integrative, and Comparative Physiology, 277*, 86–93.

Pereda, E., Gamundí, A., Rial, R., & González, J. J. (1998). Non-linear behaviour of human EEG: Fractal exponent versus correlation dimension in awake and sleep stages. *Neuroscience Letters, 250*, 91–94.

Rial, R. R., Akaaˆrir, M., Gamundí, A., Nicolau, M. C., Garau, C., Aparicio, S., . . . Esteban, S. (2010). Evolution of wakefulness, sleep and hibernation: From reptiles to mammals. *Neuroscience and Biobehavioral Review, 34*, 1144–1160.

E

Ecstasy (MDMA) Use and Sleep Problems

Methylenedioxymethamphetamine (MDMA, ecstasy) has its main effect as an indirect serotonin (5-hydroxytryptamine) agonist that induces a significant and long-lasting period of wakefulness in the recreational user (Allen, McCann, & Ricaurte, 1993). The impact of this period of wakefulness on subsequent sleep quality and especially quantity for regular users of ecstasy has received modest attention. Sleep studies in this area can be divided into laboratory studies (using sleep measurement instruments such as electroencephalograms) or prospective self-report studies (often using sleep diaries).

The first and most important study investigating the role of sleep architecture in human recreational ecstasy users was conducted by Allen et al. (1993). The researchers hypothesized that serotonin neurotoxicity from ecstasy use would manifest itself in participants' sleep. Regular ecstasy users' sleep was recorded by an electroencephalogram in a sleep laboratory, and they were only permitted to sleep for eight hours before being woken up. The findings showed that users and nonusers did not differ in amount of rapid eye movement (REM, dreaming) sleep; however, ecstasy users did have significantly less total sleep time and less stage 2 sleep. This suggested that there was an effect of ecstasy on sleep in humans, particularly during the lighter stages.

Many years later a follow-up study conducted in the same sleep laboratory noted rather different findings (McCann, Eligulashvili, & Ricaurte, 2000). This time there were no significant differences for amount of stage 2 sleep. Rather, ecstasy users had increases in stages 3 and 4, the deeper stages of sleep. The authors concluded that although sleep architecture was affected differently in both studies, sleep is still significantly disrupted in ecstasy users compared to controls. The differences between the two studies highlighted the gaps in knowledge in this area and the need for additional sleep architecture research on recreational ecstasy users.

In a recent review, McCann and Ricaurte (2007) summarized that serotonin is vital for sleep, not only for its modulation but also for its influence on circadian rhythms and airway patency. The review discussed the importance of serotonin for the opening of the tracheobronchial airway passage. This opening is significantly affected by ecstasy use, resulting in consequences for potential sleep disorders such as sleep apnea. The authors concluded that the unique role of serotonin for all these aspects of sleep and risk factors for sleep disorders indicates that any drug that disrupts serotonin will also have a profound impact on sleep quality.

In addition to studies measuring sleep, a number of important studies investigating self-rated sleep quality in the days following ecstasy use have been conducted. In one such study, Huxster, Pirona, and Morgan (2006) assessed sleep quality in ecstasy users for up to seven days after use. They found that self-rated sleep quality in ecstasy users was significantly poorer than polydrug controls across all seven days. However, after controlling for alcohol on the day of heaviest use, they found that the effect was no longer significant. It was concluded that self-reported sleep-quality problems after ecstasy use can be attributed to increased alcohol use on the night ecstasy is taken. Additionally, Jones, Callen, Blagrove, and Parrott (2008) found that ecstasy use affected all aspects of sleep, including self-reported quality, quantity, and nighttime awakenings for up to seven days after use. Additionally, ecstasy users also reported low energy and trouble concentrating for the same time period. Therefore it is unclear how long measures of sleep quality are affected after using ecstasy and also how much alcohol and polysubstance use (particularly other amphetamines such as cocaine) on the night of ecstasy use affects subsequent sleep.

Human research has demonstrated that regular ecstasy use induces wakefulness, diminishes stage 2 and REM sleep, and interrupts airway patency. All of these factors may produce a restless and disrupted night's sleep, influence subsequent energy and mood, and affect the development of sleep disorders. Much of the objective work in this area has looked at sleep for a limited time, and few have tracked the influence of other drug use, particularly cannabis, in the days following a weekend dose. New research needs to investigate the interactions between weekend ecstasy use and weekday self-medication of sleep-inducing substances, including benzodiazepines.

From the existing evidence it can be proposed that recreational weekend ecstasy use has long-lasting effects on sleep quality and quantity, which may impact daytime functioning. What we do not know is to what extent is this effect modulated by other drugs and alcohol consumed on the weekend. We also do not know what interactive effect sleep-inducing self-medication with other substances is having on long-term sleep quality. It is these questions that require further research and investigation.

Katy Alicia Jones

See also: entries related to Sleep Disorders; entries related to Sleep Physiology

References

Allen, R. P., McCann, U. D., & Ricaurte, G. A. (1993). Persistent effects of (+/-) 3, 4-methylenedioxymethamphetamine (MDMA, "ecstasy") on human sleep. *Sleep, 16*, 560–564.

Huxster, J. K., Pirona, A., & Morgan, M. J. (2006). The sub-acute effects of recreational ecstasy (MDMA) use: A controlled study in humans. *Psychopharmacology, 20*, 1–30.

Jones, K. A., Callen, F., Blagrove, M., & Parrott, A. C. (2008). Sleep, energy and self rated cognition across 7 nights following recreational ecstasy/MDMA use. *Sleep and Hypnosis, 10*, 16–28.

McCann, U. D., Eligulashvili, V., & Ricaurte, G. A. (2000). (+/-)3,4-methylenedioxymethamphetamine ("ecstasy")-induced serotonin neurotoxicity: Clinical studies. *Neuropsychobiology, 42*, 11–16.

McCann, U. D., & Ricaurte, G. A. (2007). Effects of (+/-) 3, 4-methylenedioxymethamphetamine (MDMA) on sleep and circadian rhythms. *The ScientificWorld Journal, 7,* 231–238.

Effect of Dreams on Waking Life

Whereas the number of studies investigating the effect of waking life on dreams is large, research looking into the effect of dreams on waking life has been done quite rarely. Three major topics have been studied: (1) effect of nightmares on daytime mood, (2) creative inspiration by dreams, and (3) dreams and psychotherapy.

Schredl (2000) has found that dreams affect the mood of the following day; which is the effect most often reported of dreams on waking life. Carrying out a carefully designed diary study in nightmare sufferers, Köthe and Pietrowsky (2001) reported that days after experiencing a nightmare are rated much lower on scales of anxiety, concentration, and self-esteem than days after non-nightmare nights. The hypothesis of Kathryn Belicki that the effects of nightmares on waking life are overestimated by persons with high neuroticism scores had not been supported by Schredl, Landgraf, and Zeiler (2003). The major factor contributing to nightmare distress was nightmare frequency. A recent study (Schredl & Reinhard, 2009–2010) also indicated that the effect of dreams on daytime mood is not limited to negatively toned dreams— intense positive and negative emotions affected daytime mood in a similar way.

Many examples of creative inspiration from dreams have been reported over the years (for an overview see Van de Castle, 1994): *Wild Strawberries* (a film by Ingmar Bergmann), the story of Dr. Jekyll and Mr. Hide by Robert Louis Stevenson, the pop song "Yesterday" by Paul McCartney, and the paintings of Salvador Dali all provide excellent examples. Kuiken and Sikora (1993) and Schredl (2000) found that 20 and 28 percent of the participants (student samples), respectively, reported creative inspirations from dreams at least twice a year. In a large-scaled study with more than 1,000 participants (Schredl & Erlacher, 2007), about 7.8 percent of the recalled dreams included a creative aspect. Reported were dreams stimulating art, giving an impulse to try something new (approaching a person, traveling, etc.), or helping to solve a problem (e.g., mathematical problems, etc.). The factors that are associated with the frequency of creative dreams in this study were dream-recall frequency itself, the thin boundaries personality dimension, a positive attitude toward creative activities, and visual imagination.

Although dreamwork is quite common in modern psychotherapy (Schredl, Bohusch, Kahl, Mader, & Somesan, 2000) and despite the extensive literature on case reports since Freud's *The Interpretation of Dreams,* systematic research on the efficiency of dreamwork is limited to the research efforts of one group. For more than 15 years, Clara Hill and her coworkers carried out studies to measure the effectiveness of single dream-interpretation sessions, dream groups over six weeks, or dream interpretation within short-term psychotherapy (Hill & Knox, 2010). The basis for their work is a cognitive–experiential model of dream interpretation that includes the three stages: exploration, insight, and action (Hill & Rochlen, 2004). Similar studies for other therapeutic approaches to dreamwork are overdue.

To summarize, research indicates that dreams do affect subsequent life to a considerable amount; this could also be conceptualized as continuity (Schredl & Reinhard, 2009–2010). It would be interesting to study whether the positive effects such as creative inspirations or elated mood (e.g., after lucid dreams or flying dreams) can be enhanced by training.

Michael Schredl

References

Hill, C. E., & Knox, S. (2010). The use of dreams in modern psychotherapy. *International Review of Neurobiology, 92*, 291–317.

Hill, C. E., & Rochlen, A. B. (2004). The Hill cognitive-experiential model of dream interpretation. In R. I. Rosner, W. J. Lyddon, & A. Freeman (Eds.), *Cognitive therapy and dreams* (pp. 161–178). New York: Springer.

Köthe, M., & Pietrowsky, R. (2001). Behavioral effects of nightmares and their correlations to peronality patterns. *Dreaming, 11*, 43–52.

Kuiken, D., & Sikora, S. (1993). The impact of dreams on waking thoughts and feelings. In A. Moffitt, M. Kramer, & R. Hoffmann (Eds.), *The functions of dreaming* (pp. 419–476). Albany: State University of New York Press.

Schredl, M. (2000). The effect of dreams on waking life. *Sleep and Hypnosis, 2*, 120–124.

Schredl, M., Bohusch, C., Kahl, J., Mader, A., & Somesan, A. (2000). The use of dreams in psychotherapy: A survey of psychotherapists in private practice. *Journal of Psychotherapy Practice and Research, 9*, 81–87.

Schredl, M., & Erlacher, D. (2007). Self-reported effects of dreams on waking-life creativity: An empirical study. *Journal of Psychology, 141*, 35–46.

Schredl, M., Landgraf, C., & Zeiler, O. (2003). Nightmare frequency, nightmare distress and neuroticism. *North American Journal of Psychology, 5*, 345–350.

Schredl, M., & Reinhard, I. (2009–2010). The continuity between waking mood and dream emotions: Direct and second-order effects. *Imagination, Cognition and Personality, 29*, 271–282.

Van de Castle, R. L. (1994). *Our dreaming mind.* New York: Ballentine.

Effect of Medications on Sleep and Dreaming

Many commonly used (and abused) medications are known to affect sleep. Patients and physicians need to be aware of these side effects when medications are prescribed. The most likely sleep-related side effects that patients may experience include: trouble going to sleep or staying asleep (insomnia), extreme sleepiness (hypersomnia), dreaming, and abnormal behaviors such as sleep walking, sleep talking or acting out dreams (parasomnias).

Nightmares are a particularly common side effect often associated with specific medications (Thompson & Pierce, 1999). Nightmares typically occur in REM sleep, the phase of sleep where the body is paralyzed except for eye movements and breathing. Moreover, nightmares typically occur at the end of the night, when the amount of REM sleep occupies a greater portion of the sleep cycle than at the beginning of the night. Even without medication, nightmares occur in up to 80 percent of individuals and are reported to be recurrent in 5 percent of the population (Leung & Robson, 1993). Therefore it can be difficult to separate a nightmare that is a medication side effect from a naturally occurring phenomenon.

There are several chemical messengers in the brain, known as neurotransmitters, that control sleep and waking. These neurotransmitters control REM sleep, and in turn dreaming and nightmares. Medications increase or decrease these neurotransmitters, affecting the amount of REM sleep and ultimately dreaming and nightmares. However, the relationship is not always straightforward. Many medications that decrease the amount of REM sleep may increase the likelihood of nightmares. By contrast, medications that *increase* the amount of REM sleep may have no effect or decrease the likelihood of dreaming and nightmares (Pagel & Helfter, 2003; Thompson & Pierce, 1999).

GABA

Alcohol, benzodiazepines (i.e., lorazepam), and non-benzodiazepines (i.e., zolpidem) may act at the receptor of GABA or increase GABA levels. GABA levels affect the balance of sleep and wake stages. Many of these medications determine how long it takes to fall asleep. Some of these are also believed to decrease REM sleep in the early parts of the night and, when the effects wear off, increase REM sleep at the end of the night. This can lead to a resurgence of dreams and nightmares. This is often reported as part of the alcohol-withdrawal syndrome (Pagel & Helfter, 2003; Thompson & Pierce, 1999).

Serotonin

Selective serotonin reuptake inhibitors (i.e., fluoxetine), tricyclic antidepressants (amitryptiline), and serotonin antagonist and reuptake inhibitors (nefazodone, trazadone) are used to treat depression and anxiety. These medications have various effects on sleep, REM sleep, and dreaming. Patients may report insomnia or hypersomnia, depending on the class of medication. Many of these medications increase the amount of serotonin and decrease REM sleep. There may be an increase in REM sleep or dreaming when the drug is stopped. Dream recall may be increased or decreased. There are case reports of antidepressants causing REM sleep behavior disorder, whereby patients act out their nightmares as they lose the paralysis often associated with REM sleep. Nefazodone is unique as it is known to increase REM sleep and has been reported to increase dreaming and nightmares.

Dopamine

Medications that increase dopamine (i.e., levodopa, ropinirole, pramipexole, amphetamines) can lead to various effects on sleep and dreams. These medications have been associated with insomnia, daytime sleepiness, increased amount of nightmares, night terrors, and vivid dreams. There may be reductions or increases in REM sleep depending on the dose of medication (Pagel & Helfter, 2003; Thompson & Pierce,. 1999).

Acetylcholine

Medications that increase the neurotransmitter acetylcholine (rivastigmine) increase REM sleep and those that reduce the amount of acetylcholine (amitriptyline) decrease REM sleep. Despite the opposite effects on REM sleep, both can lead to nightmares (Pagel & Helfter, 2003; Thompson & Pierce,. 1999).

Norepinephrine

Drugs that affect blood pressure often cross into the brain, leading to effects on the amount of REM sleep. Some of the beta blockers (i.e., metoprolol) used to treat high blood pressure can block the amount of norepinephrine in the brain, and have also been associated with a decrease in the amount of REM sleep (Pagel & Helfter, 2003; Thompson & Pierce, 1999). Yet, despite the decrease in REM sleep, beta blockers have been implicated in vivid dreams, hallucinations, and nightmares. Prazosin is a blood-pressure mediation that blocks the effect of norepinephrine in the brain and has been reported to also decrease the incidence of nightmares. In patients with posttraumatic stress disorder, there are reports of vivid flashbacks or nightmares of painful or traumatic experiences. Patients are often found to have higher level of norepinephrine in this condition (Miller, 2008).

When approaching a patient complaining of vivid dreams, nightmares, or sleep disturbances, a physician should review the medication list and substance abuse history in detail. It is clear that commonly prescribed medications can lead to sleep disturbances or nightmares from the mechanisms explained. It is important to realize as well that a side effect of REM sleep reduction does not always imply that nightmares or dreams will be reduced proportionally, and in fact the reverse effect may be seen.

Steven David Brass

See also: entries related to Sleep Physiology

References

Leung, A. K., & Robson, W. L. (1993). Nightmares. *Journal of the National Medical Association, 85*(3), 233–235.

Miller, L. J. (2008). Prazosin for the treatment of posttraumatic stress disorder sleep disturbances. *Pharmacotherapy, 28*(5), 656–666.

Pagel, J. F., & Helfter, P. (2003) Drug induced nightmares—An etiology based review. *Human Psychopharmacology, 18*(1), 59–67.

Thompson, D. F., & Pierce, D. R. (1999) Drug-induced nightmares. *Annals of Pharmacotherapy, 33*(1), 93–98.

Effects of Blindness and Deafness on Dream Content

Individuals with total congenital ocular blindness are frequently asked about their dreams, and they respond that they dream without visual imagery. Several articles have been written on this topic confirming this anecdotal evidence. There are three sleep laboratory studies (Amadeo & Gomez, 1966; Berger, Olley, & Oswald, 1962; Kerr, Foulkes, & Schmidt, 1982) and one dream study done at home (Hurovitz, Dunn, Domhoff, & Fiss, 1999), which stand out. Kerr and colleagues confirmed the findings of Amadeo and Gomez and that of Berger and colleagues. They studied four sighted (aged 19 to 26 years) and six severely visually impaired persons (aged 25 to 32 years) during an eight-week period in a laboratory while having simultaneous EEG recordings. The subjects with various eye conditions were all healthy and educated. In four congenitally blind persons, the visual impairment ranged from total blindness to light and form perception. The other three subjects acquired their visual loss later in life; two of them had light perception and another lost central vision due to macular degeneration. The subjects slept one night a week in the laboratory and were woken up four different times. All together during eight weeks each subject was woken up 6 times at sleep onset, 16 times in rapid eye movement sleep (REM), and on 10 occasions in nonrapid eye movement sleep (NREM). After awakening they were asked what was going through their minds. The answers were analyzed according to sensory modalities, content, and coherence. It was concluded that the visual content was absent in individuals who were totally blind since birth and completely or partially absent in those who lost their sight in early childhood, usually prior to the age of four to five years. Minimal visual content was present when an individual with congenital blindness had only form perception. Therefore, it was concluded that in almost all respects, except for the presence of visual imagery, the dreams of congenitally blind men and women were similar to those of the sighted, and the dreams of those individuals who acquired their blindness later in life were indistinguishable from the sighted.

Hurovitz and colleagues studied 372 dream reports of 15 individuals (10 females and 5 males, aged 24 to 73 years) who had congenital and acquired severe ocular visual impairment (Hurovitz et al., 1999). For two months, these well-educated and healthy subjects with various eye conditions were asked to record their dreams at home on audio tapes just after awakening. The authors studied the recordings with the Dream Research Program, which was able to find words such as see, saw, look, or watch and phrases such as I have not seen him in years. The sensory references were also divided into three categories: visual, auditory, and taste/smell/touch. These were compared to the age

when blindness was acquired, to the degree of visual impairment and to the percentage of a person's life as being blind. The authors concluded that there was continuity between dream content and waking conditions, and the dreams of the blind closely reflected the senses that were used during wakefulness. Furthermore, in those who lost their sight after early childhood, the visual imagery was gradually replaced by other sensory experiences that came to be more important in their waking lives. Caution was emphasized when interpreting the language of totally blind people, because they metaphorically use visual words and phrases, such as see, look, pretty, hope to see you, and so on.

There is another common form of visual impairment, which is caused by damage to the visual centers in the brain, rather than to the eyes. These individuals may or may not be able to receive and interpret signals from the eyes. Since they tend to have severe cognitive difficulties, their dream contents have not been studied. However, most likely the visual content is also modified in their dreams. Persons with total congenital deafness also lack auditory content in their dreams, while individuals with congenital deafness and blindness dream more about locomotion, touch, smell, taste, or proprioception, because their sensory experiences derive from their residual senses (Mendelson, Singer, & Solomon, 1960).

Memory formation and the daily deletion of memory at the synaptic level are increasingly understood. It is well known that dreaming occurs mainly during REM sleep—a state that is critical for memory formation and learning. In fact, the amount of REM sleep parallels cognitive growth of children. Memories are stored according to time, emotions, significance, and other factors, while weaker memories are deleted. Both processes are critical for our survival. Thus, a constant reorganization of new and old memories occurs daily. Indeed, there are dedicated neurological mechanisms for this reason (Meck, 2005). Studies show that it is possible to forget visual or auditory memories, especially when the sensory loss occurs early in life. Even individuals who lose their senses later in life might forget some of their weaker sensory memories. These observations clearly show that the dream content and memory formation are closely linked. Most importantly, the dream analysis of individuals with sensory deficits tells us that dreaming reflects cognitive activities in wakefulness and dreams appear to be a by-product of the complex process of memory formation. Any attempt at analyzing the meaning of dreams must consider these physiological facts.

James E. Jan

References

Amadeo, M., & Gomez, E. (1966). Eye movements, attention, and dreaming in subjects with lifelong blindness. *Canadian Psychiatric Journal, 11,* 501–507.

Berger, R., Olley, P., & Oswald, I. (1962). The EEG, eye movements, and dreams of the blind. *Quarterly Journal of Experimental Psychology, 14,* 183–186.

Hurovitz, C. S., Dunn, S., Domhoff, W. G., & Fiss, H. (1999). The dreams of blind men and women: A replication and extension of previous findings. *Dreaming, 9,* 183–193.

Kerr, N. H., Foulkes, D., & Schmidt, M. (1982). The structure of library dream reports in blind and sighted subjects. *The Journal of Nervous and Mental Disease, 170,* 286–294.

Meck, W. H. (2005). Neuropsychology of timing and time perception. *Brain and Cognition, 58,* 1–8.

Mendelson, J. H., Singer, L., & Solomon, P. (1960). Psychiatric observations on congenital and acquired deafness: Symbolic and perceptual processes in dreams. *American Journal of Psychiatry, 116,* 883–888.

Effects of Work on Sleep

There is a growing recognition that sleep deficiency and sleep disorders are having a dramatic impact on public health (Institute of Medicine, 2006). Sleep deficiency can be defined as the presence of insufficient sleep duration and/or inadequate sleep quality, such as might occur with a sleep disorder. Adequate sleep duration, typically thought to be in the range of seven to nine hours/night for most adults, can be operationalized as a lack of impairment of cognitive functions or other symptoms, or simply the lack of need for an alarm clock. In large epidemiological studies, seven to eight hours/night of sleep typically confers the least risk to health. Occupational factors are associated with sleep outcomes, including, at least, participating in the labor force at all, nonstandard schedules, long work hours, and manager characteristics.

Work, so fundamental to basic survival and health, as well as wealth, well-being, and positive social identity, has its darker and more costly side too. Work can negatively affect our health, an impact that goes well beyond the usual counts of injuries, accidents, and illnesses from exposure to toxic chemicals. The *ways in which work is organized*—particularly its pace, intensity, and the space it allows or *does not allow* for control over one's work process and for realizing a sense of self-efficacy, justice, and employment security—can be as toxic or benign to the health of workers over time as the chemicals they breathe in the workplace air. (Schnall, Dobson, & Rosskam, 2009.)

As globalization increasingly pushes toward a 24/7 economy, a growing number of workers will find themselves in a job that requires a nonstandard work schedule. Full adaptation to a nonstandard schedule, especially night work, is uncommon due to the irregularity of the sleep–wake and light–dark cycle across the workweek and the robustness of circadian rhythms. One of the central recommendations for optimizing sleep health or sleep hygiene includes maintaining a regular sleep/wake schedule as it is thought to be effective at avoiding sleep deficiency and improving health, well-being, and alertness. Inconsistently timed sleep leads to poor-quality sleep (more wake time and number of awakenings), often due to sleeping at varying circadian phases (Czeisler & Buxton, 2010).

The number of hours employees work in the United States continues to increase with profound consequences for worker health. Working long hours, including mandatory overtime, or a compressed work week including 12-hour or longer shifts, has been shown to lead to employee sleep deprivation and fatigue that can lead to decreased productivity, increased absenteeism, and poor physical and mental health (Schnall et al., 2009). Evidence from a nationally representative sample of Americans suggests that compensated work time is the most important determinant of sleep duration, with sleep duration decreasing as work time increases (Basner et al., 2007).

Work–family conflict and work-related health problems are becoming increasingly recognized as a negative consequence of exposure to unhealthy workplace policies and practices, including managerial practices. One study in the long-term health care industry found that employees with less-supportive managers slept about a half hour less a day and were more than twice as likely to have two or more cardiovascular disease risk factors than employees with managers who were more creative and open-minded with respect to the work–family issues of their employees (Berkman, Buxton, Ertel, & Okechukwu, 2010). A longitudinal intervention study of grocery store employees and managers found that employees who perceived their managers as unsupportive before training had worse job attitudes, blood pressure, heart rates, sleep quality, and overall health, and were less likely to be with the company a year later. After training to improve managers' sensitivity and ability to handle employee work–family issues, workers viewed their managers as being more supportive, and reported improvements in their overall health (Kossek & Hammer, 2008).

Escalating time pressures and work–family conflict have negative business consequences such as reduced worker productivity and increased turnover and negative long-term consequences for the economic health of organizations and, ultimately, the nation. Few studies have systematically tested the effects of workplace policies and practices on work–family conflict, individual and family health and

A. Manager Work-Family Score predicts CVD risk

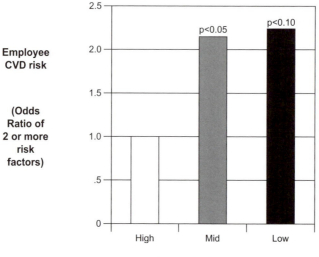

B. Manager Work-Family Score predicts hrs of sleep

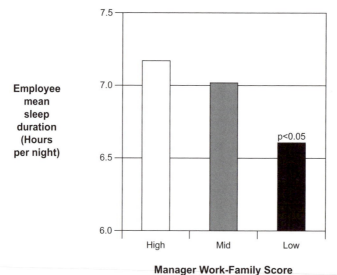

Figure 6: (A) Manager Work–Family Score Predicts CVD Risk. (B) Manager Work–Family Score predicts hrs of sleep. Manager characteristics influence employee health including sleep. Manager (n = 45) characteristics of openness, creativity, and flexibility regarding employee work–family issues was assessed in a qualitative interview and compared to the directly measured cardiovascular disease (CVD) risk and sleep duration of the employees they directly supervised (n = 393). CVD risk was assessed from measure height and weight (BMI), cholesterol, HbA1c, and self-reported chronic conditions (heart disease, diabetes diagnoses) and smoking status. Sleep was measured with wrist actigraphy (mean of 6.2 days. Models control for age, gender, wage, education, race/ethnicity, worksite. Redrawn from Berkman et al. (2010).

well-being, or organizational outcomes. Future research should focus on the implementation of initiatives that would change current working conditions in ways that reduce stressors and improve the health of workers, their families, and their employers (Kelly et al., 2008).

Orfeu Marcello Buxton

See also: Anthropology of Sleep; Increasing Sleep Complaints

References

Basner, M., Fomberstein K. M., Razavi, F. M., Banks, S., William, J. H., Rosa, R. R., & Dinges, D. F. (2007). American time use survey: Sleep time and its relationship to waking activities. *Sleep, 30*(9), 1085–1095.

Berkman, L. F., Buxton, O., Ertel, K., & Okechukwu, C. (2010). Manager's practices related to work-family balance predict employee cardiovascular risk and sleep duration in extended care settings. *Journal of Occupational Health Psychology, 115*(3), 316–329.

Czeisler, C. A., & Buxton, O. M. (2010). The human circadian timing system and sleep-wake regulation. In M. H. Kryger, T. Roth, & W. C. Dement (Eds.), *Principles and practices of sleep medicine* (5th ed., pp. 402–419). New York: Elsevier.

Institute of Medicine. (2006). *Sleep disorders and sleep deprivation: An unmet public health problem.* Washington, DC: National Academies Press.

Kelly, E. L., Kossek, E. E., Hammer, L. B., Durham, M., Dray, J., Chermack, K. . . . Kaskubar, D. (2008). Getting there from here: Research on the effects of work-family initiatives on work-family conflict and business outcomes. *The Academy of Management Annals, 2*, 305–349.

Kossek, E. E., & Hammer, L. B. (2008, November). Supervisor work/life training gets results. *Harvard Business Review.*

Schnall, P. L., Dobson, M., & Rosskam, E. (2009). *Unhealthy work: Causes, consequences, cures.* Amityville, NY: Baywood.

Electromagnetic Fields of Mobile Telephones and Sleep Parameters

The widespread use of cell phones led and still leads to concerns about possible health effects in public and research. Several studies of the last two decades dealt with potential effects of electromagnetic fields (EMF) emitted by mobile telecommunication on the human central nervous system. In most of these studies possible effects of EMF of Global System for Mobile Communications signals (GSM 900 or GSM 1800) from handsets on the electroencephalogram of the waking and sleeping brain were evaluated. Due to methodological differences in these studies, quite divergent results were reported. It is therefore important to note that the type and strength of the signal applied and the duration of exposure differed essentially between studies: duration of exposure lasted from 30 minutes up to eight hours, and exposure was either applied prior to daytime or night sleep, or subjects were exposed during the whole night. In one of the first published studies on the effects of whole-night exposure of GSM on sleep Mann and Roschke (1996) found a decreased sleep latency and a reduction of REM sleep as a percentage of sleep period time. The same research group was not able to replicate these findings in their subsequent studies. In the first of a series of studies by a Swiss research group, wake after sleep onset time was six minutes shorter in the GSM-exposure night compared to a control night (Borbely et al., 1999). This finding was not confirmed by the following studies of the same research group, either (Regel et al., 2007). In a study in which people of a broader age range (18 to 60 years) were exposed to a handset-like signal for 30 minutes prior to sleep, REM-sleep latency decreased from 107.8 minutes to 90.2 minutes (Loughran et al., 2005). The results of a recently published Swedish study demonstrated a reduction of slow-wave sleep by 9.5 minutes and an increase in stage 2 sleep by 8.3 minutes in the GSM compared to the sham condition (Lowden et al., 2011). In another recently published study, in which subjects were exposed to GSM and wideband code-division multiple access (WCDMA)/ Universal Mobile Telecommunications System (UMTS) in different nights, only few variables out of 177 characterizing the initiation and maintenance of sleep differed significantly between the EMF and the sham conditions, and these differences did not indicate a negative impact on the macrostructure of sleep (Danker-Hopfe, Dorn, Bahr, Anderer, & Sauter, 2011). From the present results there is only little evidence for modifying effect of GSM 900 MHz on sleep macrostructure, and none of WCDMA exposure. In general, the few effects seen are small and still lie within the normal physiological range. Replication studies with one and the same study designs are needed to validate or disconfirm the positive findings.

Cornelia Sauter and Heidi Danker-Hopfe

See also: entries related to Sleep Disorders

References

Borbely, A. A., Huber, R., Graf, T., Fuchs, B., Gallmann, E., & Achermann, P. (1999). Pulsed high-frequency electromagnetic field affects human sleep and sleep electroencephalogram. *Neuroscience Letters, 275,* 207–210.

Danker-Hopfe, H., Dorn, H., Bahr, A., Anderer, P., & Sauter, C. (2011). Effects of electromagnetic fields emitted by mobile phones (GSM 900 and WCDMA/UMTS) on the macrostructure of sleep. *Journal of Sleep Research, 20,* 73–81.

Loughran, S. P., Wood, A. W., Barton, J. M., Croft, R. J., Thompson, B., & Stough, C. (2005). The effect of electromagnetic fields emitted by mobile phones on human sleep. *NeuroReport, 16,* 1973–1976.

Lowden, A., Akerstedt, T., Ingre, M., Wiholm, C., Hillert, L., Kuster, N., . . . Arnetz, B. (2011). Sleep after mobile phone exposure in subjects with mobile phone-related symptoms. *Bioelectromagnetics, 32,* 4–14.

Mann, K., & Roschke, J. (1996). Effects of pulsed high-frequency electromagnetic fields on human sleep. *Neuropsychobiology, 33,* 41–47.

Regel, S. J., Tinguely, G., Schuderer, J., Adam, M., Kuster, N., Landolt, H. P., & Achermann, P. (2007). Pulsed radio-frequency electromagnetic fields: Dose-dependent effects on sleep, the sleep EEG and cognitive performance. *Journal of Sleep Research, 16,* 253–258.

Embodied Imagination

Embodied imagination (EI) is a method of working with dreams and memories that was developed by Jungian analyst Robert Bosnak in the 1970s. Currently, it is practiced with individuals, couples, and groups in psychotherapy, medicine, theater, art, and creative research. The technique draws from such disparate influences as analytic psychology, neuroscience, alchemy, ancient incubation practices, method acting, and complexity theory. EI employs artificial flashback memory to help an individual enter a hypnagogic state, a state of consciousness that naturally precedes the onset of sleep. With careful and supportive guidance, a dream or memory environment is reexperienced as a composite of its many perspectives simultaneously. Bodily responses to images, viewed as a form of intelligent communication, are integral to the technique. While new insights emerge, the process initially bypasses the intellect. Instead, an expanded body awareness, based on a change in interoception as well as a shift in the experience of external stimuli, is the catalyst for change.

One key element of EI is the exploration of ego-alien images, those with which the dreamer does not originally identify. Slow observation of the sensory details of these images facilitates a type of mimesis, through which the dreamer inhabits an unfamiliar body along with its associated subjective state. Recent studies of virtual reality confirm that people can psychologically inhabit other bodies (Yee & Bailenson, 2007, pp. 271–290), even bodies radically different from their own (Slater, Spanlang, Sanchez-Vives, & Blanke, 2010). Moreover, this research provides strong evidence that imaginal shifts in body awareness carry over into waking-life behavior. For example, after subjects left a virtual environment in which they acquired a virtual body or avatar, the quality of their social interactions varied with apparently imperceptible changes in height and attractiveness between subjects and avatars. In EI work, transits into unfamiliar images are made with dual consciousness, in which the dreamer never loses a sense of self-as-dreamer.

Increasingly, EI is used in concert with traditional medicine to help people with health concerns, a component of which is often chronic pain. Clinical examples abound in which EI work creates new states that embody health and well-being. Significant healing effects have been documented in people suffering from an array of conditions, including cancer, AIDS, arthritis, and multiple sclerosis. The following cases are illustrative: a woman diagnosed with ovarian cancer was able to sustain a renewed sense of circulation in her legs for weeks after she embodied the strong, natural stance of a Micronesian woman who appeared in her dream; a man living with an AIDS-induced facial droop and partially immobilized shoulder and chest was able to regain his range of motion for years after entering the subjective experience of a crease in a jacket he had dreamed about (Bosnak, 2007, p. 57); after practicing composites from a series of dreams, an arthritic woman found herself walking in a body that lifted her out of her painfully inflamed joints and following work for eight consecutive weeks in a form of EI called brief depth intervention, the long-term emotional and physical pain of a woman's clubfeet decreased, replaced with a new body sense of strength and movement (White, 2009).

As a theory, EI is concerned with the direct effect of imagination on the body. It is supported by the fields of psychoneuroimmunology (Sternberg, 2000), psychoneurendocrinology (Wolkowitz & Rothschild, 2003), as well as the study of the placebo effect (Benedetti, Carlino, & Pollo, 2011, pp. 339–354; Kradin, 2008; Moerman, 2002), all of which demonstrate that psychosocial changes lead to physical changes. The framework for understanding the role of EI in improving health outcomes is based on the definition of embodiment as the interface between body and meaning. The meaning a physical condition has for an individual cannot be dissociated from a unique myriad of conscious and unconscious psychosocial factors. In working with images to create new embodied states, these factors are influenced and the body's self-healing response is triggered. Flashing back into a dream, the body does not distinguish between physical reality and imaginal reality. Kosselyn and Moulton (2008, pp. 35–51) bolster this assertion by demonstrating that when people imagine performing an action, the same pattern of muscles fire in the same order as when they perform the real action. It is hypothesized that by mentally rehearsing an embodied state of wellness, the body can be convinced of its physical wellness. Repeated practice can transform new states into implicit memory, eventually making the embodiment of these states an instinctual and automatic process (Kandel, 2006, p. 132). In general, EI is thought to promote a greater capacity for embodied self-awareness, as distinct from conceptual self-awareness, which has been associated with increased creativity and openness to change (Fogel, 2009, p. 31).

As the placebo effect is often defined as the effect of the psychosocial context on the patient, it might help explain the efficacy of EI techniques. The type and quality of doctor–patient communication, for example, have been shown to reduce pain by activating the opioid mechanisms that induce the expectation of analgesia (e.g., Colloca & Benedetti, 2005, pp. 545–552). Researchers suggest that the therapist's belief in the healing potential of a particular treatment, along with other formal aspects of the therapeutic act, can change the circuitry and chemistry of the patient's brain (Benedetti et al., 2011, pp. 339–354; Moerman, 2002). A significant placebo effect has been demonstrated even when patients have been told explicitly that they are taking an inert substance (Jha, 2010). Preliminary evidence that the iatric use of imagination makes this effect more robust comes from a laboratory study (Abraham, Bosnak, Fischer, Roy, & Wager, 2010); using the EI techniques of flashback memory, transits, and composites, subjects who were immersed in a positive personal memory had significantly decreased thermal pain, even at high temperatures. Pain reduction increased over time and was greater than that for subjects assigned to a passive relaxation condition.

Opening in 2011, the Santa Barbara Healing Sanctuary (www.sbhsanctuary.com) will provide a unique setting for using EI to treat those suffering from medical conditions with EI. Inspired by the Asklepios healing centers of ancient Greece, where dreams were at the center of medicine, the integrative medical sanctuary will be subject to rigorous scientific study as it brings together the wisdom of more than 2,000 years with cutting edge practices in modern medicine.

Judith Lisa White and Jill Fischer

References

Abraham, D., Bosnak, R., Fischer, J., Roy, M., & Wager, T. (2010, April 17–20). *Memory immersion produces reduction in pain perception*. Poster session at the 17th Annual Cognitive Neuroscience Society Symposium, Montréal, Canada.

Benedetti, F., Carlino, E., & Pollo, A. (2011). How placebos change the patient's brain. *Neuropsychopharmacology, 36*(1), 339–354.

Bosnak, R. (2007). *Embodiment: Creative imagination in medicine art and travel*. London: Routledge.

Colloca, L., & Benedetti, F. (2005). Placebos and painkillers: Is mind as real as matter? *Nature Reviews Neuroscience, 6*, 545–552.

Fogel, A. (2009). *The psychophysiology of self-awareness—Rediscovering the lost art of body sense*. New York: W.W. Norton & Company.

Jha, A. (2010, December 22). Placebo effect works even if patients know they're getting a sham drug. *Guardian Weekly*. Retrieved from http://www.guardian.co.uk/science/2010/dec/22 placebo-effect-patients-sham-drug?

Kandel, E. R. (2006). *In search of memory*. New York: W. W. Norton & Company.

Kosselyn, S. M., & Moulton, S. T. (2008). Mental imagery and implicit memory. In K. D. Markman, W. M. Klein, & J. A. Suhr (Eds.), *Handbook of imagination and mental simulation* (pp. 35–51). London: Psychology Press.

Kradin, R. (2008). *The placebo response and the power of unconscious healing*. New York: Routledge.

Moerman, D. (2002). *Meaning, medicine and the "placebo effect."* Cambridge: Cambridge University Press.

Slater, M., Spanlang, B., Sanchez-Vives, M. V., & Blanke, O. (2010). First person experience of body transfer in virtual reality. *PLoS ONE, 5*(5), e10564.

Sternberg, E. M. (2000). *The balance within*. New York: W. H. Freeman & Co.

White, J. (2009). Breaking the psychic cast: The pain of forward movement. Presented at the International Association for the Study of Dreams Conference, Chicago, IL, June 26.

Wolkowitz, O. M., & Rothschild, A. J. (2003). *Psychoneuroendocrinology: The scientific basis of clinical practice*. Arlington, VA: Psychiatric Publishing.

Yee, N., & Bailenson, J. N. (2007). The proteus effect: The effect of transformed self-representation on behavior. *Human Communication Research, 33*, 271–290.

Emotional Responses to Nightmares

Do nightmares increase or decrease waking emotional distress? Some research suggests that nightmares may act as a coping mechanism to reduce levels of anxiety and depression, easing emotional overload (Picchioni et al., 2002). Other research suggests the reverse, that nightmares may add to already existing emotional distress, increasing emotional overload (Roberts, Lennings, & Herd, 2009). Various additional factors may be connected with whether nightmares increase or reduce waking emotional distress, such as prior proneness to anxiety or existing emotional support (Picchioni et al., 2002; Roberts et al., 2009). With findings supporting both sides of this question, further research is needed before definitive conclusions may be reached.

Can nightmares cause ongoing distress? Nightmares can bring about dramatic emotional responses from those who experience them. Such responses are not necessarily limited to the time the nightmares occur. Repeated frightening nightmares have been shown to be associated with substantial emotional waking distress, including elevated levels of anxiety and depression (Levin & Fireman, 2002; Roberts et al., 2009). Where a person's ability to function in social situations or at work is impaired by nightmare experience and accompanying waking distress, the *Diagnostic and Statistical Manual of Mental Disorders, Fourth Edition* refers to this condition as nightmare disorder (American Psychiatric Association, 1994, p. 580).

Is nightmare waking distress more associated with (1) the frequency of nightmares or (2) emotional responses to them in waking life? This distinction is important because any effective therapy regimes for nightmare distress need to focus on the likely cause of that distress. From the research literature it appears that treatments for people suffering nightmare waking distress tend to target a reduction in nightmare frequency, assuming frequency to be the base of the problem (Lancee, Spoormaker, Krakow, & van den Bout, 2008). However, nightmare frequency has been shown to have only a slight relationship with nightmare waking distress (Levin & Fireman, 2002). While treatments focusing on nightmare frequency have been successful in reducing frequency, they are not always successful in reducing the associated distress (Lancee et al., 2008; St-Onge, Mercier, & De Koninck, 2009). Future research into treatments that focus on reducing both frequency and waking distress may reveal that a combined approach is more consistently successful in reducing overall nightmare experience than focusing on frequency alone.

Does anything else contribute to nightmare waking distress? Waking distress may arise at least in part from the dreamer's emotional reaction to their dream. People who fear that the nightmare is a sign of serious psychological disturbance, a prophecy of disaster, or revelation of their own deeper insights may suffer more waking distress over their nightmares than others (Belicki, 1992). Future research specifically targeting the dreamer's preconceptions and interpretations about their dreams may provide further information about the links between nightmare experience and nightmare waking distress. Insights into how nightmare sufferers perceive their nightmares in relation to their own life may suggest approaches for effective treatment to reduce nightmare experience.

Jan Roberts and
Christopher J. Lennings

See also: entries related to Sleep Disorders

References

American Psychiatric Association. (1994). *Diagnostic and statistical manual of mental disorders (DSM-IV)*. Washington, DC: Author.

Belicki, K. (1992). The relationship of nightmare frequency to nightmare suffering with implications for treatment and research. *Dreaming: Journal of the Association for the Study of Dreams, 2*(3), 143–148.

Lancee, J., Spoormaker, V., Krakow, B., & van den Bout, J. (2008). A systematic review of cognitive-behavioral treatment for nightmares: Towards a well-established treatment. *Journal of Clinical Sleep Medicine, 4*(5), 475–480.

Levin, R., & Fireman, G. (2002). Nightmare prevalence, nightmare distress, and self-reported psychological disturbance. *Sleep, 25*(2), 205–212.

Picchioni, D., Goeltzenleucher, B., Green, D., Convento, M., Crittenden, R., Hallgren, M., & Hicks, R. (2002). Nightmares as a coping mechanism for stress. *Dreaming, 12*(3), 155–169.

Roberts, J., Lennings, C., & Herd, R. (2009). Nightmares, life stress, and anxiety: An examination of tension reduction. *Dreaming, 19*(1), 17–29.

St-Onge, M., Mercier, P., & De Koninck, J. (2009). Imagery rehearsal therapy for frequent nightmares in children. *Behavioral Sleep Medicine, 7*(2), 81–98.

Endocrinology of Sleep

Sleep is a time of considerable activity in various endocrine systems. Accordingly human sleep is characterized by the alternating occurrence of episodes of non-REM and REM sleep and by patterns of sleep-associated hormone secretion. The electrophysiological activity of sleep is recorded by polysomnography (sleep EEG). Collection of blood by a long catheter helps to determine plasma concentrations of various hormones throughout the night. In young normal subjects during the first half of the night the major amounts of slow-wave sleep (SWS) and growth-hormone (GH) surge occur, whereas cortisol levels reach their nadir. During the second half of the night REM sleep and cortisol secretion preponderate, whereas the amount of GH is low. This pattern of sleep-endocrine activity is the peripheral endpoint of a reciprocal interaction of the hypothalamo–pituitary–adrenocortical (HPA) and the hypothalamo–pituitary–somatotrophic (HPS) systems. A reciprocal interaction exists between sleep EEG and sleep-related hormone secretion. Changes of sleep (sleep deprivation, sleep curtailment) result in changes of hormone secretion. On the other hand, changes of endocrine activity (experimental hormone administration, transgenic animal models, endocrine disorders, depression, aging) induce sleep-EEG changes. Certain neuropeptides and steroids participate in sleep regulation. For the hormones of the HPA and of the HPS systems please see the respective entries.

Prolactin, Vasoactive Intestinale Polypeptide (VIP)

Prolactin is a circulating hormone. It acts as a neuroprotein as well. Prolactin levels rise in human subjects after sleep onset. The prolactin peak is reached during the second or the last third of the night. Prolactin is neither affected by normal aging nor by a depressive episode. This is in contrast to many other hormones. Prolactin levels increase during the recovery night after sleep deprivation.

In laboratory animals (cats, rabbits, rats) REM sleep increases after systemic and after intrahypothalamic prolactin administration. REM sleep and non-REM sleep increase in adult rats bearing juvenile rat anterior grafts under the capsule of the kidney. On the other hand the amount of REM sleep decreases after systemic or intrahypothalamic injection of antiserum to prolactin in the rat. SWS is increased, whereas REM sleep is unchanged in patients with prolactinoma in comparison to healthy volunteers.

VIP acts similar to prolactin as it enhances REM sleep in laboratory animals.

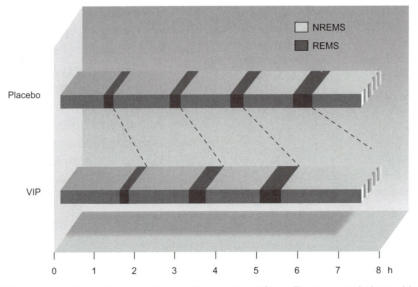

Figure 7: Summarized Sleep Cycles on Basis of Conventional Sleep Electroencephalographic Analysis after Placebo and 4 × 50 µg VIP (*n* = 10). Open bar, non-REM period; solid bar, REM period. Reprinted from Murck et al. (1996), Fig. 2 © American Physiological Society, used with permission.

Non-REM and REM sleep increase when VIP is given to rats during the dark period. Also, after VIP microinjections into the pontine reticular tegmentum and into the oral pontine tegmentum REM sleep is enhanced in rats. The REM sleep-promoting effect of systemic VIP is inhibited by immunoneutralization of circulating prolactin in rats. Stimulation of prolactin appears to be involved in promotion of REM sleep after VIP. This view is supported by the fact that VIP antibodies and a VIP antagonist diminish REM sleep in rats.

After two doses of VIP, different effects were observed in young healthy male volunteers. Pulsatile iv administration of 4 · 10 ?g VIP decreases nocturnal prolactin levels, whereas sleep EEG is not affected. After a dose of 4 · 50 ?g, VIP prolactin increases and the non-REM–REM cycles are decelerated. Each non-REM and REM period is prolonged (see Figure 7). The cortisol nadir is advanced and the GH peak is blunted. It is thought that VIP affects the circadian clock, resulting in prolonged sleep cycles and in the advanced occurrence of the cortisol nadir. The blunted GH surge may be secondary to the advanced increase of HPA activity.

Hypothalamo–Pituitary–Thyroid System

From clinical practice it is well established that changes of vigilance are major symptoms of disorders of the thyroid gland. Hyperthyroidism is linked with insomnia. Fatigue is a frequent symptom in hypothyroidism. Astonishingly there exist only a few data on sleep EEG in these diseases. Reduced SWS in patients with hypothyroidism was reported in one study in comparison to healthy volunteers. These changes normalized after therapy. After pulsatile iv injections of thyreotropin-releasing hormone, sleep efficiency decreases and the cortisol morning rise occurs earlier in young healthy male volunteers.

Galanin

The neuropeptide galanin is widely located in the mammalian brain. A cluster of GABAergic and galaninergic neurones was identified in the ventrolateral preoptic area, which stimulates non-REM sleep. SWS and the duration of REM periods increased after repetitive iv galanin injections to young normal male subjects. The secretion of GH and cortisol remained unchanged in this experiment. In the rat model sleep was not affected by intracerebroventricular administration of galanin. Deprivation of REM sleep prompts galanin gene expression. After intravenous administration of galanin to patients with depression during antidepressive therapy with trimipramine, REM latency increases and the severity of depression according to the Hamilton Depression Scale decreases. These findings suggest an acute antidepressive effect of galanin.

In one study after intracerebroventricular administration of neuropeptide Y (NPY) EEG spectral activity changed similarly to effects of benzodiazepines in the rat. The prolongation of sleep latency after corticotropin-releasing hormone (CRH) was antagonized dose dependently by NPY in rats. In contrast, in another study after intracerebroventricular injection of NPY and after bilateral microinjection of NPY in the lateral hypothalamus non-REM sleep and REM sleep were suppressed in rats during the first hour. On the other hand a sleep-promoting effect of NPY was also found after repetitive iv injections in young healthy volunteers as sleep latency and the first REM period decreased and the time spent in sleep stage 2 and the sleep period time increased. In this experiment nocturnal cortisol and ACTH levels decreased. Sleep latency was also shortened after NPY in patients with depression of both sexes with a wide age range and in matched normal control subjects. Furthermore prolactin levels increase, whereas cortisol and ACTH remained unchanged. We suggested that NPY participates in sleep regulation, particularly as a signal for sleep onset antagonizing CRH by action at the $GABA_A$ receptor.

Hypocretins/Orexins

A pair of neuropeptides synthesized in the lateral hypothalamus was discovered nearly simultaneously by two groups of researchers. These neuropeptides were named orexins or hypocretins. A lack of orexins or their receptors cause symptoms of narcolepsy in animal models. Narcolepsy is characterized by several abnormalities of the sleep–wake organization and of the sleep structure, including cataplexy, excessive daytime sleepiness, and sleep onset REM episodes (the occurrence of REM sleep during the first 10 minutes after sleep onset). Cataplexy-like behavior was found in knockout mice that do not produce orexins. A genetic form of narcolepsy in dogs is related to mutation of the gene for the orexin-B receptor. Only little amounts of orexin are found in brains of patients with narcolepsy. In these patients orexin-A levels are low, whereas the plasma levels are in the normal range. It was hypothesized that orexin stabilizes the sleep–wake pattern by preventing unwanted transitions between sleep and wake stages. In patients with narcolepsy, a lack of orexin or of orexin receptors leads to numerous transitions between vigilance states and to the intrusion of elements of REM sleep into wakefulness. In dogs, orexin-A reduces cataplexy and normalizes the sleep–wake pattern.

Gonadal Hormones

In women the menstrual cycle, pregnancy, and menopause reflect marked changes in the activity of gonadal hormones and have some influence on sleep regulation. In healthy women the percentage of REM sleep tends to be higher in the early follicular phase than in the late luteal phase. The percentage of non-REM sleep is higher in the luteal phase than in the follicular phase. EEG power density in the upper frequency range of the sleep spindles during non-REM sleep shows a large variety across the menstrual cycle with a maximum in the luteal phase.

In women EEG activity in the sigma frequency range shows a distinct decline during menopause, whereas these changes occur more gradually in men. After menopause sleep, endocrine changes associated with depression were found to be accentuated.

Administration of gonadal hormones to intact adult animals prompts only weak effects on sleep. The sleep of intact and gonadectomized female and male C57BL/6J mice was investigated in one study. This strain is useful to examine gender differences since the female animals show very little changes in sleep distribution across the menstrual cycle. The amount of wakefulness was higher in the intact female than in the intact male mice. Ovariectomy prompted a decrease in wake and a corresponding increase in non-REM sleep. In transsexual men who undergo crossgender therapy, stage 1 sleep increases during high chronic dosages of estradiol. In postmenopausal women estrogen replacement therapy by skin patch increases REM sleep and reduces intermittent wakefulness during the first two sleep cycles. The physiological decrease of SWS and slow-wave activity from the first to the second sleep cycle is restored. For the effects of progesterone replacement therapy, see the following section, "Neuroactive Steroids."

Neuroactive Steroids

Neuroactive steroids exert direct effects on neuronal membranes and thereby rapidly affect CNS excitability. The $GABA_A$-receptor complex mediates their effects on neuronal excitability. Neuroactive steroids are involved in the regulation of anxiety, memory, and sleep. Glia cells in the brain synthesize certain neuroactive steroids independently from peripheral doses. The sleep EEG of humans and rats is changed specifically after various neuroactive steroids.

Oral administration of pregnenolone to young male healthy volunteers prompts increases of SWS and decreases of EEG power in the spindle frequency range (see Figure 8). These changes are compatible

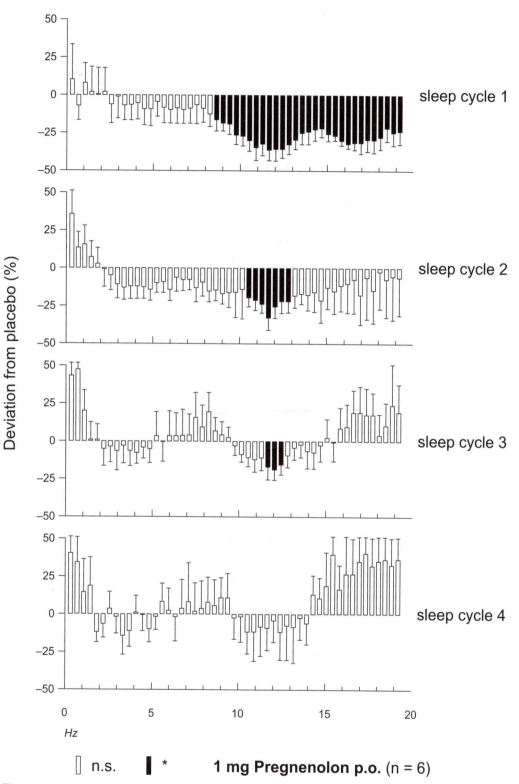

Figure 8: EEG Power Spectra (0.19.3 Hz) for Sleep Cycles 1–4 in Man ($n = 6$). Bars show deviation from placebo level (100%) in each 0.39 Hz bin (error bars: 1 S.E.M.). Solid bars denote significant differences between placebo and pregnenolone (two-sided Bonferroni t test, nominal $p < 0.05$). Reprinted from Steiger et al. (1993), Fig. 2. © (1993) with permission from Elsevier.

with partial inverse agonistic action at the GABA$_A$ receptor. Similarly, after subcutaneous pregnenolone at the beginning of the light period, SWA increases in rats, whereas after intraperitoneal pregnenolone sulfate, REM sleep increases in rats.

As early as in 1954 a dose-dependent hypnotic effect of intravenously administered progesterone was reported. In healthy young male volunteers oral progesterone prompted an increase of non-REM sleep particularly of sleep stage 2 and a decrease of SWA. Furthermore EEG power in the higher frequency range (>15 Hz) tends to be elevated. A distinct interindividual variability exists in the bioavailability of progesterone consequently in the time course of the levels of its metabolite allopregnanolone. Two subgroups of subjects were identified, one with an early peak and one with a late peak of allopregnanolone. The time course of this peak is associated with EEG-power changes. In subjects with an early allopregnanolone peak the initial increase in the EEG activity in the spindle and alpha range during the first few hours of sleep is found, whereas in those subjects with a later peak of the metabolite, a decrease of SWA is mainly found. The sleep-EEG changes after progesterone in this study were similar to those after benzodiazepines. They appear to be mediated partly by a conversion of progesterone into allopregnanolone.

Progesterone declines in women after menopause. REM sleep increases and intermittent wakefulness decreases in postmenopausal women after subchronic oral progesterone replacement. Intraperitoneal administration of three doses of progesterone to rats at the onset of the dark period

prompts decreases of non-REM-sleep latency, wakefulness and REM sleep, and increases of REM latency and of pre-REM sleep, an intermediate state between non-REM and REM sleep. In the lower frequency range, EEG activity decreases, whereas it increases in the higher frequency range. After intraperitoneal allopregnanolone non-REM-sleep latency is reduced in rats and pre-REM sleep is elevated; during non-REM sleep the EEG activity decreases in the lower frequencies and increases in the higher frequencies. These data are in line with a benzodiazepine-like effect of allopregnanolone on sleep.

Tetrahydrodeoxycorticosterone (THDOC) is a barbiturate-like ligand of the GABA-receptor complex. In rats, sleep latency is shortened and non-REM sleep is increased after THDOC. The precursor of THDOC, DOC does not affect sleep in young male healthy volunteers.

After oral administration of dehydroepiandrosterone (DHEA), REM sleep increases selectively in young healthy male subjects. This observation points to a mixed GABA$_A$ agonistic/antagonistic effect of the substance. Intraperitoneal administration of DHEA sulfate prompts a dose-dependent effect on EEG power in rats. After 50 mg/kg, DHEAS EEG power in the spindle frequency range increases, whereas opposite effects occur in 100 mg/kg DHEAS.

Axel Steiger

See also: entries related to Sleep Physiology

References

Lu, J., Sherman, D., Devor, M., & Saper, C. B. (2006). A putative flip-flop switch for control of REM sleep. *Nature, 441,* 589–594.

Manber, R., & Armitage, R. (1999). Sex, steroids and sleep: A review. *Sleep, 22*, 540–555.

Murck, H., Guldner, J., Frieboes, R. M., Schier, T., Wiedemann, K., Holsboer, F., & Steiger, A. (1996). VIP decelerates non-REM–REM cycles and modulates hormone secretion during sleep in men. *Regulatory, Integrative and Comparative Physiology, 40*, R905–R911.

Saper, C. B., Chou, T. C., & Scammell, T. E. (2001). The sleep switch: Hypothalamic control of sleep and wakefulness. *Trends in Neurosciences, 24*(12), 726–731.

Siegel, J. M. (2004). Hypocretin (orexin): Role in normal behavior and neuropathology. *Annual Review of Psychology, 55*, 125–148.

Steiger, A. (2007). Neurochemical regulation of sleep. *Journal of Psychiatric Research, 41*, 537–552.

Steiger, A., Trachsel, L., Guldner, J., Hemmeter, U., Rothe, B., Rupprecht, R., . . . Holsboer, F. (1993). Neurosteroid pregnenolone induces sleep-EEG changes in man compatible with inverse agonist GABAA-receptor modulation. *Brain Research, 615*, 267–274.

Endometriosis and Dreams

In a 1998 study of 4,000 women with endometriosis, 95 percent cited pain as the most common symptom. On average, it takes an American woman nine years to get a correct diagnosis (Ballweg & the Endometriosis Association, 2004), before which she most likely has received a variety of misdiagnoses and has even been referred to a psychologist, with the implicit assumption that it is all in her head. In spite of great advances in medical technology, the only way to make an accurate diagnosis of endometriosis is through surgery and direct observation. At present, there is no cure. For many women the pain of endometriosis is not only physical, but also a deeply emotional experience. Dreams can offer a woman struggling with endometriosis hope, a way to make meaning of her suffering and possibly offer clues about the nature of her disease, which may lead to appropriate treatment.

For one patient I followed who was suffering from endometriosis, a particular pattern seems to emerge in dreams based more than 10 years. Not only does a clear relationship between dreaming and pain emerge but also a connection between hormonal levels and dream imagery. Several studies have also noted a connection between waking day events and dream content (Schredl & Hoffman, 2003). In this patient's journals, dreams from the days of extreme pain were markedly different from dreams just before pain erupted. On the days just before pain, imagery was highly pleasurable and often blatantly erotic, with no hint whatsoever of the suffering to come. In marked contrast, dreams on the days of acute pain were often filled with violent imagery. This pattern of sensual dreams followed by disturbing nightmares echoes the increase of hormonal activity, which causes endometrial cysts to swell and finally burst, resulting in acute pain.

On the days of acute pain, typical dream imagery included physical restraint, bodily injury, and exposed sexual organs. Often there was a distressed young girl nearby, in need of care. Other images included burning and explosions together with feelings of rage, fear, and helplessness. Here is a typical example.

On the sheer rocky face of a mountain a naked woman is trapped in the center of a cold, yellowish thundering waterfall screaming and crying. A clay sewer pipe encases her torso leaving her crotch bare and exposed. Her daughter reaches up, trying to comfort her. On another wall is another woman imprisoned in grief, confined in the wall in anger. Next to her is a deep dark hole, which opens up into the basement.

Not only does imagery in this dream clearly refer to the site and intensity of abdominal pain through the image of a woman's torso trapped in a sewer pipe, but it also refers directly to the emotional suffering that often accompanies endometriosis through the image of another woman imprisoned in a wall of anger and grief. The bare crotch suggests a connection with sexuality as the little girl tries hopelessly to comfort her.

Dreams can provide validation for pain, which is often dismissed by the very people from whom a woman may be seeking guidance and relief. Medical practitioners, as well as therapists could benefit from asking about dreams and considering their possible relationship to the body, gaining clues to the origins of pain, which may have been overlooked. Nightmares in particular, can offer a tremendous source of energy, urging a woman to take action rather than falling into despair.

The body and dreaming are intimately related. When the body hurts, dreams often depict pain graphically. By including dreamwork as part of a holistic approach to endometriosis, a woman can care for herself on multiple levels while discovering new ways of being in her body that can ultimately have a positive effect on her health. Given the amount of time it takes to get a correct diagnosis of endometriosis, dreams may also offer an invaluable, untapped resource for getting help more quickly, thereby preventing unnecessary pain and infertility.

Sheila McNellis Asato

References

Ballweg, M. A., & the Endometriosis Association. (2004). *Endometriosis: The complete reference for taking charge of your health.* Chicago: Contemporary Books.

DeCicco, T. L., & King, D. B. (2007). The relationships between dream content and physical health, mood, and self-construal. *Dreaming, 17*(3), 127–139.

Schredl, M., & Hofmann, F. (2003). Continuity between waking activities and dream activities. *Consciousness and Cognition, 12*(2), 298–308.

ESP in Dreams

Extrasensory perception (ESP), also known as extended sense perception, has three components. Telepathy allows us to reach beyond the senses and ordinary reality to retrieve information about another person's mental processes. Clairvoyance will present information about ongoing activity in a distant locale. With precognition, a future event is foreshadowed that has not occurred. At one time, it was considered rare to awaken and find out that two people had exactly the same dream or discover the truth of last night's dream showing a relative being injured while traveling abroad, or even dream about an accident that had not occurred, A 10-year study relating ESP to dreaming initiated at the Brooklyn-based Maimonides Hospital in 1962 showed that ESP in dreams was not only possible but also more commonplace than formerly believed. The findings are summarized in the book *Dream Telepathy* (Ullman, Krippner, & Vaughan, 1973). A major finding of this study showed that the majority of people have ESP in their dreams. A wide variety of people with and without ESP or psychic ability participated in the Maimonides studies over the years. Out of 148 attempts, 111, or 75 percent, were successful in activating ESP in their dreams (Vaughan, 1982).

In a typical telepathy experiment, a sender focusing on a target picture in one room sends impressions to the receiver or dreamer in another room while a monitor watches the dreamer's brain waves. With the onset of the rapid eye movement, the monitor wakes the sleeping receiver to get an immediate report about the dream. After waking, the receiver is shown eight pictures, including the target, and ranks them from the most likely the target to the least likely. Eight nights of dreaming constituted one study in the Maimonides research. In 9 of the 13 major studies carried out, statistically significant results were obtained validating that telepathy in dreams was real. Robert Van de Castle, one of the telepathic dreamers in the Maimonides study, gives an account of his laboratory experiences in his book *Our Dreaming Mind* (Van de Castle, 1994).

The function of the precognitive dream is to warn or prepare the dreamer for an upcoming event. This type of compelling dream is unusually vivid and unforgettable. Days later, reality replaces reverie as an experience literally fulfills the drama originally previewed in the dream. Precognitive dreams span the range from trivial to profane and life saving. They can provide a warning about an accident, death, health challenge, calamity, or natural disaster. Precognitive dreams can also signal the more positive and significant life events such as receiving a proposal, previewing the birth of a baby, or receiving an unexpected gift. Anecdotal accounts of precognitive dreams have been collected for a long time. For example, President Lincoln had a precognitive dream in which he rose and walked into the East Room. "Who is dead in the white room?" he asked. "The President," came the answer. "He was killed by an assassin."

Malcolm Bessant, the prime precognitive dream subject in the Maimonides study was able to foresee randomly created events of the next day more than 60 percent of the time. However, most ESP dreams occur spontaneously during sleep and not under controlled laboratory conditions. Keeping a dream journal helps track the veracity of the precognitive dream. By doing this, physicist Dale Graff (2007) saw an unfolding tragedy, intervened upon waking and probably saved a life.

Anecdotal accounts and research on clairvoyance in dreams have not been as prevalent as the studies on telepathic and precognitive dreams. Clairvoyant dreams are almost always experienced exactly as the event actually happened, involving less metaphoric representation than the other ESP dreams. According to Robert Hoss (2005), some of the most memorable stories of clairvoyant dreams occur simultaneously between family members at a time of crisis or the death of a loved one.

While research on ESP in dreams has been promising, it is often difficult to control. Whether spontaneous or actively studied in the lab, boundaries between these three ESP processes are thin. In a telepathy experiment, for example, the images retrieved can actually come from a sender, or happen as the receiver uses precognition to sense the target picture. With the precognitive dream, the content can truly signal a future event or metaphorically represent a condition in the dreamer. For example, dreaming of a car crash may foreshadow such an upcoming event or symbolically represent the dreamer's body physically breaking down. There is a need to educate the public on how to recognize signals that the dream is truly precognitive and take advantage of the information provided.

Marcia Emery

References

Graff, D. E. (2007). Explorations in precognitive dreaming. *Journal of Scientific Exploration, 21*(4), 707–722.

Hoss, R. (2005). *Dream language.* Ashland, OR: Innersource.

Ullman, M., Krippner, S., & Vaughan, A. (1973). *Dream telepathy.* New York: Macmillan.

Van de Castle, R. (1994). *Our dreaming mind.* New York: Ballantine.

Vaughan, A. (1982). *The edge of tomorrow.* New York: Coward, McCann, Geoghegan.

Evaluation of Tonsils in Patients with Sleep Apnea

Sleep-disordered breathing (SDB), such as snoring and obstructive sleep apnea syndrome (OSAS), is often caused by multilevel airway obstruction, including the nasal cavity, oropharynx, and hypopharynx. Adenotonsillar hypertrophy is the main cause of airway obstruction in children with SDB. Therefore, tonsillectomy and adenoidectomy are most frequently used to correct this disorder in children. Although obesity is the main risk factor of OSAS in adults, simple tonsillectomy in properly selected adults with OSAS may be beneficial. Palate position, tonsil size, and body mass index seem to be valuable predictors of the success of uvulopalatopharyngoplasty, the most common surgical procedure performed for SDB, in adults (Friedman, Ibrahim, & Bass, 2002, pp. 13–21). Therefore, accurate evaluation of palatine tonsil size before surgery may be one of the important predictive factors for successful treatment of patients with SDB.

Radiological evaluation of objective tonsil size (OTS) using computed tomography (CT) and magnetic resonance imaging (MRI) has some limitations for clinical use (Stuck & Maurer, 2008, pp. 411–436), offers precise measurements of cross-sectional areas, three-dimensional reconstruction, and volumetric assessment of the airway, but CT use is limited by employment of ionized radiation. MRI does not use ionized radiation and offers excellent soft tissue contrast and three-dimensional assessment of tissue structures, but MRI use is limited by high cost. Clinically, we preoperatively evaluate palatine tonsils using the 0–4+ subjective tonsil size (STS) scale by asking a patient to open his or her mouth wide and then estimating the extension of the tonsil to the midline (Brodsky, Adler, & Stanievich, 1989, pp. 1–11; Friedman et al., 2002, pp. 13–21).

However, we sometimes find that preoperative STS does not reflect OTS, and there may be discordance between them.

There have been reports about the relationship between STS and OTS. Children with snoring or apnea had larger tonsil volume (TV) and length than those without obstructive symptoms in spite of the same STS.3. A recent study reported a strong correlation between TV and STS in children with SDB (Spearman's $>$ = 0.4960, p = 0.0039) (Howard & Brietzke, 2009, pp. 675–681). However, the difference of OTS according to the STS has only recently been reported by Wang, Chung, Jang, and Lee (2009, pp. 716–721). In children, STS was significantly correlated with tonsil height (TH; r = 0.281), tonsil width (TW; r = 0.345), tonsil thickness (TT; r = 0.199), and TV (r = 0.427) ($p < 0.001$ for all). In adults, STS was also significantly correlated with TH (r = 0.462), TW (r = 0.474), TT (r = 0.551), and TV (r = 0.550) ($p < 0.001$ for all). In children, TV increased from 2.17 mL for the size 1 group to 4.71 mL for the size 4 group; TH increased from 2.14 cm for the size 1 group to 2.78 cm for the size 4 group; TW increased from 1.32 cm for the size 1 group to 1.86 cm for the size 4 group; and TT increased from 1.07 cm for the size 1 group to 1.38 cm for the size 4 group. In adults, the TV of the size 3 (5.91 mL) and 4 (6.03 mL) groups was significantly higher than that of the size 1 (2.94 mL) and 2 (3.40 mL) groups, but there were no significant differences between the sizes 1 and 2 or between the size 3 and 4 groups. Tonsil height, TW, and TT also showed the same pattern as TV in adults.

However, discrepancies between STS and TV could be observed. Table 2 shows the distribution of TV according to STS in children and adults. In children, 120 tonsils (33.7%) in the size 3 group and 14 (13.0%) in the size 4 group had volumes less than 3 mL, similar to the mean volume in the size 1 and 2 groups. In contrast, 2 tonsils (8.7%) in the size 1 group and 30 (44.8%) in the size 2 group had volumes greater than 3 mL, similar to the mean volume in the size 3 and 4 groups. In adults, four (8.5%) tonsils in the size 3 group were less than 3 mL in volume, similar to the mean volume of the size 1 and 2 groups, whereas one (5.0%) tonsil in the size 1 group and six (15.8%) in the size 2 group were greater than 5 mL in volume, similar to the mean volume of the size 3 and 4 groups.

Although there is a statistical correlation in children between TV and STS, there is significant discordance in size 2 and 3 groups, thus greatly limiting the value of STS assessment in the majority of children. However, adult STS may reflect OTS and may help predict it preoperatively.

Jong Hwan Wang

See also: entries related to Sleep Disorders

References

Brodsky, L., Adler, E., & Stanievich, J.F. (1989). Naso- and oropharyngeal dimensions in children with obstructive sleep apnea. *International Journal of Pediatric Otorhinolaryngol, 17*, 1–11.

Friedman, M., Ibrahim, H., & Bass, L. (2002). Clinical staging for sleep-disordered breathing. *Otolaryngology-Head and Neck Surgery, 127*, 13–21.

Howard, N.S., & Brietzke, S.E. (2009). Pediatric tonsil size: Objective vs subjective measurements correlated to overnight polysomnogram. *Otolaryngology-Head and Neck Surgery, 140*, 675–681.

Table 2: Distribution of Tonsil Volume According to the Subjective Tonsil Size Scale in Children and Adults.

Tonsil volume (mL)	Children, no. of tonsils (%)				Adults, no. of tonsils (%)			
	Size 1	Size 2	Size 3	Size 4	Size 1	Size 2	Size 3	Size 4
≤ 1.0	1 (4.3)	2 (3.0)	0	0	1 (5.0)	0	0	0
> 1.0, ≤ 2.0	10 (43.5)	13 (19.4)	27 (7.6)	1 (0.9)	4 (20.0)	9 (23.7)	0	0
> 2.0, ≤ 3.0	10 (43.5)	22 (32.8)	93 (26.1)	13 (12.1)	7 (35.0)	10 (26.3)	5 (8.5)	0
> 3.0, ≤ 4.0	2 (8.7)	23 (34.3)	125 (35.0)	27 (25.2)	4 (20.0)	10 (26.3)	6 (10.2)	0
> 4.0, ≤ 5.0	0	4 (6.0)	67 (18.8)	31 (29.0)	3 (15.0)	3 (7.9)	10 (16.9)	2 (22.2)
> 5.0, ≤ 6.0	0	3 (4.5)	28 (7.8)	21 (19.6)	1 (5.0)	2 (5.3)	14 (23.7)	2 (22.2)
> 6.0	0	0	17 (4.8)	14 (13.1)	0	4 (10.5)	24 (40.7)	5 (55.6)
Total no.	23	67	357	107	20	38	59	9

Stuck, B.A., & Maurer, J.T. (2008). Airway evaluation in obstructive sleep apnea. *Sleep Medicine Review, 12*, 411–436.

Wang, J.H., Chung, Y.S., Jang, Y.J., & Lee, B.J. (2009). Palatine tonsil size and its correlation with subjective tonsil size in patients with sleep-disordered breathing. *Otolaryngology-Head and Neck Surgery, 141*, 716–721.

Evolution of Reptilian Sleep

Until the discovery of rapid eye movement (REM) sleep, sleep was considered to be a passive state, uniform in all animals. The viewpoint suddenly changed when the active nature of mammalian sleep and its two phases were recognized. This discovery boosted the search for two sleep phases in different animal species and groups. Most researchers understood that knowing how, when, and why sleep evolved would provide an answer to the question why we sleep.

Soon the extension of the two sleep phases to birds suggested two probable alternatives for sleep phylogeny: either the two phases appeared in an ancestor common to mammals and birds, or they could have appeared as a result of an evolutionary convergence. To clarify the issue, the obvious option was to study reptilian sleep.

Many early studies claimed that non-REM (NREM) and REM also existed in reptiles. However, careful observation dismissed the phasic events of supposed reptilian REM as artifacts. On the other hand, slow-wave EEG was never found in sleeping reptiles.

In conclusion, reptiles seemed to have behavioral sleep but lacked the typical signs of REM and NREM sleep. This prompted the search for other less-evident signs and the best candidate was the high-voltage spike (HVS), similar in morphology, neuroanatomical origin, behavioral correlations, and pharmacological profile to the hippocampal spike recorded in sleeping cats (Hartse, 1994). Additionally, a rebound in immobility and HVS frequency was observed after extended activity. An incomplete form of NREM sleep thus seemed to be primitive sleep in agreement with the alleged absence of REM in one primitive mammal, the echidna (Allyson & Goof, 1968). REM sleep would be a late comer, appearing in mammals and birds as a consequence of homeothermy.

However, this conclusion was disputed. First, some studies reported opposite results; that is, increased HVS frequency during wakefulness. Also, the cat's hippocampal spike was found to be no sound sign of sleep as it not only appeared during NREM sleep but also during grooming, eating, or drinking. What is more, the HVS hypothesis left the assumed convergent evolution of avian and mammalian REM sleep unexplained and no explanation was offered for the successive production of NREM–REM sleep cycles in a sleep episode.

This state of affairs remained unchanged until the discovery of large amounts of REM sleep in the platypus, a primitive mammal with many reptilian traits. This led to upheaval in theories on sleep phylogeny, suggesting the existence of REM sleep in reptiles.

Nowadays, there are several opinions regarding reptilian sleep. The first one supports the existence of a primitive NREM sleep with HVS but without delta EEG waves. In contrast, a number of authors affirmed that assumed reptilian sleep was not internally generated, like mammalian sleep, but was instead a passive response to environmental factors—mostly light and heat—and the assumed rebounds could be use-dependent aftereffects with no relation to sleep regulation. In fact, the regulation of reptilian sleep is contradictory with the well-known capacity for multiday continuous rest. Finally, the results for the platypus suggested the presence of some hidden form of REM sleep.

A new hypothesis, first presented in 1993 with successive amendments in 2000 and 2010 (Rial et al., 2010), introduced a new evolutionary scenario, proposing that the main change from reptiles to mammals and birds was not the development of sleep, but that of cortical waking. This new state blocked the remnants of subcortical reptilian waking, which remained as sleep. In summary, reptilian behavioral sleep was a truly passive state, only dependent on environmental and circadian factors, and it should be considered environmentally generated rest, a process quite different from mammalian sleep. This hypothesis has the added merit of explaining most gaps that earlier hypotheses left unexplained.

Rubén Victor Rial

See also: entries related to Evolution of Sleep

References

Allyson, T., & Goof, W. R. (1968). Sleep in a primitive mammal, the spiny anteater. *Psychophysiol, 5,* 200–201.

Buzsâki, G. (1986). Hippocampal sharp waves: Their origin and significance. *Brain Research, 398,* 242–252.

Flanigan Jr., W. F., Wilcox, R. H., & Rechtschaffen, A. (1973). The EEG and behavioral continuum of the crocodilian *Caiman sclerops, Electroenceph. Clinical Neurophysiology, 34,* 521–548.

Hartse, K. M. (1994). Sleep in insects and non-mammalian vertebrates. In M. H. Kryger, T. Roth, & W. C. Dement (Eds.), *Principles and practice of sleep medicine* (pp. 95–104). London: Saunders.

Rial, R. V., Akaârir, M., Gamundí, A., Nicolau, C., Garau, C., Aparicio, S., . . . Esteban, S. (2010). Evolution of wakefulness, sleep and hibernation: From reptiles to mammals. *Neuroscience and Biobehavioral Reviews, 34*, 1144–1160.

Evolutionary Approaches to Sleep

To discover the functions of sleep, we need to study sleep within an evolutionary theoretical framework. Sleep, at least non-REM sleep, undoubtedly has adaptive functions, though no one knows for sure what they are. REM sleep is also very likely adaptive, though this is hotly disputed. Indications that both forms of sleep are adaptive are as follows: Animals will sacrifice mating and foraging opportunities to sleep. Animals will also make themselves vulnerable to predation to sleep. Sleep probably promotes bodily repair processes in some way, though it is not yet clear how that function is accomplished. Sleep very likely also promotes immune competence and resistance to parasites. Most investigators, however, believe that sleep performs special functions for the brain. Finally sleep exhibits functional design; that is, sleep is associated with specific brain sites and activation patterns that are necessary to engage if sleep is to occur normally. We can safely conclude that some aspects of sleep are adaptive. But sleep's precise function is still unknown. The purpose of this short article is not to review competing theories on the adaptive functions of sleep but instead to simply sketch some basic ideas concerning existing evolutionary frameworks that can help investigators form hypotheses concerning potential adaptive functions of sleep.

Some of the evolutionarily inspired frameworks for studying sleep phenomena are as follows.

Behavioral Ecology and Life History

According to life-history theory, life-cycle traits such as gestation length, size and number of offspring, age at first reproduction, ongoing reproductive strategy, and length of life are all influenced by ecological factors and contribute to reproductive fitness. Individuals develop mechanisms or biobehavioral strategies that help them solve problems of infant survival, childhood growth, adult development, and reproduction across the life span. Perceptual-emotional information about current environmental conditions (e.g., local mortality rates) is used to make (unconscious) decisions about optimal allocation of limited resources.

Trade-offs have to be made between time and energy devoted to somatic effort (i.e., investing in growth and development of the body) versus time and energy devoted to reproductive effort (i.e., funneling effort toward producing and raising offspring). Similarly, natural selection is expected to optimize the timing of reproduction (e.g., mature early and invest in reproduction sooner or delay maturity and reproduce later). Reproductive effort has two further components: mating effort (locating, courting, and retaining a suitable mate) and parenting effort (i.e., gestating, giving birth, and engaging in postnatal care). In short, when it concerns the developing organism, life-history theory deals with how juvenile individuals unconsciously and optimally allocate somatic versus reproductive effort now versus in the future, given an assessment of current life circumstances. In adult animals, except in times of illness or injury, most effort is centered on reproductive goals (mating and parenting).

Sleep as a Scarce Resource

From a behavioral ecology and life-history framework, sleep is a resource that can be used to address the ever shifting trade-offs that need to be negotiated between somatic and reproductive effort. During development, when resources need to go to somatic growth, both sleep states can support growth and therefore should be long relative to their values in the mature organism. Similarly, during illness or injury, sleep durations should increase to support somatic repair. During the adult state, however, the two sleep states reduce (but do not eliminate) support for somatic effort and shift into greater support of reproductive effort. Given the differing brain activation profiles associated with REM and NREM sleep (REM is a highly activated desynchronized state while slow-wave sleep is a highly synchronized state), we expect that each sleep state should support reproductive effort in distinctive ways, with REM taking the lead given its apparent preference for activation of limbic-brain regions.

These simple theoretical assumptions give rise to the prediction that both REM and NREM should be similarly affected by and related to variables indexing somatic effort (metabolic rate, brain development and maintenance, and immune defense). Thus, correlations between somatic variables and individual sleep states should be weak while correlations with total sleep should be robust and positive. Ecological pressures such as predation risk will affect the two sleep states differently. When vigilance is at a premium and sleep needs to be restricted, NREM will be favored (prolonged) over REM, except when reproductive opportunities are present. Gestational period is the exception to these simple rules as it involves both reproductive and somatic effort. Here REM will play a more prominent role. REM is also expected to be more strongly related to variables indexing reproductive effort (e.g., brain volume in emotional brain centers such as the amygdala, reproductive competition, age at maturity) than NREM.

Natural selection works primarily on juveniles so I will focus next on evolutionary theories that concern juvenile development.

Sex-Ratio Determination

It is not widely appreciated that pregnant females can influence the sex of their offspring via modulation of hormonal and physiological conditions in utero. Sleep states may play a role in this process. There are good evolutionary reasons to give the mother some control over the sex of her offspring. If the cost of producing one sex is not equal to the cost of producing the other sex (and we know that it is not equal for most mammalian species), then mothers are predicted to find ways to detect the sex of the fetus she is carrying and then to make a decision as to whether to carry it to term. Of course, all of this happens in an unconscious manner.

Costs here refer to the amount of resources required to grow a fetus and then a child to reproductive age. If the lifetime reproductive success of the mother can be better enhanced by giving birth to males rather than females, she will give birth to more males than females. If, for example, a male costs twice as much to produce as a female in the context of a population of animals with a 1:1 sex ratio (though humans depart slightly from this 1:1 ratio), then the return on investment to the mother from investing in production of males will be only half that of females. She could instead produce two females for the cost of every male, thereby increasing the chances of getting her genes into the next generation.

Trivers and Willard (1973) argued that because male reproductive opportunities and male lifetime reproductive success are more variable than those of females for most mammalian species, the mother should be selected to invest in males if local conditions (in terms of resources, mortality rates, etc.) are good and in females if local conditions are poor. This argument predicts that the sex ratio should vary to some extent with the social dominance/status of the mother. Mothers high in a dominance hierarchy tend to have greater access to resources, and thus conditions for enhancing lifetime reproductive success of their offspring are good. Pregnant mothers who rank high in a dominance hierarchy should produce more male offspring than female offspring.

While there are numerous theories as to how the mother can determine the sex of the evolving fetus, the common denominator involves modulation of levels of hormones that normally maintain a pregnancy. Sleep states in the mother are known to vary with the trimester of the pregnancy and may influence circulating levels of hormones that maintain the pregnancy. Sleep states may also modulate the mother's ability to maintain a pregnancy regardless of the sex or fitness of the developing fetus.

Pregnancy and Genetic Conflict

From the point of view of sleep state biology, pregnancy is, of course, a unique physiological process wherein the sleep states of two genetically distinct individuals may interact. Haig (1993) has called attention to the fact that the placenta is genetically part of the fetus and not of the mother, and thus there is potential for a divergence of genetic interests between the fetus and the mother. Abnormal triploid fetuses with a double set of the father's genes and a single set of the mother's have a very large placenta, while abnormal fetuses with a double set of the mother's genes and one of the father's have very small placentas and show a retardation of growth. Modeling of genetic strategies of parents and their offspring suggests that with respect to the maternal–fetal interaction, the fetus is selected to extract as much resources from the mother as possible, while the mother is selected to moderate attempts to extract her resources. Her genetic interests lie not just in the present child but in whatever future children she may bear. She needs to be discriminative when it comes to investment of valuable resources in the current child. Future offspring of the mother, therefore, are in direct competition with the current fetus for resources, and the fetus thus attempts to extract as much as it can from its mother.

Given that sleep states are essentially brain states which emit electrical signals that influence an array of neuronal, hormonal, immunological, and behavioral responses, it seems reasonable to suppose that maternal sleep states will influence fetal development. If, furthermore, Haig's (1993) (genetic) conflict theory of human pregnancy is correct, then we can expect that fetal interests will include an attempt to target maternal sleep states for modification, given that these sleep states regulate or at least influence fundamental metabolic, hormonal, and immunological systems of the mother.

If the fetus wants to influence transfer of nutrients (e.g., glucose) from maternal tissues to fetal tissues, then the maternal brain (including its sleep states) should become a target for fetal manipulation, particularly in the second and third trimester, when fetal need for glucose is increasing rapidly with fetal brain development. Fetal manipulation of maternal sleep states might also allow the developing child to influence maternal waking behaviors. In many animals, for example, maternal slow-wave sleep (SWS) facilitates the milk ejection reflex when an infant suckles. Independent of fetal attempts to influence maternal sleep, the drastic physiological changes that accompany pregnancy undoubtedly influence maternal sleep states as well. For all of these reasons, we would expect alterations in maternal sleep architecture as the pregnancy progresses. Interestingly, available data suggest that time spent in SWS declines over the course of the pregnancy. As the time of birth approaches in pregnant monkeys the occasional contracture switches to contractions. This switch is related to the onset of sleep in the mother.

Parent–Offspring Conflict

Postnatal sleep states in the infant develop in the context of mother–infant interactions. From the point of view of the infant, formation of an attachment tie to the mother is all important, or else it will not thrive and may even not survive. Development of mother–infant attachment proceeds within a broader context of conflict between mother and child over amount and quality of resources to be invested in the infant. This conflict over provisioning of or investment in the infant is driven by the contrasting genetic interests of the mother versus those of the infant.

Trivers (1974; Trivers & Willard, 1973) pointed out that parents are related to their offspring by a coefficient of relatedness of 0.5; that is, the child carries only half of the maternal genomic complement. Consequently, the genetic interests of mother and child are not identical and offspring will tend to want more from their parents than their parents are willing to give. Offspring in mammals, furthermore, may not share the same father and thus their genetic interests will diverge significantly from those of their siblings. Even if they do share the same father, they are related to siblings only by 0.5 and thus their interests are not identical to those of their siblings. Offspring should therefore attempt to monopolize extraction of resources from the mother regardless of consequences to the mother or to siblings.

One arena where parent–offspring conflict plays itself out concerns sleep. When the infant or juvenile finally falls asleep the mother finally gets to rest herself. Thus, mothers want sleep durations to increase during the juvenile stage as it is easier for them to pursue their other priorities while the infant is asleep (strapped to the back or safely tucked into a sleep site, etc.), but the infant or juvenile's interest is in gaining more nutrients and attention from the mother and that is best done when awake.

Attachment Theory

Several investigators have suggested that for the neonate and the juvenile, evaluation of local ecological conditions reduces to evaluation of their experience of their caregivers. Bowlby and others in the field of attachment theory have called attention to the importance of infant–mother attachment relationships in development of infant cognitive, emotional, and social skills. If the neonate/child can form a secure emotional attachment to the mother, the child will conclude that the local environment will support a long-term reproductive strategy of delayed maturity and high investment in a few high-quality offspring. If, on the other hand, the child meets a cold, rejecting mother or faces threats of abandonment, and so on, then a strategy of rapid maturation and early reproduction with greater numbers of offspring, and so forth, will most likely obtain. Thus, development of adult reproductive strategies depends crucially on the juvenile's early experience of attachment.

Belsky, Steinberg, and Draper (1991) developed one of the first models of childhood attachment patterns as they relate to later reproductive behaviors. Belsky et al. suggested that early environmental factors in the family of origin (e.g., the amount of stress, spousal harmony, and financial resources) affect early child-rearing experiences (the level of sensitive and responsive caregiving). These child-rearing experiences then affect psychological and behavioral development of the child (e.g., patterns of attachment, the nature of internal working models of self and of others), which influences both somatic development (how quickly sexual maturation is reached) and development of reproductive effort.

Behavioral and reproductive strategies are conceived as ensembles of cognitive, brain, physiologic, and social processes and behaviors that implement a series of adaptive behaviors that increase reproductive fitness. Two developmental trajectories are conceived, eventuating in two reproductive strategies in adulthood. One strategy involves a short-term opportunistic orientation toward mating and parenting in which sexual intercourse with multiple partners occurs earlier and romantic relationships are short term and unstable. This orientation is geared toward increasing the quantity of offspring as early as possible. The second strategy involves a long-term investing orientation in which sexual intercourse occurs later in life with fewer partners, pair bonds are long term and more stable, and personal investment is greater. This orientation is associated with delayed maturity and with maximizing the quality of offspring.

These models of developmental attachment processes suggest that there must be an automatic and unconscious physiological process by which assessment of current life circumstances is made early in life. REM is a viable candidate for such a process as it involves very high activation levels of the amygdala and associated structures. Interestingly, sleep processes appear to play a crucial role in physiological mechanisms whereby early experience shapes adult reproductive strategies. In birds, paradoxical/active sleep (REM is sometimes called paradoxical sleep or PS in nonhuman species) may mediate certain aspects of sexual imprinting. There is also evidence that suggests that blocking REM early in life yields sexual dysfunction later in life in mammalian species.

Patrick McNamara

References

Belsky, J., Steinberg, L., & Draper, P. (1991). Childhood experience, interpersonal development, and reproductive strategy: An evolutionary theory of socialization. *Child Development, 62*, 647–670.

Haig, D. (1993). Genetic conflicts in human pregnancy. *Quarterly Review of Biology, 68*(4), 495–532.

Trivers, R. L. (1974). Parent offspring conflict. *American Zoologist, 14*, 249–264.

Trivers, R. L., & Willard, D. E. (1973). Natural selection of parental ability to vary the sex ratio of offspring. *Science, 179*(68), 90–92.

Evolutionary Psychology Theories of Dreams

Evolutionary psychology is interested in the universal features of the human mind. It tries to explain them as adaptations that evolved during human evolutionary history and were selected for because they helped ancestral humans to survive. Sleep and dreaming are universal features of the human mind: all humans everywhere in the world and across all times and cultures display them. Thus, to understand what functions they serve, we should place them in the evolutionary context.

Dreaming is a puzzling phenomenon whose function has long remained a mystery. Placing it in the evolutionary perspective might offer new insights into the question why we dream. Although there are countless theories of dreaming and its function, only a few have taken the evolutionary perspective into account: the sentinel theory, psychotherapeutic emotion-regulation theories, the costly signaling theory, and simulation theories of dreaming.

Sentinel Theory

The earliest theory with an evolutionary approach is called the sentinel theory (Snyder, 1966). According to this idea, REM sleep and dreaming evolved in mammals to guard the sleeping animal. If approaching dangers are detected by the brain during sleep, the highly activated brain during REM sleep prepares the animal to wake up. Simultaneously, the brain generates dreams about potential dangers to prepare the animal to face them upon awakening. If no signs of danger are detected by the brain, pleasant dreams are generated to promote the peaceful continuity of sleep. Dream-content studies on humans, however, do not lend support to the idea that dreams try to predict what is going on in the external world at the time of awakening.

Dreaming as Psychotherapy

Several theorists (e.g., Hartmann, 1998) have proposed that dreaming evolved to serve a psychotherapeutic function: dreaming helps to heal the adverse psychological effects of traumatic experiences, regulating negative emotions and preserving a positive emotional tone for the next period of wakefulness. This function is thought to have been particularly useful for our ancestors, who faced difficult conditions and traumatic experiences on a daily basis. Indeed, studies have shown that dream content is in fact often based on emotionally charged memories and the emotional state of the dreamer, which lends support to the theory that emotions are being processed or regulated during dreaming.

Costly Signaling Theory

McNamara (2004) assumes that REM sleep and dreaming constitute traits that send signals to other members of the population informing them about the fitness of the bearer of the traits. REM sleep is costly to produce, because it requires high metabolic activity in the brain and consumes energy. Dreaming is costly because it affects negatively the mood and the emotional behavior of the sleeper after waking up. If the individual functions well despite these costly handicaps, he will be accepted by the other group members and his social and communication skills have been shown to be of high quality. However, REM sleep and dreaming are themselves invisible to outsiders and do not leave any obvious signals about them for others to observe, which weakens the credibility of this theory.

Simulation Theories

Assume that dreaming is a virtual-reality simulator in the brain that produces automatically programmed mental training sessions to prepare for the future. Dreaming as simulation was selected for during evolutionary history, because when dreaming, it is possible to simulate perceptual, cognitive, and motor functions that require regular, repeated, automatic rehearsal or preparation in a completely safe environment.

The Threat-Simulation Theory

Revonsuo (2000) states that dreaming was primarily selected for its capacity to simulate dangerous events and how to perceive, avoid, and survive them efficiently. Threatening events are too dangerous to practice in real situations (because one may end up injured or dead before getting any practice); thus the safe simulated environment is the only way to prepare for them. There is new evidence showing that dreams in fact do frequently contain threat simulations (Valli & Revonsuo, 2009).

Other simulation hypotheses (see Valli & Revonsuo, 2007) include the idea that dreaming simulates social interactions, or the ability to interpret what other people are thinking or feeling. Dream-content studies show that dreams are highly social and contain much social interactions, which lend support to the social simulation hypothesis.

Recently, a developmental simulation hypothesis called protoconsciousness theory has been put forward by Hobson (2009). According to this idea, a virtual reality system is genetically encoded in humans and will be automatically installed in the developing brain during the abundant fetal REM sleep that internally activates the developing brain. If this theory is correct, we dream and thereby experience a very basic form of consciousness already before birth.

All the evolutionary theories of dreaming have both strengths and weaknesses (for an evaluation, see Valli & Revonsuo, 2007). At present, the various simulation theories as well as the emotion-regulation theories are the ones receiving greatest empirical support. Overall, the evolutionary perspective has invigorated the study of dreaming and provided new insights into the question why we dream.

Antti Revonsuo

References

Hartmann, E. (1998). *Dreams and nightmares: The new theory on the origin and meaning of dreams*. New York: Plenum Press.

Hobson, A. J. (2009). REM sleep and dreaming: Towards a theory of protoconsciousness. *Nature Reviews Neuroscience, 10*, 803–813.

McNamara, P. (2004). *An evolutionary psychology of sleep and dreams*. Westport, CT: Praeger.

Revonsuo, A. (2000b). The reinterpretation of dreams: An evolutionary hypothesis of the function of dreaming. *Behavioral and Brain Sciences, 23*, 877–901.

Snyder, F. (1966). Toward an evolutionary theory of dreaming. *The American Journal of Psychiatry, 123*, 121–142.

Valli, K., & Revonsuo, A. (2007). Evolutionary psychological approaches to dream content. In D. Barrett & P. MacNamara (Eds.), *The new science of dreaming, vol. 3: Cultural and theoretical perspectives* (pp. 95–116). Westport, CT: Praeger Publishers/Greenwood Publishing Group.

Valli, K., & Revonsuo, A. (2009). The threat simulation theory in the light of recent empirical evidence—A review. *The American Journal of Psychology, 122*, 17–38.

Existential Dreams

Systematic classificatory methods (cf. Busink & Kuiken, 1996) have repeatedly identified three types of impactful dreams: nightmares, transcendent dreams, and existential dreams. Of these, existential dreams distinctively involve sadness and despair, separation/loss, inhibition (fatigue), light/dark contrasts, affective shifts, and intense affect during the dream ending. Existential dreams are distinguishable from other impactful dream types—and from ordinary dreams—not by any single feature (e.g., sadness) but rather by a coherent profile of features involving feelings and emotions, motives and goals, sensory phenomena, movement characteristics, and dream endings. Like nightmares and transcendent dreams, existential dreams include visual discontinuities (e.g., explicit looking, sudden shifts in location); relatively intense affect, especially during dream endings; and compelling imagery that seems real to the dreamer even after awakening. However, despite such evidence of their shared intensity, their effects on waking thoughts and feeling differ. Existential dreams are distinctively followed by a shift toward self-perceptual depth. That is, after awakening—and often for hours, days, or weeks—existential dreamers report that their dream continues to influence their mood, make them sensitive to aspects of their lives they typically ignore, and make them feel like changing the way they live (Kuiken, Lee, Eng, & Singh, 2006).

These reported dream effects suggest that existential dreaming per se brings about shifts in self-perception, perhaps through the mnemonic and affective transformations that occur within the dream. This suggestion conflicts with the common assumption that deepened self-perception emerges only during dream telling and interpretation (e.g., during psychotherapy). It is consistent, however, with evidence that existential dream narratives themselves involve emerging self-awareness. For example, existential dreamers typically report that, during the dream, they become aware of themselves as if from the outside. Also, they report the spontaneous emergence of clear and distinct emotions (usually sadness) as the dream progresses. Such emerging self-awareness is not characteristic of nightmares. Thus, among the two types of impactful dreams involving negative effect, only existential dreams involve poignant self-reflection.

The contrast with nightmares is relevant also because nightmares and existential dreams emerge from rather different life circumstances. While there is ample evidence linking nightmares to the traumatic distress of PTSD, there also is evidence linking existential dreams to the separation distress of grief and bereavement. The following is an example of an existential dream that not only involves separation/loss and emerging self-awareness, but also explicit reference to bereavement:

In my dream, from my recollection, I was nowhere. I wasn't inside or outside. I was crying but I didn't know why. Then my close friends appeared and tried to take me with them. I was hesitant to follow them; I remember feeling guilty. My family members showed up, all but my Mom. Then it hit me: We were all upset because my Mom had passed away. I don't know how, when, or how; I just know I was feeling a lot of pain. Next thing I knew people kept appearing and consoling me. I was then woken up because I was crying and I had a horrible feeling in my stomach.

In this dream, guilty, unexplained sadness spontaneously becomes explicitly painful sadness as the dream reaches its conclusion. Following awakening, this dreamer's pain is realized as a previously unrecognized—or only vaguely recognized—personal truth.

In general, then, existential dreams are both disquieting and constructive, which may explain dreamers' ambivalence about them. This very ambivalence contrasts with the more nearly univocal character of nightmare distress. This contrast has important implications for clinical and research definitions of nightmares. Nightmares often are defined as abrupt awakenings from late night sleep with clear recall of a frightening dream narrative. However, according to some clinical definitions, the associated narrative may involve any kind of negative emotion. Broadening the definition of nightmares in this way may have unfortunate consequences, both clinically and in research, because nightmares and existential dreams appear to have different origins and different effects. Restricting the definition of nightmares to awakenings from late night sleep with clear recall of a (specifically) frightening dream narrative would enable more precise location of that source of largely unmitigated dream distress. It would also ensure separate consideration of the sources of existential distress that alter self-understanding and constructively affect the course of bereavement. Among empirically constrained theories of dreaming, the fear and vigilance of traumatic distress is often considered the prototypic form of dream experience. However, the sadness and self-monitoring of separation distress may be an equally fundamental source of dreaming.

Donald Kuiken

References

Busink, R., & Kuiken, D. (1996). Identifying types of impactful dreams: A replication. *Dreaming, 6*, 97–119.

Kuiken, D., Lee, M. N., Eng, T. C., & Singh, T. (2006). The influence of impactful dreams on self-perceptual depth and spiritual transformation. *Dreaming, 16*, 258–279.

External Sensory Stimulation as a Technique to Study Dreaming

Neurobiolological theories of dreaming have remained divided since the first studies investigating brain mechanisms of dreaming. This is primarily due to the ongoing debate as to whether ponto–geniculo–occipital (PGO) waves are an underlying biological mechanism of dreaming. This debate remains unresolved because PGO activity can only be directly recorded in animals using indwelling electrodes, and dream reports are only obtainable from humans. However, there are now new, novel methods available that can be used to test phenomenological relationships between inferred PGO activity in humans and dream reporting on awakening. Such methods involve the presentation of sensory stimuli, at below waking threshold, in specific ways that have been shown to manipulate PGO activity in animals.

The PGO Wave and Dream Theories

The PGO wave is one of the most controversial physiological activities occurring during sleep, which is claimed to underlie dream activity. The early identification of PGO waves arose from electrophysiological studies in the cat. These studies identified phasic neuronal activity originating from the pontine brainstem (P) that could be concurrently recorded from the lateral geniculate nucleus (G) of the thalamus and the occipital cortex (O). Given the predominance of PGO waves during REM sleep, this activity was then suggested as a correlate of dreaming. Support for this association arose from lesion and microstimulation studies demonstrating the primary role of the brainstem in the generation of both PGO waves and the REM-sleep state, in addition to findings that PGO waves were mainly measurable from visual brain regions (lateral geniculate nucleus [LGN] and occipital cortex of cats), which was consistent with the visual nature of dreaming (Callaway, Lydic, Baghdoyan, & Hobson, 1987).

The best known and most widely accepted attempt to integrate PGO waves into a model of dreaming was the activation synthesis (AS) hypothesis of Hobson and McCarley (1977), which proposed that PGO activity is a fundamental neural component underlying dreaming and accounts for the internal signal generation and sensory input characteristic of REM sleep. Based on evidence from microelectrode studies in the cat, it was proposed that the brainstem is the central generator of dreaming, assigning the forebrain a secondary passive role. It was hypothesized that the forebrain receives tonic and phasic signals from the midbrain reticular formation via the thalamus, and phasic eye movement (EM) signals from the pontine reticular formation via the LGN. The forebrain was then thought to integrate the internally generated pseudosensory information from the brainstem with previously stored sensorimotor information, resulting in the generation of dreaming. In light of new neuroimaging and lesion studies, the AS hypothesis was revised as the activation, input, modulation (AIM) model (Hobson, Pace-Schott, & Stickgold, 2000). This model proposes a similar role for PGO waves; however, to be in line with more recent neuroimaging data from REM sleep, PGO waves are purported to stimulate cortical association and limbic areas in humans, rather than randomly stimulating primary sensory areas as originally proposed in the AS hypothesis.

The Problems of Testing a PGO Model of Dreaming

Scientifically testing a PGO model of dreaming is problematic. This is because dreaming and PGO activity cannot be directly studied at the same time in the same participant. PGO waves have been investigated extensively in animals using indwelling electrode recordings of the pons, LGN, and cortex. However, observing and quantifying animal dreams is not possible. Conversely, mentation reports are easily obtained from humans, but indwelling electrode recording procedures are too invasive, and a reliable, noninvasive measure of PGO waves in humans is yet to be developed. It may be that such methods are not yet possible because the spatial and temporal resolution of current neuroimaging techniques is inadequate to accurately measure and track such specific and rapid neural activity.

Until neuroimaging methods dramatically improve, there needs to be a simple, noninvasive method to measure PGO activity in humans. Several studies have investigated possible PGO wave indicators that could be externally measured in humans. However, measures such as phasic integrated potentials and middle ear muscle activity, among a range of PGO analogues, have failed to provide a consistent relationship to either dream-recall frequency or specific features of sleep mentation (for a review, see Pivik, 1991). It seems that EMs have remained as the only accepted, reliable indicator of PGO activity, confirmed by a number of studies in animals (Callaway et al., 1987). However, the natural appearance of EMs, by definition, is restricted to REM sleep. This means that any studies of EMs as an indicator of PGO activity are confounded by the presence of REM sleep or limited to studies within REM sleep.

PGO Waves, Eye Movements, and External Stimuli

In an attempt to address the dilemma of investigating the relationship between PGO activity and dreaming in humans, Conduit, Bruck, and Coleman (1997) developed a technique derived from earlier animal research showing that a variety of external sensory stimuli, including visual flashes, touch, and auditory tones, can induce EMs and concurrent PGO spikes during sleep. Conduit et al. (1997) presented human participants with single presentations of combined light and tone stimuli of intensity just below waking threshold during stage 2 nonrapid eye movement (NREM) sleep. When a clear EM occurred in response to a presentation, signaling a PGO event, individuals were awakened and mentation reports collected. A significantly greater frequency of visual imagery reports was obtained on awakenings from the stimulus condition than the control condition without lights and tones, and it approximated the amount of dreaming after REM awakenings. This finding suggested that enhanced dreaming was linked to the generation of PGO activity during NREM sleep. However, a limitation of Conduit et al.'s (1997) study was the use of combined light and sound stimuli. It was possible that external stimulation of the light delivered during sleep could have increased visual imagery reports by means of stimulus incorporation.

In a subsequent study, Fedyszyn and Conduit (2007) presented single tones at below waking threshold during stage 2 and REM sleep to induce EMs. When at least one concurrent EM was observed in

response to a stimulus presentation, subjects were awoken and mentation reports were collected. Mentation reports following induction of EMs during stage 2 sleep contained a higher frequency of imagery and were rated as more vivid than control mentation reports. However, a further limitation of both of these studies was that stimulus presentation during stage 2 sleep also resulted in an increase in EEG arousal. In both studies this arousal was found to significantly correlate with imagery ratings during stage 2. Thus, the increase in imagery following induction of EMs during stage 2 sleep could have been a result of increased cortical arousal. Hence, a PGO hypothesis of dreaming was not adequately tested by these experiments. Fedyszyn and Conduit (2007) concluded that the induction of ocular activity during sleep via external stimulation was confounded by cortical arousal, and such PGO indicators and cortical arousal seemed to be inseparable.

Recent experiments from our laboratory anecdotally reported the suppression of EMs in response to the presentation of a repeated tone at low intensity below waking threshold. Such EM suppression during REM sleep has also been observed in response to white noise and constant photic stimulation. In a more recent fMRI study, it was also observed that continuous external tones presented during REM sleep produced a significant decrease in thalamic blood oxygen level dependent response and suppression of EMs (Wehrle et al., 2007). Therefore, Stuart and Conduit (2009) investigated the effect of low-intensity repeated auditory stimulation on EMs and subsequent dream reporting on awakening from REM sleep. Repeated low-level tone presentations resulted in a significant decrease in the amplitude and frequency of EMs and reported dream imagery on awakening. Tone presentations also resulted in a significant increase in EEG arousal. Provided one is willing to assume that the appearance of EMs correlates with PGO burst activity in humans, as it does in other mammals (such as cats and monkeys), these initial results have provided phenomenological support for PGO-based hypotheses of dream reporting, including the AIM model.

Conclusions

The use of external sensory stimulation holds great promise as a method of testing PGO-based theories of dreaming. However, research to date using such methods to study dream phenomenology has come only from one laboratory. Preliminary results appear to support PGO-based theories, but new novel application of such methods, possibly using any one of an endless array of presentation parameters, from other researchers, might challenge this initial interpretation.

Esther Sammut and Russell Conduit

References

Callaway, C. W., Lydic, R., Baghdoyan, H. A., & Hobson, J. A. (1987). Pontogeniculooccipital waves: Spontaneous visual system activity during rapid eye movement sleep. *Cellular and Molecular Neurobiology, 7*, 105–149.

Conduit, R., Bruck, D., & Coleman, G. (1997). Induction of visual imagery during NREM sleep. *Sleep, 20*, 948–956.

Fedyszyn, I. E., & Conduit, R. (2007). Tone induction of ocular activity and dream imagery from stage 2 sleep. *Dreaming, 17*, 35–47.

Hobson, J. A., & McCarley, R. W. (1977). The brain as a dream-state generator: An activation-synthesis hypothesis of the dream process. *American Journal of Psychiatry, 134*, 1335–1348.

Hobson, J. A., Pace-Schott, E. F., & Stickgold, R.. (2000). Dreaming and the brain: Toward a cognitive neuroscience of conscious states. *Behavioral and Brain Sciences, 23*, 793–842.

Pivik, R. T. (1991). Tonic states and phasic events in relation to sleep mentation. In S. J. Ellman & J. S. Antrobus (Eds.), *The mind in sleep: Psychology and physiology* (2nd ed., pp. 214–247). New York: J. Wiley.

Stuart, K., & Conduit, R. (2009). Auditory inhibition of rapid eye movements and dream recall from REM sleep. *Sleep, 32*, 399–408.

Wehrle, R., et al. (2007). Functional microstates within human REM sleep: First evidence from fMRI of a thalamocortical network specific for phasic REM periods. *European Journal of Neuroscience, 25*, 863–871.

F

False Awakenings

A false awakening is a type of dream that involves the subjective experience of waking up while remaining in the dream state. Often the false awakening will resemble the dreamer's actual waking circumstances, at times with a remarkable degree of accuracy and detail. The dreamer may then perform routine tasks in the dream typically done immediately after awakening, such as getting dressed or brushing one's teeth (Green & McCreery, 1994, p. 65).

Other false awakenings contain fantastic or unrealistic elements not associated with the dreamer's waking circumstances (Windt & Metzinger, 2007, p. 235). The dreamer may wake up in the same environment as the dream that occurred prior to the false awakening. Or the dreamer may awaken into a dream containing aspects of the dreamer's past. For example, a false awakening may entail waking up in the dreamer's childhood bedroom. Frequently, the dreamer fails to notice the incongruities associated with the unrealistic elements of the new dream environment. When these incongruities do prompt the dreamer to become aware of dreaming, the dream becomes a lucid dream.

Some dream sequences involve an entire series of false awakenings. For example, in the early 20th century, the French zoologist Yves Deluge described a dream of being awakened by a friend knocking at his door, asking for his help (Green & McCreery, 1994, p. 66). He quickly got dressed, and when he wiped his face with a cold, damp cloth he again experienced himself waking up. He went back to sleep, convinced the earlier knocking at his door was a dream. However, when he was awakened a second time by the same friend knocking at his door, asking him to hurry, he decided he had not been dreaming after all. This cycle of the knock on the door and the wet cloth waking him into parallel dream environments repeated itself four times before Yves actually awakened and realized both sets of experiences were dreams.

False awakenings often occur at the end of a lucid dream (Windt & Metzinger, 2007, p. 234). In these cases the lucid dreamer is first aware of being in a dream, then dreams of waking up, and is persuaded the dream has ended. In actuality the dream continues, although it ceases being a lucid dream, since the dreamer is no longer aware of being in a dream. False awakenings and lucid dreams share several common characteristics (Green & McCreery, 1994, p. 65). Both types of dreams are normally more realistic and stable than nonlucid dreams. The dreamer generally exhibits a higher level of rational thinking in lucid dreams as well as false awakenings. The presence or absence of lucid awareness represents the most significant distinction between the two states. The lucid dreamer is aware of being in a dream, whereas in a false awakening the dreamer mistakes the dream for a waking experience.

Besides lucid dreams, false awakenings are closely related to a variety of nonordinary sleep states and anomalous experiences. Sometime false awakenings are accompanied by an inability to move one's body. This type of experience is known as sleep paralysis. False awakenings and sleep paralysis both occur during transitional periods between waking and sleeping, and combine characteristics of both states in unusual ways (Nielsen & Zadra, 2011). There are also significant overlaps between descriptions of false awakenings and reports of out-of-body experiences, apparition sightings, and alien abductions (Rose, Blackmore, & French, 2002).

Chris Olsen

References

Green, C., & McCreery, C. (1994). *Lucid dreaming: The paradox of consciousness during sleep*. London: Routledge.

Nielsen, T., & Zadra, A. (2011). Idiopathic nightmares and dream disturbances associated with sleep-wake transitions. In M. H. Kryger, T. Roth, & W. C. Dement (Eds.), *Principles and practice of sleep medicine* (pp. 1006–1015). Philadelphia: Saunders.

Rose, N. J., Blackmore, S. J., & French, C. C. (2002). Paranormal belief and interpretations of sleep paralysis. Paper presented at the Parapsychological Association 45th Annual Convention, Paris. Retrieved from http://www.susanblackmore.co.uk/Conferences/PA2002.htm

Windt, J. M., & Metzinger, T. (2007). The philosophy of dreaming and self-consciousness: What happens to the experiential subject during the dream state? In P. McNamara & D. Barrett (Eds.), *The new science of dreaming volume III: Cultural and theoretical perspectives* (pp. 193–247). Westport, CT: Praeger.

Family Unconscious in Dreams

Family dynamics and related feelings are some of the most powerful influences on the psychological patterns of individuals. They are extraordinary in their depth and intensity. Family members are known to frequently dream about each other. The vast majority of these dreams are casual in nature in which a parent, sibling, or other relative is doing something generally recognized. Sometimes, however, family members are doing something unusual or even paradoxical. Strong feelings and images emerge, which reveal the dynamic emotions experienced about these special people in our lives. The family is the intimate fluid and dynamic matrix in which, over time, the nexus of dynamic conflicts and also personal and unconscious identity is woven. The dream, with its strange contours and story line, is the perfect field on which to project these intimate primary emotions and patterns. The dream is really a pulse taken on the heartbeat of family life.

The work of Freud, Jung, and others revealed that in addition to these primal feelings, there are great spiritual energies and messages from the collective and racial unconscious hidden in dreams. This region of the unconscious is a vast reservoir of knowledge, wisdom, and experience collected by humanity through the ages. It is collective and racial and therefore, in a very intimate way, shared.

Anomalous research has also revealed that ESP or psi occurs a great deal in certain kinds of dreams. Any number of possibilities can occur when family members are dreaming because the fluid psychological boundaries between individuals are fluid and change significantly in the dream state.

Observations of families in therapy have discovered that recurrent shared patterns of interaction and behavior are sometimes reflected in the dreams of family members. This is especially true when the families are going through a crisis or some other intense situation.

Families often live in the same place, including the same house and rooms for decades, even for generations. Family members are often in similar sleep and dream cycles. Certain coordinating tendencies can be observed. The major emotional issues in the family at times appear to be reflected in slightly different ways in each family member's inner landscape. In a sense each family member's dream life reflects and enfolds the dream life of each other family member.

In one family the following recurring dream was recorded of a 15-year-old girl. She dreamed that she escaped from her parents' house and jumped into their car. As she drove away, the father would run toward her but never manage to quite catch her. The closer he got, the faster the car went. Finally the girl fully escaped him only to run headlong into a telephone pole and kill herself. In this family's therapy sessions, the themes of autonomy and separation with a great deal of anxiety occurred repeatedly. The daughter fought continually with her parents over her own intense involvement with a young man of whom the family did not approve. She felt rebellious and dominated by her parents, in particular her father. However, when she stayed away from home too long, she began to experience somatic problems and wanted to lose herself in male companionship.

Another dream recorded by the girl's 12-year-old sister revealed a similar theme. The younger girl dreamed that a large awful man ran around screaming at her mother, her older sister, and herself. Finally, the man stepped on all three but did not kill them. The dream recurred several times. The family that provided this dream series had as its members a father who had had a manic-depressive psychosis; an extremely religious, compulsive mother; and two teenage girls. All three females in the family had psychosomatic problems, including stomach cramps, persistent gas pains, migraines, and frequent depression. There are innumerable other examples that implicate not only somatic and psychological symptoms but in some cases shared imagery.

What emerged in these observations was a field of shared images, ideas, and feelings in each individual within the family. This shared family emotional field, which we call *the family unconscious,* is a shifting, interconnected field of energy and information that does not obey the conventional rules of space and time of the waking state. This field of interconnected energy, influence, and information in many ways mimics a kind of hologram or holonomic matrix in which each part enfolds and reflects all other parts at slightly different angles.

There appears to be a subtle dimension of somatic and behavioral influence and also potentially a vast reservoir of healing located in the collected dreams and memories of the people who are most dear to us through so many important years of our lives.

Edward Bruce Bynum

References

Bynum, E. B. (1980). The use of dreams in family therapy. *Psychotherapy: Theory, Research and Practice,* 17(2), 227–231.

Bynum, E. B. (2003). *Families and the interpretation of dreams.* New York: Cosimo Books.

Bynum, E. B. (2004). *The family unconscious: "An invisible bond."* New York: Cosimo Books.

Fantasy Literature and Dreams

All fiction may be viewed as a kind of dreaming insofar as the writer conjures characters, settings, and plots out of his or her private imagination by merging aspects of ordinary life with novel details that do not actually exist. Authors of fantasy literature carry this oneiric impulse to extremes of creative counter-factuality. Stories in this genre often depart radically from present-day life as they invent alien worlds, intelligent nonhuman beings, alternative histories, and far-flung visions of the future. In many fantasy tales, however, the dreamy deviations from normality appear in subtler form, lurking just on the outskirts of conventional awareness. In psychological terms, it could be argued that all forms of fantasy literature stimulate in readers a dreamlike experience in which they become more open to new ideas, insights, and possibilities beyond the status quo of the waking world.

Defined in this way, many works of classic Western mythology may be identified as fantasy literature, with dreams frequently playing a prominent narrative role. In *The Epic of Gilgamesh,* the warrior king suffers terrible nightmares that prompt his heroic quest to conquer death. Homer's *Iliad* and *Odyssey* feature several characters who experience divine dream revelations of prophetic guidance, heavenly advice, and occasionally harmful deception. Ovid's *Metamorphoses,* Apuleius's *The Golden Ass,* and Virgil's *Aeneid* include episodes in which dreaming serves as a lively conduit between humankind and the gods. These mythological texts present dreaming as a realm of boundless transformation, alluring in its numinous potential but dangerous in its expression of dark, wild desires. The historical roots of fantasy literature can be found in these wary mythological tales of gods and heroes.

Closer to contemporary times, fantasy writers of the 19th and 20th centuries took interest in dreams as a means of exploring themes of wonder, epistemological uncertainty, and horror. Edgar Allen Poe (1809–1849) deliberately aimed at eliciting nightmarish feelings of existential dread in his readers, as seen in *A Descent into the Maelstrom, The Murders in the Rue Morgue,* and the poem "A Dream within a Dream." Robert Louis Stevenson (1850–1894) used his own dreams and nightmares to develop the plot of *The Strange Case of Dr. Jekyll and Mr. Hyde,* and he attributed much of his literary inspiration in general to the brownies, the Scottish fairies who visited him at night in his sleep. H. P. Lovecraft (1890–1937) wrote numerous short stories in which dreaming features as one of the most frequently used portals between the normal world of sanity and the unnameable horrors that prowl the shadows. In "The Circular Ruins" by Jorge Luis Borges (1899–1986), a wizard performs a long and complex ritual of dreaming to create a living being, only to discover that he himself is merely the creation of someone else's dream.

More recently, fantasy authors have written cautionary stories about efforts to control dreaming, whether by technological manipulation or simply by imposing the rationalist goals of the waking ego on dreaming experience. Ursula K. LeGuin (b. 1929) envisions in *The Word for World Is Forest* an alien planet of arboreal creatures whose waking lives are thoroughly integrated with lucid dreaming; the brutal human colonists who enslave and abuse these creatures represent all the forces of modernity that conspire to destroy dreaming. In LeGuin's *The Lathe of Heaven,* a man living in a dystopic near-future America discovers he can change reality with his dreams; when a sleep researcher tries to use the man's ability to improve the world, horrifically unintended consequences ensue. *Dreamside* by Graham Joyce (b. 1954) describes a 1970s era British university where four passionate but aimless students and a secretive psychology professor engage in an ill-conceived experiment to become conscious in their dreams and control what happens in them. The results are not what they expect. The characters in *Dreamside* are so intent on figuring out *how* to induce lucid dreaming that they never ask themselves why they want to do so in the first place.

Fantasy literature often addresses younger readers with magical stories that speak to their conflicted feelings and anxious concerns about growing up. *Alice's Adventures in Wonderland* by Lewis Carroll (1832–1898) presents an elaborate dream world filled with whimsical shape-shifting, conceptual puzzles, and occasional moments of severe alarm. Two popular book series of recent years, J. K. Rowling's (b. 1965) *Harry Potter* stories about a magical school for young wizards and witches and Stephanie Meyer's (b. 1973) *Twilight* saga about vampires, werewolves, and the human girl who loves them both, are filled with significant dreams that influence, warn, and inspire the characters. The millions of people, mostly children and teenagers, who have read these books have been well primed to accept the possibility that unusually powerful, revelatory, magical dreams can break through the boundaries of ordinary life to motivate acts of great courage and creativity. Although not intended for children, the *Sandman* series by Neil Gaiman (b. 1960) uses the comic book format to weave a darkly inventive story of Morpheus, one of the seven endless cosmic deities, who embodies dream. In Gaiman's work, fantasy literature comes full circle by reviving its historical connection to the mythology of primal dreaming creativity.

Kelly Bulkeley

Fetal Sleep

One form of sleep that has not been adequately studied is fetal sleep. It may come as a surprise that a fetus sleeps but the scientific consensus is that this is indeed the case. All mammals studied to date exhibit a period of spontaneous and mixed brain activity in the uterus known as indeterminate sleep that slowly differentiates into distinct sleep states by the middle of the pregnancy. Both quiet sleep (QS) and active sleep (AS) are thought to develop out of this indeterminate sleep.

In humans, development of individual behavioral sleep phenomena such as physiological cycles of quiescence and arousal into distinct sleep states begins at approximately 28 to 32 weeks gestational age (ga) and is complete by 36 to 40 weeks ga. At about 28 weeks ga, discrete periods characterized by REMs and respiratory movements begin alternating with periods of sustained motor quiescence with no or very low numbers of eye movements. An REM-like sleep state appears between 30 and 32 weeks ga and increases in amount until it comprises approximately 90 percent of fetal sleep. This REM-like state remains at about 90 percent of sleep until about one to two weeks of postnatal life, and then it begins a relatively rapid decline toward adult values. That decline occurs at different rates in different infants. By the end of the first year, REM-like sleep has declined to about 50 percent of total sleep. By the time adulthood is reached, REM comprises only about 20 to 25 percent of total sleep. In the human fetus, the amount of quiet, NREM-like sleep initially increases and then stabilizes by 35 to 36 weeks ga and only modest changes are noted in the postnatal period.

According to Davis, Frank, and Heller (1999), AS and QS have few features in common with adult REM and NREM. Behavioral AS, for example, is not mediated by the same brain mechanisms responsible for REM. Unlike in the adult, cholinergic blockade has no effect on behavioral AS in the rat, and the adult REM-related atonia is absent in neonatal AS. On the other hand, fetal behavioral AS is characterized in both altricial and precocial species by neck muscle atonia, REMs, and generalized muscle twitching—all signs that we are dealing with a precursor form of REM sleep.

Returning to the human case, one obvious question to ask with respect to fetal sleep is whether sleep of the mother affects the developing sleep states of the fetus. One consistent finding that emerges from the study of alterations of sleep architecture in pregnancy is that the time the mother spent in slow-wave sleep/SWS declined over the course of the pregnancy. It is not clear if the decline in SWS could be attributed to hormonal changes and physical discomfort characteristic of pregnancy. If physical discomfort alone caused the changes in sleep architecture (i.e., decline in SWS), one would expect a more global effect on sleep rather than just an effect on SWS. Lee et al.'s (Lee, McEnany, & Zaffke, 2000) longitudinal data, furthermore, show that while time spent in SWS declined overall, percentage of SWS actually increased in the second trimester relative to both the first and third trimesters.

What might explain changes in sleep architecture during pregnancy? And how do these changes affect fetal sleep and development? During the first 10 weeks of pregnancy, human chorionic gonadotopin (hCG) levels secreted from the trophoblast of the embedded zygote maintains the corpus luteum and its secretions of estrogen and progesterone. These sex steroids together with prolactin (secreted from the pituitary) foster the profound physiological changes and growth in both the mother and the fetus throughout the pregnancy. Increased levels of progesterone, furthermore, dampen or prevent uterine contractions. Progesterone and hCG falls in the second trimester as the placenta itself increases its production of placental lactogen (PL), progesterone (P), and estrogen (E). The placenta also releases human placental growth hormone.

PL acts on maternal tissues, directing them to ensure that enough nutrients are available to the fetus. It also prepares the mother's breasts for lactation after the baby is born. One possibility, therefore, is that changes in SWS in pregnancy reflect the decline in maternal P and the rise in fetal PL hormone during the same period.

All the previously mentioned sleep–hormonal interactions in the mother and the fetus, however, do not tell us whether the mother's state affects the sleep states of the fetus or whether the sleep states of the fetus affect development of the pregnancy or of the newborn. Presumably, the fetus sleeps because it needs to sleep and any dysfunction of fetal sleep patterns should impair development of the fetus itself—yet it is difficult to find direct evidence for this otherwise reasonable conjecture. There is simply not enough data available to evaluate the claim.

On the other hand, there is some evidence to suggest that sleep dysfunction in the pregnant mother does have adverse effects on the developing fetus including, fetal sleep (Chang, Pien, Duntley, & Macones, 2010). Sleep deprivation during pregnancy, for example, increases the risk of preterm delivery and postpartum depression.

It should be clear from this short review that fetal sleep remains largely unexplored territory and that we know very little about it. This lack of knowledge concerning fetal sleep undoubtedly is due to the difficulties inherent in the study of fetal sleep. New technologies such as magnetoencephalography (Haddad et al., 2011) are currently being assessed to fill this gap.

Patrick McNamara

See also: entries related to Sleep and Development

References

Chang, J.J., Pien, G.W., Duntley, S.P., & Macones, G.A. (2010). Sleep deprivation during pregnancy and maternal and fetal outcomes: Is there a relationship? *Sleep Medicine Reviews, 14*(2), 107–114.

Davis, F.C., Frank, M.G., & Heller, H.C. (1999). Ontogeny of sleep and circadian rhythms. In P.C. Zee & F.W. Turek (Eds.), *Regulation of sleep and circadian rhythms* (Vol. 133, pp. 19–80). New York: Marcel Dekker.

Haddad, N., Govindan, R.B., Vairavan, S., Siegel, E., Temple, J., Preissl, H., . . . Eswaran, H. (2011). Correlation between fetal brain activity patterns and behavioral states: An exploratory fetal magnetoencephalography study. *Experimental Neurology, 228,* 200–205.

Lee, K.A., McEnany, G., & Zaffke, M.E. (2000). REM sleep and mood state in childbearing women: Sleepy or weepy? *Sleep, 23*(7), 877–885.

Fetal Yawning

All the movements that a newborn is able to produce originate during fetal life and are performed throughout the life span. At the beginning of the third month, the embryo becomes a fetus with the occurrence of the first oral and pharyngeal motor sequences under the control of the neurological development of the brainstem, which coordinates the respiratory, cardiac, and digestive systems. Circuits that generate organized and repetitive motor patterns, such as those underlying feeding, locomotion, and respiration belong to the central pattern generators in the medulla, which are genetically determined, subserving innate motor behaviors essential for survival.

In humans, yawning is recognized as one of the movement patterns consistently present as early as 12 weeks after conception and remains relatively unchanged throughout pregnancy and life. The frequency of yawns does not change between 20 and 36 weeks' gestational age. Up to 50 to 60 fetal yawns per day have been documented. Yawning, in fact, peaks during fetal life and then gradually declines until the end of the second year of life (5 to 20 per day).

A fetal yawn is a paroxysmal cycle characterized by a standard cascade of movements over a 5- to 10-second period. The 4-D ultrasound differentiates this typical development: the fetal mouth, previously closed, opens widely for four to six seconds with simultaneous retraction of the tongue, followed by a quick closure, and usually combined with retroflexion of the head and sometimes elevation of the arms (pandiculation). This harmonious sequence is markedly different than a brief swallowing episode. Using a color Doppler technique, it is possible to observe the flow of amniotic fluid through the fetal mouth, oropharynx, pharynx, and trachea to the lungs. This movement pattern is non-repetitive in the fetus, contrarily to adults. Yawning appears to be clearly not just a matter of opening one's mouth, but a generalized stretching of muscles, especially those of the respiratory tract (diaphragm, intercostals), face, and neck.

The strong muscular contraction that represents a yawn is metabolically expensive. If we agree with the terms of Darwin's evolutionary propositions, the cost in brain activity must be outweighed by the advantages gained in terms of developmental fitness. Thus, a structural hypothesis suggests an activation in the synthesis of neurotrophins, which leads to a cascade of both new synapse formation or recruitment and activation through the diencephalon, brainstem, and spinal cord. The phenomenon of activity-dependent development has been clearly shown to be one mechanism by which early sensory or motor experience can affect the course of neural development. Activity-dependent development may be a ubiquitous process in brain maturation by which activity in one brain region can influence the developmental course of other regions. Thus, fetal yawning facilitates a harmonious progress in the development of both the brainstem and the peripheral neuromuscular function (neuromuscular rewiring).

Yawning's survival without evolutionary variations postulates a particular importance in terms of developmental needs. The ability to initiate motor behavior generated centrally and linked to arousal and respiratory function is a property of the brainstem reticular formation, which has been remarkably conserved during

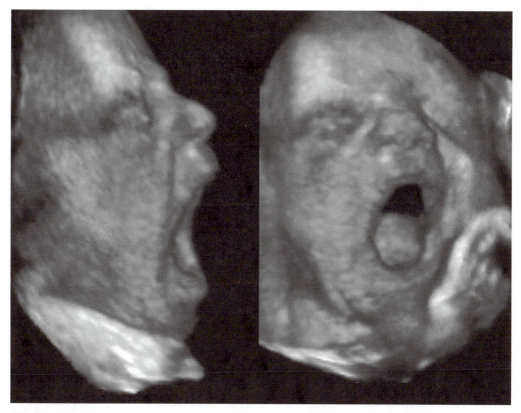

3D ultrasound image of a 23-week-old, 250-gram fetus yawning. (Olivier Walusinski)

the phylogeny of vertebrates, including agnathans, fishes, amphibians, reptiles, and birds. Thus, yawning and stretching have the traits of related phylogenetic old origins.

Olivier Nils Walusinski

See also: entries related to Sleep and Development

References

Joseph, R. (2000). Fetal brain behavior and cognitive development. *Developmental Review, 20,* 81–98.

Masuzaki, H., & Masuzaki, M. (1996). Color Doppler imaging of fetal yawning. *Ultrasound in Obstetrics and Gynecology, 8,* 355–356.

Petrikovsky, B. M., Kaplan, G. P., & Holsten, N. (1999). Fetal yawning activity in normal and high-risk fetuses: A preliminary observation. *Ultrasound in Obstetrics and Gynecology, 13,* 127–130.

Sepulvedam, W., & Mangiamarchi, M. (1995). Fetal yawning. *Ultrasound in Obstetrics and Gynecology, 5,* 57–59.

Walusinski, O. (2010). Fetal yawning. *Front Neurol Neuroscience, 28,* 32–41.

Flying Dreams

Flying without any helping means has always fascinated mankind. Flying dreams have been reported fairly often (Schredl

& Piel, 2007). In student samples, 30 to 63.5 percent of the participants reported that they had experienced flying dreams at least once (Nielsen et al., 2003; Schredl, Ciric, Götz, & Wittmann, 2004). On the other hand, the actual frequency of flying dreams is very low (1.2%, $N = 1,910$ diary dreams, student sample; Barrett, 1991). Some studies reported higher frequencies of flying dreams in men, but this was not confirmed by a large representative survey (Schredl & Piel, 2007).

Over the centuries, a large number of researchers have speculated about the etiology of flying dreams (for an overview see Schönhammer, 2004; and Schredl, 2008). In the 19th century, the analogy to *Lungenflügel* (the two lungs) and flying dreams was brought up. It was also speculated that the reduced sensory input via the skin produces the sensation of floating. This is interesting since some persons in deep relaxation report that they have the sensation of floating. A Freudian psychoanalyst, Paul Federn, linked the flying dream to penile erections, which he viewed as an overcoming of gravity. On the basis of their activation–synthesis hypothesis of dreaming, Hobson and McCarley (1977) formulated the assumption that "flying dreams may thus be a logical, direct, and unsymbolic way of synthesizing information generated endogenously by the vestibular system in D (REM) sleep" (p. 1339). The major drawback of these physiological explanations is that they did not explicitly explain why only some dreams incorporate flying while others (the vast majority) do not. Assumptions about intensity of internal stimuli, attention processes, or disposition are vaguely formulated and indicate that other factors may be playing an important role in the occurrence of flying dreams.

Freud (1987) suggested that flying dreams are remembrances of childhood memories; of games of being thrown in the air or rocking, things that almost all children enjoy very much. Whereas several authors interpreted the positive emotions often experienced in flying dreams as, for example, overcoming life difficulties, will to dominate, and expressing release and freedom, other authors associate inferior coping styles to the occurrence of flying dreams, for example, avoiding problems or impotency—flying as a metaphor that the dreamer is doing something with pleasure that is not possible in waking life (Schredl, 2008).

Empirical studies on the correlates of flying dreams are scarce. The continuity hypothesis would predict that persons with a lot of flying experiences during the day would dream more often about it. This was confirmed by an observation reported by Van de Castle (1994) who interviewed hang-glider instructors. They told him they dreamed frequently of flying without needing their hang glider. Unfortunately, larger surveys, including persons with frequent air travels (pilots, flight attendants, business people, etc.), have not yet been carried out. Brink (1979) reported that the occurrence of flying dreams was higher in creative persons, left-handers, and persons with an internal locus of control. The occurrence of flying dreams in a student sample ($N = 444$) was related to low neuroticism, openness to experience, boundary thinness, dream-recall frequency, and playing an instrument (Schredl, 2008).

To summarize, the findings in this area indicate that psychological factors play a role in the explanation of flying dreams. This does not completely rule out any of the physiological theories. The traits associated with flying dreams positively support the continuity hypothesis at the level of emotions. Future studies should measure the current frequency of flying dreams and correlate this variable with the dreamer's current emotional state in waking life.

Michael Schredl

References

Barrett, D. (1991). Flying dreams and lucidity: An empirical study of their relationship. *Dreaming, 1,* 129–134.

Brink, T. L. (1979). Flying dreams: The relationship to creativenss, handedness and locus of control factors. *Journal of Altered States of Consciousness, 5,* 153–157.

Freud, S. (1987). *Die Traumdeutung [The Interpretation of Dreams] (1900).* Frankfurt: Fischer Taschenbuch.

Hobson, J. A., & McCarley, R. W. (1977). The brain as a dream state generator: An activation-synthesis hypothesis of the dream process. *Americal Journal of Psychiatry, 134,* 1335–1348.

Nielsen, T. A., Zadra, A. L., Simard, V., Saucier, S., Stenstrom, P., Smith, C., & Kuikn, D. (2003). The typical dreams of Canadian university students. *Dreaming, 13,* 211–235.

Schönhammer, R. (2004). *Fliegen, Fallen, Flüchten: Psychologie intensiver Träume.* Tübingen: dgvt.

Schredl, M. (2008). Personality correlates of flying dreams. *Imagination, Cognition and Personality, 27,* 129–137.

Schredl, M., Ciric, P., Götz, S., & Wittmann, L. (2004). Typical dreams: Stability and gender differences. *Journal of Psychology and Christianity, 138,* 485–494.

Schredl, M., & Piel, E. (2007). Prevalence of flying dreams. *Perceptual and Motor Skills, 105,* 657–660.

Van de Castle, R. L. (1994). *Our dreaming mind.* New York: Ballantine.

Flying in Dreams: The Power of the Image

Air-Robics: The Phenomenon of Dream Flying

If, as they say, "ontogeny recapitulates phylogeny," consider this: In our primal development we all have the residual tail, gills, and wings, as well as other as yet unknown possibilities and talents, of the creatures that live in air and water. If that is so, then it is no wonder we are able to fly and breathe under water in our dreams without instructions or hesitation. We just do it like the little bird when it is ready to fledge and the little fish when it emerges from the sack.

For many years I have been collecting flying dreams. As I travel in airplanes I ask "how do you fly?" I am amazed to discover there are hundreds of flying styles, positions, conditions, and tools that help people get off the ground in their sleep. Some flyers said they can only get a few inches off the ground, but nonetheless high enough to avoid an obstacle or a threatening enemy. Some flyers who had medical operations found their body hovering above the operating table. But I have gathered an amazing collection of flying styles, and I will share them here in the hopes that my readers will enjoy some new adventures.

Styles of flying include flapping, soaring, sitting, lying, swimming, flopping, breast stroking, dolphin kicking, whale tail snapping, and yoga levitation.

Assisted flying, also called method flying, is using guide ropes to get started or taking giant strides for takeoffs. Some dreamers use sticks, magic wands, bed riding, carpet cruising, floor grabbing, back packing, and—the most original—a blood-pressure cuff and the man who flew on his refrigerator. A craft teacher I knew said in one of his dreams he invented a dream-dousing rod. By holding two cross sticks together, he found he could steer through space as though on a bicycle.

Altitude flying and barn storming seemed like a macho style. One dreamer said he could do fancy twists and turns and plunge straight toward the earth; in the nick of time he would pull out of the dead fall and he enjoyed showing his expertise as he heard the audience clapping.

Recurring Flying Nightmares

One pilot came to me for dreamwork on his recurring dream of not being able to get off the ground. After talking to the images he found that his plane was too heavy, the runway too short, and the plane too crowded. If he did not do something about his load, he was headed for the ground.

Telephone wire flying: This dreamer says she flies but never above the telephone wires because she likes to stay in contact. My oldest son said when he was little he would dream he was hovering above our heads in earshot but out of sight.

Flying at building height over populated areas was a common style because it feels safer knowing you can land on rooftops,

and old-fashioned *chicken flapping,* which uses your elbows like chicken wings, is popular but does not get you much higher than the branches of trees.

Fish tail flopping in air sounds awkward and *bottom bumping* might get you somewhere but what do you bump, the clouds?

Intention Flying and Guided Imaging

This is helpful for those dreamers who are *losing power,* and when it happens in mid-air it is so fast you have to wake up before you hit the ground. It usually means you have unfinished business. But there is also *flying in the body of others.* Since you have seen my story of the borrowed therapist, you know I recommend borrowing a helper because it works. Borrow someone else's body who does a lot of dream flying, and imagine you have permission to use his method, or you can *tandem fly* by strapping yourself to his back like the sky jumpers. I have stories of dreamers who fly on air currents like gliders. *Channel flying* they say is like hang gliding: "climb the hill where the winds are strong, wait for the right current to lift you off the ground, it is easy."

My physicist friend says he can fly weightless by sucking in his gravity sensor. That allows him to rise into outer space without any restraints. Some of these weightless dreamers know how to leave their bodies and let their spirit soar in the atmosphere like the yogis who levitate.

There are people who fly to see and those who fly to feel. Some flyers go somewhere and others like to go nowhere. In one of my dreams I found myself happily sitting

flapping

jet-propulsion

magic wand

ecstatic orgasmic

free-body flying

Flying Styles

Dream Flying styles are numerous and very inventive.

The Greeks and ancient cultures knew all about dream flying.

Beginners use bird flapping. Kids like Jet propulsion.

Spiritualists use Magic wands that make soft landings

Free-body flying just needs unencumbered brain work.

Blood pressure pumping is a modern adaptation.

Orgasmic ecstasy is very individualistic.

Many dreamers create machines, sails, atomic devices.

One dreamer found he could fly on top of his refrigerator.

blood pressure pumping

(Ann Sayre Wiseman)

on the window sill of a 10-story apartment house overlooking Central Park for no reason I could find. (But that was before I learned to work on my dreams.)

Umbrella and balloon flying does not work unless you are Mary Poppins or know how to get your mind to leave the body; in that case gurus in India call it transcendence.

While working with kids on my children's nightmare book, I found that children of the space age fly to the planets, walk in space, and some get lost in broken spaceships terrified that they will never return to earth. Emergency flying is usually propelled by the fight or flight method. My neighbor, the physicist, said he could ball-up and shoot through the astral-dome into the black hole to look around.

Emergency flying: One woman from the Midwest said she flew East in time to say goodbye to her father before he died that morning.

Some dreamers tell of floating through walls and floating down stairs head first with arms in back. One man realized he had no arms at all.

When you find yourself flying upside-down, said a woman from New Hampshire, it is important *to fly high* so you will not bump into the unseen things. She says, "risk it naked, it is delicious to just let go."

A young San Francisco dreamworker reported to the Association for the Study of Dreams that she is an expert at *orgasmic cartwheeling*. And the art of ecstatic orgasmic aerobatics. She says *tandem flying* shares the responsibility of landing on your feet. She has invented a dream pill and can teach her Olympic routine to curious customers.

Ann Sayre Wiseman

References

Wiseman, A. S. (1989). *Nightmare help: A guide for parents and teachers*. Berkeley, CA: Tricycle Press.

Wiseman, A. S. (1995). Linda's flying talk. *ASD Newsletter, 12*, 10.

Fornari, Franco

Franco Fornari (1921–1985), psychiatrist and psychoanalyst, was president of the *Italian Psychoanalytic Society* and head of the Department of Psychology at the Faculty of Philosophy and Letters of the University of Milan. Fornari studied early affective development, informed by the theory of Melanie Klein. Fornari was one of the first to introduce the subject to Italy. He was particularly interested in the application of psychoanalytic theories to social relationships and culture, believing that psychoanalysis may help resolve interpersonal, institutional, and social conflicts.

In his book *The Psychoanalysis of War* (1974), Fornari applied a psychoanalytic reading to ideological conflicts underpinning wars, seen as externalizations of intrapsychic mechanisms. In other works he proposed a psychoanalytic interpretation of literary or philosophical texts, or reports of institutional exchanges taking place in daily life, such as teachers' and parents' meetings at school.

In his theory of dreams, Fornari reinterpreted the Freudian theory by underlining the function of symbolism. In the author's view, the unconscious discovered by Freud may be seen as a capacity for affective symbolization, an unconscious way of thinking, distinguishing good from bad rather than true from false, as in cognitive symbolization. Such a capacity for symbolization expresses itself in a language for effects, where the elementary unit, similar to phoneme in language, may be called coinema (from *coiné*, the common language spoken by the Greeks). Such a language is regulated by affective codes, unconscious rules prescribing what is right and what is wrong, as functional or dysfunctional to the survival of the individual and the species.

In Fornari's view, dreams are direct manifestations of affective symbolization, and dream symbolism is the expression of a primary functioning of the mind, which may occur unconsciously. Affective thought is dominant in dreams, but it can always be found, even if in a subordinate position, in daily representations. For instance, in cognitive symbolization a house is a building (i.e., a cognitive category); in terms of affective symbolization it may represent a shelter or on the contrary, a prison (i.e., affective categories, carrying the perceived relationship of the subject with the object). The bizarre nature of dreams is not caused by censure, as in Freud's view, but by the prevailing affective categories over the cognitive ones, by prevailing affective logic on cognitive logic.

Fornari exposed his general theory in *I fondamenti di una teoria psicoanalitica del linguaggio* (1979) (Fundamentals of a psychoanalytic theory for language), and studied the interpretation of dreams in *Il codice vivente* (1981) (The living code). In the latter, a number of dreams experienced by pregnant women were symbolically analyzed, with no reference to associations from the dreamers' side. In the interpretation of dreams the author did not try, as Freud did, to trace an unconscious desire in the present or past, in conflict with a more or less unconscious prohibition or fear. The conflict lays between contrasting values systems, representing different parts of the self (called affective roles, such as father, mother, child, male, female, sibling). In the case of the pregnant women the dream's instigator is the rising maternal affective role, finding itself in conflict with other parts of the self, such as the role of the female or child.

Fornari's views about dreams are in line with recent psychoanalytic theories of the self (Fosshage, 1997), valuing the manifest content of dreams and ascribing to dream life a function in the development of the psychological organization: the dream provides schemes guiding the individual, as organizers of developmental tasks. In contrast to the views of other psychoanalysts, Fornari proposed that dreams may be seen as bottom-up, that is, created by presubjective, unconscious, and philogenetically determined structures, and that they could therefore be interpreted symbolically, without the need to use free associations relating to daily life.

In Italy, Fornari collaborated with Sergio Molinari, who proposed with Foulkes the tonic-phasic model of REM dream (Molinari & Foulkes, 1969). The emphasis on the symbolic in the manifest content of dreams informs a revisiting of typical dreams as a direct expression of affective categories (Maggiolini, Cagnin, Crippa, Persico, & Rizzi, 2010).

Alfio Maggiolini

See also: entries related to History of Dreams/Sleep

References

Fornari, F. (1975). *The psychoanalysis of war*. Bloomington: Indiana University Press. (Original work published 1970)

Fornari, F. (1979). *I fondamenti di una teoria psicoanalitica del linguaggio* [Fundamentals of a psychoanalytic theory for language]. Torino: Boringhieri.

Fornari, F. (1981). *Il codice vivente* [The living code]. Torino: Boringhieri.

Fosshage, J. (1997). The organizing functions of dream mentation. *Contemporary Psychoanalysis, 33,* 429–458.

Maggiolini, A., Cagnin, C., Crippa, F., Persico, A., & Rizzi, P. (2010). Content analysis of dreams and waking narratives. *Dreaming, 20*(1), 60–76.

Molinari, S., & Foulkes, D. (1969). Tonic and phasic events during sleep: Psychological correlates and implications. *Perceptual and Motor Skills, 29,* 343–368.

Freud, Sigmund

The dream theory of Sigmund Freud (1900) is so well known that it is at risk of being read on autopilot, if at all. Part of the problem is that psychoanalytic ideas have become so clichéd they no longer refer to anything beyond themselves. If Freud's views on dreams could be restated without recourse to psychoanalytic jargon, however, they would go something like this.

When you fall asleep, some parts of your mind are more asleep than others. Only the part of your mind that represents the outside world (and generates your everyday experiences) properly falls asleep. Another part of your mind, which represents the internal processes of your body (and reflects its biological needs) never sleeps. This is because some of the processes of the body can never be switched off; they are necessary to keep you alive.

The most basic task of the mind is to meet our needs in the outside world. But this is easier said than done; biological needs are compulsive and the external environment is indifferent to your individual needs. Sometimes it is even hostile toward us. As a result, the waking mind must contend with competing demands; the urgent needs of the body on the one hand and the frustrating constraints of reality on the other.

Fortunately, the mind has inbuilt procedures for satisfying our vital needs. We do not have to reinvent solutions to the most pressing problems of life. These inbuilt solutions are called instincts. For example, when you are hungry or thirsty, you search for food or drink. This is called foraging. We do not wait for someone to teach us to forage; we do it automatically. The same applies to reproductive needs. (If we waited for someone to teach us to do such things, we might wait until we die. Then we cannot reproduce. Thereby, inborn inclinations that meet appetitive needs are selected into the gene pool and those that do not are culled.)

Although instincts operate automatically, we can usually inhibit them . . . up to a point. All biological needs must *eventually* be assuaged; but we humans are particularly good at inhibiting instinctual responses to our needs. For this reason we are also especially adept at being able to think up novel and flexible solutions to life's problems in unpredictable and changing environments.

The part of the mind that represents the outside world is also the part that inhibits the instincts. This is the part that switches off when we fall asleep. The instincts are therefore released from inhibition during sleep, and the balance between automatic biological processes and the constraints of reality (which guide our wakeful thinking) now shifts in favor of the automatic processes. That is why we dream.

Dreaming begins when instincts are triggered during sleep. As stated, in wakefulness our instinctual urges are not simply acted on; they are replaced by goal-directed thinking and problem-solving behaviors. But this cannot happen during sleep because the reality-oriented, problem-solving part of the mind is switched off. The demands of the instincts therefore persist and eventually press for gratification. This threatens to wake us up. So, we *dream*. *Dreams are imaginary gratifications of our instincts*. This temporarily fends our needs and wants off until the morning, so that we can sleep. This is the essence of Freud's theory.

Why, then, do we not always dream of gratifying basic needs? And why do we have nightmares? Freud's answer was that although children's dreams are simple fulfillments of their needs and wants (see Colace, 2010), once social prohibitions are internalized through development, the gratification of instincts during sleep provokes anxiety. For this reason, we either wake up or we must somehow camouflage the gratifications in our dreams; we must make them acceptable. In other words we now either dream of things that only indirectly gratify our basic wishes, or we suffer nightmares and wake up. Nightmares are unsuccessful dreams, or unsuccessful attempts to camouflage instinctual

gratifications. That is why the meaning of our dreams is not transparent.

To discover the hidden meaning of your dreams, Freud recommended the following procedure. Allow your mind to wander in relation to each element of the dream, and take note of everything that occurs to you. Take care not to dismiss any line of thought, even if it seems silly or irrelevant. It is especially important not to suppress embarrassing or upsetting thoughts. (The waking mind is prone to do these things, for the reasons already explained.) To the extent that you allow yourself to do this freely, to that extent the meaning of the dream will be revealed.

Mark Solms

See also: entries related to History of Dreams/Sleep

References

Colace, C. (2010). *Children's dreams: From Freud's observations to modern dream research*. London: Karnac.

Freud, S. (1900). *The interpretation of dreams.* In J. Strachey (Ed.), *The standard edition of the complete psychological works of Sigmund Freud* (Vols. 4 & 5). London: Hogarth.

Freud's Approach to Dreams

Sigmund Freud (1856–1939) considered *The Interpretation of Dreams,* originally published in 1899–1900, to be his greatest scholarly contribution. It is surely his most famous and seminal work. The first sentence announced his intention to prove "that there is a psychological technique which makes it possible to interpret dreams, and that, if that procedure is employed, every dream reveals itself as a psychical structure which has a meaning and which can be inserted at an assignable point in the mental activities of waking life" (Freud, 1953a, p. 1). Freud illustrated his general claim with almost 200 dream examples, including, remarkably, 50 of his own. These served to show that dreams are the "royal road to a knowledge of the unconscious activities of the mind" (Freud, 1953a, p. 608). This famous quotation was based on his self-analysis, which he had begun after his father died in 1896, and particularly on the interpretation of his own dreams by the technique of free association. His fundamental supposition that even irrational and inconsistent dreams have meaning and enable insight into unconscious processes proved well-founded, as did his belief in psychic determinism.

On the morning of July 24, 1895, Freud had had a dream about one of his patients, which he wrote down immediately upon awakening. On the strength of his detailed, careful, and remarkably coherent analysis by free association to its various elements, Freud's dream about Irma's injection became the initial spark of psychoanalysis as a specific method of depth psychology. Through dream analysis Freud discovered his own feelings of guilt toward Irma, his need to justify his therapeutic failure, and how he disburdened himself in his dream by blaming a colleague of improper medical treatment due to an infected injection. Remarkably, it was Freud's insight into the meaning of his own dream that fundamentally shaped his *Interpretation of Dreams*. He summed up his groundbreaking discovery in the following words: "The dreams 'content was the fulfillment of a wish and its motive was a wish'." (Freud, 1953a, Vol. 4, p. 119). More specifically: "A dream is a (disguised) fulfillment of a (suppressed or repressed) wish" (Freud, 1953a, p. 160).

Freud differentiated between the manifest (surface level, conscious) and the latent (unconscious) content of a dream. The latent dream content consists of dynamic unconscious wishes, latent dream thoughts, and body sensations. Latent dream thoughts are connected to daytime activities and are therefore also called residues of the day. The psychic operation that turns the latent dream content into the manifest dream is called dreamwork. It eschews dream censorship and rests on a set of mechanisms and processes such as condensation, displacement, dramatization (or representation), and secondary elaboration (or revision). By the work of interpretation it is possible to remove the disguise caused by the mechanisms of repression to cancel the distortion of the dream content due to the psychic process of censorship, and to reverse the transformation into the dream. The free associations, consisting of ideas, feelings, recollections, bodily reactions, etc., point to unsettling wishes and upsetting fantasies.

Freud demystified dreams. Although he later modified his central claim (see Marinelli & Mayer, 2003) and accepted, for example, the existence of dreams that do not fulfill a wish, it remained his deep, lifelong conviction that interpreting dreams is the most efficient method to obtain insight into the processes of unconscious psychical life. In the third of his series of *Five Lectures on Psycho-Analysis,* which he delivered at Clark University, in Worcester, Massachusetts, in 1909, Freud declared: "it is the most secure foundation of psychoanalysis and the field in which every worker must acquire his convictions and seek his training. If I am asked how one can become a psychoanalyst, I reply: 'By studying one's own dreams'." (Freud, 1957, p. 33)

Isabelle Noth

See also: entries related to History of Dreams/Sleep

References

Freud, S. (1953a). The interpretation of dreams. In J. Strachey (Ed. and Trans.), *The standard edition of the complete psychological works of Sigmund Freud* (Vols. 4 & 5). London: Hogarth Press. (Originally published in 1900)

Freud, S. (1953b). On dreams. In J. Strachey (Ed. and Trans.), *The standard edition of the complete psychological works of Sigmund Freud* (Vol. 5, pp. 629–686). London: Hogarth Press. (Originally published in 1901)

Freud, S. (1957). Five lectures on psychoanalysis. In J. Strachey (Ed. and Trans.), *The standard edition of the complete psychological works of Sigmund Freud* (Vol. 11, pp. 1–56). London: Hogarth Press. (Originally published in 1910)

Marinelli, L., & Mayer, A. (2003). *Dreaming by the book: Freud's the interpretation of dreams and the history of the psychoanalytic movement* (Trans. Susan Fairfield). New York: Other Press.

Functional Neuroimaging during Human Sleep

Whereas during wakefulness, brain function is mainly driven by cognitive processes, regional brain activity during sleep is primarily organized by spontaneous sleep processes. In humans, functional neuroimaging techniques provide unique opportunities to characterize regional brain function during sleep.

During nonrapid eye movement (NREM) sleep, all markers of cerebral metabolism and hemodynamics (cerebral glucose utilization [Maquet et al., 1990, 1992] and cerebral blood flow [Braun et al., 1997; Kajimura et al., 1999] measured by positron emission tomography [PET]), cerebral oxygen metabolic rates measured by the Kety–Schmidt technique (Madsen et al., 1991b) are significantly decreased relative to wakefulness. However, capitalizing on the better temporal and spatial resolution of simultaneous electroencephalographic (EEG) and functional magnetic resonance imaging (fMRI) recordings, transient surges in regional activity can be detected in synchrony with phasic events such as spindles and slow waves.

Spindles are associated with transient activity in the thalami, paralimbic areas (anterior cingulate and insular cortices), and superior temporal gyri (Schabus et al., 2007). Multichannel EEG recordings and source-reconstruction methods showed that two types of spindles exist that differ in their functions, for example, in memory processing (Schabus, 2009), and in their topography (Schabus et al., 2007). During slow spindles (centered around 12 Hz), activity increases, particularly in the superior frontal gyrus, whereas fast spindles (centered around 14 Hz) are more prominent at parietal and mesofrontal regions, involved in sensorimotor processing, and the hippocampus, involved in memory processing. This result corresponds with the influence of fast spindles on procedural and declarative memory consolidation during sleep (Schabus, 2009).

Slow waves are associated with an activity increase in frontal regions, precuneus, and posterior cingulate cortex (Dang-Vu et al., 2008). The largest waves (>140 ?V) are associated with significant activity in the parahippocampal gyrus, cerebellum, and brainstem, whereas delta waves (75–140 ?V) are related to frontal responses (Dang-Vu et al., 2008). Source reconstruction of scalp high-density EEG recordings confirmed these findings (Murphy et al., 2009).

During rapid eye movement (REM) sleep, regional cerebral blood flow is increased in the mesopontine tegmentum and thalamic nuclei (Braun et al., 1997; Maquet et al., 1996; Nofzinger, Mintun, Wiseman, Kupfer, & Moore, 1997), in keeping with the mechanisms of REM sleep generation in animals (Steriade & McCarley, 2005). Moreover, the distribution of cerebral activity in REM sleep is usually assumed to correlate with the main characteristics of dreaming activity (Maquet & Franck, 1997; Maquet et al., 1996, 2000).

In the forebrain, REM sleep is characterized by high activity levels in limbic and paralimbic areas (amygdala, hippocampus, anterior cingulate, orbitofrontal, and insular cortices) (Braun et al., 1997; Maquet, 2000; Maquet & Franck, 1997; Maquet et al., 1996; Nofzinger et al., 1997), which

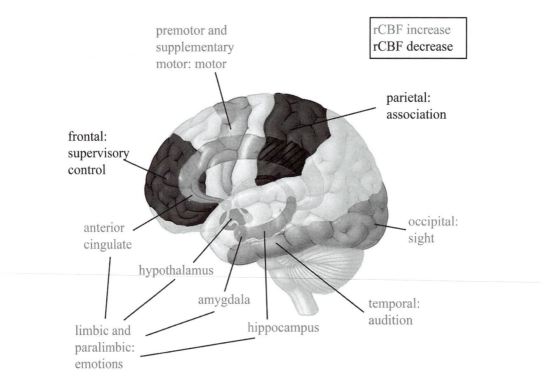

A schematic view of the regional distribution of brain activity during REM sleep in humans. (Based on reference Kussé et al. [2010]). (Caroline Kussé)

could be related to the high emotional load of dreams. Their strong perceptual character, essentially visual and auditory, might rely on the high activity on occipital and temporal cortices (Braun et al., 1997), although this result is less systematically reported (Maquet et al., 1996). Finally, motor and premotor cortices are also shown to be very active, which might account for motor behaviors during dreams (Maquet et al., 2000). These activations contrast with the relative quiescence of the associative cortices (inferior and middle frontal gyrus as well as the posterior part of the inferior parietal lobule) during REM sleep, as compared to wakefulness (Braun et al., 1997; Kajimura et al., 1999; Maquet et al., 1996). The hypoactivity of the prefrontal areas might explain other formal characteristics of dreams, such as lack of insight, temporal distortions, bizarreness (Madsen et al., 1991a), weakening of self-reflective control, and amnesia on awakening (Hobson, Pace-Schott, Stickgold, & Kahn, 1998). On the other hand, the activation of mesio-temporal areas would account for the memory content commonly found in dreams (Maquet et al., 2000).

Functional connectivity is also modified during human REM sleep. While the functional relationship between striate and extrastriate cortices is excitatory during wakefulness, it is shown inverted during REM sleep (Braun et al., 1998). Likewise, the functional relationship between the amygdala and temporal and occipital cortices is different during REM sleep as opposed to wakefulness or NREM sleep (Maquet & Phillips, 1998). The neural mechanisms underpinning this pattern of brain activity remain unclear, although they are usually attributed to specific changes in neuromodulation (Steriade & McCarley, 2005) or specific neural activities during REM sleep such as ponto–geniculo–occipital waves (so called because they are most easily recorded in the pons, lateral geniculate bodies, and occipital cortex of animals [Datta, 1997]). Several observations suggest the existence of similar waves in man as brain activity associated with bursts of saccades shows a peculiar distribution. EEG (Lim et al., 2007), magnetoencephalography (Ioannides et al., 2004), PET (Peigneux et al., 2001), and fMRI (Miyauchi, Misaki, Kan, Fukunaga, & Koike, 2009) experiments showed that activity in the right geniculate body and the primary occipital cortex increases proportionally to the density of eye movements to a larger extent during REM sleep than during wakefulness. Moreover, activity in the bilateral pons precedes REM saccades (Ioannides et al., 2004).

Finally, it was shown that regional brain activity during sleep could be modified by previous experience, suggesting that sleep is involved in memory processing (Maquet et al., 2000; Peigneux et al., 2004).

Caroline Kussé and
Pierre Maquet

See also: entries related to Sleep Assessment

References

Braun, A.R., Balkin, T.J., Wesenten, N.J., Carson, R.E., Varga, M., Baldwin, P., . . . Herscovitch, P. (1997). Regional cerebral blood flow throughout the sleep-wake cycle: An H2(15)O PET study. *Brain, 120*(Pt 7), 1173–1197.

Braun, A. R., Balkin, T. J., Wesensten, N. J., Gwadry, F., Carson, R. E., Varga, M., . . . Herscovitch, P. (1998). Dissociated pattern of activity in visual cortices and their projections during human rapid eye movement sleep. *Science, 279*(5347), 91–95.

Dang-Vu, T. T., Schabus, M., Desseilles, M., Albouy, G., Boly, M., Darsaud, A., . . . Maquet, P. (2008). Spontaneous neural activity during human slow wave sleep. *Proceedings of the National Academy of Sciences, 105*(39), 15160–15165.

Datta, S. (1997). Cellular basis of pontine ponto-geniculo-occipital wave generation and modulation. *Cellular and Molecular Neurobiology, 17*(3), 341–365.

Hobson, J. A., Pace-Schott, E. F., Stickgold, R., & Kahn, D. (1998). To dream or not to dream? Relevant data from new neuroimaging and electrophysiological studies. *Current Opinion in Neurobiology, 8*(2), 239–244.

Ioannides, A. A., Corsi-Cabrera, M., Fenwick, P. B., del Rio Portilla, Y., Laskaris, N. A., Khurshudyan, A., . . . Kostopoulos, G. K. (2004). MEG tomography of human cortex and brainstem activity in waking and REM sleep saccades. *Cerebral Cortex, 14*(1), 56–72.

Kajimura, N., Uchiyama, M., Takayama, Y., Uchida, S., Uema, T., Kato, M., . . . Takahashi, K. (1999). Activity of midbrain reticular formation and neocortex during the progression of human non-rapid eye movement sleep. *Journal of Neuroscience, 19*(22), 10065–10073.

Kussé, C., Muto, V., Mascetti, L., Matarazzo, L., Foret, A., Bourdiec, A. S., & Maquet, P. (2010). Neuroimaging of dreaming: State of the art and limitations. *International Review of Neurobioly, 92*, 87–99.

Lim, A. S., Lozano, A. M., Moro, E., Hamani, C., Hutchison, W. D., Dostrovsky, J. O., . . . Murray, B. J. (2007). Characterization of REM-sleep associated ponto-geniculo-occipital waves in the human pons. *Sleep, 30*(7), 823–827.

Madsen, P. L., Holm, S., Vorstrup, S., Friberg, L., Lassen, N. A., & Wildschiodtz, G. (1991a). Human regional cerebral blood flow during rapid-eye-movement sleep. Journal of Cerebral Blood Flow & Metabolism, 11(3), 502–507.

Madsen, P. L., Schmidt, J. F. Holm, S., Vorstrup, S., Lassen, N. A., & Wildschiodtz, G. (1991b). Cerebral oxygen metabolism and cerebral blood flow in man during light sleep (stage 2). *Brain Research, 557*(1–2), 217–220.

Maquet, P. (2000). Functional neuroimaging of normal human sleep by positron emission tomography. *Journal of Sleep Research, 9*(3), 207–231.

Maquet, P., Dive, D., Salmon, E., Sadzot, B., Franco, G., Poirrier, R., . . . Franck, G. (1990). Cerebral glucose utilization during sleep-wake cycle in man determined by positron emission tomography and [18F]2-fluoro-2-deoxy-D-glucose method. *Brain Research, 513*(1), 136–143.

Maquet, P., Dive, D., Salmon, E., Sadzot, B., Franco, G., Poirrier, R., & Franck, G. (1992). Cerebral glucose utilization during stage 2 sleep in man. Brain Research, 571(1), 149–153.

Maquet, P., & Franck, G. (1997). REM sleep and amygdala. *Molecular Psychiatry, 2*(3), 195–196.

Maquet, P., Laureys, S., Peigneux, P., Fuchs, S., Petiau, C., Phillips, C., . . . Cleeremans, A. (2000). Experience-dependent changes in cerebral activation during human REM sleep. *Nature Neuroscience, 3*(8), 831–836.

Maquet, P., Peters, J., Aerts, J., Delfiore, G., Degueldre, C., Luxen, A., & Franck, G. (1996). Functional neuroanatomy of human rapid-eye-movement sleep and dreaming. *Nature, 383*(6596), 163–166.

Maquet, P., & Phillips, C. (1998). Functional brain imaging of human sleep. *Journal of Sleep Research, 7*(Suppl. 1), 42–47.

Miyauchi, S., Misaki, M., Kan, S., Fukunaga, T., & Koike, T. (2009). Human brain activity time-locked to rapid eye movements during REM sleep. *Experimental Brain Research, 192*(4), 657–667.

Murphy, M., Riedner, B. A., Huber, R., Massimini, M., Ferrarelli, F., & Tononi, G. (2009). Source modeling sleep slow waves. *Proceedings of the National Academy of Sciences, 106*(5), 1608–1613.

Nofzinger, E. A., Mintun, M. A., Wiseman, M., Kupfer, D. J., & Moore, R. Y. (1997). Forebrain activation in REM sleep: An FDG PET study. *Brain Research, 770*(1–2), 192–201.

Peigneux, P., Laureys, S., Fuchs, S., Collette, F., Perrin, F., Reggers, J., . . . Maquet, P. (2004). Are spatial memories strengthened in the human hippocampus during slow wave sleep? *Neuron, 44*(3), 535–545.

Peigneux, P., Laureys, S., Fuchs, S., Delbeuck, X., Degueldre, C., Aerts, J., . . . Maquet, P. (2001). Generation of rapid eye movements during paradoxical sleep in humans. *Neuroimage, 14*(3), 701–708.

Schabus, M. (2009). Still missing some significant ingredients. *Sleep, 32*(3), 291–293.

Schabus, M., Dang-Vu, T. T., Albouy, G., Balteau, E., Boly, M., Carrier, J., . . . Maquet, P. (2007). Hemodynamic cerebral correlates of sleep spindles during human non-rapid eye movement sleep. *Proceedings of the National Academy of Sciences, 104*(32), 13164–13169.

Steriade, M., & McCarley, R. W. (2005). *Brain control of wakefulness and sleep*. New York: Kluwer Academic.

Functional Theories of Dreaming

Why do we dream? To say that we dream because the brain is activated in sleep is satisfying from a mechanistic point of view but this answer begs the functional question (see the entry "Activation–Synthesis Hypothesis of Dreaming"). Physiology aside, is there some psychological benefit to having the subjective experience of dreaming with or without the awareness of such experience in waking? This is a hotly debated question. I will attempt to summarize the evidence for and against dream function. I will conclude that the question is ill-posed for philosophical reasons. Furthermore, I will argue that abundant evidence suggests that the subjective experience of dreaming itself may well be an epiphenomenon and not, per se, useful to human survival. It may well be necessary to have REM and it may be probable that REM is associated with dreaming, but awareness and recollection of our dreams may not only be unnecessary but actually quite counterproductive.

Philosophical Issues

When I say that the question, "does dreaming have a function?" is ill-posed, I mean to emphasize that the scientific distinction between brain and mind is still not rigorously observed when the question is raised. The tendency to identify (not just correlate) REM sleep with dreaming has been present ever since Eugene Aserinsky and Nathaniel Kleitman (1953) first described the correlation between the brain state, REM, and the mind state, dreaming. Thus W. C. Dement (1960), wishing to test Freud's hypothesis that dreaming was an escape valve for the mind, reported their findings on the psychologically deleterious effects of REM-sleep deprivation in an article entitled "The Effect of Dream Deprivation" and published it in no less distinguished a journal than *Science*. But their results, which Kohler et al. (1969) and his group later showed were nonspecific, did not measure dreaming at all! Dement assumed, erroneously that REM sleep and dreaming were identical.

It is as devilishly difficult, it would appear, to avoid Cartesian dualism as it is to resist the blandishments of Sigmund Freud! Yet that is precisely what we must do if we are to pose the dream-function question clearly. Experimental evidence bearing on the question demands a clear distinction between brain events (e.g., REM sleep) and mind events (e.g., dreaming). To be rigorous we might even insist on a complete dissociation of the two domains, a thought experiment which I, for one, find difficult even to imagine.

Critique of Evidence in Favor of Dream Function

So convinced are we that dreaming must have a function, we succumb to unconvincing arguments. Thus whether we are considering couples undergoing divorce (Cartwright, 1996), athletes preparing for gymnastic or diving competition (Schredl & Erlacher, 2008), or geniuses solving scientific conundrums (Barrett, 2007), we are tempted to believe that it is the dreaming per se that confers one or another benefit, whereas the subjective experience of dreaming may be an epiphenomenon of REM.

Although it is difficult to conceive of a dream occurring with no brain substrate, it is important to admit that dreaming may simply be a cognitive noise that the brain makes when it is engaged in important housekeeping tasks (such as the

thermoregulation that is a prime function of REM) or even the reorganization of memory, which is tied to REM by thin but convincing threads of evidence.

The spectacular anecdotes of earth-shaking scientific insights (such as Friedrich Kekule's dream-inspired image of the benzene ring, or Otto Loewi's dream of the crossed-heart perfusion experiment that won him a Nobel Prize for the discovery of chemical neurotransmission) are clearly little more than just-so stories. Kekule was dozing on a streetcar and Loewi was about to have his scientific insight while wide awake. Most scientific insights probably occur in waking but we are never told about them. The truth is that we all want to believe that dreaming is more than a little bit revelatory.

Throughout human history dreaming—probably because of its bizarreness—has been regarded as prophetic, a tradition most recently instantiated by Freud, who declared that dreaming was the "royal road to the unconscious." What unconscious? The motivational unconscious! One hundred and ten years after the *Interpretation of Dreams* was published, this theory remains unproven and is now rightly considered scientifically dubious.

Evidence against the Dream-Function Hypothesis

Many people, among them famous scientists who I have known, deny having any dream recall whatsoever. Some of my psychologically well-adjusted friends are also persistently dream forgetters. Most people remember less than 5 percent of the dreams we suppose, with good scientific reason, they had. So, there is robust, admittedly anecdotal evidence for an almost total dissociation of mental health (on the one hand) and intellectual distinction (on the other) and dream recall. But most devastating to the dream-function hypothesis is the generally poor recall of dreaming, even in such good dream recallers as me. If dreaming—as subjective experience—is so important, why does nature go so far out of her way to hide it? To make work for the Freudians? I doubt it.

No, the evidence more strongly supports the idea that we are not supposed to remember our dreams! Sometimes we do remember them, and sometimes we may even learn something we did not otherwise know, but usually our dreams are merely fascinating talking points which I, for one, would only give up reluctantly (but that is a social consideration, not a scientific theory).

Many other eminent thinkers have arrived at a similar conclusion; David Hartley, the father of Associationism, said that, "We dream in order to forget," an idea famously echoed by the Nobel laureate Francis Crick. Neither of those scientific worthies observed the crucial REM sleep/dream distinction. Picking up that cudgel, philosopher Owen Flanagan has gone so far as to suggest that "Dreams are the spandrels of sleep." Beautiful? Yes, but functionally significant? No!

An Alternative Theory

If dream recall is not valuable, then how can we retain the commonsense view that dreaming is, somehow, important to cognition? I have recently suggested that dreaming is the subjective experience of brain activation in sleep and gone on to suggest that it is as psychologically meaningful as it is because REM sleeping/dreaming is a critical progenitor of waking consciousness. In REM we run test programs for the brain. Those test programs automatically instantiate a sense of self, of agency, of sensorimotor specificity in anticipation of the outside world, as well as to provide a template for associative memory. This virtual reality system equips the developing brain with a virtual reality predictor of the waking world in which we will behave, survive, and, hopefully, reproduce. Our dreams are good predictors and faithful reproducers of that world but only up to a point. The errors of omission and of commission that dreaming makes are a small price to pay for the flexibility and versatility of what they provide. We do not have to remember the information spun off as we run these developmental and brain-maintenance programs, we just have to remember to go to sleep!

J. Allan Hobson

See also: Activation–Synthesis Hypothesis of Dreaming

References

Aserinsky, E., & Kleitman, N. (1953). Regularly occurring periods of ocular motility and concomitant phenomena during sleep. *Science, 118,* 361–375.

Barrett, D.L. (2007). An evolutionary theory of dreams and problem-solving. In D.L. Barrett & P. McNamara (Eds.), *The new science of dreaming, Volume III: Cultural and theoretical perspectives on dreaming* (pp. 133–153). New York: Praeger/Greenwood.

Cartwright, R.D. (1996). Dreams and adaptation to divorce. In D. Barrett (Ed.), *Trauma and dreams* (pp. 179–185). Cambridge, MA: Harvard University Press.

Dement, W. C. (1960). The effect of dream deprivation. *Science, 131*(3415), 1705–1707.

Kollar, E. J., Pasnau, R. O., Rubin, R. T., Naitoh, P., Slater, G. G., & Kales, A. (1969). Psychological, psychophysiological, and biochemical correlates of prolonged sleep deprivation. *American Journal of Psychiatry, 126*(4), 488–497.

Schredl, M., & Erlacher, D. (2008). Relationship between waking sport activities, reading and dream content in sport and psychology students. *Journal of Psychology, 142,* 267–275.

G

Gender Differences in Dreaming

Gender differences have often been lively discussed in the public and in academic psychology alike. So it is not astonishing that quite a lot of dream studies focused on the differences between men and women regarding dream recall, attitude toward dreams, and dream content. A comprehensive meta-analysis (Schredl & Reinhard, 2008) showed consistent gender differences, with women tending to recall their dreams more often than men. However, this gender difference started to be evident only in children/adolescents older than 10 years, indicating that a gender-specific dream socialization might be the explanation and biological factors might not be of importance. This idea is supported by the finding that sex-role orientation (expressivity) is also related to dream-recall frequency in adults (Schredl, Lahl, & Göritz, 2010). The same pattern of gender differences can be found for nightmare frequency (Schredl & Reinhard, 2011). Marked gender differences have been also reported for the frequency of telling dreams, interest in dream interpretation, and positive attitude toward dreams (for an overview see Schredl, 2007).

Regarding dream content, the first large-scale content analytical study (Hall & Van de Castle, 1966) showed several typical gender differences. Women's dream

reports included more explicit mentioned emotions, household objects, and references to clothing, whereas men dreamed more often about sex and physical aggression. Interestingly, most of these differences had been confirmed by follow-up studies (Schredl, 2007). On the other hand, formal characteristics such as bizarreness, emotional tone, and intensity of dreams do not differ between the sexes (Schredl, 2007). A very robust finding is that men dream more often about men than women (67% male dream characters), whereas women dream equally often about men and women (48% male dream characters)—figures taken from Hall and Van de Castle (1966). Whereas some authors referred to Freud's Oedipus complex to explain this difference, Schredl and Jacob (1998) were able to show that the waking-life environment (amount of contact with women and men during the day) strongly affects the ratio of male and female characters within the dream. This study raised the question of how gender differences in dreaming are explained. According to the continuity hypothesis of dreaming, gender differences in waking life should be reflected in men's and women's dreams. Looking at the literature on gender differences in waking-life aggression and sexuality (especially frequency of masturbation and sexual fantasies), the reported and stable gender differences in dreams for these areas seem plausible (Schredl, 2007). An interesting gender difference in dream content concerns human aggressors in children's bad dreams, men (especially male strangers) are much more often dream aggressors than women. This might also be easily explained by the continuity hypothesis because most violent acts, crime, and warfare are carried out by men.

To summarize, dream research showed consistent gender differences for dream recall, nightmare frequency, dream content, and other dream variables such as dream telling. Research looking into factors explaining these differences are still scarce; for example, the differences in dream-recall frequency or nightmare frequency. It would be interesting to study whether girls and boys are socialized differently in regard to dreams; for example, encouraged to talk about dreams. Although the continuity hypothesis seems promising in explaining gender differences regarding dream recall, studies directly relating waking-life differences to typical dream differences are also still scarce. A recent study (Schredl, Desch, Röming, & Spachmann, 2009) showed, for example, that the frequency of sexual activities and sexual fantasies did not completely explain the gender difference in the frequency of erotic dreams.

Michael Schredl

References

Hall, C. S., & Van de Castle, R. L. (1966). *The content analysis of dreams.* New York: Appleton-Century-Crofts.

Schredl, M. (2007). Gender differences in dreaming. In D. Barrett & P. McNamara (Eds.), *The new science of dreaming— Volume 2: Content, recall, and personality correlates* (pp. 29–47). Westport, CT: Praeger.

Schredl, M. (2011). Gender differences in nightmare frequency: A meta-analysis. *Sleep Medicine Reviews, 15,* 115–121.

Schredl, M., Desch, S., Röming, F., & Spachmann, A. (2009). Erotic dreams and their relationship to waking-life sexuality. *Sexologies, 18,* 38–43.

Schredl, M., & Jacob, S. (1998). Ratio of male and female characters in a dream series. *Perceptual and Motor Skills, 86,* 198–200.

Schredl, M., Lahl, O., & Göritz, A. S. (2010). Gender, sex role orientation, and dream recall frequency. *Dreaming, 20,* 19–24.

Schredl, M., & Reinhard, I. (2008). Gender differences in dream recall: A meta-analysis. *Journal of Sleep Research, 17,* 125–131.

Genetics and Epigenetics of Sleep

Genes are hereditable entities that contribute to biologically complex phenomena of the organism. However, DNA information serves as chemical instructions to accomplish biological functions in a complex epigenetic environment. Sleep is one of such complex phenomena that are under genetic control, although it can be subjected to a number of additional biological and environmental factors. Indeed, the link between genotype and phenotype is not direct and the contribution that genetics exert on the quantity and quality of sleep is difficult to estimate. Pioneer investigations in humans proposed, in the 1930s and 1950s, that classical measures of sleep, such as the latency to fall asleep, the waking alpha rhythms, the duration of sleep, and the presence of paradoxical sleep were much better defined by genetic rather than environmental variables (Davis & Davis, 1936). Later on, in the 1970s, an extensive study in monozygotic (MZ) and dizygotic (DZ) twins concluded that the evidence for the heritability of sleep parameters was not so compelling (Gedda & Brenci, 1979). A number of studies followed since then and readdressed this issue. Overall, most literature agreed that genetics contribute between 40 and 50 percent to sleep. Although the quantification of the heritability in these cases is very difficult, mainly because of a considerable variation that characterizes the EEG spectrum across different individuals, the evidence remains strong across many studies that there is a much higher heritability for parameters such as alpha, delta, theta, and beta rhythms in MZ twins compared to DZ twins (Dauvilliers et al., 2004; De Gennaro et al., 2008; van Beijsterveldt, Molenaar, de Geus, & Boomsma, 1996).

The fundamental discovery, in 1992, that a prion disease caused by a mutation in *PRNP* (a gene that encodes for the major prion protein) leads to the fatal familial insomnia, FFI (Medori et al., 1992), demonstrated that a single gene modification can cause a sleep disorder. Following this discovery, both circadian and sleep abnormal phenotypes were confirmed in prion protein-deficient animal models. Since thalamic lesions seem to be pivotal in FFI, it is hypothesized that genetic factors acting on the thalamus may play a role in common insomnias (Taheri & Mignot, 2002).

Another important progress, in the field of sleep genetics, came from the discovery that a mutation in the gene encoding for hypocretin (orexin) receptors causes narcolepsy (Lin et al., 1999). Besides the question of the impact that a single gene might have on sleep, a considerable amount of evidence,

nowadays, leads to the claim that the physiology of sleep is controlled by genes.

The genetic components of sleep are of vast interest for treatment of sleep disorders such as narcolepsy, restless-leg syndrome (RLS), obstructive sleep apnea syndrome (OSAS), and insomnia. Furthermore, evidence in clinical genetics has highlighted, recently, that there is a strong relationship between sleep disorders concerning their genetics.

Narcolepsy is a complex disorder characterized by intrusive and irresistible episodes of sleep, cataplexy, hypnagogic hallucinations, and sleep paralysis. A series of loci and regions have been associated with susceptibility to narcolepsy; for example, *NRCLP1* (17q21), *NRCLP2* (4p13-q21), *NRCLP3* (21q11.2), *NLC1A*, and *MX2* (21q22.3).

RLS is characterized by a need to move the legs at time of rest, especially at night, and, as a consequence, by nocturnal insomnia and chronic sleep deprivation. This disorder is prevalent with aging and the genetic component is variable across studies, ranging between the 40 and 90 percent. Mapping studies in RLS families have revealed a considerable locus heterogeneity identifying loci such as *RLS1* (12q12-q21), *RLS2* (14q13-q31), *RLS3* (9p24-p22), *RLS4* (2q33) *RLS5* (20p13), and *RLS6* (6p21). A recent *RLS7* locus has pointed out a series of candidate genes such as *MUPP1, SLC1A1, KCNV2, MAOA, MAOB*, and *DMT1*.

The OSAS is characterized by a partial or complete repetitive collapse of the upper airways during sleep that causes snoring, sleep fragmentation, and other severe consequences on the general health of the patient. The prevalence of OSAS in the general population is approximately 5 percent for women and 7 percent for men. The apoliprotein E (*APOE*) gene, mapped within *APOC1* and *APOC2* on chromosome 19, has been indicated as a causative gene for the disease (Caylak, 2009). This gene presents three different polymorphic variations (*ApoE2, ApoE3,* and *ApoE4*), which result in three different protein isoforms. Only two of them, *ApoE-∑2* and *ApoE-∑4,* are dysfunctional. Interestingly, Zhang and colleagues (2000) have found an association between polymorphic variants of the angiotensin-converting enzyme gene and OSAS.

Recently, a growing amount of scientific evidence suggests that genomic imprinting may have a role in sleep. Genomic imprinting results in allele-specific silencing according to parental origin. Thus, imprinted genes show haploid expression even though two copies of each imprinted gene are present. It is thought that there must be a significant evolutionary advantage in monoallelic expression of imprinted genes to offset the risk of genetic diseases if the single expressed copy of an imprinted gene is lost. Imprinting starts in gametes where the allele is marked by methylation. Methyl groups occur at the so-called CpG islands and prevent the binding of transcription factors to the promoter. This process represents one of the major epigenetic mechanisms that are associated with the repression of gene expression.

Many neurodevelopmental disorders associated with imprinted genes present dramatic sleep disorders. For example, Prader–Willi syndrome (PWS) and Angelman syndrome (AS) exhibit opposing imprinting profiles and opposing sleep phenotypes. PWS is associated with maternal additions/paternal deletions of alleles on chromosome 15q11–13 and characterized by temperature-control abnormalities and excessive sleepiness. Changes in sleep architecture have also been noted in children and young adults with PWS, most specifically REM-sleep abnormalities such as sleep onset of REM periods, REM fragmentation, intrusion of REM into stage 2 sleep, and short latencies to REM (see Tucci & Nolan, 2009, for an overview). Conversely, AS is associated with paternal additions/maternal deletions on chromosome 15q11–13 and is characterized by severe mental retardation and reductions in sleep. Twenty percent of patients who show clinical symptoms of AS have mutations in one or more genes in the region 15q11–13. Within this area there are at least two strong candidate genes: *UBE3A* and *GABRB3*. Mice with a *Ube3a* deletion have shown a reduction in NREM sleep, deteriorated REM sleep, and an increased frequency of waking during the dark–light transition (Colas et al., 2005).

Imprinted genes are differentially expressed in brain regions controlling sleep/wake cycles (e.g., hypothalamus) as well as in key nuclei of the major modulatory neurotransmitters such as the locus ceruleus (e.g., Nesp55). There is evidence that supports a conflict model with regard to sleep phenotype wherein NREM expression is aligned with matriline genes and REM expression is aligned with patriline genes (Tucci & Nolan, 2009).

Glenda Lassi and Valter Tucci

See also: entries related to Sleep and Development

References

Caylak, E. (2009). The genetics of sleep disorders in humans: Narcolepsy, restless legs syndrome, and obstructive sleep apnea syndrome. *American Journal of Medical Genetics A, 149A*(11), 2612–2626.

Colas, D., Bezin, L., Gharib, A., Morales, A., Cespuglio, R., & Sarda, N. (2005). REM sleep control during aging in SAM mice: A role for inducible nitric oxide synthase. *Neurobiology of Aging, 26*(10), 1375–1384.

Dauvilliers, Y., Blouin, J. L., Neidhart, E., Carlander, B., Eliaou, J. F., Antonarakis, S. E., . . . & Tafti, M. (2004). A narcolepsy susceptibility locus maps to a 5 Mb region of chromosome 21q. *Annals of Neurology, 56*(3), 382–388.

Davis, H., & Davis, P. (1936). Action potentials of the brain in normal persons and in normal states of cerebral activity. *Archives of Neurology and Psychiatry, 36,* 1214–1224.

De Gennaro, L., Marzano, C., Fratello, F., Moroni, F., Pellicciari, M. C., Ferlazzo, F., . . . Rossini, P. M. (2008). The electroencephalographic fingerprint of sleep is genetically determined: A twin study. *Annals of Neurology, 64,* 455–460.

Gedda, L., & Brenci, G. (1979). Sleep and dream characteristics in twins. *Acta Genet Med Gemellol (Roma), 28*(3), 237–239.

Lin, L., Faraco, J., Li, R., Kadotani, H., Rogers, W., Lin, X., . . . Mignot, E. (1999). The sleep disorder canine narcolepsy is caused by a mutation in the hypocretin (orexin) receptor 2 gene. *Cell, 98,* 365–376.

Medori, R., Montagna, P., Tritschler, H. J., LeBlanc, A., Cortelli, P., Tinuper, P., . . . Gambetti, P. (1992). Fatal familial insomnia: A second kindred with mutation of prion protein gene at codon 178. *Neurology, 42*(3 Pt 1), 669–670.

Taheri, S., & Mignot, E. (2002). The genetics of sleep disorders. *Lancet Neurology, 1,* 242–250.

Tucci, V., & Nolan, P. M. (2009). Toward an understanding of the function of sleep: New insights from mouse genetics. In P. McNamara, R. A. Barton, & C. L. Nunn (Eds.), *Evolution of sleep: Phylogenetic and functional perspectives* (pp. 218–237). New York: Cambridge University Press.

van Beijsterveldt, C. E., Molenaar, P. C., de Geus, E. J., & Boomsma, D. I. (1996). Heritability of human brain functioning as assessed by electroencephalography. *American Journal of Human Genetics, 58*(3), 562–573.

Zhang, J., Zhao, B., Gesongluobu, S. Y., Wu, Y., Pei, W., Ye, J., . . . & Liu, L. (2000). Angiotensin-converting enzyme gene insertion/deletion (I/D) polymorphism in hypertensive patients with different degrees of obstructive sleep apnea. *Hypertension Research, 23*(5), 407–411.

Genetics of Mouse Sleep Physiology

The main challenge for modern sleep research is to understand the functional genes of sleep. Sleep genetics promises to unravel fundamental mechanisms that cause sleep in many species. A powerful genetic approach is always based on an informative and flexible animal model. As the genome of a number of species can be explored extensively in *silico* and, then, manipulated to create animal models for targeted human phenotypes, it becomes relevant to identify species with informative phenotypes for human traits. Many animal models are commonly used in genetics, and nowadays in sleep genetics, according to different characteristics. Evolutionary conserved genetic elements are thought to exert a crucial role in sleep across many species, ranging from mammals to arthropods (Tobler, 2005); all these organisms show a regulation of sleep-associated processes, such as timing of sleep onset, depth of sleep, and average duration (Crocker & Sehgal, 2010), that seem to account for a conservation of DNA elements regulating sleep and its features. For example, mice share with humans both a rich physiology and genetics, and this makes this species suitable for the investigation of human sleep. Furthermore, mice are small and are prolific breeders. A female has a litter of 5 to 10 mice per year, giving birth to more than 100 mice during this time. They exploit complex behaviors and their physiology is regulated by a complex central nervous system; for these reasons, they are much appreciated by geneticists who investigate complex phenotypes. The mouse is considered a suitable animal model for studying the genetics of sleep homeostasis and circadian mechanisms as we do in humans. However, compared to other species, also commonly used in genetics, such as *Caenorhabditis elegans, Drosophila melanogaster,* and *Zebrafish* (*Danio rerio*), the mouse presents bigger size and longer reproductive times as well as a complex and highly redundant genome. As a consequence, there is the drawback that for those genes that are crucial both for sleep and survival, the current research in the mouse may fail to identify them.

Current technological advances aim to improve the throughput of measurement technologies that allow the monitoring of bio-signals during wakefulness and sleep in freely moving mice. Thus, the use of this species for genetic and pharmacological screens is progressively increasing.

Like humans, mice have sleep architecture in which it is possible to identify a slow-wave sleep and a paradoxical sleep. Indeed, wakefulness, nonrapid eye movement (NREM), and rapid eye movement (REM) states in mice have been widely documented (see Tucci & Nolan, 2009, for an overview). Interestingly, mice are nocturnal animals; they sleep during the light phase of the day, and when sleeping, move close to one another for warmth. Studies, focused on electrophysiological (EEG) parameters in different inbred mouse strains, have found the main differences being in delta and theta frequencies of the EEG depending on the genotypes. For example, Balb/cByJ mice present characteristic slow theta frequencies whereas classical C57Bl/6J mice, one of the most popular mouse strains used in research, have much faster theta rhythms. Starting from these observations, it was possible to carry out quantitative trait loci (QTL) mapping studies, which took advantage of the genetic isomorphism (within strain)/polymorphism (between strains) and of the diverse sleep phenotypes of different inbred strains, and have identified candidate genes that determine the variation within this specific EEG trait (Tafti et al., 2003). In particular, the mapping process brought the authors to highlight a specific genomic region that holds the *Acads* (short-chain acyl-coenzyme A dehydrogenase) gene. To reinforce the evidence that this is the candidate gene for the regulation of theta rhythms in mice, it was pivotal that the observation that *Acads* is downregulated in Balb/cByJ mice (Tafti et al., 2003). Mechanisms that regulate sleep duration have been associated to loci of chromosomes 4, 5, 9, and 15 and aspects of REM sleep have been associated to loci of chromosome 1,

17, and 19 of the mouse. QTLs, identified on chromosome 13 (DPS1: Delta Power in SWS 1) and 14 (*Rarb* gene), have been linked to changes of delta activity (Franken, Chollet, & Tafti, 2001; Maret et al., 2005). In particular, *Rarb* is involved in specific pathways (e.g., retinoic acid signaling) that modulate cortical synchrony during NREM sleep in mice.

Another approach to address questions about sleep mechanisms and genes is to investigate the consequences of sleep deprivation on EEG measures but also on gene expression in mice. Pioneer experimental work by Pompeiano, Cirelli, and Tononi (1994) have reported a differential state-dependent (sleep vs. wakefulness) expression of the immediate early genes, IEGs (Cirelli, 2002). More recently, Mackiewicz et al. (2007), by means of microarray analysis, have identified in mice, 2,090 genes in the cerebral cortex and 409 genes in the hypothalamus that show a sleep specific expression. Many transcripts were observed to change their expression level between wakefulness and sleep in specific brain areas such as the cerebral cortex, cerebellum, and hypothalamus. Genes such as *Arc, NGFI-A, c-Fos, Zif-268,* and *Homer1a,* which are considered biomarkers of neuronal activity, are generally upregulated during wakefulness. Further investigation in mouse genomic data, by exploring the *Dps1* QTL, has suggested that the expression levels of *Homer1a* could be a strong biological candidate to mimic sleep homeostasis (Mackiewicz, Paigen, Naidoo, & Pack, 2008; Maret et al., 2007). In particular, it has been reported that *Homer1a* expression is increased by sleep deprivation (Maret et al., 2007). Main studies of *Zif-268* gene have indicated a main role for this gene in brain plasticity since it turned out to be upregulated during REM sleep when mice have been exposed to an enriched environment (Ribeiro, Goyal, Mello, & Pavlides, 1999).

Increasing genetic evidence from mouse circadian models supports the lack of independency of the homeostatic and circadian processes. Although not all circadian genes affect the homeostasis of sleep, genes such as *Npas2, Dbp,* and *Prok2* seem to have a role in keeping the length of the sleep/wake cycle and *period* genes are modulated during homeostatic processes (Andretic, Franken, & Tafti, 2008; Franken & Dijk, 2009). Also *Rab3a* mutants show a shortening of the sleep–wake cycle and increased NREM sleep (Kapfhamer et al., 2002).

Great efforts are in place to unravel the mechanisms of sleep by means of reverse and forward genetics. These methods and techniques are applied to animal models with simple genomes and low redundancy such as fruit flies and the zebrafish, and to models genetically nearer to human beings such as mice and rats. Sleep is a complex phenomenon with a wide involvement of genes and epigenetic phenomena that, in turn, play a role in other mechanisms (i.e., metabolism and immune response) and this renders the genetics of sleep a vast field of study.

Glenda Lassi and Valter Tucci

See also: entries related to Sleep Physiology

References

Andretic, R., Franken, P., & Tafti, M. (2008). Genetics of sleep. *Annual Review of Genetics, 42,* 361–388.

Cirelli, C. (2002). How sleep deprivation affects gene expression in the brain: A review of recent findings. *Journal of Applied Physiology, 92*(1), 394–400.

Crocker, A., & Sehgal, A. (2010). *Genes and development, 24*(12), 1220–1235.

Franken, P., Chollet, D., & Tafti, M. (2001). The homeostatic regulation of sleep need is under genetic control. *Journal of Neuroscience, 21*(8), 2610–2621.

Franken, P., & Dijk, D.J. (2009). Circadian clock genes and sleep homeostasis. *European Journal of Neuroscience, 29*(9), 1820–1829.

Kapfhamer, D., Valladares, O., Sun, Y., Nolan, P.M., Rux, J.J., Arnold, S.E., . . . Bucan, M. (2002). Mutations in Rab3a alter circadian period and homeostatic response to sleep loss in the mouse. *Nature Genetics, 32*(2), 290–295.

Mackiewicz, M., Paigen, B., Naidoo, N., & Pack, A.I. (2008). Analysis of the QTL for sleep homeostasis in mice: Homer1a is a likely candidate. *Physiological Genomics, 33,* 91–99.

Mackiewicz, M., Shockley, K.R., Romer, M.A., Galante, R.J., Zimmerman, J.E., Naidoo, N., . . . Pack, A.I. (2007). Macromolecule biosynthesis: A key function of sleep. *Physiol Genomics, 31*(3), 441–457.

Maret, S., Dorsaz, S., Gurcel, L., Pradervand, S., Petit, B., Pfister, C., . . . Tafti, M. (2007). Homer1a is a core brain molecular correlate of sleep loss. *Proceedings of the National Academy of Science, 104,* 20090–20095.

Maret, S., Franken, P., Dauvilliers, Y., Ghyselinck, N.B., Chambon, P., & Tafti, M. (2005). Retinoic acid signaling affects cortical synchrony during sleep. *Science, 310,* 111–113.

Pompeiano, M., Cirelli, C., & Tononi, G. (1994). Immediate-early genes in spontaneous wakefulness and sleep: Expression of c-fos and NGFI-A mRNA and protein. *Journal of Sleep Research, 3*(2), 80–96.

Ribeiro, S., Goyal, V., Mello, C.V., & Pavlides, C. (1999). Brain gene expression during rem sleep depends on prior waking experience. *Learning and Memory, 6,* 500–508.

Tafti, M., Petit, B., Chollet, D., Neidhart, E., de Bilbao, F., Kiss, J.Z., . . . Franken, P. (2003). Deficiency in short-chain fatty acid b-oxidation affects theta oscillations during sleep. *Nature Genetics, 34,* 320–325.

Tobler, I. (2005). Phylogeny of sleep regulation. In M.H. Kryger, T. Roth, & W. Dement (Eds.), *Principles and practice of sleep medicine* (pp. 77–90). Philadelphia, PA: Elsevier/Saunders.

Tucci, V. & Nolan, P.M. (2009). Toward an understanding of the function of sleep: New insights from mouse genetics. In P. McNamara, R.A. Barton, & C.L. Nunn (Eds.), *Evolution of sleep: Phylogenetic and functional perspectives* (pp. 218–237). New York: Cambridge University Press.

Gestalt Dreamwork

Dreams usually serve only as a vehicle for starting Gestalt work; however, Gestalt is ideally suited to in-depth dreamwork, because it is an experiential approach that deals directly with the emotional experience within the environmental and social contexts of a person's life, much as dreams do. Gestalt therapy employs a role-play technique for experiencing the elements in a dream directly and emotionally, and it is therefore valuable for surfacing the emotions at the core of an issue that the dream and dreamer may be dealing with.

Gestalt therapy was developed by Fritz and Laura Perls in the 1940s and 1950s, with influence from and collaboration with others (Perls, 1976, pp. 237–257), and gained in popularity during the 1960s and 1970s Humanistic Movement. It has been recently applied to coaching and a unified program of human development called Gestalt practice (Brownell, 2010). Gestalt means whole, reflecting the principle that we are a total organism functioning as a whole and that self-actualization can be achieved by viewing the self as part of a greater whole. The therapeutic process is aimed at gaining self-awareness and insight, closing unfinished Gestalts (unfinished business) by working through impasses, and/or re-owning disowned parts of ourselves. A few of the key principles of Gestalt therapy application include: putting aside expectations, assumptions, and an authoritative role to establish an environment of open dialogue; surrendering to what takes place versus attempting to control it; creating a corrective growth-enhancing environment open to the unpredictable; observing and describing and supporting what is experienced instead of explaining or interpreting it; emphasizing action versus talk therapy with a focus on experiencing the here and now versus talking about possibilities; focusing on what and how and avoidance of why; and treating each item of expression as significant and owned by the person.

Fritz Perls considered the dream as the most spontaneous expression of our existence and that all the different parts of the dream are fragments of our personality (Perls, 1969, pp. 71, 72). To become a whole person without conflicts we need to re-own these alienated or disowned dream fragments or projections, and put them back together. The approach is to recall every element in the dream (character, thing, or mood) and become each one of them, "really become that thing in the dream" as Fritz would say (Perls, 1969,

p. 74). During this role-play, the person may be asked to become aware of verbal and nonverbal clues and exaggerate them, or to have encounters with other elements in the dream, a dialog between the opposing parts. Rather than talking about a person's oppressive spouse in a dream, the therapist might ask the person to imagine they are present (perhaps sitting in an opposing chair) and to dialog with them directly. New insight emerges as the dreamer becomes aware of what he or she is doing and feeling. As the often stormy interaction proceeds, a mutual understanding and appreciation between differences eventually brings about a oneness or integration of the opposing parts. The therapist does not interpret the dream, but observes and provides questions and feedback on the expressions and actions of the dreamer, with the aim being to lead them through a self discovery.

One of the most powerful applications of Gestalt therapy to dreamwork is the role-play, becoming that thing in the dream and letting it express itself. It can be a relatively uncomplicated and spontaneous activity that can be done to quickly reveal inner feelings and conflicting emotions and to surface emotional content associated with something you see or experience in a dream. Offered further on is a simple to administer yet impactful script, developed by Robert Hoss (2005, pp. 143–146) for introducing the power of Gestalt role-play into dreamwork. While a clinician might want to go deeper and broader, the scripting is found useful for self-help, beginning group or client work, or for research where a standard protocol is desired. It is derived from experience with questions that have proven generally effective when guiding subjects through a Gestalt role-play. The statements are designed in pairs to explore role identity, conflicts or impasses, and motivational factors, respectively.

After selecting something in the dream to work on (the dream image), imagine as best you can that you are that thing in the dream, immersing yourself in the role that it plays in the dream. Once you have become it (as best you can) finish the following six statements as that dream image would state them. Stay in role by speaking in the first person present tense.

1. "I am . . . (describe yourself as the dream image, and how you feel in that role)"
2. "My purpose is . . ."
3. "What I like is . . ."
4. "What I dislike is . . ."
5. "What I fear most is . . ."
6. "What I desire most is . . ."

Now read the statements as if they came from you describing feelings and situations in your life. Ask yourself, "does this sound like a way I feel, a situation or conflict I am dealing with in my waking life?" Explore any new insights, perhaps feelings surrounding your situation that you have not fully expressed or motivations that might be affecting your actions and thoughts.

Robert J. Hoss

See also: entries related to Dreams and Therapy

References

Brownell, P. (2010). *Gestalt therapy: A guide to contemporary practice*. New York: Springer Publishing.

Hoss, R. (2005). *Dream language: Self-understanding through imagery and color*. Ashland, OR: Innersource.

Perls, F. (1969). *Gestalt therapy verbatim*. Moab, UT: Real People Press.

Perls, F. (1976). *The handbook of Gestalt therapy* (Eds. C. Hatcher & P. Himelstein). New York: Jason Aronson.

Graphic Novels and Dreams

As Rick Veitch, the indefatigable creator of the long-running dream comic book *Rare Bit Fiend*, says, "The comic strip is the best way to render the dynamic, visual/verbal, time-slipping experience of a dream into easily sharable form." The interconnected series of comic strip panels, and the impact of the comic book page as a whole, offer an exciting, expressively flexible, dynamic, and universally recognizable form—available to everyone on the planet who has access to a pencil and a piece of paper. Comics can be published and distributed by the author/artist (or the team of author, editor, pencil artist, inker, letterer, colorist, and so forth) to as large, geographically wide, and culturally diverse an audience as he/she/they are able to interest and capture—particularly in these days of inexpensive instantaneous Internet communication.

In addition, the proliferation of newly developed, user-friendly computer graphics and print technologies has also put very sophisticated creative graphic tools and techniques directly into the hands of would-be comics artists, and more and more of them are taking advantage of the inspiration and expressive freedom these tools provide. A growing number of these postmodern artists are using these new art tools particularly for bringing their dream experiences to life on the page and on the screen.

In light of this boom in comics production, and the consequent liberation of comics from traditional limits on the sale and distribution of print media, it is especially interesting to note that functional magnetic resonance imaging (fMRI) studies of people reading comic books show that the process of perusing and absorbing a comic book page activates and stimulates both the visual and verbal areas of the cortex simultaneously—noticeably more so than either reading or looking at pictures alone appear to do. This simultaneous stimulation across brain hemispheres while absorbing the intertwined verbal/visual meanings of comics parallels the experience of dreaming itself, which also tends to stimulate both hemispheres as well as multiple dedicated areas of the cortex at the same time in fMRI studies. (See Sharpley & Bitsika, in press, among others.)

This particularly compelling power of comics has not gone unnoticed. As Neil Gaiman points out in his introduction to *The Best American Comics of 2010*, "comics, of course, are the easiest way to assimilate information, at least according to a study done by the CIA back in the 1980s" (Gaiman, Abel, & Madden, 2010, p. xiii).

Here is an example of the ability of the comic book/graphic novel form to evoke the experience of a classic, archetypal dream. It comes from Rick Veitch's *Rabid Eye* graphic novel (1995, p. 69).

(Yes, the "Neil" in this graphic novel version of Rick Veitch's dream is that same Neil Gaiman who authored the quote in the preceding text. They have known each other for years.) So, in eight panels on a single page, this unique version of the classic dream of "driving up the increasingly steep slope, (most often, but not always a bridge), until it becomes vertical" is conveyed much more vividly, with many more resonances and allusions, in graphic novel form than a simple written narrative or a single visual image could possibly have achieved. True, Rick Veitch is a consummately skilled artist, working professionally in the comic book arts field for decades, and yet this same quality of vividness and emotional/visual power can also achieved to a surprising extent, and with reliable regularity by even the crudest little sequential stick-figure drawings of dreams.

Making dream comics, and absorbing dream comics that others have made, honors and stimulates the deep unconscious source from which the dreams spring by imitating the form and structure of dreaming itself. The activation of both the visual and verbal limbic systems simultaneously by making and absorbing comics engages human consciousness and facilitates the evolution of human awareness, just as the dreams themselves are always striving to do, whether they are helped by consciously rendering them into an expressive, shareable form or not.

Another professional dream comics artist, Jesse Reklaw, even offers his considerable artistic skills to other dreamers in his ongoing dream comic strip, *Slow Wave,* where he renders dreams sent in to him by readers into classic four-panel strips. In his graphic novel *Dreamtoons* he gives us a rendition of wonderful, ironic, transformative dream of the night sky (Reklaw, 2000, p. 33). (In looking at this deceptively simple four-panel page, it is worth

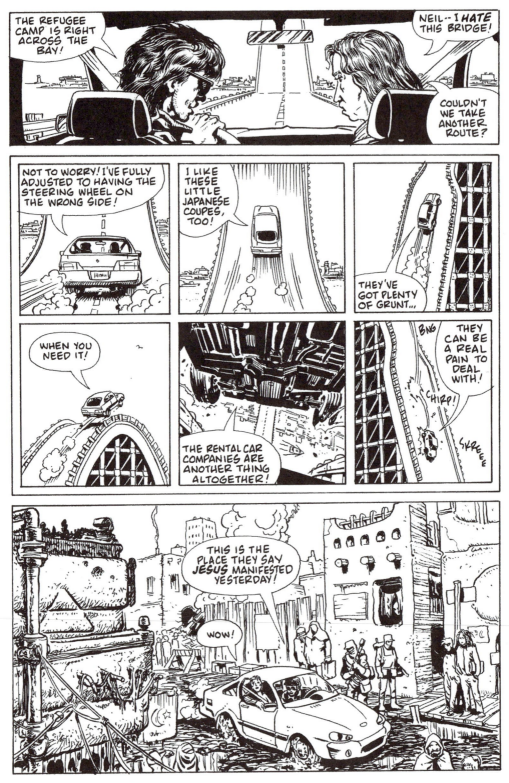

(Veitch, R. [1995]. *Rabid Eye.* King Hell Press.)

(Reklaw, J. [2000]. *Dreamtoons.* Shambhala, Boston, MA.)

remembering that the longest view we humans ever get in the waking world is our view of the night sky, since in the daytime, the sky, big as it is, is still literally the limit of how far we can see.)

With any luck, these two examples (chosen from among thousands of possibilities culled from the work of scores of graphic dream novelists) will help make it more immediately clear, than mere words unaccompanied by sequential visual images would be able to do, what a vital role the graphic novel is playing in the development of popular appreciation and deeper understanding of the universal phenomenon of dreaming.

Jeremy Taylor

References

Gaiman, N., Abel, J., & Madden, M. (Eds.). (2010). *The best American comics of 2010.* Boston: Houghton Mifflin Harcourt.

Reklaw, J. (2000). *Dreamtoons.* Boston, MA: Shambhala.

Sharpley, C.F., & Bitsika, V. (in press). The diverse neurogeography of emotional experience: Form follows function. *Behavioural Brain Research.* Published online July 14, 2010.

Veitch, R. (1995). *Rabid eye.* West Townsend, VT: King Hell Press.

Group Work with Dreams

At the close of the 20th century the group dreamwork movement was well established in North America, and was well on its way to becoming a worldwide phenomenon, having spread from Britain and the United States to postcolonial Central and South America, Asia, Africa, Australia, and the Pacific Islands, as well as across Europe and the former Soviet Union. In several of these postcolonial areas, the contemporary dreamwork movement grew directly out of earlier, indigenous traditions of dream interpretation, while in other, more industrialized areas, the movement evolved anew from a widening appreciation of the value of psychotherapy in general, and in particular, the value of the insights into dreams and other unconscious processes offered by Sigmund Freud, Carl Jung, Wilfred Bion, Melanie Klien, Susanne Langer, Abraham Maslo, Fritz Perls, and Carl Rogers (to name only some of the more influential and well-known and respected psychological pioneers in the English speaking world).

All of this growing interest led to the formation of the International Association for the Study of Dreams (IASD), in San Francisco, in 1983. This organization has been instrumental in professionalizing and affirming the legitimacy of many styles and types of dream exploration, particularly the various forms of lay–led and leaderless (that is to say, shared leadership) group dreamwork.

In the first decade of the 21st century, the group dreamwork movement has accelerated its growth in response to the growing need expressed in postmodern global society for spiritual practices not affiliated with any particular organized religion. An ever-increasing number of people are seeking ways to share their intimate, interior lives with one another in a conscious search for deeper patterns of meaning and significance in their individual lives and collective endeavors.

Some large and relatively well-organized religious traditions, particularly Judaism, Buddhism, Christianity, and Islam have also begun to develop their own styles of group dreamwork with congregations and communities, as these institutional groupings begin to search more actively for practices that reveal the potential of renewing the vitality of the spiritual lives of their members in ways that remain in harmony with their particular traditions. The sacred narratives of these traditions (and many others besides) all give particularly privileged place to dreams and dreaming as a means of direct apprehension of and communication with the Divine.

This development of lay–led group and individual dreamwork emphasizes and to a great extent grows out of the fact that the sacred narratives of *all* the world's religious traditions are all filled with stories, parables, and (particularly in the case of Islam) direct assertions regarding the Divine revelations appearing in the dreams of particular individual people genuine and binding for the community of faith as a whole.

Over the centuries, this archetypally privileged status granted to dream experience as divine revelation has also meant that these religions *also* exhibit a tendency to disparage and attempt to control who is allowed to interpret dreams, and in some cases even forbid the practice of group dream discussion altogether. The archetypally special status granted to dreams and dreaming as a means of direct communion with the Divine in all the sacred narratives of the world also offers a challenge to merely human ecclesiastical authority in any given religious gathering, making

it difficult for local religious authorities to oppose the dream pronouncements and revelations of inspired individuals (the scruffier and more malcontent the better, since there is an aspect of the archetypal figure of the prophet that also favors scruffiness and malcontentedness).

For this reason, to preserve the state of communal peace and cheerful calm that Presbyterians like to call decency and good order, many religious communities and central religious governing authorities have withdrawn support for the practice of group dream sharing and discussion, even (and particularly) when it is clearly enshrined in their most sacred cannons and traditions.

One consequence of this popular postmodern resurgent dreamwork movement is that many institutions of higher learning—in an ongoing search for new revenue streams, as well as the desire to keep pace with popular interest in continuing education—have begun to institutionalize dream studies in their regular curricula, particularly for returning students and life-long learners. At the moment, Anglophone academic institutions appear to be at the forefront of this worldwide trend.

At this point, the evidence is growing that the liberal Western belief in scientific and technological progress as an assurance of a better life for all that characterized the 20th century is fading—in the face of two world wars, increasing ecological degradation, and the rise of irrational, ideological terrorism (both socioeconomic and religious). It has always been the case, and appears to be so again, that in moments of fundamental cultural crisis and transition in foundational shared assumptions, there

is an instinctive turning back to more traditional, nonrational sources of wisdom,
authority, and discernment. Dreams have
always played this role, and once again
the popular interest in dreams appears to
be growing, in part at least, in direct proportion to people's anxieties and generally
wavering confidence in the exclusively rational materialistic worldview that characterized the industrial nations in the 20th
century.

In light of this, it seems likely that the
resurgent worldwide interesting dreams
and dreaming, and exploring their deeper
meaning and implications in the company
of other like-minded people, will only
grow.

Jeremy Taylor

References

Bulkeley, K. (2003). *Dreams of healing: Transforming nightmares into visions of hope*. Mahwah, NJ: Paulist Press.

Taylor, J. (2009). *The wisdom of your dreams: Using dreams to tap into your unconscious and transform your life*. New York: Penguin/Tarcher.

H

Hall and Van de Castle System for the Study of Dream Content

The Hall and Van de Castle (1966) coding system is an instance of the general methodology of content analysis, a quantitative approach to the search for meaningful regularities in any kind of written text. Content analysis has four basic steps, all easier said than done: (1) creating clearly defined categories that can be understood and applied in a reliable way by any investigator, which takes many hours of trial-and-error work; (2) tabulating frequencies for the categories, which is very labor intensive; (3) using percentages, ratios, or other statistics to transform raw frequencies into meaningful data, which was time consuming until the advent of computers; and (4) making comparisons with normative samples or control groups, which are not always easy to create (e.g., Krippendorff, 2004; Smith, 2000).

The Hall and Van de Castle system has 11 general coding categories: settings, objects, characters (animals, humans, and mythical figures/creatures), social interactions (aggressive, friendly, and sexual), activities, emotions (confusion, anger, apprehension, sadness, and happiness), good fortunes and misfortunes, successes and failures, food and eating elements, elements from the past, and descriptive elements. These categories encompass those

used in other coding systems, as shown by a comparison of Hall and Van de Castle categories with the results of a factor analysis revealing five general categories in other dream content systems (Domhoff, 1996, pp. 34–35; Hauri, 1975).

The coding system can be used for descriptive empirical studies or to test inferences derived from any theory. It is strictly a methodology and has no theoretical biases built into it, except the assumption that the quantification of dream elements might prove as useful as quantification has in many other areas of inquiry. In that regard, it yields findings, not interpretations. Inferences drawn from the findings about the person or group that provided the dream reports are most convincing when the content analyst knows nothing about the dreamers beforehand (blind analysis). Investigators in Canada, Europe, India, Japan, and the United States have used the system to study dream reports from college students (e.g., Lortie-Lussier, Cote, & Vachon, 2000; Prasad, 1982; Strauch & Meier, 1996; Waterman, Dejong, & Magdelijns, 1988; Yamanaka, Morita, & Matsumoto, 1982). Researchers in Italy, Spain, Switzerland, and the United States have used it to study dream reports from children (Avila-White, Schneider, & Domhoff, 1999; Crugnola, Maggiolini, Caprin, Martini, & Giudici, 2008; Oberst, Charles, & Chamarro, 2005; Strauch, 2004). American investigators have employed it to study dream reports collected by anthropologists in more than a dozen small traditional societies (e.g., Domhoff, 1996, Chapter 6, for a summary of findings; Gregor, 1981).

The coding system rests on the nominal level of measurement to avoid serious problems of reliability and psychological validity with most rating systems for dream content, which use the ordinal level of measurement, although rating systems are useful for characteristics of dream reports with degrees of intensity in waking life, such as activity level, or for aspects of dreams without specific content, such as vividness. The system has high reliability by the percentage of agreement method, which consists of dividing the total number of similar codings by two raters by the number of agreements plus disagreements. The system uses percentages and ratios to correct for differences in the length of dream reports and other methodological problems that need not be discussed here. These percentages and ratios make possible a wide range of readily understood content indicators, such as animal percent (the percentage of all characters that are animals), which is as high as 30 to 40 percent in young children, but only 6 percent for men and 4 percent for women in American society, and as high as 30 percent in some hunting and gathering societies, exceeding the American level in all of the dream samples collected by anthropologists. Aggressive and friendly social interactions are analyzed by determining rates per character, which provide a control for the number of characters. The total number of friendly or aggressive interactions divided by the total number of characters provides ratios

called the F/C and A/C indexes. These indexes can be figured for specific characters or types of characters in dreams, leading to F/C and A/C ratios with; for example, father, mother, specific friends, animals, or the general category of male strangers.

Because of the distortions and mistakes created by the use of parametric statistics with nominal data, and by the skewed distributions and nonrandom samples that are frequent in dream research, p values are determined using the formula for the significance of differences between two proportions, which has the added virtue of providing the same results as a $2 \cdot 2$ chi square and the correlational statistic r when two groups are compared using data expressed in percentages. Effect sizes are determined by the use of Cohen's h, which uses an arcsine transformation calculated for the two samples to correct for the fact that standard deviations cannot be computed for data expressed in percentages. The p and h values for the content indicators are computed automatically when codings are entered into the Dream-SAT software, available at www.dreamresearch.net. Results are displayed as either bar graphs (called h profiles) or tables (Domhoff, 1996, Appendix D; Domhoff & Schneider, 2008).

The Hall and Van de Castle coding system includes normative gender findings based on five dream reports, which range in length from 50 to 300 words, from each of 100 American college men and 100 American college women, for a total of 1,000 dream reports. These norms have been replicated several times (Domhoff, 1996, Chapter 4). They provide a basis for cross-cultural comparisons and for finding individual differences in dream content. All of the dream reports used in creating the norms, along with the original codings for them, can be found at www.dreambank. net. Studies based on subsamples drawn from the large normative samples show that it takes 100 to 125 dream reports to achieve replicable results. The large number is because most dream elements appear in less than half of all dream reports.

Studies using the Hall and Van de Castle system have yielded findings on age, gender, and cross-cultural similarities and differences that fit with what has been found in studies of waking psychological variables. It is also notable and worthy of further study that there are fewer friends and friendly interactions in the dreams of hospitalized mental patients, a child molester, and a neurotic young man in psychotherapy than in the dreams of the male normative sample (Domhoff, 1996, Chapter 8; Hall, 1966). These two findings, which are the major differences between the dreams of the patients and the male norms, are separate issues, because it is possible for friends to be present in dreams without there being friendly interactions with them and for friendly interactions to occur with people other than friends, such as parents and strangers.

Research on lengthy individual dream series reveals that most people are consistent in what they dream about over months, years, or even decades in a few cases. In addition, the most frequent characters, social interactions, and activities in their dreams are continuous with their waking interests and preoccupations, as determined by asking the dreamer or the dreamer's friends to

corroborate or reject the inferences based on blind content analyses.

Perhaps the major contribution of the Hall and Van de Castle coding system has been to demonstrate that there is psychological meaning in dreams in terms of (1) the coherency of most individual dreams, (2) the consistency of dream content over long time periods, and (3) the many correspondences between dream content indicators and waking psychological variables.

G. William Domhoff

References

Avila-White, D., Schneider, A., & Domhoff, G. W. (1999). The most recent dreams of 12–13-year-old boys and girls: A methodological contribution to the study of dream content in teenagers. *Dreaming, 9*, 163–171.

Crugnola, C., Maggiolini, A., Caprin, C., Martini, C., & Giudici, F. (2008). Dream content of 10- to 11-year-old preadolescent boys and girls. *Dreaming, 18*, 201–218.

Domhoff, G. W. (1996). *Finding meaning in dreams: A quantitative approach*. New York: Plenum.

Domhoff, G. W., & Schneider, A. (2008). Similarities and differences in dream content at the cross-cultural, gender, and individual levels. *Consciousness and Cognition, 17*, 1257–1265.

Gregor, T. (1981). A content analysis of Mehinaku dreams. *Ethos, 9*, 353–390.

Hall, C. (1966). A comparison of the dreams of four groups of hospitalized mental patients with each other and with a normal population. *Journal of Nervous and Mental Diseases, 143*, 135–139.

Hall, C., & Van de Castle, R. (1966). *The content analysis of dreams*. New York: Appleton-Century-Crofts.

Hauri, P. (1975). Categorization of sleep mental activity for psychophysiological studies. In G. Lairy & P. Salzarulo (Eds.), *The experimental study of sleep: Methodological problems*. New York: Elsevier Scientific Publishing.

Krippendorff, K. (2004). *Content analysis: An introduction to its methodology*. Thousand Oaks, CA: Sage Publications.

Lortie-Lussier, M., Cote, L., & Vachon, J. (2000). The consistency and continuity hypotheses revisited through the dreams of women at two periods of their lives. *Dreaming, 10*, 67–76.

Oberst, U., Charles, C., & Chamarro, A. (2005). Influence of gender and age in aggressive dream content in Spanish children and adolescents. *Dreaming, 15*, 170–177.

Prasad, B. (1982). Content analysis of dreams of Indian and American college students: A cultural comparison. *Journal of Indian Psychology, 4*, 54–64.

Smith, C. (2000). Content analysis and narrative analysis. In H. Reis & C. Judd (Eds.), *Handbook of research methods in social and personality psychology*. New York: Cambridge University Press.

Strauch, I. (2004). *Traume im ubergang von der kindheit ins jugendalter: Ergebnisse einer langzeitstudie [Dreams in childhood and adolescence: The results of a longitudinal study]*. Bern: Huber.

Strauch, I., & Meier, B. (1996). *In search of dreams: Results of experimental dream research*. Albany: State University of New York Press.

Waterman, D., Dejong, M., & Magdelijns, R. (1988). Gender, sex role orientation and dream content. In W. Koella, W. Obai, H. Schaltz, & P. Visser (Eds.), *Sleep '86* (pp. 385–387). New York: Gustav Fischer Verlag.

Yamanaka, T., Morita, Y., & Matsumoto, J. (1982). Analysis of the dream contents in college students by REM-awakening technique. *Folia Psychiatrica et Neurologica Japonica, 36*, 33–52.

Handedness: A New Look at the Effects on Dream Recall and Content

Why might one person have a vivid, fantastical dream, and another a less vivid, realistic one? Why do some people remember many dreams, while others remember few or even none? Do people differ in some characteristic, for example, brain organization, that predisposes them to experience dreams in particular manners? Light can be shed on these questions by examining individual differences that influence the nature of dreams. One such potential individual difference is hand preference.

Hand preference may be a marker for systematic differences in cerebral organization, with inconsistent handedness (IH), relative to consistent right-handedness (CRH), being associated with a larger corpus callosum, the part of the brain responsible for connecting the cerebral hemispheres (e.g., Denenberg, Kertesz, & Cowell, 1991; Witelson & Goldsmith, 1991). It is important to note that this approach to handedness differs from the traditional classification into 85 to 90 percent right-handers versus 10 to 15 percent left-handers. Instead, research shows that about 50 percent of humans are CRH and 50 percent are IH (e.g., Christman & Propper, 2010a).

The left and right hemispheres of the brain are also more similar in their structure in IH compared with CRH. For example, language-related left- and right-hemisphere brain structures tend to be more symmetrical in IH relative to CRH (e.g., Propper et al., 2010). IH and CRH also differ in the functional organization of the brain (Hellige, 2001). For example, IH is more likely to have language located in the right hemisphere, or even bilaterally (e.g., Knecht et al., 2000), compared with CRH. To the extent dream formation involves brain structures and functions similar to those that differ between IH and CRH, the handedness groups will differ in their dreams. Comparisons of dream characteristics between handedness groups can therefore inform us about the functional neuroanatomy involved in the dreaming brain.

It is worth briefly noting that handedness differences exist in general aspects of sleep architecture. Compared to IH, CRH is associated with increased time spent in REM sleep, fewer REM episodes per night, increased right-hemisphere activation, and decreased interhemispheric EEG coherence during sleep (Christman & Propper, 2010b).

Unfortunately, only a limited number of studies have examined handedness and dreaming. The research itself tends to be concerned with either dream-recall frequency or with specific dream characteristics. With regard to dream recall, Violani, De Gennaro, and Solano (1988) reported increased self-reported dream recall in CRH compared to left- and mixed-handers in a study using a seven-day home sleep diary. On the other hand, Van Nuys (1984) reported no handedness differences in dream recall, although left-handed participants who may have had greater right-hemisphere activity stated they recalled more dreams on average than left-handed participants without this bias. Hicks, Bautista, and Hicks (1999) reported greater

recall of vivid dreams in left- compared to mixed- and right-handers. Finally, Christman (2007) reported increased dream recall in inconsistent relative to consistent right-handers.

However, given the existence of methodological complications in the measurement of dream recall (e.g., Schredl, 2002), as well as in the measurement of handedness, the nature and existence of handedness differences in dream recall remain an open question. It is worth noting that individuals with lesser degrees of functional cerebral asymmetry report higher levels of dream recall (Doricchi, Milana, & Violani, 1993). IH is associated with lesser cerebral asymmetry (Hellige, 2001), suggesting the possibility that, with appropriate methodologies, IH may ultimately be associated with increased dream recall.

With regard to dream content characteristics, again only a small number of studies have looked at any potential individual differences in handedness effects, although the pattern in the literature seems clearer. Cohen (1977) found that, among CRH, dream content across a night's sleep progressively shifted toward greater left-hemisphere involvement (assessed both behaviorally and electrophysiologically), but this did not occur in left-handers. Hicks et al. (1999) reported greater dream vividness among left-, relative to mixed- or right-handers. Specifically, Hicks et al. divided dreams into seven distinct types: lucid dreams, archetypal dreams, fantastic nightmares, prelucid dreams, control dreams, posttraumatic nightmares, and night terrors. Left-handers were more likely than mixed- or right-handers to recall having had more vivid types of dreams, in particular lucid dreams and fantastic nightmares. The other dream types did not differ as a function of handedness.

Similarly, McNamara, Clark, and Hartmann (1998) reported that the dreams of left-handers were characterized by increased imagery and affective content. Specifically, left-handers included more high-imagery nouns and affective words in their dream reports, compared to CRH. Additionally, left-handers also reported that their dreams were less likely to reflect everyday life experiences. The literature therefore points to the possibility that IH is associated with increased dream vividness and fantastical imagery, relative to CRH.

These handedness differences may reflect differences in connectivity between the two hemispheres. In fact, there is greater connectivity between the hemispheres over the occipital lobe during both wake and REM sleep in left-handers compared to right-handers (Nielsen, Abel, Lorrain, & Montplaisir, 1988). Additionally, Nielsen and Chenier (1999) reported that a measure associated with increased communication between the cerebral hemispheres via the corpus callosum was associated with an increased proportion of dream characters whose faces were explicitly represented in the dream. Interestingly, IH is associated with increased communication between the hemispheres; this raises the possibility that detailed analyses of dream content may demonstrate consistent differences between the handedness groups.

Thus, there is tantalizing evidence of individual differences in handedness effects on dreaming. The picture is somewhat clouded by methodological variations in assessment of dream recall and handedness, but further research is clearly merited, given the pervasive handedness differences found in overall sleep architecture. For example, the paradoxical fact that CRH is associated with both increased time spent in REM sleep and decreased number of REM sleep episodes per night suggests the existence of both quantitative and qualitative differences in dreaming substrates between CRH and IH. As reviewed previously, nonright-handers' dreams appear to be more vivid and less realistic than right-handers; this difference between handedness groups in dream qualities may reflect differences between the handedness groups in cortical connectivity via the corpus callosum, with IH being associated with increased connectivity. For example, the tentative evidence of increased dream recall among persons with IH may be related to evidence of increased interhemispherically mediated waking memory retrieval in IH (Christman & Propper, 2010b).

Ruth E. Propper, Stephen D. Christman, and Tracy N. Iacovelli

See also: entries related to Sleep and the Brain

References

Christman, S. D. (2007). *Individual differences in déjà vu and jamais vu experiences: Degree of handedness and access to the right hemisphere.* Presented at the 19th Annual Meeting of the Association for Psychological Science, May 24–28, Washington, DC.

Christman, S., & Propper, R. (2010a). Episodic memory and hemispheric interaction: Handedness and eye movements. In G. Davies & D. Wright (Eds.), *Current issues in applied memory* (pp. 185–205). London: Psychology Press.

Christman, S.D., & Propper, R.E. (2010b). Handedness, REM sleep, and dreaming: Interhemispheric mechanisms. *International Review of Neurobiology, 92*, 215–232.

Cohen, D.B. (1977). Changes in REM dream content during the night: Implications for a hypothesis about changes in cerebral dominance across REM periods. *Perceptual and Motor Skills, 44*, 1267–1277.

Denenberg, V.H., Kertesz, A., & Cowell, P.E. (1991). A factor analysis of the human's corpus callosum. *Brain Research, 548*, 126–132.

Doricchi, F., Milana, I., & Violani, C. (1993). Patterns of hemispheric lateralization in dream recallers and non-dream recallers. *International Journal of Neuroscience, 69*, 105–117.

Hellige, J.B. (2001). *Hemispheric asymmetry: What's right and what's left.* Cambridge, MA: Harvard University Press.

Hicks, R.A., Bautista, J., & Hicks, G.J. (1999). Handedness and the vividness of dreams. *Dreaming, 9*(4), 265–269.

Knecht, S., Dräger, B., Deppe, M., Bobe, L., Lohmann, H., Flöel, A., . . . Henninsen, H. (2000). Handedness and hemispheric language dominance in healthy humans. *Brain, 123*, 2512–2518.

McNamara, P., Clark, J., & Hartmann, E. (1988). Handedness and dream content. *Dreaming, 8*, 15–22.

Nielsen, T., Abel, A., Lorrain, D., & Montplaisir, J. (1988). Interhemispheric EEG coherence during sleep and wakefulness in left- and right-handed subjects. *Brain and Cognition, 14*, 113–115.

Nielsen, T.A., & Chenier, V. (1999). Variations in EEG coherence as an index of the affective content of dreams from REM sleep: Relationships with face imagery. *Brain and Cognition, 41*, 200–212.

Propper, R.E., O'Donnell, L.J., Whalen, S., Tie, Y., Norton, I.H., Suarez, R.O., . . . Golby, A. (2010). A combined fMRI and DTI examination of functional language lateralization and arcuate fasciculus structure:

Effects of degree versus direction of hand preference. *Brain and Cognition, 73*, 85–92.

Schredl, M. (2002). Questionnaires and diaries as research instruments in dream research: Methodological issues. *Dreaming, 12*(1), 17–26.

Van Nuys, D.W. (1984). Lateral eye movement and dream recall: II. Sex differences and handedness. *International Journal of Psychosomatics, 31*, 3–7.

Violani, C., De Gennaro, L., & Solano, L. (1988). Hemispheric differentiation and dream recall: Subjective estimates of sleep and dreams in different handedness groups. *International Journal of Neuroscience, 39*, 9–14.

Witelson, S.F., & Goldsmith, C.H. (1991). The relationship of hand preference to anatomy of the corpus callosum in men. *Brain Research, 545*, 175–182.

Healing and Dreams

Ancient as well as modern cultures have believed that dreaming is restorative and innately healing and that dreams can guide the conscious mind—in symbolic language—about the directions best followed to achieve health and wholeness.

The first written mention of healing and dreams is found in *The Yellow Emperor's Classic of Internal Medicine* (approximately 2600 BCE). Hippocrates (ca. 460–380 BCE) similarly recognized that dreams can provide important information about the healing process:

> Inductions to be derived from natural dreams, from which to attain knowledge of the good or bad state of the body . . . To see the earth level and well tilled, tree that are luxuriant, covered with fruit and cultivated, rivers flowing naturally, with water that is pure. (Hippocrates, 1931, p. 423)

In the time period surrounding Hippocrates—for a thousand years—supplicants in Greece would make a pilgrimage to the temples of Asclepius to incubate dreams, to have healing dreams in a special chamber specifically built for this purpose. The process included bathing, fasting, music, and other ritualistic activities; all of these increased the likelihood of a healing dream.

Carl Jung (1875–1961), the preeminent Swiss psychiatrist, devoted considerable attention to dreams; they were a cornerstone of his treatment method. He concluded:

> The general function of dreams is to try to restore our psychological balance by producing dream material that re-establishes, in a subtle way, the total psychic equilibrium. (Jung, 1968, p. 50)

Patricia Garfield's *The Healing Power of Dreams* is the book that contains the most examples and information about healing dreams. Her views about these dreams include:

> Your dreams can keep you healthy, warn you when you are at risk, diagnose incipient physical problems, support you during physical crises, forecast your recuperation, suggest treatment, heal your body, and signal your return to wellness. (Garfield, 1991, p. 17)

Similar to Garfield's work but much more wide ranging and philosophical, Mark Barasch's *Healing Dreams* is based on 15 years of research about such dreams. He also uses his own remarkable dreams when he was dealing with thyroid cancer to illustrate the dream healing process.

Healing dream after a heart attack. (Stephen Parker)

One of the more promising directions of using dreams in the healing process is being pioneered by Wendy Pannier and Tallulah Lyons (Lyons & Pannier, 2010). Working with cancer survivors and using guided imagery and relaxation techniques, they help the person reenter the dream, explore the dream, and, if necessary, transform the dream.

With *lucid dreaming*, in research pioneered by Scott Sparrow and Stephen LaBerge, the dreamer is aware that she is dreaming and controls the dreaming and healing process, at least to some extent. This is somewhat similar to image rehearsal and re-scripting dreams, only in a much more altered state of consciousness.

In the 2009 film documentary *The Edge of Dreaming*, Scottish film director Amy Hardie experiences a vivid dream that tells her she is going to die before her next birthday. She believes that she has to reenter the nightmare to change this prophecy; she is assisted in this by a shamanic healer, Claudia Goncalve.

Similarly, there is promising research (Lu, Wagner, Male, Whitehead, & Boehnlein, 2009, pp. 236–239) involving reducing nightmares of war veterans through image rehearsal and re-scripting their nightmares. Since nightmares are one of the defining characteristics of posttraumatic stress disorder, the reduction of nightmares can provide a quantifiable measure of healing

In a different vein than quantifiable research, and illustrative of dream healing imagery throughout the centuries, Ernest Rossi, PhD, wrote a memoir of his dreams after having a stroke. In his fifth week of recovery, he dreamed:

I enjoy the numinous beauty and wonderment of looking through a new clear crystal cover on our swim spa seeing the delightful light blue, clean water in the sparkling sunlight. (Rossi, 2004, pp. 215–227)

This dream is strikingly similar to the dreams Hippocrates described at the beginning of this article: healing imagery in dreams is part of an ancient process.

Stephen Bixby Parker

References

Garfield, P. (1991). *The healing power of dreams.* New York: Simon and Schuster.

Hippocrates. (1931). *Regimen IV: On dreams* (Trans. W.H.S. Jones, Loeb ed., Vol. IV). Cambridge, MA: Harvard University Press.

Jung, C. (1968). *Man and his symbols.* New York: Random House.

Lu, M., Wagner, Male, L., Whitehead, A., & Boehnlein, J. (2009). Imagery rehearsal therapy for posttraumatic nightmares in U.S. veterans. *Journal of Traumatic Stress, 22,* 236–239.

Lyons, T., & Pannier, W. (2010, August 30). The healing power of dreams and nightmares. Retrieved from http://www.healing powerofdreams.com/Pannier_Lyons%5B1%5D.pdf

Rossi, E. (2004). Gene expression and brain plasticity in stroke rehabilitation. *American Journal of Clinical Hypnosis, 46*(3), 215–227.

Hill Dream Model

The Hill Dream model (Hill, 1996, 2004), developed by Clara E. Hill at the University of Maryland, is based on the following assumptions: dreams reflect waking life, the meaning of dreams is personal, and clients must come up with their own understandings of dreams but working with a therapist can be helpful. The model integrates client-centered, Gestalt, psychodynamic (Jungian, Freudian), and behavioral theories of dreamwork and involves three stages. In the exploration stage, the therapist asks the client to retell the dream in the first person present tense and then works with the client to choose several key images. The client is then encouraged to explore these key images sequentially in great depth through description ("Paint me a picture of this image in words"), reexperiencing ("What are you feeling at this moment in the dream?"), association ("What is the first thing that comes into your mind as you think about this image?" "What memories do you have of this?"), and waking-life triggers ("What has happened recently that might have sparked this image?"). In the insight stage, the therapist works with the client to construct a meaning of the dream, focusing on the experience itself, waking life, or inner personality dynamics (in terms of parts of self, inner conflicts, or spiritual/existential concerns). In the action stage, the therapist and client work together to decide if and how the client would like to do differently in waking life based on the new understanding of the dream. Steps of the action stage include changing the dream in fantasy (with special steps taken for working with nightmares), and then restating the possible changes and bridging these changes to waking life. The model is collaborative, such that the therapist is an expert on the process of working with dreams but not the expert on the interpretation of the dream (the new understanding of the dream should be a surprise to both the therapist and client). A single dream session using this model typically takes about 90 minutes.

More than 25 studies have been conducted on the Hill Dream model (see Hill, 2004; Hill & Knox, in press; Hill & Spangler, 2007). Dreamwork using this model has been shown to be more effective than regular therapy sessions. Specifically, clients rate dream sessions high in terms of ratings of session quality, working alliance, gains from dream interpretation, and mastery insight. They also show gains in insight into specific dreams, clarification and implementation of action ideas for specific dreams, change in target problems identified in dreams, and improved attitudes toward dreams. Clients who benefit from dreamwork are those who are able to become very involved in the dreamwork, but such variables as attitudes toward dreams, openness, gender, and dream recall do not seem to be related to outcome. Clients have indicated that what they found to be particularly helpful about the model were the associations, links to waking life, catharsis, having an objective perspective, and working with a therapist. Other findings include that working with therapists is more effective than self-help, all of the stages and components of the model have been shown to be effective, and probes for insight appear to be particularly effective therapist interventions. We are currently investigating how therapists who have been trained in this model use dreams in ongoing psychodynamic psychotherapy sessions. Future challenges for research involve comparisons of this model with other dream models (e.g., Freudian, Jungian), other evocative therapeutic approaches (e.g., sand tray, psychodrama), and modifying the model for specific populations (e.g., people with posttraumatic stress syndrome, children).

From this body of research, it can be recommended that therapists use this model in therapy, especially when clients are psychologically minded, have troubling dreams, or want to understand their dreams. Therapists can use the model as a sole intervention in one to two sessions with healthy clients or as one component of ongoing psychotherapy, although the model needs to be modified to fit into a 50-minute session.

Clara Hill

See also: entries related to Dreams and Therapy

References

Hill, C. E. (1996). *Working with dreams in psychotherapy*. New York: Guilford Press.

Hill, C. E. (Ed.). (2004). *Dream work in therapy: Facilitating exploration, insight, and action*. Washington, DC: American Psychological Association.

Hill, C. E., & Knox, S. (in press). The use of dreams in modern psychotherapy. In P. McNamara & A. Chow (Eds.), *International Review of Neurobiology*. New York: Elsevier.

Hill, C. E., & Spangler, P. (2007). Dreams and psychotherapy. In D. Barrett & P. McNamara (Eds.), *The new science of dreaming* (pp. 159–186). Westport, CT: Greenwood Publishers.

Hypnagogic Imagery

The term *hypnagogic imagery* was coined by early dream researcher Alfred Maury in 1848, to describe the unique hallucinatory experiences that occur during sleep onset, or stage 1 sleep. *Hypnagogic experience* might be a better term, since these experiences are not exclusively visual, but may occur in any sensory modality: visual, auditory, tactile, olfactory, or kinesthetic. Typical hypnagogic experiences are visual or auditory, and most often consist of abrupt, disjointed impressions of near-hallucinatory vividness, including shapes, objects, or faces suddenly flying into view; images not connected to any larger narrative; sounds (often harsh or grating); and phrases uttered by disembodied voices. *Hypnagogia* (a term proposed by Mavromatis, 1987) may also include fleeting thoughts, physical sensations, and brief REM-like dreams. Hypnopompic experiences are similar to hypnagogia, but occur during the transition from sleep to waking.

Mavromatis (1987) made the first serious attempt to catalog the variety of hypnagogic phenomena. He found that hypnagogic experience tends to unfold in four stages, with vividness, luminosity, and intensity of color increasing as one goes deeper. The first or light stage includes flashes of light, colors, and moving geometric shapes. The second or middle stage includes faces and scenes, usually in swift succession, as well as bodily sensations and distortions (e.g., swelling, floating). The third or deep stage consists of autosymbolic phenomena, that is, dreamlike images that seem charged with significance and may symbolically represent the condition or thoughts of the subject. For example, the subject is trying to follow a line of thought but becomes distracted, and suddenly sees himself walking on a mountain path with no idea how he strayed from the main trail. The fourth stage is characterized by hypnagogic dreams: brief, vivid, intense dreams with loss of awareness of the waking environment. Hypnagogic dreams generally differ from REM dreams in several ways: if REM dreams are complex, multimodal, sequential experiences of being immersed in a perceived environment, hypnagogic dreams tend to be brief, disjointed (not connected to form a larger narrative), uni- or bimodal, and experienced at a remove (the dreamer is looking *at* the images, rather than being immersed in the world of the dream).

The variety of hypnagogic experience may relate to variations in brain states during sleep onset, a transitional state that generally lasts only a few minutes but may go on much longer. The progression from waking to stage 1 to stage 2 sleep is not necessarily smooth and continuous; some sleepers may move back and forth between waking and stage 1 several times before passing into stage 2 sleep. Furthermore, stage 1 is not unitary; variations within stage 1 may include the temporary resurgence of alpha waves, fluctuations in theta rhythms, and miscellaneous humps, spikes, or partial spindles (not yet the full sleep spindles associated with stage 2). More research is needed to establish possible correlations between hypnagogic phenomena and brain states.

The intermediate nature of sleep onset results in a dreamy softening of boundaries while retaining to some degree the critical faculties of waking consciousness, which proves to be fertile ground for developing new ideas and perspectives. Many artists and writers have experimented with hypnagogic experience as a source of creative inspiration. Perhaps the best known was the surrealist painter Salvador Dali, who developed his own method for mining hypnagogia: he would sit upright in a chair holding a key between the thumb and forefinger of his left hand, having previously placed a plate on the floor directly below the key. He would then let himself drift off to sleep, to be wakened abruptly by the loud noise when his grip relaxed and the key fell against the plate. In this way he was able to recall a high percentage of hypnagogic images.

Richard A. Russo

References

Maury, A. (1848). Des hallucinations hypnagogiques ou des erreurs des sens dans l'état intermédiare entre la veille et le sommeil. *Annals de Medico-Psychologie System Nerveux, 11,* 26–40.

Mavromatis, A. (1987). *Hypnagogia: The unique state of consciousness between wakefulness and sleep.* London: Routledge & Kegan Paul.

Nielson, T. (1995). Describing and modeling hypnagogic imagery using a systematic self observation procedure. *Dreaming, 5,* 74–94.

Hypocretin Gene Transfer in Mice Models of Narcolepsy

In the last few years significant gains have been made in the use of gene therapy to successfully treat specific diseases (Aiuti et al., 2009; Cartier et al., 2009; Maguire et al., 2009). Now that some disorders have been linked to specific genes it is important for sleep researchers to explore the use of genetic pharmacology in sleep medicine. The sleep disorder narcolepsy is especially suited for gene therapy since it is characterized by the specific loss of neurons containing the neuropeptide hypocretin, also known as orexin (Peyron et al., 1998; Thannickal et al., 2000). The gene for hypocretin can be transferred into specific brain regions and its effects on behavior studied. Mouse and canine models for the disease exist, which permit reliable tests of the strategy. Recent advances in viral vectors have made it possible to transfer specific genes of interest even at the clinical level. These viral vectors have little or no cytotoxicity and are not tumerogenic. However, long-term consequences are still not known.

The gene transfer approach can rapidly identify the optimal site for reversing symptoms. Moreover, the gene transfer can be tailored to specific phenotypes of neurons so that the gene is expressed in only those neurons. Site and phenotype specific gene transfer will identify which function (EEG, sleep onset REM periods, cataplexy) is restored at each injection site, thereby revealing the hypocretin (HCRT) circuit responsible for the function. This is very cost efficient in the drug-discovery process as it permits investigators to rapidly test specific hypotheses regarding the HCRT network in regulating sleep and wakefulness. The method can be also be transferred for use in canine narcolepsy without any added cost to make new materials. Rescuing canine narcolepsy is an important step as it will not only provide confirmation of the narcolepsy circuit but also speed public approval of the use of gene therapy for sleep disorders.

Our group was the first to recognize the importance of gene therapy in sleep medicine and published the first proof of principle that it works in mice models of narcolepsy (Liu et al., 2008). We have answered several critical questions: (1) Can the gene for hypocretin be placed anywhere in the brain for it to be effective? We have determined that there is indeed site specificity. Placing the gene into the striatum does not affect any narcolepsy symptom. On the other hand, placing the hypocretin gene into neurons of the zona incerta is very effective in blocking cataplexy; (2) Does hypocretin gene transfer rescue some or all of the symptoms of narcolepsy? We have found that cataplexy can be blocked but not excessive daytime sleepiness, sleep fragmentation, or sleep attacks. This suggests that there are specific circuits regulating cataplexy whereas the other symptoms might be regulated by diffuse hypocretin innervations; (3) How long do the effects last? This depends on the life of the virus used to transfer the gene. In one study, the effects lasted for only four days, which was the life of the herpes simplex virus used to insert the gene (Liu et al., 2008). In the newer study (unpublished study), a recombinant adeno-associated viral (rAAV) vector was used and the effects lasted for at least 21 days. rAAV does last for months and we are currently exploring if the cataplexy continues to be blocked; (4) Can hypocretin release be regulated by optogenetic stimulation and does this block narcoleptic symptoms? This will mechanistically control cataplexy and serve as a translational tool. Overall, gene therapy shows promise as a method to treat sleep disorders.

Priyattam J. Shiromani

See also: entries related to Hormones in Sleep

Note

This work was supported in part by the Department of Veterans Affairs, Veterans Health Administration, Office of Research Development (BLR&D), and NIH grants NS030140, NS052287, MH55772, and HL091363.

References

Aiuti, A., Cattaneo, F., Galimberti, S., Benninghoff, U., Cassani, B., Callegaro, L., . . . Roncarolo, M. G. (2009). Gene therapy for immunodeficiency due to adenosine deaminase deficiency. *New England Journal of Medicine, 360*, 447–458.

Cartier, N., Hacein-Bey-Abina, S., Bartholomae, C. C., Veres, G., Schmidt, M., Kutschera, I., . . . Aubourg, P. (2009). Hematopoietic stem cell gene therapy with a lentiviral vector in X-linked adrenoleukodystrophy. *Science, 326*, 818–823.

Liu, M., Thankachan, S., Kaur, S., Begum, S., Blanco-Centurion, C., Sakurai, T., . . . Shiromani, P. J. (2008). Orexin (hypocretin) gene transfer diminishes narcoleptic sleep behavior in mice. *European Journal of Neuroscience, 28*, 1382–1393.

Maguire, A. M., High, K. A., Auricchio, A., Wright, J. F., Pierce, E. A., Testa, F., . . . Bennett, J. (2009). Age-dependent effects of RPE65 gene therapy for Leber's congenital amaurosis: A phase 1 dose-escalation trial. *Lancet, 374*, 1597–1605.

Peyron, C., Tighe, D. K., Van den Pol, A. N., De Lecea, L., Heller, H. C., Sutcliffe, J. G., & Kilduff, T. S. (1998). Neurons containing hypocretin (orexin) project to multiple neuronal systems. *Journal of Neuroscience, 18*, 9996–10015.

Thannickal, T. C., Moore, R. Y., Nienhuis, R., Ramanathan, L., Gulyani, S., Aldrich, M., . . . Siegel, J. M. (2000). Reduced number of hypocretin neurons in human narcolepsy. *Neuron, 27*, 469–474.

Hypothalamo–Pituitary–Adrenocortical (HPA) System and Sleep

The HPA system is essential for the individual's survival. It mediates the reaction to acute physical or psychological stress. The stress reaction starts with the release of corticotropin-releasing hormone (CRH) from the parvocellular neurons of the paraventricular nucleus of the hypothalamus. This is followed by secretion of corticotropin (ACTH) from the anterior pituitary, which results in the secretion of cortisol (in humans) or corticosterone (in rats) from the adrenocortex. In humans, during sleep, both the nadir and the acrophase of ACTH and cortisol secretion occur. During the first few hours of the night the quiescent period of the HPA hormones is found. At the same time the maxima of slow-wave sleep (SWS) and growth-hormone (GH) secretion occur (see the entry "Hypothalamo–Pituitary–Somatotrophic [HPS] System and Sleep"). During the early morning hours, between 02:00 and 03:00 A.M., the first pulse of cortisol is observed, which is followed by further pulses until awakening. During the second half of the night GH levels are low. This pattern points to a reciprocal interaction between HPA and HPS systems (see Figure 9). The pattern of cortisol secretion is widely dependent on a circadian rhythm. However, manipulation of the sleep–wake pattern results in subtle changes in HPA secretion. In rats during the dark period, when these animals are active, CRH gene-transcription levels increase. They decrease in the morning and throughout the light period.

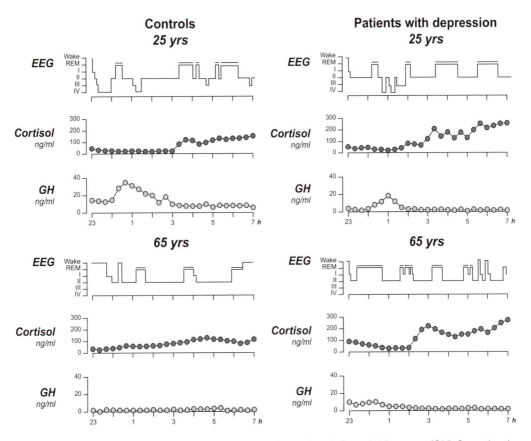

Figure 9: Hypnogramm and Pattern of Nocturnal Cortisol and Growth-Hormone (GH) Secretion in Young and Old Healthy Volunteers and Patients with Depression. Abbreviations: REM—rapid eye movement sleep, I–IV—stages of non-REM sleep. Fig. XXIV-3.1 from Steiger (2002a), © with permission from Wiley.

Corticotropin-Releasing Hormone

Sleep of conditional mouse mutants that overexpress CRH in the entire central nervous system (CNS) or only in the forebrain, including limbic structures, was compared to sleep in wild-type mice. In both strains of homozygous CRH-overexpressing mice REM sleep was elevated constantly. Only in the strain overexpressing CRH in the entire CNS was non-REM sleep suppressed slightly during the light period. After

six hours of sleep deprivation, elevated amounts of REM sleep were also found in heterozygous CRH-overexpressing mice during recovery sleep. This effect was reversed by treatment with a CRH receptor type 1 antagonist in heterozygous and homozygous CRH-overexpressing mice. The peripheral stress hormone levels were not elevated at baseline or after sleep deprivation. Since the stress axis was not changed in these animals, the sleep-EEG changes, particularly the increase in REM sleep, are most likely induced by the elevated fore-brain CRH through activation of CRH receptor type I. In Lewis rats the synthesis and the release of CRH is reduced due to a hypothalamic gene defect. These rats show more time in SWS and less time awake than intact rat strains. Conversely, spontaneous wakefulness of rats is diminished after a CRH antisense oligodeoxynucleotide. The latter study supports a role of maintenance of wakefulness and sleep-disturbing effects of CRH.

Intracerebroventricular administration of CRH decreases SWS in rats and rabbits. Decrease of SWS by CRH is even found after 72 hours of sleep deprivation. In addition sleep latency and the amount of REM sleep increase. After repetitive hourly intravenous injections of CRH (4 · 50 ?g, between 2200 and 0100 hours) in young normal male subjects, SWS and REM sleep decrease, the GH peak is blunted, and cortisol levels increase during the first half of the night. In young healthy women a partly different effect of the same dose of CRH was observed; as REM sleep increased during the first third of the night, the intermittent time spent awake was elevated and SWS decreased. The sleep-EEG effects in young normal subjects, particularly in women and in the animal models resemble sleep-EEG changes in patients with depression. Therefore it appears likely that CRH overactivity participates in the alterations of sleep in depressed patients. This view is supported by a study on the effects of a CRH receptor-1-antagonist on sleep EEG in patients with depression. After four weeks treatment with the substance R121919 (a receptor antagonist)

the characteristical sleep-EEG changes of depressed patients are counteracted, as SWS increases and the number of awakenings and REM density decrease.

The effect of CRH appears to depend on age as a dose of CRH was not effective in young healthy men, which impairs sleep in middle-aged healthy male subjects.

Vasopressin

Vasopressin is the major cofactor of CRH in the activation of the stress axis. After intracerebroventricular vasopressin administration, wakefulness increases in the rat. Chronic intranasal administration of vasopressin improves sleep in healthy elderly subjects. The total sleep time, SWS, and REM sleep increase. It was hypothesized that this treatment may compensate age-related decreases of vasopressin content of the suprachiasmatic nucleus, or that vasopressin could act by stimulating the expression of central corticosteroid receptors.

ACTH

After nocturnal infusion of ACTH, cortisol and GH increase in healthy volunteers. Ebiratide, a synthetic ACTH(4–9) analogue, shares several behavioral effects of ACTH in the absence of changes of peripheral hormone secretion. As expected after repetitive intravenous ebiratide, cortisol and GH levels remained unchanged in young male subjects, whereas sleep latency and, during the first third of the night, wakefulness increases and SWS decreases. These findings suggest that the blood–brain interface is no obstacle for CNS effects of intravenously given neuropeptides.

Cortisol, Synthetic Glucocorticoid, and Mineralocorticoid Receptor Ligands

In young male healthy volunteers, SWS and slow-wave activity (SWA) increase and REM sleep decreases after administration of cortisol by infusion or by repetitive nocturnal injections. In the latter study, GH increases after cortisol. Also in healthy elderly men and in patients with depression, SWS, SWA, and GH increase and REM sleep decreases in analogue protocols with repetitive intravenous administration of cortisol. Since CRH and cortisol exert opposite effects on SWS and GH it appears unlikely that the sleep-endocrine changes after CRH are mediated by increased cortisol levels. These changes may be induced by negative feedback inhibition of endogenous CRH. Similarly, inhibition of cortisol synthesis by metyrapone diminishes SWS and cortisol in healthy volunteers, whereas REM sleep remains unchanged. Since ACTH is enhanced in this experiment it appears likely that endogenous CRH is enhanced. The effects of acute and chronic glucocorticoid treatment on sleep are different. Subchronic treatment of female patients with multiple sclerosis with the glucocorticoid receptor agonist methylprednisolone induces a shortened REM latency, an elevated REM density, and a shift of the major portion of SWS from the first to the second non-REM sleep period. These changes resemble the sleep-EEG disturbances in patients with depression. Therefore, it is likely that a synergism between elevated CRH and cortisol results in the characteristical sleep-EEG changes in depressed patients. In a single case study the oral administration of mifepristone, a mixed glucocorticoid- and progesterone-receptor antagonist, disrupted sleep distinctly.

Sleep in Disorders with HPA-Activity Changes

The capacity of the adrenal glands to produce corticosteroids is distinctly diminished in Addison's disease. No major sleep-EEG changes were found in these patients. In one study Addison's patients were compared under two conditions. They either received continuous hydrocortisone replacement or short-time withdrawal of hydrocortisone. In comparison to withdrawal, REM latency decreases and REM time and intermittent wakefulness increase after replacement. This finding suggests that cortisol is necessary to initiate and to maintain REM sleep. In Cushing's disease, and in depression as well, hypercortisolism and disturbed sleep are frequent symptoms. Cortisol levels are excessive in Cushing's disease, either central or peripheral origin. Increased SWS, impaired sleep continuity, and disinhibition of REM sleep were reported in these patients. Similar sleep-EEG findings are frequently found in patients with depression, whereas dysregulation of the HPA system is more subtle. Characteristic sleep-EEG alterations in depressed patients include disturbed sleep continuity (prolonged sleep latency, increased number of awakenings, early morning awakening), decreased non-REM sleep (decreases of stage 2 and SWS, in younger patients the major portion of SWS is shifted from the first to the second cycle), and disinhibition of REM sleep (shortened REM latency, prolonged first REM period, elevated REM density, a measure for the amount of rapid eye movements during REM sleep). ACTH and cortisol levels are enhanced in most sleep-endocrine studies throughout the night or throughout 24 hours, respectively, when compared to healthy volunteers. In most, but not all, studies GH levels are blunted in patients with depression (see Figure 10). These observations suggest a strong relationship between shallow sleep, a low GH, and ACTH overactivity in depression. Furthermore there exist similarities in the sleep-endocrine changes during depression and during normal ageing. The longitudinal comparison of ACTH and cortisol between acute depression and recovery in adult depressed patients showed a decrease of HPA hormone levels during 24 hours or during the night, respectively. As of now one study is available comparing adult patients, intra-individually, with depression and who were drug free at least 14 days before each examination between acute depression and full recovery. Whereas cortisol levels decreased after remission, sleep-EEG changes and low GH levels persisted. It appears that HPA hypersecretion is a state marker of depression in adult patients. The persistence of most sleep-EEG and GH changes after recovery was confirmed over a period of three years. Cortisol appears to normalize independently from sleep. Therefore it is unlikely that hypercortisolism in acute depression is secondary to shallow sleep. The metabolic disturbances during acute depression may result in a biological scar, which is reflected by persisting changes of sleep and of GH in the remitted patients.

This hypothesis is further supported by a study in survivors of severe brain injury. Several months after the injury cortisol levels of these patients were in normal range. However, their GH and time spent in sleep stage 2 were reduced. Despite normal cortisol levels at the time of examination, in this study either HPA overactivity related to stress under intensive-care situation after brain injury or glucocorticoid treatment in some patients may contribute to the observed changes of sleep EEG and GH levels. Elevated HPA hormones were observed in some, but not all studies in patients with primary insomnia.

Conclusions

A reciprocal interaction of the HPA and the HPS system appears to play a key role in sleep regulation. CRH stimulates ACTH, cortisol, and REM sleep, and induces more shallow non-REM sleep. A balance exists between GHRH and CRH. During depression (CRH overactivity) and normal aging (decline of GHRH activity) similar changes of sleep-endocrine activity occur (see Figure 10).

Axel Steiger

See also: Hypothalamo–Pituitary–Somatotrophic (HPS) System and Sleep; entries related to Sleep Physiology

References

Kimura, M., Müller-Preuss, P., Lu, A., Wiesner, E., Flachskamm, C., Wurst, W., . . . Deussing, J.M. (2010). Conditional corticotropin-releasing hormone overexpression in the mouse forebrain enhances rapid eye movement sleep. *Molecular Psychiatry, 15*, 154–165.

Steiger, A. (1995). Schlafendokrinologie. *Der Nervenarzt, 66*, 15–27.

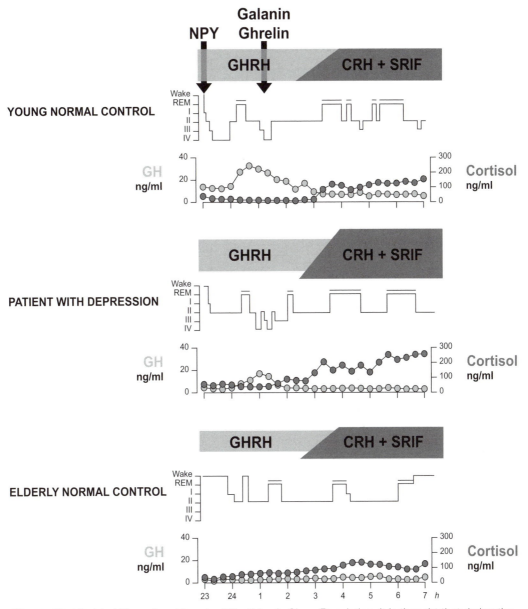

Figure 10: Model of Normal and Impaired Peptidergic Sleep Regulation. It is thought that during the first half of the night the influence of GHRH preponderates resulting in the high amounts of SWS and GH. Galanin and ghrelin may be co-factors to GHRH. NPY influences timing of sleep onset. During the second half of the night CRH and its co-factors somatostatin dominate. Changes in the GHRH/ CRH balance during depression and ageing result in similar alternations of sleep-endocrine activity. Abbreviations: GHRH—growth hormone-releasing hormone, CRH—corticotropin-releasing hormone, SRIF—somatostatin, NPY—neuropeptide Y. From Steiger (1995), © Springer Verlag Heidelberg.

Steiger, A. (2002a). Neuroendocrinology of sleep disorders. In H. D'haenen, J. A. den Boer, H. Westenberg, & P. Willner (Eds.), *Textbook of biological psychiatry* (pp. 1229–1246). London: John Wiley & Sons

Steiger, A. (2002b). Sleep and the hypothalamo-pituitary-adrenocortical system. *Sleep Medicine Reviews*, 6, 125–138.

Steiger, A. (2007). Neurochemical regulation of sleep. *Journal of Psychiatric Research*, 41, 537–552.

Hypothalamo–Pituitary–Somatotrophic (HPS) System and Sleep

The growth-hormone (GH) surge is the major amount of GH that is released during 24 hours. It occurs near to sleep onset, in temporal association with the first period of slow-wave sleep (SWS) (see Figure 11). This observation points to a strong interaction between GH and sleep. Changes of sleep result in changes of GH secretion. On the other hand all components of the HPS system participate in sleep regulation.

The physiological role of GH is to stimulate tissue growth and protein anabolism. The peptides GH-releasing hormone (GHRH) and ghrelin stimulate the synthesis and secretion of GH from the pituitary, whereas somatostatin inhibits GH. The observation that the GH surge is suppressed during sleep deprivation shows that the GH surge is widely sleep dependent, whereas GH release prior to sleep onset may occur in healthy subjects. In very young healthy male subjects who are sleep deprived, but relaxed, an unchanged nocturnal GH peak was found. In subjects who were at least 25 years old the GH peak was blunted during sleep deprivation. Lying relaxed appears to be sufficient to trigger the nocturnal GH peak in very young healthy subjects. The pattern of nocturnal GH release shows a sexual dimorphism. A single GH surge is found in

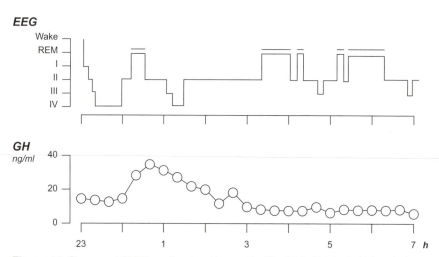

Figure 11: Sleep and GH Secretion in a Young Healthy Male Subject. Abbreviations: REM—rapid eye movement sleep, I–IV—stages of non-REM sleep. Steiger (1995), Fig. 1 © Springer Verlag Heidelberg.

male subjects. In contrast, in women, after a first GH peak, which is smaller than in male subjects, further peaks occur. In patients with isolated GH deficiency, the amount of SWS and of slow-wave activity (SWA) (EEG delta power, which occurs predominantly during SWS) are reduced in comparison to normal controls.

Growth Hormone Releasing Hormone

GHRH is the one neuropeptide in which its sleep-promoting effect is best documented. In the mouse, in the region of chromosome 13 linked to SWA, the GHRH receptor gene is found. A circadian rhythm appears to drive hypothalamic GHRHmRNA. When sleep propensity reaches its maximum at the onset of the light period, hypothalamic GHRHmRNA peaks. GHRH levels are low in the morning, increase in the afternoon, and decline at night. Many hypothalamic GHRH responsive neurons appear to be GABAergic. Calcium levels in GABAergic neurons cultured from rat fetal hypothalamus increase during perfusion with GHRH. Many hypothalamic GHRH responsive neurons appear to be GABAergic. GABAergic neurons in the median preoptic nucleus and in the ventrolateral preoptic nucleus were identified as potential targets of the sleep-regulatory actions of GHRH. Furthermore it was shown that GHRH may also act in the cortex to influence sleep.

Non-REM sleep is enhanced when GHRH is administered variously to male laboratory animals and to male human subjects. In detail, non-REM sleep increases after intracerebroventricular administration of GHRH in rats and rabbits, after its intravenous administration to rats, and after its injection into the medial preoptic area of rats. Similarly, SWS and the nocturnal secretion of GH increases after repetitive hourly iv injections of GHRH between 2200 and 0100 hours to young normal male subjects via long catheter, whereas cortisol decreases. It appears to be crucial to mimic the pulsatile endogenous release of peptides by repetitive injections, because sleep EEG remained unchanged after GHRH infusion. Also, intranasal administration of GHRH promotes sleep. The effect of GHRH to sleep appears to be influenced by time of administration, age, and gender. When GHRH was given intravenously during the early morning hours to young normal men, no major changes of sleep EEG were found. In elderly women and men the sleep-promoting effects of intravenous GHRH is weak. In drug-free depressed patients of both sexes of a wide age range and in matched controls, a sexual dimorphism in the sleep-endocrine response to GHRH was found. ACTH and cortisol levels decrease in male patients and controls after GHRH. In females, however, these hormones are enhanced after GHRH. Similarly, in male patients and control subjects the amount of non-REM sleep increases and wakefulness decreases after GHRH, whereas sleep is changed in the opposite fashion in female patients and controls. Sleep-impairing effects of GHRH were confirmed in young healthy women. These data corroborate a reciprocal interaction of GHRH and corticotropin-releasing hormone (see the entry "Hypothalamo–Pituitary–Adrenocortical [HPA] System and Sleep"), whereas their synergistic sleep-impairing effect is suggested in females.

Generally sleep appears to be impaired when GHRH levels are low, whereas sleep is promoted when GHRH levels are high. In detail, in the rat, non-REM sleep is diminished after GHRH receptor antagonists and after antibodies to GHRH. Conversely, in the so-called super mice, the giant transgenic mice, GH levels are increased and, during the light period, non-REM sleep is elevated and REM sleep is almost doubled compared to the wild type. Also during recovery sleep following sleep deprivation, the super mice sleep more than the control mice. In dwarf rats, deficits in the central GHRHergic transmission exist and hypothalamic GHRH levels are reduced. In these rats the amount of non-REM sleep is reduced in comparison to control rats. Also in dwarf homocygous (lit/lit) mice the amounts of non-REM sleep and REM sleep are diminished. The GHRH receptors of these mice are nonfunctional.

The major stimulus for sleep is sleep deprivation. During the recovery night after sleep deprivation, non-REM sleep, SWS, and REM sleep increase, whereas intermittent wakefulness decreases. GHRH appears to be involved in this effect. Sleep promotion after sleep deprivation is inhibited by GHRH antibodies and by microinjections of a GHRH antagonist into the preoptic area in rats. Sleep deprivation induces a depletion of hypothalamic GHRH and low hypothalamic GHRH contents in rats. After sleep deprivation, hypothalamic GHRHmRNA is elevated, whereas hypothalamic somatostatin is diminished. During the recovery night after sleep deprivation, the non-REM sleep-promoting effect of sleep deprivation was augmented after repetitive intravenous GHRH administration in healthy male and female subjects. Interestingly, this effect is shared by corticotropin-releasing hormone.

Somatostatin

Intracerebroventricular administration of somatostatin results in selective increases of REM sleep in the rat. After systemic and after intracerebroventricular administration of octreotide, a somatostatin analogue, non-REM sleep, and GH decrease. Similarly, after subcutaneous octreotide, SWS decreases and intermittent wakefulness increases in young healthy volunteers. After intravenous administration of somatostatin to young healthy subjects, sleep remained unchanged, whereas the same dose impairs sleep in elderly women and men. This finding suggests that the vulnerability for sleep-impairing effects of somatostatin increases during ageing. A reciprocal interaction of GHRH and somatostatin in sleep regulation, resembling the opposite effects on GH release, appears likely.

Growth Hormone; Insulin-Like Growth Factor-1 (IGF-1)

When GHRH is inhibited via negative feedback by administration of GH in humans and laboratory animals or by higher intracerebroventricular dosages of IGF-1, non-REM sleep decreases. On the other hand sleep was impaired after a GH antagonist. The latter finding suggests that beside of GHRH also GH promotes sleep. In patients with acquired GH deficiency, sleep remained unchanged after chronic GH substitution.

GH Secretagogues and Ghrelin

Ghrelin is the only known endogenous ligand of the GH secretagogue receptor. Synthetic ligands of this receptor were already known in the 1970s. After GH-releasing peptide-6 administration (GHRP-6), sleep stage 2 increases. GH and, during the first half of the night, cortisol increase after GHRP-6. A similar endocrine response is found after hexarelin, whereas sleep stage 2 increases after GHRP-6, SWS and SWA decreases after this substance. This may be explained by a change of the GHRH–corticotropin-releasing hormone (CRH) ratio in favor of CRH, due to inhibition of endogenous GHRH after distinct stimulation of GH following hexarelin.

In mice, after systemic ghrelin administration, non-REM sleep increases. In mice with nonfunctional GHRH receptors, sleep remains unchanged. This observation suggests that an intact GHRH receptor is a prerequisite for this effect. Oral administration of the GH secretagogue MK-677 for one week exerts marked sleep-promoting effects in young men, whereas only weak effects were found in elderly subjects.

Similar to the effects of GHRH after repetitive intravenous ghrelin administration, SWS, SWA, and GH increase in young men. Cortisol is blunted after GHRH in young men, the hypothalamo–pituitary–adrenocortical (HPA) hormones ACTH and cortisol are elevated after ghrelin administration. After the first injection of ghrelin, the GH levels showed the highest response, whereas the increase of cortisol was relatively low. In contrast, after the last injection, the highest response of cortisol and the lowest of GH were found. These observations suggest that ghrelin acts as an interface between the HPA and the HPS systems. In a series of studies, the influence of time of administration, age, gender, and depression on the sleep-endocrine effects of ghrelin were tested. In young normal men ghrelin had no effects on sleep EEG when given during the early morning. In young and in elder healthy women, sleep remained unchanged after ghrelin, whereas the changes in GH and cortisol levels were similar to those in male subjects. In elder healthy men and in male patients with depression, sleep promotion after ghrelin was preserved as the amount of non-REM sleep increased. In female patients with depression, the amount of REM sleep decreased.

In contrast to the findings in humans and mice after intracerebroventricular and after intrahypothalamic ghrelin administration, wakefulness and feeding increased in rats. It was hypothesized that decreased wakefulness and increased feeding are two parallel outputs of the hypothalamic ghrelin-sensitive circuitry. Its activation may trigger the behavior during the first three hours of the activity period of rats, the dark onset syndrome. One should keep in mind a possible delayed sleep-promoting action of ghrelin following the feeding period in some of the experiments in rats. In favor of a sleep-promoting effect of ghrelin is the observation that ghrelin knockout mice sleep less than the wild type. Furthermore nocturnal ghrelin levels are reduced in patients with insomnia compared to normal controls. Finally an advanced increase of ghrelin during the recovery night after sleep deprivation was found. In the

Wisconsin Sleep Cohort Study, a positive correlation between short sleep time and elevated ghrelin levels was observed.

Axel Steiger

See also: entries related to Sleep Physiology

References

Liao, F., Taishi, P., Churchill, L., Urza, M. J., & Krueger, J. M. (2010). Localized suppression of cortical growth hormone-releasing hormone receptors state-specifically attenuates electroencephalographic delta waves. *Journal of Neuroscience, 30,* 4151–4159.

Obál, F., Jr., & Krueger, J. M. (2004). GHRH and sleep. *Sleep Medicine Reviews, 8,* 367–377.

Steiger, A. (1995). Schlafendokrinologie. *Der Nervenarzt, 66,* 15–27.

Steiger, A., Dresler, M., Schüssler, P., & Kluge, M. (2011). Ghrelin in mental health, sleep, memory. *Mollecular Cell Endocrinology, 34,* 88–96.

Van Cauter, E., Latta, F., Nedeltcheva, A., Spiegel, K., Leproult, R., Vandenbril, C., . . . Copinschi, G. (2004). Reciprocal interactions between the GH axis and sleep. *Growth Hormone & IGF Research,* 14(Suppl. A), S10–S17.

I

Illness and Dreams

Many cultures throughout history have recognized how dreams can contribute to understanding and treating illness. In the healing arts traditions of ancient Greece, from which modern medical and psychological practices derive, dreams played a central role. Galen and Hippocrates consulted patients' dreams regularly for diagnostic and prognostic information. Plato and Aristotle believed dreams had a faculty of inner perception by which the workings of body and soul were observable.

That dreams have access to information in advance of any manifest or detectable symptoms has been corroborated by modern observation and research. In Freud's famous Irma or specimen dream, he was examining white patches on the inside of a patient's mouth; this dream image has been considered prodromal of the debilitating jaw cancer he developed later in life. Jung reported that he had dealt with 44 cases in which dreams referred to existing organic conditions; he discussed several of these in his 1935 Tavistock lectures to a medical audience (Jung, 1968). King and DeCicco (2007) found that patients with lower levels of physical health and physical functioning reported dreams of medical themes, injuries and illnesses, and bodily misfortunes.

Dreams come in conjunction with illness because it is an archetypal, or universal, situation to which the deep core of our being responds—as it does to all major life events—by producing dreams that help facilitate an individual's understanding and development. A dream may reflect the patient's subjective attitude toward or personal feelings about an illness; or they may contain factually accurate information not consciously known. Dreams in which an individual appears who *in reality* had or has the same symptoms or condition that the dreamer develops can be especially revelatory: a correspondence may exist between the disposition of the known case and the outcome of the dreamer's. Dreams related to an existing or emerging condition may come not only to the sufferer but to family members, close friends, or professionals involved in the case. If there is a question of differential diagnosis or if a condition is psychosomatic, dreams also can be of value in crafting appropriate treatment plans.

Studies have been made of dreams using medical categories in order to elucidate the psychological and imagistic themes in them. A more direct approach of asking individuals with existing somatic complaints, organic or psychogenic, if they have ever dreamed about them, has yielded hundreds of dreams, which have been sorted according to the mode in which the symptom is represented. The human body's systems are frequently symbolized by parallel structures and processes in animals, vehicles, and houses (Sabini, 1981).

Unfortunately, little systematic work has been done to collect the initial, recurring, or ongoing dreams of either general medical or psychosomatic patients. Psychosomatic research, well established in the 1940s and 1950s, declined between 1960 and 1980, and has not yet picked up again despite the current trend toward holistic healing.

Dreaming of an illness does not necessarily imply that an organic condition exists, but may point to a psychic malaise that has not and may not be somaticized. Dreams arise from the interstices between mind and body, spirit and matter, and are thus positioned to bridge these two fundamental aspects of our being, illuminating their interplay.

Meredith Sabini

References

Jung. C. G. (1968). *Analytical psychology: Its theory and practice*. The Tavistock Lectures. New York: Random House.

King, D., & DeCicco, T. (2007). The relationships between dream content and physical health, mood, and self-construal. *Dreaming, 17*(3), 127–151.

Sabini, M. (1981). Imagery in dreams of illness. *Quadrant, 14, 2*.

Illusory Contents in Dreams

Dreams accompany certain activities of the sleeping brain. They occur primarily when spontaneous electrical oscillations activate neural circuits that process memories. Much of dream fantasies and ambiguities owe to weakened brain-nerve connections (synapses). This entry relates to this weakening influence, as illustrated by children's dreams, which are minimally exposed to aging. During nonrapid eye movement (NREM) sleep, recently acquired short-term hippocampal memories become stored in the neocortex for the long term (hippocampal replay). Additionally, enormous numbers of already-stored memory fragments become strengthened. During rapid eye movement (REM) sleep, many already-stored, long-term memories are strengthened.

Since dreams usually are highly visual, visual-memory storage is illustrated. Storage is sparse and distributed in both the hippocampus and neocortex; sparse, because only a memory fragment is represented at any single location; distributed, because the various fragments exist at separate locations. Fragments of an object's memory (for color, texture, orientation, position, etc.), for example, may be clustered together at these separate locations.

Activations by both fast and slow brain waves contribute to the sleep strengthening of stored memories. Activation often is accompanied by an unconscious awareness of the corresponding memories as static dreams; that is, isolated thoughts and perceptions. Without such periodic strengthening, memories would deteriorate by continuous weakening of their synapses (by molecular turnover). Specific strengths for any given memory become established and maintained either by use or spontaneous, periodic activations during sleep. Since sufficient numbers of molecules are required to preserve specific synaptic strengths, if lost molecules were not replaced periodically, memories would gradually deteriorate. For infrequently used memories, most strengthening occurs during sleep.

During REM sleep, spontaneous gamma oscillations (30 to 100 cycles/second) trigger a process known as temporal binding (binding by synchrony), in which neurons of distributed memory fragments are activated synchronously, transiently combining their features. Certain slow brain waves of REM sleep—presumably the hippocampal theta waves (four to eight cycles per second)—trigger the serial linking of individual memories, to form connected, narrative dreams. Activation without binding probably merely maintains and increases synaptic strengths.

From 85 to 95 percent of REM dreams are ordinary and mundane, with authentic contents. Our main thesis here is that the illusory, ambiguous contents of many dreams have a single cause—effective synaptic strengths. It is most relevant, then, to ask, what occurs when only a small fraction of memory synapses are weakened? For example, one would not expect a scene to be degraded beyond recognition. A face still would still be a face, but possibly unrecognizable. Thus, temporal binding of small numbers of memory neurons, with weakened synapses might lead only to minor discrepancies.

Illusory dreams with faulty thoughts and perceptions probably trace to the inclusion of old, variously incompetent memories with significant numbers of defective synapses. Dreams with unlinked memories are said to be static or thoughtful. They typically occur during adult NREM sleep, in children up to about five years old, and in some seizures and artificial brain stimulation. Any influence that tended to randomize temporal binding and serial linking would favor illusory dreams.

Whereas bound memories always exist in dreams, serial linking of them may fail. For example, up to five years old, children's dreams often consist of static images of familiar animals, suggesting that serial linking is not fully developed. Inasmuch as Foulkes reported dreams in only 15 percent of REM awakenings of typical three- to five-year-old children, and none from their NREM sleep, it appears that temporal-binding mechanisms are infrequently present at these ages during REM sleep, and absent during NREM sleep. In a dramatic change, a story-like format begins to appear at five years old, in which characters move about and interact in a dynamic dream world, often with the dreamer participating. This contrasts with earlier static dream content, lacking in social interactions and dreamer presence. These changes accompany the well-known 5-to-7 shift in cognitive competence. Since defective synapses accumulate with age, there should be relatively few, or even none in young children, whose dreams should reflect minimal memory-recall failures.

These deductions conform to Foulkes's findings with 3- to 15-year-old children. Although they reported no illusory dream, dream distortions were common. These did not begin to occur until five to seven years. But almost without exception, dream contents at three to five years were authentic, suggesting that relatively few synapses were weakened. Mere dream distortions at five to seven years reflect the expected minimal weakening of synapses. The frequency of occurrence of unknown people and places generally increases with age through (and beyond) adolescence. It follows that the much lesser interference with the dream process in children is largely a consequence of lesser time having transpired for progression of interfering influences.

J. Lee Kavanau

See also: entries related to Dream Theories

References

Foulkes, D. (1982). *Children's dreams: Longitudinal studies.* New York: Wiley and Sons.

Kavanau, J. L. (2002). Dream contents and failing memories. *Archives Italiennes de Biologie, 140,* 109–127.

Impactful Dreams

Impactful dreams are those that continue to influence the dreamer's thoughts and feelings even after awakening. Their impact often includes changes in attitude, shifts in self-perception, and even adjustments in worldview. Such far-reaching and enduring changes contrast with REM carry-over effects, which include transient changes in perception (e.g., altered tactile sensitivity), cognition (e.g., divergent thinking), and mood (e.g., lingering apprehension) immediately after awakening. Instead, the effects of impactful dreams often last hours, days, or weeks and involve alteration of the dreamer's core convictions and commitments.

Because of their capacity to induce change, impactful dreams often acquire status and standing within a culture—or subculture—that values those changes. So, people may give special attention to—and perhaps even try to bring about—the

types of impactful dreams that reflect a valued cultural pattern or tradition. Also, because of their intensity and cultural significance, impactful dreams have attracted the attention of researchers with very different scholarly agendas (e.g., understanding therapeutic change, understanding religious change). For both cultural and scholarly reasons, then, discussions of impactful dreams involve considerable theoretical and conceptual diversity, as is evident in the terminology used to identify such big dreams (e.g., nightmares, titanic dreams, retrieval dreams, archetypal dreams, prophetic dreams, lucid dreams, reality dreams).

In their attempts to address this diversity and empirically identify different classes (or types) of impactful dreams, researchers with different theoretical and cultural commitments have usually focused on single diagnostic features. For example, lucid dreams may be defined simply in terms of awareness of dreaming while dreaming, and nightmares may be defined simply in terms of sleep-disturbing negative dream emotion. In contrast, systematic classificatory studies, such as are commonplace in biology, draw attention to natural kinds, that is, classes that (such as animal species) maximize the number of features shared by members of a class and manifest coherent patterns of features across several levels of analysis. Because these classificatory criteria are seldom invoked in dream studies, dream classification often has been driven by cultural biases, disciplinary priorities, or utilitarian objectives.

However, when systematic classificatory methods have been adopted (cf. Busink &

Kuiken, 1996), they have provided identification of three types of impactful dreams, distinguishable not by any single feature (e.g., sleep disrupting emotion) but rather by coherent profiles of features involving feelings and emotions, motives and goals, sensory phenomena, movement characteristics, and dream endings. One type, nightmares, involves fear, harm avoidance, vigorous activity, auditory anomalies, physical metamorphoses, and intense affect during the dream ending. A second type, existential dreams, involves sadness and despair, separation/loss, inhibition (fatigue), light/dark contrast, affective shifts, and intense affect during the dream ending. A third type, transcendent dreams, involves ecstasy and awe, magical success, vigorous activity, extraordinary sources of light, shifts in perspective, and intense affect during the dream ending.

Nightmares, existential dreams, and transcendent dreams all include visual discontinuities (e.g., explicit looking, sudden shifts in location); all three types involve relatively intense affect, especially during dream endings; and the imagery of all three types seems real to their dreamers even after awakening. Despite such evidence of their shared intensity, there is evidence that these three types of dreams have very different effects on waking thoughts and feelings. Dreamers report that (1) nightmares are followed by lingering environmental vigilance (e.g., apprehension about invisible dangers); (2) existential dreams are followed by self-perceptual depth (e.g., reflection on feelings that the dreamer was previously reluctant to acknowledge; and (3) transcendent dreams are followed by consideration of previously ignored spiritual possibilities (e.g., attunement to preternatural phenomena; Kuiken, Lee, Eng, & Singh, 2006).

The identification of three different impactful dream types, each with a distinctive effect on waking thoughts and feelings, has implications for theories of dream function. Some contemporary models of dream function present the nightmare as the prototypic impactful dream. That approach makes threat, fear, and lingering vigilance pivotal, potentially obscuring the affective—and perhaps adaptive—heterogeneity of dreams. Repeated observation of three primary types of impactful dreams, including nightmares, existential dreams, and transcendent dreams, suggests that nightmares are no more prototypic of dreaming in general than are existential dreams (with their emphasis on separation, sadness, and self-perceptual shifts) or transcendent dreams (with their emphasis on magical accomplishment, ecstasy, and spiritual possibilities). It is often assumed that dreaming is a sufficiently uniform phenomenon to serve consistently some function or set of functions. However, perhaps dreaming is only apparently uniform when differences among dream types—and among the functions of different dream types—are ignored.

Donald Kuiken

References

Busink, R., & Kuiken, D. (1996). Identifying types of impactful dreams: A replication. *Dreaming, 6,* 97–119.

Kuiken, D., Lee, M. N., Eng, T. C., & Singh, T. (2006). The influence of impactful dreams on self-perceptual depth and spiritual transformation. *Dreaming, 16,* 258–279.

Importance of Sleep Health for Children

In recent years, worldwide concerns have been expressed about the increasing number of children whose sleep is inadequate or disturbed. An international task force declared that inadequate sleep in children is an epidemic and a major health concern. The growing tendency to sleep less is due to the gradual erosion of normal sleep habits related to the complexity of modern life. As a result of electrical lighting, children are able to stay active later in the evening. They may be busy with school assignments in front of their computers, watch television, talk on the telephone, or listen to music. They are also expected to perform better in school and have numerous extracurricular activities. At the same time many children wake up earlier in the morning than previously, because they are expected to participate in various sports or deliver newspapers and then go to school. It is estimated that up to 30 percent of healthy children may experience significant sleep loss, which adversely affects their learning, mood, and behavior and may even cause school failure. Health consequences of inadequate sleep can be quite severe and include increased accidents, obesity, and low resistance to infections, cardiovascular difficulties, mood disorders, depression, and a number of other problems. It is now realized that children and adults who persistently have inadequate sleep pay a price for it. Hard work is admirable but cutting back on sleep is a bad mistake, because sleep is a critical restorative brain function. As an extreme example, severe persistent sleep loss leads to neuronal loss, and with the complete absence of sleep, humans die in a couple of weeks.

The body exhibits day–night rhythms that modulate wakefulness, sleep, temperature, cognition, behaviors and a very large number of metabolic functions. These circadian rhythms are under the influence of an endogenous clock, the suprachiasmatic nucleus in the hypothalamus. This anatomical region receives light–dark input from the eyes and also constant environmental information from the brain about the day/night changes. These cues influence the timing, duration, and quality of sleep and make sure that sleep–wake patters are aligned with the day/night environmental changes.

Because sleep is a complex neurological function, the prevalence of sleep disturbances in children with neurodevelopmental problems is much higher than for typical children and may be as high as 80 percent. Parents often think that poor sleep is just an inevitable part of their neurological problems, but most sleep disorders are treatable. In fact persistent sleep disturbances should never be ignored.

There are many medical conditions that can cause sleep disturbances, but when children are referred for medical help, promotion of healthy sleep habits are always requested. This is because poor sleep habits may interfere with healthy sleep. For instance, exposure to bright light, vigorous physical or mental activities prior to bedtime, anxiety, worrying, or emotional problems delay sleep onset while relaxing activities do the opposite. Good sleep health (sleep hygiene) exposes children and adults to activities and cues that promote appropriately timed and more effective sleep through a set of sleep-related behaviors. These activities may be grouped into four basic categories. A few examples are given here for typical children.

The *sleep environment* should be comfortable, noise free, and safe with appropriate temperature control. While bright light disrupts sleep, a dim night light may still benefit children who have anxieties. Children should be proud of their bedrooms, which should never be used for punishment.

Sleep scheduling, including bedtimes and naps, should be organized in accordance with developmental, health, social, cultural, and economic considerations. The regulation of the timing of sleep is most important and every attempt should be made that there is not more than one hour's difference in bedtimes and wake-up times during the week and during the weekends.

For *healthy sleep practices,* calming bedtime activities must be carefully planned. The enforcement of rules, structure, and routine activities are important for the promotion of healthy sleep. Parents should not allow their children to get involved in any activity they wish to do. For example, difficult homework prior to sleep will invariably delay sleep onset.

Physiological controls include proper timing of meals and exercise, and avoiding stimulants such as caffeine in soft drinks or chocolate milk. Even nighttime medications may interfere with sleep.

Sleep-promoting activities apply to typical and special needs children, but for the latter group, individual sleep-hygiene practices need to be planned depending on their abilities and disabilities. Furthermore, with increasing cognitive impairment, the sleep-hygiene interventions are less effective and may not work. For such children, melatonin therapy may offer significant benefits (Jan et al., 2007).

There are numerous publications on the promotion of sleep health for children, but the following references are selected because they contain useful and practical sleep-hygiene intervention techniques (Jan et al., 2008; Mindell & Owens, 2003; Owens & Witmans, 2004).

James E. Jan

See also: entries related to Sleep and Development

References

Jan, J. E., Owens, J. A., Weiss, M. D., Johnson, K. P., Wasdell, M. P., Freeman, R. D., & Ipsiroglu, O. S. (2008). Sleep hygiene for children with neurodevelopmental disabilities. *Pediatrics, 122,* 1343–1350.

Jan, J. E., Wasdell, M. B., Reiter, R. J., Weiss, M. D., Johnson, K. P., Ivanenko, A., & Freeman, R. D. (2007). Melatonin therapy of pediatric sleep disorders: Recent advances, why it works, who are the candidates and how to treat. *Current Pediatric Reviews, 3,* 214–224.

Mindell, J. A., & Owens, J. A. (2003). *A clinical guide to pediatric sleep: Diagnosis and management of sleep problems.* Philadelphia: Lippincott Williams and Wilkins.

Owens, J. A., & Witmans, M. (2004). Sleep problems. *Current Problems in Pediatric and Adolescent Health Care, 34,* 154–179.

Increasing Sleep Complaints

Chronic sleep loss is increasingly common in industrialized societies, affecting about 45 percent of adults. This issue is important because of the known increased risk of mortality and health risks associated with sleep duration deviating from seven to eight hours.

There is an extensively distributed belief that the prevalence of sleep-related symptoms is increasing, but evidence for this is even sparser. Most of the reported epidemiological sleep studies use a cohort design but, reviewing the current literature, surveys that analyze secular trends in sleep complaints and disorders are still limited. Cross-sectional studies analyzing sample of population in a single point in time show a high prevalence of sleep complaints.

Grandner and colleagues analyzed 159,856 participants from the Behavioral Risk Factor Surveillance System. Sleep complaints were measured with a telephone survey. They found that lower income and educational attainment was associated with more sleep complaints. Employment was associated with less sleep complaints. Married individuals reported the least sleep complaints (Grandner et al., 2010).

Another survey was done to investigate the prevalence of sleep complaints in a randomized cluster sample of 2,110 subjects from the Brazilian population. Of all interviewed subjects, 63 percent reported at least one sleep-related complaint (61% for snoring, 35% for insomnia, 17% for nightmares, 53% for leg kicking, and 37% for breathing pauses). Sleep complaint prevalence increased with age and was similar among inhabitants of different Brazilian regions. Insomnia and nightmares were significantly more prevalent in women (40% and 25%, respectively), and snoring was more prevalent in men (35%) (Bittencourt et al., 2009).

Data presented from the National Sleep Foundation's 2007 Sleep in America Poll that included 959 women (18 to 64 years of age) surveyed over telephone showed that poor sleep quality was reported by 27 percent and daytime sleepiness was reported by 21 percent of respondents. These complaints were associated with health-related, as well as sociodemographic factors (Baker, Wolfson, & Lee, 2009).

To reveal possible trends in self-reported sleep duration and insomnia-related symptoms, Kronholm and colleagues reanalyzed all available data from surveys carried out in Finland from 1972 to 2005. The main result was a minor decrease of self-reported sleep duration, especially among working aged men. However, the size of the reduction (about 4%) was relatively small, approximately 5.5 minutes per each 10 years during the 33 years' time interval under study (Kronholm et al., 2008).

A study was done to compare the prevalence of sleep habits and complaints and estimate the secular trends among three population-based surveys carried out in 1987, 1995, and 2007 in the general adult population of the city of Sao Paulo, Brazil. Sample sizes included 1,000 volunteers in the 1987 and 1995 surveys and 1,101 volunteers in the 2007 survey. Difficulty initiating sleep, difficulty maintaining sleep, and early morning awakening increased in the general population over time, mostly in women. Habitual snoring was the most commonly reported complaint across decades and was more prevalent in men; however, a significant increase was noted only in 2007 (Santos-Silva et al., 2010)

Some investigations have shown that information, education, and communication strategies have been effective in raising awareness and improving self-reporting. Furthermore, these findings support the need for development of health care and educational strategies to supply the population's increased need for information on sleep disorders and their consequences.

Lia Rita Azeredo Bittencourt, Rogerio Santos-Silva, and Sergio Tufik

See also: Anthropology of Sleep; Effects of Work on Sleep

Note

Financial support came from the Associação Fundo de Incentivo a Psicofarmacologia (AFIP), FAPESP, and CNPq.

References

Baker, F. C., Wolfson, A. R., & Lee, K. A. (2009). Association of sociodemographic, lifestyle, and health factors with sleep quality and daytime sleepiness in women: Findings from the 2007 National Sleep Foundation "Sleep in America Poll." *Journal of Women's Health, 18*(6), 841–849.

Bittencourt, L. R., Santos-Silva, R., Taddei, J. A., Andersen, M. L., de Mell, M. T., & Tufik, S. (2009). Sleep complaints in the adult Brazilian population: A national survey based on screening questions. *Journal of Clinical Sleep Medicine, 5*(5), 459–463.

Grandner, M. A., Patel, N. P., Gehrman, P. R., Xie, D., Sha, D., Weaver, T., & Gooneratne, N. (2010). Who gets the best sleep? Ethnic and socioeconomic factors related to sleep complaints. *Sleep Medicine,* 11(5), 470–478.

Kronholm, E., Partonen, T., Laatikainen, T., Peltonen, M., Härmä, M., Hublin, C., . . . Sutela, H. (2008). Trends in self-reported sleep duration and insomnia-related symptoms in Finland from 1972 to 2005: A comparative review and re-analysis of Finnish population samples. *Journal of Sleep Research, 17*(1), 54–62.

Santos-Silva, R., Bittencourt, L. R., Pires, M. L., de Mello, M. T., Taddei, J. A., Benedito-Silva, A. A., . . . Tufik, S. (2010). Increasing trends of sleep complaints in the city of Sao Paulo, Brazil. *Sleep Medicine,* 11(6), 520–524.

Incubation of Dreams

Dream incubation is the practice of going to sleep with the intention of having a dream for a specific purpose.

The incubation method may be culturally specific and ritualistic, as in Native American vision quests (Reed, 2005a). Incubation may be informal, as in a creative person anticipating to dream about an ongoing project (Barrett, 1993) or someone with a concern repeating a bedtime affirmation expressing the intention to dream about it (Delaney, 1998). Incubation may be practiced as a spiritual enactment, involving symbolic experiences to prepare for transformative dreaming, with or without a skilled practitioner guiding the process (Reed, 2005a; Tick, 2001). Finally, incubation may be enacted as the focus of a scientific exploration, where a researcher provides specific context for the study's participants to seek a dream and the results are examined (Barrett, 1993; Reed, 2005b).

The purpose of dream incubation may vary from a need for healing, creative problem solving, or inspiration. The assumed source of the incubated dream may vary according to the worldview of the practitioner: to come from new combinations of old experiences and ideas, from the transpersonal areas of the mind, from deceased relatives or saints, from a god, or from God himself.

The earliest record of dream incubation dates back to Greece eons before Hippocrates. The Father of Medicine attributes all his knowledge and skills to the god Asklepios, whose dream temples provided healing to those who slept there. These dreams were visionary in nature, seeming to occur in the temple where the person was sleeping. Asklepios often performed the healing himself. These miraculous cures gradually devolved into symbolic dreams that temple attendants (*therapeutes*) would interpret to develop a treatment. The collection of reports of such healings, or the remedies developed from the dreams, became Hippocrates's working medicine (Reed, 2005a; Tick, 2001).

A modern attempt to recreate the phenomenon of dream incubation involved the use of psychodrama, employing the universal symbols of visionary quests—the sacred sanctuary and the encounter with the spiritual benefactor—and a specially constructed, imaginary dream-incubation temple (a tent) to provide an experience analogous to the ancient Greek dreamer (Reed, 2005a). A related approach used a variety of therapeutic methodologies to stimulate dreaming while actually sleeping in one of the Asklepian dream temples (Tick, 2001).

Intense incubation rituals are not necessary to incubate dreams. Delaney (1998) found that having a person repeat an affirmation regarding the intention for dreaming can produce results. Barrett (2001) asked students to incubate a dream on a topic of their choice, but without providing a specific method for incubation. Half the students incubated dreams that independent judges evaluated as relevant and helpful. Personal problems, especially related to health, were the majority of successful incubation topics. Hypothetical questions rarely stimulated pertinent dreams. Another modern incubation procedure involved asking a group of people to incubate dreams to resolve the undisclosed problem of a stranger in distress (Reed, 2005a). In this method, no instructions were given for how to perform vicarious dream incubation; rather the evoking of the altruistic motive was the dynamic factor behind the method's success. Another successful method, employing personal motivation amplified by sustained effort, involved using a programmed textbook to guide the person through a series of incubation attempts toward the same goal. The active principle, attributed to Edgar Cayce, is that a person may act on an insight from a dream while intending that this action incubate another dream that provides improved insight (Reed, 2005b). These studies show that dream incubation can occur with minimal effort or method, but that personal motivation is critical—intention trumps technique.

Only the intense, psychotherapeutic dream-incubation methods have resulted in dreams that have been healing in and of themselves. The other methods have yielded pertinent results; however, it has been through the interpretation of these dreams that their payoff was realized. Thus modern research has replicated the two versions of the Greek dream-incubation tradition.

Henry Reed

References

Barrett, D.L. (1993). The "Committee of Sleep": A study of dream incubation for problem solving. *Dreaming, 3*, 115–123.

Barrett, D.L. (2001). *The committee of sleep: How artists, scientists, and athletes use their dreams for creative problem solving—and how you can too.* New York: Crown Books/ Random House.

Delaney, G. (1998). *All about dreams.* San Francisco: HarperSanFrancisco.

Reed, H. (2005a). *Dream medicine: Learning how to get help from our dreams.* Mouth of Wilson, VA: Hermes Home Press.

Reed, H. (2005b). *Dream solutions: The original dream quest guidebook trailblazing intuitive dream guidance.* Mouth of Wilson, VA: Hermes Home Press.

Tick, E. (2001). *The practice of dream healing: Bringing ancient Greek mysteries into modern medicine.* Wheaton, IL: Quest Books.

Incubus/Succubus

The incubus and succubus are Latin-derived mythological terms for male and female demons, respectively, who assault sleepers in their bed and sexually molest them. Also known as supernatural assault, the incubus encounter is medically associated with the parasomnia known as *sleep paralysis*, which can be defined as the awareness of REM paralysis that is sometimes accompanied by realistic hypnagogic hallucinations.

The historical distinction between nightmare and incubus accounts is largely emotional: terror predominates with the mare demon but incubus accounts include dread mingled with pleasure. On this point, medical anthropologist David Hufford (1982) suggests that the incubus tradition may be a subset of the classic waking nightmare or may be a different phenomenon altogether.

Psychoanalyst Ernest Jones (1931[1951]) outlined narratives of the incubus in early ecclesiastical documents, as well as other historical traditions around the world, and connected them to the modern nightmare, which he defines as an agonizing dream that includes intense terror, a sense of pressure on the chest, and the conviction of paralysis. Jones noted the erotic qualities of these historical accounts and argued, in line with the Freudian tradition, that the fantasy is the result of psychosexual repression that is experienced convincingly as sexual assault by a lewd demon. Jones's term nightmare later came to mean any terrifying dream, in part because Jones did not distinguish between ordinary sleeping dreams and the distinct waking awareness that comes with sleep-related paralysis hallucinations.

In general, mid-20th century psychologists and psychiatrists interpreted supernatural assault claims as rooted in various psychological issues, including passive–aggressive conflicts, neurosis, and latent homosexuality. American psychiatrist Sim Liddon (1976) linked the historic tales of supernatural assault and Jones's nightmare to the hallucinatory symptoms of sleep paralysis, arguing that the experience of sleep paralysis has no hidden meaning itself; rather, the patient supplies the interpretation after the event occurs. The depathologization of sleep paralysis and its incubus hallucinations continued as psychiatrists discovered that many healthy people have the experience, as well as those suffering from narcolepsy and other sleep ailments.

The biblical tradition of Lilith, Adam's first wife, is derived from Babylonian succubus narratives extending back to the second century BCE. *Lilith* by John Collier, 1892. (The Bridgeman Art Library International)

Supernatural assault by the incubus or succubus can be considered a multi-sensory REM hallucination occurring at sleep onset or while waking up. The encounter has several components. First, the victim feels paralyzed, due to the atonia of skeletal muscles that occurs during REM sleep. Secondly, a feeling of pressure or weight is felt on the chest, throat, or belly of the sleeper. Thirdly, the victim feels panic or intense fear, which is sometimes mixed with erotic feelings and pleasure. Fourthly, a sensed presence in the sleeping quarters is discerned, which may alarm the sleeper more. Finally, the victim may see, hear, and even smell a fully formed hallucination of a human or human-hybrid creature sitting on their chest or hovering nearby, which, in its fully formed manifestation, can touch, assault, and sexually violate the victim. Afterward, victims have clear memories of the event and often proclaim that the experience was real, and not a dream or hallucination.

History and Myth

Sexual-contact hallucinations have been noted since ancient times, the first of which may be accounts of the Babylonian demoness Lilith, who stalked men to breed with them. Descriptions of Lilith as a demon seductress who comes only at night can be found in the *Talmud* as well as Aramaic inscriptions on ritual pottery vessels. In ancient Greece, the imp Pan was known to sit on his victims and sometimes copulate with them, according to the writings of dream interpreter Artemidorus in his second-century *Oneirocritica*.

The term incubus means to lay on top of; succubus translates to lie underneath. However, the terms came to denote the male and female genders of the offending entity, as both lay on the victim. Even in the early centuries of the Common Era, the incubus/succubus had erotic connotations, and Christian monks believed that sexual dreams were directly inspired by demons. According to anthropologist Charles Stewart (2002), erotic dreams were increasingly demonized by the Christian laity as well, due to the belief that control of one's inner sexual urges was a component of spiritual purity. Augustine of Hippo verified the existence of incubi, associating their wanton sexuality with nature spirits such as sylvans and fauns. Interestingly, fifth-century Roman physician Caelius Aurelianus wrote about the incubus attack in a decidedly psychoanalytic tone as an attempt to gratify a shameful lust, and did not consider it unhealthy unless it occurred repeatedly.

The most infamous historical use of the incubus narrative occurred during the late witch trials of the 15th century. Many women were declared heretics and put to death after admitting, often under torture, that they had willful sex with the Devil in the form of an incubus or succubus. *Malleus Maleficarum*, an influential witch-hunting manual written in 1487, concluded that while incubi are likely to come to any woman, witches are those who willingly submit and enjoy the demonic subjugation. This trend continued in Colonial America during the Salem Witch Trials of 1692, when several men testified that they were victims of succubi attacks, who they argued were the spirit doubles of the accused women Susanna Martin and Bridget Bishop. Court testimonies from this trial clearly depict the main symptoms of the succubus attack, including paralysis, full visual hallucinations, and the sensation of being laid upon.

Modern Narratives

Supernatural assault narratives have continued into the modern era, but the characteristics of the incubi have changed over time. While some still report molestation by demons, others report being oppressed by invisible beings, zombies, vampires, and malevolent ghosts. Perhaps the most prevalent modern visitor is the alien, who paralyzes his victims and sexually abuses them, violates them with metallic probes, or extracts semen. Positive or pleasurable accounts of incubus encounters may be under-reported due to stigma and taboo, although modern accounts have been reported (Cheyne, 2001), some of which also include the sensation of orgasmic release.

Lucid dreams, another REM phenomenon marked by high levels of self-awareness, have been studied in the laboratory in relationship to genital arousal with the conclusion that dreamed orgasms match physiological responses. Work in this vein could be extended to isolated sleep-paralysis-related incubus encounters, as, currently, the sexual physiology of this unique experience is unknown. Modern brain mapping during the incubus attack could further be of interest, especially as it may reveal unique characteristics of erotic fantasies with elements of terror and submission.

In the human sciences, sociological and feminist literary analysis could compare the incubus encounter with modern tabooed fantasies and possibly shed some light on human sexuality and its expression during imaginal states of consciousness. Finally, more narrative research, in the West as well as cross-culturally, is needed to more precisely delineate the components of the incubus encounter from classic waking nightmares that are also associated with sleep paralysis and hypnagogic hallucinations.

Ryan Hurd

See also: entries related to History of Dreams/Sleep

References

Cheyne, J. A. (2001). The ominous numinous: Sensed presence and "other" hallucinations. *Journal of Consciousness Studies, 8*(5–7), 133–150.

Hufford, D. (1982). *The terror that comes in the night: An experience-centered study of supernatural traditions*. Philadelphia: University of Pennsylvania Press.

Jones, E. (1931[1951]). *On the nightmare*. London: Hogarth Press.

Liddon, S. C. (1976). Sleep paralysis and hypnagogic hallucinations: Their relationship to the nightmare. *Archives of General Psychiatry, 17*(1), 88–96.

Stewart, C. (2002). Erotic dreams and nightmares from antiquity to the present. *Journal of the Royal Anthropological Institute, 8*(2), 279–309.

Infant Sleep and Parenting

The evolution of sleep consolidation (sleeping through the night) during the first year of life is a complex process, driven by underlying biological forces (e.g., maturational, medical, and temperamental factors) and environmental influences (e.g., cultural influence, parenting, and parent–infant interactions). Among the psychosocial factors influencing the development of sleep, parenting factors, such as parental sleep-related behaviors, cognitions, and maternal psychopathology, have received the most scientific attention.

Parental behaviors, particularly those related to parent–infant bedtime interactions, are closely related to infant sleep. Numerous studies have demonstrated that active parental involvement and soothing at bedtime (e.g., feeding, holding, rocking) is strongly associated with frequent and/or prolonged infant night-wakings, whereas parental interventions encouraging infant self-soothing at night (e.g., letting the infant fall asleep independently) are associated with more consolidated sleep. Breast feeding is one of the most common maternal soothing methods during the night. Although breast feeding has many advantages for infant development, it is important to note that nighttime breast feeding has been found to be associated with more frequent infant night-wakings. It seems likely that when settled to sleep by their parents (by breast feeding or by other means) infants learn to associate falling asleep with parental assistance and thus continue to rely on parental help when waking up during the night. In fact, brief awakenings during the night are a natural phenomenon characterizing the sleep of most infants and children. Thus, even though sleep disturbed infants tend to wake up more than controls, their main problem is their inability to self-sooth and resume sleep without parental help.

Though most studies in the field suggest that parental practices influence the development of infant sleep, it is also possible that infants with more problematic sleep patterns require more parental involvement. Therefore, the development of infant sleep could be best conceptualized in the context of a transactional model that assumes complex and bidirectional relationships between parenting and infant sleep.

Recent studies attempting to explore the underlying factors leading to different levels of parental involvement at night suggest that parental cognitions (e.g., perceptions, beliefs, expectations, and interpretations) may play an important role. Specifically, parental cognitions reflecting difficulties with limit setting have been found to be associated with increased parental assistance in settling the infant to sleep. For example, in two different longitudinal studies it was found that maternal cognitions reflecting difficulties in limiting parental involvement during the night, predicted higher active physical nighttime soothing, and these soothing methods predicted more infant night-wakings. Parents who are concerned that infant night-wakings are a sign of infant distress, and who perceive the encouragement of infant self-soothing as an insensitive and even harmful practice, are more likely to become actively involved in helping their infant to fall asleep.

Maternal psychopathology, especially maternal depression is another important parenting factor that has been associated with infant sleep problems. The findings in this field demonstrate that anxious and depressed pregnant women are at increased risk of having children with reported sleep problems and that infants of depressed mothers have lower sleep quality in comparison to controls. Though the underlying mechanisms explaining these links are not clear, the findings support the hypothesis that maternal depression contributes negatively to infant sleep development. However, findings demonstrating that treating infant sleep problems can lead to improvement in maternal emotional distress suggest that infant sleep problems may influence maternal mood.

The majority of studies on infant sleep and parenting used a naturalistic correlational design. There is a need for controlled and longitudinal studies to better understand the causal relations and the mechanisms underlying the links between parental factors and infant sleep. In addition, future research should explore the role of fathers' sleep-related practices and cognition in infant sleep development. Lastly, most of the research on infant sleep and parenting has been conducted on Western cultures and on parents representing the middle–upper socioeconomic status. Because parental practices are influenced by ethnicity and cultural norms and values, the links between infant sleep and parenting should be further explored in more diverse populations.

Liat Tikotzky

See also: entries related to Sleep and Development

References

Morrell, J., & Steele, H. (2003). The role of attachment security, temperament, maternal perception, and care-giving behavior in persistent infant sleeping problems. *Infant Mental Health Journal, 24*(5), 447–468.

Sadeh, A., Tikotzky, L., & Scher, A. (2010). Parenting and infant sleep. *Sleep Medicine Reviews, 14*(2), 89–96.

Tikotzky, L., & Sadeh, A. (2009). Maternal sleep-related cognitions and infant sleep: A longitudinal study from pregnancy through the first year. *Child Development, 80*(3), 860–874.

Warren, S.L., Howe, G., Simmens, S.J., & Dahl, R.E. (2006). Maternal depressive symptoms and child sleep: Models of mutual influence over time. *Development and Psychopathology, 18*(1), 1–16.

Infant Sleep Interventions

Infant sleep problems are among the most common complaints parents present to child-care professionals. Frequent night-wakings and the inability to resume sleep without parental help characterize 20 to 30 percent of all children between the age of six months and three years. The importance of early interventions aimed at treating infant night-waking problems is highlighted by findings demonstrating that these problems may be quite persistent if left untreated. Moreover, sleep problems are correlated with poor cognitive and emotional functioning of children and with family stress and parental psychopathology. However, interventions are usually not considered for infants under the age of six months because multiple night-wakings and nighttime feeding are developmentally appropriate during the first months of life.

Studies in the field of infant sleep and parenting have consistently demonstrated that active parental involvement (e.g., feeding, rocking) at bedtime is significantly associated with frequent infant night-wakings. Infants who are settled to sleep by their parents, probably learn to associate falling asleep with parental assistance and therefore may fail to develop self-soothing skills necessary for resuming sleep (see the entry "Infant Sleep and Parenting"). Therefore, *cognitive-behavioral interventions* for infant sleep problems are mainly focused on changing parental sleep-related perceptions and reducing parental nighttime involvement (i.e., removal of the reinforcement) to facilitate the development of infant self-soothing skills. However, prior to implementing these interventions, assessment should include screening for physiological factors that may contribute to the sleep problem (e.g., allergies, breathing problems). If present, these problems should be addressed before or in combination with the psychologically oriented interventions.

The most common sleep interventions are: (1) Early parental education programs (during pregnancy or early postpartum) focusing on guiding parents how to promote healthy sleep habits; (2) unmodified extinction—parents are asked to put the infant awake in bed, leave the room, and ignore night-wakings. It is expected that after a while, the infant will learn that crying behavior is not followed by parental attention and therefore will cease signaling and learn to self-soothe. Though randomized controlled studies have found this method to be efficient, many parents find it extremely difficult to comply and to consistently ignore their children's cry; (3) Graduated extinction (e.g., checking)—parents are instructed to put the child awake in bed and shortly visit the infant in fixed or gradually increasing intervals if the infant is crying. The aim of the visit is to assure the infant about parental presence and at the same time to transfer a clear message that the infant is expected to sleep. A related technique, parental presence, is based on the same principles but starts with guiding the parents to sleep in the infant's room to alleviate concerns about separation anxiety;

(4) Faded bedtime focuses on delaying bedtime thereby creating a physiological pressure to sleep. Parents are guided to devote the time before bedtime to calming activities with the child (positive routine). A consistent bedtime routine (e.g., bath, massage) is also recommended. When infants learn to fall asleep independently, bedtime is gradually advanced. The change at bedtime is supposed to lead to more consolidated sleep.

Behavioral sleep interventions based on withdrawing parental involvement involve some level of infant protest and crying because of the changes in the infant's usual routines. Many parents find it very difficult to tolerate infant crying because of their concerns that ignoring infant signals would harm the child. Therefore, to prepare the parents toward the behavioral intervention, clinicians should educate parents on realistic expectations and address their cognitions and concerns regarding the intervention, before guiding them on how to implement behavioral techniques. This process is often necessary to facilitate parental cooperation. In addition, since sociocultural factors have significant impact on parental perceptions and values regarding sleep-related practices, behavioral interventions should be culturally sensitive and should take into account specific family characteristics.

Though many studies documented the efficacy of behavioral sleep intervention that are based on minimizing parental nighttime involvement, future research should address the long-term effects of these interventions on child–parent attachment and on the child's sense of security. In addition, replication of findings regarding the positive results of these interventions is needed with families of greater ethnic and socioeconomic diversity.

Liat Tikotzky

See also: entries related to Sleep and Development

References
Kuhn, B. R., & Elliott, A. J. (2003). Treatment efficacy in behavioral pediatric sleep medicine. *Journal of Psychosomatic Research, 54,* 587–597.

Mindell, J. A., Kuhn, B., Lewin, D. S., Meltzer, L. J., & Sadeh, A. (2006). Behavioral treatment of bedtime problems and night wakings in infants and young children: An American Academy of Sleep Medicine review. *Sleep, 29,* 1263–1276.

Ramchandani, P., Wiggs, L., Webb, V., & Stores, G. (2000). A systematic review of treatments for settling problems and night waking in young children. *British Medical Journal, 320,* 209–213.

Sadeh, A. (2005). Cognitive-behavioral treatment for childhood sleep disorders. C*linical Psychology Review, 25,* 612–628.

Tikotzky, L., & Sadeh, A. (in press). The role of cognitive–behavioral therapy in behavioral childhood insomnia. *Sleep Medicine.*

Insomnia in Chronic Renal Failure

Insomnia is a very common disease in chronic renal patients. Insomnia is primarily a clinical diagnosis based on data obtained from the patient's history and sleep diaries. History should include a review of sleep habits, sleep environment, drugs and alcohol consumption, pain, and coexisting medical and psychiatric conditions. Duration of the symptoms is also important. Insomnia is considered transitory if it has lasted for less than one month, subacute if it has lasted for one to six months, and chronic if the complaint has persisted for more than six months. Insomnia is manifested by one or more of the following symptoms: difficulty falling asleep (sleep onset insomnia), difficulty staying asleep (sleep maintenance insomnia), earlier than expected awakening, or poor sleep quality (nonrestorative sleep) (Meyer, 1998; Oyahon, 2002). Insomnia can be classified as primary or idiopathic where no underlying cause can be identified. The term secondary insomnia or comorbid insomnia is used when a patient experiences the features of insomnia in relation to medical and psychiatric conditions or drugs. Early-morning awakenings are frequently caused by anxiety or depression or due to drug withdrawal. Frequent awakenings may be due to an associated restless legs syndrome or to obstructive sleep apnea. Insomnia may contribute to impaired daytime functioning, tiredness, fatigue, and sleepiness symptoms. Insomnia is a common sleep problem. Its prevalence in the general population ranges from 4 to 64 percent (Leger,Guilleminault, DeFrance, Domont, & Paillard, 2000; Terzano et al., 2004). The prevalence is much higher in patients with chronic renal failure and reported to range from 45 to 59 percent of the patients (Sabbatini et al., 2002). Insomnia in chronic renal patients is associated with greater daytime consequences than in the general population. There are many etiologies for insomnia in chronic renal failure, including uremia, other associated medical problems such as restless legs syndrome, diabetic neuropathy, pain, underlying electrolyte imbalance, psychiatric illness and medications. Dialysis efficacy is a contributing factor for insomnia in patient undergoing dialysis. Elderly patients and those with a longer time on dialysis and with high levels of parathyroid hormone are at higher risk of insomnia. Insomnia has direct and indirect costs. It may cause personal distress as well as adverse social and economic consequences, leading to a number of deleterious effects on behavior, health, sense of well-being, enjoyment of interpersonal relationships, and personal safety (Imanshahidi & Hosseinzadeh, 2006; Sabbatini et al., 2008). The management of insomnia depends on its etiology. If the patient has a medical, or other sleep disorder, treatment should be directed at the disorder. In dialysis patient's electrolytes balance, correcting anemia, adequate dialysis is essential. In case of a psychiatric disorder, treatment should be directed at the disorder. This may involve medications, psychotherapy, and even referral to a psychiatrist, psychologist. Behavior therapy is also very important role in therapy this includes good sleep hygiene, relaxation, biofeedback techniques, and cognitive-behavior therapy are very useful therapy for insomnia. Drug therapy with sedative-hypnotic medications does not cure insomnia but may provide symptomatic relief. If these medications are to be used then it should be prescribed in combination with nonpharmacological treatment (Grunstein, 2002).

Hamdan Al-Jahdali

See also: entries related to Sleep Disorders

References

Grunstein, R. (2002). Insomnia: Diagnosis and management. *Australian Family Physician, 31*(11), 995–1000.

Imanshahidi, M., & Hosseinzadeh, H. (2006). The pharmacological effects of Salvia species on the central nervous system. *Phytotherapy Research, 20*(6), 427–437.

Leger, D., Guilleminault, C., DeFrance, R., Domont, A., & Paillard, M. (2000). Prevalence of insomnia in a survey of 12,778 adults in France. *Journal of Sleep Research, 9*(1), 35–42.

Meyer, T.J. (1998). Evaluation and management of insomnia. *Hospital Practice, 33*(12), 75–78, 83–86.

Ohayon, M.M. (2002). Epidemiology of insomnia: What we know and what we still need to learn. *Sleep Medicine Reviews, 6*(2), 97–111.

Sabbatini, M., et al. (2002). Insomnia in maintenance haemodialysis patients. *Nephrol Dial Transplant, 17*(5), 852–856.

Sabbatini, M., et al. (2008) Sleep quality in patients with chronic renal failure: A 3-year longitudinal study. *Sleep Medicine, 9*(3), 240–246.

Terzano, M.G., et al. (2004). Studio Morfeo: Insomnia in primary care, a survey conducted on the Italian population. *Sleep Medicine, 5*(1), 67–75.

International Association for the Study of Dreams

The International Association for the Study of Dreams (IASD) is a nonprofit, international, multidisciplinary organization focused on the study of dreams and the dissemination of knowledge about them. Its activities are designed to promote an awareness and appreciation of dreams in both professional and public arenas, and to encourage research into the nature, function, and significance of dreaming. It was founded in 1982 and held its first conference in 1983.

IASD is open to both professionals and nonprofessionals who are interested in dreaming. Its membership has representatives from dozens of countries and from a broad range of backgrounds, including clinical practice, academic research, laboratory experimentation, classroom teaching, community organizing, group dreamwork, artistic and literary creativity, and personal study. Among its academic members, a variety of academic disciplines and theoretical perspectives are represented, including anthropology, medicine, psychology, history, education, art, sociology, business administration, comparative literature, language studies, religion and spirituality, social work, and nursing.

IASD provides a number of forums for the discussion and study of dreams. It holds

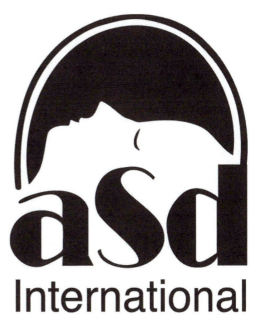

International Association for the Study of Dreams logo (International Association for the Study of Dreams)

annual conferences every summer where research findings on dreams, workshops on dreamwork techniques, dream-related performances, and dream art are featured. These are often held in the United States, but also in other locations throughout the world. IASD sponsors regional meetings with a similar range of papers, workshops, experiential events, social gatherings, art exhibitions, and training in a variety of dream-work techniques. These regional meetings provide opportunities for networking among people in a particular geographical area who study dreams.

IASD publishes *Dreaming,* a professional journal that presents articles from a variety of scholarly disciplines. It also publishes a magazine, *Dream Time,* which includes interviews, book excerpts, and articles of interest to people leading dream groups and working with their own dreams. Members receive a monthly e-newsletter, *Dream News.* The organization maintains an extensive Web site accessible to nonmembers with pages providing basic educational information about topics such as dream recall, dream interpretation, children's dreams, lucid dreams, and nightmares. Other pages contain abstracts of past conference presentations, selected articles from *Dreaming,* and *Dream Time,* and bulletin boards and e-study groups for ongoing discussion of specialized dream topics.

IASD promotes a broad variety of approaches to working with dreams but emphasizes that all legitimate ones recognize the dreamer as the ultimate authority and the decision maker regarding the significance of the dream. Their Statement on Ethics of Dreamwork says in part,

Speaker Ernest Hartmann, MD, in front of Doris Becke's art piece titled *Dream Session,* at the 2011 IASD conference in the Netherlands. (Richard C. Wilkerson)

Systems of dreamwork that assign authority or knowledge of the dream's meanings to someone other than the dreamer can be misleading, incorrect, and harmful. Ethical dreamwork helps the dreamer work with his/her own dream images, feelings, and associations, and guides the dreamer to more fully experience, appreciate, and understand the dream. Every dream may have multiple meanings, and different techniques may be reasonably employed to touch these multiple layers of significance.

Deirdre Barrett

See also: *Dreaming*: The Journal of the Association for the Studies of Dreams

Reference

International Association for the Study of Dreams. (n.d.). Retrieved from http://www.asdreams.org/2008menu.htm

Intersubjective Dreams

The dreams healers and clients have about each other and about the healing process go to the heart of the endeavor. Recognized for their singular importance by Hippocrates and Galen, by the Asklepian tradition, and by indigenous cultures with shamanistic practices, such dreams fell into disrepute after Freud labeled a doctor's dream about a patient as a sure sign of a neurotic problem (Lippmann, 2000). The clinical literature reflects this negative attitude: from 1900 until the mid-1980s, only one or two papers on this topic per decade were published.

The emergence of intersubjectivity and a more nuanced understanding of countertransference have opened the way for increased interest in the dreams that therapists and clients have about each other. Research done in the 1980s provided baseline estimates about when and how often these dreams take place. In two separate surveys of analytic patients' dreams, 1 out of 10 was found to contain undisguised figures of the therapist (Rosenbaum, 1965). To this can be added the various ways the therapist can be depicted—as a nurse, contractor, plumber, midwife, private eye, dentist, archaeologist—thus making the frequency of such dreams much greater than 10 percent.

A recent doctoral dissertation on therapists in training found that they dream about their patients and/or supervisors as often as once a week (Degani, 2001). A survey of Canadian psychoanalysts and candidates determined that dreaming about patients was most likely to take place when the clinical material was highly charged with erotic or aggressive themes; this was true for all phases of treatment. The survey also found that experienced analysts were just as likely to have dreams about patients as were novice candidates (Lester, 1989).

It may be either the therapist or the client who has a dream about the interactive field between them. The dream can open up new territory where both intrapsychic and intersubjective conflicts can be explored more fully. Psychiatrist C. G. Jung had more interest in the interpersonal dimension than Freud did, citing many examples of dreams he and his patients had about each other. In his 1929 dream seminar, he told of a dream in which the patient and his analyst had established a joint checking account. This exemplifies the pool of shared resources that is created by the mutual healing endeavor. In 1934, Jung wrote to a young psychiatrist, "In the deepest sense we all dream *not out of ourselves* but out of what lies *between us and the other*" (Adler, 1973, p. 172).

This simple statement, far ahead of its time, provides the theoretical foundation for a new model of understanding of the fact that mutual dreaming takes place. Intersubjective dreams can be seen as a consultant in the room, whose task is to monitor the treatment, keep it on course, and move it forward. Such dreams are like a third thing that emerges from the interstitial space between one individual and another, drawing both into the healing matrix.

Meredith Sabini

References

Adler, G. (1973). *C.G. Jung letters I.* Princeton, NJ: Princeton University Press.

Berenholz, D. (2007). Countertransference dreams: An intersubjectivist theory perspective. *Dissertation Abstracts International, 68*(5-B), 3386.

Degani, H. (2001). Therapists' dreams about patients and supervisors. *Dissertation Abstracts International, 62*(3-B), 1570.

Jung, C.G. (1984). *Dream analysis: Notes on the seminar given in 1928–1930.* Princeton, NJ: Princeton University Press.

Lester, E. (1989) Countertransference dreams reconsidered: A survey. *International Review of Psychoanalysis, 16,* 305–314.

Lippmann, P. (2000). Dreams and psychoanalysis: A love-hate story. P*sychoanalytic Psychology, 17*(4), 627–650.

Rosenbaum, M. (1965). Dreams in which the analyst appears undisguised: A clinical and statistical study. *International Journal of Psychoanalysis, 46,* 429–437.

Intuition in Dreams

Using intuition in dreams will capture the wisdom embedded in the dream. Alternate names for this ability to bypass the logical mind and go beyond ordinary consciousness to retrieve information are gut feeling, premonition, hunch, sixth sense, or instinct. The noise of the day silences the intuitive voice, which gets a chance to speak through a dream providing a warning, guidance, or creative breakthrough. Intuition and dreams speak the same metaphoric language, communicating in pictures, symbols, and images.

Intuition in dreams has varying functions such as heightening creativity and invention, foreshadowing the future, and retrieving rapid insights in the dream analysis. The intuitive mind invents and creates in the dream. Many inventors find that dreams can help them solve problems while artists and writers often get creative ideas from them. Thomas Edison used to keep a pencil and paper on his bed stand and would write down the ideas that came to him while he was sleeping. Dmitri Mendeleev saw the periodic table of elements roll out for him in a dream. Robert Louis Stevenson wrote the classic thriller *Dr. Jekyll and Mr. Hyde* after seeing the story in a nightmare.

Intuition will use a dream to preview an upcoming event. These precognitive or foreshadowing dreams that come true are discussed under the "ESP in Dreams" entry. Covering the range from trivial to life altering, these red flag alerts can provide a warning about an accident, death, health challenge, calamity, or natural disaster. Precognitive dreams can also be practical reminding you of an upcoming appointment, signal a significant event such as a promotion, proposal, baby birth, new friendship, or unexpected gift of money.

Intuition can be used in dream analysis to retrieve rapid insights and clarify the meaning of the dream. For example, dreaming of being robbed at gunpoint may not be ominous but provide a quick reminder from the intuitive mind that an anticipated document is being held up.

Each dream symbol has a very personal meaning and is custom designed for the dreamer. The DreamShift process (Emery, 2001) connects with the intuitive mind to delve deeper into the dream's meaning. Using the intuitive antenna will also help with the dream decoding. Each person receives intuitive information in a unique way. By extending the five senses, this may happen in a number of ways, such as seeing the words visually, hearing them, getting a feel for the symbols, having a taste in the mouth, sensing a good or bad smell, or just knowing.

The key with this particular intuitive dreamwork technique is to identify and then unravel a major symbol or two in the dream that reflects the underlying message. Since this method is the major one employing intuition in dreamwork, a brief example will illustrate this process.

Dream Background

Roz was questioning her wavering friendship with Nelly and had this illuminating dream. *I was in a social setting and Nelly was being strong and intimidating. She pulled out a gun and shot someone. Then she pointed the gun at me and was going to shoot me. Then Nelly said she'll decide whether to spare me. I wasn't completely afraid. Then another woman came along who held a gun over Nelly.*

Here are the steps of the DreamShift process to decode the underlying dream message.

First, *Give the dream* a title. Gun Control.

Second, *Become centered and receptive.* Roz listened to her wind chimes and affirmed, "My intuitive mind will help me understand the dream."

Third, *Identify the major symbols choosing a maximum of three.* The major symbol is the gun.

Fourth, *Interpret these symbols using amplification or word association.* Freely associating to the gun elicits the following words: hunting, power, protection, fire, and weapon. The intuitive hit comes when the dreamer says, "calling the shots."

Fifth, *Engage the symbol artistically through art, dance, music, or drama.* She moves her body to drum music.

Sixth, *Implement the dream discovery using the logical mind.* Focusing on the pivotal gun symbol Roz saw how controlling Nelly was in their relationship because she always called the shots. Roz was uncomfortable with this one-sided relationship and planned to talk to Nelly about creating more give and take interaction in their relationship.

Since intuition is so challenging to calibrate, research using this modality in dreamwork is very limited. However, a direction for future research would be comparing the DreamShift technique with other nonintuitive methods to discern which route gets to the heart of the dream not only faster but more accurately.

Marcia Emery

Reference

Emery, M. (2001). *PowerHunch! Living an intuitive life*. Hillsboro, OR: Beyond Words Publishing.

Involuntary Nature of Dreaming

One of the most obvious characteristics of the process of dreaming is that it is involuntary—yet this feature has only rarely been commented on. While there may be some individuals who dream very little or not at all, these are the exceptions rather than the rule. As far as we know the vast majority of the human race dreams every night and does so whether they want to or not. Indeed, attempts to prevent REM sleep and dreaming have all proven fruitless. Even pharmacological treatments that are thought to partially suppress REM sleep are not associated with loss of dreaming. Dreaming we can safely conclude is involuntary. We dream whether we like it or not.

Why is dreaming involuntary? We also think whether we like it or not, as long as we are conscious, the mind appears to be constantly productive as long as it is activated. Since it is activated in REM sleep and in some stages of light sleep we can expect the mind to be productive there as well. When the mind produces its thoughts during REM we call the thoughts dreams. While this explanation of the involuntariness of dreams is reasonable, as far as it goes dreams cannot be considered simple cases of thinking while asleep. That is because dreams are very specialized cognitive events or products. They are produced by specialized cognitive machinery that happens to be most engaged during REM sleep. Cognitive models of the content of dreams tend to assume that dreams utilize existing memory images to construct new images that more or less successfully simulate features of the dreamer's life world. Certainly that seems to be partially true but dreams also produce thoughts, images, and scenes that cannot be traced back to memories and cannot be conceived as constructions cobbled together from preexisting memory images. Dreams are capable of producing brand-new images—images never before encountered by the dreamer. And they do this on a regular basis. Dreams also virtually never produce images or scenes of things we do or see nearly every day—such as reading, writing, and other prosaic daily activities. Dreams, in short, cannot be considered mere reflections of our everyday concerns and affairs. Instead they are the special creative products of a special cognitive operation that engages most fully when we are in REM. The involuntary nature of the dreaming process may be related to these specialized cognitive creations of REM sleep. Whether or not that is the case the involuntary nature of dreaming supports the idea that dreaming itself, not just REM sleep, may have a vital or crucial function. That function, however, remains unknown.

Patrick McNamara

Islam and Dreams

The importance of dreams has been emphasized in the Islamic Holy Scriptures (Qur'an and Hadith). Twenty-four verses of the Holy Qur'an discuss dreams in five chapters. The Hadith is the collection of accounts given by the Prophet Muhammad (PBUH) and are gathered in Hadith books. In Hadith books these accounts are classified according to categories, and one of these categories is devoted to accounts related to dreams. Around 100 prophetic accounts refer to dreams and dreaming.

According to the Islamic teachings, dreams are classified into three subtypes.

The first group is called Ru'ya; meaning truthful dreams or visions, which are dreams of divine origin and are either glad tidings from God, or premonitions. The warning dream is a message to the dreamer to warn him/her of some impending threat or danger in the near future, or to prepare him/her for some bad news.

The second group is called self-talk, which reflects the dreamer's concerns and preoccupations.

The third group comprises the bizarre and jumbled dreams that are of no significance.

According to Islamic teachings, truthful dreams are a human faculty that occur to believers and nonbelievers alike (Twaijry, 1992).

Tabir is the Muslim science of dream interpretation, which emerged very early in the history of Islam. Following the dawn prayer in the mosque, the Prophet used to ask his followers whether anyone had seen a dream. He would then provide an interpretation of the images and symbols of their dreams, and also of his own. The dream should be recounted accurately and truthfully, as there is a warning to those who lie about their dreams. If someone sees a bad dream he is advised to say a certain prayer.

A dream in which the Prophet Muhammad appears as a character is a true dream because Satan does not have the power to assume the shape of God's Prophet. The only restriction is that his figure in the dream should be similar to his known reported physical description.

Word association was one of the Prophet's techniques in interpreting some dreams.

From approximately the ninth-century AD, dream interpretation, known as Tabir materialized as a dynamic body of knowledge integrating Islamic faith with the classical heritage of the Greeks and Romans.

These interpreting principles continue to guide the dream practices of present-day Muslims. It is interesting to note that Muslims' insights and observations have many significant points of contact with the theories developed by Western psychologists over the past 150 years (Bulkeley, 2002).

Ibn Khaldun (1332–1402), in his work "An Introduction to History," postulated that God created sleep as an opportunity for humans to "lift the veil of the senses" and gain access to divine realities and higher forms of knowing. So, when sleep becomes deeper, the soul can be liberated from the constraints of the external sensations and receive reflections from the unseen spiritual world. When that veil is lifted, the soul is ready to learn the things it desires. At times, it catches a glimpse of what it seeks. The more clear the reflections, the more literal the dream would be.

This begs the question: could this liberation of the soul correspond to the states of rapid eye movement (REM) sleep episodes, when most dreams occur? Also, science does not tell us why REM occurs during this type of sleep; however, one of the Prophet's sayings (Hadith) can give an explanation. This Hadith mentions that: "the eyes follow the movement of the soul." So, it has been postulated that these eye movements could be following the vibration of the soul during its spiritual journey (Salem, 2010).

V. J. Hoffman's (1997) work on the role of visions in contemporary Egypt offers striking evidence that dreams continue to play an important part in the religious lives of present-day modernized Muslims. According to Hoffman, dreams provide Muslims with direct experiential affirmation for their faith, connecting them with divine powers and realities and reassuring them of the living presence of God in their lives.

Mohamed Omar Salem

References

Bulkeley, K. (2002). Reflections on the dream traditions of Islam. *Sleep and Hypnosis, 4*(1), 4–14.

Hoffman, V. J. (1997). The role of visions in contemporary Egyptian religious life. *Religion, 27*(1), 53.

Ibn Khaldun. (1967). *The muqaddimah* (Trans. Franz Rosenthal). Princeton, NJ: Princeton University Press.

Salem, M. O. (2010). Function of dreams: An integrated approach. *The Journal of the Islamic Medical Association of North America (JIMA), 42*(1), 15–22.

Twaijry, H. (1992). *The dream book*. Riyadh: Al-Liwa Publishers.

Isolated Sleep Paralysis

Isolated sleep paralysis (ISP) is a common parasoma defined by the chief symptom of muscular paralysis experienced consciously either at sleep onset or when waking from sleep. Isolated refers to the lack of symptoms of another primary sleep disorder, notably narcolepsy and sleep apnea, which are also associated with sleep-paralysis occurrences. When ISP occurs multiple times a night for extended periods, a diagnosis of repetitive ISP may be given. ISP can be treated pharmaceutically as well as managed by attending to lifestyle choices, but there is no known cure.

ISP has several major characteristics shared by individuals from many cultures around the world. First, the paralysis can feel like being held down, being crushed by a weight or an invisible person, as well as related difficulty breathing. Second, the paralysis sometimes occurs with vivid hallucinations that can include all sense modalities and which can be fully incorporated into the sleeping environment. In particular, the hallucination of a sensed presence is frequently felt in the room, which is the uncanny feeling that someone or something is watching. Third, in a minority of cases, the sleeper claims to be physically, and even sexually, assaulted by the hallucinated other. While this assault does not actually occur in consensual reality, it can have a long-lasting psychological effect. Fourth, there are bizarre kinesthetic feelings, including bodily sensations such as floating, falling, rotating, or the sensed separation of one's vantage point from the body, also known as an *out-of-body experience*. Fifth, the paralysis and other symptoms are accompanied by strong emotions. Not just fear, but terror, horror, and even death anxiety are commonly reported. A subset of reports includes strong feelings of love, bliss, and transcendence. Finally, all of the symptoms of this episode are witnessed consciously, often with eyes open, so that the incident appears to be vivid, realistic, and easily remembered for many years, unlike many other kinds of sleep-related phenomena. Sufferers often say, "this was not a dream."

ISP is sometimes confused with night terrors, or *pavor nocturnus*, which is a frightening experience that occurs when awakening from deep sleep. Unlike ISP, night terrors are not usually remembered clearly. Also, ISP is not the same as the nightmare, or the bad dream that causes

Eighteenth-century painter John Henry Fuseli's incubus depictions were some of his most popular themes. *The Nightmare* by John Henry Fuseli, 1781. (Getty Images)

the dreamer to wake up from fear or other strong emotions.

Confusingly, what today is called sleep paralysis was originally referred to as a *nightmare,* defined by early 20th-century psychologist Ernest Jones, who, as a student of Sigmund Freud, interpreted sleep-paralysis symptoms as dreams that showed evidence of sexual dysfunction. The confusion between sleep paralysis and dreams continues through much of the medical and psychiatric literature as over the years nightmare came to mean bad dreams in general. In the 1960s, psychiatrists noticed that narrative accounts of Jones's classic nightmare were related to the symptoms of sleep paralysis with hallucinations. In 1976, medical folklorist David Hufford demonstrated that the cultural tradition

of the "Old Hag" spirit in Newfoundland also has the major calling cards of sleep-paralysis symptoms, exhibiting the parasoma's robust phenomenology across cultures. Today, despite the common occurrence of ISP in normal subjects, the parasoma is often misdiagnosed by the medical community as mental illness.

Physical Correlates

ISP occurs at the boundaries of wakefulness, or Stage 1 sleep, but has been determined in the lab to also include brain-activity characteristics of REM sleep. Therefore, sleep paralysis can be described biologically as consciousness during REM intrusion into light sleep. The paralysis is a natural part of REM sleep in which major muscle groups are targeted by the brain to go limp, a process called *REM muscle atonia.* When muscle atonia is consciously experienced, it may be interpreted as being held down. Furthermore, breathing is commonly restricted in REM sleep, leaving the ISP experience with the sensation of not being able to breathe if sudden attempts are made to gulp in air, a fear response that can heighten to panic. Leading sleep-paralysis researcher Allan Cheyne (2003) also argues that the sensed presence may be formed when the brain's threat-activated vigilance system cannot resolve the ambiguity of threatening imagery caused by REM dreaming intrusion into waking life. Physiological arousal of the genitals can occur during sleep paralysis, playing a role in the sexual nature of some hallucinations. Interestingly, most sleep-paralysis encounters happen when the sleeper is lying in the supine position, on one's back, although they can occur in any sleeping position.

Immediate causes of ISP are unknown, although a genetic link is assumed. For those susceptible of ISP, many psychiatrists and psychologists have noted that the single biggest factor for triggering the parasoma is interrupted or broken sleep. A second important contributing factor is generalized stress or anxiety. Together, these two variables reliably predict that individuals with high levels of ISP will be students, nurses, truck drivers, new parents, soldiers, and other individuals who suffer from poor sleep hygiene or consistent sleep restriction. Other demographics with higher-than-normal levels of reported ISP include refugees, sufferers of posttraumatic stress disorder, as well as individuals with social anxiety or a history of childhood sexual abuse.

Sleep paralysis with hallucinations occur only some of the time, and not for all sufferers, although exact prevalence statistics are heavily debated. These fully sensed and apprehended visions are collectively called *hypnagogic hallucinations*. When hypnagogic hallucinations combine with the sensed presence, the result can include the viewing of a horrific anthropomorphic figure that is interpreted as the instigator of the feelings of paralysis. Full-contact hallucinations can combine with bodily sensations, including the common hallucination of the human-like entity sitting on, strangling, or having forcible sex with the sleeper. The visage of the malevolent entity is sometimes shrouded from view. Other reports showcase a number of horrific creatures, including vampires, zombies, red-eyed demons, aliens, insects, and other nightmarish figures.

More positive night visitors include angels, family members who have passed on, unknown human figures dressed in period clothing, gnomes, fairies, and other beautiful and sensual figures, highlighting that not all sleep-paralysis hallucinations are necessarily nightmarish in character.

Role in History and Myth

The symptoms of ISP can be seen throughout Western letters as well as in regional folklore, fairytales, sculptures, and other visual arts. The narrative dramatizations generally focus on the paralysis of the individual who is set upon by a malevolent demon, ghost, pressing spirit, or seducer in the middle of the night. In Sumerian Babylon, the female seducing spirit Lilith pounced on men while they slept alone and bred demonic offspring. In ancient Greece, the male Ephialtes was feared as an entity that jumps on the chest and tries to suffocate women. The earliest surviving work of English fiction, *Beowulf*, concerns the conquest of Grendel, a *mara* (Welch for crusher) who attacks sleeping men at night. Mara is the root of the modern word *nightmare* as well. European myths of vampires, werewolves, and witches involve tales of paralysis and supernatural assault, as do many accounts of fairies and elves, which paralyze their victims before abducting them.

In the Christian West, sexual hallucinations related to paralysis incidents at night were caused by the succubus and incubus, who were female and male demons, respectively, who sat on the sleeper's chest. Sadly, many women in the Middle Ages were put to death after being accused of having sex with these demonic figures during the night. During the Salem Witch Trials in the American colonies, women were burned at the stake due to the spectral evidence of men's testimonies that the accused women or their spirits climbed into bed with men and seduced them against their will.

Psychological and Cultural Co-Creation

ISP represents a unique opportunity for dream and consciousness studies as the experience is incompletely described unless biological, psychological, and cultural systems are simultaneously sourced. Biologically, ISP has a strong natural expression regardless of supporting cultural frameworks, as is the case in much of Europe today and the United States. However, cultural myths, folklore, and beliefs can overlay the experience and give rise to expectant visions of particular creatures, horrors, and malevolent entities. As medical anthropologist Shelley Adler (2010) argues, some cultural expressions of ISP may even induce serious physical harm, as the case may be with Hmong refugees in the United State who believe that the ghost attacks of ISP can kill. During the 1980s, Hmong refugees also suffered from sudden unexplained nocturnal death syndrome, a deadly genetic heart condition that may be exacerbated by extreme psychological stress that is stirred up by refugee life, broken family structures, and the disturbed sleep patterns that further give rise to high levels of ISP.

Conversely, dreamwork with sleep-paralysis sufferers (Hurd, 2011; Sevilla, 2006) has illustrated how having a positive outlook, or a stabilized psychological set, can also be enough for Western sufferers to turn sleep-paralysis encounters away from the nightmare narrative and toward positive transpersonal events, lucid dreaming, sexual ecstasy, and opportunities to face, work with, and accept unconscious psychological material.

Sleep-paralysis research is in its infancy in many regards. Little is known about its genetics, as well as the markers of susceptibility in individuals. Psychiatrically, many suffering sleepers await a pharmaceutical cure for ISP and repetitive ISP. Psychologically, the links between ISP, alien abduction narratives, and the dynamics of recovered memories are a rich area of future study. Also, the interpersonal dynamics between the sleeper and the self-like other are little explored from any camp, be it behavioral, cognitive, or depth psychology. Anthropologically and historically, the as-yet-unrecognized evidence of sleep-paralysis symptoms await in many aged ethnographic and historical source materials.

Ryan Hurd

See also: entries related to Sleep Physiology

References

Adler, S. (2010). *Sleep paralysis: Night-mares, nocebos and the mind-body connection.* New Brunswick, NJ: Rutgers University Press.

Cheyne, J. A. (2003). Sleep paralysis and the structure of waking-nightmare hallucinations. *Dreaming, 13*(3), 163–179.

Hufford, D. (1982). *The terror that comes in the night: An experience-centered study of supernatural traditions*. Philadelphia: University of Pennsylvania Press.

Hurd, R. (2011). *Sleep paralysis: A guide to hypnagogic hallucinations and visitors of the night*. Los Altos, CA: Hyena Press.

Sevilla, J.C. (2006). *Wrestling with ghosts: A personal and scientific account of sleep paralysis*. Bloomington, IN: Xlibris.

Istikhara: Islamic Dream Incubation

An important part of dream practice in Islam is the little-known phenomena of Istikhara. Istikhara has one main practice with either a focus on consequent daytime guidance or guidance through dream symbolism. In my research I have focused on Istikhara using dreams in the Islamic tradition (Edgar & Henig, 2010). I have found that Istikhara is a significant feature particularly in marriage choice but also sometimes in political and business decision making. Also, Istikhara was found in these studies to be practiced by young and old alike. Istikhara may have evolved from the Ancient Greeks in their *Asclepion* temples, where dream incubation and consequent interpretation was practiced particularly with regard to medical conditions. Social anthropologists have found variants of dream Istikhara in North and West African countries over the past 40 years.

Istikhara is typically learnt from family members and, although the practice varies between countries and individuals, a follower would typically say two additional, specific prayers at night during which they would focus on the big question. They would then lie on their right side and attempt to hold the question as they sleep. Some followers would look for an answer the following morning, but in different traditions Istikhara would be done for seven nights. People who practice Istikhara rely on symbolism to make their decisions. The colors white or green, imagery of important religious figures, or beautiful things would indicate that the proposed action was positive. The colors black, yellow, or red, an unpleasant person, or ugly things are viewed as negative. Once followers get an answer, they are bound to use the advice as it is viewed as the will of Allah.

Although Istikhara as daytime prayer for guidance for right action is sanctioned in Islam as the Prophet Mohammed is reported to have taught the practice to his followers, its adoption into dream incubation is arguable a widespread additional cultural practice thought to be legitimized for Muslims by the Prophet's deep respect for potentially true dreams, *al-ruya,* from Allah.

Both Hidayet Aydar (2009) and myself have found the dream version of Istikhara practice widespread across Islamic countries and communities. My research has focused on interviewing members of the Pakistani community in the United Kingdom and in Pakistan, Turkey, North Cyprus, and Bosnia. In some cultural settings today locally noted Muslims offer to do Istikhara, via dreaming, for others rather than just for themselves. In Bosnia, we found Istikhara practitioners advertising for paying clients. In Sarajevo, we interviewed a 70-year-old female Istikhara practitioner who specialized in helping people with marriage choices and who reported a guide in her dreams, a young handsome man dressed in white, who assisted her.

One Pakistani woman in the United Kingdom who did Istikhara about her daughter's future marriage, dreamt of a good looking bowl of dates, which in the event did not taste very nice. She reported how this imagery anticipated the outcome of the marriage. A Pakistani female student in her 20s studying in the United Kingdom told me how she did Istikhara to finally make a marriage choice. Her parents were opposed to the marriage, but she had known him for five years and was keen to continue the relationship. Her two friends and her mother also did Istikhara, as did a male family friend in the United States. The student dreamt of losing control of her car and crashing into the side of the mountain while the weather was bad. This nightmare experience and the other negative dreams and feelings of her friends and family convinced her that she should not marry this man. Likewise, regarding her brother's marriage, her grandmother did Istikhara and dreamt of her brother and his potential bride in a field with the woman wearing a green bridal scarf. This dream image was seen as a good sign and the marriage went ahead.

Typically, following the advice of an Istikhara experience the person gains confidence in his/her choice of action, and, as we know through the idea of the self-fulfilling prophecy, a positive approach to any endeavor may beneficially affect the outcome.

Iain Ross Edgar

References

Aydar, H. (2009). Istikhara and dreams: Learning about the future through *dreaming In K. Bulkeley, K. Adams, & P. Davis (Eds.), Dreaming in Christianity and Islam: Culture, conflict, and creativity* (pp. 123–136). Piscataway, NJ: Rutgers University Press.

Edgar, I., & Henig, D. (2010). Istikhara: The guidance and practice of Islamic dream incubation through ethnographic comparison. *History and Anthropology, 21*(3), 251–262.

J

Journaling of Dreams

Because dreams are so fleeting—easily forgotten within moments of waking—recording dreams in some fashion is vital to studying them and using them. When a person records his or her dreams on a regular basis over time, the result is a dream journal, or dream diary.

Although most commonly created in handwritten, narrative form, dream journals have been kept in databases and on websites, recorded as digital audio, and sketched, painted, and collaged. Many dream journalers annotate their dream records with information about the waking-life context in which each dream occurred, as well as other associations and memories evoked by the images, actions, and feelings in each dream. Dozens of popular books about dreaming have included tips for remembering and journaling dreams. Among the most common are keeping a pen and notebook next to one's bed; reminding oneself before sleep of the intention to remember dreams; using strategies (such as setting an alarm) to encourage waking during rapid eye movement (REM) sleep; describing the action in the present tense; and composing a title for each dream. (One must always remember that an account of a dream is not the dream itself. However, a carefully kept journal can help the dreamer relive the dream experience.)

Among the diverse and prominent people whose dream journals have been published are authors Franz Kafka, Graham Greene, Jack Kerouac, and William S. Burroughs; scientist and theologian Emmanuel Swedenborg; filmmaker Federico Fellini; and Swiss psychologist Carl G. Jung, whose journal (published in 2009 as *The Red Book*) was a major source for the development of his psychoanalytic theory.

In psychotherapy, the dream journal is often the basis for exploration and reflection. During the second half of the 20th century, formal traditions of early psychoanalysis were crafted by many practitioners into an array of approaches, from Gestalt to group dream sharing, that employ the dream journal to provide insight, guidance, and inspiration.

Academic researchers sometimes employ dreamers' journals to perform studies about the nature of dreaming. In some cases, researchers have asked volunteers to write down their dreams in full detail and answer questions about them. This was how pioneer Calvin Hall began the work that led to the Hall–Van de Castle Scales, a well-known system for classifying and scoring dream elements. In other cases, dreamers donate their existing journals for study; a repository of more than 20,000 dreams from a variety of short-term and long-term journals exists at DreamBank.net.

Content analysis, often based on the Hall–Van de Castle Scales, quantifies what people dream about. It can be adapted to many types of inquiry across a number of fields and allows researchers to make inferences about dreamers in general as well as about individual dreamers. Although content analysis is usually applied by academics to other people's dreams, some individual dreamers have successfully applied it to their own journals. (One, Kelly Bulkeley, reported that indeed the norms established in the Hall–Van de Castle Scales supported the waking-life preoccupations that came to light in his own dreams.)

When the International Association for the Study of Dreams (IASD) first established its annual conferences in 1984, most research based on dream journals was the domain of academics. But soon individual dream journalers began to report their own observations. Their research, using the personal relevance of associated meaning and waking context, is particularly consistent with the ethics statement of IASD, "which recognizes the dreamer as the decision-maker regarding the significance of the dream."

The biggest challenge in doing this sort of research is that, over time, reviewing a growing collection of records requires ever more patience and perseverance. Yet it is only over time that some of the most meaningful phenomena, and the most complex, can be observed. (Among the methods in use for accessing dream journal records are a simple computer operating system search of dreams that have been typed as electronic documents; several types of software developed specifically to contain one's dream journal; and, most recently,

social-networking websites and blogs.) Challenges also ensue when reporting one's findings: the more complex an observation, the more difficult it is to convey to others. In addition, a dreamer may naturally resist sharing deeply personal material publicly.

A concentrated forum for this dreamer-centered research has been the panels on long-term journal keeping (LTJK), presented almost every year since 1996, at IASD's annual conferences. These sessions were initiated by Bulkeley and Dennis Schmidt. At the inaugural session, Schmidt summarized the justification for including independent study by dreamers themselves in this field: "In the tradition of the naturalists whose patient observations prepared the ways to elegant understandings of physics, chemistry, and biology, home journal keepers record and discover events and regularities that astonish and enlighten . . . the personal journal is a uniquely sensitive instrument that may enlighten not only the individual dreamer but the whole field of dream study."

In the years since, LTJK panelists have presented research that covers a wide range of issues and concerns, from creative process to health maintenance to personal guidance to life span passages to Jung's concept of *synchronicity*, or meaningful coincidence (something experienced by a great many of these naturalist dreamers). The quality and breadth of their work suggest that the vast amount to be learned from dream journaling has barely been addressed. A sizeable subset of the presentations has reported findings that point to the far edges of what dream science might be expected to explore in the future.

One example is the "Dreamatarian Diet" documented by Ed Kellogg, whose doctoral dissertation in biochemistry at Duke University was on the subject of longevity. In the 1970s, he began to pay attention to when and how foods showed up in his dreams. He sorted them into five categories ranging from super to poisonous. There were surprises—for example, his dreams recommended foods high in monounsaturated fat at a time when both science and the media promoted polyunsaturates. But later research showed monounsaturated fats to be the most heart healthy. Other research that appeared years, even decades, after the dreams confirmed the general value for many of Kellogg's dream diet recommendations— including recent research that has identified toxic compounds advanced glycoltion end-products (AGEs) and longevity-gene activators found in foods. Following up on his LTJK paper, Kellogg (2007) discovered that the dream foods rated poorest on his scale had very high levels of AGEs and low levels of longevity-gene activators, whereas so-called super foods had the reverse. Kellogg concludes that despite his PhD and staying informed of the latest research, his dreaming self knew much more than his waking self.

Systematic methods for taking a longer view of one's journal, as Kellogg did, might be partially responsible for the growing number of LTJK reports of complexity far beyond what is apparent in working with solitary dreams. Many of the threads of this complexity have normal cause-and-effect connections (either physical or psychological), and serious researchers do their best to consider all such possible explanations before labeling the many remaining connections as synchronistic. While Jung's definition of synchronicity referred to meaningful coincidences between a single internal concern of the psyche and a single external event, LTJK often reveals knots and webs of synchronicity extending across long periods and many people, some of them not previously known to the dreamer. Schmidt, Cynthia Pearson, and Gloria Sturzenacker have focused their independent research on these webs, which give the clear impression of information transfer outside the everyday experience of space and time.

Pearson has labeled these webs *arabesques* after the intricately patterned designs of that name. She noted a number of these as she entered keywords from hundreds of dreams into a database. One example: In 1996, Pearson entered keywords from dreams recorded in 1991, including one titled "Snake Kills Henry's Puppy." In waking life, Henry is her brother, and at the time of the dream, his daughter, Pearson's beloved niece, was dying of a brain tumor. Pearson's notes recognized the symbolism at the time of the dream, but almost five years later, as Pearson entered this snakebite dream in the database, she had just finished reading a book on the unlikely subject of snakes and snakebites that Henry had lent to her. The wonder she felt at this synchronicity was, in turn, synchronistically expressed by a quote she had written down from the book itself: "Mystery . . . is not the absence of meaning, but the presence of more meaning than we can understand" (Covington, 1995, pp. 203–204).

Sturzenacker has developed a graphical system, inner guide mapping, for summarizing long, complex arabesques visually for quick review. This has helped her identify a variety of metapatterns linking her journaled dreams and new waking events, and a single narrative might contain many of these.

Several types appeared in the "Museum Day arabesque" that Sturzenacker reported on the LTJK panel. A simple one, the specific time separation, refers to events on similar dates of different months or years; a subtype is anniversary dreams. The parallel story lines metapattern consists of two completely unrelated events or interests that become meaningfully connected by something unexpected. A third metapattern, the triangle, is a series of three links tracing the order in which correspondences are noticed leading from the present to the past back to the present.

The central dream in the Museum Day arabesque involved a specific time separation: it was on the birthday of the person who would be revealed, only at the very end, as the central figure of the arabesque.

The parallel story lines began as a visit to a museum exhibit titled Art & Auschwitz and, later that day in 2003, a news item that mentioned the actor Steve Buscemi.

The Auschwitz and actor story lines were brought together by two triangles. The first side of the first triangle was drawn when the title *13 Moons* in Buscemi's filmography reminded Sturzenacker (in 2003) of a dream she had titled "12 Moons" (from 1996; the birthday dream). The second side of this triangle extended to M., an acquaintance recorded as being in the dream. M. was the unexpected connection to the

present and, so, the triangle's third side: Sturzenacker had not had contact with M. since the 1996 dream—until she had heard, two weeks before reading Buscemi's filmography in 2003, that M. had undergone dangerous surgery. The other triangle then formed when Sturzenacker searched her journal and found that M. appeared in just two other records. One was a 1997 dream, with which she had recorded multiple associations to the Holocaust—the context of the 2003 art exhibit. Thus the actor and Auschwitz parallel story lines converged into one narrative.

As often happens, the attention-getting weirdness of such developments led to further research and further correspondences. The Museum Day arabesque grew to include eight dreams from 1998 or before. It culminated in an insight combining journal content and waking research that had a tremendous and lasting emotional impact on the dreamer.

Many long-term narratives of this sort (hidden stories, Schmidt has called them) skim bits from widely dispersed dreams and waking events. And while the arabesques may have as much psychological impact as depth work with the dreams that underlie them, the focus might be quite different.

The considerable involvement of complex synchronicity revealed in long-term journals has led LTJK researchers to speculate on possible new sciences implications. Sturzenacker has suggested that features of an unknown cosmological topography may be showing through into everyday waking life. Pearson suggests that in dreams we are not subject to the constraints of space–time that we recognize in our waking lives. This, she notes, seems to dovetail with ongoing developments in physics and the concept of the multiverse—the hypothesized existence of many different universes parallel to our own.

The possibilities for further research are as vast as the dreaming and waking lives our journals document, and perhaps a multiverse beyond. From a technical viewpoint, journal keepers could benefit from more advanced yet less time-consuming technology to record, index, digest, summarize, classify, and access their records, as well as to meticulously distinguish between connections that have explainable causes and those that do not. From the human side, journal keepers could be surveyed about their experiences of those distinctions, and about whether and how dreaming has influenced their view of their own lives and the nature of reality.

Gloria Sturzenacker and
Cynthia Pearson

Note

Abstracts of all the Long-Term Journal-Keeping panels that have been presented at International Association for the Study of Dreams conferences appear at DreamJournalist.com.

References

Covington, D. (1995). *Salvation on Sand Mountain*. New York: Penguin.

International Association for the Study of Dreams. (n.d.). *IASD ethical guidelines.* IASD Dreamwork ethics statement. http://www.asdreams.org/ethics.htm#ethics1

Kellogg, E. (2007). Mind–body healing through dreamwork. Presented at the IASD annual conference, Sonoma, CA. http://www.asdreams.org/psi2007/papers/edkellogg.htm

Schmidt, D. (1999). Stretched dream science: The essential contribution of long-term naturalistic studies. *Dreaming, 9*(1), 43–69. http://www.dreamjournalist.com/

Jung's Dream Theory

Born in 1875 in a country village near Basel, Switzerland, Carl Gustav Jung was the son of a stern Lutheran pastor and a minister's daughter. He took an early interest in his dreams, wondering about their strange power, frightening imagery, and sacrilegious themes. The Protestant theology of his parents could not explain these experiences, but Jung felt strongly they were important and meaningful, and thus began a lifelong study of dreaming and dream interpretation.

After completing medical school, Jung focused his early career on psychiatry. In 1900, he began working as a clinician at the Burholzi Mental Hospital in Zurich. That same year, Sigmund Freud published *The Interpretation of Dreams*, and in 1906 Jung initiated a correspondence with Freud that soon blossomed into a close working relationship. For many years Jung was Freud's greatest champion, but in 1914 they angrily broke off their friendship— Jung thought Freud was too dictatorial, and Freud thought Jung was too mystical. Whatever the cause, Jung was deeply wounded by his exile from the psychoanalytic community. For the next several years he suffered severe mental and emotional distress, which he labored to analyze as he would one of his patients. He wrote down all his dreams and fantasies, painted personal images of mandalas and other religious symbols (recently published in The *Red Book*), and slowly reconstructed his identity on a firmer foundation of self-understanding. The rupture of his relationship with Freud was, by his own account, a decisive catalyst in the creation of his later system of thought and clinical practice.

Jung shared with Freud and other depth psychologists the premise that the conscious mind emerges over time from a primal state of unconsciousness. Both Jung and Freud agreed that dreams offer a window into the unconscious, but they disagreed about what can be seen through that window. Jung emphasized the direct and natural expressiveness of dreaming. Dreams give us an honest portrayal of who we are and who we might become. One of the important functions of dreams, according to Jung, is a prospective anticipation of future growth. While Freud looked for insights into the dreamer's past, Jung sought visions of possible development in the future. Jung did not mean that dreams make predictions, but rather that dreaming uses the psyche's vast powers of imagination and symbolic creativity to speculate about where one's life may be leading. The other major function Jung identifies is the compensation of psychological imbalance. Dreaming helps preserve a healthy and well-integrated personality by bringing important feelings, memories, and intuitions from the unconscious into the conscious mind.

The interpretation of dreams does not lead, in Jung's view, to a specific answer or rational translation. The goal is rather to open the individual's conscious mind to new meanings and deeper self-understanding. His approach is pragmatic in the sense that the dreamer's beneficial response is the primary test of an interpretation. If it helps the patient get better, it is a good interpretation. Jung took special interest in highly memorable dreams from early childhood, as these types of dreams reveal with special clarity the unconscious dynamics of the human psyche. Jung used the term big dreams to refer to these and other types of rare but intensely meaningful dream experiences. To help interpret big dreams Jung tried to amplify the imagery and emotions by connecting them with symbolic parallels in world mythology and religious history. He said most dreams have a dramatic structure, like a theatrical play, and one ought to interpret a dream by first analyzing it in terms of four dramatic categories: the characters and setting (locale), the basic problem (exposition), what happens to change the problem (peripeteia), and the result of the actions (lysis).

Over the course of his career Jung developed a complex theory of archetypal symbols; that is, recurrent patterns of meaning that reflect innate features of human development. In big dreams, the most important archetypes Jung identifies are the shadow, representing unconscious elements that have been neglected by the conscious personality; the anima and animus, symbolizing the unconscious aspects of the opposite sex in each person; and the self, representing the human potential to achieve wholeness and self-integration. Every person follows his or her own lifelong path of individuation toward the self, toward the potential wholeness that lies dormant within the unconscious. Jung valued dreams because they offer personal guidance and inspiration in following that path.

Kelly Bulkeley

References

Jung, C.G. (1965). *Memories, dreams, reflections* (Trans. R. Winston & C. Winston). New York: Vintage Books.

Jung, C.G. (1968). *Man and his symbols*. New York: Dell.

Jung, C.G. (1974). *Dreams* (Trans. R.F.C. Hull). Princeton, NJ: Princeton University Press.

Jung, C.G. (2008). *Children's dreams: Notes from the seminar given in 1936–1940* (Trans. E. Falzeder & T. Woolfson). Princeton, NJ: Princeton University Press.

Jung, C.G. (2009). *The red book* (Trans. S. Shamdasani). New York: W.W. Norton.

Jung's *The Red Book*

Jung's *The Red Book* is the edited record of Swiss psychiatrist C.G. Jung's (1875–1961) dreams, inner visions, and inner dialogues occurring from November 13, 1913, to February 8, 1916, the period during World War I. *The Red Book* contains three sections: Liber Primus (November 13 to December 25, 1913), Liber Secundus (December 26, 1913, to April 19, 1914), and Scrutinies (April 19, 1914, to February 8, 1916). Throughout the following 14 years, Jung drew from his personal journals known as the *Black Books*, and edited and elaborated on each section until the work's final completion in 1930.

Jung's The *Red Book* is an exact reproduction of the original German manuscripts. It includes an English translation and historical footnotes by the volume's editor, historian of science, Sonu Shamdasani. The text is written in calligraphy in the style of an illuminated manuscript, and is accompanied by illuminated images.

Detailed historical footnotes connect Jung's text with extant letters, journal entries, lectures, articles, and publications, as well as with references to literary, philosophical, and scientific works as notated in Jung's personal library. The experiences recorded in *The Red Book* became the foundation for Jung's theories of individuation, the self, ego, the collective unconscious, archetype, shadow, anima and animus, the transcendent function, the psychological influence of Christianity, and psychological studies of symbolism, mythology, and culture.

The Red Book was prompted by Jung's search for his soul in a time of personal professional success but inner emptiness. His search reflects his particular Germanic European cultural ethos, as he investigates questions posed by Goethe, Nietzsche, the Bible, Gnostic scriptures, pre-Christian Germanic mythology, and the medieval Grail legend. His questions addressed the nature of God, good and evil, the cultural wounds contained within Christianity, modern spiritual redemption, and creative individual existence.

Jung termed his method of exploration the way, *der Weg*. During the day he committed himself to his professional work in the spirit of the times; during the night he focused on his inner work, the spirit of the depths. He tracked his dreams and engaged in imagination and inner dialogue, a method that he termed *active imagination*. He used his mind to focus on a particular area—for an extended time, his focus was his soul—and then engaged in creative dialogue with the inner figures he encountered.

Jung discovered distinctive multivalent iconographies of his soul in his explorations.

His inner images include the prophet Elijah, the blinded Salome, the desert anchorite, Christ, Satan, the serpent, the lion, the white bird, the phallus, the tree of life, the star, the magician, the wise man, the child, the frog-king. These imagoes constitute some of the valorized and the devalued, the ignored and unknown parts of his self. His confrontations with these figures catalyzed transformation and successive surrendering of parts of his ego identity. With this sacrifice came an experience of numinous sacred energy—a release of divine light as well as darkness within him. While these states may have brought about a *mana*-identification with god-energy, they were balanced by repeated descents into abject misery; he states at the end of *The Red Book* that the person who follows *der Weg* must embrace suffering at its core.

Jung's inner explorations in *The Red Book* comprise a methodology—a way, ein Weg—of psychological transformation. Jung witnessed the successive differentiations and transformations of his inner figures as he related to them over time. He termed the essential transformative force within the psyche that guided this growth the *self*: the psyche's directing monadic intelligence. In the process of *der Weg*, the path of individuation, the self directs each person individually to find and connect to its essential monadic presence. This is effected through successively relating to new and increasingly numinous aspects within oneself, and in so doing, successively surrendering accustomed ego identifications so that new, more conscious adaptations might be born.

While Jung's work demonstrates that one's ancestral traditions and one's collective cultural ethos delimit the language and the images of engagement in individuation, it also shows how a new spiritual impulse is born within a historical age. For Jung, the unanswered and unredeemed questions in Christianity became the foundation for his own psychological and spiritual growth. These experiences led him to believe that the individual exploration of God experienced in *der Weg* would provide the next spiritual experience for mankind—a path of individual suffering, yes, but ultimately a path of collective wholeness.

Laurel M. McCabe

See also: Jung's Transcendent Function: Neurological Support

Reference

Jung, C.G. (2009). *The red book* (Trans. S. Shamdasani). New York: Norton.

Jung's Transcendent Function: Neurological Support

Carl Jung, the eminent Swiss psychologist and one of the founders of analytical psychology, stated that the unconscious is an "independent productive activity, constantly supplying us with contents" and claimed dreams to be its most readily accessible expression (Jung, 1971, p. 135). Furthermore, he saw dreams as having a purposeful structure, an underlying intention, with the general function being to restore psychological balance (Jung, 1973, p. 127). Jung contended that the dream recognizes personal motives and compensates for our misconceptions and the deficiencies of our personalities, the aim being to bring the conscious and unconscious together to transition to or arrive at a new attitude (Jung, 1971, p. 279). This is a release from one attitude or pattern of existence to a more mature one he called the transcendent function (Jung, 1973, p. 149). Jung describes transcendence as a part of the individuation process, an unconsciously driven process of becoming an individual with a focus on self-actualization, considering the personality as a whole or greater self (Jung, 1971, p. 296).

Whereas Jung supported these theories with his observations, there is some evidence from more recent neurological studies of the waking and dreaming brain that the capacity for such unconscious processing might exist in the dream state. Recent rapid eye movement (REM) studies, by various neuroimaging groups, have provided an understanding that a unique combination of active and inactive brain centers appears to account for the unusual characteristics of dreams as well as some of the functions that Jung and many other dream psychology theorists attribute to dreaming (Hobson, Pace-Schott, & Stickgold, 2003, p. 32, Pace-Schott, 2007, pp. 115–142). Areas of the brain that process information at a relatively unconscious level are activated during REM, including the limbic regions, which are believed to selectively process emotionally relevant memories (Dang-Vu, Schabus, Desseilles, Schwarz, & Maquet, 2007, p. 102); the visual association cortex, which processes visual meaning; and the anterior cingulate and basal forebrain regions involved in processing internal information for decision making. In contrast, areas more related to conscious processing, rational thought, and episodic memory, remain relatively inactive—leaving

the unconscious to orchestrate the dream plot. Activation of unconscious processing centers, which deal with memories and the emotional impact of an event, accompanied by the creation of visual associations, with little access to the memory of the waking episode, is supportive of Jung's contention that the "unconscious aspect of any event is revealed to us in dreams where it appears not as a rational thought but as a symbolic image," an "emotionally charged pictorial language" (Jung, 1973, p. 30).

The REM-state activity in the frontal cortical and subcortical areas is of potential interest to what Jung observed as a transcendent function in dreams since these areas have been shown to be involved in unconscious decision making and attitude change. Recent studies show the anterior cingulate is involved in conflict monitoring and mediating problem solving. It receives information about a stimulus and selects an appropriate response (Apps, Balsters, & Ramnani, 2009) based on past experience and observed or imagined outcomes (Hayden, Pearson, & Platt, 2009, pp. 948–950). It then monitors the consequences of actions and changes or adapts our behavior if the outcome is not as expected (Luu & Pederson, 2004). The projecting and testing of imagined outcomes to adapt new behaviors is also not unlike the threat simulation theory that Revonsuo attributes to dreams (Dang-Vu et al., 2007, p. 98). The anterior cingulate does not achieve this alone but typically networks with other adjacent structures, many found to be active in the REM state. The basal ganglion is active in detecting errors, anomalies, and novel situations as well as deciding which of several possible behaviors to execute based on reward learning. The orbitofrontal cortex also works with the amygdale to process emotional information (Pace-Schott, 2007, p. 119) and is also involved in decision making, expectation, and regulating our planning behavior based on reward and punishment (Bechara, Damasio, Damasio, & Anderson, 1994, pp. 7–15; Kringelbach, 2005, pp. 691–702) so as to change our ongoing behavior (Kringelbach & Rolls, 2004, pp. 341–372). Perhaps the goal-driven focus toward individuation and self-actualization, with its sense of unconscious inner direction, is a contribution of the active medial prefrontal cortex, which involves social processing and self-referential mental activity (Pace-Schott), as well as goal-directed behavior (Gusnard, Akbudak, Shulman, & Raichle, 2001, pp. 4259–4264), self-monitoring of learning, and our sense of knowing (Marley, 2009).

These unconscious processing centers, which become active during REM sleep, give support to Jung's theory that the unconscious has the capability to become independently productive and mediate a transcendence as Jung describes it. To what degree these centers interoperate in the dream state to bring about change is yet to be fully discovered, but the capability appears to exist for the dreaming mind to recognize inconsistencies in our perceptions (errors and anomalies), anticipate the consequences of our actions, and compensate for them by mediating a subsequent change in attitude with a sense of knowing that it is appropriate to the circumstances.

Robert J. Hoss

References

Apps, M., Balsters, J., & Ramnani, N. (2009, February 24). Anterior cingulate cortex: Monitoring the outcomes of others' decisions. *Medical News Today*. Retrieved from www.medicalnewstoday.com/articles/153472.php

Bechara, A., Damasio, A. R., Damasio, H., & Anderson, S. W. (1994). Insensitivity to future consequences following damage to human prefrontal cortex. *Cognition, 50*, 7–15.

Dang-Vu, T. T., Schabus, M., Desseilles, M., Schwarz, S., & Maquet, P. (2007). Neuroimaging of REM sleep and dreaming. In D. Barrett & P. McNamara (Eds.), *The new science of dreaming* (Vol. 1, pp. 95–113). Westport, CT: Praeger.

Gusnard, D., Akbudak, E., Shulman, G., & Raichle, M. (2001). Medial prefrontal cortex and self-referential mental activity: Relation to a default mode of brain function. *Proceedings of the National Academy of Science, 98*, 4259–4264.

Hayden, B., Pearson, J., & Platt, M. (2009). Fictive reward signals in the anterior cingulate cortex. *Science, 324*(5929), 948–950.

Hobson, J. A., Pace-Schott, E. F., & Stickgold, R. (2003). *Sleep and dreaming* (Eds. E. F. Pace-Schott, M. Solms, M. Blagrove, & S. Harnad). New York: Cambridge University Press.

Jung, C. G. (1971). *The portable Jung* (Ed. J. Campbell). New York: The Viking Press.

Jung, C. G. (1973). *Man and his symbols*. New York: Dell Publishing.

Kringelbach, M. L. (2005). The orbitofrontal cortex: Linking reward to hedonic experience. *Nature Reviews Neuroscience, 6*, 691–702.

Kringelbach, M. L., & Rolls, E. T. (2004). The functional neuroanatomy of the human orbitofrontal cortex: Evidence from neuroimaging and neuropsychology. *Progress in Neurobiology Journal, 72*, 341–372.

Luu, P., & Pederson, S. M. (2004). The anterior cingulate cortex: Regulating actions in context. In M. I. Posner (Ed.), *Cognitive neuroscience of attention* (pp. 213–231). New York: Guilford Press.

Marley J. (2009, February 24). Medial prefrontal cortex plays a critical and selective role in "feeling of knowing" meta-memory judgements. *The Amazing World of Psychiatry: A Psychiatry Blog*. Retrieved from http://theamazingworldofpsychiatry.word press.com/2009/02/24/

Pace-Schott, E. (2007). The frontal lobes and dreaming. In D. Barrett & P. McNamara (Eds.), *The new science of dreaming* (Vol. 1, pp. 115–154). Westport, CT: Praeger.

K

Kleine–Levin Syndrome

Kleine–Levin syndrome (KLS) is a periodic hypersomnia characterized by recurrent episodes of hypersomnia and other behavioral and cognitive symptoms. It mainly affects teenage boys. It is sometimes associated with hyperphagia and, in some cases, hypersexuality. Each episode is of brief duration lasting about a month. Patients are entirely asymptomatic between episodes. No definite cause has been identified, and no effective treatments are available. The International Classification of Sleep Disorders diagnostic criteria for KLS include: (1) episodes of excessive sleepiness lasting more than two days and less than four weeks, occurring at least once a year; (2) intermixed with long intervals of normal alertness, mood, cognition, and behavior lasting usually months to years; (3) recurring at least every year interspersed with long periods of normal sleep; (4) not better explained by a sleep disorder, a neurological disorder (e.g., idiopathic recurrent stupor, epilepsy), a mental disorder (e.g., bipolar disorder, psychiatric hypersomnia, depression), or the use of drugs (e.g., benzodiazepines, alcohol). In addition to these recurrent episodes of hypersomnia, KLS patients should experience at least one of these symptoms: hyperphagia, hypersexuality, odd behavior, or cognitive disturbances (e.g., confusion, feeling of de-realization, or hallucinations).

While it is generally agreed that KLS is associated with neurocognitive changes in addition to the characteristic sleep and behavioral problems, very little is known about the cognitive sequelae of KLS. Results of the Arnulf et al. (2008) survey of some 108 cases demonstrated marked apathy, exhaustion, memory problems, temporal disorientation, de-realization, dreamy state, and impaired speech among other cognitive and perceptual symptoms.

Consistent with the supposition that KLS may carry long-term cognitive consequences, Landtblom, Dige, Schwerdt, Safstrom, and Granerus (2002) studied neuropsychological functions in an individual who suffered his first KLS episode at age18. Neuropsychological and neuroimaging data were collected on the patient at the time of the first episode and then seven years later, long after hypersomnolent crisis periods had ceased. At retesting, Landtblom et al. found a normalized frontal perfusion but a persistent slight hypoperfusion affecting mainly the left temporal lobe. Relative to baseline testing, there was also a decline in short-term verbal and visual memory abilities. Fontenelle, Mendlowicz, Gillin, Mattos, and Versiani (2000) pointed out that Landtblom's data are consistent with one of their KLS patients who exhibited academic decline over time as well as the cases of Sagar, Khandelwal, and Gupta (1990), who described three KLS patients who exhibited academic decline after the onset of the illness. In summary, it appears that at least some KLS patients are vulnerable to progressive cognitive decline secondary to KLS. These individuals need to be identified so that early intervention can arrest or stop that decline in intellectual abilities.

Patrick McNamara

See also: entries related to Sleep Disorders

References

Arnulf, I., Ling, L., Gadoth, N., File, J., Lecendreux, M., Franco, P., . . . Mignot, E. (2008). Kleine-Levin syndrome: A systematic study of 108 patients. *Annals of Neurology, 63*(4), 482–493.

Fontenelle, L., Mendlowicz, M. V., Gillin, J. C., Mattos, P., & Versiani, M. (2000). Neuropsychological sequelae in Kleine-Levin syndrome. *Arquivos de Neuro-Psiquiatria, 58,* 531–534.

Huang, Y. S., Guilleminault, C., Kao, P. F., & Liu, F. Y. (2005). SPECT findings in the Kleine-Levin syndrome. *Sleep, 28,* 955–960.

Huang, Y. S., Lakkis, C., & Guilleminault, C. (2010). Kleine-Levin syndrome: Current status. *Medical Clinics of North America, 94*(3), 557–562.

Landtblom, A. M., Dige, N., Schwerdt, K., Safstrom, P., & Granerus, G. (2002). A case of Kleine-Levin syndrome examined with SPECT and neuropsychological testing. *Acta Neurologica Scandinavica, 105,* 318–321.

Miller, B. L., & Cummings, J. L. (Eds.). (2007). *The human frontal lobes: Functions and disorders.* New York: The Guilford Press.

Sagar, R. S., Khandelwal, S. K., & Gupta, S. (1990). Interepisodic morbidity in Kleine-Levin syndrome. *British Journal of Psychiatry, 157,* 139–141.

L

Leading Dream Groups

Independent groups that come together for dreamwork (outside of a clinical setting) most frequently operate under the leadership of a single individual whose roles include being a teacher, guide, and facilitator. Some group leaders are counselors, psychologists, ministers, or health care professionals with degrees and other certification, while other leaders are qualified by an accumulation of experience as participants in dream groups.

Depending on the leader's training and experience, the issues brought forth in the group may be examined at a variety of psychological levels. Leaders of all backgrounds may benefit from participation in dream-group leadership programs.

The leader must use good judgment in accepting members into the dream group. Under no circumstances should the group include anyone who may have a psychological disorder, as such a person is likely to be disruptive to the group. (Even if the leader is a trained and certified psychologist, his/her role is to guide the group's dreamwork, not to function as a psychological counselor.)

The dream-group leader's primary responsibility is to provide a safe and confidential setting in which all participants can reveal the content of their dreams and the waking-life circumstances that may contribute to understanding those dreams.

The leader ensures this central objective by establishing rules and ethical practices that will be observed within the group; these guidelines may be developed independently by the group leader, and/or may be based on those suggested by the International Association for the Study of Dreams in their *IASD Ethical Guidelines*. Although dream groups differ significantly from other psychological encounter groups, the principles of established psychological group process are encouraged and helpful in group dreamwork. The leader of the group must be aware of group dynamics, such as projection and bring it to the attention of the group.

Elemental to providing a safe environment for dreamwork is the tenet that each dreamer has final authority over his/her dream. The leader and group members alike must accept the premise that the dreamer is the only one who can know for certain the truths revealed by his/her dream; the meaning of the dream is relative to the dreamer's personal experience. It is also vital to clarify that the group as a whole must accept and respect differing personalities, beliefs, and values.

Having created a safe, confidential, and comfortable environment, the leader's fundamental purpose is to conduct the dreamwork in such a way that participants are able to forge their own individual paths to self-awareness and development. The function of the leader and other group members in this process is to ask questions that help the dreamer uncover the dream's meaning and message.

The leader's teaching role within the group includes presenting information about, and drawing distinctions between, various dream theories (Jungian, Freudian, Gestalt), providing a body of thought from which participants may draw as they approach their own dreams. In addition to explaining details of these theories and the possible meanings of dream symbols brought up in group discussion, the leader may wish to recommend outside reading material.

In the role of dream-work guide, the group leader determines and conveys to the participants the procedures that the group will use in their work. For example, the leader might instruct participants to: (1) write down their dreams in advance of the meeting; (2) present dreams to the group in the present tense (to more readily reexperience the action and emotions of the dream); (3) refrain from asking questions or otherwise speaking until the dreamer is finished presenting his/her dream; (4) frame remarks about others' dreams in language such as "If it were my dream"; and (5) pay close attention to emotional and physiological responses.

As facilitator of the group's dreamwork, the leader is responsible for meeting several specific goals: (1) organize the group (e.g., membership, meeting place, time, format, fees); (2) encourage all group members to share their dreams and participate in discussion of dreams presented by others; (3) ensure that participants are respectful toward one another and the dreams themselves; (4) maintain the group's focus on the dreamwork (limiting off-topic discussion and conversation); (5) make observations about dream content and possible meaning that the dreamer has not yet vocalized; (6) interject theoretical background that may be of help to the dreamer and the group in general; (7) listen carefully; refrain from being too vocal, but continually lead the group forward.

The leader sets the tone for the group, encouraging responsibility to oneself and the group as a whole, and fostering respect for one's own dreams as well as the dreams of others. Throughout the dream-work process, the leader must remain aware of group members' individual needs, and ensure that each individual has a proportionately fair share of time in which to present and work on dreams. It is also vital to encourage group members to take risks, admit fears, embrace change, and attend to their own intuition.

The group leader will be presented with many challenges which, when approached with openness and wisdom, provide opportunities for growth for the leader, as well as group members. It is vital to listen to members' concerns without being defensive or judgmental and be willing to lead the group into discussion to reach a solution for whatever situation arises.

A final imperative for the group leader is to model an active and healthy approach to dreamwork and the personal growth that can result from bringing the dream's messages into one's daily life. Intrinsic to this goal are the modeling of: (1) commitment to the dream-work process and to the group itself; (2) trust and honesty within the group; (3) willingness to take risks and face change in one's own life; and

(4) sharing personal growth experienced as a result of his/her own dreamwork.

Justina Lasley

References

International Association for the Study of Dreams. (n.d.). *IASD ethical guidelines.* Retrieved from http://www.asdreams.org/ethics.htm#ethics2

Lasley, J. (2004). *Honoring the dream: A handbook for dream group leaders.* Mount Pleasant, SC: DreamsWork Publications.

Taylor, J. (1983). *Dreamwork: Techniques for discovering the creative power in dreams.* Mahwah, NJ: Paulist Press.

Ullman, M. (1996). *Appreciating dreams: A group approach.* Thousand Oaks, CA: Sage Publications.

Yalom, I.D. (1995). *The theory and practice of group psychotherapy.* New York: Basic Books.

Literature and Dreams

Since dream reports appear among the first-preserved human records in many cultures, dreaming itself may be the earliest known form of human creativity. When a society moves out of an exclusively oral tradition with the invention of writing, texts emerge that can only be called *literary*; like dream reports, they have narrative forms, a metaphorical tenor, imagery that functions symbolically, and other figurative (nonliteral) uses of language. They share what has been called "the felt presence of secondary meaning" and therefore require interpretation.

More than 5,000 years ago, one of the first accounts of the dreaming process occurred in a narrative poem inscribed in cuneiform (wedge-shaped) writing on clay tablets. In the preserved fragments of this poem, a major dream episode displays many characteristics of contemporary literary texts and dream reports. The often accompanying urge to share dreams, as represented in this earliest text, turns dreamers into storytellers and invites the participation of others in a search for meaning. There is an assumption of societal as well as individual significance. "My sister, listen to my dream: …/My drinking cup falls from its peg./My shepherd's crook has disappeared./An eagle seizes a lamb from the sheepfold./A falcon catches a sparrow on the reed fence" (Wolkstein & Kramer, 1983, pp. 75–76).

The dreamer, Dumuzi, shares his dream with his sister, Gesthinanna, not just for pleasure, but also because he depends on her to provide him with an interpretation. "My sister who knows the meaning of words,/My wise woman who knows the meaning of dreams" (Wolkstein & Kramer, 1983, p. 75). Thus a text composed in Mesopotamia near the Persian Gulf area, transliterated from the now-extinct Sumerian writing system, and translated into modern English, already contains the drama of a life-altering nightmare. It is central to this story of the goddess, Inanna. The poem's kinship to the better-known Babylonian epic, *Gilgamesh*, is also rooted in dreaming, since *Gilgamesh* contains several dream episodes crucial to that story's development and revelatory of the individual characters who appear in it. Since earliest times, then, dream reports and literary texts, dreaming and creative writing, have been interpenetrating spheres of human experience.

An ancient term, oneirocriticism, has been revived to name the interdisciplinary study of these often converging phenomena. (*Oneiros* is from the Greek word for one kind of dream and now refers generically to any dream phenomena; criticism is another term for poetics as the study of literature and language.) More than 1,500 years ago, for example, a Greek bishop, Synesius of Cyrene (circa 400s CE), wrote a treatise in Latin, *De Insomniis* (*On Dreams*), praising dreams for the way they stimulated the imagination. He recommended the keeping of a dream journal (night book), since transcribing dreams would improve one's writing style, public speaking skills, and general use of language.

Such dream books are a fascinating phenomenon central to understanding the long history of dreaming in its relation to the writing and reading of literature. They turn up everywhere, comprising ongoing cross-fertilization of cultural knowledge and a melding of belief systems of vastly different times and places. A 10th-century-CE book on dreams, *The Oneirocriticon of Achmet*, is subtitled, "A Christian-Greek adaption [*sic*] of Islamic, Arabic material." Another such book takes syncretism even further: it is titled *Apomazar* and subtitled the "doctrine of the Indians, Persians, & Egyptians. Taken from the library of Jean Sambucus. Then turned from the Greek into Latin by Jean Leunclais. And put again into French in Paris 1581." These books are ancestors to contemporary self-help books about remembering, recording, and even controlling your dreams just as they are predecessors for the dream theorizing of later experts.

Ultimately, the most facile travelers between the realms of dreaming and literature are creative writers themselves. They often claim that their own dreaming has revitalized their creative energy in writer's block periods. They credit life-changing big dreams for making it impossible to ignore the links between their dreaming and creating processes (British poet William Blake, 1757–1827). They find dreaming a resource for solving problems that arise with a work in progress (Chilean novelist Isabel Allende, b. 1942). Some writers import, intact, their own dreams into their texts (U.S. horror-fiction writer Stephen King, b. 1947). King even admits to the ancient practice of incubation: presleep reflection on a topic of concern accompanied by a request for assistance from the dream world.

Many classic or culture-embodying texts—as well as texts that become valued for their challenge to the classics—feature dreaming and dreamlikeness (China's *Dream of the Red Chamber*, mid-18th century); Spain's *Don Quixote*, by Miguel Cervantes, 1547–1616). Many authors have achieved fame through an imagination so infused with dreaming that they also kept dream diaries and directed some of their talent to nonfiction commentary on the subject (British author Samuel Taylor Coleridge, 1772–1834; Austrian novelist Franz Kafka, 1883–1924; Argentinean author Jorge Luis Borges, 1899–1986). Even some single dream episodes from various literary traditions have had sufficient power to take on a global life of their own outside their original texts (Raskolnikov's horse-beating nightmare in Dostoevsky's *Crime and Punishment* [1866]; the narrator's initial dreams in Emily Bronte's *Wuthering Heights* [1847]).

All genres of literature have been susceptible to the influence of dreaming. One of the most memorable of *The Canterbury Tales* of Geoffrey Chaucer (British, 14th century) is a beast fable centered on an intense debate, between a hen and a rooster, about the origins, nature, and meaning of dreams. Maurice Sendak (United States, b. 1928) wrote and illustrated a trilogy of children's picture books on dreams, which included the much translated and globally known tale, *Where the Wild Things Are*. A Chicano coming-of-age novel, *Bless me, Ultima* (1972), by Rudolfo Anaya is suffused with dreaming that enables a young boy to reconcile attachment to his ancestral Mexican heritage with the modernized ways of his family in the United States.

Dreaming in literature performs many of the same functions that traditionally recognized and labeled literary devices, authorial strategies, and formal properties have always done, but with distinctive characteristics. Anthropologist-poet Paul Friedrich (United States, b. 1927) coined the term *oneiremes* to describe dreaming elements in literature and the unique ways they reinvent the creation, content, and form of literary texts. Dreams provoke an instant bond and sense of recognition for readers, all of whom are dreamers themselves. Through incorporation of dreams, authors can give readers access to a full 24 hours of any day in the lives of their fictional figures. Since dreaming traverses three territories simultaneously—the uniquely individual, the culturally specific, and the universally human—a depth of understanding of character, circumstance, or allusion can be quickly conveyed. Furthermore, since dreaming emanates from

a kinetic fusion of brain–mind and bodily processes, both mental and somatic dimensions of human experience are available for representation.

All these qualities proved particularly valuable in the 20th century with writers seeking to chronicle the special circumstances of previously marginalized and disenfranchised people, to express the inexpressibility of some extreme human conditions such as apartheid and the Holocaust, or to represent the multilayered complexity in immigrant/diaspora/post-colonial experience. Further, oneirically informed literary criticism is illuminating these fluid interactions among dreaming, literature, and the reading mind. For example, while exploring the novels of African American author Richard Wright (1908–1960), Mikko Tuhkanen observes that dreaming extends to authors, characters, and readers "possibilities—often figured as *speeds*—that are unavailable within the extant phenomenological horizon" of their lives (2010, p. 155). Taking an interpretive stance he calls oneiropolitical, Tuhkanen shows how dreaming, through its atemporality, offers the dreamer temporary release from oppression and time to imagine a future of freedom and to awake to the option of revolutionary change.

Similarly, Maggi Phillips finds dreaming a rare avenue by which the silenced gain a voice in the works of post-colonial African women writers such as Flora Nwapa, Buchi Emecheta, Bessie Head, Tsitsi Dangarembga, and Ama Ata Aidoo whose tragic drama, *Anowa*, depicts the agonizing cost of the social repression of dreaming. Their history enables these writers "to command such a spectrum of possibilities that it is impossible to say how many dreaming realms they access" (Phillips, 1994, p. 91). They draw from all those realms to bridge the radical disjunctions between their past and present: "Their writing evokes spiritual compensation, historical revenge, and the means of moral transmission" (Phillips, 1994, p. 102).

Jenni Adams (2009) describes the emerging importance of dreaming, along with other altered states of being and consciousness, in literature of the Holocaust. This tendency, falling within the rubric of magic realism, enables writers like Jonathan Safran Foer to translate the unspeakable into accessible language as well as to depict convincingly the paradoxical coexistence—just as it is regularly depicted in dreaming and accepted without question by dreamers—of the rational and the irrational, the unthinkable and the readily knowable. The vividness of a dream's psychic reality carries over, often in a deeply sensory way, into the material reality of waking life. Thus dreaming forces confrontation with such fundamental questions as what is real and what is illusory, what is true and what is false, what can we know and how do we come to know it.

Once having glimpsed the scope of dreaming in world literature, how does the interested general reader proceed? Promising avenues of discovery include reading widely in a single author (see the entry "Shakespeare and Dreams"); in emerging genres (see the entry "Graphic Novels and Dreams"); in varieties of genre fiction (see the entry "Fantasy Literature and Dreams"). One can choose to explore certain literary movements that have been especially hospitable to dreaming: surrealism, European romanticism, magic realism. Further special opportunities can be found in literature growing out of unusual dream-and-culture configurations such as that in the Australian aboriginals' dreamtime. Finally, the experience of dreams in literature may intensify awareness of the reader's own dreaming. Even in the 21st century many readers can profit from Synesius's advice and keep a dream journal of their own, returning to the first source of human creativity from which so much of the literary imagination has sprung.

Carol S. Rupprecht

See also: Fantasy Literature and Dreams; Graphic Novels and Dreams; Shakespeare and Dreams

References

Adams, J. (2009). The dream of the end of the world: Magic realism and Holocaust history in Jonathan Safran Foer's *Everything Is Illuminated. CLIO: A Journal of Literature, History, and the Philosophy of History, 39*(1), 53–77.

Phillips, M. (1994). Engaging dreams: Alternative perspectives on flora Nwapa, Buchi Emecheta, Ama Ata Aidoo, Bessie Head, and Tsitsi Dangarembga's writing. *Research in African Literatures, 25*(4), 89–103.

Rupprecht, C. S. (2007). Dreaming, language, literature. In D. Barrett & P. McNamara (Eds.), *The new science of dreaming* (Vol. 3, pp. 1–34). Westport, CT: Praeger.

Tuhkanen, M. (2010). Richard Wright's oneiropolitics. *American Literature, 82*(1), 151–179.

Wolkstein, D., & Kramer, S. N. (1983). *Inanna: Queen of heaven and earth.* New York: Harper & Row.

Little Dreams

There is no question that *big dreams,* such as dreams of dead loved ones coming back to life or momentous ones that you think about for days on end, are important to one's understanding of self and the world. Carl Jung (1974) said they "are often remembered for a lifetime, and not infrequently prove to be the richest jewel in the treasure house of psychic experience" (p. 76). It is no wonder that they have attracted so much research and therapeutic attention.

And what about that dream you had last night? That fragment you barely remember? The dreams that make up the majority of the entries in any dream journal? Jung rather condescendingly called these insignificant. He said little dreams "are the nightly fragments of fantasy coming from the subjective and personal sphere, and their meaning is limited to the affairs of everyday life" (Jung, 1974, p. 76).

But many therapists and others working with dreams find their very value in the connections little dreams have with the affairs of everyday life. Forty years ago, Ann Faraday (1972) provided a multitiered structure for gaining insight from dreams that involves first examining them for factual or objective information about the dreamer's waking life, then looking for clues to the dreamer's attitudes and conflicts and how these affect the dreamer in the world (she called this *Through the Looking Glass*), and finally looking at the representation in the dream of the deepest, most powerful inner self. And she made no hierarchical distinction between these types of dreams: the latter is not somehow more important than the former.

With her Dream Interview Method, Gayle Delaney (1991) raised to a high art the gleaning of meaning from the most ordinary dream. This method asks the dreamer,

in an open-ended way, to describe in detail the dream setting, people or characters, animals, objects, feelings, and action or plot. Then the dreamer is asked to bridge to waking life, by considering how various descriptions of dream elements remind the dreamer of some event or person or situation, etc., outside the dream. This nonintrusive but nevertheless sophisticated method allows the dreamer to garner information from even a fragment of a dream.

One of the most interesting ways in which little dreams can provide very big meaning is through the examination of dream series. This is the material at hand for anyone who keeps a dream journal. Jung actually preferred to look at long series: "a long dream-series no longer appears as a senseless string of incoherent and isolated happenings, but resembles the successive steps in a planned and orderly process of development" (1974, p. 75).

A compelling example is Robert Bosnak's 1989 account of his analysis of a man who lived with AIDS, became progressively more ill, and finally died. Christopher (as he is named in the book) kept a dream diary in a notebook covered in brown corduroy. Over the course of the 46 reported dreams, the core characters, activities, and preoccupations in Christopher's life appear in sharp and poignant relief. Bosnak makes no distinction between big and little dreams, but gives each one his concerned and indeed loving attention. And each one helps bring Christopher to a deeper understanding of himself and his difficult life path.

Over the course of decades, Bill Domhoff (1996) and his colleagues (notably Calvin Hall and Robert Van de Castle) have collected dream series from a wide variety of people, ranging from Freud and Jung and a child molester to ordinary people. Rather than examining each dream narrative, as clinicians and others working with dreams tend to do, they took a seemingly dry and statistical approach, and coded each dream for discrete elements such as characters, social interactions, and emotions. By comparing the patterns in each person's series to norms based on large numbers of dreamers, they have been able to compile remarkably accurate profiles of the person's preoccupations, worries, interactive style, and emotional tone.

Therefore, little dreams should not be relegated to the insignificant. Rather they should be treasured and held close for the special view they provide of the dreamer's relationships, worries and preoccupations, and place in the world.

Johanna King

See also: Big Dreams

References

Bosnak, R. (1989). *Dreaming with an AIDS patient.* Boston: Shambhala.

Delaney, G. (1991). *Breakthrough dreaming: How to tap the power of your 24-hour mind.* New York: Bantam Books.

Domhoff, G.W. (1996). *Finding meaning in dreams: A quantitative approach.* New York: Springer.

Faraday, A. (1972). *Dream power.* New York: Berkley Medallion Books.

Jung, C. (1974). *Dreams* (Trans. R.F.C. Hull). Princeton, NJ: Princeton University Press.

Logical Structure of Dreams and Their Relation to Reality

Through most of the long history of reflection and commentary on dreams, the nature and significance of their logic has not been substantially explored. Until fairly recently, dreams have mostly been seen as logically incoherent. For example, dreams appear indifferent to contradictions (one thing in a dream, for instance, can also be another, incompatible thing) and to non-sequitur leaps in continuity. The logical character of dreams has therefore seemed obviously unrelated to that of waking reality. As a result, it is only their content that has been seen as sometimes reflecting, revealing, and even predicting the events of waking reality.

In contrast, during the last century in Western research, dreams have often been defended as generally logically coherent in essentially the same way as waking life. Despite this new appraisal, however, their logical structure has mostly still not been explored in its own right as a significant part of the connection dreams have with waking reality. Perhaps this is because, being similar to that of waking life, it has now seemed unremarkable. The various sources of this newer appraisal may be roughly divided into the work of Carl Jung, phenomenological philosophy, humanistic psychology, structuralist anthropology, cognitive psychology, and narrative theory.

Jung understands dream images and occurrences as symbolic of coherent psychological needs and processes, so that an apparently contradictory image, for example, may express a need for or the fact of undergoing a transformation from one perspective on one's life to another. Phenomenological dream theorists see the kinds of contradictions and non sequiturs that occur in dreams as in fact equally present in waking life, and as only apparent in both contexts. When we suddenly feel close to someone in waking life, for example, that person's nearness is at least in some sense real even though it is not physically real. This area or dimension of reality does not obey the same laws as physical reality: for instance, we can be at a new felt distance from someone without intervening travel. When dreams exhibit variations from the logic of physical reality, they are the same variations that waking life exhibits, variations that coherently and validly express the character of their corresponding areas of reality. As a result, dreams are really just another mode of inhabiting the same world as waking life (see, e.g., Boss, 1957).

Humanistic psychologists consider dreams to be problem-solving processes of essentially the same kind as those in waking life, but conducted with the more limited, but also in some ways less readily self-deceiving, resources available during sleep. A seminal example is Hall (1953). Fromm, unlike many of these theorists, notes the comparatively bizarre logic of dreams, but argues that many of the constraints that are crucial to waking thinking are irrelevant to the thinking in our dreams, since these constraints derive from the potential consequences of our actions and we do not act during sleep (Fromm, 1951, p. 28). The otherwise bizarre logic of dreams is therefore appropriate for the conditions of sleep. A structuralist approach to dreams treats them as "modes of argument in which a problem is resolved through a series of rule-governed transformations of an initial dream situation" (Kuper, 1979, p. 645). Unlike the other approaches, this is a focus on the logic of dreams in its own right; but the logical rules it explores are "not [those] of logic but of mytho-logic"

(p. 647). That is, it is not a logic of consequence, in which the transformations entail or follow from each other, but a set of rules for reshaping the dream materials to match a pre-given, desired outcome.

Cognitive researchers, such as humanistic psychologists, argue that dreams are not especially nonsensical but "are, rather, reasonable projections of what we might expect if waking cognition were operating under the somewhat dissociated circumstances generally accompanying sleep" (Cavallero & Foulkes, 1993, p. 11). Finally, States (1993) has drawn on narrative theory to develop an account of the coherence of dreams in terms of the techniques that characterize coherent storytelling: for example, shifting scenes without showing the transitions and combining different characters into one.

Some longstanding Asian traditions see dream life and waking life as equally real whatever their similarities or differences, so that the logical character of dreams, including whatever incoherence they may involve, is directly part of the logical character of reality. Here again the logic of their structure has not been a focus of reflection in its own right. These traditions have, however, emphasized the different issue of the logical paradoxes of interaction *between* dream and waking reality that are involved; for instance, in the idea that what we take to be reality may *be* a dream in a larger reality, and so on for this reality in turn. These traditions have taken seriously the significance of these paradoxes for the nature of reality itself (see, e.g., O'Flaherty, 1984).

It mostly remains for the future to explore the possible connections of the logical structure of dreams in its own right with waking reality. A recent first step in this direction is the proposal that, while dreams do characteristically involve moments of logical incoherence, the deepest dimensions of waking reality also violate logic in the same kinds of ways, as various types of metaphysics, mysticism, and art attest, and that the logical incoherence of dreams sometimes expresses the nature of those deep dimensions of reality (Barris, 2010). These dimensions are those in which we confront the sense of our lives or of reality as a whole, as we do when asking metaphysical and existential questions, or when we are faced with fundamental and global differences of outlook. In general, when we reflect on something, we take up a position outside it from which to survey it: similarly, in reflecting on the nature of sense as a whole, or on our own idea of sense as a whole, we take up a position at least partly outside sense or outside our current interpretation of it. By our own standards, this is not a position that makes sense. It is self-contradictory to try to make sense outside the constraints of sense. But this is the only position in which we can have any understanding of what sense itself, as a whole, is, let alone deepen our understanding of it; and it is the only position in which we can come to understand alternative frameworks for sense as a whole. This partly incoherent reflection is therefore the deepest kind of thinking we can undertake. The proposal is that dreams consist sometimes or partly in this kind of confrontation with the sense of things as a whole, and that at least some aspects of their incoherence expresses the logic of this deepest kind of thought.

A more limited but related type of incoherence occurs when we acquire a new concept, or when we move from understanding a particular thing in terms of one concept to understanding it in terms of another. Since a concept constitutes or frames the whole of the sense of its content, this kind of shift also begins or steps outside the whole possible sense of something either to establish or to reconstitute that same sense. As a result, it involves the same kind of incoherence as reflection on sense as a whole. When we gain a new perspective on some aspect of our lives, that perspective sometimes involves acquiring a new concept or a change of the concepts in whose terms we understand the issues, and therefore involves this kind of incoherence. This kind of transition, too, may be part of what is expressed in the logic of dreams (Barris, 2010, p. 11, note 6).

Jeremy Barris

References

Barris, J. (2010). The logical structure of dreams and their relation to reality. *Dreaming, 20*(1), 1–18.

Boss, M. (1957). *The analysis of dreams* (Trans. A. J. Pomerans). London: Rider.

Cavallero, C., & Foulkes, D. (Eds.). (1993). *Dreaming as cognition.* London: Harvester Wheatsheaf.

Fromm, E. (1951). *The forgotten language: An introduction to the understanding of dreams, fairy tales, and myths.* New York: Grove Press.

Hall, C.S. (1953). *The meaning of dreams.* New York: Harper & Row.

Kuper, A. (1979). A structural approach to dreams. *Man, 14*, 645–662.

O'Flaherty, W.D. (1984). *Dreams, illusion, and other realities.* Chicago: University of Chicago Press.

States, B.O. (1993). *Dreaming and storytelling*. Ithaca, NY: Cornell University Press.

Lucid Dreaming

Lucid dreaming is the experience of achieving conscious awareness of dreaming while still asleep. It is a hybrid state because part of the brain performs wake-like functions and part of the brain remains asleep. The most prominent phenomenon indicating lucidity in a dream is conscious awareness or conscious insight into the fact that one is dreaming while the dream continues. Experienced lucid dreamers are sometimes able to change the dream plot and/or carry out certain predetermined movements. Lucid dreams are thought to arise from nonlucid dreams in REM sleep. As our studies have shown, however, lucid dreaming itself is not an REM-sleep phenomenon.

The first-known reports of lucid dreams go back to the second half of the 19th century, when Marquis d'Hervey de Saint-Denis, a French nobleman and explorer of China, systematically collected his dream recalls noting that he was often successful in a volitional control of dream content. However, he also noted that it is difficult to dream to order. The term lucid dreaming was coined by the Dutch psychiatrist van Eeden (1913), who had allegedly tried to persuade Sigmund Freud to comment on lucid dreaming, however, to no avail. Scientifically, lucid dreaming was first investigated by Paul Tholey and Steven LaBerge. Brigitte Holzinger (Holzinger & Klosch, 2008) has focused on the clinical relevance of lucid dreams in the treatment of nightmares, for example. My own research group has investigated the changes in brain electrophysiology that accompany lucid dreams. Many questions, however, have not yet been addressed. It is unclear, for example, at what age lucidity peaks. Is lucid dreaming related to brain development? We would also like to know whether lucidity in dreams is in any way related to personality traits, or whether lucid dreaming has any adverse effects on performance during the day. Can lucid dreaming be used to practice difficult motor tasks and thereby improve motor performance in the wake state, such as suggested by some authors?

The scientific study of lucid dreaming is hampered by several methodological challenges; for example, the lack of a clear definition of lucidity in dreams, its dependence on introspective reports (Voss, 2010), and its rare occurrence. An experimental advantage is that subjects can signal that they have become lucid by making a sequence of voluntary eye movements that can be used as a behavioral indication of lucidity in the sleeping, dreaming subject, as evidenced by EEG and EMG tracings of sleep. Because lucidity can be self-induced, it constitutes not only an opportunity to study the brain basis of conscious states but also demonstrates how a voluntary intervention can change those states.

Definition of Lucid Dreams

Different authors define lucidity in dreams more or less restrictively. Whereas LaBerge (1985) considers lucid insight into the fact that one is dreaming sufficient to label a dream as lucid, others apply a much broader definition, which, in addition to lucid insight, includes full intellectual clarity, the availability of autobiographic memory sources, the ability to actively control the dream, as well as an overall increase in the intensity of multimodal hallucinatory imagery (Tart, 1988; Windt & Metzinger, 2007).

In collaboration with researchers from philosophy, psychology, and psychiatry we have recently constructed a lucidity scale to empirically determine the defining elements of lucid dreams. Results from preliminary factor analysis yield six factors, the strongest of which is reflective insight into the fact that one is dreaming. Other factors (in the order of descending factor strength) are logical thought, access to waking memory, supernatural abilities, volitional control of dream plot, and dissociative elements, such as, for example, perceptions of depersonalization or derealization. By contrast to nonlucid dreams, lucid dreams are thus characterized by lucid insight, the ability to think rather logically, the ability to access memory sources, a capacity to volitionally carry out actions and movements that are not possible in waking (e.g., walking through walls), a certain degree of control over the dream plot, and the ability to take on a third-person perspective in the dream.

Brain Physiologic Correlates of Lucid Dreams

Several studies have documented that lucid dreams have a distinct electrophysiology. Our own data show that, while lucidity often occurs out of REM sleep, lucid dreams are not REM-sleep phenomena. Rather, lucidity occurs in a hybrid state, with amplified elements of waking, evidenced by increased power in upper-frequency bands and improved cortical networking. An important characteristic distinguishing lucid dreaming from waking with eyes closed is the alpha band activity (power) and coherences present in the wake but not the lucid-dreaming condition. By contrast, lucid dreaming shows REM-sleep-like activity in low-frequency bands delta and theta. Figures 12–14 show typical coherences for waking with eyes closed (WEC), lucid dreaming, and REM sleep.

Differences between REM sleep and lucid dreaming were most prominent in the 40-Hz-frequency band. We found evidence of increased power as well as heightened cortical networking, across short as well as long ranges. The increase in 40-Hz coherence was especially strong at frontal sites. However, since REM sleep is typically less synchronized in frontal regions, this increase in frontal and dorsolateral frontal areas may be secondary to the increase in global networking. These results suggest that 40-Hz activity holds a functional role in the modulation of conscious awareness across different conscious states. It also supports theories linking 40-Hz synchronization with perceptual binding and the integration of cognitive processes.

Ursula Voss

References

Holzinger, B., & Klosch, G. (2008). Cognition during sleep: A therapeutic intervention in nightmares. *Journal of Sleep Research, 17*, 93.

LaBerge, S. (1985). *Lucid dreaming*. New York: Ballantine Books.

Tart, C. (1988). From spontaneous event to lucidity—A review of attempts to consciously control nocturnal dreaming. In

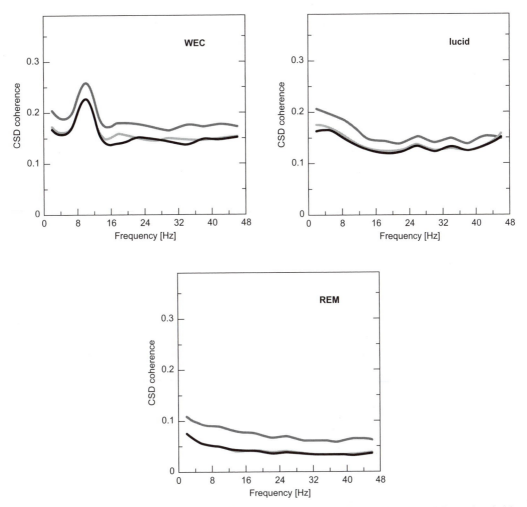

Figure 12–14: Short- and Long-Range Coherences Obtained for Waking (top), Lucid Dreaming (middle) and REM Sleep (bottom). Coherences are indications of interscalp networking and synchronization. Coherences are averaged across electrode pairs in four-second epochs. Short-range (55 pairs) was defined as less than 10 cm and long range (65 pairs) as larger than 15-cm interelectrode distance. Coherences are lowest in REM sleep and strongly enhanced in lucid dreaming (Courtesy Ursula Voss).

J. Gackenbach & S. LaBerge (Eds.), *Conscious mind, sleeping brain* (pp. 67–103). New York: Plenum Press.

van Eeden, F. W. (1913). A study of dreams. *Proceedings of the Society for Psychical Research, 26*. Retrieved from http://www. lucidity.com/vanEeden.html

Voss, U. (2010). Lucid dreaming: Reflections of the role of introspection. *International Journal of Dream Research, 3*, 52–53.

Voss, U., Holzmann, R., Tuin, I., & Hobson, J. A. (2009). Lucid dreaming: A state of consciousness with features of both waking and non-lucid dreaming. *Sleep, 32*, 1191–1200.

Windt, J. M., & Metzinger, T. (2007). The philosophy of dreaming and self-consciousness: What happens to the experiential subject during the dream state? In P. McNamara & D. Barrett (Eds.), *The new science of dreaming*. Westport, CT: Praeger Perspectives.

Lucid Dreaming in Sports

The dreaming brain provides a simulation of the real world and a lucid dreamer is able to act deliberately within this simulation (Erlacher & Chapin, 2010). Different applications of lucid dreaming have been discussed in the literature. One possible application is to practice movements in a lucid dream to enhance the performance in the waking state. Practice in lucid dreams is defined as a type of mental rehearsal, whereby a person is using the dream state to consciously practice specific motor tasks without waking up (Erlacher, 2007). Even though this kind of mental rehearsal is not novel (Tholey, 1990), it is a rather unknown technique to enhance motor skills.

It seems that at least some athletes have already been using lucid-dream practice in sports to improve their waking performance (Erlacher, 2007; LaBerge & Rheingold, 1990; Tholey, 1990). LaBerge and Rheingold (1990), for example, report of a long-distance runner who practiced his running technique or a tennis novice who learned his tennis serve, while Erlacher (2007) provides an account of one female high diver who described that she practiced complex twists and somersaults in her lucid dreams and reported that the movements felt real, and she could also slow down the entire sequence to focus on important details of her dive.

In a questionnaire study, Erlacher, Stumbrys, and Schredl (submitted) asked 840 German elite athletes from various sports about their experience with lucid dreams. About 57 percent of the athletes stated that they experienced a lucid dream at least once in their lives, 24 percent are frequent lucid dreamers (having one or more lucid dreams per month). Nine percent of the lucid dreamers used this dream state to practice sport skills and the majority of those athletes had an impression that the rehearsal within their lucid dreams improved their performance in wakefulness.

In a qualitative study, Tholey (1981) instructed six proficient lucid dreamers to perform different complex sport skills in their lucid dreams, such as skiing or gymnastics. The participants reported that they had no difficulties in performing those complex sport skills during their lucid dreams. Furthermore, the participants reported that the movements were accompanied by a pleasant feeling in the dream and, due to the practice, their movements improved in both the dream state and the waking state.

To test the effects of lucid-dream practice in a quasi-experimental field study, Erlacher and Schredl (2010) assigned 40 participants to a lucid-dream practice group, a physical practice group, and a control group. The waking performance of the motor task (coin tossing) was measured in the evening and on the next morning by the participants at home. Twenty participants from the lucid-dream practice group attempted to carry out the motor task in a lucid dream on a single night. Seven participants succeeded in having a lucid dream and practicing the experimental task. This group of 7 participants showed a significant enhancement, while the other 13 subjects showed no improvement. Comparing all groups, the physical practice group demonstrated the highest increase in performance followed by the successful lucid-dream practice group. Both groups had statistically significant higher improvements in contrast to those participants who did not practice the task.

Further evidences for the effectiveness of lucid-dream practice come from sleep laboratory studies that demonstrated a strong correlation between lucid-dreamed actions and physiological measurement (e.g., EEG, EMG, heart rate) (Erlacher & Schredl, 2008a, 2008b).

Daniel Erlacher

See also: entries related to Lucid Dreaming

References

Erlacher, D. (2007). *Motorisches Lernen im luziden Traum: Phänomenologische und experimentelle Betrachtungen*. Saarbrücken: VDM.

Erlacher, D., & Chapin, H. (2010). Lucid dreaming: Neural virtual reality as a mechanism for performance enhancement. *International Journal of Dream Research, 3*(1), 7–10.

Erlacher, D., & Schredl, M. (2008a). Cardiovascular responses to dreamed physical exercise during REM lucid dreaming. *Dreaming, 18*, 112–121.

Erlacher, D., & Schredl, M. (2008b). Do REM (lucid) dreamed and executed actions share the same neural substrate? *International Journal of Dream Research, 1*(1), 7–13.

Erlacher, D., & Schredl, M. (2010). Practicing a motor task in a lucid dream enhances subsequent performance: A pilot study. *The Sport Psychologist, 24*(2), 157–167.

Erlacher, D., Stumbrys, T., & Schredl, M. (in press). Frequency of lucid dreams and lucid dream practice in German athletes. *Imagination, Cognition and Personality*.

LaBerge, S., & Rheingold, H. (1990). *Exploring the world of lucid dreaming*. New York: Ballentine Books.

Tholey, P. (1981). Empirische Untersuchungen ueber Klarträume. *Gestalt Theory, 3*, 21–62.

Tholey, P. (1990). Applications of lucid dreaming in sports. *Lucidity Letter, 9*, 6–17.

Lucid Dreaming Therapy for Nightmares

Nightmares are a common disorder affecting 2 to 5 percent of the general population (Spoormaker, Schredl, & van den Bout, 2006). The clinical definition of nightmares in the Diagnostic and Statistical Manual for Mental Disorders is: "extremely frightening dreams that lead to awakening," yet various emotions have been reported in nightmares and direct awakening seems not to be associated with increased distress (Blagrove, Farmer, & Williams, 2004). Nightmares disturb the sleep, inflict daytime distress, and can be part of posttraumatic stress disorder (PTSD). Furthermore, nightmares are associated with higher psychopathology scores, although it seems that nightmare distress rather than nightmare frequency is related to these psychopathology scores (Blagrove et al., 2004; Spoormaker et al., 2006). These findings suggest that nightmares could be viewed as a sleep disorder that should receive specific diagnosis and treatment.

Nightmares can be adequately treated with cognitive-behavioral therapy: Imagery rehearsal therapy (IRT) and exposure are the two most thoroughly empirically tested treatments for nightmares (Lancee, Spoormaker, & van den Bout, 2010a). In both treatments the nightmares are imagined during the day. In exposure, desensitization occurs by imagining the original nightmare; IRT employs exposure as well but the nightmare is imagined in a changed format.

These treatments are also effective in self-help format (Lancee et al., 2010a), although a majority of participants still suffered from residual nightmares after treatment.

This is an argument for the search for alternative treatment strategies, also for those persons who suffer from nonrepetitive nightmares. Lucid dreaming, realizing in a dream that one is dreaming, may be such an alternative treatment. Lucid dreaming has been physiologically verified by volitional eye movements on the electrooculogram during rapid eye movement sleep (e.g., LaBerge, Nagel, Dement, & Zarcone, 1981), and as lucid-dreaming frequency is moderately correlated with nightmare frequency (Schredl & Erlacher, 2004), it seems plausible that nightmares can trigger lucid dreaming. With lucid-dreaming treatment for nightmares, participants imagine their (changed) nightmare during the day while thinking that they are only dreaming (thereby triggering lucidity in the real nightmare). Alternatively, they can perform lucidity exercises such as the reality test to increase the chances of lucidity when one experiences intense fear, which is most likely to happen in a nightmare.

A few case studies and one randomized controlled pilot (Spoormaker & van den Bout, 2006) have studied this treatment; all indicated that lucid dreaming was an effective treatment of nightmares even when sometimes nightmares spontaneously changed without lucidity. In the controlled study, lucid-dreaming treatment was superior to a waiting list on nightmare frequency but did not have an effect on secondary measures such as subjective sleep quality and PTSD complaints. However, adding lucid-dreaming treatment to the self-help manual based on imagery rehearsal (i.e., following all standard imagery rehearsal exercises yet adding one lucidity exercise during imagination of the nightmare) counterintuitively reduced the efficacy of the treatment (Lancee, van den Bout, & Spoormaker, 2010b), presumably because the treatment and its goals became too complex for a self-help format. Future lucid-dreaming research should use a face-to-face setting to compare original IRT with original lucid dreaming therapy.

As lucid-dreaming treatment is a demanding treatment that requires much motivation and openness for cognitive experiences, the recommendation is to use this treatment when well-established treatments such as imagery rehearsal or exposure therapy are not an option. Having posttraumatic nightmares should be a contraindication against the use of lucid-dreaming treatment, as lucidity without the ability to change dream imagery may make the experience of replicative posttraumatic nightmares worse. Moreover, lucid dreaming is not an appropriate treatment strategy for persons with psychotic symptoms and/or difficulties to distinguish reality from internal stimuli. In short, lucid dreaming is indicated for those nightmare sufferers with few comorbid psychiatric complaints and nonrepetitive idiopathic nightmares, for which the other treatments are not feasible.

Victor I. Spoormaker and Jaap Lancee

References

Blagrove, M., Farmer, L., & Williams, E. (2004). The relationship of nightmare frequency and nightmare distress to well-being. *Journal of Sleep Research, 13,* 129–136.

LaBerge, S., Nagel, L. E., Dement, W. C., & Zarcone, V. P. (1981). Lucid dreaming verified by volitional communication during REM sleep. *Perceptual and Motor Skills, 52,* 727–732.

Lancee, J., Spoormaker, V. I., & van den Bout, J. (2010a). Cognitive behavioral self-help treatment for nightmares: A randomized controlled trial. *Psychotherapy and Psychosomatics, 79,* 371–377.

Lancee, J., van den Bout, J., & Spoormaker, V. I. (2010b). Expanding self-help imagery rehearsal therapy with sleep hygiene and lucid dreaming: A waiting-list controlled trial. *International Journal of Dream Research, 3,* 111–120.

Schredl, M., & Erlacher, D. (2004). Lucid dreaming frequency and personality. *Personality and Individual Differences, 37,* 1463–1473.

Spoormaker, V. I., Schredl, M., & van den Bout, J. (2006). Nightmares: From anxiety symptom to sleep disorder. *Sleep Medicine Reviews, 10*(1), 53–59.

Spoormaker, V. I., & van den Bout, J. (2006). Lucid dreaming treatment for nightmares: A pilot-study. *Psychotherapy and Psychosomatics, 75,* 389–394.

Lucid Nightmares

Many dreams with emergent properties of self-awareness begin as anxiety dreams or dreams characterized by intense negative affect such as fear or terror. Lucid nightmares are self-described disturbing dreams in which the dreamer becomes self-aware, leading to awakening. The prevalence of lucid nightmares today is unknown, although several researchers are testing lucid-dreaming techniques to reduce and transform nightmares.

Lucid nightmares in normal sleepers without clinically defined trauma are a marginalized topic within the field of lucid-dreaming research, perhaps due to the conflation of self-awareness with dream control, leading to a gap in the literature regarding lucid-dream experiences that cannot be emotionally managed by the dreamer. Lucid nightmares are often viewed as a failed lucid dream. However, while dream control and self-awareness are often correlated, these two dimensions can be experienced separately.

Many scholars have mentioned nightmares with self-awareness in passing. Most of these accounts describe how self-awareness can lead to detachment from the emotions of the nightmare, leading to an escape from or alteration in the narrative. For example, 19th-century French dream enthusiast Hervey de Saint-Denys details how his frequent nightmares sometimes led to dreams with awareness, in which curiosity overcame strong emotion. Similarly, philosopher Thomas Reid recounts how he learned to use self-awareness to overcome the fright of his nightmares as a teenager. On the other hand, a minority of accounts describe a combination of self-awareness and ongoing fear. Dutch psychoanalyst Frederick Willem Van Eeden, who coined the phrase *lucid dreaming* in 1914, best represents this view. Van Eeden mentions demon dreams as well as a type of false-awakening dreams he called wrong waking-up dreams. Both dream types are marked by self-awareness and

Frederik Willem Van Eeden, who was the first to use the phrase "lucid dream" in English, was haunted equally by what he called "demon dreams." *Frederik Van Eeden*, 1918. ([The Dutch Labour Movement till 1918], International Institute of Social History, Amsterdam)

vivid imagery, an unsettling atmosphere and demonic dream figures that lead to a fitful struggle to wake up. Furthermore, Van Eeden (1972) claims that his demon dreams seem to follow his lucid control dreams (p. 158).

Lucid dreams and nightmares have formal similarities that naturally lead to a blending of their features. Both lucid dreams and nightmares have vivid imagery, intense emotions and more kinesthetic description than ordinary dreams. Both

can disturb sleep by leading directly to awakening. Nightmares have more instances of metacognition than ordinary dreams, including self-questioning, even if formal self-reference is not achieved. Last, anxiety in dreams often leads to spontaneous lucid dreams.

The phenomenology of lucid nightmares is not well developed, and its characteristics are preliminary at best. Primarily, lucid nightmares cannot be controlled or modified by the dreamer, although there may be attempts to do so. The dreams often include dream figures who may look threatening, demonic, undead, or in a perceived state of suffering or intense emotionality. These dream figures also attempt to interact with the dream ego, and appear to have their own motivations, autonomy, and intelligence. Other confrontations that cannot be escaped include images of death and decay, human skeletal remains, mutant creatures, monsters, fire and other hellish scenery, sickly lighting and shadows, and other forms of putrescence and pestilence. Physical pain may be present, including wounds, energetic shocks, burning sensations, piercing, mutilation, and even destruction of the dream body. The full emotional range is possible, including anger, rage, grief, anxiety, fear, and terror. A subset of these experiences may also be marked by detachment and clarity within the dream and afterward.

By way of example, licensed counselor Gregory Scott Sparrow (1991) discusses how, in the height of his experimentation of lucid dreaming, he encountered terrifying dreams, including angry dream figures that sometimes turned demonic despite his self-assurance that he could not be hurt in the dream. This modern account mirrors Van Eeden's description from 1914, and suggests that more is going on psychologically than a failure to stay in control.

Similar typologies to lucid nightmares can be found in initiation dreams and initiation visions, which also involve the themes of sacrifice, death, mutilation, and rebirth while the dreamer takes the attitude of surrender or the role of witness. Relatedly, frightening near-death experiences, which can occur during sleep and may also be an REM phenomenon, have comparable characteristics, including self-awareness, autonomously generated imagery and disturbing encounters, and a confusing emotional mixture of terror and detachment. One important difference between these two states of consciousness is their effects on the dreamer. While initiation dreams can result in the empowerment of the dreamer to take on new roles in life, often frightening near-death experiences result in increased fear and disappointment.

In comparison, lucid nightmares seem to have a wide spectrum of aftereffects, from feelings of peace and harmony to bewilderment, emotional sensitivity, ecstasy, catharsis, and feelings of renewal. Given the stressful nature of lucid nightmares, in combination with their potential for self-understanding and the establishment of new self-constructs, lucid nightmares fit in well with Stanislav and Christina Grof's (1989) spiritual emergency, which has been included in the diagnostic manual for the American Psychiatric Association as a religious or spiritual problem characterized by a nonpathological altered structure of experience.

Lucid Dreaming Re-Scripting Techniques for Nightmares

In the 1970s, during the beginnings of the modern dream-work movement, a method of conquering nightmares using active lucid dreaming was inspired by the Senoi tribal society in Malaysia, although scholars have since disputed the anthropological accuracy of its tribal namesake. German psychologist Paul Tholey (1988) also developed a confrontational model of lucidity training in which he sought out disturbing dream scenarios to face threatening figures.

Other techniques for using self-awareness to transform nightmares include a cognitive approach, based on the ability of dreamers to remind themselves to lose their fear and achieve a degree of emotional distance in the midst of terrifying dreams. Pilot studies in nightmare intervention by teaching lucid dreaming as a means to rescript the dream narrative have more recently been applied to post-traumatic stress disorder (PTSD) sufferers, although these techniques have not yet shown success in reducing PTSD nightmares. A 2010 review of lucid-dreaming treatments (Gavie & Revonsuo, 2010) suggests that lucid-dreaming induction is in fact effective for reducing nightmares in non-PTSD cases, perhaps because the thought of more self-control reduces anxiety in waking life, which further reduces nightmare frequency.

New Frontiers

From an existential perspective, nightmares can be seen as opportunities to create new meanings and explore new possibilities. As such, lucid nightmares may be more than an indicator of ill health but rather the healing process in action. As such, lucid nightmares in nontraumatized individuals may have their own healing trajectory. In some cases, witnessing the imagery unfold rather than manipulating the dream content may facilitate growth precisely through facing and sitting with these spontaneous experiences of suffering. In lucid-dreaming scholarship, dream witnessing is discussed as a balance between active participation and the attitude of detached receptivity, not as complete submission to the dream. Retaining the power to choose is essential. Some lucid nightmares result in the destruction of the dream body and rebirth into a new dream body, along with new emotional frontiers and a new existential viewpoint. Confronting terror with equanimity is at the heart of Eastern approaches to suffering, and also can be seen in the West in the *mysterium tremendum*, as outlined by religion scholar Rudolph Otto, as well as the private and personal Christian initiation known as the dark night of the soul.

More research with lucid-dreaming treatments is needed with regard to PTSD as well as nontraumatized sufferers of nightmares. Further clinical, psychoanalytical, and phenomenological work with lucid nightmares could distinguish the most effective and appropriate paths for guided healing and self-healing, including dream re-scripting techniques, promoting dream witnessing, choosing surrender and dream body annihilation, and combinations of these conscious decisions in the face of disturbing dream scenarios.

The most important results in any exploration involving lucid nightmares are establishing increased feelings of safety and security when facing the past, more confidence in expressing oneself in the present, and instilling a sense of hope and empowerment when envisioning the future.

Ryan Hurd

See also: entries related to Lucid Dreaming

References

Gavie, J., & Revonsuo, A. (2010). The future of lucid dreaming treatment. *International Journal of Dream Eesearch, 3*(1), 13–15.

Grof, S., & Grof, C. (1989). *Spiritual emergency: When personal transformation becomes a crisis.* Los Angeles: Tarcher.

Sparrow, G. S. (1991). Letter from Scott Sparrow. *Lucidity, 10*(1/2), 421–424.

Tholey, P. (1988). A model of lucidity training as a means of self-healing and psychological growth. In J. Gackenbach & S. LaBerge (Eds.), *Conscious mind, sleeping brain* (pp. 263–287). New York: Plenum Press.

Van Eeden, F. (1972). A study of dreams. In C. Tart (Ed.), *Altered states of consciousness* (pp. 147–160). New York: Double Day Press.